# TEXTS FOR PREACHING

## YEAR C

Also published by Westminster John Knox Press

*Texts for Preaching:*
*A Lectionary Commentary Based on the NRSV—*
*Year B*

by Walter Brueggemann, Charles B. Cousar,
Beverly R. Gaventa, and James D. Newsome

# TEXTS FOR PREACHING

*A Lectionary Commentary
Based on the NRSV*

## YEAR C

Charles B. Cousar, Beverly R. Gaventa,
J. Clinton McCann, Jr., James D. Newsome

Westminster John Knox Press
Louisville, Kentucky

© 1994 Westminster John Knox Press

Acknowledgments will be found on page ix.

*Book design by Drew Stevens*

*First edition*

Published by Westminster John Knox Press
Louisville, Kentucky

This book is printed on acid-free paper that meets the American National Standards Institute Z39.48 standard. ♾

PRINTED IN THE UNITED STATES OF AMERICA
9   8   7   6   5   4

**Library of Congress Cataloging-in-Publication Data**
(Revised for vol. 3)

Texts for preaching.

    Includes index.
    Contents:     [2] Year B / Walter Brueggemann . . . [et al.] — [3] Year C / Charles B. Cousar . . . [et al.]
    1. Lectionary preaching.  2. Bible—Commentaries.
I. Brueggemann, Walter.  II. Cousar, Charles B.
BV4235.L43T488  1993      251        93-8023
ISBN 0-664-21970-5 (v. 2)
ISBN 0-664-22000-2 (v. 3)

# Contents

Preface     vii
Acknowledgments     ix

First Sunday of Advent     1
Second Sunday of Advent     10
Third Sunday of Advent     19
Fourth Sunday of Advent     29

Christmas, First Proper     39
Christmas, Second Proper     48
Christmas, Third Proper     57
First Sunday After Christmas     66
Second Sunday After Christmas     75

Epiphany     84
First Sunday After Epiphany
   (Baptism of the Lord)     Ordinary Time 1     93
Second Sunday After Epiphany     Ordinary Time 2     103
Third Sunday After Epiphany     Ordinary Time 3     112
Fourth Sunday After Epiphany     Ordinary Time 4     122
Fifth Sunday After Epiphany     Ordinary Time 5     132
Sixth Sunday After Epiphany     Proper 1     Ordinary Time 6     141
Seventh Sunday After Epiphany     Proper 2     Ordinary Time 7     151
Eighth Sunday After Epiphany     Proper 3     Ordinary Time 8     160
Last Sunday After Epiphany
   (Transfiguration Sunday)     170

Ash Wednesday     180
First Sunday in Lent     189
Second Sunday in Lent     199
Third Sunday in Lent     209
Fourth Sunday in Lent     219
Fifth Sunday in Lent     228
Sixth Sunday in Lent
   (Palm Sunday or Passion Sunday)     238
Holy Thursday     248

| | | | |
|---|---|---|---|
| Good Friday | | | 257 |
| Easter | | | 266 |
| Second Sunday of Easter | | | 275 |
| Third Sunday of Easter | | | 285 |
| Fourth Sunday of Easter | | | 295 |
| Fifth Sunday of Easter | | | 305 |
| Sixth Sunday of Easter | | | 313 |
| Ascension | | | 322 |
| Seventh Sunday of Easter | | | 331 |
| Pentecost | | | 341 |
| | | | |
| Trinity Sunday | | | 351 |
| Proper 4 | Ordinary Time 9 | May 29–June 4 *(if after Trinity)* | 361 |
| Proper 5 | Ordinary Time 10 | June 5–11 *(if after Trinity)* | 371 |
| Proper 6 | Ordinary Time 11 | June 12–18 *(if after Trinity)* | 381 |
| Proper 7 | Ordinary Time 12 | June 19–25 *(if after Trinity)* | 391 |
| Proper 8 | Ordinary Time 13 | June 26–July 2 | 401 |
| Proper 9 | Ordinary Time 14 | July 3–9 | 411 |
| Proper 10 | Ordinary Time 15 | July 10–16 | 419 |
| Proper 11 | Ordinary Time 16 | July 17–23 | 429 |
| Proper 12 | Ordinary Time 17 | July 24–30 | 439 |
| Proper 13 | Ordinary Time 18 | July 31–August 6 | 449 |
| Proper 14 | Ordinary Time 19 | August 7–13 | 459 |
| Proper 15 | Ordinary Time 20 | August 14–20 | 469 |
| Proper 16 | Ordinary Time 21 | August 21–27 | 479 |
| Proper 17 | Ordinary Time 22 | August 28–September 3 | 487 |
| Proper 18 | Ordinary Time 23 | September 4–10 | 497 |
| Proper 19 | Ordinary Time 24 | September 11–17 | 507 |
| Proper 20 | Ordinary Time 25 | September 18–24 | 517 |
| Proper 21 | Ordinary Time 26 | September 25–October 1 | 527 |
| Proper 22 | Ordinary Time 27 | October 2–8 | 535 |
| Proper 23 | Ordinary Time 28 | October 9–15 | 546 |
| Proper 24 | Ordinary Time 29 | October 16–22 | 556 |
| Proper 25 | Ordinary Time 30 | October 23–29 | 566 |
| Proper 26 | Ordinary Time 31 | October 30–November 5 | 576 |
| Proper 27 | Ordinary Time 32 | November 6–12 | 585 |
| Proper 28 | Ordinary Time 33 | November 13–19 | 596 |
| Proper 29 | Ordinary Time 34 | November 20–26 | |
| *(Christ the King or Reign of Christ)* | | | 603 |
| All Saints | | November 1 | |
| | | *(or first Sunday in November)* | 609 |
| | | | |
| Index of Lectionary Readings | | | 619 |

# PREFACE

These are not easy days for preachers. The demands made on the pulpit seem unceasing—to bring the biblical texts to bear upon the critical experiences of parishioners, upon their joys, griefs, and suffering; to shed light on the local or global crisis of the moment; to support the program of the church; to address the burning social issues of the day; to instruct disciples in the thought and life of a long tradition; to evangelize and re-evangelize; in a word, to nurture a community of faith. That congregations these days are often unfamiliar with the language of the Bible, its narratives, parables, songs, and letters, makes the task of preaching even more complex.

These studies of lectionary texts are offered as a resource to colleagues whose vocation it is to preach week in and week out. While diverse in form and style, the studies seek to fill that space between a critical commentary and the sermon itself. They provide an orientation to the text and offer theological reflections that are meant to spark the imaginations of those who prepare and deliver sermons.

For Year C, the studies of all the Old Testament texts have been contributed by James D. Newsome and the studies of all the Psalms texts by J. Clinton McCann, Jr. The only exception has come on days when the designated readings are the same for all three years of the lectionary cycle (A, B, C). In such cases, the material of Walter Brueggemann has been used from the previously published volume on Year B. Beverly R. Gaventa has written the studies on the Gospel texts from the beginning of the year through Good Friday and the studies on the Epistle texts from Easter until the end of the year. Charles B. Cousar has contributed the studies on the Epistles from Advent through Good Friday and thereafter the studies on the Gospel texts. All have contributed to the Introductions.

We are grateful to the editors and staff of Westminster John Knox Press for their patient guidance throughout the project, and, in particular, to Harold L. Twiss, who has kept us moving toward the day of publication. We are also indebted in countless ways to the administrators, colleagues, and students in the three institutions in which we teach—Columbia, Eden, and Princeton—who have supported our efforts and to long-suffering family members who have contributed in more ways than they know.

CHARLES B. COUSAR
Editor, Year C

# ACKNOWLEDGMENTS

Unless otherwise noted, scripture quotations are from the New Revised Standard Version of the Bible, copyright © 1989 by the Division of Christian Education of the National Council of the Churches of Christ in the U.S.A., and are used by permission.

Scripture quotations from the Revised Standard Version of the Bible are copyright 1946, 1952, © 1971, 1973 by the Division of Christian Education of the National Council of the Churches of Christ in the U.S.A. and are used by permission.

Scripture quotations from *The New English Bible* are copyright © 1961, 1970 by The Delegates of the Oxford University Press and The Syndics of the Cambridge University Press and are used by permission.

Scripture quotations from *The Revised English Bible* are copyright © 1989 by Oxford University Press and Cambridge University Press and are used by permission.

Scripture references for the lectionary readings are from the *Revised Common Lectionary*, copyright © 1992, the Consultation on Common Texts. Used with permission.

# First Sunday of Advent

Advent has two faces, two orientations. It looks to the past in the sense that it is a recapitulation of the longing with which women and men of faith living in a bygone era anticipated the coming of God's Messiah. But Advent also looks to the future in an attitude of expectancy over what God has yet to do in the life of humankind.

Advent's face toward the past is usually the one we seek. How very wonderful that a gracious God broke in upon the life of humankind through the birth of Jesus, God's very own Son! But Advent's face to the future is one that also deserves our attention. The coming of the Babe to Bethlehem, for all of its miraculous grace, is but hint and suggestion of the Second Advent when this same Jesus, now Risen Lord and Savior, will return to claim the world that is his.

While the lectionary texts for this day help us look in both directions, the emphasis is clearly on "Advent again," Christ's return to rule with compassion and power. The passage from Jeremiah draws heavily on the language of prophetic judgment to make an important statement about God's grace to come "in those days." The "day of wrath" pictured by a prophet like Zephaniah has become a time of restoration and of salvation.

Psalm 25, a psalm of distress, emphasizes the weakness of men and women and the redemptive qualities of God's grace. Relying on language reminiscent of the book of Exodus, the psalmist sings of a God whose basic nature is to forgive.

First Thessalonians 3:9–13 looks forward to "the coming of our Lord Jesus" as the climax of human experience and urges love and holiness on all who wait for that climax of human history. Yet, while both love and holiness are worthy goals toward which to strive, in the end they are the gifts of a gracious God.

The passage from Luke 21 is heavy in apocalyptic imagery. It

anticipates the Second Advent with the admonitions "Be on guard,"
"Be alert." Watch!

## Jeremiah 33:14–16

The coming of Advent jolts the church out of its "ordinary time"
with the invasive good news that God's grace is impending—that it
is about to present fresh possibilities for deliverance and wholeness.
Understandably, those who receive this word are joyfully curious as
to just what God is about, and we strain to know the shape and
dimensions of God's new initiatives in human life. The texts satisfy
our hunger for knowledge of God's ways only partially, in that
while we are given the larger form and direction of God's intentions,
we are left wanting more of the details.

In order adequately to portray the new realities of God's love, the
prophet here turns to the literature of God's judgment. As early as
the time of Amos, the deliverers of God's prophetic word had
promised a day of retribution to come. "Why do you want the day of
the LORD [to arrive]?" Amos had asked his mid-eighth-century
listeners. "It is darkness, not light," he promised, going on to
compare this day to a mauling by a bear or a bite from a snake (Amos
5:18–20). Shortly before the time when Jeremiah was active, the
prophet Zephaniah repeated this theme. The day of the Lord

> will be a day of wrath,
> a day of distress and anguish,
> a day of ruin and devastation,
> a day of darkness and gloom,
> a day of clouds and thick darkness.
>                                (Zeph. 1:15)

Who could possibly want to be present to participate in such a
terrible day as this?

Quite astonishingly Jeremiah seizes upon just this moment in
God's time to proclaim a message of great joy. (One will want to
consult a good, recent commentary on the question of the authorship
of Jer. 33:14–26, as well as on the issue of the relation of this text to
Jer. 23:5–6.) In the prophets' hands that which was understood in the
past to be a time of great suffering is now transformed into an
occasion of redemption and joy. "The days are surely coming . . ."
are the words that begin our passage, and one cannot possibly miss
the point: that which was intended for judgment is now purposed by

God to be a moment of salvation. "In those days . . .," v. 15 reminds the reader. "In those days . . .," echoes v. 16.

The joyous thing that is to transpire in the coming time is nothing less than the fulfillment of Yahweh's promise to revive the house of David. The image is, of course, that of a great, felled tree from which a new shoot is to emerge (compare Isa. 11:1)—an image that itself is a paradigm of life-out-of-death and thus is one that affirms the larger image of days-of-evil now become days-of-good. But the shoot is no ordinary sucker, feebly attempting to preserve a last vestige of the once-mighty oak or cedar. "This is a "righteous Branch," one who will fulfill the ancient model of Israelite kingship by executing justice and righteousness. The Branch will become a mighty Tree in its own right.

Psalm 72 is perhaps the most lyrical of the several expressions within the Old Testament of the biblical ideal of the king as the bringer of God's justice and righteousness. Note particularly there the concern that the king protect those who are unable to protect themselves, and it is quite likely that this special emphasis is implied in Jer. 33:14–16. In the coming days, with the arrival of this new member of the Davidic family, the people "will be saved" and "will live in safety" (v. 16). That the work of this king is to be nothing other than the work of Israel's very God is made emphatic by the name to be given to this new Branch: Yahweh Is Our Righteousness.

The beginning of Advent is a time of great gladness in the hearts of God's people for the obvious reason that Advent is a time for remembering the "coming" (that is, the "advent") of God's Son. The new David is about to appear in the Babe of Bethlehem, and all the carols of the season are about to burst forth. And while the reasons for our joy are well grounded, the Old Testament lection for this day also reminds us that not all is sweetness and light, for grace and judgment are closely connected in the thought of the prophets, in that God's judgment is the tragic side of God's just response to the reality of human sinfulness. Thus, there is also a quality of awe to Advent. The love of God finds its desired fulfillment in the redemption of the people, but this same love also results in judgment on human sinfulness. The Babe of Bethlehem who came so long ago to save is also the risen, victorious Christ who will come again, in the words of the Creed, "to judge the living and the dead."

The Advent season is a breaking into our "ordinary" days to remind us that the Babe who came will come again, that the First Advent is prelude to the Second. "The days are surely coming, says the LORD."

## Psalm 25:1–10

Psalm 25 is an acrostic poem. This form, in which each line starts with a successive letter of the Hebrew alphabet, is often accused of being rigid and artificial; however, it artistically conveys the concept of completeness. In this regard, it is revealing that the very middle letter in the acrostic pattern begins v. 10 with a word that itself conveys comprehensiveness: "*All* the paths of the LORD are steadfast love and faithfulness" (emphasis added).

The centrality of v. 10, or perhaps vs. 10–11 together, is reinforced by other features of the psalm. For instance, the repetition of two key words near the beginning and end of the psalm serves as a sort of frame, which directs attention toward the center (see "shame" in vs. 2, 3, 20; "wait" in vs. 3, 5, 21). Focusing toward the center is also achieved by the change in person. Verses 1–7 are in the first person (except v. 3), as are vs. 15–21. In contrast, vs. 8–14 are in the third person, except v. 11. The effect is to draw attention to the central section, especially to v. 11. Since vs. 10 and 11 are linked conceptually (see below), they form a theological center for the psalm. While Ps. 25 is a prayer, it is also a source of instruction about God, whose character it is to be faithful and steadfastly loving toward sinful humanity.

The first line of Ps. 25 anticipates the fundamental affirmation and plea of vs. 10–11. Because God is faithful and loving, the psalmist entrusts his or her life to God. The verse could also be translated, "To you, O Lord, I offer my life" (see Ps. 96:8; Ezek. 20:31 where the verb "lift up" means to bring an offering). To offer one's life to God involves trusting God amid threatening circumstances (Ps. 25:2). As is always the case, faith and hope are inseparable. To offer one's life to God means to live with hope, to "wait" for the Lord (v. 3; see vs. 5, 21). In God is the psalmist's only hope of not being defeated or "put to shame" by enemies or circumstances (vs. 2–3; see v. 20).

In two other psalms the psalmist also says, "I lift up my soul" to God (86:4; 143:8). In both of these contexts, as in Ps. 25, the psalmist affirms his or her trust in God (86:2; 143:8) and appeals to God's steadfast love (86:5, 13, 15; 143:8, 12) as the basis for trust. As in Ps. 25:4, 5 (see vs. 8, 9, 12), the offering of the self to God is accompanied by the request that God teach the psalmist God's way (86:11; 143:8, 10). Faith and hope in God are characterized by openness to God's instruction and God's leading. The word "way(s)" occurs four times (Ps. 25:4, 8, 9, 12), and the same Hebrew root underlies the English "lead(s)" in vs. 5 and 9. "Way" connotes "way of life" or lifestyle, and in this regard v. 9 is particularly interesting. Its chiastic structure ("leads . . . humble . . . humble . . . way") has the visual effect of surrounding the humble with God's "way" or God's leading. The lifestyle of those who trust God will be characterized by humility— openness to God's teaching and reliance not on the self but on God.

The psalmist is confident that God does teach and lead (vs. 8–9, 12), but is also very aware of his or her failure to follow (vs. 7, 11, 18). Thus, the basis of the offering of the self to God (v. 1) is not the psalmist's own worthiness, but rather the need for forgiveness. In vs. 6–7, the appeal is to God's "mercy" (or "motherly compassion"; the word is related to the Hebrew word that means "womb") and "steadfast love." The word "remember" occurs three times (NRSV "Be mindful" in v. 6). What the psalmist requests is that God not remember sins, but rather remember God's own character (v. 6): "according to your steadfast love remember me" (v. 7).

The mention of "mercy," "steadfast love," "sins," and "transgressions" in vs. 6–7 anticipates the theological center in vs. 10–11. The vocabulary in these four verses is strongly reminiscent of Ex. 34:6–9, the revelation of God's self to Moses and Moses' response at the conclusion of the golden calf episode which begins in Ex. 32:1 (see "steadfast love" in Ps. 25:6, 7, 10, and Ex. 34:6–7; "faithfulness" in Ps. 25:10 and Ex. 34:6; "pardon" in Ps. 25:11 and Ex. 34:9; "guilt"/"iniquity" in Ps. 25:11 and Ex. 34:7, 9; "sin(s)" and "transgression(s)" in Ps. 25:7 and Ex. 34:7). Especially when heard against the narrative background of Ex. 32—34, Ps. 25 is an eloquent testimony to the character of God, a God whose commitment to sinful people requires that God's fundamental attributes be steadfast love, mercy, and grace (Ps. 25:16; see Ex. 34:6). These attributes take concrete form in God's willingness to forgive (Ps. 25:11, 18), which is the good news that enables the psalmist to offer his or her life to God (v. 1).

The author and/or editors of Ps. 25 clearly had been instructed by and knew the stories of God's past faithfulness and forgiveness (the Jewish designation for the books of Genesis—Deuteronomy is the Torah, which means "instruction"). They were also open to God's ongoing instruction ("instructs" and "teach" in Ps. 25:8 and 12 are translations of the Hebrew root from which the noun "torah" is derived); and their testimony to God takes the form of a prayer that begins and ends with a commitment to wait for the Lord (vs. 3, 5, 21). Such testimony is appropriate for Advent, during which we both celebrate God's past faithfulness (Christ's birth, or first coming) and continue to wait for the Lord (see Luke 21:25–36, which directs attention to Christ's second coming). Like the psalmist, we wait penitently, offering our lives to God to receive forgiveness. And we wait both confidently and humbly, requesting God's instruction and trusting that God will empower us to learn and do new things.

## 1 Thessalonians 3:9–13

While epistles are not narratives in the strict sense of the word (like Gospels), they nevertheless have stories to tell. They often relate what has happened in the past involving the writer and the audience as actors, what is going on in the present, and what might be anticipated in the future. Occasionally the story gets so enmeshed in the "message" of the letter that it is hard to piece it out. Invariably, however, a plot emerges, and the letter itself becomes a critical event in the very story being told. Sometimes we are left wondering how it all turns out in the end.

The lection for this first Sunday of the year from 1 Thessalonians (3:9–13) makes sense as we read it in light of the letter's story. The plot begins with Paul's ministry in Thessalonica, coming on the heels of the rough treatment he had received from opponents in the neighboring city of Philippi (2:2). The first chapter of the letter relates the diligence, gentleness, and steadfastness of Paul's work and the model response of the readers. We learn that Paul, after leaving Thessalonica, becomes anxious for the struggling Christian community because of persecutions they are having to endure and grieves that he cannot come to see them. But he sends his trusted coworker Timothy to encourage them and to bring a report of their situation (2:17–3:5).

The letter, then, is written in light of Timothy's report, a report that is basically positive and encouraging (though we learn that some readers are despondent over the delay of Jesus' return and the deaths of friends, while others have quit supporting themselves in their enthusiastic pursuit of spiritual matters [4:13–5:14]). The text for this Sunday is a particular expression of delight and gratitude for the progress of the believers at Thessalonica and a petition to God in their behalf for their continued growth.

What gives the passage an appropriate "Advent" setting is the sensitivity that everything the actors in the story do is done in anticipation of "the coming of our Lord Jesus with all his saints" (3:13). The plot has a projected closure, and the closure gives meaning to all the events that occur along the way. The return of Jesus is not posed as a threat to keep the troops in line, but as a conclusion to the human story, when the faithful life of the believers will come to light.

Two words occur in the petition made in behalf of the readers that appear (with their cognates) frequently throughout the letter and that immediately get our attention: love and holiness. Love has characterized the life of the Christian community at Thessalonica from its very beginnings. Paul remembers their "work of faith and labor of love and steadfastness of hope" (1:3). Timothy's report reinforces that perception and prompts Paul to ask God that their love may "increase and abound" (3:12).

What is striking about the reference is the double community to which the love relates. On the one hand, there is to be "love for one another." Within the Christian congregation there are relationships to be nurtured, the despondent to be encouraged, the idle to be prodded. The mutual needs and tensions of church members are not to be ignored in a greater cause of evangelism or social action. The internal life of the community, whether profound or superficial, whether peaceful or strife-ridden, will in fact make a witness, and the critical question is what kind of witness.

On the other hand, the petition asks for love "for all." The line between the church and the world is not one that tells us whom to love and whom to ignore or disdain. The circles God draws are inclusive, not exclusive, and they direct the compassion of the Christian community beyond itself and its own needs.

The second word of prominence in the text is holiness, a word that with its cognates occurs six times in this brief letter. Holiness names the quality of life that distinguishes the Christian community from the world. "The saints" (or "the holy ones") are the people chosen and set apart by God, who at the coming of Jesus will prove to be blameless.

The notion of holiness often connotes a rigid style of life that follows a clearly definable code of ethics. One is holy if one does this or that, or refrains from doing this or that. Such a connotation is reinforced by 1 Thessalonians, which some commentators have labeled "a letter of moral exhortation." What is particularly noteworthy in this letter is that twice holiness is mentioned in a petitionary prayer (3:13; and 5:23, where "sanctify" could be rendered "make holy"). We discover that God alone makes people holy and qualifies them as blameless at the coming of Jesus. All one's valiant efforts to follow the moral exhortations do not produce holiness. It is the gift of a gracious God, whose Son comes at Christmas and yet once again.

## Luke 21:25–36

With its warning about the day that may "catch you unexpectedly, like a trap" (Luke 21:34–35), this Gospel reading could seem painfully appropriate for Christians who know that the First Sunday of Advent carries in its wake the customary if much-lamented December frenzy. The awareness that the annual "trap" of holiday preparation is about to spring once again brings with it all the usual anxiety and excitement.

Behind the wry smiles that may greet admonitions to alertness, however, many may find the presence of this passage in the Advent readings somewhat odd. The church's traditional connection between the first coming of Jesus at his birth and his second coming at the Parousia is more acknowledged than understood. What possible connection can there be between the anticipated birth of one tiny infant and the "roaring of the sea" or the shaking of the "powers of the heavens"? How can this advent be said to "come upon all who live on the face of the whole earth"?

The immediate problem of interpreting the connection between First and Second Advents is complicated, of course, by the difficulties many modern readers have with apocalyptic language. Those who cannot anticipate a literal fulfillment of passages such as this one find themselves skipping over them entirely or muttering vague phrases that never quite satisfy anyone.

The language of the text itself is anything but vague. Catastrophe among human beings follows upon cosmic uproar in the heavens and on earth. Such fear seizes people that they actually faint. Even the heavens are shaken. Finally, the Son of Man himself appears in a cloud.

For the reader acquainted with Scripture, this passage may not appear all that odd. To identify a few examples, Joel 2:30 refers to "portents in the heavens and on the earth" (see the use of the same passage in Acts 2:17–21). Isaiah 24:19 says, "The earth is violently shaken." Psalm 46:6 comments on the "uproar" of the nations and Ps. 89:9 on the "raging of the sea." In fact, the passage can be thought of as a veritable patchwork quilt of phrases from the Old Testament.

For the reader acquainted with Scripture, this passage conjures up an expectation about divine intervention into the way the world is rather than some specific event that can be predicted and described. This language will remain larger than life, for that is what apocalyptic language does: it uses unimaginably large language to anticipate unimaginably important events.

Precisely because vs. 25–28 do anticipate divine intervention in the way things are, the remainder of the passage concerns itself with the appropriate human attitude to that inevitable intervention. First, vs. 29–33 insist that these signs of the future have become, in fact, signs of the present day. Just as the coming of new leaves always and inevitably indicates that summer will soon be at hand, so Jesus' words indicate that the kingdom of God lies close at hand (vs. 29–31). Verses 32–33 provide solemn assurances of the faithfulness of Jesus' promise. The first response of human beings, then, is to trust. Just as Scripture can be trusted, so may the words of Jesus.

The final verses of the lection admonish wariness. Other concerns ought not lead the faithful to be forgetful about the day that is to come (v. 34). No one can escape it (v. 35). Therefore, all should be "alert," "praying that you may have the strength to escape . . . and to stand before the Son of Man" (v. 36).

Watchfulness, wariness, vigilance—these attitudes come to the fore in this passage. The initial depiction of the apocalyptic signs concludes with the admonition to "stand up and raise your heads" in anticipation of the coming redemption (v. 28). Again in v. 31, the kingdom is near and believers should be on the alert. Verses 34 and 36 bring that warning to the foreground.

Waiting and watching are not easy, precisely because other things do interfere. If not all Christians are overcome by "dissipation and drunkenness," most do find themselves threatened by "the worries of this life." Provisions for family, difficulties related to work, concerns about the affairs of government, clamoring after power and status—both things worthy and things trivial have a way of clouding the vision so that the impending kingdom of God remains somehow just out of sight. One way of summarizing this passage might be to say that "things are not necessarily what they appear to be." To look only at things that seem to be close at hand is to miss the larger picture.

At just that point this passage becomes particularly appropriate for the First Sunday of Advent. Things are not what they seem. Normalcy and predictability have disappeared forever. The pregnancy of one more teenager is no longer an ordinary matter; indeed, the pregnancy of this particular teenager provides the overture to a cosmic event. In the birth of a helpless baby all the powers of the universe find that the days of their own power are numbered. Nothing will again be the same. Watch!

# SECOND SUNDAY OF ADVENT

At Advent something is afoot in God's world. There is a terrible, hopeful newness about life: terrible because it promises to overthrow all our old, comfortable, sinful ways; and hopeful for the very same reason. We know its shape, and yet we do not know it. It is the working of the same God who, in ancient times, brought Israel out of Egypt, established Israel in the land, forced Israel into exile and reestablished Israel in the land. But this "old" God is breaking in upon human life in awesomely new ways—a Babe in a manger, a crucified, risen Lord, a triumphant return.

The texts for this day capture something of this terrible hope, this ancient newness. In a passage that the church from earliest times has associated with the Christ-event (Mal. 3:1–4), the prophet Malachi (Hebrew for "my messenger") speaks of a coming messenger of Yahweh who will accomplish the purification of Yahweh's people by means of judgment. As the fire of the metallurgist separates the precious metal from the dross, as the launderer's soap purges the grime, so the messenger of Yahweh will banish sin from the life of the people. "But who can endure the day of his coming?"

The "Psalm" for this day is the Benedictus from Luke 1:68–79, the song of Zechariah on the occasion of the birth and circumcision of his John (soon, the Baptist). It is, among other things, a recital of God's saving intervention in the history of Israel. The God who "has remembered his holy convenant" (v. 72) is now making good on the promise of the prophets of old "that we would be saved from our enemies" (v. 71). John is the messenger of the Lord who, in language that recalls the promise of Malachi, "will go before the Lord to prepare his ways" (v. 76).

The passage from Philippians (1:3–11) is a prayer in which Paul reminds his readers that a trustworthy God will bring to fruition the work of salvation that was begun so long ago (that astonishing "ancient newness"). And what is the consummation of that work?

10

Nothing other than "the day of Jesus Christ" (vs. 6, 10), which will not only signal the completion of God's work of redemption, but will also—so Paul hopes—find his Philippian friends morally and spiritually whole before God.

The Gospel lection (Luke 3:1–6) is a brief introduction, in prose and in poetry, to the narrative concerning the work of John the Baptist. After identifying, in typical Lukan fashion, the moment in time by means of reference to powerful political and religious figures in John's world, Luke draws on the Old Testament prophetic tradition for words by which to validate the ministry of John. Although the Old Testament quotation is from Isa. 40, it nonetheless echoes the phrases of Mal. 3:1–4. John is clearly the one who has come to "prepare the way of the LORD" (Isa. 40:3; Mal. 3:1), the one who, in defiance of those who *apparently* exercise power, is on hand to proclaim the kingdom of the *truly* powerful, Jesus Christ.

## Malachi 3:1–4

That Advent is a time of preparation is clear to all who take the season seriously, especially to all who take seriously the biblical texts associated with Advent. Yet the sense of preparation with which many Christians approach these first four weeks in the church's liturgical year consists of the joyful anticipation of the events of the Bethlehem manger. "For God so loved the world that he gave his only Son" is perhaps as apt a text as any to summarize our Advent readiness. "Joy to the world" is as appropriate a hymn as any. Love and joy thus become the watchwords of the season.

While there is no denying the persistent reality of these qualities as Advent themes, it is easy to overlook another reality, and that is that Advent is also a season of anticipation, or even apprehension, over the coming of Christ the Judge, the One who will set straight all the world's wrongs by presiding in glory and in justice over a sinful humankind. In other words, Advent is the season of preparation not only for the first coming of our Lord, but also for the second.

The lection from Mal. 3 brings to the forefront of our thinking these "other" images of Advent.

Because we have virtually no idea of the historical context in which Malachi lived and worked (or, indeed, whether "Malachi" is a person's name or simply a euphemism ["my messenger"] for some anonymous prophet or prophets), we are in the dark concerning the immediate object of the prophetic words. Perhaps Malachi is expecting some military figure to be raised up by God to purge evil out of the life of God's people. Or perhaps—and more likely—the prophet is describing some eschatological agent of God who will usher in a final, righteous era in the history of Israel and of humankind.

Be that as it may, the church has traditionally interpreted these verses as a statement about John the Baptist and has linked them with Mal. 4:5. A new Elijah will arise, or, in the view of the church, has already arisen in order to judge the people and in order to usher in the coming kingdom of God.

In spite of the fact that John himself is recorded as denying this association (John 1:21), and in spite of other early interpretations that connected the Elijah role with Jesus himself (Matt. 16:14; Luke 9:8), the church has continued to consider the ministry of John as fulfillment of the words of Mal. 3:1–4; 4:5–6.

Our text for this day begins on a note of great good news: the messenger of Yahweh of hosts, the God of Israel, is about to appear. The coming of this noble figure is by no means unexpected, for this is the one "whom you seek," the one "in whom you [the people] delight." (Note carefully here that the "Lord" ['Adōn] of Mal. 3:1 is not the same as the "LORD [YHWH] of hosts" of that same verse. The first figure is the messenger of Yahweh, the second is the very God of Israel.) Nevertheless, he comes "suddenly," and his role is that of the "messenger of the covenant." Whatever else this title may represent, it is surely a sign that the work of this messenger, this 'Adōn, involves the life of the community of faith, for it is with none other than the faithful people that Yahweh holds covenant.

But the glad tidings with which the lection opens are soon transformed into a mood of apprehension. The messenger may be a news bringer, but the news that he brings is a word of judgment. The justice of God, which this coming one represents, is so thorough in its determination that it is doubtful that any may survive unscathed. "Who can endure the day?" "Who can stand?" (v. 2). The reason for this tension is announced without equivocation. (The manner in which NRSV divides v. 2 into parts of two paragraphs is not sustained by the Hebrew text nor by the conceptual flow of the passage. It would be preferable to include all of v. 2 in the second paragraph of our lection.) The messenger of the covenant, as Yahweh's agent, will consume human impurities in the same manner in which a metallurgist's fire consumes the dross, and in the same way that a strong detergent eliminates contaminants. The people of God will be reshaped into the image that Yahweh intends for them, an image of righteousness. Then and only then will they be able to present righteous offerings to their Lord.

(The specific object of Yahweh's judgment would seem to be the

priesthood, the "descendants of Levi" of v. 3. But it is likely that in
the prophet's mind the priests are representatives of all Israel.)

Thus, in this text the church is confronted by the reality that the
Advent expectation is not just a longing for the "sweet little Jesus
boy" of the wonderful old spiritual. It is also the anticipation that
with the coming of God's messenger the world is put on notice that
things are about to change, that old wrongs are about to be uprooted
and replaced with the values of God. This new day will, in reality, be
a return to a former time, the "days of old" of v. 4, when the world
was younger and human life was lived nearer the heart of God.

## Luke 1:68–79

Instead of a reading from the Psalter, the lectionary appropriately
proposes for the Second Sunday of Advent the song of Zechariah,
sometimes called the Benedictus (from the initial word of the Latin
text) but more accurately defined as a "berakah" (the Jewish prayer
of blessing). The song/prayer is one of the several canticles that
appear in the midst of Luke's long and carefully organized birth
narrative. As in a Broadway musical, characters break into song at
critical moments, each a hymn of praise for the marvelous activity of
God.

The introductory verse (Luke 1:67) indicates that this song of
praise is also a prophecy. The reader is told ahead of time where the
narrative will lead. Not unlike the music of many Broadway scores,
the lyrics provide an all-important interpretation of the story—
what's *really* happening and what is going to happen.

Three observations about the content of the canticle: First, the role
of John is defined by the role of Jesus. In light of the strange
circumstances regarding the choice of his name, the question is
raised about John by Elizabeth and Zechariah's neighbors. "What
then will this child become?" (1:66). But the song/prayer, instead of
giving an immediate response, launches into a blessing of God for
the visitation and redemption of Israel through "a horn of salvation"
(RSV), who comes in the Davidic line (1:68–75). The redemptive agent
is depicted as a fulfillment of the ancestral hope, one whom the
people are to serve without fear. Only after God is praised for the
coming deliverance does the focus turn to John—and then only for
two verses (1:76–77)—before returning to the theme of God's mercy
and salvation.

John's importance lies in who he is and what he does in relation to
Jesus: a prophet to go before the Lord to prepare his ways (an

allusion to Mal. 3:1). His story really matters because it is encompassed by the larger story of God's compassion for Israel. As in the Fourth Gospel, John becomes a model for the church and its members, whose identity and individuality lie not in an isolated uniqueness but in their role as players in the divine drama of the salvation of the world. Their autobiographies make sense when they engage and are engaged by God's story.

Second, the canticle serves as a brief history of salvation. The numerous allusions and echoes of Old Testament passages undergird what is explicitly affirmed in the text—that God is beginning to fulfill promises and honor oaths made long ago. The saving story did not begin with John and Jesus, but with Abraham, later involving David and the prophets. Though the people of Israel often forgot the undergirding promises, God did not, and now in a time of depression they are recalled and their initial fulfillment announced.

Christmas, then, is first and foremost a celebration of the faithfulness of God, a reminder that the chosen people have not been abandoned, that the commitments made and frequently renewed have not slipped God's mind. The RSV translation of Luke 1:68 puts it nicely in saying that God "has *visited* and redeemed his people" (emphasis added).

Third, the language used in the canticle to depict the coming salvation is intriguing. On the one hand, it is shockingly this-worldly and political. The kingship of David is recalled, and the hope is "that we would be saved from our enemies and from the hand of all who hate us" (1:71). There is no hint that the salvation will consist of an escape from the human arena, from the world of conflict and tribulation, from a time of risks and uncertainties. No doubt the continued domination of the Romans made the original readers pause and wonder. For them (and for us), the ancient promises were only beginning to be completed and much still awaited (and awaits) divine resolution.

On the other hand, the language of salvation is highly religious. Deliverance comes not by the military defeat of the oppressors, but by the forgiveness of sins, by the light that illuminates darkness and death, by walking in the way of peace (1:75–79).

Both the this-worldly expressions and the religious expressions seem critical; neither are to be avoided. In the Lukan narrative, in fact, the two types belong together. Salvation is not a purely spiritual matter, but neither is it equated with political freedom. It consists in the service of God without fear, a service that entails both holiness and righteousness (1:74–75). A "saved" people is characterized by a distinctive piety *and* a passion for justice.

## Philippians 1:3–11

It may seem strange to find this prayer of thanksgiving that opens Paul's letter to the Philippians designated as a reading for the Advent season. Normally such prayers represent Paul's adaptation of the traditional letter form of the Greco-Roman period and are often expressed in stereotypical phrases intended as a rhetorical device to build a base with the readers. The prayers anticipate the more meaty matters to come in the body of a letter.

The prayer that begins Philippians clearly telegraphs at least two critical themes of the letter—the reliable God who will see to the completion of what has been begun, and the importance of discernment in the moral life. And yet these two motifs gain their significance because of their setting between the advents, between "the first day"(1:5) and "the day of Jesus Christ" (1:6, 10). The eschatological language provides a dynamic framework in which to reflect on God's activity and the demands laid on the Christian community.

The use of "day" as an eschatological symbol goes back at least as far as the time of Amos, who warns a presumptuous Israel that "the day of the LORD" can turn out to be darkness and not light (Amos 5:18–20). In the prayer of thanksgiving, "day" occurs in two ways. The initial reception of the gospel is designated as "the first day" (Phil. 1:5). Hearing the word of God's grace and sharing with others in its power is like Eden all over again. It is the beginning of life, the creation of something entirely new. But the final day, the day toward which life is aimed, is "the day of Jesus Christ" (1:6, 10). It is the point of Jesus' return, when the veil will be removed and the good beginnings will be completed.

The church lives between the two days. The first day is not to be confused with the last day. The personal and moral ambiguities that continually confront us result from the fact that "the day of Jesus Christ" remains in the future. We live in an expectant, but unfulfilled, world. And yet our confidence in God's promise and our growth in discernment are more than pipe dreams because of "the first day" and the light it casts on those in-between days in which we find ourselves.

Look at two of the themes developed in this context. First, the great affirmation of 1:6 reminds the readers that the present is a time for God's activity in a venture that God, not the readers, has begun. God ultimately leaves no buildings unfinished, no battles in doubt, no chaos unresolved. The fact that the morning headlines and the nightly news do not always provide obvious reassurance of such a conviction would come as no surprise to Paul or his readers. He is in prison (1:12–14), and they are anticipating suffering (1:29–30). Yet the certainty about God's intentions makes possible a positive interpretation of their situations, even seeing them as gifts of divine grace.

Verse 6 has been understood at various times in the church's history as implying that the circumstances of people in the world are going to get better and better until they reach an omega-point, the day of Christ, and that it is the task of Christians and other like-minded folk to work for that moment. We are under commission to build the kingdom of God, and its growth can be plotted like an upward-moving line on a graph. The problem with such a reading is that it overlooks the fact that the subject of the sentence is God (and the fact that life does not confirm it). *God* will bring to completion the good work already begun. God may use believers as agents in the divine mission, but the burden of finishing and the timetable for completion are God's, not the church's. In this letter at least, the responsibility of believers is much more modest—growth in perception, living in unity, coping with anxiety, demonstrating a servant vocation.

The "good work" already begun is not to be reduced to what is happening in the life of the individual. The second-person pronouns used throughout the passage are all plural, suggesting that what God has begun is a communal project expressed in the corporate body of believers. To the modern church faced with a bleak future because of the erosion of membership, the affirmation of 1:6 becomes a word of hope.

The second critical theme emerges in the petition for a love that will "overflow more and more with knowledge and full insight" to enable the readers "to determine what is best" (1:9–10). The delay of "the day of Christ" means that believers are confronted with all manner of moral ambiguities and decisions that demand clear discernment. What is prayed for is not so much a matter of determining right from wrong as a setting of priorities, of distinguishing ultimate from penultimate matters, of sorting out what is important from what is trivial.

Some things in life make a great difference; much is at stake (v. 10). Other matters are relatively inconsequential. Paul later in this letter cites wealth as a matter of little significance (4:11–12). He prays for his readers that they may develop the gift of discernment and do the things that really matter. A Pauline scholar has written, "Love fills up one's life and informs all moral knowing and doing in such a way that one sorts out and does the things that really matter. . . . Living thus, believers confidently arrive at the day of Christ with no fear of judgment" (J. Paul Sampley, *Walking Between the Times;* Minneapolis: Fortress, 1991, p. 83).

## Luke 3:1–6

This lesson begins somewhat abruptly. No word of transition helps the reader connect chapter 3 with the infancy narrative that precedes it. Once again Luke sets the stage by indicating the names of those who are in charge of the world. It appears that Luke begins his story all over again with the opening of this lesson (3:1).

On the other hand, certain features of this passage do connect it with what has come before, although subtly. John comes on the scene as "John son of Zechariah" (3:2), ensuring that the reader knows that this is the grown-up child of the astonished Zechariah and Elizabeth. More important, Luke depicts John in a way that unmistakably identifies him as a prophet, indicating that he is now fulfilling the words that were spoken concerning him even prior to his birth (Luke 1:13–17; see also 1:67–80). The one who was intended "to make ready a people prepared for the Lord" (1:17) stands poised to do just that.

Given these important connections between the infant John and the prophet John, why the elaborate introduction of the rulers' names in 3:1–2—an introduction that appears to threaten the sense of continuity and begin the story all over again? First, Luke here follows a pattern established in a number of Old Testament prophetic writings, in which the book itself begins by reference to the ruler's name (see, for example, Jer. 1:2; Micah 1:1; Zeph. 1:1). Second, this introduction follows a pattern Luke has already employed twice in the infancy narrative itself. He introduces Zechariah with "In the days of King Herod of Judea" (1:5), and he begins the story of Jesus' birth with reference to the emperor Augustus and the governor Quirinius. Third, this most elaborate of the three introductions allows Luke a presentation of figures who will be important later in the Gospel—Pilate and Herod.

This introduction does more than simply fulfill formal expectations or anticipate characters whose real work comes later in Luke's story. By elaborating this list of rulers, Luke provides some indication of who is—or who appears to be—in charge of things. He begins with the most formidable figure of Tiberius, emperor of Rome. Then he lists the governors of various territories in the vicinity of the ministry of Jesus—Pilate, Herod, Philip, and Lysanias. Then he moves on to religious authorities, Annas and Caiaphas (although how both can oe said to be high priest remains a problem, as the commentaries will indicate). The rulers of the earth are in their places.

But wait! In the midst of the status quo, Luke writes that "the word of God came to John son of Zechariah in the wilderness." John is neither emperor nor governor nor priest, but it is to John that the "word of God" comes. And it comes not in Rome nor in any other seat of power, but "in the wilderness," an unexpected place indeed.

Within the announcement of this prophetic call and its interpretation by means of the quotation from Isa. 40:3–5, three themes emerge that will be important throughout Luke-Acts: the word of God, repentance, and the salvation of God. The "word of God" (*rēma tou theou*) that comes to John consists, in the first instance, of his prophetic call and the proclamation that follows (see also Acts 2:14; 5:20). In the book of Acts, however, a closely related phrase (*logos tou theou*) becomes a way of referring to the gospel and its embodiment in the church. The apostles proclaim the "word of God" (Acts 6:2); it grows and multiplies despite persecution (12:24).

John's proclamation concerns "a baptism of repentance for the forgiveness of sins." This proclamation not only prepares the way for the coming of Jesus, but anticipates the work of the church. John's action serves as a prototype of the church's preaching of baptism and its declaration that in Jesus, God forgives human sins.

What is at stake in the prophetic activity of John is nothing less than "the salvation of God." Already the infancy narratives of chapters 1 and 2 have sounded this central Lukan theme of salvation. Zechariah declares that John's role will be "to give knowledge of salvation" (Luke 1:77), and Simeon addresses God concerning Jesus as "your salvation" (2:30). As late as Paul's final words in Acts, the "salvation of God" dominates Luke's concerns (Acts 28:28).

Within Luke's two volumes, then, John "son of Zechariah" serves as an able "forerunner" for Luke's theology of the word of God, the preaching of forgiveness, and the salvation of all people. In the context of Advent, John serves as the one who reminds Christians of the need to be prepared for the Christ who is to come. The task of making the highways workable again, repairing them so that "all flesh" can indeed see God's salvation, is a task that the church dare not neglect.

At the same time, the selection of John as the vehicle of God's word reminds the church that the word of God does emerge in unlikely places. The rulers of the world and the rulers of the church continue in their ways, content with things as they are, perhaps lulled into believing that they are in fact the "rulers." The advent of the infant Jesus will demonstrate that real power lies elsewhere.

# THIRD SUNDAY OF ADVENT

A single theme dominates the lections for this day: joy over what the Lord has done and will do. But it is not a giddy, senseless type of joy, unaware of the harsh realities of the human situation. Rather it is a joy that is anchored to an acknowledgment of God's love and presence in human life. Because this joy takes seriously the distance between God's hopes for human life, on the one hand, and the realities of that life as it is actually lived, on the other, it is all the more wonderful. It is also a joy that is all the more intense because it is kindled amid circumstances in which joy is least expected.

The text from Zephaniah (3:14–20) is quite astonishing. Some of the gloomiest passages in all of the Old Testament appear in Zephaniah, the book of a prophet who was apparently driven to near-despair over the sorry conditions of Judah's life in the years following the reign of evil King Manasseh. But almost without warning the night clouds dissipate and the day breaks. The prophet's imperative, "Rejoice and exult with all your heart" (3:14), displaces the earlier "wail from the Second Quarter" (1:10). The reason that joy has overtaken deep despondency is quite simple: "The king of Israel, [Yahweh], is in your midst" (3:15).

Isaiah 12:2–6 serves as the Psalm lection for this day, and it too sings of great joy. The text is a pivotal one in the structure of the book of Isaiah because it brings to a close that unit (chaps. 1—12) which contains some of the most important oracles of Isaiah of Jerusalem. The impression thus given is that this insightful personality, having seen all that he has of Judah's waywardness before God, emphasizes the joyful consequences of God's presence in the nation's life. It is a joy that compels faith and trust, a joy that insists that the people wait for the gracious outpouring of God's mercy.

The brief imperative to joy in Phil. 4:4–7 makes quite evident a reality present in the Zephaniah and Isaiah passages, but less emphasized there. That is that the joy which results from the presence of the Lord changes and reorients the life of the believer. Because women and men of faith have reason to rejoice, they are to live gently, holding anxiety at bay, as they pray and give thanks to the Lord. It all sounds very much like Pollyanna, until one realizes the reason for this life-changing joy: "The Lord is near" (Phil. 4:5).

The lection from Luke 3:7–18 does not appear very joyful on its face, for it is a summary narrative of the preaching of John the Baptist, a preaching that is thoroughly eschatological. But even here the theology flows in much the same currents as the other texts for the day. The presence of the Lord (the "one who . . . is coming" [3:16]) changes the nature of human life, so that justice, compassion, and honesty take the place of their opposites. Only by means of reordered lives can men and women escape "from the wrath to come" (3:7). This is clearly the "good news" (3:18) of the coming Lord.

## Zephaniah 3:14–20

No emotion is more welcomed into human life than that of joy. Joy is the realization that deeply held hopes have been or shortly will be fulfilled. Joy is also the dawning of an understanding that those events which have been most feared will not occur. But if joy is always one of the sweeter sensations of life, especially exultant is that joy which is completely unexpected, or which breaks suddenly into the midst of our gloom.

The present lection from Zephaniah speaks of such joy. Surely those scholars are correct who view Zeph. 3:14–20 as a postexilic addition to the corpus of sayings (or writings) of a prophetic individual who lived early in the reign of King Josiah (c. 640–609 B.C.). Yet in its canonical setting this passage stands as a sudden and not completely anticipated shout of great gladness. It is as if a deep and imponderable cloud has been pierced by a ray of sunlight! a funeral dirge punctuated by a carol of hope!

Would that the historical record had left us more information about the person whose name is associated with this brief anthology. The suggestion of the editorial introduction to the book (Zeph. 1:1) is that Zephaniah was the great-grandson of Judean King Hezekiah (c. 715–687 B.C.), of whom the Deuteronomistic historians record that "he did what was right in the sight of [Yahweh]" (2 Kings 18:3). But things had deteriorated to a sorry state by the time of the accession to the throne of Hezekiah's descendant (and thus Zephaniah's cousin) Josiah. During the interim, evil Manasseh had occupied the throne for almost half a century (c. 687–642 B.C.), with a resulting decay in faithfulness and morality (note 2 Kings 21:1–16). To be sure, Josiah would eventually set things straight (2 Kings 22—23), but that would take time. For the moment, faithful persons like Zephaniah could only lament the terrible realities of their world.

Those realities were so dreadful that the prophet concludes that Yahweh has no option but to destroy all creation (Zeph. 1:2–9). Yahweh will invade the darkness of Judah's heart like a person with lamps who ferrets out secret and hidden sins (1:12). The result will be a terrible day of judgment, a "bitter" day "of distress and anguish," "of ruin and devastation," "of darkness and gloom," "of clouds and thick darkness," "of trumpet blast and battle cry" (1:14–16)!

How astonishing, then, to reach the climax of this prophetic anthology and to discover words, not of despair, but of hope and great joy. It is as if the prophet, or someone writing in the prophet's name, has drawn us back from the chasm of judgment at the very last minute, so that our joy is rendered all the more intense because of the hopelessness out of which it has come. In historical terms, it would be more accurate to say that the joy of which 3:14–20 speaks has been generated by the sense that a terrible price has now been paid for the sinfulness of the nation, for almost surely our lection was written from the standpoint of a nation that had survived and recovered from exile. Yet, to return to the shape of the text as the tradition has presented it to us, we cannot escape the remarkable conclusion that that word from God which began as irredeemable judgment has been transformed into transcendent gladness. That which once anticipated the silence of the people (1:7) or, worse, their cries of sorrow (1:11) now celebrates their choruses of joy (3:14)!

It goes without saying that the roots of this joy do not lie in the strength or sudden goodness of the people. It is, rather, vested in the grace and benevolence of God. The God who is Israel's judge is also Israel's lover and partner in covenant. "The king of Israel, [Yahweh], is in your midst" (v. 15). The people should replace their fear with confidence and strength (v. 16), because Yahweh is like a mighty warrior who has championed the cause of the people (v. 17). Since Israel's warrior-God will now "rejoice" and "exult," so may Israel be caught up in the same emotions. Since Yahweh will "renew" Israel "in his love" (to follow the NRSV rendition, based on the Septuagint text), Israel may accept this love in gladness.

The power of this text as an Advent lection lies not only in its words of joy, but in the particular context in which these words are found. The church's "ordinary time," that extended season observed before Advent, is, among other things, a reminder of the mundane character of much of life. "Ordinary time" exists—in part, at least—as a paradigm of a sinful world to which the church is called by God to minister and to witness. The painful reality is, however, that the work of the kingdom is shot through with our own incompetence and sin and, if we were left to our own devices, we would be trapped in the midst of those very forces of darkness against which the church labors.

Advent, then, is the signal that in the midst of human darkness the light shines. The coming One draws near not to condemn the people, but to redeem them and to cast their lives into new patterns and shapes. "The king of Israel . . . is in your midst" (v. 15) is as sure a message for those who anticipate the birth of the Child as it was for those to whom the prophet spoke long ago.

The result is identical: profound joy and gladness!

## Isaiah 12:2–6

Isaiah 12:2–6 is a song of praise or thanksgiving that concludes chapters 1—12, a major unit within the book of Isaiah. Historical critics generally assign chapters 1—12 to the early career of eighth-century Isaiah of Jerusalem, who is portrayed primarily as announcing judgment on Judah. While this may be correct historically, it is clear that the book of Isaiah is much more complex. The opening chapters do contain announcements of judgment (1:2–31; 2:5–5:30; 9:8–21), but interspersed are several oracles of salvation that envision peace for Judah, Jerusalem, and indeed all the earth. These include 2:2–4, which some scholars suggest serves a programmatic function for the entire book of Isaiah, as well as the hope-filled messianic passages in 9:2–7 and 11:1–10 traditionally used during Advent. In fact, the phrase "in that day" in 12:4 (see also 12:1) links 12:2–6 to 11:10 (see also 2:2; 11:11); that is, 12:2–6 is presented as the song of those who await the promised salvific activity of God on behalf of Judah, Jerusalem, and all the earth.

As such, 12:2–6 represents the response invited by the whole book of Isaiah, which is addressed to people in waiting. The promised deliverance from Assyria (10:5–11:16) is actually narrated in the book of Isaiah (chs. 36—39); however, deliverance from Babylon (chs. 40—66) is promised (and even announced) but *not* narrated. This promised deliverance can be read in a historical context as return from exile, or it may be interpreted symbolically (see Edgar W. Conrad, *Reading Isaiah;* Minneapolis: Fortress Press, 1991, esp. pp. 49–51, 79–80, 158–68). In any case, readers of the entire book of Isaiah are left to await a new act of deliverance. They can wait faithfully and hopefully, because they know God has acted in the past to deliver the people. For the book of Isaiah as a whole, then, waiting involves an eye to the past as much as it does an eye to the future. The same is true for 12:2–6. Because it reveals to us what is involved in waiting for God, 12:2–6 is an appropriate text for Advent, a season that faces us toward the past (Christ's first coming) and toward the future (Christ's second coming).

Our passage begins with an affirmation of faith. Waiting for God inevitably involves faith, trust (see Heb. 11:1). The reference to "my salvation" envelops Isa. 12:2. Life is to be found in God, and the faith and courage with which the people await the future is rooted in God's past activity. The second half of v. 2 is a quotation of Ex. 15:2a, a line of the song that Moses and the Israelites sang immediately after being delivered from the Egyptians. The song in Ex. 15 culminates in the affirmation that "the LORD will reign forever and ever" (v. 18). Ultimately, hope is rooted in the conviction that God rules the world and that life depends on God. God is "my salvation," "my strength," "my might."

The affirmation of God's sovereignty is reinforced by the series of invitations in Isa. 12:4–5. The first three imperatives in v. 4 recall the beginning of Ps. 105, which rehearses God's deeds, especially the exodus (vs. 23–38). The final imperative in Isa. 12:4 recalls Ps. 148:13. Psalm 148 invites the recognition of God's sovereignty not only by all the peoples of the earth (v. 11), but also by everything in heaven and on earth (see vs. 1, 7). The affirmation that God "has done gloriously" (Isa. 12:5) recalls Ex. 15:7 (see the word "majesty"); and the repetition of "name" in Isa. 12:4 recalls the purpose of the exodus—to make "my name resound through all the earth" (Ex. 9:16).

Waiting for God, grounded in the conviction that God rules the world, will also involve joy (Isa. 12:3, 6). To be sure, God's future saving activity will be a source of joy (see Isa. 35:1, 10; 65:18), but those awaiting God's activity can already be joyful. This joy is not a superficial happiness, but rather partakes of suffering in the hope of glorification (see Rom. 8:17–25). In short, it is an eschatological joy, not unlike that of Jesus "who for the sake of the joy that was set before him endured the cross" (Heb. 12:2). This joy in waiting is an appropriate posture for Advent, especially for the Third Sunday of Advent, "Joy Sunday."

A final dimension of waiting for God involves praise and proclamation. To "give thanks" (Isa. 12:4) and to "sing praises" (v. 5) involves the proclamation of God's activity. What God has done is to be "known" (vs. 4, 5) both "among the nations" (v. 4) and "in all the earth" (v. 5). Those who wait for God are to be witnesses. As was the case with joy, God's future saving activity will form the content of praise and proclamation, but those awaiting God's new activity can already be witnesses. Again, this witness by those awaiting God's activity is especially appropriate for Advent, a season in which the people of God are invited both to anticipate God's new activity and to prepare to announce again to the world the good news of God's incarnation, in essence, that "great in your midst is the Holy One of Israel" (v. 6).

## Philippians 4:4–7

The all-important story behind these injunctions at the end of Philippians (4:4–7) is the situation of the author incarcerated somewhere in the Greco-Roman world—Rome, Ephesus, or Caesarea— and the readers either already experiencing or about to experience some form of persecution (1:12–14, 29–30). Jerked out of their literary and historical contexts, the exhortations connote an unrealistic attitude toward life, a Pollyanna religion that ignores the harsh tragedies and calls for a stoiclike serenity. But the stories of the author and the readers force us to take the injunctions with utmost seriousness. They emerge from and are directed to what some would call the dark side of human experience.

Verses 2–3 contain advice given to a specific situation in the congregation. Verses 4–7, however, are general exhortations, directed to the whole community, collectively and individually. The paragraph is composed of three injunctions:

Rejoice in the Lord. . . .

Let your gentleness be known. . . .

Do not worry about anything.

The first two are simply stated; the third includes a contrasting, positive exhortation to make requests to God with thanksgiving. At the close of the injunctions is a promise that God's peace will guard the hearts of those who pray. Between the first two injunctions and the third is the brief but surprising affirmation, "The Lord is near." Its intrusion into an otherwise neatly structured section breaks the pattern and serves to get our attention.

"The Lord is near" can be taken in two (not necessarily mutually exclusive) ways: temporally or spatially. If "near" is read as a temporal adverb, then the impending return of Jesus undergirds the injunctions. Believers are to rejoice, live gently, and be free of anxiety because the advent of the Lord is just around the corner, an advent that will right the wrongs of the present and fulfill God's purposes for the world.

If "near" is read as a spatial adverb, then it likely reflects the language of the psalms, where the Lord's constant nearness is offered as reassurance to the brokenhearted and those who seek him (Ps. 34:18; 119:151; 145:18). Whichever reading is chosen, the phrase sets the tone for the sermon during the Advent season. The presence of Jesus, whether thought of as historical or spiritual, creates the motivation for rejoicing, for gentleness, and for a life unburdened by anxiety.

The third injunction warrants special attention, since it speaks an immediate word to most people. Like Jesus' words in the Sermon on the Mount (Matt. 6:25–33), it tends to evoke a rejoinder—"Not worry? But you don't have children to rear, bills to pay, elderly parents to look out for, tension-filled jobs to do. There is no such thing as an anxiety-free life."

The text does not promise that the readers will be spared hard times or pressure-packed lives. Neither does it minimize those hard times as if the readers might be inclined to exaggerate, to make mountains out of molehills. The hard times are vividly detailed elsewhere in this letter. The text simply enjoins the readers in light of the nearness of the Lord not to be overcome with anxiety, as if events were out of control and the ultimate outcome of things were in doubt.

The antidote to worry is prayer—petitionary prayer and thanksgiving. In the midst of the hard times ("in everything"), people are to keep on making their requests of God, not forgetting to surround their petitions with thanksgiving. If the Lord is near, then the prayers do not go unheard, and that is more than enough reason for gratitude.

Notice that there is no promise here that our petitions will be granted in just the way we (or Paul or the Philippians) would like, such as release from prison or avoiding suffering. What is promised is the peace of God to stand guard, like a sentry, at the doors of our lives (both hearts and minds). In place of paralyzing anxiety is God's shalom, given in the midst of and perhaps in spite of the hard times. Such a promise is hard to fathom, since our tendency is to connect peace with the absence of strife, with a pressureless moment. Thus the reminder—the peace that "surpasses all understanding."

The text offers a particularly apt word for the Advent season, especially the harried, frantic days preceding Christmas, often so filled with anxiety that many are left with little joy and deep depression. The nearness of the Lord invites us to experience the time differently, to meet worry with prayer and thanksgiving, and to discover our lives protected by God's inscrutable peace.

## Luke 3:7–18

The habitual, predictable character of Advent makes it easy to think of this time of preparation as essentially benign. Music, exchange of gifts, decorations—various aspects of Advent celebrations suggest that the event that lies ahead is to be welcomed without hesitation or anxiety.

From beginning to end, Luke's report about the ministry of John the Baptist contradicts this cheery picture of what it means to prepare for the arrival of Jesus. The tone here is thoroughly eschatological, opening with the address of the crowds as "You brood of vipers!" (3:7) and concluding with the promise that Jesus will destroy the "chaff" with an "unquenchable fire" (3:17).

While all the report of John's preaching is eschatological, it contains three distinct sections: eschatological indictment (3:7–9), ethical preparation (3:10–14), and messianic promise (3:15–18).

That the first section of John's preaching is an indictment is unmistakable, as anyone who is addressed as a "viper" would surely agree! Nevertheless, the primary thrust of this section consists, not of a presentation of the specific faults of the audience, but of an announcement of the imminence of God's judgment. Here, as elsewhere, "the wrath to come" is an eschatological phrase that refers to the wrath of God, who will no longer withhold judgment (Isa. 13:9; Ezek. 7:19; Rom. 1:18). Luke 3:9 reinforces this aspect of the passage with its insistence that the ax is "even now" ready to strike.

The crowds respond in the way that the crowds at Pentecost will later respond to Peter's proclamation of the resurrected Jesus (Acts 2:37). "What then should we do?" implicitly acknowledges their guilt and opens the door for instruction. Each element in the instruction is concrete and specific (Luke 3:10–14). First, John tells the group as a whole that they must share food and clothing. Then, "even" the tax collectors repeat the question and receive a parallel response. That they must be told not to take more than is prescribed reflects the Roman tax system, which tacitly encouraged abuse of the local population. Finally, soldiers ask what they must do, and they also are instructed not to abuse the people. Since both the tax collectors and the soldiers would be Romans, or Jews who cooperate with Romans, John's call to repentance has here reached well beyond the confines of Israel.

When the crowds begin to speculate that John might himself be the Messiah, John responds swiftly with a promise about the one who is to come. Here again the element of eschatological judgment comes to the foreground, as the Messiah is depicted as the harvester who will "gather the wheat into his granary; but the chaff he will burn with unquenchable fire" (3:17). This strong echo of v. 9 connects the judgment of the Messiah directly to that of God.

This passage, with its language of unmitigated and impending judgment, seems at first glance to be out of place in Luke's Gospel. Luke, after all, is the evangelist who emphasizes the tender, forgiving character of Jesus. It is Luke who explains that the disciples fall asleep at the Mount of Olives "because of grief" (22:45); Luke also depicts Jesus as healing the ear of the high priest's slave when a disciple cuts it off at Jesus' arrest (22:51).

The distinctive character of John's preaching should not allow us to lose sight of the fundamental Lukan themes that appear in the passage, however. First, John insists that "God is able from these stones to raise up children to Abraham" (3:8). The power of God, already enacted in the miraculous births of John the Baptist and of Jesus, here serves to remind the people that they exist only as a direct result of God's will.

Second, each of the specific ethical instructions in vs. 10–14 concerns possessions, either the sharing of possessions or the prohibition against extortion and greed. The demand for justice in the handling of possessions runs throughout Luke, of course, beginning even in the Magnificat's emphasis on justice for the poor and the downfall of the mighty (1:46–55). Several of the stories in Acts depict the harm that befalls those who are attached to possessions (for example, Acts 5:1–11; 8:9–24). The threefold repetition of the demand for generosity within this one brief passage indicates how strong a concern it is for Luke.

Third, when John speaks about the Messiah who is to come, he does so in terms of baptism "with the Holy Spirit and fire." The coming of the Holy Spirit in the fiery tongues of Pentecost and the subsequent guidance of the church by the Spirit fulfills this promise for the church. In Luke's story, however, the Spirit is active even before Jesus' birth, assisting those who interpret the remarkable events that are unfolding (Luke 1:41; 2:27–32).

The lection concludes with the narrator's comment that John preached to the people with "many other exhortations," but it would be inappropriate to stop reading with v. 18. Verses 19–20, after all, indicate that John the Baptist and Jesus have one more experience in common. Both are rejected for their proclamation. The One whose coming Advent anticipates is also the One the world continues to reject.

# FOURTH SUNDAY OF ADVENT

The final Sunday in Advent is a time of heightened expectation, as it moves the church from the anticipation of God's promised fulfill-ment to a realization of that fulfillment. The realization is, of course, only partial and fragmentary. The Babe is to be born in Bethlehem's manger, but much suffering and struggle lie ahead for him until the completion of his earthly mission. And much suffering and struggle lie ahead for the people of God, in that the final fulfillment of all that God has promised will not be realized until the Second Advent, the return of him who was a Babe but is now reigning Savior and Lord.

The texts for this Sunday capture something of this flavor of "already, but not yet." Micah 5:2–5a appears in a context that reflects difficult times for the people of God, perhaps the fall of Jerusalem in 587 B.C. Suddenly, however, the prophet begins to speak in tones of joy. Little Bethlehem, of small consequence in so many ways, will give to Israel the One who will rule in peace. And this is to be no ordinary ruler of the house of David, but one whose origins are "from ancient days" and who "shall be great to the ends of the earth." The rule of this wonderful King is yet to come, but its joyful effect is already felt in the hearts of those who are aware of his nearness.

The Psalm lection, Ps. 80:1–7, is a prayer that pleads for the advent of Yahweh, the "Shepherd of Israel." The psalmist is deeply aware that the people's resources are inadequate to meet the demands placed on them and that, without Yahweh's intervention in their lives, they are lost. The text reverberates with urgent imperatives: "Give ear" (v. 1), "save us" (v. 2), "let your face shine, that we may be saved" (vs. 3, 7)! The passage is a moving reminder that, unless Yahweh brings divine grace to bear on the human condition, there is no hope.

Hebrews 10:5–10 may appear to be a surprising Advent text, focusing as it does on the sacrificial death of Christ. But the passage serves as an important reminder that Advent and Christmas are not

29

meant to be times of romantic sentimentality. Rather the First
Advent had a larger purpose, which extended all the way to Good
Friday and Easter. Jesus was born in order that the crucified, risen
Christ might redeem sinful men and women.

The Gospel lection, Luke 1:39–45, is the narrative of the meeting of
Mary and Elizabeth, the pregnant mothers-to-be of Jesus and John, a
text that highlights the special nature of Mary and her child. Mary
receives a warm affirmation from Elizabeth ("Blessed are you
among women"), and Jesus is recognized as the unique person that
he is ("my Lord," Elizabeth calls him). Even the unborn John salutes
Jesus, leaping in his mother's womb at the approach of Mary and her
child.

The time is at hand. The birth of the Lord is near.


## Micah 5:2–5a

The God of Israel is a God of shimmering surprises, of outlandish
innovation and renewal. At precisely that moment when God's
people have determined the shape of the future and have measured
themselves according to its dimensions, God intervenes and so
disturbs our orientation that we are forced to begin again in the
construction of our dreams. If our hopes are molded to conform to
some unrealistic and prideful vision of ourselves and of our tomor-
rows, God unfailingly whittles us and our false confidence down to
size. If, on the other hand, we have steeped ourselves in the waters of
despair, God intrudes to point us beyond our pessimism to God's
vision of new life.

Scholars are at a loss to discover the precise background of
chapters 5 and 6 of the book of Micah. Yet it seems probable that,
while much within this unit of material is in harmony with the
"genuine" Micah oracles of chapters 1—3, chapters 4 and 5 reached
their present form at a time subsequent to the destruction of
Jerusalem in 587 B.C. The person(s) who wrote chapter 5, of which the
present lection is a part, speaks so poignantly of a Jerusalem under
siege that that person either had experienced the terrors of such a
siege directly or had read (heard) about them from others. In all
likelihood the siege in question is that which Nebuchadnezzar laid
to Jerusalem and which ended in the city's complete destruction in
the second decade of the sixth century B.C. But it is possible that
Sennacherib's invasion of 701 B.C. is the point of reference (if we read
"Assyrians" and "Assyria" of vs. 5b–6 in a literal fashion), or even

that any of the several invasions of Judea by Seleucid forces in the second century B.C. could be behind the text.

Micah 5:1, although not part of the lection for this day, sadly describes the predicament of the people. The citizens are penned up in the city and the king has been humiliated, or shortly will be (Zedekiah was savagely abused by the Babylonians: see 2 Kings 25:6–7). In such a situation, there is little reason to hope that the future will be anything other than filled with gloom. Indeed, there is little reason to hope that there even will be a tomorrow.

However, the future of the people of God is not so hopeless as it appears. Bethlehem, the ancestral home of the family of David, will yet bring forth another ruler who shall redeem the people (Micah 5:2). The proclamation of God's good news is couched in such a manner as to capture the ironies of God's most unexpected visitation, for insignificant Bethlehem will serve to unseat Israel's mightiest enemy. Moreover, while the action—whose roots are very ancient—is described as yet to occur, its very proclamation is intended to dispel the terror of the present moment, so that both past and future serve as God's vehicles to liberate the present. The abused king will be replaced and vindicated by the king to come, the "one who is to rule in Israel."

Verse 3 is obscure, but it appears to take realistic account of the Babylonian exile, which initially began in 597 B.C., but which reached new depths of suffering as a result of the tragedy of 587 B.C. Yet the historical exile with all of its oppression becomes here a paradigm of the bondage of the nation to its sin. The new and coming king will liberate the people of God from this bondage, the birth of the royal child serving to signal an end to the people's servitude. When the mother has borne her child, those who are lost will be restored to the household of faith.

The final full verse of the lection (v. 4) serves to describe the function of this new Davidic king. "Strength" and "majesty" are attributes that he brings to his task of shepherding the people, qualities that he derives from none other than Yahweh, Israel's God. "Peace" is also his nature (v. 5a), and as a result of these realities, the people will enjoy security, even as the Davidic king is "great to the ends of the earth" (v. 4d).

As mentioned above, just which group of defeated Jews first heard or read the sparkling promises of our lectionary text is unknown, but it is quite likely that they regarded this brightly lit tomorrow as too beautiful to be genuine. Indeed, when read literally, these words *are* too good to have been true, for no Davidic king ever arose to liberate his people from the bondage of Babylonian (or

Assyrian, as in vs. 5b–6) servitude. When the people trooped back to Jerusalem from Babylon near the end of the sixth century B.C., they were not acting independently, but were led by Jews in the service of the Persian king Cyrus, who styled himself "ruler of all the world" and "ruler of the four rims of the earth."

And so the promise of Micah 5:2–5a would be nothing more than a historical curiosity, nothing more than a gorgeous pipe dream, if it were not for the birth of Mary's son in Bethlehem's stable. Into the besieged city he comes—the city of the human heart—with the majesty and strength of God. And he comes with priceless gifts to those who receive him, gifts of security and peace.

## Psalm 80:1–7

Although scholars are unanimous in categorizing Ps. 80 as a communal lament, there is widespread disagreement concerning the particular calamity that the psalm describes. Regardless of the origin of Ps. 80, it is likely that the psalm in its present literary context represents a response to the catastrophic experience of exile. Several scholars have recently suggested that the Psalter as a whole may have been shaped in response to the exile, so it is helpful to keep the exile in mind as at least the kind of catastrophe that may have led to the creation of Ps. 80.

Psalm 80 opens with a series of imperatives that begin to suggest the dimensions of the problem. "Give ear" is often accompanied by the object "my prayer" (Pss. 17:1; 55:1; 86:6; see also 84:8; 141:1–2). The need for this opening imperative suggests that the people think that Yahweh is inattentive. The specific mention of the "people's prayers" in Ps. 80:4 lends additional support.

"Shine forth" is the language of theophany; it is twice associated with God's appearing on mountains (Deut. 33:2; Ps. 50:2). The plea for God's appearance suggests that the people thought God was absent (see also Ps. 94:1, another communal lament that begins with "shine forth"). The two additional pleas in Ps. 80:2 also convey the urgency of the situation. To be saved in Old Testament terms is to remain alive. If God remains inattentive, inactive, or absent, then the people will die (see the plea in v. 18, "give us life"). The remarkable thing about vs. 1 and 2 is that they are addressed to the very God whom the people perceive is inattentive and inactive, if not entirely absent. If God is the problem, God is also the solution. This inattentive, inactive God is addressed in the most exalted of terms. God is the "Shepherd of Israel" (v. 1). "Shepherd" is a royal title (see 2 Sam. 7:7;

Ezek. 34; Ps. 78:70–72); and God's kingship is emphasized by the designation of God as the one who is "enthroned upon the cherubim" (see 1 Sam. 4:4; 2 Sam. 6:2; Ps. 99:1). Even when all appearances suggest the contrary, the people still affirm that God reigns.

Psalm 80:3 continues the imperative series and is also related thematically to vs. 1–2. It stands out, though, because it is the first occurrence of a refrain (see vs. 7, 19, and a variation in v. 14). "Restore us" is more literally "cause us to return," and the word suggests several dimensions of meaning that are appropriate for Ps. 80. For instance, the word is used elsewhere for God's causing the people to return from exile (1 Kings 8:34; Jer. 27:22; see also Dan. 9:25). It is also used of causing people to return to God, that is, repent (see Neh. 9:26; Lam. 5:21), and of causing someone to return to life (2 Sam. 12:23; Job 33:30). All these dimensions may be contained in the translation "restore us" (also, see below on Ps. 80:5). "Let your face shine" suggests much the same thing as the "shine forth" of v. 1; that is, "be present for us." In Num. 6:24–26, the parallels to this plea are "bless," "keep," "be gracious," and "give peace."

The problems implicit in the pleas of Ps. 80:1–3 are made explicit in vs. 4–6. The question "How long?" is characteristic of both individual and communal laments (see Pss. 13:1; 74:10; 94:3). Instead of hearing the people (see 80:1), God is angry with (literally, "smokes against"; see Deut. 29:20; Ps. 74:1) their prayers. In a different way, Ps. 80:5 also recalls v. 1. The word for "shepherd" more literally means "one who pastures" or "one who feeds." It was the role of a shepherd to feed the flock, and it was the role of the king as shepherd to feed the people (see Ezek. 34). The lament of Ps. 80:5 is all the more poignant when we consider the plea of the refrain, "let your face shine," and consider the existence in the Temple of the "bread of the face" (NRSV, "bread of the Presence"; see Ex. 25:30; 1 Sam. 21:6; 1 Kings 7:48). The bread of God's face, the reality of God's sustaining presence, has been replaced by the bread of tears.

The lament is concluded in Ps. 80:6 with characteristic language. The word translated "laugh" underlies the NRSV's "mocked" in 79:4 and "derision" in 44:13; both psalms are communal laments. The word that NRSV translates "scorn" is more accurately "strife, contention," which may be a preferable translation in light of the similarity between the refrain of Ps. 80 and the priestly benediction of Num. 6:22–26. The same Hebrew verb underlies the word "give" in the phrase "give you peace" (Num. 6:26) and "make" in the phrase "make us the contention" (Ps. 80:6). In short, the people are experiencing precisely the opposite of the priestly benediction.

With the exception of the longer divine name, v. 7 is identical to v.

3. The repetition has the effect of expressing the urgency of the plea after the problems have been more explicitly stated in the lament of vs. 4–6. The echo of the refrain in v. 14 and the concluding occurrence in v. 19 mean that Ps. 80 begins, ends, and is permeated, structurally and theologically, by the plea for God to restore the people.

The conviction of confronting God in every circumstance lies at the heart of the laments. This is the paradox of the laments. That we have to do with God in matters of suffering and death as well as in matters of prosperity and life is a remarkable affirmation, especially in a world where the most overtly religious folk are inclined to view suffering as evidence of alienation from God and secular folk are inclined to locate the source of prosperity and life anywhere but in God. As we celebrate the advent of God incarnate, there is no better way to witness to God's reign than by continuing to address God out of our individual and corporate afflictions and by continuing to look to God as the only source of light and life.

## Hebrews 10:5–10

It is intriguing to speculate why certain texts came to be the designated readings for Sundays during the church year. Certainly, at first blush, the choice of Heb. 10:5–10 as the lection for the last Sunday of Advent prompts such wonderings. It does not immediately suggest a lot of themes normally associated with the coming of Christmas, such as incarnation or the fulfillment of messianic intentions. The passage primarily consists of an interpretation of a nonmessianic psalm that is not otherwise associated with Jesus, and occurs in the midst of a discussion about the sacrificial system, more reminiscent of Lent than Advent. No doubt the first words of the text ("when Christ came into the world") led to its selection for this Sunday, and perhaps they can provide the basis for our thinking of the meaning of the incarnation in a different way.

What we are *not* invited to do by the text is either to retreat into the romance and sentimentality of the Christmas season or to ponder philosophically how the divine is expressed in a human figure. Instead, we are directed to the purpose of Jesus' coming into the world—to do the will of God. The incarnation is unique because Jesus so radically obeys the divine intentions that he makes all previous means of dealing with sin passé. His utter faithfulness creates "the new and living way" (10:20), by which our approach to God is redefined.

The background for 10:5–10 comes in the earlier discussion about the incapacity of the cultic system to deal ultimately with human sin (10:1–4). The fact that sacrifices have to be offered repeatedly indicates that the offenses are not finally atoned for by the sacrifices. The best they can do is to serve as a reminder to worshipers of the reality of sin. The weakness of the cultic system, then ("consequently"), sets the stage for understanding what happens in the incarnation.

Psalm 40:6–8 is placed on the lips of Jesus as a statement of what he accomplishes in coming into the world. Before attending to the content of the psalm, we note this unusual literary method of making a point. In the midst of an argument for the discontinuity between the old and the new, between the traditional sacrificial system and the once-and-for-all sacrifice of Jesus, a continuity is affirmed. A psalm from the old covenant provides the language to describe the unique activity of the new covenant. In obeying the will of God, Jesus completes a divine intention that has been there from the beginning. His abolishing of the first in order to establish the second (Heb. 10:9) is not an iconoclastic action but a fulfillment, a doing of the unchanging will of God. In reading Hebrews, it becomes critical to discover the continuities between the old and the new affirmed in the text, alongside the discontinuities.

As the commentaries note, the citation of Ps. 40 comes from the Septuagint rather than the Hebrew text, and there occurs an interesting diversion (perhaps an interpretation) from the Hebrew. In Ps. 40:6, instead of reading "but you have given me an open ear," the Septuagint reads (and Hebrews quotes) "but a body you have prepared for me" (Heb. 10:5). The new alternative to the incapacity of the cult is God's preparing and sending Jesus, who does the divine will and effects what the cult could never accomplish. The word "body" becomes the writer's convenient way of saying that Jesus' obedience is physical and worldly. It comes to expression in the concrete realities of human life, in the specific choices that face people living in a fallen world. The incarnation in fact is depicted as "the offering of the body of Jesus," meaning not merely in death but in life as well (10:10). The character of the new, then, is not to be construed in ways that ignore the earthy and agonizing dimensions of obedience.

If the character of the incarnation is the obedience of Jesus to the divine will, the benefit of the incarnation is our sanctification. The perfect tense of the verb "have been sanctified" in 10:10 underscores the element of completion. The dishonoring of the divine-human relationship caused by our sin and unsatisfied by the offering of animal sacrifices has been rectified by Jesus' obedience.

The concluding adverb ("once for all") in 10:10 is an important one in this epistle. On the one hand, it declares an end to the repetitive practices of the ancient cult. On the other hand, it announces that in this age where such animal sacrifices would be disdained anyway, there is nothing we can do to make ourselves accepted by God. The ineffectiveness of the various sin-offerings has its counterpart in our subtle (and not so subtle) ways of trying to win God over, ways that at times result in frantic religious activity but not sanctification. The Letter to the Hebrews reminds us that the coming into the world that we celebrate at Christmas is exactly what the adverb says, "once for all." It accomplishes what has never been done before and will never be done again.

## Luke 1:39–45

Much about Mary's visit to Elizabeth remains unclear. First, Luke, who often precisely locates events, provides scant indication of either time or place. "In those days" and "a Judean town in the hill country" give only the vaguest sense of when and where these events occur. The explanation that Mary enters "the house of Zechariah" is almost ironic, since Zechariah himself makes no appearance and is not at the moment capable of the conversation that Mary and Elizabeth share with each other (see Luke 1:19–20). Second, Luke never indicates the reason for Mary's visit. Following as it does on Gabriel's announcement, Mary's visit might be a way of testing out the accuracy of Gabriel's words. Or perhaps Mary simply seeks the company of another woman whose pregnancy will set the neighbors' tongues in rapid motion.

What is clear, of course, is that Mary has come to see Elizabeth. This brief exchange between the two of them serves to introduce Mary's extended speech in 1:46–55. It also, however, provides a reinforcement of Gabriel's announcement. In fact, virtually every word of Elizabeth's confirms Gabriel's words to Mary. And, because she speaks by virtue of the Holy Spirit (1:41), Elizabeth may be regarded as a trustworthy witness.

First, Elizabeth cries out, "Blessed are you among women, and blessed is the fruit of your womb." With these words, Elizabeth confirms Gabriel's initial address, "Greetings, favored one! The Lord is with you." Both salutations announce that God is acting in a way that will bless Mary.

Second, Elizabeth asks why it is that "the mother of my Lord" (1:43) should visit her. With this phrase (and the previous reference to the "fruit of your womb"), Elizabeth recalls the promise of Gabriel that Mary would give birth. While Elizabeth does not speak of the child with the messianic titles preferred by Gabriel, her reference to him as "my Lord" nevertheless acknowledges his role in God's plan.

Finally, Elizabeth pronounces a blessing on Mary "who believed that there would be a fulfillment of what was spoken to her by the Lord" (1:45). Here Elizabeth does not reinforce Gabriel's speech, but she does reinforce and reinterpret Mary's own words in 1:38: "Here am I, the servant of the Lord; let it be with me according to your word." What might have been understood earlier as mere acquiescence, a resignation to the more powerful will of God, here emerges as active confidence that God would bring God's promise into reality.

Taken as a whole, this scene confirms that the unbelievable words of Gabriel are indeed to be believed. The aged and barren Elizabeth carries within her the child who will become John the Baptist. Mary is referred to as "the mother of my Lord." She herself trusts God, as will become dramatically apparent in the Magnificat.

This scene does not merely repeat earlier themes, however. What distinguishes Elizabeth's comments from those of Gabriel is that, where Gabriel drew attention to the greatness of the child Mary would bear, Elizabeth draws attention to the maternity of Mary. Here it is as "blessed . . . among women" that Mary is greeted. Here she is identified as "the mother" of Jesus.

The attention given to Mary in this passage reinforces questions about the selection of Mary. Luke provides not a word that indicates why she was chosen or what her attributes might be. (Readers learn far more about Zechariah and Elizabeth than they do about Mary!) To put the question pointedly: Does Mary's selection suggest that she is particularly worthy of this honor? Is the "favor" Mary finds with God (1:28) a response to her own goodness?

Knowing the sensitive nature of this issue for some Christian traditions, in which the virtues of Mary are recalled and celebrated, it is important to deal with it carefully. The words of Gabriel can, in fact, be read as suggesting that Mary warrants this blessing, although much less is said about her own merits than those of Simeon, for example (2:25–35). What seems more significant here is the grace shown to Mary, the inexplicable gift of this impossible birth.

Certainly the emphasis of the text, already in the annunciation of Gabriel and especially here with the greeting of Elizabeth, lies on the faithful response of Mary. She warrants praise because she assents to become God's servant, because she trusts the words spoken to her. In Catholic circles since Vatican II, Mary is often spoken of as the first disciple. The greeting of Elizabeth gives ample reason for such a designation.

Because of our tendency to see women as models only for other women, and because of our tendency to praise passivity and acquiescence in women, a word of caution is in order here. If Mary trusts God's word, she does nothing more or less than is expected of every believer, male or female. It is in that sense that she becomes the first disciple of Jesus.

# CHRISTMAS, FIRST PROPER

The themes of the rule of God and of the divinely appointed monarch, so prominent in Advent texts, also figure in large measure in these lections for Christmas Eve/Day. In certain ways, these texts are predictable, in that they not only announce the coming of the King, but also project the nature of the divine rule. The two lections from the Old Testament, Isa. 9:2–7 and Ps. 96, are closely related to the political ideology of the Davidic monarch in ancient Israel and, in the view of many scholars, functioned in the life of the people in a political sense, before their transpolitical authority was understood. The Gospel lection is the engaging story from Luke 2:1–20, without a reading of which Christmas could simply not be Christmas at all.

But in other respects these texts are startling and intrusive. In Isa. 9:2–7, the new king is welcomed with all the trumpetry surrounding an important royal birth or coronation, but the text then points not to a triumph of the new king's armies (as one might expect), but to the ascendancy of "justice" and "righteousness." Psalm 96 echoes that expectation, even as it looks beyond any human king to the rule of King Yahweh. Luke 2, for all its familiarity to ears that have heard it over and over again, jolts us by its juxtaposition of the figures of King Jesus, wrapped in swaddling cloths, and the Emperor Augustus, ordering the census of the people. We who have read beyond Luke 2 know which king will truly and ultimately reign, but of that the text itself only hints. And Titus 2:11–14, while perhaps not striking the reader immediately as a royal text, outdistances the other lections for this day, in that it not only celebrates the King who has come, but him who will come again, "our great God and Savior, Jesus Christ" (v. 13).

Thus there are common threads that bind these lections together, but there is also a sense of theological "movement." And together, the texts express that which goes beyond the boundaries of any single one of them. For they urge those who read them and who hear

39

them read not only to celebrate the coming of the King and the dawning of the special qualities of the kingdom, but to prepare for the return of Him whose rule is both "already" and "not yet," both present and still to come.

## Isaiah 9:2–7                                                    (A B C)

This well-known oracle is apparently a public decree from the royal palace. It concerns the emergence of a new king in Jerusalem. Two scholarly hypotheses are usual concerning the oracle. First, it may be the *birth announcement* of a new heir to the Davidic throne. Second, the oracle may be a *coronation announcement* when the prince succeeds his father on the throne. In either case, the celebrative rhetoric proclaims the new heir as the fulfillment of all the long-standing hopes and expectations of the realm.

The oracle persists in its "power" voice long after any concrete reference to a specific king has been given up. The oracle has become an announcement of God's faithful gift of newness through a new ruler, in response to sore need in the community. The newness mediated by the oracle is that the realm has come under new governance. That oracle then may have had repeated use in the royal court, as each new king is thought to be at last the one who will establish a right government. Moreover, if the oracle had taken on a life of its own in the political-liturgical rhetoric of ancient Israel, then it is not surprising that the church found the oracle useful and appropriate for its announcement of Jesus.

That indeed is the role of the angels in the Bethlehem story (Luke 2:10–14). They are making an announcement (either birth or coronation) on behalf of the court. A new heir has been designated, who will faithfully inaugurate a new creation. Thus Jesus is not announced in a rhetorical vacuum, but the tradition utilizes the common royal language of newness.

The oracle begins with *a general expression of joy* at the profound transformation that is just under way (Isa. 9:1–2). The joy at the newness is characterized by two references. It is joy as in the time of a good harvest (v. 3). The joy of harvest comes when anxiety about crops is nullified and economic prosperity is assured for another year. Or it is joy as at the end of the battle, when the enemy has been routed (vs. 4–5). The poem anticipates an utter newness, which overcomes all the harsh reality of the recent past.

Future well-being depends on *defeat of the enemy* that has been threatening (vs. 4–5). These verses are commonly skipped over in church reading. They are, however, crucial to the development of the poem. They indicate that the newness is concretely related to the realities of power. The community has lived under the boot of oppression, exploitation, and humiliation. Now, however, in the form of the new king comes rescue!

The anticipated rescue will be brutal and violent. The coming "light" is powerful enough to seize all the boots of the enemy soldiers, all their uniforms, which are soaked in their blood, to burn them in a huge fire (compare Ps. 46:8–9). This is disarmament, but it is disarmament by a victor. The fire is an act of triumph and defiance that nullifies the enemy, to eliminate his threat and to destroy his myth of invincibility. No wonder the folk cheered, for the occupying enemy had generated deep and abiding hatred.

Only now do we learn the cause of the joy (Isa. 9:2–3) and the reason for victory (vs. 4–5). The turn of the future is because *there is an heir*, a son (vs. 6–7)! He will head the government, which has been desolate and irrelevant. In the announcement of birth or of coronation, the new heir is given names that assert Judah's best memories and deepest hopes. The new king will be utterly sagacious in dispensing justice ("Wonderful Counselor"), will have the power, prowess, and potency of a god ("Mighty God"), will be as reassuring and protective as a great tribal leader ("Everlasting Father"), and will be a bringer of peace and prosperity ("Prince of Peace").

The oracle ends with two theological affirmations (v. 7). First, the coming rule is marked by "justice" and "righteousness," by care for people and mercy toward the weak. The new rule is not one of self-aggrandizing power, but it will enact and embody the best hopes of the old Mosaic covenant. Jerusalem had long neglected justice and righteousness (compare 1:21–23; 5:7), but now it will be rehabilitated (compare 56:1). The king will at last do what the prophets had always hoped. Second, the newness embodied by the new heir is the work of Yahweh, wrought by the passion and faithfulness of God. This faithful king is no self-starter. Israel's daily hope is rooted in the reality of this covenant-making, world-transforming, justice-working God!

## Psalm 96                                              (A B C)

This psalm, with its expansive mood of joy and celebration, is an exclamation of praise perfectly appropriate for Christmas Eve or Christmas Day. Like other psalms of praise, Ps. 96 reads as if it were written with an eye toward its use in public worship, the worshiping congregation (v. 7) and the temple of God (v. 6) being almost tangible objects within the poem. Whether, as some scholars argue, it was originally an enthronement psalm for ancient Judean kings or, as others propose, a song in celebration of the ark of the covenant, this psalm has been changed and spoken at festive moments in the life of the people of God over the centuries. Indeed, it is striking that it is the people who are addressed directly throughout this psalm, as Yahweh, the God of Israel, is consistently referred to in the third person.

Perhaps the initial feature of this psalm to attract the reader's attention is the triple imperative that begins the psalm: Sing! (vs. 1–2). The imperative is plural in Hebrew, a feature that, once more, underscores the psalm's interest in the worshiping congregation. Furthermore, this imperative (šîrû) is strengthened by the cognate noun "song" (šîr), which appears in the very first line of the psalm. An additional note of emphasis is the triple use of the phrase "to the LORD." In other words, the poet has used the very effective devices of repetition and similarity of sound to urge the worshiping people: "Praise the LORD!"

As is often the case in psalms of praise, Ps. 96 soon addresses the reasons for praising God. In the first part of the psalm, these are at least two in number: first, Yahweh is an actual God and not, like the deities of other nations, a nonentity (v. 5a). Second, it is Yahweh, Israel's God, who created the heavens (v. 5b) and who is encountered as a living Reality in the house of worship (v. 6). (It is interesting that 1 Chron. 16, which provides a somewhat different version of Ps. 96, reads for 96:6b, "strength and *joy* are in his [holy] place," 1 Chron. 16:27, emphasis added).

The structure of Ps. 96:1–6—the imperative to praise Yahweh followed by the reasons for doing so—is repeated in vs. 7–13. Here the imperative is "Give [NRSV "Ascribe"] glory to Yahweh!" a call to worship that is linked with a very specific act of self-giving: "Bring an offering" (v. 8).

In vs. 7–13 the reason for praising Yahweh is as straightforward as it is profound: "The LORD is king!" (v. 10), and here we come to what is perhaps the central affirmation of the psalm. The kingship of God, which was revealed at creation (v. 10b), is further expressed in Yahweh's role as the administrator of justice (vs. 10c, 13). Verse 13, in fact, might be translated, instead of NRSV's "judge," as "bring justice." And v. 13 goes on to detail the means by which Yahweh's justice is to be expressed: "with righteousness" and "with his truth." Thus, as do a number of the psalms that refer to the rule of God or to that of the God-appointed Davidic monarch, the justice of Yahweh the King is linked to the divine expression of other moral values.

And because Yahweh is a king of justice, righteousness, and peace, all creation rejoices (vs. 11–12):

> the heavens,
> the earth,
> the sea and its creatures,
> the field and its creatures,
> the trees of the woods.

All join in praising the coming of the King!

And it is of great significance that the King *is coming* (or has come—the Hebrew is ambiguous). Whatever the original significance of this phrase (v. 13a) within the liturgy of ancient Israel may have been—and we cannot be sure—it deepens our understanding that the psalmist sang not of some distant God, remote and unconcerned. Rather, the God who reigns over Israel and over the world is a God who cares, who insists on justice, righteousness, and peace in the lives of the people, and who is personally present to see that these qualities mold the nature of human life. Thus, the ultimate reason for this song of joy is not simply that the God of justice reigns, but that that God is here. Now.

This is, of course, the story of Christmas: the Babe of Bethlehem and the regnant God are one. That the story is one of mystery and wonder is, of course, a part of its power. Yet the mystery and wonder are not limited to the question of the incarnation: "How in the world could God become a human being?" The mystery and wonder also extend to the prior question, "How could the Maker and Ruler of the universe care whether life is just?" We cannot fathom the answer to either question, of course. But just as the lection from Luke 2 affirms that God assumed human flesh at Bethlehem, so Ps. 96, in lyric tones, insists that God cares how men and women live. When we are seized by the joy of which the psalmist sings, we begin to understand—however dimly—the full meaning of the birth of Mary's Son.

## Titus 2:11–14                                        (A B C)

In common with the other readings assigned for this day, Titus 2:11–14 celebrates the glorious appearance of God's grace. What distinguishes this lesson from the others is the explicit connection the writer makes between that grace and the ethical response it entails.

Warnings about appropriate behavior run throughout this letter.

Even the salutation identifies Paul's apostleship with the furtherance of "godliness" (1:1). The bulk of the first chapter concerns qualifications for Christian leadership, and dominating those qualifications is the need for moral and upright behavior. Chapter 2 continues instructions about what Titus is to teach various groups within the community regarding their Christian behavior. While specific admonitions in Titus sharply offend late-twentieth-century Christians (for example, the expectation that women are to be submissive to their husbands and slaves to their masters), the need for discipline and identity within the Christian community emerges as a crucial issue in our own time.

Titus 2:11 shows that the disciplined behavior urged by the author of Titus has a profoundly theological root: "For the grace of God has appeared, bringing salvation to all." In this single verse we find an apt summary of the Christmas story. First, it is about God's grace. In common with other New Testament writings, the event of the birth, death, and resurrection of Jesus Christ is subsumed under the single title "grace."

English translations necessarily obscure the fact that the Greek verb here is *epiphainein*, from the root of which we get our English noun, epiphany. God's grace makes its appearance in Jesus Christ. Notice the way in which what we sometimes think of as an attribute of God—that is, grace—is anthropomorphized by its use with a verb.

The appearance of grace has its purpose in the salvation of all people. It is worth pondering what alternative purpose there might be for the epiphany of God's grace. Perhaps God's grace might find its purpose in self-glorification or in the sheer awe of human acknowledgment of God. The testimony of scripture, however, is that God's intent in the epiphany is to save humankind.

No qualifications limit those who are the object of God's salvation. The noun used in the Greek text, *anthrōpos*, includes both men and women, although it is often translated as "man." "All people" surely includes the well-known categories of human beings Paul uses in Gal. 3:28 (Jew and Greek, slave and free, male and female). It also includes sinner and penitent, persecutor and persecuted, "insiders" and "outsiders" of every type. God's salvific grace knows no limits.

God's grace does, however, have an impact on the way people live their lives. Following v. 11's powerful statement of the Christmas message, vs. 12–14 explain how grace "trains" or, better, "disciplines" human beings in three distinct but related ways. The first discipline of grace is stated in negative terms. Believers are to "renounce impiety and worldly passions," terms that may well reflect the Gentile origins of the writer and his audience. A Gentile who became a Christian was said to have turned away from the worship of idols, things that are not God (Gal. 4:8–9; 1 Thess. 1:9). The same claim would not be made about Jewish Christians, who had always worshiped the true and only God.

It is not enough, of course, merely to renounce things that are bad, although perhaps some early Christians, like some latter-day Christians, regarded Christian behavior simply as a list of prohibitions. The second discipline of grace consists of living "lives that are self-controlled, upright, and godly." This wording has an austere, nearly puritanical connotation that is unnecessarily harsh. To be "self-controlled" (*sōphronōs*) is to show moderation. The word has to do with being reasonable or sensible. "Upright" translates the familiar *dikaiōs*, which pertains to living justly or rightly. To live a "godly" (*eusebōs*) life pertains to devotion or awe that one addresses to God. The first word pertains to the way one deals with oneself (with control), the second to the way one deals with others (justly), and the third to the way one deals with God (with reverence).

While these first two disciplines of grace are confined to life in "this world," that is, in the present, the third discipline results in expectation. Grace teaches believers to wait for "the blessed hope and the manifestation of the glory of our great God and Savior, Jesus Christ. He it is who gave himself for us that he might redeem us from all iniquity and purify for himself a people of his own who are zealous for good deeds" (Titus 2:13–14). This summary of Christian confidence in the future reminds us that our celebration of the first advent of God's grace in Jesus Christ is a celebration of the promised Second Advent as well.

## Luke 2:1–14 (15–20)                                      (A B C)

Luke's account of the birth of Jesus appears as the Gospel lesson for both the First and Second Propers of Christmas. Since the reading for the Second Proper is limited to vs. 8–20, we shall concentrate the commentary on vs. 1–7 for the First Proper and deal with the remainder of the story under the Second Proper.

This passage, so beautifully crafted in Luke's narrative, certainly counts among the most familiar passages in the Bible. Dramatizations of the Christmas story as well as repeated readings make it a well-known text. People in North America who know little or nothing about the Christian faith know about the shepherds and the angelic chorus. For that reason, the text presents a challenge to the preacher to hear and declare a fresh word that probes the familiar and yet moves beyond it.

What immediately emerges from the early portion of this story is the political context in which the birth of Jesus is recounted. We are told that Emperor Augustus had ordered an enrollment and that Quirinius was governor of Syria. Despite the problems surrounding the historical accuracy of this beginning (dealt with in most commentaries), the narrative setting cannot be ignored. It is not against the background of the reign of Herod, the local ruler who is known for his heavy-handed and brutal ways, that the story of Jesus' birth is told (as in Matthew's Gospel), but against the background of the Roman Empire.

The emperor Octavian was a prominent figure, who solidified the somewhat divided loyalties of the various regions of the empire and ushered in the famous Pax Romana. In 27 B.C., the Roman senate gave him the title "the August One." Poets wrote of his peaceful ideals and anticipated that his reign would signal a golden age based on virtue. Ancient monuments even ascribed to him the title "savior." He represented a high and hopeful moment in Roman history.

Luke gives Octavian his familiar title and recognizes his authority by noting that "all the world" (actually the Roman Empire) is encompassed by his decree. Often in ancient times the demand for a census evoked rebellion and opposition, but Luke records a dutiful response: "All went to their own towns to be registered." The mention of Augustus not only provides an indispensable time reference to help readers date the events that are being narrated, but also enables Luke to explain how Mary and Joseph, who lived in Nazareth, had a baby born in Bethlehem.

The introduction, however, provides a much more important function than this. It sets the stage for the birth of one who is Savior, Christ the Lord. Octavian is not pictured as an evil, oppressive tyrant, a bloody beast "uttering haughty and blasphemous words" (Rev. 13:5). The Roman state in Luke's narrative simply does not represent the enemy against which Christians must fight. The backdrop for Jesus' birth is rather a relatively humane and stable structure, the best of ancient governments, which led to dreams of a peaceful era and aspirations of a new and wonderful age. The decades between the time of Jesus' birth and the time of Luke's narrative, however, exposed the failed hopes and the doused aspirations. Octavian is succeeded by caesars who turn the imperial dreams into nightmares.

Against the horizon of disillusionment, we read of the birth of another ruler, from the lineage of David, whose meager beginnings, on the surface, do not compare with the promise and hope of Augustus. All the world obeys the caesar, but Jesus' parents are rejected and relegated to a cattle stall. Yet the birth of Jesus is good news for all the people, ensuring a new and lasting promise of peace and goodwill.

The narrative does not present us with a confrontation between Augustus and Jesus, but with a contrast between vain expectations and true hope, between the disappointment that follows misplaced anticipations and the energy born of a divine promise, between the imposing but short-lived power of Caesar's rule and the humble manifestation of the eternal dominion of God, between the peace of Rome and the peace of Christ. The titles for Jesus, found later in the narrative (Luke 2:11)—Savior, Christ, and Lord—stand out starkly against the claims made for Augustus, and in the ensuing story become titles interpreted in fresh and surprising ways.

The setting for Luke's birth narrative clarifies for us the distinction between false hopes and true ones. Relatively humane, stable structures that contribute to the well-being of others often tend to promise more than they can deliver. Their very positive nature becomes seductive and generates impossible expectations. In contrast, Jesus is the anchor for reliable hope, for dependable promises, for anticipations that are more than fulfilled.

# CHRISTMAS, SECOND PROPER

A variety of perspectives characterizes this collection of Christmas lections, and a variety of emotions as well, ranging from hope over what God has promised to do to joy over what God has done. The verses from Isa. 62 express the people's sense of expectation that God will complete that which God has already promised. But this expectation is couched in terms that suggest that God's people—and the hope they cherish—are vulnerable and cannot forever endure God's apparent need to be reminded of what God has promised to do. Psalm 97, on the other hand, knows nothing of vulnerability but is a straightforward celebration of the presence of God, a presence that all creation affirms and that results in righteousness and justice drawn to dimensions that are both cosmic and human.

The tender story of the visitation to the shepherds in Luke 2:8–20 is but an extension of the royal theology of Ps. 97. But what an extension! Here there are no melting mountains giving witness to the rule of God, but a chorus of angels who testify that the King of kings is to be found in a most unkingly milieu—a manger. Finally, the lection from the epistles, Titus 3:4–7, adds to this theological and emotional mix the important element of grace: the good news of God's intervention in human life is a declaration not of that which men and women deserve, but of what God has freely given.

In a significant manner, therefore, the four lections rehearse the drama of redemption, beginning with human need, moving through an acknowledgment of God's concern and power, and culminating in a declaration of God's compassion out of which issues God's saving initiative. They thereby formulate a history of salvation for women and men everywhere who have found in Jesus Christ the expression of all that God is and does.

Christmas is an acknowledgment of that history and, as any meaningful celebration must be, a rehearsal of it. But it is a rehearsal that views the history of salvation, not as chronological increments, but as a progression of events all of which happen simultaneously. Even we who rejoice over a gracious God's gift of the Son and our acceptance of this gift—the latter stages of the drama—must acknowledge that in certain ways we are still mired in the earlier stages in that we are vulnerable and must pray daily for God's presence and affirmation.

That view of Christmas, therefore, which tends to emphasize the triumphalist aspects of the occasion to the exclusion of its statements concerning human weakness and need is only partially on target. The diversity of these four lections helps us to hear the many voices with which Christmas speaks and sings.

## Isaiah 62:6–12 (A B C)

This poem is set in the context of exiles who have returned to Jerusalem. They found the city to which they returned less than honored. Indeed, the city, which had been destroyed by the Babylonians, is still pitiful in its desolation, a source of embarrassment. God had promised a transformation, but has not yet worked it. The poem concerns the expectation and insistence of the faithful that God must be moved to act for the sake of the beloved city.

The problem is to compel God to act as God has promised to act. The poet does not reflect on why God has not acted; he only knows that there has been none of the saving action promised by God. For that reason, the poet devises a strategy to secure from God a rescued, restored city (vs. 6–7). "Sentinels" will be stationed on the walls around the city. They will be endlessly diligent in their work; they have only one task, a most peculiar task. They are to speak, not be silent. They are to speak incessantly. Their speech is to remind God of God's promises, to alert God to the needs of the city, to nag God, to invoke God, to move God to act.

The prayer on behalf of the city is an act of passionate hope. The hope is governed by the particle "until" (see v. 1). The city of Jerusalem waits eagerly under the influence of God's "until." The community is in expectation, waiting until God will keep God's promise. Thus the "until" of hoping faith stands between the passionate prayer of Israel and God's own faithful action. It is the conviction of the poet that God can be forced to enact that "until" by persuasive intercession. That, however, can happen only if God is endlessly reminded to be faithful.

The affirmation of these verses is that God has indeed heeded the "reminders" of vs. 6–7, has acted to restore Jerusalem; the city is assured a future of joy and well-being (vs. 10–12). Thus, vs. 6–7 have "worked," and Jerusalem has received its "until" from God.

God's spectacular presence will give the city a new name. The city had appeared to observers to be pitiful and abandoned, called "Forsaken" (see v. 4). Now the ones in the city are a holy people, believing utterly in God. They are Yahweh's redeemed, Yahweh's special project, and recipient of God's staggering care.

As anyone can see, the city is no longer "forsaken," but can be called "Sought Out," cared for, valued, treasured. Thus, what is a hope in vs. 6–7 now has become a reality. The poem asserts that the God who seemed not to care can be mobilized to act.

This poem testifies to God's faithfulness, which transforms Jerusalem. The difficult question is how to treat a Jerusalem text in terms of the rule of Jesus, as the opening of the new age.

It is most plausible to take "Jerusalem" as a metaphor, but as a metaphor for what? We may suggest three ways in which the metaphor might function in rethinking the larger impact of Jesus' birth:

1. Calvin takes "Jerusalem" to be *the church*, God's beloved community, which God shelters and for which God cares. On this reading, the text promises that the church will be healed of its disarray and will become an adequate habitat for the power and ministry of God.

2. "Jerusalem" is no doubt linked to creation in the tradition, so that "new Jerusalem" bespeaks *new creation* (compare Isa. 65:17–18; Rev. 21:1–4). On this reading, the text anticipates the renovation of a needy, distraught world.

3. "Jerusalem" functions in the Gospel narratives in relation to the notion of *kingdom*. Thus the kingdom of David becomes the kingdom of Jesus, which is the kingdom of God (compare Mark 1:14–15). On this reading, "Jerusalem" is a reference to the new society, the new socioeconomic arrangement that makes human, humane life possible.

It is odd that Jerusalem is "invaded" by Jesus in ways that threaten the authorities (Luke 9:51). The same Jesus, however, weeps over and yearns for Jerusalem, waiting with this text for God's promises to be kept (Luke 13:33–35; 19:41–44). Our reading of this text must not be so freely metaphorical that we miss the actual flesh-and-blood reality of the city, a reality enmeshed in dismay, but only "until"—until God acts. When God acts, Jerusalem is "sought out," as is the church, as is every city, as is creation, as is humanity, sought out by God for love, care, healing, forgiveness, and finally newness. The preachable point is God's "until."

## Psalm 97 (A B C)

A celebration of the kingship of God, a belief that figures prominently in the faith of ancient Israel, is at the heart of this psalm. The first half of the psalm (vs. 1–6) describes the majesty of the divine King, while the last half (vs. 7–12) raises implications for the life of the people concerning God's rule.

Yahweh's majesty is portrayed primarily by means of figures of speech associated with a thunderstorm: clouds, darkness, fire, and lightning. The presence of Yahweh is so awesome that Yahweh's enemies are reduced to ashes, and even the otherwise solid mountains melt. Hyperbole, to be sure (for similar uses of these figures, see especially Ps. 29). Yet nestled among the metaphors are straightforward statements concerning the personal qualities of Yahweh. Yahweh's rule is based on righteousness and justice (v. 2b), a moral order built into the very fabric of the universe (v. 6).

As to what the rule of God means in the lives of people, the psalm notes that idolatry inevitably leads to despair, whereas Yahweh's presence sustains and supports Yahweh's people (vs. 7–10). Light and joy await those for whom the righteousness of the King has become a personal moral order (v. 11).

The final verse of the psalm (v. 12) is a call to these righteous ones to rejoice and give thanks to the Lord!

The relevance of this text to Christmas lies, first, in its celebration of the royal presence of God. In some ways the fire and lightning of the first half of the psalm may seem out of place in the celebration of the birth of a Babe, the "gentle Jesus, meek and mild" of the familiar hymn. But the church has maintained from its earliest beginnings that the Infant of Bethlehem is but one aspect of the nature of the incarnate Son, that he who "was conceived by the Holy Spirit" and "born of the Virgin Mary" will also "come to judge the living and the dead." And thus this Psalm lection recalls for us that the God who, in the Holy Child, comes to us in vulnerability and weakness is also the One who presides over the affairs of the universe and who insists that justice be done. If the violent language of the thunderstorm seems to the modern mind an unusual means of expressing the nature of God—to say nothing of the concept of the annihilation of God's enemies (v. 3b)—it may be helpful to remember that the language of the biblical poets is often extravagant, in that they frequently used the most intense human experiences to convey the nature of a God whom ordinary words cannot contain (compare Ex. 15:3, "The LORD is a warrior").

Beyond its celebration of the presence of Yahweh the King, this Psalm lection is consistent with other Advent and Christmas texts in its declaration that the rule of God is based on righteousness and justice. The manner in which these qualities are described here makes it clear that they are not incidental to human life, but are part of the tissue that God has woven into the universe. To act unjustly or unrighteously—to be an unjust or unrighteous person or society—is to repudiate the purposes for which all life exists. And it is, of course, to repudiate God.

Thus the value of this psalm as a Christmas lection lies in its ability to project the larger dimensions of the incarnation. It is tempting on this day to be occupied with the image of the helpless child in the manger and, therefore, to orient our festival around the children in our families and around the childishness in us all. To be sure, that is an important quality to be preserved, because it helps us to come to terms with our own weakness and vulnerability. It also brings us nearer to Jesus' teaching that the kingdom of God is a kingdom of children (Mark 9:36–37 and parallels).

But a more comprehensive understanding of Christmas includes the acknowledgment that Jesus' weakness—evident not only at Bethlehem, but at Calvary as well—is complemented by his role as King and divine Lord. At the heart of Christian belief is the affirmation that the infant son of Mary and the crucified Galilean peasant is also the Sovereign of the universe, who was present at the beginning (John 1:1) and who will preside over the end (Rev. 1:4–8). His rule is one of justice, righteousness, and peace, and those who would prepare themselves to be the citizens of his kingdom will dedicate themselves to these qualities now, as they/we try to create of the present time an anticipation of the time yet to come.

To celebrate Christmas without embracing this larger meaning is to sentimentalize and trivialize the festival. Christ's presence in human life is intended to change us, to reshape our commitments and our priorities so that they reflect the values of the kingdom of God. We may meet Christ at this season as the pink and cuddly Babe who reminds us of the innocence with which life begins. But when we follow him from the manger into the harsh and struggling world, we are asked to follow him to a cross. Our Christmas joy, however, derives from our knowing that not even a cross could defeat the just and peaceable kingdom over which he will preside at the end of time.


## Titus 3:4–7                                                                (A B C)

This text appropriately stands coupled with the angelic visitation to the shepherds in Luke 2:8–20, for what Luke conveys in narrative, the epistle to Titus asserts in the form of a creed—namely, that the inbreaking of God through Jesus Christ results entirely from God's decision.

In Titus, this assertion begins with a striking contrast between human existence before and after the Christ-event. Verse 3 details a catalog of evils to which human beings are susceptible, in order to show the profound character of God's salvation. Verse 4 introduces the advent of Jesus Christ as an event of radical discontinuity ("But when . . .").

Here the coming of Jesus Christ, the Christmas event, is described as "the goodness and loving kindness of God our Savior." As in Titus 2:11–14 and elsewhere in the New Testament, God's action stems not from self-glorification but from God's profound love of humankind. This attribute of God "appears" in human history, and the verb used here is the same one from which we derive our term "epiphany" (see 2:11).

The verses that follow characterize the meaning of this epiphany for humankind. Titus 3:5 introduces an important contrast, which can best be seen through a somewhat literal translation:

> not from works on the basis of righteousness
>> that *we* did
> but on the basis of *his* mercy
>> he saved *us.*

Several pairs of opposites give emphasis to the contrast here. The first and third lines contrast the means by which salvation has been accomplished—that is, not righteousness but mercy. The second and fourth lines contrast the agents of salvation—not human beings but God alone. The pronouns underscore this contrast, and the result of the whole is a denial of any notion that the salvation of human beings results from their own virtue.

The end of v. 5 amplifies God's salvation. It comes about as a result of his mercy and "by the water of rebirth and renewal by the Holy Spirit." Probably "water" refers to the practice of baptism, which Christians early on associated with renewal and the gift of the Holy Spirit. "Rebirth" (*paliggenesia*), of course, is a concept that many religious traditions associate with conversion. In the context of Titus, rebirth refers specifically to moral rebirth. The gift of God in Jesus Christ enables human beings to turn from their former lives and to live in conformity with God's will.

At first glance, v. 6 adds little to what has already been said, but it is nevertheless a significant part of the text. First, the statement that

God "poured out [this Spirit] on us richly" characterizes God's gift as a generous one. This imagery of pouring out water rather than measuring a minimal amount sufficient for the task conveys the extravagance of God's salvation. Second, the reference to Jesus Christ as the agent of God's salvation tells in concrete terms the means by which God's salvation made its epiphany. Through a human being, God has embraced all of humankind.

Verse 7 recalls the goal of salvation in terms of justification and the eschatological hope. Having been justified by the grace of Christ, believers become heirs "to the hope of eternal life." This statement carefully avoids asserting that believers *already* possess eternal life, for that final gift stands as the culmination of God's acts of salvation. Nevertheless, believers live out of their hope, their confidence, in God's power over death itself.

The opening words of v. 8 ("The saying is sure") suggest that what precedes in vs. 4–7 is taken from an early Christian tradition which the author quotes. These opening words also reinforce the trustworthiness of the claims that have just been made. God may be relied on to complete the salvation begun in Jesus Christ.

As a reading for Christmas Day, this text reminds us of the fact that the birth of Jesus Christ takes place as sheer gift. No human act imagined it, willed it, brought it about. It results solely from the generous, even outrageous, love of God for humankind. This text, with its strong assertions about the salvation accomplished in Jesus Christ, also reminds us that the events of Christmas occur *on our behalf*. The celebration of Christmas as a wonderful story about the lowly birth of a great hero completely misses the point that the Savior who is born is born for us. Here Titus 3:4–7 announces the message of the angels: "To you is born this day in the city of David a Savior. . . ."


## Luke 2:(1–7) 8–20                                        (A B C)

The birth of Jesus is the center of Christmas. What one learns about Jesus from the narratives that relate his birth comes, however, from the actions and words of the other characters of Christmas—in Luke, from the shepherds, the angelic messenger, the heavenly chorus, the mysterious bystanders (2:18), and Mary; in Matthew, from repeated angelic messengers, Joseph, the Wise Men, Herod, the chief priests and scribes. Nowhere is that more evident than in the Lukan story, where a bare statement of the birth of Jesus is followed by the intriguing account of the nameless shepherds. They are traced from their location in the field tending their flock through their visit to Bethlehem and back to where they originated. From their actions and their interactions with the angelic messenger and the heavenly host, we learn about the character and significance of Jesus' birth.

We first meet the shepherds doing what shepherds are supposed to be doing—tending their flocks. They no doubt remind Luke's readers of the shepherding done once in these same regions by Jesus' famous ancestor, David. The routineness of these shepherds' lives is abruptly interrupted by the appearance of the angelic messenger. Their world, circumscribed at night by the wandering of the sheep, is exploded by the awesome presence of this one who brings news of Jesus' birth. The manifestation of the divine glory, the shepherds' fright, the announcement of the messenger disrupt their order and uniformity and set them on a journey to hear and see earth-changing events.

Three things we note about the intrusive announcement of the messenger. First, the good news includes great joy for "all the people." It is not merely the shepherds' small world that is changed by the word of Jesus' birth, but it is Israel's world. While Luke sets the story of the birth in the context of the Roman Empire (2:1–2), he has a primary interest in the destiny of Israel and "the falling and the rising of many" for whom this baby is set (v. 34). Jesus' relevance for the world, in fact, begins in the city of David as the fulfillment of Jewish expectations. It includes the acceptance of Jewish traditions (vs. 21, 22–40, 41–52), and only from this very particular origin does its universal character emerge.

Second, the announcement focuses on three astounding titles this baby is to carry—Savior, Messiah, and Lord. "Savior" has meaning in the narrative because original readers would recognize that such a title the exalted Emperor Augustus had borne. Unfortunately, the eager anticipations for a brighter, more peaceful day stirred by his rule were long since dashed by the brutality and weakness of his successors. Now a true and promise-fulfilling Savior appears. "Messiah" (or "Christ") reminds us of Israel's hope for the anointed figure and God's grand design which he will inaugurate. "Lord," interestingly, occurs four times in our passage, and in the other three instances is used for God (2:9 [twice], 15). It is inescapable in such a context, then, that divine associations be attached to Jesus (in v. 11).

Third, the angelic announcement designates the sign that will assure the shepherds that they have found "a Savior, who is the Messiah, the Lord." But such a strange sign! Hardly fitting for one bearing such honored titles! The babe "wrapped in bands of cloth and lying in a manger," however, is only the beginning of the story

of God's unusual ways in accomplishing the divine rule. Not by
might or coercive tactics, but in submission and humbleness, Jesus
fulfills his vocation.

Perhaps it is the perplexity caused by such a menial sign for such
an exalted baby that evokes the immediate confirmation of the
heavenly chorus, who join the angelic messenger in a doxology. God
is praised for the birth of this child because the birth begins God's
reign of peace on earth. The creatures of the heavenly world, in a
context of praise, announce God's good plans for this world.

Having heard the heavenly witnesses, the shepherds now decide
to go to Bethlehem and "see" this revelation. Like other disciples
who abruptly leave fishing boats and tax tables, they go "with
haste." We are not told what happened to the flocks, apparently left
in the fields. The shepherds' old world has been shattered by the
appearance of the messenger, and now they are in search of a new
one, one centered in the event that has occurred in Bethlehem.

When the shepherds find Mary, Joseph, and Jesus, the narrator
records that they report the message that had been made known to
them about the baby. To whom did they give their report? To Mary
and Joseph? Perhaps. Perhaps the shepherds in responding to the
angelic messenger in fact become a confirmation to Mary and Joseph
of the significance of this baby so unusually born. But there must
have been a wider audience for the shepherds' report too, since "all
who heard it" were astonished—not believing or thoughtful or
adoring, just "amazed." Apparently nothing spurred them to ask
questions or pursue the matter further. In contrast, Mary clings to
what has happened. She continues to ponder the events and the
words (the Greek word is inclusive of both) of the shepherds' visit.

Finally, the shepherds go back to where they came from, apparently back to fields and to flocks, but not back to business as usual.
What was told them by the angelic messenger has been confirmed.
They have heard and seen for themselves. Their old world is gone,
replaced by a new world. Whatever the structure and order of life
before, their world now is centered in the praise and glorifying of
God. The nights in the field will never be the same.

# CHRISTMAS, THIRD PROPER

Ecstasy over the Christmas miracle is the theme that binds these lections together—unrestrained joy over what God has done and over who God is. Yet it is a clearly focused, informed ecstasy, whose very power is generated by the precision with which events are viewed. The God whom these texts celebrate is a God who, in the royalist imagery of the day, reigns in strength, and whose activity on behalf of humankind is timelessly ancient, coinciding with the initial impulses of creation. Yet the eternal Monarch is not distant and remote, qualities that might be suggested by the terms of majesty in which the king is described. Rather this God is near and immediate, a participant in the human struggle for light and salvation.

The texts begin in a mode of transcendency, but move quickly to one of immediacy. As worshipers, we join in rejoicing over the coming of the messenger "who says to Zion, 'Your God reigns' " (Isa. 52:7). We also celebrate "the Lord, for he is coming to judge the earth . . . with righteousness, and . . . equity" (Ps. 98:9). Then the note of immediacy is struck by the focus on what God has done just now, in these "last days," in which "he has spoken to us by a Son" (Heb. 1:2). The One who was present at creation, the eternal Word, "became flesh and lived among us" (John 1:14).

In reading these texts, one is reminded again of the difficulty that all human wordsmiths—be they preachers or whoever—have in articulating the depth of emotion that accompanies Christmas. For all four of these texts are songs, which rhapsodize rather than explain that which happened at Christmas. Perhaps the one exception is the lection from Heb. 1. Yet even this text, which begins as sober prose, soon breaks into song, as if unable, when faced with the limits of simple narration, to restrain its enthusiasm and joy. Small wonder that worshipers on Christmas Day are more likely to leave the church whistling the anthem sung exuberantly by the choir than repeating to one another phrases from the minister's sermon.

Yet the preacher cannot abdicate the task of proclaiming the Christmas good news to the "musicians" who constitute the church, but must wrestle with the impossible challenge of capturing the meaning of Christ's nativity in the frailty of words. These texts are of incomparable value as she or he attempts to meet the challenge.

## Isaiah 52:7–10                                                     (A B C)

This poetic unit is the pivotal statement in "the gospel to exiles" in Isa. 40—55. The poet creates a wondrous scenario in which there are four characters in the dramatic moment of homecoming.

The first character is *"the messenger"* (v. 7). He is the one who hurries across the desert of the Fertile Crescent with news about the titanic battle between Yahweh and the powers of the empire. He has the first news—in a pre-electronic mode—of the outcome of the battle. The term "messenger" is the biblical word for gospel, so that he is the "carrier of the gospel." His way of running already signals that the news is good. Messengers with bad news do not run as well, or as lightly or buoyantly.

The poet piles up words to summarize the message he carries. He announces *"shalom."* He asserts *"good."* He declares *rescue* ("salvation"). Then finally, excited, out of breath, the messenger blurts out the outcome of the contest: "Your God has become king!" The gods have battled for control of the future. The news, the gospel, is the victory of Yahweh. This means for "Zion" a new, joyous, holy governance.

Enter the second voice, *"the sentinel"* (v. 8). On the walls of destroyed Jerusalem, in despair yet still yearning, are sentries. They watch, and they call out what they see. Over the horizon, according to this poetic scenario, they see the runner of v. 7 approaching with a message. They see how he runs. They notice how light and eager are his feet. They conclude immediately that he runs with good news, or he would not run so eagerly. The sentries watch and see only the messenger. They are able, however, to extrapolate from what they see. As they look at the runner and the horizon, they are able to translate both the messenger and the message. What they really see, in a bold act of imagination, is nothing other than victorious Yahweh.

The watchmen sing for joy. They are jubilant because Yahweh is coming. The God long held exile by the empire, the God held as captive as were the Jews, has broken free and is coming home.

The third character in this dramatic scenario is *wounded, defeated,*

*fearful Jerusalem* (v. 9a). The poet imagines that the city, left desolate by the Babylonians, still consists of shattered walls and gates,
defeated doors, broken-up streets, all disheveled, despondent, despairing (compare Neh. 1:3).

Then, however, the watchmen on the wall call down into the city.
Yahweh is victorious; Yahweh is coming home. The watchmen then
invite the broken, forlorn city to change its mood. It is time to sing
and dance, because decisive help is on the way. The fate of the city
has been broken.

This sequence of messenger (Isa. 52:7), watchmen (v. 8), broken
city (v. 9a) is all stage setting for the central character of the plot. The
central character, Yahweh, enters the action at this point (vs. 9b–10).
There had been anticipation of Yahweh as the messenger announced
Yahweh's rule (v. 7), as the sentries see Yahweh's return (v. 8).

Now the poet pays careful attention to Yahweh's dramatic entrance into the poem and into the city. Four statements characterize
Yahweh in this moment of triumphal entry.

(*a*) "Yahweh has comforted Yahweh's people" (v. 9b). Since Isa.
40:1, the poet has taken "comfort" as the central yearning of the
exiles. "Comfort" does not mean simply resigned consolation, but
active intervention, which alters the circumstances of the community.

(*b*) "Yahweh has redeemed Jerusalem." Some texts, instead of
"Jerusalem," read "Israel." Either way, Yahweh has gotten the
special object of love out of hock, permitted it again to live its own
life in freedom.

(*c*) Yahweh has rolled up sleeves as a powerful, strong, intimidating warrior (v. 10). The empires of the world notice Yahweh's
power and back off from their dehumanizing policies. In this
particular text, the poet finds it necessary to utilize a machismo
metaphor to make the claim of power. (Notice elsewhere the use of
maternal metaphors to make a very different point: 40:11; 49:14–15.)

(*d*) The culmination of the entire dramatic scenario concerns the
salvation and homecoming wrought by Yahweh. God is indeed a
God who liberates. Moreover, this is "our God," the God who is "for
us," whose whole life is given over to "us." This poem is relentlessly
good news for the faithful who are defeated.

## Psalm 98                                                    (A B C)

Like the Psalm lections for the first two propers of Christmas, this
text is also a psalm of praise to God. Moreover, its primary images are

similar to Pss. 96 and 97: God as the victorious warrior and as the
creator of the world. The first image is found in vs. 1–3, where the
language reminds us of the exodus narrative, especially Ex. 15.
Yahweh is portrayed here as the defender of the people of God who,
by means of "his right hand and his holy arm" (that is, without human
aid), has achieved the people's liberation. In doing this, Yahweh has
communicated a basic truth concerning the divine nature in that "he
has revealed his vindication." In other words, Yahweh *is* Savior, so
that not to have saved the people would have been a fundamental
violation of who Yahweh is. And in achieving this liberation, Yahweh
has acted in public and demonstrative ways, so that "all the ends of
the earth" have witnessed these mighty deeds.

The image of God as reigning creator dominates vs. 4–8, and in
the background one detects ancient Israel's memory of the old
Creation myths of the ancient Near East in which a hostile primeval
ocean was tamed by the power of God (compare Ps. 93:3–4). But if
the "sea" once rumbled in anger as Yahweh's enemy, it and all
creation (the "world" of v. 7b) now roars its praise of the majestic
Lord who rules over it, and it claps its hands in joy (v. 8). Only this
cosmological dimension to Israel's understanding of God's activity
can account for the universal scope of the imperative in v. 4: All the
earth is to sing before the Lord in joy. Israel is to join in this
outpouring of praise, of course, with lyre, trumpets, horn, and—
needless to say—the human voice.

In all these things, echoes of the Second Isaiah may be detected,
since that prophet also compares Yahweh to a warrior and makes
frequent use of the Creation as a model for God's other acts of
salvation (that is, re-creation). Isaiah 42:10–13 is especially close to
our psalm, the first words of Isa. 42:10 and Ps. 98:1 being identical.

But there is a third section to this psalm, and the transition into it
is so subtle that it may easily be missed. The One who is Victor-
Creator-King is also Judge, and the climax of the text is achieved in
the proclamation that the past is but prologue to the coming of this
divine Judge (v. 9). Yahweh now comes to judge both creation and
those who inhabit it, and to do so by means of righteousness and
equity (the Hebrew noun for "equity" is related to an adjective
meaning "straight" or "upright"). Verse 9 prevents the psalm from
being simply a celebration of what Yahweh *has* done, and decisively
shifts the focus of the celebration to what Yahweh *is* doing now.

The relevance of this text to Christmas is obvious, for at Christ-
mastide we reflexively look backward in time, remembering the
manger, the Holy Family, the angels and shepherds, and so on. The
temptation is to allow our celebration to be lodged there, in the past.

To be sure, our joy is motivated by our profession that the Infant is also the risen Christ, through whose death and resurrection we are reconciled to God. And yet, our thoughts tend to remain focused on a scene long ago and far away.

The force of this psalm is to move us away from the past into the present, into the now. And there are at least two words in the psalm that compel this redirection of our attention. The first of these is the word "new" in the first line of v. 1 (compare Ps. 96:1). The implication is that the old songs will no longer do, in that they are incapable of capturing the human response to what God is doing now. (In the mind of the psalmist these "old" songs were likely the laments over Israel's past disasters; see Ps. 74 or the book of Lamentations.) So it seems clear that the Hebrew poet intends to urge the people to adopt fresh expressions of joy commensurate with the present outbreak of Yahweh's activity. God, who is now working in original and primal ways, must be praised in songs similarly cast.

The second term that calls our attention to the contemporary nature of God's activity is the verb "to come," in v. 9. It is true that there is a certain ambiguity in the Hebrew ($b\bar{a}$'), in that the perfect indicative ("he comes") and the active participle ("is coming") have the same form. But one may argue for the sense "is coming" (NRSV) because of the parallel verb "will judge" ($yi\check{s}p\bar{o}t$), which is imperfect (compare Ps. 96:13). Thus God is in the act of coming now to set things right, and God's former acts of creation and re-creation, although fascinating and wonderful, are but preliminary to what God is in the process of doing at the present moment.

Christmas, while commemorating what God did in the long ago at Bethlehem, is in reality the joyful celebration of what God is doing here and now. God is judging creation, specifically the human family, in the sense that God is at work to set things right. Therefore, the contribution of this psalm to the anthology of Christmas lections is to redirect our Christmas wonder. Our carols of great gladness are not just over what God did at Bethlehem, but over what the reigning Christ does today to straighten that which is crooked in human life and to set right that which has fallen.

## Hebrews 1:1–4 (5–12)                                    (A B C)

In these opening lines, the author of Hebrews draws upon considerable rhetorical skill to produce one of the most elegant passages in the New Testament. The first four verses, rich in alliteration and imagery, announce the major themes of the book as a whole: Christ is both the exalted Son of God and the one whose sacrifice atoned for human sin. Verses 1–2 introduce the theme of the exalted Son by contrasting him with God's messages to humanity in previous generations, and the contrast between Christ and God's angels runs throughout Heb. 1 and 2. This contrast between Christ and the prophets, or between Christ and the angels, does not cancel out the deep continuity that Hebrews affirms. The God who "spoke to our ancestors . . . by the prophets" is identical with the God who "has spoken to us by a Son." God's action in Jesus Christ is absolutely superior to God's earlier actions on behalf of humankind, but former history is in no way denied or negated, as becomes clear when Hebrews draws on Israel's scripture and history throughout.

Verse 2 identifies God's Son as both the "heir of all things" and the one through whom the world was created. Christ stands at both ends of cosmic history. As the writer of Revelation puts it, he is both Alpha and Omega (Rev. 22:13). The world has its origin and its destiny in Christ. This language bears a striking resemblance to Jewish wisdom literature, in which similar claims appear about the figure of Lady Wisdom. Its use here and elsewhere in early Christianity reflects not only the Jewish "background" to Christian thought but the perennial need to portray Christ in language that people can understand.

With its assertions about Christ reflecting God's glory and his role in purification, Heb. 1:3 introduces the dialectic that is at the heart of Christian faith. Jesus is said to be "the exact imprint" of God's nature—that is, Jesus is in every way like God. And Jesus is simultaneously the one who sacrificed himself as a human being for other human beings.

Verse 4 introduces the motif of Christ's superiority to angels, which continues in the quotations from scripture in vs. 5–12. In common with other New Testament writers, the author of Hebrews displays no concern for the original context of the passages he cites. What matters is that scripture lends itself to the claims being made about Christ. In v. 5, the quotations (Ps. 2:7 and 2 Sam. 7:14) reinforce the assertion of Heb. 1:1–2, that Jesus is indeed the Son of God. Similarly, vs. 6–7 reinforce the contrast between God's Son and God's angels (v. 4) by showing that the angels are instructed to worship God's Son.

God may make "his angels winds, and his servants flames," but the Son is destined to rule forever (v. 8). Verse 9 introduces the notion of the goodness of Christ. He exemplifies faithfulness to God by his righteousness, and thereby demonstrates his fitness for reign.

Verses 10–12 continue the contrast with angels by reinforcing the earlier claim that God's Son stands both at the beginning of history and at its end. Christ is God's agent in creation. Christ will always remain the same: "and your years will never end."

The primary thrust of this opening section of Hebrews appears to be doxological. God's eschatological gift of the Son merits human thanks and praise. Within this doxology, the major themes of the book are sounded, and they will be developed in the course of the text. Perhaps there is also a polemical thrust to the contrast between God's Son and God's angels. For example, it could be that some Christians are interpreting Jesus as simply one of God's messengers or that some are actually worshiping angels. Such theories are very difficult to support because of the absence of any explicit polemic.

Whatever the thrust of this text in its own day, the reading of it on Christmas presents several possibilities. With its powerful insistence on Christ as the beginning and end of all things, this text stands as a corrective to any tendency to romanticize the infant Jesus. Just as the theme of Christ's sacrifice stands in tension with his majesty (1:3), so that helplessness of the babe in a manger stands in tension with Christ as the agent and goal of all creation. While the christological language of Hebrews may sound foreign indeed to many contemporary Christians, the proclamation that God's Son stands, unchanging and unchanged, both at the beginning and at the end, may be gospel indeed to people who experience change as the only constant in their lives and who seek frantically for something that abides.

## John 1:1–14                                                      (A B C)

The prologue to John's Gospel has perhaps had more influence on the church's doctrine of the incarnation than any other passage. It affirms in carefully stated language the preexistence of the Word, who is identified with and yet distinct from God, who is the divine agent in creation and yet incarnate in the flesh. But when the congregation gathers for worship on Christmas Day, it does not want or need to hear about the precise distinctions of the church's doctrine. The mood of the season hardly calls for a didactic sermon. It is rather the time to celebrate the birth at Bethlehem and to ask about its meaning, its implications for the congregation, for the church, and for the world. Therefore, the question to ask of the Gospel reading for this service is: How does John 1:1–14 interpret Christmas? What can we learn from it about the baby born in the manger and the meaning of that birth for human life?

First and foremost, from the prologue to John's Gospel *we learn that in Jesus Christ we meet nothing less than the revelation of God.* Word (or Logos), the subject of all the verbs in vs. 1–2, has a rich and illustrious heritage in both Hellenistic and Jewish circles. What is most important, however, is the simple notion of communication. When one speaks or writes a word, one is communicating. "The word of the Lord came to the prophet"—and we through the prophet hear God's message. Now we discover that in Jesus Christ the word identified with God from the very beginning (1:1–3) has taken human form (v. 14), and Christmas is the story of the birth of God's self-communication to the world.

Rather than speaking in Johannine terms, it is perhaps more popular today to think of a "Christology from below," that is, to begin with the historical figure who walked the dusty roads of Galilee, who associated with tax collectors and sinners, who was like us in every respect, and then to speak of his special relationship to God. John's "Christology from above," however, still has its place. It provides us with the healthy reminder of God's distance, that we can only know God as God is *given* to us in an act of revelation. Not our best aspirations or fondest longings or even most sincere service can precipitate such an event. Christmas is first of all the celebration of a gracious decision on God's part to become human in the baby of Bethlehem.

Second, from John's prologue *we learn that God's revelation in Jesus Christ is not altogether obvious.* The Word came to a world that should have known him. After all, he had created the world. In particular, he came to a special people chosen from all the nations to be his own and to a land that was his heritage, but he was rejected. Jesus was not universally acclaimed as the revelation of God, nor worshiped as the one in whom we touch ultimate reality. In fact, the rest of John's Gospel relates story after story of how prominent religious people not only did not recognize Jesus but found him offensive, accused him of blasphemy, charged him with being demon-possessed. Those who confidently thought that they saw things rightly in fact turned out to be blind.

John simply will not let his readers off the hook. He confronts us with a divine self-disclosure that does not document itself with foolproof evidence. We are not provided with irrefutable grounds for faith. We are asked to believe that a particular individual, living in a buffer state in the Middle East, powerless before a Roman governor, is the One in whom we meet the Creator of heaven and earth. The fact that the genuinely religious people who should have received him in fact rejected him leaves readers even more uneasy.

But rejection is not the whole story. There are those who received Jesus, who trusted him, who found themselves by a creative act of God reborn, empowered to be children of God. On the surface they hardly seem potential candidates for the divine family—a Samaritan woman, an unnamed Roman official, a man born blind, an extravagant Mary of Bethany. They are a somewhat unlikely group to become that community called into being and nurtured by the revelation of God in Jesus. But that in itself tells us something about the character of God and God's intentions in Jesus.

Third, from John's prologue *we learn that there is continuity between God's works of creation and revelation.* It begins with language reminiscent of Gen. 1:1, recalling the ancient account of Creation. Then readers are told that the Word enfleshed at Bethlehem is the agent in creation, the one by whom all things were made. There were those in the early church (as there have been those in the modern church) who drove a wedge between nature and grace. The material world for various reasons was thought to be evil, a place from which to escape to a realm of the spirit. Redemption meant freedom from the earthly, the historical, the sensual.

The prologue will have none of this. Salvation is the fulfillment, not the negation, of creation. Jesus does not rescue God's people from a dark and dangerous world. Rather the one who was God's partner in creation has made God concretely known by becoming "flesh." Such a connection between nature and grace certainly underscores the Christian responsibility to care for the earth.

# FIRST SUNDAY AFTER CHRISTMAS

The First Sunday After Christmas is often dubbed a low Sunday. The excitement of the season has waned. Favorite carols have been sung and resung, some more times than we would prefer. For many church members it is a time to withdraw and recoup for the new year ahead. Certainly the mood demands a move beyond the familiar sights and sounds of the season to the coming year.

The texts assigned for the Sunday curiously pair themselves, and in differing ways provide a rich resource for reflection in this post-Christmas pre–New Year period. On the one hand, 1 Sam. 2 and Luke 2 both relate striking encounters between mothers and sons in the context of the religious life of Israel. One son arises in a dark time in Israel's history and as an adult becomes the one who identifies and anoints David as king. The other son fulfills the promise of the first David, both by continuing the traditions of his ancestors and by living out a calling that transcends traditions ("Did you not know that I must be about my Father's interests?" Luke 2:49, marginal reading). Both sons usher in new eras. Both mothers respond in their own fashion to the mysterious ways God has worked in their lives. Their lives provide models for the human response to the strange events of Christmas.

On the other hand, Ps. 148 and Col. 3 agree on the critical role of worship in the life of the people of God. The psalm calls for an unbounded praise that encompasses both heaven and earth. People, animals, angels, and all of nature are caught up in a grand celebration of the divine glory. Colossians 3 more pointedly locates worship as an essential characteristic of God's chosen ones, who have put off the old humanity and who seek in love to live the new life in Christ. Alongside the marks of kindness, humility, patience, and forgiveness, they are to be taught by the word of Christ and to nurture gratitude, peace, and joyful singing. Worship is an appropriate theme for the new year.

## 1 Samuel 2:18–20, 26

The Old Testament lection for this day has been chosen because it is part of the story of young Samuel upon which Luke drew in order to tell the story of young Jesus, with 1 Sam. 2:18–20, 26 anticipating the Gospel lection for this day, Luke 2:41–52.

Samuel's birth occurred at an important juncture in Israel's history. In the hands of the Deuteronomistic historians, the books of Samuel followed immediately upon the closing verses of Judges— that is, without the presence of the book of Ruth, which was inserted at a later time. The final verse of Judges (21:25) makes it clear that the position of the nation, in spite of God's frequent intervention to save the people, was quite precarious. The threats from external enemies, primarily the Philistines, were serious enough in themselves, but the discordant note on which the book of Judges closes suggests strongly that internal tensions and immorality were a major problem as well. In its reference to the fact that "there was no king in Israel" the verse also hints at the nature of the ultimate solution: the house of David.

Notice that the book of Ruth has been introduced at this point in the canonical order of the Old Testament (but not the Hebrew Bible!), not just because it "fits" the chronological sweep of the biblical narrative, but because it too resonates to the anticipation within the text over the coming Davidic king. The book of Ruth colors the subtlety of Judg. 21:25 by introducing the name of David (Ruth 4:17), even as it tells the beautiful story of how a courageous woman, David's great-grandmother, came to Israel.

And so the larger story of Samuel's birth (1 Sam. 1:1–2:26) is told against a background of pessimism generated by the lack of a royal figure in Israel's life and by both intimidation from the outside and lawlessness within. When Hannah prays to the Lord at Shiloh (1 Sam. 1:9–18) it is most immediately because she is childless, a condition that in ancient Israel was viewed as especially ruinous. But the larger dimensions of the text tell us that her prayer was lifted in an Israel devoid of a savior and a king. Samuel, God's answer to Hannah's prayer, is not that savior-king, but his life will ultimately be the bridge between Israel's kingless past and its Davidic future (note 1 Sam. 8:1–22). Thus, the pessimism of Judg. 21:25 is muted by the anticipation of the coming anointed ruler.

First Samuel 2:18 emphasizes the priestly role of young Samuel, the ephod being a liturgical garment worn by Israelite priests. But the text seems not so much interested in Samuel's sacramental office as in the devotion of his mother and father. The reader will already have learned that the earnest prayer of Hannah was uttered on the occasion of one of the family's annual pilgrimages to the sacred Yahweh shrine at Shiloh (1 Sam. 1:9–18). In the present lection, the faithfulness of Samuel's mother is reemphasized, as is the loving attention she pays to her son. Each year (again, it is stated, at the time of the family's pilgrimage) Hannah came to Shiloh with a fresh ephod for her son, an act that not only symbolized her devotion to Samuel, but also stood as a reaffirmation of her earlier vow to dedicate the lad to Yahweh (1:11).

Notice how this characteristic of the text is both similar to and different from Luke 2:41–51: whereas the devotion to God of Mary and Joseph is also expressed by means of their pilgrimage at festival time, their own faithfulness stands in weak anticipation of the faithfulness of Jesus (Luke 2:50). In the case of Samuel's parents, or at least in the case of Hannah, parental faithfulness incubates and sustains the faithfulness of the son.

Elkanah, whose profile is subdued throughout the story of Samuel's youth, is found in the company of Hannah and is described as being the nominal recipient of Eli's blessing: "May [Yahweh] repay you [the pronoun is masculine singular] with children by this woman" (1 Sam. 2:20). But it is really Hannah who is being blessed. Samuel is *her* gift to Yahweh, and Yahweh's gift in return is that she be the mother of other children. Verse 21, which is not included in the lection, provides details concerning the carrying out of this promise.

One recalls the Lukan literature, in which God's blessing on Mary is celebrated (Luke 1:42–45, 48–49).

First Samuel 2:26, included in the present lection because of its obvious inspiration of Luke 2:52, serves as a summary statement which proclaims the result of the Spirit's work in the life of young Samuel. The NRSV phrases Luke 2:52 so that its close parallel to 1 Sam. 2:26 is somewhat obscured, and for that reason the preacher may prefer the RSV for the Lukan lection.

In a moment of need in the life of the people, God's mercy has intervened to send a savior. That statement characterizes both the Old Testament and Gospel lections for this Sunday. The primary difference between the texts is that the subject of 1 Sam. 2:18–20, 26 is not himself the royal savior, but is the one by whom that savior, David, will be identified and invested with his office. Yet in both instances the people of God rejoice, for in their weakness God's mercy has raised up the one (or the One) who comes to deliver and to redeem.

## Psalm 148

In a sense, Ps. 148 displays the typical structure of a hymn or song of praise—an invitation to praise (vs. 1–5a, 7–13a) followed by reasons for praise (vs. 5b–6, 13b–14). At the same time, the typical structure is utilized in a unique way. The invitation to praise, for instance, is greatly elaborated. Every half-line of the psalm up through v. 4a begins with a summons to praise. The word "praise" occurs no less than eleven times as a verb and once as a noun (v. 14).

What is striking too is the identity of those invited to praise God. While the songs of praise generally push toward universality (see Pss. 67:1–7; 100:1; 103:20–22; 117:1, for example), Ps. 148 takes inclusivity to the limit. The Lord is to be praised "from the heavens" (v. 1) by the beings and objects that inhabit the heavens (vs. 2–4), and the Lord is to be praised "from the earth" (v. 7a) by the beings and elements that inhabit the earth (vs. 7b–12). In other words, praising God is the vocation and goal of all creation. Not only are people of all genders, ages, and stations in life to praise God (vs. 11–12); but also invited to praise God are the heavenly host (v. 2; see Ps. 103:20–21) and the heavenly bodies (Ps. 148:3–4; see Ps. 19:1–6) and the chaotic deeps with their inhabitants (Ps. 148:7b; see Isa. 51:9–10) and the weather (Ps. 148:8) and geographical formations (v. 9a; see Isa. 44:23; 49:13; 55:12) and plants (Ps. 148:9b) and all kinds of animals (v. 10). Psalm 148 is even more inclusive than the climactic final verse of the Psalter, for in Ps. 148 it is not just a matter of "everything that breathes" praising God (Ps. 150:6). Rather, it is a matter of everything that *is* praising God.

The list of those invited to praise God is reminiscent of Gen. 1—2: "heavens" and "earth" (Ps. 148:1, 7; Gen. 1:1; 2:1); "host" (Ps. 148:2; Gen. 2:1, NRSV "multitude"); "stars" (Ps. 148:3; Gen. 1:16); "sea monsters" (Ps. 148:7; Gen. 1:21); "fruit trees" (Ps. 148:9; Gen. 1:11); "wild animals and all cattle, creeping things and flying birds" (Ps. 148:10; Gen. 1:21, 24–25). The inclusiveness of this list has profound ecological implications. We human beings are partners in creation with God and with a multitude of other living and inanimate things. Psalm 148 also recalls Gen. 9, where the covenant after the flood is established not just with Noah and his descendants (Gen. 9:9), but also with "every living creature" (9:10, 12, 15, 16) and indeed with "the earth" (9:13). The all-inclusive invitation to praise suggests that the human vocation of "dominion" (Gen. 1:26, 28) involves not just a stewardship of creation but also a partnership with creation. Saint Francis of Assisi had it right when, on the basis of Ps. 148, he composed his Canticle of the Sun, in which he addresses the sun and wind and fire as brother, and the moon and waters and earth as sister (see Hos. 4:1–3, which also suggests the interrelatedness and well-being of humankind and the creation).

Verses 5a and 13a conclude each series of invitations to praise with an identical formulation. The repetition of the phrase "the name of the LORD" directs attention to God's identity and character, which are the subject of the reasons for praise in vs. 5b–6 and 13b–14. In vs. 5b–6, God is creator. God's sovereign word brings things into being and defines their place in the cosmic system (see Prov. 8:27–31; Job 38:4–11; the Hebrew word translated "bounds" in Ps. 148:6 also occurs in Prov. 8:29 and Job 38:10). God's creative work is also in view in v. 13bc with the mention of "earth and heaven," the two realms from which praise has been invited.

In keeping with several psalms at the end of the Psalter that address God as king or affirm God's reign (see Pss. 145:1; 146:10; 149:2), v. 13 also articulates God's sovereignty. In particular, "glory" is an attribute that is elsewhere specifically associated with God's reign (Ps. 96:6, NRSV "honor"; Ps. 145:5, NRSV "majesty"). Like Ps. 148, several of the hymns that specifically affirm God's kingship invite heaven and earth and the beings and objects therein to praise God (Pss. 29:1; 96:11–12; 97:1; 98:4, 7–8). Indeed, the movement of Ps. 148 is similar to that of Ps. 29 (see First Sunday After Epiphany); that is, the praise of heavenly beings (Pss. 29:1–2, 9; 148:2–4) is accompanied by a prayer for or the affirmation of God's strengthening or blessing of God's people (Pss. 29:11; 148:14).

The same movement is also found in Luke 2:13–14, where heavenly beings proclaim both God's glory and peace on earth. The angels' song communicates Luke's conviction that the birth of Jesus represents God's enthronement, and it suggests the appropriateness of Ps. 148 for the season of Christmas. The church affirms that Jesus the Christ not only announced but also embodied the reign of God. Therefore Jesus is to be exalted; and

> at the name of Jesus
> every knee should bend,
> in heaven and on earth and under the earth."
> (Phil. 2:9–10; see Ps. 148:13)

Also quite appropriately, one of the church's cherished Christmas hymns, "Joy to the World," is a paraphrase of Ps. 98, another psalm that celebrates God's enthronement. To greet Jesus as Lord is to recognize God's sovereign claim on our lives and the whole created order, a claim that is clearly articulated in Ps. 148.

## Colossians 3:12–17

The reading from Colossians for this Sunday provides a wonderful text with which to address the coming new year. It appears as the second half of a series of injunctions marking the end of the old humanity and the inbreaking of the new. Using the imagery of undressing and dressing, the text first lists the negative features of life that are to be "stripped off" (3:5–9), the old humanity with its practices. Then it turns to the positive characteristics of the new humanity with which the readers are told they are to "clothe" themselves (3:10–17). While the imagery no doubt derives from the baptismal experience of disrobing before going into the water and taking a new robe when coming out of the water, the various descriptions of the new life provide rich content for a Christian reflection on the life of a new year.

What does it mean to live as a Christian in what some label a post-Christian era, when the prominence of the church in the broader culture has diminished, when Christian values and commitments are not readily acknowledged? It may be that simply raising the question will remind us of our kinship with the early Christians, who operated as a tiny minority in a society that found their ways strange and at times offensive.

The distinctiveness of the church is clearly affirmed in 3:12a. Readers are reminded that they are special—"God's chosen ones, holy and beloved." The text does not lay out a set of moral maxims for the broader culture, but addresses this peculiar group of people who have discovered themselves called and graced by God. The following verses provide vignettes of what the life of such special people is to look like, what characteristics are to distinguish them from neighbors who may not have (yet) discovered themselves called and graced by God. There are both descriptive and proscriptive dimensions to the injunctions. They tell readers what the Christian life is like, but as imperatives they make demands and stake out claims that cannot be avoided.

We note that the injunctions are rather broad in scope (as are most of the ethical imperatives in the New Testament). While they are addressed to a specific audience that has a distinctive set of problems, they make an impact on all Christian readers. They can be applied in a wide range of contexts, and in fact force readers to inquire about their peculiar meanings in changed surroundings.

The five virtues listed in 3:12b (paralleled by five vices in 3:5) are elsewhere in the New Testament all attributed to God or Jesus. As specifically noted in 3:13 regarding forgiveness, the character of God determines the character of God's people. Since God is compassionate, kind, humble, meek, patient, forgiving, loving, and peaceful, God's people are to be and live in like manner. They take their cues for life not from their innate constitution as humans or from what seems to work best in the world, but from the character of God's self-revelation in Jesus Christ.

Some observations about the detailed injunctions: Forgiveness is depicted as an ongoing mark of Christians. The tenses of the verbs in 3:13 make it clear that what is being advocated is not a single occasion of offense and pardon, but a life of forgiving, albeit rooted in the once-and-for-all act of divine forgiveness. Love is given a primary place ("above all"). As Paul writes in 1 Cor. 13, love is the particular reality that has eschatological force, that lasts when all other virtues fade. Here it is singled out as the secret to unity in the community.

The peace of Christ is to "rule in your hearts" (Col. 3:15). The verb appears only this once in the New Testament, but it comes from the actions of the judge (*brabeus*) who makes decisions in contests and assigns the prizes. To put it colloquially, the peace of Christ functions as the umpire who arbitrates the issues and who has full authority to determine how the game is to be played. While peace is God's gift, it also is meant to be an ongoing experience, to become the controller of decisions and the shaper of visions.

In the midst of the ethical injunctions come the words about worship—the active presence of the gospel, teaching, admonition, and singing (3:16). The Christian community is to be distinguished not merely by the quality of its life in the world but also by its regular worship, not only by special interpersonal relations but also by its vocal praise of God.

Finally, the note of thankfulness is sounded three times in the text, perhaps to be sure that the readers do not ignore it (3:15, 16, 17). The repeated reminder touches the issue of motivation. The lives of Christians are driven not by a need to repay God for their offenses previously committed, nor by an effort to stay in good with God as an insurance policy against possible disaster—feelings that are naturally entertained from time to time. Gratitude for both the special and common gifts of grace generates the distinctive life that sets Christians apart as God's chosen ones, holy, beloved.

## Luke 2:41–52

Given the normal human curiosity about the youth of revered or honored figures, it is perhaps surprising that the canonical Gospels contain only this single story about the youth of Jesus. The apocryphal gospels supplement, of course, with astonishing stories about the boy Jesus striking down difficult playmates and raising them up again or shaping sparrows out of clay and bringing them to life. If Luke's story of the boy Jesus in the Temple seems tame by comparison with those later legends, it nevertheless shares with them the desire to explain that Jesus' greatness could be seen already in his childhood. The unknown boy from Nazareth demonstrates such prodigious wisdom that he amazes the teachers in the Temple precincts and bewilders his parents!

In its Lukan setting, the story does more than simply glorify Jesus, however. First, its setting in the Temple continues the Lukan motif of Jesus' continuity with the traditions of Israel. His parents' piety has already been demonstrated in their offering of 2:22–38 and in the narrator's note that they went to Jerusalem annually to celebrate the Passover. Here we find Jesus himself in the Temple and engaged in discussion with Israel's teachers.

Second, the story anticipates the radical commitment that Jesus' teaching will later demand of his hearers. What the adult Jesus asks of his followers, the child Jesus here enacts. He concerns himself with the things that matter to the extent that fundamental family relations are treated as secondary matters. The meaning of the phrase the NRSV translates as "in my Father's house" is quite ambiguous, as the commentaries on this passage will explain. Whatever the phrase means, it claims as first priority the connection of Jesus with the God who is indeed his father. This statement becomes even more impressive when we recall the high priority Jesus' contemporaries assigned to loyalty to family connections.

Third, in spite of the distance between Jesus and his parents that is implied by his question, "Why were you searching for me?" and in spite of their inability to understand his behavior, he demonstrates the appropriate obedience by returning to Nazareth with them. This feature of the text is closely linked with the first two, for the piety of Jesus' family and his own profound sense of connection to God are reflected in his obedience to the Fifth Commandment.

As long as we read this passage as a praiseworthy incident in the life of the young Jesus, it remains largely innocuous. If we change our lenses, however, and read it through the experience of Jesus' human parents, particularly Mary, it becomes much more troubling. In addition to the theme of Jesus' wisdom and devotion, another theme that appears here and continues throughout the Gospel is the inability of others to comprehend Jesus and his message. No one, not even Mary, fully understands who Jesus is or what his mission will involve.

The way in which Luke tells the story invites readers to consider it along with the parents, for the action of the story revolves around their experience. They leave Jerusalem, they travel, they discover that their child is missing, they begin a frantic search to find him, they eventually find him in the Temple. It is difficult not to be moved by the fierce worry that must surely accompany such a journey.

The discovery of Jesus engaged in dialogue with the teachers of Israel may lead to astonishment, but it does not diminish the anxiety of his parents. The NRSV considerably understates the intensity of Mary's question, which betrays that she and Joseph have been in the grip of a terrible anguish. That it is Mary rather than Joseph who asks the question arouses the attention of interpreters, for in the Mediterranean culture of that era the father would be expected to take the initiative in confronting a son. One reason often given for the change here is that the scene itself concerns the Heavenly Father of Jesus, a point that might be confused were Joseph to speak. Throughout the infancy narrative, however, Luke draws attention to Mary and her responses to events (for example, 1:26–38, 46–56; 2:6–7, 19, 34). That he does so here also should not be surprising.

Two further comments by the narrator focus our attention on the human parents of Jesus, and especially Mary. The first comment (Luke 2:50) indicates that "they did not understand what he said to them." The second comment is that Mary "treasured all these things in her heart" (v. 51), but this translation in the NRSV is somewhat misleading. Mary "keeps" these things, much as Jacob kept events surrounding the troublesome Joseph (Gen. 37:11) or Daniel kept his visions (Dan. 7:28). These events perplex and trouble Mary, who turns them over again and again and again.

What Luke conveys here is something far more significant than a mere mental or emotional scrapbook of the infant Jesus. Despite Gabriel's announcement (or even because of it?), Mary does not understand what she sees and hears. In common with all other followers of Jesus, she must wait and see what will unfold, who he will become, and where his Father will lead him. She stands with the church itself, trusting that this child comes from God, consenting to obedience, and straining to comprehend.

# SECOND SUNDAY AFTER CHRISTMAS

With a variety of striking images, the readings for the Second Sunday After Christmas invoke praise and thanksgiving to God for God's outrageous generosity in the gift of Jesus Christ. The first three readings all contrast that generosity with the situation of humanity apart from God's intervention. Jeremiah 31:7–14 portrays for us a people in exile, a people for whom despair and grief seem to be the only option. The apparent eternity of winter's grasp dominates Ps. 147:12–20, with its picture of God sending "snow like wool" and "frost like ashes." John's prologue conjures up the hopelessness of life lived out in a dark world, a powerful place in which humans cannot even see how to proceed for themselves.

Common to all these texts is not only the assertion of human helplessness and hopelessness apart from God, but also the proclamation that God has already invaded the world and caused a new world to come into being. God invades and overturns the exile, replacing mourning with exuberant joy. God's gift of spring occurs even without our request for aid, simply because God is one who rescues. The incarnation of Jesus Christ powerfully breaks in as God's Light triumphs over against all darkness. Ephesians 1 asserts the soteriological consequences of God's invasion and proclaims those consequences to have been part of God's will even from the beginning. The gospel is not God's afterthought in response to a problem: it is deeply rooted in God's nature to act on behalf of creation.

Another element common to these texts is their assertion of praise and thanksgiving to God. In response to this proclamation of the gospel, the only right action for human beings is to sing the doxology.

## Jeremiah 31:7–14                                          (A B C)

The exile of Israel smells of defeat, despair, and abandonment. Moreover, it is a place of deadly silence. All the voices of possibility have been crushed and nullified. Our capacity to make this text available depends on making two daring connections.

1. The *deadliness of exile* is the context into which *Jesus is born* and in which Christmas is celebrated. Christmas is an act against exile.

2. The *deadliness of exile* continues to be a metaphor through which to understand *our own social, cultural situation* of defeat, dehumanization, and despair.

Thus all three settings, in the exile of Jer. 31, in the New Testament, and in our time, are closely parallel in their silent hopelessness. Into all three scenes, the gospel flings this strident speech of God.

In the first part of our text, God addresses the exilic community and invites it to a new reality, which is rooted only in God's faithful resolve (vs. 7–9).

1. God issues an invitation to Israel in exile filled with glad imperatives (v. 7). In characteristic hymnic fashion, Israel is invited to sing aloud, raise shouts, proclaim, praise, say. These are all acts of joyous assertion which muted Israel thought it could never voice. The reason for the rejoicing is in the substance of the saying, which might be paraphrased: "Yahweh has *saved* the covenant partner!" God intervenes to liberate and new life begins, new life that was not at all expected. The reason for singing is that the deathly grip of Babylon is broken!

2. Verses 8–9 give the reason for the singing. The introductory "see" invites Israel to notice something utterly new. Now God speaks in the first person. Moreover, God is the willing subject of active verbs that will transform the life of Israel: "I am going to bring, I will gather, I will lead, I will let them walk." The poet conjures a great pilgrimage of people headed home, the ones who thought they would never have a home. In that pilgrimage are included the ones who are vulnerable and dependent, the blind, the lame, the pregnant women. These are the ones who are always at risk. Now, however, that risk is ended; they are safe, kept, and guarded on the way.

Now God addresses the nations (vs. 10–14).

1. The speech of God puts the nations on notice (vs. 10–11). They will have to yield to God's deep resolve. They will have to release their hostages and forgo their supply of cheap labor. God will be the faithful shepherd who values every sheep, even the lost, even the

ones in exile. The nations can do nothing to stop God from this daring resolve.

2. The poet then conjures for us what new life will be like when the exiles come home and the power of fear and death is broken (vs. 12–14).

(a) Creation will flourish; there will be extravagant material goods (v. 12). In an arid climate that has only marginal supplies of water, to be by reliable "brooks of water" (see v. 9) is a powerful image of material well-being. Death is fended off.

(b) Social life will resume (v. 13a). Young people can have their loud, boisterous parties. No one will mind; older people will join in, because such noise is a song of confidence, stability, freedom, and well-being.

(c) Restored creation (v. 12) and restored community (v. 13a) are rooted in God's transformative power. It is God, only God, but surely God, who transforms mourning to joy, exile to homecoming, death to life, sorrow to gladness (v. 13b; compare John 16:20).

(d) An ordained religious community will live in utter well-being (v. 14). People will prosper, priests will prosper. Priests and people together will live in well-being, where blessings abound.

In every season, including ours, the oracle of God breaks the dread of exile. Exiles are those who live in resignation, believing no newness is possible. That gripping hopelessness is not explained by the psychology of modernity, but is a deep theological crisis. The only ground for newness is God. Here God speaks unambiguously, against all our presumed death. It is by the power and faithfulness of God that life begins again.

## Psalm 147:12–20 (A B C)

The ability of this lection to stand independently of the rest of the psalm of which it is a part is illustrated by the fact that in the Septuagint it is a distinct psalm, Ps. 147 in the Septuagint enumeration (vs. 1–11 of this psalm constituting the Septuagint's Ps. 146). It consists of two basic parts, of which the first is vs. 12–14. These lines urge the people to praise God (v. 12) because God has endowed the nation with peace (the first lines of vs. 13 and 14, respectively) and prosperity (the second lines of these same verses).

The second part of the psalm, vs. 15–20, celebrates the power of God's word. This theme is announced in v. 15, where the Hebrew wordplay goes undetected in most English translations. The Hebrew behind "his command" (NRSV, REB) is 'imĕrātô, and literally means something like "his utterance," since it is related to the root '*āmar*, "to utter" or "to say." This term is paralleled by "word" (*děbārô*) of v. 15b, and the effect of the whole verse is to remind the reader that God is in an ongoing conversation with creation. The action verbs "send out" and "run swiftly" imply incessant dialogue (not monologue, as we shall note below) between God and the people of God (compare v. 19), a continuing hum of communication.

The nature of God's word—that part of the dialogue which originates with the Deity—is described metaphorically in vs. 16–18. It is perhaps coincidental that this description of the wintry blast in ancient Israel is appointed to be read in North American churches at the coldest time of year in the northern temperate zone, and the articulation of these verses will be strengthened in those congregations whose houses of worship lie under blankets of snow on this day. NRSV's "Who can stand before his cold?" in v. 17b is an accurate translation of the Masoretic Text as it stands, but a slight change in the Hebrew letters yields "before his cold the waters stand still," that is, "freeze," perhaps a preferred rendering (see REB).

If vs. 16–17 portray God's deep freeze, v. 18 describes God's thaw. Here is found another wordplay. "Word" of 18a echoes the same term (*děbārô*) in 15b, but here it is paralleled not by '*iměrātô*, but by *rûhô*, which may mean either "his wind" (NRSV), "his breath," or "his Spirit." The ambiguity is probably not accidental, for another Hebrew poet has written an extended play on this very word in Ezek. 37:1–14, an ingenious creation in which the power of language to speak on several levels at once is remarkably demonstrated. Psalm 147:18 seems to be an intriguing way of saying, "As the warm spring winds blow to melt the ice and snow of winter, so the Spirit of God melts all that is frozen in human life."

As noted above, the statement in v. 15 concerning the presence of God in human life is balanced by a similar statement in v. 19, a pair of "brackets" around the metaphor of vs. 16–18. Yet in v. 19 the application to human life of God's word is given a sharper focus than in v. 15, for here it is applied in a special way to Israel, a thought that is extended into the first two lines of v. 20.

The entire text is climaxed by a final *halělû-yāh*, which not only echoes similar imperatives in v. 12, but balances the psalm's opening *halělû-yāh*, in v. 1.

The heart of this text is, of course, the metaphor of winter and spring. It limits the power of this passage to see it as a simple statement of God's power over the world of nature, although it does make such a statement. But beyond that it portrays God's role in the movement of the individual person (or human community) from death to life, from desolation to hope, from meaninglessness to purpose. Verses 16–17 may be compared to many of the psalms of lament and of thanksgiving, which describe the human condition of alienation and estrangement in the language of imagery. Psalm 30:9, for example, complains that if the psalmist (or reader of the psalm) is allowed to die, God will be the loser, since the dead are incapable of praise. But "death" is no more the final word in Ps. 30 than is "winter" in Ps. 147:12–20. In vs. 11–12 of Ps. 30 God responds to the human plea for help by restoring the helpless one to life:

> You have turned my mourning into dancing; . . .
> so that my soul may praise you and not be silent.

Yet it is significant that in this lection God intervenes to restore the helpless even though there is no stated plea for help. The warm winds of spring do not thaw the frozen water because of human intercession, but simply because it is God's nature to restore and redeem. The same God who rebukes the ice and snow also rebukes sin and evil, because that's the kind of being God is. Men and women may cry to God for help, but it is God's nature to help whether or not men and women cry.

This reality brings forth the human response of praise, that part of the divine-human dialogue referred to above that originates with men and women. The God of Israel is the Lord of both freezing and thawing, of both death and life, of both alienation and fellowship. And because this God is always at work moving life from the one to the other, the community of faith sings in joyful response: Hallelujah!

## Ephesians 1:3–14                                        (A B C)

Paul customarily opens his letters with an expression of thanksgiving for God's action in the lives of the congregation he addresses. Ephesians, which was probably written by a disciple of Paul rather than by Paul himself, not only continues that practice but expands it. Virtually the whole of chapters 1—3 is taken up with expressions of praise and thanksgiving. Ephesians 1:3 introduces this dominant mood of doxology with an ascription of praise to God for God's gifts to humankind. Since the word "blessing" in Greek can refer both to an act of thanksgiving or praise and to an act of bestowing some gift on another, the play on the word in this verse sets the tone for what follows: God is to be blessed for God's blessings. The extent of these blessings comes to expression in the phrase "every spiritual blessing in the heavenly places." God's goodness takes every conceivable form.

Verses 4–14 detail the form of God's blessings and focus on God's choosing of the elect. First, the author points to the agelessness of God's election: "He chose us in Christ before the foundation of the world." This bit of eloquence need not be turned into a literal proposition about God's act of election. Instead, the author asserts that God's choosing has no beginning. Just as it is impossible to identify the beginning of God's Christ (John 1:1), so it is impossible to conceive of a time when God did not choose on behalf of humankind.

God's election creates a people who are "holy and blameless before him." Verse 5 elaborates this characterization of God's people. They become God's children through Jesus Christ, but always what happens is "according to the good pleasure of his will." Everything that has occurred comes as a result of God's will and results in "the praise of his glorious grace that he freely bestowed on us in the Beloved." In the face of God's eternal choice on behalf of humankind, in the face of God's revelation of his Son, Jesus Christ, in the face of God's grace, the only appropriate response is one of praise (v. 6).

Verses 7–14 continue the exposition of God's gifts to human-kind—redemption, forgiveness, wisdom, faith. The exposition culminates with repeated references to the inheritance believers receive through Christ (vs. 11, 14). That inheritance carries with it the responsibility already articulated in v. 6, which is to praise God's glory. Primary among the Christian's responsibilities is the giving of praise to God. With v. 15, the writer moves from this general expression of thanksgiving for God's actions on behalf of human-kind to particular expressions of thanks relevant to his context. He constantly keeps the Ephesians in his prayers, asking for them "a spirit of wisdom and of revelation as you come to know [God]" (v. 17). The prayer continues in v. 18 with the petition that believers might be enlightened so that they know the hope to which they have been called and the riches that are part of God's inheritance. This mood of doxology continues throughout chapter 2 and most of chapter 3, as the author celebrates the nature of God's action in Christ Jesus.

For Christians in the West, particularly for those in North America, these words may have an alien and perhaps even an exotic tone. They run counter to at least two of our most deeply held values.

First, these verses insist over and over again that humankind is utterly dependent on God. To assert that God creates, God destines, God wills, God reveals, God accomplishes God's own plan means that human beings, in and of themselves, accomplish nothing. This assault on the Western sense of independence and autonomy poses not only a challenge, but also a significant opportunity for preaching.

The second way in which this text cuts against the grain of Christianity in a North American context derives from its insistence on the obligation to praise God. Our thoroughgoing pragmatism inclines us to respond to the claim that God has acted on our behalf with the question, "What are we to *do?*" If we stand in God's debt, then we understand ourselves to be obliged to pay back the amount owed. The text, however, stipulates no repayment, for the debt can never be paid. Instead, the exhortation is to give God thanks and praise. To our way of thinking, this is no response at all, and yet it is fundamental to our existence as God's creatures. The reading of Ephesians should prompt us to recall the words of the Westminster Larger Catechism, that the chief end of human life is "to glorify God and enjoy him forever."

## John 1:(1–9) 10–18                                    (A B C)

A portion of the prologue to the Fourth Gospel appeared as the Gospel reading for the Third Proper of Christmas, and the commentary on that lesson focused on Jesus as the revelation of God. Beyond the sentimentality and romance of Christmas, we encounter in the baby born at Bethlehem, so the passage tells us, nothing less than God's decision to become human. The full prologue (if one chooses) now occurs as the reading for the Second Sunday After Christmas, and provides us with the opportunity to reflect on further dimensions of God's incarnation as they emerge from the text.

One notable feature of the prologue is the prominence of visual language (a particularly relevant feature for the Epiphany season). "Light" and "glory" are terms associated with the Word, and "seeing" (alongside "receiving" and "believing") is the verb used for the perception of faith. Even before a statement of the incarnation, we read that the life found in the Word illuminates human experience, that the light continually shines in the darkness, and that the darkness has neither understood nor succeeded in extinguishing the light. (The Greek verb in 1:5 translated in the NRSV as "overcome" has a double meaning: "comprehend" and "seize with hostile intent." Perhaps an appropriate English word retaining the ambiguity would be "grasp," or "apprehend.")

The mention of John the Baptist, who is a kind of lesser luminary or reflected light (5:35) and is contrasted with the true light, signals the movement from a preincarnate lumination to the historic advent of the light in Jesus. It is in this context that we understand that the coming of the light into the world "enlightens everyone" (1:9). This universal reference has sometimes been taken to refer to the ancient notion that every individual possesses a spark of the divine, a measure of a universal conscience. The function of religion (any religion?) is to nurture the inextinguishable spark until it glows with understanding, so the argument goes. But such a reading hardly coheres with the evangelist's use of the image of light throughout the Gospel. Jesus claims in a specific way to be the light of the world (8:12), without whom people grope in the darkness (12:35). The coming of the light entails judgment, because it discloses that people prefer darkness to light (3:19). What seems to be implied in the prologue is that all people, whether they believe it or not, live in a world illuminated by the light just as they live in a world created by the Word. What they are called to do is to trust the light, to walk in it, and thereby to become children of light (12:36).

Whether as a bolt of lightning in a dark sky, or as a distant beam toward which one moves, or as the dawn that chases the night, what light does is to push back darkness. The prologue, however, gives no hint that the light has totally banished the darkness, that life now is a perpetual day. In fact, the story John tells reiterates the powerful opposition of the darkness in the ministry of Jesus and beyond. But the promise of the prologue is that the darkness, despite its best efforts, including even a crucifixion, has not put out the light.

The last paragraph of the prologue has to be understood in terms of the many references to the book of Exodus, which it reflects. In a sense its background is the statement that "no one has ever seen God" (1:18). Though in fact there are places in the Hebrew Bible where people "see" God (for example, Ex. 24:9–11; Isa. 6:1), the statement seems to recall the occasion where Moses, eager to behold the divine glory, is not allowed to view the face of God, only God's backside (Ex. 33:23). In contrast, now God is seen in "the only Son."

Furthermore, the seeing of the divine glory is made possible by the incarnation of the Word, who "tabernacled among us." The Greek verb translated in the NRSV (John 1:14) as "lived" more specifically means "tented" or "tabernacled," and recalls the theme of God's dwelling with Israel, in the tabernacle of the wilderness wanderings and the Temple at Jerusalem. In the humanity of Jesus, the Christian community has beheld the very divine glory Moses wished to see, that unique and specific presence of God that hovered over the tabernacle as a cloud by day and a fire by night.

Terms like "light" and "glory" tend toward abstractions and become very difficult to communicate in concrete language to a contemporary congregation. What, then, does it mean to "see" God, to behold the divine glory? Two other words repeated in the prologue help in the translation: grace and truth. To behold God is to be a recipient of wave after wave of the divine generosity (grace) and to experience God's faithfulness to the ancient promises (truth). "Seeing" includes but goes beyond mere sense perception; it has to do with becoming children of God, with discovering the divine benevolence and reliability. Revelation in the Fourth Gospel has a strongly soteriological cast (17:3).

# EPIPHANY

As the reading of Isa. 60:1–6 in the context of the celebration of Epiphany recalls, the coming of God into the world is often understood as the coming of a brilliant light. That light, the gift of God, carries with it the power to transform Israel so that Israel is restored and also those outside Israel are inevitably drawn to the light seen in Israel. While the social context differs dramatically, Eph. 3:1–12 makes a similar point: part of the mystery of the Epiphany is the mysterious inclusion of Gentiles among God's people. Submission to God's gift of light carries with it the obligation to accept and proclaim the inclusion of all outsiders within this mystery.

Psalm 72:1–7, 10–14 and Matt. 2:1–12 draw on imagery of the king and his enthronement, rather than the appearance of light. For the psalmist, the king's power and longevity must serve the purpose of the people's good. Prominent among the king's obligations is his responsibility to protect and liberate those who are not able to protect and liberate themselves. Ironically, Matt. 2:1–12 concerns the birth of an infant king whose power and longevity are severely threatened by another king, who acts only to protect himself. The Magi, outsiders drawn by the light that marks the infant king's birth, mark the beginning of the procession of those outsiders who see in the gospel the mystery of salvation. The juxtaposition of the enthronement psalm and the story of the infant Jesus, already King, dramatically poses the question of where authentic power lies and what constitutes genuine kingship.

## Isaiah 60:1–6                                          (A B C)

Israel has had a long season of darkness (the despair of exile). Now comes its season of light. The light is not self-generated by Israel. It is a gift given by Yahweh. In the liturgical life of Israel,

God's powerful coming is often presented as the coming of light, though the word used for such light is "glory." God's glory "shines." And when God's glory (powerful, magisterial presence) "shines," Israel lives in the glow, and is itself a presence of light in the world. Thus the text that moves Israel from darkness to light is a dramatic move from absence to presence, from despair to hope, from dismay to well-being.

God's coming will decisively transform Israel's circumstance of despondency (Isa. 60:1–2). Israel is addressed with an imperative: "Arise." The imperative, however, is in fact an invitation. The imperative is not a burden, but good news. The imperative is an invitation for Israel to return to the land of the living.

The ground for the imperative is introduced by "for" (= because). Israel can arise because "your light has come." The words are wondrously and deliberately ambiguous. "Your light" is in fact Yahweh, who is Israel's only source of hope and possibility. At the same time, however, "your light" refers to Israel's own "glow," which is a gift from Yahweh that changes the very character of Israel. Thus "your light" is both *intrusion from Yahweh* and *restored Israel.*

These poetic lines are constructed so that an affirmation of "God's glory" is stated in v. 1b and reiterated in v. 2d. Between these two affirmations is a statement about darkness and thick darkness, gloom and despair. Thus the "glory" brackets and comprehends, contains and overwhelms, the darkness.

The poet waxes eloquent and extravagant about the magnet of Jerusalem among the nations (vs. 4–7). Something new is happening that Israel could not have expected or believed. When Israel finally lifts its eyes from its despair, it will not believe what it sees! There is a huge procession from all over the known world. Jerusalem had thought itself abandoned; now all the others are making the journey to be in Jerusalem.

On the one hand, "your sons" and "your daughters" will come, cared for, protected, valued (v. 4). These are the exiles that have been scattered far from Jerusalem. They had remained scattered long after the "official return," either because they were restrained by their "hosts" from coming home, or because they had lost their will and desire and resolve to come home. The light ends the exile. The poet imagines a world in which the abused and nearly forgotten now are drawn back to their proper habitat among God's beloved people.

On the other hand, the procession also includes more than the scattered Jewish exiles. It also includes the "wealth of the nations" (v. 5). Israel was rarely if ever one of the affluent nations. Most often Israel, in its disadvantage, stood in awe of its more powerful, prosperous neighbors. The poet plays on Israel's long-established sense of disadvantage, of being a rather second-rate people. Now, in this scenario, realities are reversed. The exotic material of the nations, long coveted from a distance, is given to Israel, who is the locus of the light in the world. The exiles are not coming home empty-handed. The exiles bring all that the nations can offer— camels, gold, frankincense, and flocks. Damaged Jerusalem has become the pivot and possibility for a new world.

The rhetoric of the poem is double-focused, in a quite careful way. On the one hand, there is no doubt that Israel gains as a political, economic power and is assured security and prosperity. On the other hand, that assurance is passionately theological. The exiles bring this much wealth, not to prosper Jerusalem, but to worship Yahweh (v. 7). The passage begins in God's glory (vs. 1–2) and ends in God's glory (v. 7). Israel's new reality of prosperity exists exactly in the envelope of God's glory.

Whenever the nations bring such exotic gifts, they are in fact submitting themselves to God's new future. That is what is happening with the bringing of "gold, frankincense, and myrrh" (Matt. 2:11). When God is thus worshiped, Israel prospers, Jerusalem glows, the nations come to their proper existence, all bask in the glow of God's well-being. God's presence creates newness for the entire world. In this poem, all—Jerusalem, the exiles, the nations— receive the gift of life.


## Psalm 72:1–7, 10–14                                          (A B C)

A widely held scholarly view sees this psalm as a hymn sung at the time of the enthronement of the Davidic king, or if ancient Israel possessed an annual ceremony of reenthronement, as did ancient Babylon, a hymn devoted to that occasion. In either event, there is a sense in which the king is entering (or reentering) the public life of the nation, and the psalm expresses the hopes that the people have vested in this monarch, who is also the representative of God. Therefore it is an appropriate text for the Epiphany observance, a celebration of the entrance of the messianic ruler, Jesus Christ, into the life of humankind.

The opening (vs. 1–4) constitutes a prayer to God that the king will establish a right social order. Prominent in these lines are terms that were often found on the lips of the prophets: righteousness (vs. 1, 2, 3), justice (vs. 1, 2), and peace (v. 3, NRSV "prosperity"). They are also found in certain of the psalms of praise, where they refer not only to qualities characteristic of God, but to the nature of human life before God (Pss. 97:2; 98:9). For the author of Ps. 72, these qualities are not abstractions, but are moral ideals which have become incarnate in the Davidic king. Those qualities which began with God ("*your* justice, . . . *your* righteousness," v. 1, emphasis added) have become the standards by which the human king is to rule. His role is to help those who cannot help themselves (v. 4).

The following section (vs. 5–7) begins as a prayer for the king's long life, the kind of ritualistic formula that has been a part of coronation ceremonies ancient and modern ("Long live the king!"). Yet it is of the nature of this psalm that it will not dwell on the king's good health, but returns to the larger question of the health of the community. As in the first section, "righteousness" and "peace" (v. 7) are the standards by which the well-being of the people is judged, and it is they, not just the heartbeat of the king, that must be preserved past the end of the moon (v. 7, compare v. 5).

The discourse soon turns to the urgent affairs of the society: the well-being (*šālôm* of vs. 3, 7) of the poorest, most helpless citizens. Notice the verbs: "delivers" (v. 12), "has pity" (v. 13), "saves" (v. 13), "redeems" (v. 14). Clearly God's king is to bring the same energies to bear on the quality of the nation's domestic life as on foreign affairs. And—if the literary form means anything—since the king's concern for domestic matters is placed in a climactic position within the psalm, this aspect of his duties is to weigh more heavily upon him than his military adventures.

This lection ends with an affirmation of the value of human life in the king's eyes: "Precious is their blood in his sight" (v. 14).

The most often remarked emphasis of Epiphany is on the appearance of the messianic king, Jesus Christ, and it is in this connection that other lections for this day emphasize light (Isa. 60:1; Matt. 2:2) and the ability of men and women to see God's work (Isa. 60:2; Eph. 1:9, 18). But this Psalm lection contributes an added dimension to the Epiphany observance by celebrating not only the appearance of the king, but the nature of the king's rule as the liberator of those who are unable to liberate themselves. To be sure, the same note is struck in other texts that describe the birth and infancy of Jesus (notably Luke 1:52–53), but few texts draw so tightly the connection between God's act of sending a king and the responsibilities of the king as protector of the poor and the weak.

There is an irony in this theme when it is applied to Epiphany, for Epiphany is the celebration of the visit of the Magi, bearers of precious gifts to the boy-king Jesus. The description of wealth in the traditional Gospel lection for Epiphany (Matt. 2:1–12) is to be found in the gold, frankincense, and myrrh, the treasures of the Magi. In that narrative the messianic King is a weak and vulnerable child, under threat from the tyrannical Herod. His one kingly act is a passive one of receiving the tokens of royalty bestowed by others.

But in the Epiphany Psalm lection, all of that is turned around. Here the royal office itself is that which has been bestowed, not just its tokens. And the giver is not some earthly seer or potentate, but the one true King, Israel's God. As for the theme of wealth in the psalm, while there is some traditional language of empire, the real wealth consists in šālôm (vs. 3, 7). This is more than "peace" in the sense of an absence of warfare. It is also more than "prosperity," as the NRSV—with some justification—has it (v. 3). Šālôm in this case is the total well-being of the people (compare NEB's "peace and prosperity"), their ability to live free from "oppression and violence" imposed by others (v. 14) and free from the devastating effects of poverty.

Thus the Epiphany celebration is the joyous proclamation of a kingdom like no other. It is the joyous acceptance of a King who has come to set us free.

## Ephesians 3:1–12                                                      (A B C)

Following the first two chapters of Ephesians, with their extensive thanksgiving to God, in 3:1 the author takes up Paul's ministry in the context of God's mystery. Verses 1–3 characterize Paul's calling as his "commission." Verses 4–6 elaborate on the nature of God's mystery that is now revealed, and this section provides the most obvious entrance into a discussion of the Epiphany. In vs. 7–9, the focus is once again on Paul's ministry concerning that mystery, and in vs. 10–12 it is on the ministry of the church as a whole.

The opening statement breaks off awkwardly after the identification of Paul as "a prisoner for Christ Jesus for the sake of you Gentiles." Verse 2 verifies Paul's calling as prisoner on behalf of the Gentiles by referring to the gift of God's grace which bestowed on him a "commission" on behalf of Gentiles. Verse 3 makes specific the nature of this gift of grace, in that the mystery became known to Paul through revelation. In common with all believers, Paul's knowledge of God's action comes to him solely through God's own free gift.

Verse 4 returns to the term "mystery," which is initially described only as a "mystery of Christ." The newness of the revelation of this mystery emerges in v. 5, which emphasizes that only in the present time has the mystery been revealed. This assertion stands in tension with statements elsewhere in the Pauline corpus regarding the witness of the prophets to God's action in Jesus Christ (for example, Rom. 1:2; 16:26). What the author celebrates is the present revelation of God's mystery, and the contrast with the past helps to emphasize that fact but should not become a critique or rejection of past generations. Similarly, the second part of v. 5 identifies the "holy apostles and prophets" as recipients of revelation, not because revelation confines itself to those individuals but because of their central role in proclamation.

Verse 6 identifies the "mystery of Christ": "the Gentiles have become fellow heirs, members of the same body, and sharers in the promise in Christ Jesus through the gospel." Given the previous few verses, we might anticipate that the "mystery" refers to the mystery of Jesus' advent. For this letter, however, the "mystery of Christ" has a very specific connotation, namely, the inclusion of the Gentiles. Each word identifying the Gentiles in v. 6 begins with the prefix *syn*, "together," emphasizing the oneness created through the mystery. We might convey this phrase in English as "heirs together, a body together, sharers together." For the writer of Ephesians, central to the "mystery of Christ" is the oneness of Jew and Gentile.

The emphasis here on the social dimension of the gospel, the unification of human beings, needs specific attention. Certainly Ephesians does not limit the mystery to its social component, as if the only characteristic of the gospel is its impact on human relations. The extensive praise of God and of Jesus Christ in chapters 1 and 2 prevents us from reductionism. Nevertheless, here the radical oneness of Jew and Gentile who become one new humanity (2:15) becomes a necessary ingredient in the larger reconciliation of humankind to God (2:16). Any separation between "vertical" and "horizontal" dimensions of faith here stands exposed as inadequate.

Verses 7–9 return us to Paul's role with respect to the gospel. He, despite his own standing as "the very least of all the saints," receives the gift of preaching among the Gentiles and, indeed, among all people (v. 9). Proclamation of the gospel comes not from Paul and his fellow apostles alone, however. Verse 10 identifies the role of the whole church in proclamation. The church, both through its verbal proclamation and through its actions, makes known God's wisdom. Here that wisdom is addressed to "the rulers and authorities in the heavenly places." The gospel addresses not only human beings but all of God's creation.

Verses 11–12 affirm once again the purpose of God in the proclamation of Paul and of the church. God's purpose has its final goal in Christ Jesus our Lord, "in whom we have access to God in boldness and confidence through faith in him." These last terms connote more in Greek than the English translations can convey. To speak "boldly" (*parrēsia*) is to speak without regard for the consequences, and to have "access" (*prosagōgē*) is to have, through Jesus Christ, a means of drawing near to God. In other words, the revelation, or epiphany, of Jesus Christ carries with it both the obligation of proclaiming the gospel and the strength needed for carrying out that obligation.

## Matthew 2:1–12                                                     (A B C)

The story of the Magi coming from the East to bring gifts to the infant Jesus is associated in the minds of most churchgoers with Christmas. It is a piece of the scene usually enacted at the Christmas service or pageant. The story, however, with its strong connections with the Hebrew scriptures and its prominent depiction of these non-Jewish worshipers, fits more appropriately the celebration of Epiphany. It telegraphs for the reader of Matthew's narrative the opening of the gospel beyond Jewish boundaries and the reminder of the worldwide mission of the church.

We shall examine the passage in terms of its three primary characters. First are the Magi. The Greek term *magoi* suggests that the "wise men" were priestly sages from Persia, who were experts in astrology and the interpretation of dreams. What distinguishes them in the narrative is *their sincere and persistent search* for the baby "born king of the Jews." While one might suppose them to have been veteran, sophisticated travelers, what is striking is their candor and openness. Almost naive, they seem to anticipate no difficulty in inquiring of Herod the king about the birth of a rival king. Their inquisitiveness forces a troubled Herod to seek help from the chief priests and scribes, who, though aligned with Herod, ironically produce the decisive clue that finally leads to Bethlehem.

Throughout their journeys, the Magi are *patently guided by God*. It is, first, a star in the East and then a text from Micah that lead them to their goal. When the time comes for them to leave Bethlehem, they are warned in a dream to take a different route home to avoid Herod. These strange outsiders do not stumble onto the Messiah as if by accident. They search with purpose and are directed each step of the way by a divine hand.

The Magi's stay in Bethlehem is *marked by great joy, by the worship of the infant Jesus, and by the giving of gifts*. They come prepared and seem to know what to do when they arrive. The narrative is specific about the gifts—gold, frankincense, and myrrh—expensive gifts suitable for royalty. We are not given any clues about the motivations of the Magi, why they came and why they worshiped. The narrator only seems interested in the response they made, the proper response to the King of Israel.

Now the remarkable fact that undergirds the entire portrait of the Magi—their searching, their guidance, their worship—is its character as the fulfillment of scripture. Isaiah 60:1–6 and Ps. 72:1–7, 10–14, two other texts for Epiphany, speak of the time of restoration when

> the wealth of the nations shall come to you. . . .
> They shall bring gold and frankincense,
> and shall proclaim the praise of the LORD.
>
> (Isa. 60:5–6)

The arrival of the non-Jews at Bethlehem turns out to be a part of the divine plan, an accomplishment of the promises made long ago. The Magi, as representatives of all non-Jews, belong here in the company of those worshiping the infant Messiah. In a sense they pave the way for the command the risen Christ gives to the Eleven at the end of Matthew's narrative: make disciples of all the nations.

A second key figure in our text is Herod the king. He also plays a prominent role in the latter half of Matt. 2, a passage that serves as the Gospel reading for the First Sunday After Christmas in the A cycle. Suffice it here to say that the scheming of the troubled and cruel Herod turns out to be no match for the guileless Magi, guided by the hand of God. Herod's plot to have the Magi search out and identify his rival for him backfires when they are directed in a dream to go home a different way. If the Magi represent the presence of non-Jews who appropriately worship Jesus, Herod represents the imperial powers, imposing and conspiring but threatened and ultimately frustrated by King Jesus.

Third, we turn to the figure of Jesus, who in this narrative says and does nothing, but nevertheless is the chief protagonist. The entire plot revolves around the affirmation that Jesus is King of Israel. The text from Micah that the chief priests and scribes uncover identifies him as "a ruler who is to shepherd my people Israel" (2:6). The Greek verb translated as "shepherd" actually depicts what shepherds do with their flocks—tend, protect, guide, nurture. Jesus' rule is distinguished from Herod's rule by his gentle guardianship, his compassionate care for his people. But it is just this shepherd-king who is finally rejected and mocked by the same chief priests and scribes who, at the crucifixion, say, "He is the King of Israel; let him come down from the cross now" (27:42).

The account of the Magi's visit to Bethlehem and their worship of the King of the Jews becomes a critical episode in the larger story of God's redemptive plan for humankind. Salvation comes through Jesus the Jew, the fulfillment of the prophetic dreams, but it reaches far beyond to strangers from the East, to a Roman centurion, and to a Canaanite woman. At the end of the story it is no longer a matter of non-Jews coming to Bethlehem, but of Jewish disciples going out to all the nations.

# FIRST SUNDAY AFTER EPIPHANY

## (BAPTISM OF THE LORD)
### Ordinary Time 1

Baptism for most Christian communities is the sacrament by which new converts are received into communing fellowship, the sign and seal of their incorporation into Christ. Some baptize infants on the basis of the covenant promise made to Abraham ("to you and to your offspring"). Others reserve baptism for those who make a personal and public profession of faith in Christ. For each tradition, baptism carries immense significance and its observance marks one of the most sacred moments in the church's life.

The texts for this Sunday offer a unique opportunity to reflect on the meaning of baptism, particularly as it is rooted in Jesus' own baptism by John and as it resonates in the assigned lections from the Old Testament. For one thing, the New Testament texts connect the presence of the Spirit with baptism. The single narrative of Luke and Acts by no means yields an unambiguous answer to the temporal relation between the two, but they belong together. Baptism is then not to be confused with an initiatory ceremony for joining a social club (a sorority or a fraternity), a bit of ritual as a rite of passage. The text claims that the very divine presence that came upon Jesus that day in the Jordan comes upon Jesus' followers. As Simon Magus learns, the Spirit is a powerful reality that cannot be domesticated or bought and sold like a commodity on the market.

Baptism is also an acknowledgment of one's belonging to God. The voice from heaven at Jesus' baptism declares him to be God's own Son. It is the similar claim made about Israel in the oracle of Isaiah, when the Lord says, "Do not fear, for I have redeemed you; I have called you by name, you are mine" (43:1).

But the voice from heaven in ascribing to Jesus titles such as "Son" and "Beloved" commissions him for a special vocation. He is the servant, the agent of God's reign, a sovereignty so eloquently praised in Ps. 29. His followers in baptism are also commissioned to be subjects of God's rule and empowered agents of reconciliation.

93

## Isaiah 43:1–7

A sense of euphoria characterizes the oracles of the Second Isaiah, especially those recorded in the opening chapters of the "book" (Isa. 40—55) associated with this anonymous prophet of the exile. It is a spirit of great gladness coming from the realization that the long night of exile is about to come to an end. Yet, it is not a joy provoked simply by the prospect of freedom, although that news in itself would be sufficient to generate great excitement. Rather this euphoria issues out of the realization that the liberation that is soon to come will be the result of Yahweh's intervention in the affairs of the nation.

Already the prophet has insisted that the dark night of the people is about to end, for Jerusalem "has served her term," "her penalty is paid" (Isa. 40:2). As a conquering monarch proceeds in majesty across the countryside, so the ultimate king, Yahweh, will proceed across the landscape of human life in such a manner that creation itself will acknowledge this marvelous event (40:3–5). Not that Yahweh will be seen directly. His "glory" will be revealed through the work of the mighty Cyrus, the imposing "victor from the east" (41:2) whose mastery of the known world (known to the Israelites, at least) is nothing other than the will of Yahweh. Cyrus is so much the agent of Yahweh's will that the prophet goes on to refer to him as Yahweh's "shepherd" (44:28) and "anointed" one (45:1). Thus the liberation that is proclaimed is no ethereal or otherworldly thing; it is a liberation from a very concrete and specific oppression.

The lection for this day celebrates with great exuberance this wonderful salvation of God. Notice may be given to the manner in which the opening lines of the passage (43:1) describe Yahweh's redemptive activity in Israel's life by means of an increasingly narrow focus. It is Yahweh who has "created" and "formed you" and who, as Creator, has then "redeemed you." But this Yahweh is not content simply to save, but insists on clinging in love to the redeemed people: "I have called you by name" (compare the phrase "called by *my* name" in v. 7, emphasis added) so that "you are mine." Those who have been saved by God have also been claimed by God.

Not even the greatest dangers in the nation's past can intimidate Yahweh's people (v. 2). The reference to "waters" and "rivers" not only recalls the threats presented by the waters of the Red Sea (Ex. 14—15), but by the primeval chaos waters that were thought to surround the heavens and the earth (note Gen. 7:11). The "fire" and "flame" of more recent memory represent the horrors of military destruction, such as the conflagration that destroyed Jerusalem and sent the prophet's generation into exile (2 Kings 25:8–17). Not even these terrors are capable of undoing Yahweh's people, because "I *presence* will be with you."

The references to Egypt, Ethiopia, and Seba (Arabia?) are not entirely clear, but these nations seem to represent areas about to be drawn into Cyrus' orbit (although they were not actually conquered by him). Perhaps the idea is that their political fate is a price that must be paid for the liberation of Israel; they become, in other words, "your ransom" (compare Isa. 43:4). Yahweh, by whose very name Israel is called (vs. 1, 7), is identified as "your God," your "Holy One," "Your Savior." Since captive Israel lived in the midst of a society in which gods competed for allegiance, the fact of Yahweh's name was especially important. It is Yahweh who is doing this great thing, and no other deity (compare 42:8).

The reason for Yahweh's saving intervention is quite uncomplicated: Israel is Yahweh's beloved people. The thought of the Second Isaiah is remarkable for its universalism, in that the prophet elsewhere spells out the view that Israel's redemption is to be accomplished in order that Israel may become a vehicle for the dissemination of the knowledge of Yahweh among the nations of the earth (compare 42:6; 49:6). But not even the prophet's extensive worldview can compel him to place Israel and other nations on an equal footing. The future of other peoples will be determined by Yahweh's will for Israel (43:4b), because Israel, in a way that is true of no other people, is Yahweh's beloved.

Therefore, the prophet urges the nation to take courage (note the repeated phrase "do not fear," in 40:9; 41:13, 14; 43:1, 5), for Yahweh is engaged, is active in the life of the people. Notice may be given of the repeated use of the first person singular pronoun (more than a dozen times in the NRSV translation), as if to signal Yahweh's personal commitment to the issue of Israel's redemption. The exiles will be returned to their land (43:5–6), for they are those who bear Yahweh's name (v. 7).

Thus the text ends on a note similar to that on which it began, in that the three creation verbs in the final two lines of v. 7 recall the creation verbs of v. 1. The God who created the heavens and the earth is about to (re-)create Israel. So vast is the compassion of this Yahweh God.

## Psalm 29

Psalm 29 is usually judged to be among the oldest of the psalms, primarily because of the observation that it seems to be a Yahwistic adaptation of an ancient Canaanite hymn to Baal-hadad, the weather god (see below). In terms of structure, Ps. 29 is a hymn or song of praise, and it is usually included among the enthronement psalms (Ps. 47; 93; 95—99) that celebrate Yahweh's kingship (see vs. 10–11). While Ps. 29 shares several features typical of other hymns and enthronement psalms, there is much about it that is unique.

The uniqueness of Ps. 29 is evident in vs. 1–2. The invitation to praise is addressed not to Israel nor to any other earthly congregation but rather to "heavenly beings" (v. 1). These beings may be understood as angels, but more likely should be understood as the deposed gods of the Canaanite pantheon. In either case, the ancient conception of a divine council is clearly in view (see Ps. 82:1; Gen. 1:26); and its members are called upon to acknowledge (which is the sense of "ascribe to") the absolute sovereignty of Yahweh— Yahweh's "glory" and "strength." "Glory" is the key word in Ps. 29:1–2 and the entire psalm (see vs. 3, 9). It consists of God's "strength" (v. 1; see Ps. 24:8 where the title "King of glory" is associated with God's strength and might) and "holy splendor" (Ps. 29:2), although this latter phrase is difficult to translate and could refer to the attitude or even the attire of those called on to "worship the LORD" (v. 2).

Verses 1–2 anticipate and prepare for the remaining two sections of the psalm. The word "glory" frames the central section (vs. 3, 9), at the end of which the heavenly beings proclaim what they have been invited to proclaim in vs. 1–2: "Glory!" That Yahweh's glory is indeed related to Yahweh's sovereignty is evident in vs. 10–11, the final section, where it is said that Yahweh "sits enthroned as king forever." This explicit affirmation has been anticipated in v. 2 by the invitation to "worship," which literally means to bow down before a monarch or superior. Verses 1–2 are already at least implicitly polemical; that is, the invitation to acknowledge Yahweh's sovereignty means the denial of sovereignty to other gods. It is not surprising that the invitation in v. 2 involves the acknowledgment of "the glory of [Yahweh's] name." The name "Yahweh" (NRSV "LORD") occurs no less than eighteen times in Ps. 29; the effect is to reinforce the exclusive claim of Yahweh.

The polemical thrust of Ps. 29 is even clearer in vs. 3–9, where the key phrase "the voice of the LORD" occurs seven times. The number seven symbolizes fullness or completion; Yahweh's power, which is represented by the voice, is all-encompassing; Yahweh's sovereignty is absolute. The "voice of the LORD" is thunder, and vs. 5–9 describe poetically the effects of a violent thunderstorm. Trees are destroyed (vs. 5, 9ab); the earth seems to shake (vs. 6, 8); lightning flashes like fire (v. 7). In Canaanite conceptuality, the effects of such a storm were attributed to Baal-hadad. Psalm 29, however, denies any power to Baal-hadad; the awesome power of the storm is testimony to Yahweh's sovereignty.

In v. 3, "the waters" could be a reference to the Mediterranean Sea, over which the storm gathers force before crashing into the coast of Palestine. More likely, however, the reference is to the cosmic waters above and below the earth, as in v. 10 (see Gen. 6:17; 7:6, 7, 10). In other words, the effects of the storm are to be understood as testimony to Yahweh's sovereignty over all creation. This is what is affirmed in Ps. 29:9c when "in his temple all say, 'Glory!' " The temple in v. 9c seems to be God's heavenly abode, where the heavenly beings would have gathered (see Pss. 11:4; 18:6; Isa. 63:15); however, the meaning is ambiguous. In all likelihood, human worshipers who would have gathered in the Jerusalem Temple are invited to join in acknowledging Yahweh's reign.

This latter direction of interpretation is reinforced by the first explicit mention of human beings, in the conclusion of the psalm (Ps. 29:10–11). Because Yahweh is the eternal ruler of all creation (v. 10), it is Yahweh who is in a position to provide "strength" (see v. 1) and the blessing of peace to Yahweh's people. As it was the rule of the earthly king to provide peace for the people (see Ps. 72:1–7), so it is with Yahweh, the heavenly king.

Psalm 29 affirms essentially what we affirm regularly as we pray the conclusion to the Lord's Prayer: "For thine is the kingdom and the power and the glory, forever." Its use on the First Sunday After Epiphany is appropriate. Epiphany follows upon Christmas, and Ps. 29 effectively bridges the two seasons. The movement of Ps. 29 recalls Luke's account of Jesus' birth, in which heavenly beings proclaim "Glory to God" (Luke 2:13–14; Ps. 29:9c) and peace on earth (Luke 2:13–14; Ps. 29:11). In the birth of Jesus, God's reign is manifest. The cosmic proclamation of God's reign in Ps. 29 is also fitting for Epiphany, which means "manifestation." At Jesus' baptism, which is celebrated on the First Sunday After Epiphany (Luke 3:21–22), a heavenly voice proclaims him "my Son" (Luke 3:22), publicly manifesting Jesus as an agent of God's reign. Jesus would soon proclaim and enact "the good news of the kingdom of God" (Luke 4:43–44).

Whether in Old Testament times, in the first century A.D., or in our day, the proclamation of God's reign always has a polemical thrust. We may not be inclined to worship Baal, but we are persistently tempted to claim the earth as our own and to assert our sovereignty rather than to acknowledge God's claim on us. The earth is suffering and human life is being diminished by our selfishness. Psalm 29 reminds us that the earth and our lives belong to God (see Ps. 24:1). Enduring strength and peace derive from joining the heavenly beings as they cry, "Glory!" (Ps. 29:9c). Or, to paraphrase the Westminster Shorter Catechism, the chief end of humankind is to glorify and enjoy God forever.

## Acts 8:14–17

There are at least two ways to approach this text with an eye to preaching on the Sunday called the "Baptism of the Lord." The first is to move beyond the limits of the designated passage and focus on what is clearly the literary center of the passage—the figure of Simon the Magician. The second is to stick with the four verses recommended (Acts 8:14–17), giving attention to the visit of Peter and John with the Samaritans and the relation of baptism and Spirit. Both ways are appropriate to the liturgical theme of the Sunday.

The first approach calls attention to the context—Philip's mission to Samaria and the encounter with Simon. Simon's magical feats attracted great attention among the Samaritans. His claims that he was the greatest brought a chorus of amens from his attentive audiences. They listened eagerly and spoke the appropriate response. "This man is the power of God that is called Great." Whether or not Simon also profited financially from his exploits (as did other magicians of the time), we are not told. The narrator seems more interested in the way Simon mesmerized the crowd (8:9–11).

Verse 12 begins with a critical "But." Over against the celebrated popularity of Simon is set the preaching of Philip, accompanied by the working of "signs and great miracles" (8:13). The very ones who had been attracted to Simon now became believers and received baptism. Curiously, Simon too believed and was baptized, signifying the triumph of the gospel over the practice of magic.

What is the difference between "the signs and great miracles" Philip did and the magic of Simon? It may be to the naked eye they look the same, eventuate in similar results. But the text clearly perceives a difference between the two. While magic thrives on devices intended to control divine forces and often succeeds by tricking a gullible audience, the miracles of Philip are powerful signs pointing to the reign of God, the very content of his preaching. Simon's magic drew attention to himself; Philip's miracles bore witness to One greater than he, in whose mission he was deeply engaged. The text celebrates the overcoming of the former by the latter.

After the arrival of Peter and John from Jerusalem, Simon became enamored with the powerful demonstration of the Spirit that happened when the apostles laid hands on the Samaritan believers (8:17–18). He offered to pay the apostles if they would grant him the same authority. Peter's sharp rebuke and Simon's plea for intercessory prayer for himself underscore yet another message of the text—the Spirit is not for sale.

Simon understood the logic of the marketplace, where commodities are purchased. "You get what you pay for." But the Spirit is not a commodity to be made the personal possession of any individual or group, whether the price be large donations or immense religious and social activity. "The spirit blows where it chooses" (John 3:8, NRSV margin). Every effort to domesticate the Spirit and harness the divine power ends in frustration, because the Spirit above all else symbolizes the freedom of God. Whatever ultimately happened to Simon is not clear, except that he became the patron saint of those who bought and sold ecclesiastical favors ("simony").

The second approach to the text for this Sunday centers on the delegation from the Jerusalem church, who come to the baptized believers of Samaria, pray with them, and lay their hands on them, enabling them to receive the Holy Spirit (Acts 8:14–17). The parenthetical explanation of 8:16 raises the difficult theological question about the relation between baptism in the name of the Lord Jesus and the reception of the Spirit.

The verse has spawned a variety of interpretations. Is the giving of the Spirit to be separated from the rite of baptism, a second and fuller stage in God's blessing? Is Philip's preaching somehow inadequate, needing to be supplemented? Does the text imply that the apostles must be present for the Spirit to be given in such a dramatic way? All these interpretations (and others) have been proposed.

Perhaps the best explanation of 8:14–17 (and certainly consistent with the broader narrative of Acts) is that it celebrates the movement of the gospel to the Samaritans (see Acts 1:8) and through the presence of Peter and John as emissaries from Jerusalem affirms the inclusiveness of the gospel. The Samaritans are given the very same gift of the Spirit earlier experienced by the Jerusalem church, and the distinction in the narrative between baptism and the reception of the Spirit makes this possible. There are not two churches, one Samaritan and one Jewish, but one people of God, blessed by the one Spirit. Verse 25 confirms the unity of otherwise disparate and hostile peoples by noting that as Peter and John returned to Jerusalem they preached "to many villages of the Samaritans."

The narrative's somewhat irregular deviation of separating baptism from the giving of the Spirit does not finally contradict the pattern established in Jesus' own baptism (Luke 3:21–22).

## Luke 3:15–17, 21–22

All the Synoptic Gospels include the baptism of Jesus, and each of them connects Jesus' baptism with John the Baptist and also labors to show Jesus' superiority to John (presumably as a result of some challenge from disciples of John). Mark is content to have John assert his inferiority to the one who will follow him (Mark 1:7–8), but Matthew takes matters a bit farther, having John initially demur from the task of baptizing Jesus (Matt. 3:13–15). Luke takes matters yet a step farther, placing the notice of John's arrest and imprisonment just before Jesus' baptism (Luke 3:18–20) and announcing Jesus' baptism with no reference whatsoever to the name of the one who baptized him. Placing Jesus' baptism in the context of John's ministry suggests that Jesus is baptized as part of that ministry, but Luke provides no details. The Gospel of John does not include a story of Jesus' baptism by John, although John there functions as a powerful witness to Jesus.

If the Synoptics share a story of Jesus' baptism, they also connect that baptism closely with the Holy Spirit. John's prophetic announcement about the one who will follow him includes a reference to a future baptism with the Holy Spirit (Mark 1:8; Matt. 3:11; Luke 3:16; compare John 1:19–34), and Jesus' own baptism is marked by the descent of the Spirit (Mark 1:10; Matt. 3:16; Luke 3:22). These references to the activity of the Spirit are significant in all the Gospels, of course, but they take on a heightened significance in Luke because the Spirit has already been exceedingly active in the early chapters of Luke's Gospel.

Luke's story begins with an announcement of John the Baptist's birth, in which Gabriel proclaims that "even before his birth he will be filled with the Holy Spirit" (1:15). In response to Mary's bewildered question about how she will bear a child, she learns that "the Holy Spirit will come upon" her (1:35). Elizabeth suddenly breaks forth in praise of Mary at the instigation of the Spirit (1:41–42), and Simeon visits the Temple at the precise moment when Mary and Joseph arrive with Jesus because the Spirit prompts him to do so

(2:27). Small wonder that interpreters have sometimes referred to Luke-Acts as the "book of the Holy Spirit."

These early actions of the Holy Spirit have been the sort that readers would easily identify as gospel in the sense of "good news." Even if the experience of being overcome by the Holy Spirit may have terrified Mary or Elizabeth, readers will surely welcome these manifestations of God on behalf of God's people. In the proclamation of John the Baptist, however, a new element enters the picture: baptism "with the Holy Spirit and fire" (3:16). John's description of this form of baptism sounds like anything but good news: "His winnowing fork is in his hand, to clear his threshing floor and to gather the wheat into his granary; but the chaff he will burn with unquenchable fire" (3:17). To be sure, Luke also includes the more congenial motif of the Spirit's descent upon Jesus in a form like that of a dove and the heavenly declaration of Jesus as God's Son (3:22), but that provides little comfort for those who anticipate the "winnowing fork" that is to follow!

Contemplating these and other Lukan references to the Holy Spirit can produce a multitude of bewildering questions. Is the descent of the Spirit on Jesus different from the church's reception of the Spirit at Pentecost? How does the Spirit-inspired speech of John the Baptist or Elizabeth differ from that later granted to Peter or Paul? What exactly is baptism with the Holy Spirit, and how is it connected with water baptism, with church membership, with prophecy?

In this writer's judgment, attempts to produce a systematic statement of Luke's understanding of the Holy Spirit inevitably fail. The evidence simply does not lend itself to logical generalizations. Luke draws on language about the Holy Spirit in a variety of contexts, and he is more concerned with asserting the presence and activity of the Spirit than with charting the Spirit's moves.

In this particular passage, the first reference to the Spirit serves to reinforce the prophetic motif already introduced in the Magnificat and in the oracles of Simeon. The coming of Jesus Christ does not baptize the status quo; rather, it overthrows every power and undermines all that seems certain in the world's eyes. Many among Jesus' hearers will find this most unwelcome news. If Luke's is a gospel of mercy, it is also very much a gospel in the prophetic mode.

The second reference to the Spirit connects Jesus both with the Spirit and with God. In the complexity of Luke 3:21–22, we can see why the church later employed Trinitarian language to give voice to the relationship among the three, Father, Son and Spirit. For Luke, however, the scene ensures that Jesus' ministry itself derives from the Holy Spirit, that Jesus himself is God's Son.

The editor's decision to exclude 3:18–20 from the reading for this Sunday is understandable, given the way in which John's arrest seems to intrude upon an otherwise clear move from the baptism practiced by John to the baptism of Jesus. The inclusion of John's arrest is important, however, for it recalls that the price paid by those who act at the behest of the Spirit is often a high one.

# SECOND SUNDAY AFTER EPIPHANY

## Ordinary Time 2

The four texts for this Sunday were not chosen to "go together" in the strictest sense. The Old Testament texts contain references to "dawn," "burning torch" (Isa. 62:1), and "light" (Ps. 36:9), which are familiar symbols for the Epiphany season, and the miracle of changing the water to wine at Cana is a traditional text for this part of the Christian calendar. First Corinthians 12, on the other hand, begins an extended series of lections from that epistle and seemingly has no connection with any of the other texts.

And yet there is a common theme: the incredible generosity of God. The psalmist sings of it in terms of God's "steadfast love," which comes in times of opposition and threat. "With you is the fountain of life" (Ps. 36:9). The voice of Isa. 62 can hardly contain itself. Jerusalem's vindication is at hand. A new name is to be given. As a young man delights in and marries a young woman, so God rejoices over Jerusalem and shows off his bride to all the nations.

The story at Cana in John 2 depicts Jesus as the generous giver par excellence. He answers the emergency of a depleted wine supply with provisions that both quantitatively and qualitatively go beyond what the original host could supply. First Corinthians 12 reminds us of the abundant gifts of the Spirit, leading first to a confession of Jesus as Lord and then to a variety of services for the common good of the church.

Whatever is to be said about the particular interpretation of each of the four lessons, it cannot ignore the ultimate source "from whom all blessings flow."

## Isaiah 62:1–5

If those scholars are correct who view Isa. 60—62 as forming the original core around which the larger work of the "Third Isaiah" was constructed, the present text may be understood as a continuation of that proclamation of good news first announced in Isa. 60:1–6 (see Epiphany). The mood of this entire section is decidedly joyful in that it declares new deeds of great and astonishing mercy on the part of Israel's God. In many ways this enthusiasm is a continuation of the optimism that characterized the work of the "Second Isaiah," yet Isa. 60—62 presumably comes from a later hand(s) and a somewhat different historical context than does Isa. 40—55. It is likely that by now the exiles have returned to Judea and have begun to reweave the fabric of the nation's life in the devastated land. Thus, the exuberant joyfulness in the face of so much present and future hardship is quite remarkable. The text, in fact, is quite aware of the great gulf that separates "what has been" from "what will be," and the manner in which it contrasts the realities of the past with the promise of the future is one of the sources of hope within the passage.

The initial impression the reader receives from this text is that its author is so brimming with exuberance over the impending outburst of God's grace that he or she simply cannot hold it all in. The image is that of the child who bursts into the house, exploding with excitement over some great turn of events at school that day, who cannot restrain herself until she has told the whole incredible story. Or it is the image of the adult, one whose life is perhaps surrounded by the drab and humdrum routine of his job, who experiences some hoped-for but improbable good fortune and cannot resist rushing to the telephone to share the news with anyone who will listen. "I will not keep silent, . . . I will not rest, until . . . " (v. 1) are words of one who is beside him- or herself with overflowing happiness.

Yet the reason for this impatience is not that some great and marvelous thing is happening to the speaker, but that it is happening to those who hear this announcement. The "I" of this passage is clearly some divinely appointed messenger. One would assume that this is the same individual who is referred to by the first-person pronoun throughout most of chapter 61, the one on whom the "spirit of [Yahweh]" rests (61:1). The fact that Jesus understands these words to be fulfilled by means of his own ministry (Luke 4:16–21) does not obviate the possibility that, in the prophet's mind, they also described the prophet's own role as the deliverer of Yahweh's word.

(On the matter of the pronouns in ch. 61, notice should be taken of the difference of perspective between v. 8, where "I" is clearly Yahweh, and other points in the text, such as v. 10, where "I" unmistakably refers to Yahweh's designated agent.)

If "I" is the speaker of these words in 62:1–5, then "you" and "your" (vs. 2–5) is unquestionably Jerusalem, or in other words, the community of God, but note "her" of v. 1. So that the very important difference between this text and the images suggested above is that what is about to happen will most profoundly impact not the life of the speaker (although that possibility should not be ruled out), but the lives of those who hear (read!) this message. This reality makes the uncontainable joy of the messenger all the more remarkable!

The heart of the messenger's declaration is contained in v. 2: "You shall be called by a new name." Perhaps the author of this passage had in mind Abraham, whose name was changed from Abram at an important juncture in his life (Gen. 17:5); or perhaps Jacob, who underwent a similar experience (Gen. 32:28). This new name is not to be conferred by other peoples, even though "nations" and "kings" will be amazed witnesses to this transformation. This new name is to come from none other than God.

There are actually two new names for God's people: Hephzibah ("My Delight Is in Her") and Beulah ("Married"). (Perhaps "crown of beauty" and "royal diadem" of v. 3 are also to be considered new names.) Hephzibah is contrasted with Jerusalem's *old* name, Azubah ("Forsaken"); Beulah, with Shemamah ("Desolate"). The focus in both of these names is now on *God's* joy over what is about to happen in that, as in Hosea (2:16 and elsewhere), the imagery is that of Yahweh's claiming Israel as a groom claims a bride. Now it becomes clear that the reason for all this joy—God's joy and prophet's joy alike—is that a new day is about to dawn in the relationship between God and the people.

(The portrait of Yahweh as groom is strengthened in the NRSV by the change to "builder" in v. 5 from the improbable "sons" of the RSV.)

The text, then, makes the bold affirmation that that joy which is truly worthy of the name, that joy which endures, is joy over communion and community with God. How tempting it would have been for the text to focus on the end of the captivity as the supreme reason for the people's joy, or the prospects of the splendid fresh bricks and mortar that, in time, would characterize the new Jerusalem. But this is not the new Jerusalem of bricks and mortar; this is the new Jerusalem of the Spirit of God. This is the new Jerusalem where joy is not only a feature of human life, but a feature of God's life as well. If "your God [shall] rejoice over you" (v. 5), can it be conceivable that the objects of that joy can do otherwise than be caught up in a transforming joy of their own?

## Psalm 36:5-10

The lectionary represents the central section of a psalm that commentators identify as an individual lament or prayer for help. While vs. 5–9 are addressed to God, they have the character of a profession of faith. The actual petition or prayer for help begins in v. 10 and continues in v. 11. Numerous commentators have treated Ps. 36 as two separate psalms, vs. 1–4 and 12 and vs. 5–11, an approach that the lectionary reinforces. It is better, however, to treat the psalm as a unity. When not eliminated, the references to the wicked in vs. 1–4 and 11–12 provide a framework for hearing the psalmist's profession of faith and prayer for help. This framework makes it clear that the psalmist's praise and prayer arise not from circumstances of prosperity and outward peace, but are offered rather in the midst of opposition and threat.

The theme of the psalmist's profession, praise, and prayer is God's "steadfast love" (vs. 5, 7, 10). While acutely aware of the character of the wicked and their threatening deeds (vs. 1–4), the psalmist chooses to take his or her stand on the character of God. There is no other word in the Old Testament that serves so well to describe the character of God as does *ḥesed*, "steadfast love" (see Ex. 34:6–7 where it forms the heart of God's self-revelation to Moses). God's love is unbounded. God can be trusted never to let go of God's people ("your faithfulness," Ps. 36:5; see Pss. 89:24; 92:2; 98:3, for example, where "steadfast love" and "faithfulness" are also paired, as also in Ex. 34:6). God can be trusted to set things right for God's people ("your righteousness," v. 6). God can be trusted to pursue justice inexhaustibly ("your judgments," v. 6). To be noted is that each of these attributes of God is described in cosmic terms that are arranged in descending order according to the ancient understanding of the cosmos: "heavens" above all else, "clouds" above the earth, "mighty mountains" as the highest earthly features, and "the great deep" below the earth. In short, the character of God is built into the very structure of the universe. All creation and all creatures depend on God for life. Like Ps. 29 for the First Sunday After Epiphany, Ps. 36 has far-reaching ecological implications. That God "save[s] humans and animals alike" (v. 6c) calls for a reverence for all creatures and their habitats that is seldom evidenced in our relentless desire for progress and development.

Because the life of the world depends on the love of God, the psalmist describes God's steadfast love as "precious" (v. 7). To "take refuge in the shadow of your wings" (see Pss. 17:8; 57:1; 63:7) means to acknowledge dependence on God. This is the precise opposite of the wicked, who consider themselves self-sufficient (vs. 1–2) and who pursue their own selfish ways (vs. 3–4). Psalm 36 ends by professing the faith that the way of the wicked will ultimately be fleeting and futile (v. 12). Psalm 36 thus recalls the beginning of the Psalter, which affirms that "the way of the wicked will perish" (1:6) and "happy are all who take refuge in [God]" (2:11; see also 5:11; 7:1; 11:1; 16:1, for example).

Psalm 36:8 portrays the way God provides life for people: they are fed and given drink. God's "house" may designate the Temple and indicate an original liturgical setting for the psalm, but the meaning need not be completely literal. As James L. Mays suggests, the language is symbolic and intends to express poetically the conviction that life is a gift received and nurtured by God: "It is this receiving from God that occurs in complex and related ways—through common life, liturgy, and the inner world of the spirit—that the psalm seeks to describe" (James L. Mays, *Psalms*, Interpretation series; Louisville, Ky.: John Knox Press, 1994). The affirmation is similar to that of Ps. 23:5–6.

The psalmist's profession culminates with the memorable v. 9: "with you" is to be found the source and sustenance of life and light. Again the language is richly symbolic. The same imagery is used by the Gospel of John, which locates God's presence in Jesus Christ, in whom "was life, and the life was the light of all people" (1.4). The prologue of John goes on to acknowledge the presence of darkness, but affirms that God's presence in Christ affords a light that cannot be overcome. In effect, Ps. 36 ends the same way; the psalmist prays in v. 10 for the continuation of God's steadfast love and righteousness (NRSV "salvation"), acknowledging the presence of evil (v. 11) but affirming that God's presence (the "there" of v. 12) affords a power that the wicked cannot overcome (v. 12).

Like Ps. 36, the Gospel of John also uses images of feeding. Jesus provides "living water" (John 4:10; see Ps. 36:8b) and is "the bread of life" (John 6:35; see Ps. 36:8a). Those who believe in him have "eternal life" (John 3:16). The affirmation is eschatological. Life in Christ is effective now and the joy is real (John 16:24); but it is experienced amid persistent opposition from "the world" (17:14–19). The same dynamic is present in Ps. 36. Those who belong to God ("who know you," v. 10a) already experience refuge and abundant provision (vs. 5–9) even amid persistent opposition by "the wicked" (vs. 1–4, 11–12). That life is a gift which God has given and will ultimately secure for the faithful is one of the central affirmations of the Psalter and of the entire Bible (see Ps. 73:25–26).

## 1 Corinthians 12:1–11

This Sunday brings the first of seven selections for the epistolary readings drawn from the later chapters of 1 Corinthians (chs. 12; 13; and 15). They provide an excellent opportunity for the preacher to engage in a series of sermons addressing some critical issues facing the church at large and no doubt many individual congregations within the church, issues such as the importance of diversity within the one body of Christ (three Sundays) and the meaning of Jesus' resurrection for the people of God (four Sundays).

First Corinthians 12:1–11 neatly divides into two sections: 12:1–3, dealing with the Spirit's role in leading people to affirm Jesus as Lord, and vs. 4–11, dealing with the diversity of gifts bestowed by the one Spirit. But the two sections go together, and the interpreter must not hurry over 12:1–3 to get to the latter, more familiar section. The initial statement, "Now concerning spiritual gifts [better, "spiritual matters" or "spiritual persons"], I do not want you to be uninformed," serves as an introduction to the whole section that runs through 14:40, making 12:2–4 the critical beginning of the argument.

Immediately a contrast is established between the previous life of the readers, before they became believers, and their life now as spiritual people. The real point of the contrast is between idols who have no voice and the Spirit who speaks through believers to confess the Lordship of Jesus. Paul's view of idols as deaf and dumb follows frequent texts in the Old Testament, where idols are mocked because they have no ears with which to listen to prayers and no tongue with which to utter words of truth and hope (see Ps. 115:4–8; Hab. 2:18–19). The worshipers of idols may (and in the first century did) engage in inspired speech that parallels speaking in tongues, but such activity is no proof that the idol itself speaks. The contrast has its contemporary counterpart in many of our modern objects of worship that are accompanied by feverish religious activity but, like all idols, remain mute and helpless.

The Spirit of God, however, gives believers a voice to declare "Jesus is Lord." The text does not imply a mere mouthing of the words, but a confession that entails the absolute allegiance of the confessor to the Deity. A priority is established: the first action of the Spirit is not to produce gifts such as eloquent preaching or persuasive teaching or speaking in tongues, but to evoke the basic commitment to Jesus' Lordship that undergirds the Christian experience. Only on the basis of such a common confession can the community go on to think about the rich diversity of spiritual gifts.

The obvious structure of the second section of the passage (1 Cor.

12:4–11) underlines the affirmation of v. 4 that there are a diversity of spiritual gifts but the same Giver. While a later argument will address the mutual working of the gifts (vs. 12–31) and another will stress the need for order (14:26–40), the point scored in 12:4–11 is that of diversity rather than uniformity. The Spirit should not be expected to produce sameness, all Christians looking and acting alike. The Corinthian community needed such a pointed reminder because of the abuse of the practice of speaking in tongues. The modern church more often needs such a reminder because of its growing pluralism and the threat posed by groups who have not previously had a say in the important decisions of the church. A healthy diversity may be hard to come by, but our text makes it an essential activity of the Spirit.

Two features of the argument need underscoring. First, the diversity of gifts in the church is rooted in the character of God (vs. 4–6). The Trinitarian flavor of Paul's language (Spirit, Lord, God) is neither philosophical nor calculated, and there is little profit in trying to fathom what Paul may have meant by each term. The point is that different words are used for the Giver of gifts, implying that the varieties of spiritual expressions come from one Source, who is known as Spirit, Lord, and God. Diversity is not an unfortunate accident or a cultural phenomenon that needs to be eliminated. It is inherent in the divine nature.

The second phrase in the text not to be overlooked appears in 12:7. The variety of gifts are "for the common good." The Greek word carries the notion of usefulness, of profitability for others. The gifts given to individual believers are not intended for their private benefit, nor are they to be reserved for an inner circle that may take particular delight in the exercise of a friend's gift. Chapters 13 and 14 will further develop the importance of mutual edification that lies at the heart of gift-giving.

This notion of broad usefulness calls into question an approach to diversity within the church whereby various groups keep to themselves and nurture their own growth apart from the rich gifts others bring and apart from the contributions they may make to others. For culturally diverse Corinth, the text envisions a single community in which the gifts of God are used for the service of all.

## John 2:1–11

Much in the Gospel of John eludes our understanding—the prologue with its unfamiliar language about the Word that was part of creation itself, the frequent speeches of Jesus about his relationship to God, the significance of the "beloved disciple." The particular miracle story in today's section, however, surely belongs among the more mystifying scenes in the Gospels. Here Jesus performs an astounding miracle, but the miracle does not permit any blind person sight, restore an ailing child to the parents, or rescue those imperiled by a storm. The Cana miracle provides a vast quantity of wine for a wedding feast, as each of the six stone jars would hold twenty to thirty gallons of wine. This act has provoked more than one otherwise conservative interpreter to identify at least this one miracle as a symbolic rather than a historically accurate account!

Even those readers who are not troubled by the notion of Jesus as wine purveyor find that the story presents other difficulties. What are we to make of the exchange between Jesus and his mother? Does her initial statement to Jesus ("They have no wine," v. 3) indicate that she anticipates that Jesus can supply that need? Since nothing has been said of her prior to this point, the question remains mystifying.

And what of Jesus' response to his mother: "Woman, what concern is that to you and to me? My hour has not yet come" (v. 4)? Literally, the question Jesus asks is, "What to me and to you, woman?" It remains entirely unclear whether he is rejecting her right to make this implied demand on him, rejecting the notion that the wedding feast concerns the two of them, or even rejecting all relationship with her. What the question does accomplish, of course, is to hold the reader's attention.

In fact the story very effectively holds the reader's attention, precisely because it continues to pose challenges. Jesus' miracles usually occur in plain sight, with everyone present aware of what takes place and responding to events. This miracle, by contrast, unfolds in such a convoluted way that it becomes somewhat ironic. At no point does the narrator *tell the reader* that Jesus has turned the water into wine. As a result, the steward knows he is sampling good wine, but he does not know where it came from. The servants know where it came from, but they do not know that it is wine, at least not from their own experience. Do the wedding guests even know that a miracle has occurred? Only v. 11 suggests that the disciples know.

Because of these questions raised by the story, and because of the features in the story that frequently elicit symbolic interpretation (water, wine, the wedding and its characters), exegetes often interpret this story symbolically. The variation among these interpretations is great, as the critical commentaries will attest. Turning the water of purification into wine becomes a rejection of Jewish purification rites. The mother of Jesus represents the church, or the new Eve, or the new Israel, who has no role in the ministry of Jesus. The wedding itself represents the arrival of a new age in Israel's history.

Although I would not reject any one of these interpretations, they occasionally border on a kind of allegorical exegesis, in which each part of the story stands for something outside the story itself and the story as a whole almost dissolves before our eyes. Instead of looking at the story as a puzzle to be "solved," we might regard the elusive, vexatious, enigmatic character of the story as one of its primary functions. As "the first of his signs" (v. 11), the Cana miracle points ahead toward the mysterious story that is unfolding. It warns us that this Gospel does not play by the rules of our expectations.

In that sense, the symbolism of the wedding at Cana centers, not in various details of the story, but in the larger theme of the unimaginable generosity of Jesus. The gifts of Jesus extend well beyond meeting the needs of the moment for health or safety or food. In this story, those gifts encompass the celebration of life itself. That is to say, the sheer abundance of the gifts Jesus brings to humankind extends beyond what any human being can ask or think or comprehend.

Not all will find the gifts of Jesus to be welcome. Already the Johannine prologue has anticipated those of Jesus' "own people" who would not accept him (1:11). Here that theme sounds again, this time in the statement of Jesus, "My hour has not yet come" (v. 4). Our familiarity with the Fourth Gospel alerts us immediately to the fact that he is speaking of the hour of his death, as often in this story (12:23, 27; 13:1; 16:2; 17:1). This is the first such reference in the Gospel, however, and first readers could not be expected to know what it means. Only as further references emerge and at the crucifixion itself will readers understand that this is a reference to Jesus' passion. Yet even here, with the first of Jesus' "signs," the hour that is to come makes its appearance.

Proclaiming this text challenges the preacher to resist the need to tie up the loose ends of the story into a neat package of meanings. Biblical stories generally undermine our best efforts to reduce them, and this one proves to be especially difficult to wrest into manageable form. Better to allow the loose ends, the puzzles, the uncertainties to shine forth, recalling that this is but the beginning of the story!

# Third Sunday After Epiphany

## Ordinary Time 3

The word of God read, heard, interpreted, satisfying the basic intentions for human life, challenging to the point of provoking rage, and creating a community of diversity—it is all here in the four lessons for this Sunday. It is appropriate that the people of God be reminded time and again that they live by the divine word, ancient but ever new. In hearing and obeying it there is "great consequence."

Nehemiah 8 records the beautiful story of the people of the reconstituted community of Israel gathered as one listening to Ezra read the *torah*. As the words of the text are explained, the people begin to weep, only to be told by Nehemiah and Ezra that the day is holy, a day for celebration and not for mourning, "for the joy of the LORD is your strength" (Neh. 8:10).

It is that same delight in the *torah* that makes it the object of praise in Ps. 19. It renews the soul, instructs the ignorant, brings joy to the heart and enlightenment to the eye. But it functions also to expose secret and proud sins so that God's servants can live in total dependence on divine mercy.

The lection from the Gospel reminds us that the word of God can also bring rejection and rage as well as delight (Luke 4). As Jesus reads from the scroll of Isaiah in the synagogue at Nazareth, the initial response of the hearers is amazement at the gracious words he speaks. However, when he interprets the text and explains that the promise of liberation is for the non-Jew as well as the Jew, he is met with hostility and threatened violence. As another biblical writer put it, "The word of God is living and active, sharper than any two-edged sword, piercing until it divides soul from spirit, joints from marrow; it is able to judge the thoughts and intentions of the heart" (Heb. 4:12).

The Epistle lesson from 1 Corinthians does not focus immediately on the word of God, but it depicts for us a community constituted by the word, a community grappling with the very diversity Jesus explained from the Isaiah text.

## Nehemiah 8:1–3, 5–6, 8–10

"Joy over the rediscovery of the Word of God" would be one apt summary of this text.

The events related in the books of Ezra and Nehemiah are difficult to reconstruct in terms of historical detail, and even in terms of the sequence in which individual occurrences transpire. Because of the vagueness of the date of Ezra's coming (in Ezra 7:1; is it Artaxerxes I, 465–425 B.C., or Artaxerxes II, 404–359?) it is not even possible to be sure that the work of Ezra precedes that of Nehemiah. But such problems need not detract from the force of this passage. What is clear here is that (1) there is at this juncture an important step forward in the formation of a Hebrew canon of Scripture, and (2) also the rediscovery of the Word empowers those who interpret it as well as the people who hear it read and interpreted.

The idea that the will of God is preserved in a body of literature— an idea that modern Jews, Christians, and Muslims take quite for granted—was found nowhere in the ancient world outside Israel, at least not in the sense in which we now understand the nature of the Bible. It is true that various gods were understood to have guided their people through the gift of codes of law (for example, Shamash's gift of the now-famous Hammurabi Code). It is also true that important epics and hymns described the activities of the gods and/or implored their intervention in human life (the Baal poems from Ras Shamra). But the idea of a divinely inspired anthology of literature that purports to declare the universal will of God is found nowhere outside ancient Israel, and it is not even found firmly rooted in Israel until the very late stages of antiquity, that is, from about 400 B.C.

Although Ezra's reading of the "law [Torah] of Moses" (v. 1) was not the first step toward the recognition of the power of the written Word of God (compare 2 Kings 22:8–13), it nevertheless constitutes an important movement in that direction. In other words, when one reads Neh. 8, one is looking in on one of those crucial moments in the history of God's dealing with Israel and with all humankind, a moment when the Spirit speaks through the words on the page (or in this case, on the scroll) and, in so doing, touches and changes human hearts.

This event is also a milestone in understanding the authority of the written word, in that it is not only read but interpreted (v. 8). This act of interpretation is undoubtedly connected with the fact that, whereas Ezra's text was in Hebrew, the people understood only Aramaic. But more than translation from one language to another is involved here, for in the last few centuries before the birth of Christ, the tradition of the Targum arises in Jewish worship, the Targum being an Aramaic rendering of the biblical text which is more concerned with giving the *meaning* of the Hebrew original than with transmitting its exact words. Thus, the "sermon" is born.

Precisely what Ezra read to the people is not clear, but since he read, and his helpers interpreted, "from early morning until midday" (v. 3) it must have been an extended lection. The quotation in v. 15 is not found in this form anywhere else in the Old Testament, but Ezra's emphasis on the celebration of the Festival of Booths implies a knowledge of a tradition also found in Lev. 23:33–36 and Deut. 16:13–15.

To the restored Jerusalem community this "Torah of Moses" was energizing and liberating. Their mood was not one of celebration at the beginning of this event. The reasons for the people's sadness (Neh. 8:9) are not clear, unless this event is somehow related to an earlier condemnation by Ezra of their sinful ways (note Ezra 10:1). Or perhaps their weeping results from the obvious distance between God's promises concerning their life in the land (compare, for example, Deut. 30:6–10), as described in the "Torah of Moses," and what they are actually experiencing in impoverished Jerusalem.

However that may have been, Ezra and those with him understand the joyful and liberating nature of the moment. "Do not mourn or weep" (Neh. 8:9) is followed by, "Go your way, eat the fat and drink sweet wine" (v. 10). That their joy is not to be simply a matter of self-indulgence is emphasized by the injunction to share their bounty with other members of the community who have little or nothing (v. 10). If the preacher wishes to extend the lection to include vs. 11–12 (a recommended procedure!), the results of the reading of the "Torah of Moses" are made all the more explicit: there was "great rejoicing, because they had understood the words that had been declared to them."

## Psalm 19

Like Pss. 29 and 36:5–10 for the First and Second Sundays After Epiphany, Ps. 19 testifies to the inseparable involvement of God both with the cosmos and with humanity. Psalm 19 is often treated by commentators as two separate psalms—Ps. 19A (vs. 1–6), which deals with creation, and Ps. 19B (vs. 7–14), which deals with the *torah* (NRSV "law"). But to treat these sections separately is to miss the essential message about the revelation of God and God's involvement with the world.

To be sure, vs. 1–6 do focus on creation. The actors or speakers are the created entities from Gen. 1—the heavens, the firmament, day and night, the sun. The chiastic structure of v. 1 anticipates the message of vs. 1–6. The first word in the verse is "heavens" and the last is "firmament," so as to reinforce structurally what the words themselves communicate: God's praiseworthy works fill the universe. Without literally speaking, the universe itself offers eloquent testimony, consisting both of praise to God ("glory," v. 1; see Ps. 29:1–3, 9) and instruction to humanity ("knowledge," v. 2). No place is unreached. The silent but powerful testimony of day and night extends "to the end of the world" (v. 4), and the sun's witness reaches both "end[s] of the heavens" (v. 6, where "end" occurs twice).

The sun was an object of worship in several ancient Near Eastern cultures, and it is probable that an original hymn to the sun lies in the background of vs. 1–6. But if so, it is clear that all traces of pantheism have been erased by the psalmist. The sun is not a god, but rather testifies to God. The creation testifies to the existence of its sovereign Creator. Not surprisingly, the vocabulary of vs. 1–6 recalls other psalms that specifically affirm God's sovereignty. The word "glory" (v. 1) appears in Pss. 24:7–10, 29:1–3, 9; and 145:5, 12; and the word for "world" in Ps. 19:4 frequently designates Yahweh's domain in the psalms that celebrate Yahweh's reign (Pss. 93:1; 96:10; 97:4; 98:7, 9).

It is the movement from Ps. 19:6 to v. 7 that causes problems for many commentators, but the transition is not as abrupt as it seems. It is the privilege and responsibility of a sovereign to provide guidance and instruction for his or her servants (see vs. 11, 13); and it is precisely this *torah*, "instruction," to which the psalm turns in vs. 7–11. When vs. 7–11 are heard in the context of vs. 1–6, their message about *torah* takes on a cosmic dimension. Verse 7a would be better translated as follows: "The instruction of the LORD is all-encompassing, restoring human life." As vs. 4b–6 have described the all-encompassing circuit of the sun, so v. 7a affirms that God's instruction is all-encompassing. Because "nothing is hid from its heat" (v. 6b), the sun constantly energizes the earth and the life it supports. So it is, the psalmist boldly claims, with God's instruction; it is responsible for restoring human life (see v. 7). It is a radical affirmation, for it means we live not by our ability to earn, achieve, or possess (see v. 10, where it is suggested that God's instruction is more important than money or the richest food), but rather we live "by every word that comes from the mouth of God" (Matt. 4:4; see Deut. 8:3).

Following the mention of *torah* in Ps. 19:7a are five more words that describe God's revelation, each of which is accompanied by a phrase that either indicates the effect of God's word upon humanity (vs. 7b–8) or further elaborates the nature of God's word (v. 9). The word of God accomplishes what God intends for human existence—wisdom (see Ps. 2:10), joy (see Ps. 4:7), enlightenment (see Ps. 36:9). The "fear of the LORD" in Ps. 19:9a actually describes not so much God's revelation itself but the human response of conformity to God's word. Living by the word of God is also in view in v. 11; there is "great reward" for those who conform their lives to God's instruction. The phrase would be better translated "great consequence," in order to avoid the implication that God's instruction represents a mechanistic system of reward or punishment for obedience or disobedience. The "great consequence" of living by the word of God is that one's life is in accordance with the way God has structured the universe and with God's intention for human life.

Verses 7–11 address a fundamental theological question: Is "natural revelation" (vs. 1–6) sufficient to know God (see Rom. 1:20)? Ultimately the answer is no. While the creation does offer "knowledge" (v. 2), God has also addressed a personal word to humanity. Interestingly, the personal name for God, Yahweh, appears six times in vs. 7–9, while it had not occurred at all in vs. 1–6. Finally, however, even God's personal instruction to humanity is not sufficient. There will inevitably be "errors" and "hidden faults," from which the psalmist asks to be cleansed (v. 12). The psalmist can be whole (v. 13, NRSV "blameless"; the same root underlies the word "perfect" in v. 7) because God is graceful. This abundant life (see John 10:10) results not from human achievement. Rather, it depends on God. To be "perfect" or "blameless" or "whole" is not to be sinless, but to live in dependence on God.

To be open to God's instruction, to live in dependence on God rather than self, is what makes one's words and thoughts "acceptable" to God (v. 14). The "words" of v. 14 is the same Hebrew word as "speech" in vs. 2–3. In short, dependence on God by way of openness to God's instruction and forgiveness puts one in accordance with the very structure of the universe. In other contexts, "acceptable" designates a worthy sacrifice. Our lives—our words and our thoughts—will be acceptable offerings to God when lived in dependence on God (see Rom. 12:1–2).

In concluding, the psalmist addresses God as "my rock and my redeemer." "Rock" connotes the power and strength necessary to structure a universe, while "redeemer" is a term of intimacy, sometimes translated "next of kin" (see Ruth 4:1, 3). The form of address is itself good news: the God who flung the stars into galaxies is the God who calls us by name, bids us to follow, and forgives us when we fail.

## 1 Corinthians 12:12–31a

The lection from the Epistle for this Sunday picks up where the one from last Sunday leaves of—in the midst of the stress on diversity as a necessary and enriching facet of the unity of the church. The presenting problem in the initial readers apparently concerns a division over the relative importance of spiritual gifts in the Corinthian congregation. Some members seem to push for a uniformity that stresses one gift (perhaps speaking in tongues) over all the rest, a uniformity bound to lead to disunion and division. Over against such a one-sidedness the text argues for the appropriateness of diversity, employing the well-known image of the human body.

Though the issue of the text concerns a very specific situation in a particular community, the rich imagery invites the interpreter in reflecting on the text not to be limited to the matter of spiritual gifts. In 1 Cor. 12:13 Paul himself mentions ethnic and sociological categories, no doubt forms of diversity most obvious to the modern church.

Let us look at four observations about the unfolding of the argument. First, even more emphatically than in the earlier section of the chapter (12:1–11), God is singled out as the source of the variety of spiritual gifts. Three times, using a different Greek verb each time, the text declares that God arranged it so that all members would not have the same gifts, but that within the unity there would be diversity. "God arranged the members in the body, each one of them, as he chose" (12:18; see vs. 24, 28). Diversity does not just happen, but is a part of God's gift to the church.

The stress on the divine origin and intention of diversity comes as an appropriate word in those moments when pluralism threatens to tear the church apart, when diversity results in intense power struggles. We are tempted then to think of differences as barriers to unity, as obstacles to be overcome. But by making diversity a gift of God, the text reorders the issue of power in the church. Differences are neither ignored nor viewed as limitations, "for in the one Spirit we were all baptized into one body . . . and we were all made to drink of one Spirit" (12:13).

The second observation grows out of the first. The members of the body need one another. Paul's literary strategy is a tour de force. First, he gives the foot and the ear a voice to speak their feelings, but their speech is absurd and has no effect on the appropriate part they have to play within the body (vs. 15–16). The foot's envy of the hand and the ear's envy of the eye turn out to be ridiculous words and can only be mocked. Then Paul gives a voice to the eye and the head, each to speak its word of disdain to an apparently lesser member of the body, but their voice is disallowed (v. 21), "I have no need of you" is simply ruled out as illegitimate speech. Being a member of the body renders such voice unauthorized. The point is that what keeps the body functioning properly is precisely the "need" of each member for the others.

The third observation grows out of the second. There is to be no hierarchy of gifts within the church. The imagery here is not so clear as in the earlier sections of the passage, and thus the "explanation" is more direct. In vs. 23–24 Paul seems to refer to the sexual organs as those "less respectable" (or "shameful," "less presentable") members, to which we show greater decorum by covering them, in contrast to the "more respectable" members (such as the eye or the ear) which need no covering. God arranges things so that those apparently less worthy are accorded appropriate honor. They have indispensable functions to perform.

The effect of the analogy is to neutralize the categories of "more" and "less." The total needs of the body eliminate any notion that some gifts are more essential than others. "The members of the body that seem to be weaker are indispensable" (v. 22). Thus are established a mutuality and interdependence that make hierarchical structures inappropriate.

The fourth observation depends on the previous three. The summation drawn is that in place of dissension and strife there is to be a mutual care for one another (vs. 25–26). The effect of the imagery of v. 26 is powerful. A migraine headache makes it impossible to read, to run, to appreciate good music. The suffering of one part of the body affects the whole body. The only possible conclusion is serious attention to and care for one another. The Greek word translated as "care" in v. 25 in other contexts signifies anxiety and worry and fittingly accompanies the mention of mutual suffering as well as mutual rejoicing.

One of the problems of preaching from this passage ironically is the very effectiveness of its imagery. In fact, the language of the body is so universal and illuminating that much "explanation" can hinder its impact and divert rather than assist listeners. As in preaching on many of Jesus' parables, the preacher's task in a sense is to get out of the way and let the imagery work its own effect with the congregation.

## Luke 4:14–21

By contrast with the fanfare of the infancy narratives, complete with canticles of praise and an angel chorus, the bombast of John's preaching, and the dramatic confrontation with the devil, Luke's account of the beginning of Jesus' ministry sounds a rather quiet note. After all this prologue, Jesus goes home to Galilee, "and a report about him spread through all the surrounding country" (Luke 4:14). The report apparently concerns his teaching and the praise it receives from "everyone" (v. 15).

In one sense, vs. 14–15 merely provide a transition from the temptation scene to the synagogue scene. The point is to announce that Jesus is now at work and then to show what that work entails. These transitional verses serve an additional function, however, in that they suggest a positive and warm response to Jesus' teaching, a response that unravels even in the initial proclamation in Nazareth. The ominous note in Simeon's canticle cannot be forgotten (Luke 2:34–35).

The importance Luke attaches to the Nazareth scene is revealed in the care with which he constructs it. Apparently he begins with a brief story about Jesus' return home, a story that both Mark and Matthew place much later in the ministry (Mark 6:1–6; Matt. 13:54–58). He highlights the story by moving it to the beginning of Jesus' ministry and, more important, by the addition of the quotations from Isa. 61:1–2 and 58:6. The changes convert a short story of confrontation into a programmatic announcement that concerns both the nature of Jesus' ministry and the character of the church that will follow from that ministry.

In a word, the ministry of Jesus is prophetic. That should surprise no reader who has followed Luke's story carefully. The prophetic theme announced here already appears in Mary's Magnificat, with its celebration of God's grace to the lowly and God's scorn for the proud and mighty. Although couched in different language, John the Baptist's preaching also anticipates the prophetic theme of Jesus' ministry with his warning about the judgment that accompanies the arrival of Jesus.

The quotations from Isaiah in 4:18–19 concentrate the prophetic theme on the person of Jesus. Those gathered in the synagogue may not yet understand that the quotation applies to Jesus himself, but the reader surely knows that the Spirit is indeed "upon" Jesus and that he is one anointed to preach or, as the NRSV puts it, "to bring good news." The claim of Luke 4:21 certainly identifies the passage with present events, namely, with the ministry of Jesus.

What it means to "bring good news to the poor" takes on specificity in the second half of v. 18 and in v. 19:

> to proclaim release to the captives
> and recovery of sight to the blind,
> to let the oppressed go free,
> to proclaim the year of the Lord's favor.

The language of liberation has become so commonplace in North American society in recent decades that we may not hear the urgency and the daring of this call. To declare that the captives and the oppressed should go free, and that this action results directly from the will of God, suggests already that the kingdom of God is at hand. Luke again and again calls up this theme with his stories of Jesus' inclusion of the outcasts and with later stories in Acts that portray the divine release of early Christian prisoners.

The "recovery of sight" likewise figures large in Luke-Acts, for Jesus not only gives sight to the physically blind (Luke 18:35–43) but enables others to see what has been hidden (Luke 24:31). By the same token, those who thought they could see find themselves blinded (Acts 9:8–9), and still others refuse to see what is put before their eyes (Acts 28:26–27).

The "year of the Lord's favor" or, more literally, "the acceptable year of the Lord" (RSV) may refer to the jubilee year. If so, what Luke here signals is the claim that the gospel demands a certain attitude about possessions. Followers of Jesus will find that they are expected to share possessions with others. Luke reserves some of his harshest words for those who use money irresponsibly, especially for those who might use the gospel for financial gain.

The lection ends with v. 21. Verses 21–30 are the Gospel reading for the following Sunday. To omit all discussion of these verses, however, simply distorts the passage. The response of the synagogue has only begun when all present stare at Jesus following his reading from Isaiah.

The worshipers are initially amazed and a bit perplexed by what they hear from the mouth of "Joseph's son" (v. 22). He assists them by recalling two events from Israel's history. Elijah acted to save the widow at Zarephath instead of some Israelite widow, and Elisha healed the leprosy of Naaman the Syrian rather than that of another Israelite. The implication is clear to those who drive Jesus out of town and attempt to kill him: those who are included in the liberation of Jesus' ministry come from within *and from outside* Israel. It is not the theme of liberation per se that offends the good folk of Nazareth, but the awareness that liberation includes those outside their own circle.

# FOURTH SUNDAY AFTER EPIPHANY

## Ordinary Time 4

All the lessons for today affirm the reality and illustrate the remarkable results of being known, claimed, called by God. God "knew" Jeremiah even before he was "formed . . . in the womb" (Jer. 1:5). Paul's teaching to the Corinthians about love is grounded in the affirmation that "I have been fully known" (1 Cor. 13:12). In language reminiscent of Jeremiah, the psalmist professes that it was God "who took me from my mother's womb" (Ps. 71:6). The fulfillment of the scripture that Jesus announces in Luke 4:21 involves the claim of God on his life: "The Spirit of the Lord is upon me" (4:18).

To be known, claimed, called by God means to be equipped "to accomplish abundantly far more than all we can ask or imagine" (Eph. 3:20). It means to be empowered to proclaim God's word and embody God's will. Jeremiah, for instance, despite his objections (Jer. 1:6), becomes "a prophet to the nations" (1:5). The psalmist, despite being in "the grasp of the unjust and cruel" (Ps. 71:4), "will tell of your righteous acts" (v. 15) and "talk of your righteous help" (v. 24). Amid similar opposition that is already reflected in Luke 4:21–30, Jesus will proclaim and embody God's righteousness. God's gracious claim will even enable the Corinthians to love one another in the seemingly impossible manner described in 1 Cor. 13.

The lessons offer an opportunity for us to consider God's claim on us as well. In effect, as is appropriate during the season of Epiphany, we remember our baptisms. We remember that we are known, claimed, called by God. We belong to God. From our mother's womb, our primary identity is as God's children. In the kind of world in which we live, our representation of this claim will certainly arouse opposition, as it did for the psalmist and for Jeremiah and for Paul and for Jesus. The good news is that a share of God's Spirit is ours as well, to equip and empower us in every circumstance to live and love in accordance with God's righteous purposes for us and the world.

## Jeremiah 1:4–10

In one fashion or another, each of the "major" prophetic books in the Old Testament, Daniel excepted, contains an account of the Lord's call to the personality whose name the book bears. Isaiah 6:1–8 and Ezek. 1:1–3:3 thus offer intriguing parallels to the present passage—the account of Jeremiah's call—and, while exhibiting a number of important differences, these texts also present several arresting similarities. These include (1) an initial statement by Yahweh in which the individual is summoned to speak the prophetic word, (2) a negative reaction by the individual that stresses his weakness or sin, and (3) an infusion of the Spirit of God, symbolized by Yahweh's energizing of the lips or mouth of the new prophet. (Only in Ezekiel—who is largely a passive personality in the account of his call—is the second feature somewhat muted.)

Yahweh's opening statement to the lad Jeremiah would certainly be intimidating to almost anyone. Given what we gather from other passages (see Jer. 15:17–18), Jeremiah appears to have been the kind of reflective, private person for whom the hard public life of a Yahweh prophet was absolutely repulsive. So it is little wonder that he shrank from Yahweh's terrifying summons and from the knowledge that the very God of Israel has intended the prophetic role for him even before the moment of his conception. Yet it was doubtless this cosmic dimension to his self-understanding that enabled Jeremiah to withstand the sufferings and deprivations that were to come (note Jer. 20:9).

In some ways, the idea that God has ordained a person for a particular function or vocation strikes a dissonant note in many modern ears. It appears to be the kind of predestination that stifles personal freedom and that portrays God as relating to individuals primarily in terms of their functions in life. Most women and men feel the need to exercise much more initiative in their responses to God's call and, what is more, feel that God has many roles for the faithful person to play over a lifetime. Even ordination to the ministry no longer possesses the kind of finality for many Protestants that it once had.

So how, then, does a modern reader or hearer of this text understand the uncompromising nature of God's call to Jeremiah?

Perhaps two propositions may be offered as food for thought. The first is that some persons are indeed so inextricably connected with what they do in life that their function, their vocation, is an essential—perhaps *the* essential—expression of their inner being. It is also an outpouring of their very freedom! Can one imagine

Leonard Bernstein *not* writing music or conducting an orchestra? or Bob Hope *not* telling jokes before howling audiences? or Chuck Yeager *not* flying an airplane? If some persons appear to be "born" artists or scientists or whatever, those individuals who believe in the power of the Spirit of God would not be surprised to discover that, assuming their work contributes to human well-being, these persons have been "called" to do what they do by that very Spirit—even if they themselves may not be aware of the work of the Spirit. (Compare the statement about Cyrus's call in Isa. 45:4–7.)

A second matter is that even though freedom-loving modern women and men often view lifelong commitments with suspicion, this is precisely the nature of the commitments to which God calls us. This is not to suggest that one must hold the same job all one's life or, even less, to suggest that God so "programs" individuals that our own wishes and goals are of little importance. It is to suggest, however, that (1) God's ideals for human life—justice and compassion, notably—are also to be the lifelong ideals for God's women and men and that, by whatever vocation we earn our bread, we are to shape our lives and to help shape the life of our world according to those ideals. It also means that (2) a life oriented toward justice and compassion is also a life committed to certain persons: God, family, others within the community of faith, and others within communities of our nation and our world. In the thought of the prophets, commitment to ideals and commitment to persons cannot be separated:

> And what does the LORD require of you
> but to do justice, and to love kindness,
> and to walk humbly with your God?
>                               (Micah 6:8)

If, then, we are not surprised that Jeremiah shrank from God's call, we should not be surprised that God persisted. In Jer. 1:4–10, as well as in the texts from Isaiah and Ezekiel mentioned above, the prophet submits to an act of God that not only symbolizes the prophet's new ability to do the work of God, but also symbolizes the internal presence of God's word in the prophet's life. Yahweh touches Jeremiah's mouth (v. 9), the seraph brands Isaiah's lips with a hot altar coal (Isa. 6:6–7), and the unidentified bearer of the divine voice offers Ezekiel a scroll to eat (Ezek. 3:1–3). In no case has Yahweh violated the free will of the individual; Yahweh has simply summoned the individual to make his will Yahweh's own.

The matter of one's personal call from God will always have

about it the aura of mystery, in that we can no more explain why God summons certain persons to do and be what they are than we can explain God's very nature. But there can be no mystery about the reality that God embraces certain hopes for each person and, if we are willing to listen, God will share with us what those hopes are.

## Psalm 71:1–6

Psalm 71 is usually categorized as an individual lament, and it does contain the typical elements of this genre: petition (vs. 1–4, 9, 12–13, 18), complaint (vs. 10–11), and expressions of trust (vs. 5–6, 17, 20–21) and praise (vs. 14–16, 19, 22–24). Indeed, some commentators view Ps. 71 as a sort of collage of quotations from other psalms, especially Ps. 22 (compare Ps. 71:6 with 22:9–10; 71:12 with 22:11, 19; 71:18b with 22:30–31) and Ps. 31 (compare Ps. 71:1–3 with 31:1–3; 71:9b with 31:10; 71:13 with 31:17). Because Pss. 22 and 31 are quoted by Jesus from the cross (see Mark 15:34; Luke 23:46), Ps. 71 has also become associated with Jesus' passion and is traditionally used during Holy Week. It is also quite appropriate for Epiphany, especially its theme of the proclamation of God's righteous deeds (vs. 15–19, 24).

While Ps. 71 contains the typical elements of a lament, its arrangement of them is unique. Like most laments, Ps. 71 moves from petition/complaint to praise, but it does so *three* times:

| | |
|---|---|
| Verses 1–4 | petition |
| Verses 5–8 | trust/praise |
| Verses 9–13 | petition/complaint |
| Verses 14–17 | trust/praise |
| Verse 18 | petition |
| Verses 19–24 | trust/praise |

This structure has theological significance. Without minimizing the reality of trouble and opposition, the psalmist displays pervasive trust (v. 14a) and persistent praise (v. 6c; note the word "continually" in vs. 6c and 14a). Faith lives amid adversity. Praise is not the celebration of the powerful and prosperous, but rather the language of those who know at all times and in every circumstance that their lives belong to God and their futures depend on God. As H.-J. Kraus puts it, "The psalm radiates tremendous assurance" (*Psalms 60–150*, trans. H. C. Oswald; Minneapolis: Augsburg, 1989; p. 73).

This assurance is evident from the opening words of the psalm.

The psalmist "take[s] refuge" in God. It is unclear whether the ancient practice of seeking asylum in the Temple from accusers or persecutors is reflected in this affirmation (see 1 Kings 1:49–53). In any case, the psalmist professes that his or her life depends on God. The same word recurs in Ps. 71:7, while v. 3 contains two synonyms, one of which NRSV also renders as "refuge." The assurance of belonging to God will also be expressed in other ways later in the psalm (see vs. 20–21, 24).

The psalmist's assurance rests on his or her trust that God is righteous. This trust is introduced in v. 2 and becomes the major theme of the psalm, as the psalmist repeatedly proclaims or praises God's righteousness (vs. 15, 16, 19, 24). The psalmist is convinced that God will set things right by shaming those persons who are seeking to shame him or her (see "shame" in vs. 1, 13, 24). In fact, v. 24 sounds as if God has already shamed the enemies. It is unclear whether an actual reversal of fortunes has occurred or whether the psalmist is so certain of God's help that he or she can already speak of it as having arrived. What is clear is that faith in God's righteousness exists amid opposition, at least for most of the psalm. It will be the same for us. Indeed, when we read Ps. 71 in conjunction with the Gospel lesson for the day (Luke 4:21–30), we are reminded that genuine faith in God will arouse opposition. The wicked (Ps. 71:4)—those who view themselves as self-sufficient rather than dependent on God—are as persistent a reality in our world as they are in Ps. 71 (see vs. 10–11, 13, 24).

Verse 5 begins with the personal pronoun "you," which is emphatic in Hebrew. It occurs also in vs. 3, 6, and 7, effectively focusing attention on God. The psalmist's confidence is not self-confidence; it is trust in God. Verses 5–6 introduce another major theme of Ps. 71—youth (vs. 5, 17) and old age (vs. 9, 18). It certainly seems that the psalmist is elderly, although the imagery may be metaphorical. In any case, it expresses the psalmist's conviction that he or she has belonged to God from the day of birth and that he or she will always belong to God. In effect, the psalmist does the equivalent of what Christians traditionally do during the season of Epiphany—namely, we remember our baptisms. To remember our baptisms is to profess to the world that God claimed us at birth and that we shall always belong to God. In the *self*-centered and achievement-oriented culture in which we live, our simple profession is remarkable and radical. Like the psalmist, we proclaim what God has taught us (v. 17): life is not a reward to be achieved but a gift to be received (see vs. 20–21).

For those who know that their lives belong to God, praise

becomes not only a liturgical act offered in church but also a lifestyle offered "continually" (v. 6c; see also v. 14, as well as the phrase "all day long" in vs. 8, 15, 24). For the psalmist, praise is a lifelong calling, from birth to old age. It is the ability, even in the face of adversity, to look back and say, "it was you who took me from my mother's womb" (v. 6), and to look forward and say, "You will . . . comfort me once again" (v. 21). As A. Hale Schroer has put it, "Praise is to declare even when the evidence seems stacked against it that this is God's world. . . . Praise is the posture of Epiphany for it keeps us open to the new ways God is manifesting Godself in our world" (*No Other Foundation* 9/2 [Winter 1988–89]: 16).

The psalmist may have grown old, but he or she clearly expected new things, and indeed was already intent on proclaiming God's deeds to "generations to come" (v. 18). Commentators speculate that the psalmist may have been a poet or songwriter in one of the Temple guilds. Be that as it may, we in our day and time cannot afford to leave the educational task to specialists. It is the calling of all the baptized—all who belong to God—to praise God continually (v. 6) in joyful gratitude for God's faithfulness (vs. 22–23) and as a witness "to all the generations to come" (v. 18) that ultimately nothing "will be able to separate us from the love of God" (Rom. 8:39).


## 1 Corinthians 13

The third consecutive reading from 1 Corinthians brings us to the lovely and familiar thirteenth chapter. Its rhythmic cadences and simple but expressive language make it a favorite of people within and without the church. Of all Paul's writings, it is the most likely selection to be chosen for an anthology of great literature. Its middle paragraph (13:4–7) often can be found inscribed in lovely calligraphy, suitably framed, hanging in homes and offices. "A hymn to love" it is called.

Such reverence for the passage creates problems for the preacher. The text is regularly lifted out of its context, and love becomes an abstraction, an ideal, something on a level with the "purple patches" in Kahlil Gibran's *The Prophet*. The beauty of the language obscures the practical, exhortative force of the words. The setting of a conflicted congregation, caught up in a distorted spirituality, engaged in intense power struggles, is overlooked in the admiration of the poetry.

Thus the preacher's first task is to return the text to its original context—to the dispute in Corinth over spiritual gifts—and to recognize that these are words of exhortation for a confused congregation. To be sure, they are beautiful words, but they are not written to idealize the quality of love and praise its virtues. They have an earthy, practical force to them, precisely because they are sent to a quarrelsome people who need to know that their fervent religiosity isn't worth a tinker's damn apart from a new relationship to one another, apart from love.

The chapter neatly divides itself into three paragraphs, and readers are led, step-by-step, through a powerful argument as to why their common life needs reorientation and a description (which serves as an exhortation) of what love entails.

First, it is clear that love is essential (13:1–3). Without love, speaking in tongues turns a person into a noisy and incoherent nuisance; people with profound theological insight and total faith amount to nothing; even extravagant benefactors of the poor and those who have sufferings to boast of gain nothing. (Note the very difficult textual problem in 13:3 that leads the NRSV to choose the word "boast," rather than the more familiar "be burned." It is easy to understand how the variation occurred in the process of copying manuscripts, but it is not at all clear which is the original reading.)

The first-person language underscores the personal direction of the argument. It is not that the spiritual gifts are useless or that dramatic sacrifice is to be disdained. The exercise of the gifts and the practice of sacrifice in themselves simply do nothing for the doer. It is love that makes these actions meaningful, more than displays of selfish pride or deeds of daring. And, of course, the overtones for the community are obvious. The conflicts at Corinth, the power struggles and confusion, are caused by a loveless spirituality. The antidote is not a further honing of the gifts or a call for sacrifice, but the practice of "a still more excellent way" (12:31).

The second paragraph declares that love is practical (13:4–7). The structure of the paragraph is informative. First, two positive statements (13:4a–b), then a string of eight negatives (13:4c–6a), the last of which has a positive opposite (13:6b). The paragraph closes with four parallel affirmations (13:7). The composite is a picture of love in action.

Love becomes the subject of all the verbs (fifteen of them in Greek, all more vivid than the static "is" used in translation). Love does some things and resists doing other things. It is not an abstract idea: it acts. It expresses itself in down-to-earth contexts, where it refuses to stoop to petty retaliation, demonstrates patience, shuns competitiveness, resists keeping a scorecard, remains hopeful. The impression one gets is that love primarily functions in situations of stress and conflict, anything but the romanticized version so popularly held.

The third paragraph affirms the permanence of love (13:7–13). The contrast is drawn between the transient and incomplete present and the permanent and fulfilled future. The images are forceful—like the difference between a child and an adult, the difference between the distorted reflection in a polished, bronze mirror and a face-to-face meeting.

The spiritual gifts belong to the present. They have their appropriate part to play, but their end will come. Love, on the other hand, is the supreme feature of the future age and thus enduring. It is to be pursued above all else. It makes the exercise of spiritual gifts a positive endeavor (14:1).

All this exhortation becomes exhausting. How can one ever love in the way this passage describes? There is a clue tucked away in the contrast of 13:12. "I will know fully, *even as I have been fully known*" (emphasis added). God is the unstated one, whose thorough knowledge of the community of faith now makes human love possible. The readers are not left as autonomous selves to love as best they can; they are reminded of God's gracious claim on them.

## Luke 4:21–30

"Today this scripture has been fulfilled in your hearing" (Luke 4:21). Just as the Gospel reading assigned to the previous week remains incomplete without considering this passage, so this opening statement sounds an awkward note unless 4:14–20 is taken into account (see the Third Sunday After Epiphany). According to Luke's story, Jesus' audience also found this an awkward saying, and v. 22 depicts their mixture of amazement and confusion.

"All spoke well of him and were amazed at the gracious words that came from his mouth" (4:22a). Initially, at least, the synagogue audience finds itself simply dazzled by this local boy. He has read well, and his comment about the fulfillment of the passage from Isaiah appeals to them. Who could be anything but pleased by the news of freedom, of sight, of liberation?

A question arises: "Is not this Joseph's son?" (v. 22b). The question tantalizes modern readers, for it can be heard as a somewhat hostile comment about the possibility that Joseph's child, someone so familiar to them, could actually have such wisdom and insight. That Jesus is referred to as "Joseph's son" may even reflect the raised eyebrows of neighbors who recall certain rumors about Jesus' birth. On the other hand, the question may be a friendly one, expressing in concrete terms the astonishment the narrator has already reported: "How can Joseph's son be so impressive?"

Translation alone cannot resolve the ambiguity. Given the positive response that has accompanied Jesus to date (4:14–15, 22a), it appears that the question is straightforward. Only with Jesus' subsequent remarks does he provoke the crowd to anger. What is significant here, of course, is that the crowd *assumes* that it knows who Jesus is and, therefore, what might be (and what might not be) expected of him.

With the statements of vs. 23–24, Jesus succeeds in throwing dust in the eyes of those present. The three disconnected sayings challenge the audience, but none of them is focused in such a way as to make clear what the conflict is (or will be) between Jesus and the synagogue crowd. First, he adduces a proverb attested in both Greek and Jewish writings: "Doctor, cure yourself!" Presumably the proverb, in this context, anticipates that Jesus should deal with his own faults before addressing those of others. Since he has not made any charge, however, the proverb remains somewhat unclear. Second, he anticipates that they will demand from him the same "things," probably miracles, he has done at Capernaum. That Luke has not yet told of Jesus' stay in Capernaum makes for some confusion (see 4:31; compare Mark 1:21 and 6:1–6). The third saying, also traditional, moves somewhat closer to the conflict: "No prophet is accepted in the prophet's hometown" (v. 24).

Only with the stories of vs. 25–27 does Jesus identify the cause of the conflict and thereby precipitate it! That he has reached the heart of the matter we can see in the introductory words, "But the truth is," or, more literally, "I say to you truly" (v. 25). Here he recalls two stories involving earlier prophets of Israel, Elijah and Elisha. During the famine that afflicted all of Israel, Elijah was sent to dwell with a widow. Because of her obedience, she and her household were saved. She was not, however, an Israelite but a Gentile (v. 26). Similarly, from among all the cases of leprosy that surely afflicted Israel during the time of Elisha, he brought about the healing of only one man. That one man was not an Israelite but a Syrian by the name of Naaman.

"None of them" received the assistance of Elijah (v. 26). "None of them" was healed by Elisha (v. 27). The repetition of that phrase makes the point clear. The prophets rescued, not the hometown folk, but those regarded as outsiders, those who could not call themselves God's people. Suddenly the point becomes painfully clear to those present, as vs. 28–30 explain. They are no longer spellbound by Jesus' presence or confused as to how to understand him. He has ceased to be a friendly, benign presence and has become the enemy. Only by acting quickly does Jesus escape their rage.

The beginning of Jesus' ministry also marks the beginning of hostility to him. He teaches and later heals. The crowds find him pleasant and welcome his skills. When the teaching turns threatening, however, suggesting that they themselves need repentance or suggesting the inclusion of the excluded and marginalized, the response becomes anything but one of welcome.

This lection also reflects an important facet of Luke's understanding of the fulfillment of prophecy. Unlike Matthew, who somewhat woodenly quotes specific biblical passages and indicates how they are fulfilled in the life of Jesus, Luke's understanding is more subtle. He is more inclined to *show* the fulfillment of prophecy than to *tell* it. Luke also sees events within the life of Jesus or the activity of the church as themselves forming prophecy that will be fulfilled. For example, Stephen's speech recalls Israel's resistance to its prophets, and that speech is immediately followed by another such instance, the killing of Stephen himself (Acts 7:51–8:1). Here, Jesus announces that prophets are not welcome in their hometowns, and that statement is enacted immediately by those who hear him! This small feature of Luke's style of composition contributes to his larger theme of the gospel as the fulfillment of God's own plan and will.

# FIFTH SUNDAY AFTER EPIPHANY

## Ordinary Time 5

Isaiah's experience of the presence and power of God in the Temple (Isa. 6:1–8) and Simon Peter's experience of the presence and power of God in Jesus' mighty work (Luke 5:1–11) produced in these men a profound sense of awe. Both were immediately struck by their unworthiness. "Woe is me! I am lost," says the prophet (6:5). And Peter says, "I am a sinful man!" (5:8). Paul's encounter with the risen Christ also produced in him a continuing awareness that he was "unfit to be called an apostle" (1 Cor. 15:9).

But God encounters human beings not to condemn and terrify, but rather to transform and call. Isaiah is forgiven, emboldened, and given a word to deliver to God's people. Peter is told not to fear and is assured that he henceforth "will be catching people" (Luke 5:10). By the time he wrote to the Corinthians, Paul had already become "by the grace of God" (1 Cor. 15:10) a powerful proclaimer of the gospel among the Gentiles.

The psalmist does not as clearly conform to this pattern, but he or she too has a lively awareness of the majesty of God. The psalmist, like the seraphim in the Temple, knew the pervasive influence of God's "glory" (138:5; see Isa. 6:3). And what the psalmist celebrates lies at the heart of what we celebrate during Epiphany—the manifestation of God's power and presence throughout the earth (Ps. 138:4–5). The good news is that the fulfillment of God's cosmic purpose involves the individual human beings whom God chooses to encounter. The psalmist's concluding affirmation of trust could have been voiced as well by Isaiah or Simon Peter or Paul, and we can claim it as our faith as well: "The LORD will fulfill his purpose for me" (v. 8).

## Isaiah 6:1–8 (9–13)

The account of Jeremiah's call to the prophetic office, the Old Testament lection for last week, is now followed by a similar account

132

of God's call to Isaiah of Jerusalem. There is an important sense in which the present text from Isaiah 6 is so familiar a paradigm of God's call to faithful people that it may fail to speak with the freshness of some other texts. Yet it is a key passage in this regard and deserves repeated use, for it transmits quintessential elements in the ongoing story of God's imperatives directed to people of faith.

The purpose for dating the prophet's experience of call to the final year of Judean King Uzziah (742 B.C.) is not clear (v. 1). Perhaps this is intended to be a chronological reference and no more, similar to those found in the Deuteronomistic History (note, for example, 2 Kings 15:1) among other places. But such language is rare in prophetic discourse, and the suspicion is raised that it is somehow *as a result of* the king's death that the prophet is roused to activity by the Spirit of God. The passing of Uzziah, one of Judah's last truly powerful monarchs, may have been a signal to perceptive persons that changes in the fortunes of the nation were on their way and that, in significant ways, Judah would stand in special need of God's grace in the years ahead. If so, the opening lines of this pericope stand as a reminder that the Spirit of God often works through the events of our days to draw our attention to God's will for human life.

If one word were to be employed to express the mood of our text, it would be "awe." A holy God has taken the initiative to address a weak and sinful mortal, and the prophet—quite rightly so!—is almost paralyzed with a sense of God's power and his own inadequacy. This response to God's nature permeates the outlook not only of Isaiah of Jerusalem, whose work is recalled in chapters 1—39, but of others who lived at a later time and who spoke or wrote in the tradition of Isaiah (note Isa. 41:20 and 57:15). It is clear from this text that the sense of mission on the part of God's people flows directly out of an understanding of who God is—both in and of God's self and in relation to God's world. The seraphim must shield their faces before God's awful majesty (6:2), and when they sing their words are of God's otherness (v. 3). Only the live coal (v. 6), symbol of the justice and compassion of God, can serve to purify the profit and render him fit for service to this King of majesty.

This "otherness" of God, that which sets God apart from the created world, operates both in a theological and in a moral context. Theologically, God's holiness implies that, while creation is dependent on its Creator, the reverse is far from true. God is holy in the sense that God is external to creation and presides in sovereignty over it.

The moral sense of holiness is affirmed in our text also. That is to say, a moral God is one who—unlike the gods of the human imagination—is consistent and reliable in dealing with humankind. This is a God of justice and love, who is characterized by these qualities day in and day out, in good times and in bad. What is more, this holy God summons the people of God to live lives characterized by the same persistent principles. This view is not that of Isaiah alone (compare, for example, Lev. 22:32), but it certainly lies at the heart of the prophet's proclamation. Thus it is that Isaiah feels inadequate, until the application of the live coal to his lips by one of the seraphim (literally, "burning ones").

Central to the reality projected by this text is not only that which pertains to the nature of God, but also that which has to do with the transforming power of God's presence. Attention should be given to the interesting interplay in vs. 7–8 among words that refer to the power of speech: "mouth," "lips," "voice," "saying," and "said" (twice). The act of cleansing not only restores the condition of wholeness to a sinful person (in this case the prophet), but also releases that person's power to hear God's speech and, in turn, to speak God's words to a sinful people. Often, when we read v. 8 of this text, our attention is focused on the act of *going forth* in the name of God (the etymological basis of the word "mission" is, after all, a Latin word meaning "to send out"). "Whom shall I send?" is answered by "Here am I; send me!"

But this emphasis on motion should not be allowed to obscure an equal emphasis on speech. The prophet has been released not just to go, but to go as the bearer of God's word. That reality is emphasized by the inclusion in this lection, in parenthesis, of vs. 9–13: the terrible words that Isaiah was ordained by God to deliver. If the preacher wishes to include this part of the text in his or her consideration, it would be well to remember that the prophetic words of judgment are best understood as part of a larger prophetic statement concerning God's burning (com)passion for Israel and for all humankind (compare Hos. 11:8–9).

(See also Trinity Sunday, Year B.)


## Psalm 138

Psalm 138 is usually categorized as an individual thanksgiving psalm. The mention of "your holy temple" (v. 2) suggests a possible setting. Having been delivered from distress, the psalmist comes to the Temple to offer his or her praise, perhaps along with a sacrifice of thanksgiving. While this proposed setting is reasonable, it does not fully address the uniqueness of Psalm 138, nor does it explain a fundamental ambiguity. Namely, while it seems that the psalmist has already been delivered (v. 3a), the psalmist continues to pray for deliverance (v. 8c). This apparent ambiguity is actually a representation of the reality of the life of faith. As faithful people we know that experiences of grace do not alter our essential and perpetual neediness. As a whole, Ps. 138 instructs us about our fundamental dependence on God, and it invites us, like the psalmist, to offer ourselves to God.

The first section of the psalm, vs. 1–3, begins with the psalmist presenting his or her whole self to God in thanks, "with my whole heart" (v. 1a). A unique feature of Ps. 138 is that this offering is made not simply before the congregation of Israel but rather "before the gods" (v. 1b). The verse has a polemical tone, which is perhaps best captured by a literal translating that yields the contemporary idiom "in your face." The psalmist offers his or her praise "in the face of the gods," almost contemptuously denying them sovereignty (see Pss. 58:1–2; 82:1). By stating that "I bow down toward your holy temple" (or, "palace"), the psalmist professes that Yahweh alone is sovereign, the sole provider for his or her life (v. 2a; see also v. 7).

The psalmist is able to submit his or her life to God because of trust that it is God's character (see "name," which can mean character, reputation, v. 2) to manifest "steadfast love" and "faithfulness." These same two words are used by Yahweh in the self-revelation to Moses (Ex. 34:6–7) and become a sort of basic profession of Israel's faith. They are paired frequently in the psalms as the basis for an appeal to God for help (Pss. 40:11–12; 115:1–2), or as a profession of trust (Pss. 57:3; 85:10–13). The dependability of Yahweh is also emphasized in v. 2c. The Hebrew is difficult (see NRSV margin), but could perhaps be construed as "your promises surpass even your fame" (NJB). However God's "word" is construed—as God's revelation or God's promises in written form (see, for example, Ps. 119:11, 38, 41)—it constitutes in this case a very personal address: "you answered me" (v. 3a). The psalmist is strengthened; the word gives life (see Deut. 8:3; Matt. 4:4).

The second section of the psalm, vs. 4–6, suggests that the psalmist's experience is universal. "All the kings of the earth" have been reached by God's "words" (v. 4; see "word" in v. 2), and they join the psalmist in offering themselves to God ("praise" in v. 4 translates the same Hebrew word as "give thanks" in vs. 1 and 2). Verse 5 suggests the kings yield their sovereignty in recognition of God's sovereignty. They celebrate "the ways of the LORD" rather than exercising their own wills. This is precisely what Ps. 2 at the beginning of the Psalter admonished the kings of the earth to do in order not to perish (2:10–12). For the kings of the earth as for the psalmist, the word of God gives life.

Not surprisingly, "glory" (v. 5) elsewhere is specifically associated with the recognition and celebration of God's reign (see Isa. 6:1–8; Pss. 24:7–10; 29:1–3, 9–11; 97:1, 6; 145:10–13). Lest the kings of the earth or anyone else misunderstand, the nature of God's strange sovereignty is clarified in 138:6. The exalted God "regards the lowly" and keeps the arrogant at a distance. Verse 6 is reminiscent of Ps. 113:4–9 and 1 Sam. 2:1–10, Hannah's prayer, which is taken up by Mary in anticipation of the birth and ministry of Jesus (Luke 1:46–55, especially vs. 51–53). Jesus embodied God's strange sovereignty, distancing himself from the proud and powerful in favor of the lowly. Psalm 138:6 is thus expressive of the topsy-turvy values that prevail in the reign of God.

The final section of the psalm, vs. 7–8, focuses again on the psalmist. Those who eschew self-sufficiency and commit themselves to the values of the reign of God will undoubtedly have enemies, as does the psalmist and as did Jesus. The psalmist affirms that God "gives me life" (NRSV "you preserve me") in the midst of the struggle, not beyond the struggle. Deliverance/salvation/life is at once a present reality and yet something that awaits fulfillment: "The LORD will fulfill his purpose for me" (v. 8; see Ps. 57:2–3, where the same affirmation is made in the context of trust in God's "steadfast love" and "faithfulness" as in Ps. 138). As in v. 2, the psalmist's ability to submit his or her life and future to God is grounded in God's "steadfast love."

The "not yet" dimension of deliverance is evident in the final petition (v. 8c). The Hebrew word translated "forsake" more literally means to let fall, to drop, which is appropriate in a context that refers to hands three times (vs. 7–8). The petition implicitly affirms the psalmist's conviction that he or she is in God's hands. The "work [or "works": the Hebrew is plural] of your hands" certainly includes the psalmist (see Job 14:15, where an individual person is so designated), but should probably be understood more inclusively. Elsewhere, God's "works" include all the creatures and indeed the whole creation (Ps. 104:24–26). In short, the final petition implicitly affirms what we affirm in the words of a well-known spiritual: God's got the whole world in God's hands. Like the psalmist, we make this affirmation in the midst of all kinds of trouble, opposition, and apparent evidence to the contrary. Amid the "not-yetness," it is our way of professing that God will fulfill God's purposes for us and for our world. The profession is clearly appropriate for Epiphany and invites us to join the psalmist and the kings of the earth in offering ourselves to God with our "whole heart" (Ps. 138:1; see Rom. 12:1–2).

## 1 Corinthians 15:1–11

The epistolary readings for this Sunday and the three following Sundays come from 1 Cor. 15, which includes the rather elaborate and yet critical argument Paul makes regarding the future resurrection of the dead. Unfortunately, there are several difficult exegetical points in the chapter about which commentators disagree, and the preacher can easily become discouraged and seek a less formidable passage. The issue of the future resurrection of believers remains, however, an existential question for people who sit in the pews. The reality of death is close to every family, if not to every individual, and people need to hear what Paul says about the resurrection.

Even in facing 15:1–11, we need to keep in mind the audience Paul is addressing—those who accept Jesus' resurrection from the dead, but reject a future resurrection for themselves (v. 12). Exactly why they deny a future resurrection is one of those questions about which there is not a unanimous agreement. Apparently the philosophical orientation of some and their rather triumphalistic Christology has led them to assume that they have reached the goal of salvation, that they are already living a heavenly, spiritual existence and thus have no reason to anticipate the future God has in store for them. Whatever the cause of their resistance to a future resurrection, Paul's argument begins with a reaffirmation of Jesus' resurrection, which he later argues is but the beginning of a general resurrection of the dead. He offers no "proof" of the resurrection that might satisfy commonly held canons of historical investigation. He simply states afresh the church's witness.

We should make three observations about the beginning of Paul's case and the character of the gospel (15:1–11). First, there is the creedal statement preached previously among the readers and which they themselves have accepted. It is not just Paul's personal interpretation, but a commonly held gospel, a tradition, in fact, that predates Paul and that includes a wide range of authorities— Cephas, the Twelve, five hundred brothers and sisters, James, and all the apostles, as well as Paul. The fundamental Christian message is not a complicated system peculiar to one ancient theologian, an idiosyncratic word tied to a single eccentric preacher. The core content of the gospel is a plain and simple declaration, shared by the whole church—the death of Christ for our sins according to the scriptures, his burial, and his resurrection on the third day according to the scriptures.

The gospel has far-reaching ramifications, and throughout history complex theological systems have developed to understand the ramifications, but it all begins with an unambiguous story about the deeds of the Messiah and their transformative impact on human sins. The simplicity is mind-boggling.

The second observation has to do with Paul's participation in the gospel. The creedal statement does not remain simply a piece of tradition heard and mechanically repeated. Paul lists himself as one to whom the risen Christ appeared, one unfit to serve because he had persecuted the church but whom divine grace has made into a diligent apostle (15:8–10). No doubt the inclusion of himself among the list of those to whom Christ appeared adds weight to his own authority with the Corinthian readers, but the point for us is that the gospel turns out to be more than a story. It is a transformative power. It is the divine activity by which people are drawn into the circle of God's grace and made new creatures. Correct theology, even about the resurrection, soon becomes barren apart from the life-changing dynamic of the gospel.

The third observation to be made about the gospel arises from what is said specifically to the readers. They are reminded that they have already accepted this message, and yet a disturbing caveat is placed alongside the reminder: "if you hold firmly to the message . . . unless you have come to believe in vain" (15:2). How is it that they might let go of the gospel or believe it in vain? The caveat prepares for the crucial link to be drawn later in the argument between the gospel and the future resurrection of the dead, a ramification being offered not merely as a possible implication that *might* be drawn but as essential to the saving character of the gospel itself (so 15:14–18). If readers agree that Jesus' resurrection ensures a future resurrection for all believers, then they will have held fast to the gospel and believed it to a good end. If they reject the argument and persist in saying there is no future resurrection, then, ironically, their believing will have been in vain.

While the gospel can be simply stated and demonstrates a power to transform human lives, it also carries with it certain theological and moral implications that cannot be ignored. In 1 Cor. 15 the implications have to do with the overcoming of death and the future completion of God's resurrecting activity, implications that give stability and confidence to life in the present (v. 58).

## Luke 5:1–11

The miracles of Jesus provide human beings with some benefit. They meet some human need, whether for healing or for deliverance from the fearsome powers of the sea. Despite the way it has troubled some interpreters, even the miracle at Cana provides the need of wine for those who celebrate a wedding (see comment on the Second Sunday After Epiphany). At first glance, the miracle depicted in Luke 5:1–11 follows the customary pattern in which Jesus miraculously supplies some human need, precipitating awe and, of course, puzzlement over his identity. This particular miracle, however, is more complicated than it seems on an initial reading.

Much in the ordering of the story cries out for further explanation. Why does Jesus instruct Simon to cast the nets once again, when nothing has been said that indicates Simon and his colleagues are in need of assistance? If Jesus' intent is to supply their need, why is the abundance of the catch such as to become a threat to the boats? Although we refer to this passage as the "calling" of the disciples, Jesus does not actually issue a call here. In fact, it is not clear why Simon and the others follow him or what Simon understands by "catching people" instead of fish.

Despite these questions, or perhaps because of them, several important Lukan concerns emerge in this passage. First, the passage depicts Simon as one who is obedient to Jesus' word. When Jesus instructs him to put down the nets again, he does so. His own reasoning tells him that this is one more futile effort ("Master, we have worked all night long but have caught nothing," 5:5a); his statement to that effect also underscores the impossibility of the dramatic catch that is to follow. Nevertheless, having warned Jesus, Simon Peter obeys ("Yet if you say so, I will let down the nets," 5:5b). Like Mary before him, who reminds Gabriel that she cannot have a child and yet submits to God's will (Luke 1:34, 38), Simon Peter obeys even what seems ridiculous. There will be others also who follow this pattern, as does Ananias when he instructs God that Paul is not to be trusted, but then follows the order of God just the same (Acts 9:13–17). The followers of Jesus are not necessarily expected to understand, but they are expected to obey.

A second Lukan theme that plays an important role in this lection is that of abundance, or even superabundance! Simon does not ask Jesus for assistance with the fishing, but the catch that comes is nevertheless so large that even all the available hands and both boats cannot deal with it. This aspect of the story recalls the charismatic rabbinic figure referred to as "Honi the Circle Maker." On one occasion, Honi prayed for rain, only to find that the rain came down in such torrents that he finally had to pray that the rain cease from the earth. All the Gospels, of course, associate Jesus with supplying abundance for God's people, whether that abundance takes the form of food for a hungry multitude or wine for a wedding or fish for the fishers.

With its attention to Simon, this story deals with yet another kind of abundance. When Jesus says to Simon, "from now on you will be catching people" (v. 10), he anticipates the role Simon Peter will play in Acts, where his initial preaching not only "catches" people, but astonishingly large numbers of people.

A third Lukan theme in this passage concerns the use of possessions. The story ends with the dramatic and abrupt note that "When they had brought their boats to shore, they left everything and followed him" (v. 11). In view of the vast load of fish included in that word "everything," we can imagine the rotten stench that would pervade the shore along Gennesaret a few days later, but that is not Luke's concern. What he portrays here is the radical unconcern for possessions that is integrally connected with discipleship. The disciples leave their boats, their workers, presumably even this astonishing catch, and go off after someone they cannot comprehend on a mission they do not understand.

Later Luke will tell of the early church's practice of sharing possessions with one another, of the selling of property and distribution of food to the widows. Later also he will demonstrate what happens to those whose own greed prevents them from hearing the gospel and prompts them even to stand in the way of others who wish to hear. For now, the point is more subtle and suggestive: whoever Jesus is and wherever he leads, he merits the casting aside even of one's livelihood.

The fourth Lukan theme dominates the story, and that concerns the presence of God. In some circles, Jesus' action would have led to debates about who Jesus is and what is the source of his power. Simon Peter rightly recognizes Jesus, even if he does not understand fully: "Go away from me, Lord, for I am a sinful man!" (5:8). His sinfulness plays a role here, not because he has particular sins to confess, but because he is simply human. He recognizes that the power of Jesus is God's own power, and he responds with the awe that is appropriate before that power. With Isaiah, he knows the fear of God (Isa. 6:5).

# Sixth Sunday After Epiphany

Proper 1
Ordinary Time 6

Three of the four lessons for today contain a beatitude. At first sight, the content of these beatitudes seems to differ. For Jeremiah, "Blessed are those who trust in the LORD" (Jer. 17:7). For the psalmist, "Happy are those . . . [whose] delight is in the law of the LORD" (Ps. 1:1–2). For Luke, "Blessed are" the poor, the hungry, the grieving, the persecuted. In essence, however, the three texts make the same affirmation: Blessed are those who live in dependence on God rather than in dependence on self. Blessed are those who live under God's reign.

It is obvious that the biblical definition of happiness differs from what our contemporary culture promotes as happiness, which is fundamentally self centered rather than God-centered. To be happy in biblical terms is to entrust one's life to God, to conform one's life to God's values, to depend on God as the sufficient resource for facing life's worst. In short, happiness is not a reward but, rather, is the result of choosing to live for God. In fact, the denial of self in dependence on God actually invites opposition and suffering, as the psalmists knew (see Ps. 3:1–2) and as Jeremiah knew (see Jer. 12:1–13; 15:10–21; 17:14–18) and as Jesus knew (see Luke 6:22–23). But to lose one's self or life in this manner is truly to find one's life (see Mark 8:35).

First Corinthians 15 is essentially too an affirmation that our lives and futures belong ultimately to God. Present strife and suffering are real (see 1 Cor. 15:24–28), but to believe in the resurrection is to entrust ourselves to God, both for now and forever. Such trust constitutes the true blessedness or happiness of which the prophet, the psalmist, and the evangelist speak.

## Jeremiah 17:5–10

Human happiness—or, for that matter, human misery— is inextricably bound to the commitments of our hearts. This appears to be

141

the principal thrust of Jer. 17:5–10, but the point is driven home in at least two different ways.

For the first part of our passage, vs. 5–8, the prophet relies on an ancient formula that frames both the negative and the positive results of certain courses of action ("curses" and "blessings"). The origins of this literary construction are not entirely clear (perhaps early military or political treaties), but it occupies a prominent place in certain Old Testament texts, such as Deut. 27—28. Thus it was venerable with age by the late seventh and early sixth centuries B.C. the time of Jeremiah. In the prophet's hands the purpose of this literary formulation is quite clear: to portray human well-being as the result of trust in God, and human misery as the result of misplaced allegiances.

The curse comes first (vs. 5–6). Those "mortals" and "mere flesh" on whom Jeremiah's listeners are tempted to depend may be connected in some manner to the practice of idolatry—more specifically, to some fertility cult such as the worship of Baal. That would seem to be the implication, if we read vs. 5–8 as a continuation of vs. 1–4. The Second Isaiah would later have much the same point to make, but with more mocking irony (Isa. 44:9–20). On the other hand, Jeremiah's great predecessor, Isaiah of Jerusalem, had pointed to the folly of reliance on brute human force as a means of ensuring happiness and tranquility (Isa. 31:1–3). Egyptian war chariots had failed the generations of Kings Ahaz and Hezekiah, as surely as all war chariots fail when they are counted on as a sole source of security.

Whatever their formulation, the seductions of human self-sufficiency are compelling and they must have nibbled away at the hearts of Jeremiah's contemporaries as persistently as they do to those in our own time. Those who yield to this form of self-deception are compared to plants struggling for life in the desert (v. 6). They exist, but where is the joy? The parallels between Jer. 17:5–8 and Ps. 1 (also a lection for this day) are striking, and there may indeed be some direct literary dependence, as many scholars have suggested. But the images of drought and watery abundance are so persistent in Israel/Palestine that the metaphor must have occurred independently to many persons.

After the curse comes the blessing (vs. 7–8). In v. 7 it is not just for the sake of poetic symmetry but also for the sake of emphasis that the phrase "trust in the LORD" is repeated ("whose trust is the LORD"). There is a universe between, on the one hand, "mortals" and "mere flesh" of v. 5 and, on the other, Yahweh, the living God of Israel. And those who understand this distinction and who stake their lives on it will experience benefits unknown to those who do not.

If the latter are to be compared to the parched growth of the desert, faithful men and women are to be conceptualized as verdant vegetation, luxuriating in the paradise of the riverbank (this stream could only be the Jordan). There is no fear. Neither heat nor drought is menacing, and both leaves and fruit are persistent (notice in the last four lines of v. 8 the alternation of evil/good/evil/good).

The obvious problem with texts like Jer. 17:5–8 is that, when read in isolation, they fail the test of empirical observation. The tragic reality is that many persons who trust God not at all *appear*, at least, to flourish, while many faithful persons suffer enormously. Job knew that, and so did Jesus. Thus the values in such a passage as the present lection become evident only when it is read in connection with others. Although the Gospel lection for this day bears noteworthy literary parallels to Jer. 17:5–8, the lection from 1 Cor. 15 also broadens the perspective from which the present text may be understood.

The second part of today's Old Testament lection (vs. 9–10) makes much the same point as the first, yet with differences. Jeremiah is noted for his attention to the heart as the seat of human affections. More than other prophets he brings the symbol of the heart to the center of consideration, where he employs it as a figure for both all that is right and all that is wrong with the human will and with human conduct. "Circumcise yourselves to the LORD,/remove the foreskin of your hearts" (Jer. 4:4) is not simply the prophet's way of saying that inner commitment is more important than external ritual. It also represents his argument that, when all is said and done, the nature of our commitments is the most significant thing about us. About anyone!

For Jeremiah the heart is permeated with evil, infinitely capable of deceiving others—and even of deceiving itself! The heart represents all those efforts by individuals to place themselves, each and every one of us, at the center of things, even as we camouflage our selfishness with false words and deceptive deeds intended to convey our selflessness. Such deviousness comes quite easily to the heart, quite naturally.

Yet God is not confused, for God and only God reads the heart. God and only God understands who we are—much more thoroughly than we understand ourselves. Samuel's often-quoted statement to the family of Jesse during the search for Israel's new king that "[mortals] look on the outward appearance, but the LORD looks on the heart" (1 Sam. 16:7) is a positive application of the idea, but

Jeremiah wants his hearers (readers) to understand the negative as well.

God responds to persons as persons respond to God, might be a précis of vs. 9–10. That message has much the same strength, and something of the same limitations, as that in vs. 5–8.

## Psalm 1

The nearly unanimous consensus of Psalms scholarship is that Ps. 1 has been placed at the beginning of the Psalter as an introduction or preface to the entire collection. The effect is to suggest that all the psalms will somehow be involved in the contrast between those who are "happy" and those who are described in v. 1 as "wicked," "sinners," and "scoffers." It will be crucial to understand what Ps. 1 and the rest of the book mean by "happy." As suggested below, the biblical understanding is the antithesis of what our culture generally promotes as happiness.

The contrast that is introduced in v. 1 is reinforced throughout the psalm in a variety of ways—the repetition of the adversative particle "but" (vs. 2, 4b); the emphatic "not so," which occurs near the center of the psalm (v. 4a); the contrasting similes of tree and chaff at the heart of the psalm (vs. 3–4); and finally the explicit contrast between the "way of the righteous" and "the way of the wicked" (v. 6). Indeed, Ps. 1 has often been titled "The Two Ways."

The contrast of the two ways is accompanied by the contrast of results. The way of the righteous results in one's being "happy"— the first word of the psalm. The way of the wicked leads one to "perish"—the last word of the psalm. In short, the difference between the two ways is the difference between life and death. The comprehensiveness of this claim may be reinforced poetically by the fact that the Hebrew word for "happy" begins with the first letter of the alphabet, while the Hebrew word for "perish" begins with the last letter of the alphabet. This artistic device suggests that Ps. 1 says it all: it is an all-encompassing presentation about what it means to be happy or, even more fundamentally, what it means to live.

In fact, the sharpness of the contrast between the two ways and their outcomes has often led commentators to view Ps. 1 as naive. In the so-called "real world," it certainly does not seem as if the righteous "prosper" (v. 3) and the wicked get blown away (v. 4). Of course, the rest of the Psalter makes the same observation (see Ps. 73:1–3, or as early in the book as Ps. 3:1–2!). What, then, does Ps. 1 mean by "happy," "prosper," "righteous," and "wicked"?

The righteous are defined in terms of their delight in and atten-
tiveness to the "law" (v. 2). This too has caused problems for
commentators, who tend to hear "law" in Pauline terms, in which case
the "happy" seem to be self-righteous persons. Actually, Ps. 1 points
in precisely the opposite direction. The Hebrew word *torah*, which is
traditionally translated "law," essentially means "instruction." In
contrast to "scoffers" (who are specifically defined elsewhere as those
who are unwilling to accept instruction; see, for example, Prov. 1:22
and 9:7–8), the "happy" person is the one who is open to God's
instruction, which should be understood to include scripture (including the psalms themselves), tradition, and contemporary words and
events that continue to reveal God among humans. The "happy" or
"righteous" person, then, is anything but *self*-righteous. Rather, he or
she is consistently open to God's teaching and direction.

Such openness is what for Ps. 1 and the rest of the Psalter
constitutes happiness, prosperity, life. Like trees planted beside a
stream (v. 3a), those who are open to God's teaching are never
without a resource to sustain their lives. Verse 3 is often misunderstood to suggest that obedience is materially rewarded. But to
"prosper" in "all that they do" (v. 3c) should not be interpreted in
terms of reward/punishment. Rather, v. 3c affirms that those who
trust God have a reliable resource for living under any circumstances. As James L. Mays explains, the way of the righteous is "not
so much a reward as a result of life's connection with the source of
life" (*Psalms*, Interpretation series; Louisville, Ky.: John Knox Press,
1994).

The simile for the wicked portrays just the opposite of the stable
rootedness of the righteous. The wicked, in effect, have no foundation.
The wind can drive them away (v. 4); they will not be able to "stand in
the judgment" (v. 5). That the wicked "perish" (v. 6), however, is not
so much a punishment as it is the inevitable outcome of their own
choice not to be related to God. They refuse to be connected to the
source of life. In other words, wickedness in Ps. 1 and throughout the
Psalter means to be self-centered and self-directed rather than God-
centered and God-directed. In a word, wickedness is autonomy,
which literally means "a law unto oneself."

To a culture that consistently promotes autonomy, Ps. 1 offers a
crucial alternative. Psalm 1 suggests that happiness is more than
enjoying ourselves, that the goal of life is greater than self-
fulfillment, and that prosperity is more than getting all we want.
Psalm 1 calls for a decision—the decision to find happiness in God's
direction rather than in self-assertion; the decision to seek the goal of
life by offering ourselves to God (see Ps. 138 for the Fifth Sunday

After Epiphany), the decision to find prosperity by connecting ourselves to the source of life. Psalm 1 turns the world's values upside down. Its call to decision is fundamentally the same as Jesus' call to repent and enter the realm of God (Mark 1:14–15). Like Ps. 1, Jesus promised that his followers would be "happy" or "blessed" (see Matt. 5:3–11; Luke 6:20–26), and as in the psalms this happiness is not incompatible with persecution and suffering (Matt. 5:10–11; Ps. 3:1–2, for example). The happiness of the righteous is the assurance that their lives are known by God (Ps. 1:6) and that God is their refuge in the midst of the best and the worst that human life can bring (see Ps. 2:12c).

## 1 Corinthians 15:12–20

We continue this Sunday to trace the argument Paul makes in 1 Cor. 15 about the resurrection of the dead. Though couched in the apocalyptic structure of an ancient world and complex in its logic, the chapter nevertheless probes the heart of the Christian faith—the nature of hope. It speaks to the critical questions that inevitably arise when we stand by the open grave of a friend or a loved one, and it offers a ray of light to deal with the deep, dark shadow death continually threatens to cast over the whole of our living. No issue is more urgent in the parish.

We recognize, of course, that the argument of the chapter is not directed immediately to grieving people, but to people who for various philosophical and theological reasons reject the notion of a resurrection of the dead (15:12). That is why the chapter moves in a logical rather than a pastoral mode. It appeals more to the head than to the heart. But if the case for hope is going to weather life's storms, it has to give a reason for itself. Christians must have some inkling of the ground on which they stand, and 1 Cor. 15 explores that grounding.

First, in vs. 12–19 Paul assumes the position of those who deny the resurrection of the dead and proceeds to draw out the implications of such a position. Then, in vs. 20–28, he begins to make his own case, and we suddenly discover the significance of 15:1–11—why the readers have been reminded of the basic gospel they have heard and believed.

What if it were true that there would be no resurrection of the dead? What would be the implications for Christian existence, now and in the future? The consequences are laid out with frightening force: "Christ has not been raised" (vs. 13, 16); "our proclamation has been in vain" (v. 14); "your faith has been in vain" (vs. 14, 17); God has been misrepresented (v. 15); "you are still in your sins" (v. 17); and "we are . . . most to be pitied" (v. 19). Employing a two-directional logic, Paul moves in 15:12 from Jesus' resurrection to the resurrection of the dead and in vs. 13 and 16 from the resurrection of the dead back to Jesus' resurrection. The point is that the two resurrections cannot be isolated from each another in such a way that one can be accepted and the other denied. The future resurrection cannot be denied without enormous theological consequences.

The effect of Paul's logic is to place hope in God's future squarely at the heart of the Christian experience. Hope is not a virtue practiced only by the naïve and simpleminded who do not realize how desperate things really are. To be a Christian is to hope—to believe that the death and resurrection of Jesus point beyond themselves to the completion of what has only been begun. This has nothing to do with plotting future events or setting timetables, but simply with the conviction that the future lies securely in the hands of a gracious God.

The positive side of Paul's case is enriched by the lively symbol of "first fruits" (15:20, 23). The risen Christ, whom the intended readers apparently affirm, is the initial installment, who inaugurates and pledges the ultimate offering of the total crop. The symbol signifies both something incomplete and yet something hopeful. Christ's resurrection is *only* the firstfruits, but as firstfruits it *guarantees* the whole. The two resurrections are seen as only one, revealed in two temporal stages.

Paul, of course, is trading in apocalyptic coinage here, and with it he makes the point that Jesus' resurrection is not the concluding event in the Christ-story (that is, incarnation, life on earth, crucifixion, and resurrection), but the dawning of a new and final day. It does not end something—it begins something. What it begins is an era of hope that acknowledges the fragmented and incomplete character of the present, but dares to trust in God's plans for the future.

While the assigned lesson ends at 15:20, the remainder of the paragraph (vs. 21–28) cannot be ignored. Hope does not imply a blindness to the dark moments of the present nor a passive resignation to things the way they are. Between his resurrection and the final resurrection, Christ is at work contending with and subduing the opposing principalities and powers (vs. 24–28). Again, it is apocalyptic language for saying that the present is fraught with conflict and strife—social, political, economic, and religious—and Christians cannot, like Rip Van Winkle, sleep through a revolution.

Hope, in fact, becomes a reality as the community takes its part in the warfare and, amid the hard fighting, discovers it is on the winning side.

## Luke 6:17–26

Because Luke's "Sermon on the Plain," from which this and the following two Gospel lections are taken, has drawn less attention than Matthew's "Sermon on the Mount," interpreters may not bring to the text quite the same exaggerated expectations that accompany reading of the Matthean version. Nevertheless, the temptation to see the sermon as providing us with direct access to "Jesus' message" or "Jesus' teachings" is serious. A careful reading of the passage, together with a comparison of Luke's version with that of Matthew, should confirm that both evangelists have shaped the material very much to address the needs of their own communities. That, after all, is a fundamental task of preaching.

In its Lukan setting, the sermon takes place just after Jesus calls the Twelve, here referred to as apostles (6:12–16), and in the context of a multitude of disciples who have come to hear Jesus and to be touched by him (6:17–19). When Jesus speaks, he addresses himself specifically to the disciples, to those who have committed them- selves to follow him.

The Lukan version of the Beatitudes differs from the Matthean form in that Luke's is shorter, in the sense both that the list of beatitudes is shorter and also that each individual beatitude is more briefly expressed. In addition, of course, Luke differs from Matthew by including the accompanying list of "woes" in vs. 24–26.

The care with which these beatitudes and woes are constructed emphasizes their importance. Each of the beatitudes is contrasted with a parallel woe as follows:

| *Beatitude* | | *Woe* | |
|---|---|---|---|
| v. 20 | the poor | v. 24 | the rich |
| v. 21 | the hungry | v. 25 | the full |
| v. 21 | those who weep | v. 25 | those who laugh |
| v. 22 | those who are hated | v. 26 | those of whom people speak well |

"Blessed" are the poor, the hungry, the grieved, the hated. In Greek literature outside the Bible, this word (*makarios*) could carry connotations of happiness. In the Septuagint, however, to be "blessed" is not so much to be subjectively happy as to be regarded as righteous, to be blessed in God's sight (see, for example, Deut. 33:29; Ps. 1:1; 40:4). Particularly in our contemporary context, with its preoccupation with the achievement of personal happiness, this distinction is an important one. The Septuagint likewise employs the "woe" form to indicate God's displeasure and the grief that will follow from that displeasure (see, for example, Isa. 5:18–23, where the NRSV reads "Ah").

The fourth beatitude warrants particular attention because it is more developed than any of the others. (That is not to say that the others are insignificant, especially since Luke's concerns with the poor and oppressed are clearly articulated as early as the Magnificat.) Even acknowledging all the problems with reading Luke's community situation off the pages of his Gospel, it is difficult not to read this lengthy promise of God's favor for those who are despised as a reflection of the context of Luke's church. Here, as in the Stephen speech in Acts 7, the treatment of Jesus' followers is likened to that of Israel's prophets (see Acts 7:51–53).

Running through the passage is a contrast between the present and the future. Those who "are hungry now" will be filled in the future (Luke 6:21). Those who "weep now" will laugh (v. 21). The "rich," by contrast, have already received their consolation (v. 24). Those who are "full now" will be hungry in the future, and those who "are laughing now" will find their laughter turned to mourning (v. 25).

Along with this contrast between the present and the future runs a contrast between human assessment and the assessment of God. In three of the beatitudes and their corresponding woes, this contrast is implicit rather than explicit; by human standards, the poor, the hungry, and the sorrowful are anything but the possessors of God's kingdom. In the fourth beatitude, however, this contrast becomes explicit. Those who are rejected by human beings have a great reward "in heaven." Luke's use of that phrase elsewhere strongly suggests that it is a circumlocution for "from God." Rather than a place, "heaven" refers to God's own assessment, God's judgment (see, for example, 15:7, 18, 21).

An initial reading of the Lukan Beatitudes might prompt us to accuse Luke of a "pie in the sky by and by" attitude; that is, he encourages people to endure their present suffering by holding out hope for rewards sometime in the indefinite future. When we take into account both the time element ("now" versus the future) and the issue of divine versus human assessment, however, something more complex emerges from this passage. A crude paraphrase might be, "Things are not always what they seem." Those who seem to be prospering may not be, not in God's sight. Those who seem to be suffering may be blessed, at least in God's sight. Paul puts it somewhat differently in 1 Cor. 1:25: "God's foolishness is wiser than human wisdom, and God's weakness is stronger than human strength."

# SEVENTH SUNDAY AFTER EPIPHANY

Proper 2
Ordinary Time 7

The Gospel lesson for today continues Jesus' Sermon on the Plain with the seemingly impossible exhortation to "Love your enemies" (v. 27; see v. 35). The text goes on to suggest that this means doing good to, blessing, and praying for one's opponents (v. 28); and then it gives several concrete illustrations, leading up to another general exhortation in v. 31. The text offers an opportunity for the preacher to compare the kind of love that God intends with the ways that love is defined in our culture. The love God intends is not feeling-oriented or self-centered. Rather, it involves the merciful treatment of others, and is grounded in and motivated by God's character—God "is merciful" (v. 36). Underlying the exhortation to love enemies is the conviction that God will mercifully provide for God's people.

The Joseph story clearly articulates the conviction of God's provide-ance. God was mysteriously at work through the hostile actions of Joseph's brothers. As Joseph puts it repeatedly, "God sent me" (Gen. 45:5, 7; see v. 8 and 50:20). This conviction of God's merciful provide-ance enables Joseph to, in effect, love his enemies. Passing up a perfect opportunity for revenge, Joseph instead forgives his brothers, blesses them, and does good to them. In short, Joseph is merciful as God is merciful, providing for others as God provides (see Gen. 50:21).

It is the same sort of trust in God's provide-ance that enables the psalmist to say, "Do not fret because of the wicked" (Ps. 37:1; see vs. 7, 8). Because "those who wait for the LORD shall inherit the land" (v. 9)—that is to say, because God will provide—the psalmist can advise goodness (vs. 3, 27) and generosity (vs. 21, 26). For the psalmist, an assured future transforms the present.

The same theme is present in 1 Cor. 15. Belief in the resurrection assures a future that transforms the present. It is faith in God's provide-ance of life even beyond the barrier of death that enables the

Corinthians to "know that in the Lord [their] labor is not in vain" (v. 58).

## Genesis 45:3–11, 15

Avarice and greed, jealousy and sibling rivalry, sex, politics, and palace intrigue—such are the ingredients of the story of Joseph! Small wonder that this section of the book of Genesis (chs. 37—47) has been favorite reading for Jews and Christians over the centuries, for it mirrors human nature in every age. Yet to concentrate on these characteristics exclusively is to lose sight of the central thrust of the cycle of Joseph stories, namely, that in and through all the events of Joseph's life God was at work to save the people. Most immediately, the people who benefit from God's grace are old Jacob and his family, but the ultimate object of God's loving intervention in Joseph's life is all humankind.

In terms of the development of the plot of the Joseph stories, this lection from Gen. 45 is crucial. Joseph has now become the virtual ruler of all Egypt, having survived threats to his life and well-being which are familiar to everyone who knows this tale, including a murderous plot by his brothers, attempted seduction by the wife of a powerful Egyptian, and the forgetfulness of the royal cupbearer. The famine that has ravaged Egypt has also desolated Palestine, so that Joseph's brothers, in their efforts to find food, have come face-to-face with the brother whom they earlier sold into slavery. Yet, in an ironic twist, while Joseph recognizes them they are ignorant of the identity of this powerful vizier with whom they have been negotiating and before whom they now stand condemned of theft. In purely literary terms, what could be a juicier turn of events? Joseph, with one wave of his hand, may now avenge the terrible wrong done to him so long ago by snuffing out the life or the liberty of these trembling sons of Jacob.

But that is not Joseph's way, because that is not God's way and Joseph is—first, last, and always—God's man (notice v. 8). (The exclusion of vs. 1–2 of Gen. 45 robs this lection of much of its emotional energy, so the preacher will wish to include them in her or his consideration.) Joseph's virtual collapse in the presence of his brothers reveals his awareness of God's role in his life as much as it reveals his humanity. Only the Egyptians are meant to be excluded from this catharsis, lest they misinterpret Joseph's tears for weakness.

The emotional energy displayed by Joseph is countered by the awestruck dumbness of the eleven. Are they unable to speak simply because they find this revelation hard to believe, or is it out of terror over what might soon happen to them at the hands of their long-lost but now powerful brother? Probably both, but it is their terror for their lives that Joseph addresses by attempting to calm them (v. 5). The reason for the comfort Joseph extends has nothing directly to do with his own emotions, although his concern for his father (v. 3) would doubtless have ruled out any violence against his brothers, even if Joseph had been so inclined. His brothers are to be at peace because "God sent me before you to preserve life" (v. 5). Notice that the phrase "God sent me" (or its equivalent) is repeated in vs. 7 and 8. (Compare v. 8: "God . . . made me a father to Pharaoh" and v. 9: "God has made me lord of all Egypt.") Not only does Joseph want to reassure his astonished brothers, but those who are responsible for the text, in the shape that it has reached us, want to be sure that we, the readers, do not miss the whole point of the narrative: behind all the events of Joseph's life God was at work to bring good out of evil.

The arrangements for the family's comfort that Joseph outlines in vs. 10–11 provide a kind of denouement to the drama. The blood still races with excitement over Joseph's startling self-disclosure, but Joseph pushes forward to other things. After urging the inclusion of their father in this new life, Joseph outlines to the eleven what kind of life it will be. In spite of the five years the famine still has to run, theirs will be a time of peace and plenty under Joseph's personal protection. Their families, including children and grandchildren, will be secure, even their flocks and herds. Only then, after Joseph has hugged and kissed them all, are the brothers' tongues unlocked and they begin to talk to him (v. 15).

It is as difficult for modern people as it was for ancient people to believe that God is at work even in the dark and destructive moments of life. One of the great obstacles to faith is that, no matter how hard one tries, it simply is not possible to identify grace or redemption in many human experiences. And it is easy—some would say, compelling—to extrapolate from that that God is *never* present in human suffering and defeat. But the Joseph stories lead us to a different conclusion, which is that, in spite of the awful tragedies from which God seems irretrievably absent, the Ruler of the universe is a caring friend and will ultimately have a friend's way.

So, in the Joseph stories, Joseph is a paradigm of what the grace of God can do in human life: transform a curse into a blessing. Joseph is himself a metaphor for God: the One who has every reason to reject a wayward human family, but instead loves them even to the point of the One's own participation in their suffering.

## Psalm 37:1–11, 39–40

Psalm 37 is usually categorized as a wisdom psalm. Its acrostic structure (that is, every second line begins with the succeeding letter of the alphabet) suggests careful reflection as well as the intent to instruct. It is appropriate that Ps. 37 be read the week following the reading of Ps. 1, for it involves the same sharp contrast between the righteous (vs. 16, 17, 21, 25, 28, 29, 30, 39) and the wicked (vs. 10, 12, 13, 14, 16, 17, 20, 21, 28, 32, 34, 35, 38, 40; plus vs. 1 and 9, where a different Hebrew word is used). As in Ps. 1, the righteous are attentive to God's instruction (Ps. 37:31; see Ps. 1:2) and are known by God (Ps. 37:18; see Ps. 1:6). Consequently, they "shall inherit the land" (Ps. 37:9, 11, 22, 29; see also vs. 3, 34). While this affirmation can be understood literally, it is better to understand it symbolically. Possession of the land meant access to the resources for sustaining life. In short, the righteous shall live, while the wicked "perish" (v. 20; see Ps. 1:6). The wicked "shall be cut off" (Ps. 37:9, 22, 28, 38; compare v. 34, where "destruction" translates the same Hebrew word).

The future tense is significant—"*shall* inherit" and "*shall* be cut off" (emphases added). In other words, for *now*, the righteous must be reminded, "Do not fret" (vs. 1, 7, 8). This admonition in itself is indicative that for *now*, the wicked *do* "prosper" (v. 7), at least in some sense. This is problematic, especially in light of Ps. 1:3, which suggested that only the righteous "prosper." This apparent contradiction leads us to distinguish between two senses of "prosper." If prosperity means material wealth, then indeed the wicked prosper (see Ps. 37:16). But if prosperity means being in touch with the true source of life, then indeed only the righteous prosper. It is they whom the Lord "upholds" (v. 17; see "holds," v. 24), "knows" (v. 18), and "will not forsake" (v. 28; see v. 33).

The contrast between what is *now* and what *shall be*—what is present and what is future—means that the imperatives as in (vs. 1, 3–5, 7–8) and affirmations as in (vs. 2, 6, 9–11) in Ps. 37 are eschatological. The righteous live in the present on the basis of what they know is assured in the future. The first positively framed invitation in the psalm is to trust in Yahweh (v. 3; see v. 5). In short, the righteous live by faith, and by what is always inseparable from faith—hope (vs. 7, 9; see Rom. 8:24–25; Heb. 11:1).

To live eschatologically, however, does not mean simply to live *for* the future. Rather, it means to live *by* the future. Thus, to live by faith and hope has a profound impact on the present. Trusting God enables one to live *now*, amid opposition and trouble, with integrity (vs. 18–19) and serenity (v. 7) and peace of mind and heart ("Do not fret," vs. 1, 7, 8). In short, while "prosperity" (v. 11; Hebrew *shalom)* remains in some sense a future endowment, it is also very much a present possession. Consequently, the righteous are able, amid opposition and trouble (vs. 19, 39), to live constructively (see "do good," in vs. 3, 27) justly (v. 30), and generously (vs. 21, 26). For those who commit their lives to God (v. 5), God is *already* a "refuge" (v. 40). The end of Ps. 37 recalls Ps. 2:12, where to "take refuge in" God is to be "happy."

To trust God, to wait for God, to take refuge in God is to affirm ultimately the conviction that God rules the world. This conviction, which underlies everything in Ps. 37, is perhaps expressed most clearly by the assertion that "the LORD laughs at the wicked" (v. 13). This too recalls Ps. 2 (see 2:4), which is fundamentally an affirmation of God's sovereignty over the nations and rulers of the earth (see 2:10–12). The affirmation of God's sovereignty is not and never has been an easy one to make in view of injustice in the world and the prosperity of the wicked (see the book of Job); however, Ps. 37, along with Pss. 1 and 2 and the entire Psalter, invites us to choose the difficult way that leads to life. The fundamental message of the psalm and the Psalter is expressed in the words of a familiar hymn: "That though the wrong seem oft so strong, God is the ruler yet."

To be sure, this message is not restricted to Ps. 37 or to the Psalter as a whole. It lies at the heart of Jesus' teaching as well: "The kingdom of God has come near; repent, and believe in the good news" (Mark 1:15). In other words, God rules the world; "Commit your way to the LORD; trust in him" (Ps. 37:5). Because God rules the world, everything has changed; "Power is made perfect in weakness" (2 Cor. 12:9). Right makes might. The greatest is a servant (Mark 10:42–45). The King of kings rules from a cross. The "future" (NRSV "posterity") belongs to "the peaceable," not the so-called powerful (Ps. 37:37–38). In a world ruled by God, it is even possible to say "the meek shall inherit the land" (Ps. 37:11). Or, as Jesus put it in his teaching about the reign of God, "Blessed are the meek, for they will inherit the earth" (Matt. 5:5).

## 1 Corinthians 15:35–38, 42–50

"I believe in . . . the resurrection of the body." The familiar words of the creed have their roots in the passage for this Sunday. But what do they mean? How can one conceptualize this affirmation regularly recited by the church? What can Christians anticipate regarding the future beyond death?

Two words by way of preface to the text: First, our human language is inadequate to deal with the realities we are struggling to understand. Paul in this text ventures some claims about the future existence of believers, but the claims are not born out of speculation or idle curiosity, nor do they answer all our human questions. They are addressed to a congregation that clearly has got it all wrong, and are offered as a corrective. The claims are labeled a "mystery" (1 Cor. 15:51), and much mystery still remains. We do well to acknowledge that and not say too much. Not surprisingly, this section is concluded (beyond today's lection) with a liturgical word of praise, the appropriate end of all theology (15:54–55).

Second, the controlling factor in the text is the resurrection of Christ. Since Christ was raised, a conviction Paul's readers apparently share with him, not only are believers assured a genuine future, but Christ's resurrection becomes the pattern for their resurrection. The nature of resurrection as "bodily" derives from the basic Christian message that the risen Jesus was "seen" by a host of witnesses (15:5–8).

The questions raised in v. 35 are not hypothetical. They evidently come from "someone," who is likely one of the "some of you" who say there is no resurrection of the dead (v. 12). Paul offers an answer in two stages. First, people have to die. All the embalming in the world cannot hide the grim reality of death. (The obviousness of this perhaps accounts for Paul's sharp retort, "Fool!") "What you sow does not come to life unless it dies." Death is not to be denied or taken lightly. It remains a lingering power, an enemy yet to be conquered (v. 26) and an unavoidable step in the believers' future. Whatever Paul's misguided readers may have thought, he does not allow them to ignore the inevitability of dying.

The second half of the response to the questions of v. 35, however, is more critical. There will also be a transformation. "God gives" the seed a new body. The perishable takes on the imperishable. The weak becomes powerful. The dishonorable is made glorious. The "physical body" is transformed into a "spiritual body." It is not that the old corpse with its decaying cells and worn-out muscles will be resuscitated. Something new happens. God provides the imperishable, the powerful, the glorious, the spiritual—a reality that is not there prior to death. And the new gift is precisely the substance of resurrection.

Since the notion of the immortality of the soul is often mistakenly offered as the explanation for the Christian hope for life beyond the grave, attention needs to be drawn to the text's stress on transformation. There is no hint in 1 Cor. 15 that humans bear an inextinguishable spark, called the "soul," which at death survives the discarding of the body. That seems a more logical explanation to some people, since there is no need for a miracle. In the text, however, the line of continuity between the "now" and the "then" actually lies in the word "body" (not "soul"), but a changed body (v. 44). What God chooses to resurrect is not a disembodied echo of an individual as that individual was prior to dying, but a thoroughly transformed self fit for the new world.

The contrast between a "physical body" and a "spiritual body" warrants careful consideration. The Greek adjective translated "physical" (psychikos) is not to be construed as something material that at the resurrection is then transformed into something non-material. The adjective simply denotes the life of the natural world and whatever belongs to it. "Flesh and blood cannot inherit the kingdom of God" acknowledges that there is no unbroken continuity between this life and the next. The self of the one is ill suited for the life of the other. In turn, "spiritual" (pneumatikos) characterizes the eschatological life that is controlled by the Spirit. A "spiritual body" is a body appropriate to the consummation of God's new age, without any suggestion about its substantial nature.

Despite the "mystery" of the text and its claims, the preacher dares not shy away from such a passage as this, because it carries such liberating ramifications. The "shades of the prison-house," as Wordsworth described it, that "begin to close upon the growing boy" are dispelled by the promise of the resurrection, not by a confidence in an immortal soul. Only then can life, freed from the terror and threat of death, be fully embraced and enjoyed.

## Luke 6:27–38

To love an enemy is simply impossible, for an enemy is by definition someone hated rather than loved. An enemy who is loved is no longer an enemy. So great is the contradiction implicit in the opening words of this passage that Christians, perhaps inevitably, resort to any available means to wrest the passage into some manageable form. The Pelagians of every generation will insist that enemies can be loved if only people will try harder. Others will opt for a more spiritualized interpretation of what it means to "love" an enemy. Still others will attempt to bury the demand beneath a mound of references to ancient attitudes toward the enemy.

Nothing will reduce the demand of this passage, but attention to the context and the larger argument may help us to understand it.

Luke 6:27 marks a transition in the Sermon on the Plain, away from the beatitudes and woes and toward specific concerns regarding treatment of the enemy. The opening of v. 27 ("But I say to you that listen") recalls the earlier setting of the sermon ("They had come to hear him," 6:18) and anticipates the closing of the sermon (6:47). Jesus addresses the disciples, those who are committed to hearing even what they cannot fully comprehend.

The topic of one's treatment of enemies resumes the concern of vs. 22–23 of the Beatitudes and probably again reflects Luke's knowledge of Christians who are in fact experiencing rejection because of their discipleship. How would the Christian community respond to those who ostracized them for their faith? The response to this question in vs. 27–36 (vs. 37–38 take up a different topic) moves from demand (vs. 27–31) to explanation (vs. 32–34) and finally to the theological basis for the demand (vs. 35–36).

"Love your enemies, do good to those who hate you, bless those who curse you, pray for those who abuse you." The active, verbal character of these demands is crucial. "Love" in this passage is less a noun, a characteristic, an emotional state, than it is an action. While it may be impossible to *feel* love for the enemy, it is not impossible to *act* in certain ways, even for those whom experience has shown to be the most entrenched of opponents. What Jesus means by the love of enemies becomes clear in the three verbal demands that follow and that explicate the initial demand: "Do good," "bless," "pray."

Several concrete examples provide additional clarity about what it means to love the enemy. A disciple who is struck should offer the other cheek; a disciple whose coat is taken should offer the next layer of clothing as well; no beggar should be turned away; no one who takes away possessions should be asked to return them. With the exception of the first, all these specific examples concern possessions, not surprising given Luke's emphasis elsewhere on the handling of possessions as profoundly revealing of one's capacity for discipleship.

The series of demands culminates in the so-called Golden Rule. As the commentaries will amply illustrate, this principle is well known in antiquity in a variety of forms. Searching for something unique to Jesus' formulation that somehow makes it superior to other formulations is beside the point. What v. 31 offers in this context is a general principle, probably one that was familiar to Luke's audience, that would help to explain how to go about the difficult task of loving the enemy.

At the end of v. 31, however, that demand still cries out for an explanation. Why should it be the case that disciples of Jesus must love their enemies? Significantly, no promise is made that this action will convert the enemy into a friend, will modify the enemy's behavior, or even alter one's own feelings toward that enemy! Instead, Jesus explores the established alternative behavior of equitable exchange—loving only those who love in return (vs. 32–34).

Loving only those who love us is not a credit (literally, a "grace"), for "even sinners" can do that. Again, at least in v. 34, the specific example concerns the treatment of possessions. Why lend only to those who will lend in return? "Even sinners" can do that. Here, of course, "sinners" refers to those outside the Christian community, not to the theological conviction that all people remain sinners. Even those who are the enemies of the faith can act with a minimal kind of equity, returning tit for tat. Surely disciples of Jesus should hold themselves to a higher standard.

With vs. 35–36 we come to the final restatement of this demand and then the underlying reason: "Your reward will be great, and you will be children of the Most High; for he is kind to the ungrateful and the wicked. Be merciful, just as your Father is merciful." All of this is demanded by virtue of God's own graciousness and mercy. Christians behave lovingly to their enemies not as a ploy to outmaneuver them, not even because they anticipate a reward (although the language of reward is used here), but finally because God is a God of mercy. God is kind even to the undeserving, and that kindness must be found also in the lives of God's children.

With vs. 37–38, the sermon takes up yet another topic, that of behavior within the fellowship of disciples. Here again, however, the implied standard is that of God's own behavior. Judgment and condemnation should be withheld, for God will not judge or condemn. The example of measurement, such as the measurement of the marketplace, provides a final reminder that God's measure is not justice, but mercy.

# EIGHTH SUNDAY AFTER EPIPHANY

## Proper 3
## Ordinary Time 8

With the exception of the Gospel lection, the readings for this Sunday converge on the theme of the abiding trustworthiness of Israel's God. Second Isaiah knows that God's own word cannot fail. What God intends will certainly come to pass (Isa. 55:11), as surely as rain and snow accomplish their tasks (v. 10). The result of God's own faithfulness in the case of Israel can be witnessed as Israel returns "in joy" and "in peace" from its long exile (v. 12). Nature itself breaks forth (the "cypress" and the "myrtle" of v. 13) into a memorial to God's enduring faithfulness.

Psalm 92 opens with explicit praise of God's trustworthiness. Celebration of God's "steadfast love" and "faithfulness" marks the beginning and the end of each day (v. 2). God's reliability may be seen in God's dealings with humankind. Those who are God's enemies find themselves defeated, but those who trust in God "flourish like the palm tree" (v. 12). The concluding image of God as a rock aptly conveys the thrust of the psalm: God is utterly reliable.

While Second Isaiah and the psalmist celebrate God's trustworthiness in the present, Paul strains to describe what that trustworthiness will produce in the eschatological future—the final mystery, the unimaginable transformation, the defeat of death itself. Ironically, the resurrection of Jesus Christ, by which all the "normal" rules of nature are overturned, provides the means for vindicating the ultimate "rule," that of God even over death itself.

Luke 6:39–49 does not celebrate God's trustworthiness, but it does explore the consequences of living out of that trustworthiness. The one who builds on rock (compare Ps. 92:15) is the one who hears and trusts and lives out of Jesus' words. The integrity of God is thereby mirrored in the integrity of believers, as individuals and in their dealings with one another.

## Isaiah 55:10–13

The scholarly identification of chapters 40—55 of the book of Isaiah as the work of an anonymous Jew who was active toward the end of the Babylonian captivity has not been received without controversy within the church. Echoes of the early battles may still be heard today in some church circles, where, unfortunately, the position one takes on the matter has become a test for orthodoxy. These pages are not the place to rehash that debate, but simply to point to the irony that, by denying the sixth-century provenance of this literature, some Christians rob Isa. 40—55 of much of its power. Other theological considerations aside, the understanding of the words as being issued by someone who was actually experiencing the realities that the words reflect heightens their relevance and power for readers in every age. How much less emotive and theological force they would have if they had been somewhat mechanically recorded by Isaiah of Jerusalem almost two centuries before the liberation of Babylon's captive Jews. These are songs of joy, not just of the mind, but of the viscera!

The poetic/prophetic lines that constitute this lection are the climax of that extensive song of gladness that modern scholarship associates with the Second Isaiah. To be sure, the theological underpinning of Second Isaiah's work is "mainstream" Hebrew prophecy: the people have sinned against Israel's righteous God, and their present captivity is the fruit of that sin. But that is water over the dam. A new day is at hand, in that Yahweh is graciously breaking in upon the life of the people in such a manner that all creation will join in the celebration (Isa. 42:9–13). The old penalty has been paid (40:2); now stand aside and watch in terror and in joy Yahweh's restoration of the people (41:2–10).

Verses 10–13 of Isa. 55 represent a colophon to the message of Second Isaiah, the first part (vs. 10–11) directed toward the very words that have contained the prophet's great, glad tidings; the second part (vs. 12–13) toward the people who are the objects of this extensive anthem of gladness.

The obvious analogy in vs. 10–11 is between the life-sustaining properties of rain and snow (especially important in lands such as Babylonia and Israel, where precipitation is often scarce) and the similar properties of God's word. It is remarkable that, in a prescientific age when the rhythms of nature were only partly understood (they are *still* imperfectly understood), the cyclical pattern of precipitation and evaporation should be expressed, as in v. 10. One is reminded of the lines from Shelley's "The Cloud":

> I bring fresh showers for the thirsting flowers
>    From the seas and the streams;
> . . . . . . . . . . . . . . . . . . . . . . . . . . . .
> I am the daughter of Earth and Water,
>    And the nursling of the Sky;
> I pass through the pores of oceans and shores;
>    I change, but I cannot die.

The prophet is aware not only that water is necessary to life but also that it is indestructible. Its form may change, but never its substance. So it is with "my word . . . that goes out from my mouth."

The second part of our text (vs. 12–13) focuses, as has much of Isa. 40—55, on the people of God and their future. They may have been brought into this teeming heart of Nebuchadnezzar's empire as the downcast flotsam of a devastating war. They are now to return in "joy" and in "peace." Even the natural order will, metaphorically at least, participate in their ecstacy, with singing hills and applauding trees. Briers and thorns will be banished to make way for the majestic cypress and the fragrant myrtle.

But what is the "it" (the word may also be translated "he") in the final two lines of this passage that is to serve as a "memorial" (literally: "name") to Yahweh and as an "everlasting sign"? The text is not clear about this, and some confusion has existed. The Septuagint, for example, renders this sentence "The Lord will be for a name and an eternal sign, and he will not fail," but that hardly seems to be the sense of the Hebrew.

Probably the subject of these lines, the "it," is to be understood as the saving activity of Yahweh. The very fact that Israel has been returned to its land is to be a witness to the truthfulness and mercy of Israel's God. So the REB reads:

> All this will be a memorial for the LORD,
>    a sign that for all time will not be cut off.

Another possibility, a somewhat more frightening one, is that the people themselves are to be Yahweh's enduring witness, the "name" and the "sign." (The Hebrew word for "people." 'am, although not directly employed in this passage, is singular and thus, if it were implied, would be consistent with the singular verb "[it] will be.") The celebrated passage Isa. 42:5–9 suggests that the community of faith is to be the means by which all nations are to know the liberating, redemptive power of Yahweh ("people" of 42:6 appears, in this case, to be humankind). If that meaning is also to be understood here (55:13), it places a burden on the members of the community of faith to so embody the presence of a loving, redemptive God that they themselves become God's "name" and "sign."

Perhaps, when all is said, both realities are true, in that, while God's great acts of redemption are witnesses to the divine grace, so is the faith of the people who have benefited from this grace.

## Psalm 92:1–4, 12–15

Psalm 92 is the only psalm that is designated "for the Sabbath Day." Exactly why it was singled out is unclear. Perhaps it is because the references to God's "work"/"works" in vs. 4–5 can be understood as a reference to creation, and the Sabbath was also associated with creation (see Gen. 2:1–3; Ex. 20:8–11). Or perhaps it is because the Sabbath was to be a day totally devoted to praising God (vs. 1–2), a day on which the people of God were to gather for worship (v. 13). Or perhaps it is because the name "Yahweh" occurs *seven* times.

Psalm 92 is usually categorized as an individual song of thanksgiving. In vs. 1–4, the psalmist at least implicitly invites others to share in thanksgiving for his or her having been "made . . . glad" (v. 4). Verses 10–11 sound like a description of the psalmist's deliverance, in which case they too would be characteristic of a thanksgiving song. But it is unclear whether the verbs in vs. 10–11 should be translated in the past tense (NRSV) or the future tense. In other words, has the psalmist already been exalted and the enemies defeated, or are these events still in the future? This uncertainty highlights another major aspect of Ps. 92, that is, it is concerned with the life and future of the righteous (vs. 12–15) and the wicked (vs. 7, 9, 11), as were Pss. 1 and 37 (Sixth and Seventh Sundays After Epiphany). Because v. 7 recognizes that the wicked do flourish temporarily, and because it is likely that the verbs in vs. 10–11 should be translated in the future tense (as in v. 9), it is best to approach Ps. 92 not so much as a song that celebrates a particular deliverance, but rather as a psalm that affirms the ultimate triumph of God's sovereignty and the deliverance of God's people.

While the wicked may and indeed do flourish *for now*, they "shall perish" (v. 9; see Pss. 1:6; 37:20). This assurance, as in Pss. 1 and 37, is founded on the conviction that is highlighted in Ps. 92:8, the exact center of the psalm: Yahweh is "on high forever." In other words, God rules the world (see "on high" in Ps. 93:4; Ps. 93:1 specifically affirms that God reigns, as do the following Pss. 95–99). Verse 8 of Ps. 92 is sandwiched between two verses that focus on the wicked, or the "evildoers" (vs. 7, 9). In terms of the structure of the psalm and in terms of the reality of the psalmist's world, the affirmation of God's rule is made in the very midst of evil. The perspective is eschatological. The good news is that *even now*, in the midst of evil, praise and joy are possible (vs. 1–4) and the righteous "flourish" (vs. 12–13) and are fruitful (v. 14) in an enduring way that declares that God is upright, loving, and faithful (vs. 2, 15; "declare" in v. 2 and "showing" in v. 15 translate the same Hebrew verb).

The theme of declaring makes Ps. 92 especially appropriate for Epiphany. What is to be declared gets at the very heart of God's character—"steadfast love" and "faithfulness" (see, for example, Ex. 34:6–7; Pss. 98:3; 138:2). The declaration is to be made throughout every day (see "morning" and "night" in 92:2) and throughout a lifetime (see "old age" in v. 14). It involves both liturgical activity (v. 3) and style of life (vs. 12–14). By their worship and by their work, the righteous declare that their lives and futures belong not to themselves but to God. This affirmation is particularly effective at this point in the Psalter. Psalm 90 opened Book IV of the Psalter with a portrayal of human transience (vs. 3–12) accompanied by a plea for God's favor (90:13–17). It is as if Ps. 92, especially vs. 1–4, affirms that the plea of Ps. 90 has been answered: the psalmist has been made glad (92:4; see Ps. 90:14–15), "sing[s] for joy" (92:4; see "that we may rejoice" in Ps. 90:14), and celebrates God's "steadfast love in the morning" (92:2; see Ps. 90:14). God's "work" has been made manifest to the psalmist (92:4; see 90:16). Confronted with general human transience (Ps. 90) and at least the temporary prosperity of the wicked (92:7; the language here is reminiscent of that applied to all humanity in 90:5–6), the psalmist declares the reality of divine protection (see "rock" in 92:15) and faithfulness (v. 2).

Verse 12 specifically recalls v. 7. Whereas the wicked "flourish" only briefly, "like grass," the righteous "flourish" (vs. 12–13) like fruitful, stately trees that are "planted" in God's garden (see Ps. 1:3; Jer. 17:7–8). With God as both foundation and source of nourishment, the righteous are able to take root, grow, and be fruitful (see Luke 6:43–49). As the similar text in Jer. 17 suggests, the real difference between the righteous and the wicked is that the righteous trust God and the wicked trust themselves (see esp. Jer. 17:5, 7). Psalm 92 affirms that trusting ourselves alone is illusory and ultimately destructive (vs. 7, 9). It is thus a sobering warning to a generation like ours that generally "cannot understand this" (v. 6). As much as any generation before us in the history of the world, we are inclined to trust our own intelligence, strength, and technology more than we trust God, one another, or anything else. A renewed sense of the greatness of God's works and the productivity of God's design for the world is urgently needed (see v. 5).

Thus, like Pss. 1 and 37, the eschatological affirmation of God's rule calls for a decision. The decision to find our security in God rather than self suggests another possible dimension to Ps. 92 as a Sabbath song. The Heidelberg Catechism states that the Fourth Commandment requires "that I cease from my evil works all the days of my life, allow the Lord to work in me through his Spirit, and thus begin in this life the eternal Sabbath" (Question 103). Psalm 92 affirms that in recognizing and yielding ourselves to God's rule (v. 8), we experience even now the measure of life and peace—"the eternal sabbath"—that God intends and will accomplish for the world and its creatures (see Isa. 55:10–13).

## 1 Corinthians 15:51–58

The last of the four epistolary selections from 1 Cor. 15 brings the chapter to a climax, both in a grand word of celebration at the defeat of death and in a pointed exhortation for life in the present. The powerful rhetoric of the passage becomes obvious in its frequent reading at funeral and memorial services, where commentary often detracts from the confident, triumphant affirmation made in the text. Precisely because it is a "mystery" revealed, a secret made known, the resurrection defies logical explanation.

Three motifs dominate the passage. First is the vivid insistence on transformation, a theme begun in 15:35–50. While the "here and now" is linked to the "there and then" by a continuity (a "body"), it is no natural evolution from one to the other. The resurrection entails something brand-new.

Two verbs, both repeated in the paragraph, describe the transformation. One is "change," a strong verb that in some contexts can even be translated "exchange" (Rom. 1:23). "We will all be changed" (2 Cor. 15:51, 52). The resurrection of the dead, then, is not to be compared to the evolution of the caterpillar into the butterfly nor to the maturation of the unruly child into the responsible adult. Death brings an abrupt break that necessitates a new beginning.

The second verb describing the transformation is "put on," as in dressing. Something not there previously is donned, specifically the robes of imperishability and immortality (15:53–54). They become the promised attire given at the resurrection to distinguish those who inherit the kingdom of God. This heavy stress on transformation no doubt has a particular relevance to some of the intended readers of this letter, who apparently assume that they have already arrived, that baptism has ushered them into a heavenly existence on earth. The insistence on future transformation for them provides quite a jolt.

Another way to treat this transformation is to note that death means the end of perishability and mortality. All in our present existence that marks our aging, degeneration, and decline, all evidence of sin's impact in our world, its threat and devastation, will be done away with. The *via negativa* is a characteristically apocalyptic way of referring to the future (Rev. 21:4, 22–27).

The second prominent motif in the passage is the defeat of death. Quotations from Isa. 25:8 and Hos. 13:14 are loosely drawn together in 1 Cor. 15:54–55 to express confidence about the future. So certain is the demise of "the last enemy" (15:26) that even now death can be mocked with taunting questions (15:55).

It is striking that death is not thought of here, as it is other places in the Bible, as a natural phenomenon, the result of the winding down of our physical forces. Death comes as the venom of sin, empowered by the law, and any doing away with death must include also the defeat of sin. (Verse 56 sounds as if it belongs in Rom. 5 or 7 rather than 1 Corinthians!) This has happened in the death and resurrection of Jesus, depicted here as the victory God has given us and the ground for celebrating ahead of time.

This brings the argument of 1 Cor. 15 back to where it started in the beginning, namely, with the tradition about Jesus (15:3–5). Talk about the future, even confident claims and the language of goading contempt, is rooted in what has already happened—the death and resurrection of Jesus, who is the firstfruits for all who belong to Christ.

The third powerful motif in the passage is the final exhortation (15:58), a consequence of all that has gone before. The readers, addressed as "beloved" brothers and sisters, are urged to face the present in the light of the future. A resurrection faith is depicted, through the imperatives, as an existence that is paradoxically sturdy and immovable amid the winds of change, and at the same time growing in the work of the Lord. Though not specific, the language seems to call for stability and persistence in the life and ministry of the community.

Throughout 1 Cor. 15, the phrase "in vain" (translating two different Greek words) occurs. In 15:2 a caveat is raised about the readers' faith: "unless you have come to believe in vain." For Paul

himself, God's grace had not turned out "in vain" (15:10), but for the
Corinthians who deny the future resurrection both his preaching
and their faith will have been "in vain" (15:14). The final clause of
15:58, however, concludes the chapter on an encouraging note. It
anticipates that the readers' faith will not continue to depend on a
fully "realized" resurrection, subject to the vicissitudes of experience and certain to turn up empty, but will ultimately trust in the
certainty of God's future. "You know that in the Lord your labor is
not in vain."

## Luke 6:39–49

In this final lection from the Lukan Sermon on the Plain, Jesus
turns his attention specifically to the behavior of disciples toward
others in the community of faith. (The concluding section of the
Sermon actually begins with Luke 6:37, but vs. 37–38 are assigned as
part of the reading for the Seventh Sunday After Epiphany.) The
variety of sayings and the shifts in the analogies make the passage
seem a hodgepodge, but it is united by the conviction that behavior
and character cannot be separated. What one does stems inevitably
from what one is. What one is necessarily reveals itself in what one
does.

Verses 39–42 introduce this theme by means of sayings that
address the issue of appropriate self-criticism and integrity. A
person who attempts to correct another's flaws without understanding his or her own is not sufficiently self-aware. If judgment ought
not to be leveled at others within the community, it can and must be
brought to bear on one's own behavior (vs. 37–38).

Significantly, the analogies employed in vs. 39–42 have to do with
seeing. The blind person cannot see to lead another blind person
down the road. The one whose own eye contains a log cannot
possibly see well enough to correct another's vision. Luke's fondness
for imagery related to light and to sight comes into play here (see, for
example, Luke 1:79; 4:18; Acts 9:8–9, 17–18). Given contemporary—
and justifiable—sensitivity to the needs of the blind for independence, preachers will want to treat the saying about the blind
leading the blind with some care, perhaps connecting it with the
larger Lukan concern for the gospel as the giving of light and for the
right kind of vision.

In the middle of these sayings about sight, Luke 6:40 stands
somewhat isolated: "A disciple is not above the teacher, but
everyone who is fully qualified will be like the teacher." Clearly here

Jesus addresses the nature of the Christian community as a teaching community. Its teachers remain disciples or students of Jesus, so that they never rise "above the teacher." Nevertheless, their behavior must be like his own. The implicit warning here about the significance of Christian teaching and the responsibility of those who teach is serious indeed.

With v. 43, the analogies change from those related to sight to those related to agriculture, and the topic shifts slightly from that of integrity to the more underlying issue of general character. Just as it is obvious that good trees do not yield bad fruit, so it ought to be obvious that the "produce" of a good person will be good and that of an evil person will be evil.

Verses 46–49 make explicit what has been implicit in vs. 43–45. The one who hears, really hears, the words of Jesus will necessarily act on those words. By doing so, that person erects a house that will withstand any storm that comes. The one who hears but does not act builds a house with no foundation at all, subject to destruction by any storm. The consequences envisioned in v. 49 are severe: "Great was the ruin of that house." If Luke shies away from explicitly eschatological language here, the implication is nevertheless clear. Those who do not follow Jesus' teaching are subject to the wrath of God in some final and devastating manner.

Verses 46–47 form a kind of challenge that brings to a culmination not simply this section, but all of the sermon. The one who calls Jesus "Lord" must also behave as Jesus teaches. To come to Jesus, as the multitude does in v. 17, is not enough. Nor is it enough to listen to Jesus' teaching. Being present and listening must end in action, in obedience.

In one sense the concerns of this passage seem quite contemporary. One recent trend in ethics has emphasized the importance of character in shaping ethical behavior. Rather than being preoccupied with instructing people in how to behave in given situations or with providing rules of behavior, the argument runs, we need to work toward the shaping of character.

Of course, the roots for this emphasis on character are ancient. Luke's Sermon on the Plain does not so much provide new instruction about character as it reflects what would have been found in any Greco-Roman moralist. The good person inevitably acts in ways that are appropriate and fair-minded and just. In that sense, Luke's congregation would hear nothing particularly new or unique.

What does make the sermon distinctively Christian is the way Luke grounds the appeal he makes. *Christian* character stems from the awareness that Jesus is indeed Lord (v. 46) and from the overwhelming experience of the mercy of God (v. 36). What is being served here by a "good" character (by the healthy tree) is not the city-state, the corporation, or even the family. Instead, the Christian serves the one named "Lord."

In connection with this larger sense of the Christian character, v. 48 cries out for an allegorical interpretation along the lines of Eph. 2:20, in which Christ is the cornerstone and the apostles and prophets become the foundation. The analogy does not work, of course, as is clear immediately in Luke from the difficulty that arises when we read that the man in the story himself "laid the foundation." Nevertheless, in some profound sense the sermon recalls that it is God's own action in Jesus Christ that enables the development of a character that will act in accord with Jesus' will.

# Last Sunday After Epiphany

## (TRANSFIGURATION SUNDAY)

"Glory." The word has become a bit tarnished by associations with false and, especially, self-seeking glory. In the human sphere, it connotes glitz and glamour, the cheap glory of those who achieve Andy Warhol's predicted fifteen-minutes worth of fame. Even reference to the glory of God, however, may not mean what it once did, as some people articulate a discomfort with the notion of God's glory. They fear that speaking of God's glory makes God too remote from human experience.

The texts for Transfiguration Sunday insist that glory is, whether comfortable or not, the right word for God and even for those who are touched by God's presence. The psalmist praises precisely the exaltation of God above all people. God is "enthroned upon the cherubim" (Ps. 99:1). All peoples should tremble before God and praise God's name (vs. 1, 3). The second half of the psalm makes it clear that this glory of God does not remove God from the needs of God's people. God speaks to the people through the priests and through the "pillar of cloud" (vs. 6–7). God forgives, and God avenges (v. 8).

Exodus 34:29–35 depicts God's glory and its consequences for human beings. Moses, by virtue of speaking with God, undergoes a change so dramatic that the people of Israel cannot even look on his face. That this change is not Moses' possession or accomplishment, however, the account makes evident by its insistence that "Moses did not know that the skin of his face shone" (v. 29).

In the exceedingly difficult passage from 2 Corinthians, Paul draws on this story of Moses to make the radical point that, in the Christ-event, God enables all to participate in the glory of God. All are able to see the glory of God (3:18) and, indeed, as Paul states in a verse that follows our lection, all believers have "knowledge of the glory of God" in Jesus' face (4:6).

The specific instance of God's glory that we celebrate on this

170

Sunday is, of course, the transfiguration of Jesus. Like countless interpreters since that event, Peter wishes to reduce the terrifying glory of Christ to something he can understand, a dwelling that might be visited from time to time. He learns the lesson that must continually be reinforced, that God's glory can be neither reduced nor controlled.

## Exodus 34:29–35

A large part of the power of religious faith, in whatever age and in whatever cultural context, has been its ability to lift persons and communities out of themselves and to place them in contact with more expansive, more enduring realities. For all the very necessary and appropriate appeals to make religious faith "relevant" to the moral issues of the day, the transcendent aspects of the God–human dialogue cannot be sacrificed without reducing faith to something other than itself. The Old Testament text for this day, indeed Transfiguration Sunday itself, stands as a reminder of this basic truth.

Exodus 34:29–35 forms something of a conclusion to the story of the Sinai covenant begun in Ex. 19. The Commandments have been given by God, broken by the people, and given by God again. In the midst of this drama, there has been the sometimes towering, sometimes cowering figure of Moses the mediator: bridge between Yahweh, Israel's righteous God, and Israel, Yahweh's sinful people. But now Moses has carved new tablets of the Law, as directed by Yahweh (vs. 1–28), and these he presents to the people.

But without his knowing it, Moses' appearance has changed. The text makes it quite clear that the reason for the change is Moses' continued contact with Yahweh: "The skin of his face shone because he had been talking with God" (v. 29). Something of God's holiness has been absorbed by Moses and, just as the people had earlier been terrified by Yahweh, so now they are afraid of this leader of theirs in whom the presence of God is so evident. Thus, after delivering the new tablets of the Law to the people (through their leaders, including Aaron), Moses covers his face with a veil in order to shield the people from this new terror. Yet as the dialogue with Yahweh continues, Moses removes the veil when in God's presence, only to resume it again when in the presence of the people.

It would be easy to misread this passage as an example of a primitive belief in magic of the kind so often found in early human societies. And, to be sure, the Old Testament is not devoid of that element (compare 2 Sam. 6:1–11). But to dismiss this text on those grounds would be to mistake the form of the text for its meaning. For while it may resemble superstition, the heart of this passage is a statement about the transcendence of a holy God. It is an effort to describe what some have called the "numinous" and the power of that reality in human life. Yahweh, the God of Israel, is considered here to be a Being like no other, and that very quality of the divine nature reshapes the lives of those who are touched by it.

In the thought of ancient Israel this quality of "otherness"—or to use the biblical term, this quality of "holiness"—has at least two dimensions. One may be thought of as philosophical, in that it is intended to describe a state of being. Yahweh is holy in the sense that Yahweh is absolutely distinct from that creation which Yahweh has brought forth. That is the real reason for the Second Commandment (Ex. 20:4–6; Deut. 5:8–10). Because Yahweh is absolutely unique, there should be no mistaking Yahweh for other forms of being.

Another aspect of the holiness of Yahweh in the thought of the Old Testament is moral. Yahweh is absolutely distinct from all other beings in that Yahweh alone is morally right and morally consistent. All Yahweh's relationships with creation, including humankind, are characterized by the principles of justice and compassion, and that claim can be made for no one else. It can be made for no human being; it can be made for no other god.

Those parts of the Old Testament which emphasize Yahweh's holiness then go on to insist that the community of faith reflect that holiness (notice the so-called Holiness Code in Lev. 17—26), and it is in this regard that what might otherwise be a dry, theological construct becomes a beating heart. It is also in this regard that the transcendent and the moral make contact. Israel is to reflect Yahweh's holiness in that it too is to be a community where human life is lived justly and compassionately. Ultimately, there is no other reason for God's people to care about the moral quality of their lives, since morality does not necessarily produce its own rewards (as Job well knew). God's people are to be just and loving because God is just and loving. They are to be "holy" because God is holy.

The terms "holy" and "righteous," especially when applied to human belief and behavior, have become tarnished because they are easily confused with "holier-than-thou-ness" and "self-righteousness." Obviously, any interpretation of the passage will want to be clear about this.

Thus, while this text reminds readers in every generation that there is an aspect to human life that transcends the world of experience around us, that very transcendence frames life within a moral context. And that very transcendence injects into human life a joyous freedom, which may come from no other source:

> Do not fear, for I have redeemed you;
> I have called you by name, you are mine.
> . . . . . . . . . . . . . . . . . . . . . . . . . . . . . . . . .
> For I am [Yahweh] your God,
> the Holy One of Israel, your Savior.
> (Isa. 43:1, 3)

## Psalm 99

Psalm 99 explicitly proclaims, "The LORD is king" (v. 1). Ps. 99 and the collection of which it is a part (Pss. 93; 95—99, the so-called enthronement psalms; see also Pss. 29; 47) form "the theological 'heart' " of the Psalter (G. H. Wilson, "The Use of Royal Psalms at the 'Seams' of the Psalter," *Journal for the Study of the Old Testament* [1986]: 92). They appear to be strategically placed to respond to the failure of the Davidic covenant (Ps. 89:38–51); and they do so in part by offering a pre-Davidic, Mosaic perspective. It was Moses who proclaimed the reign of God (Ex. 15:18) before there was land, temple, or monarchy. Thus the loss of land, temple, and monarchy should not be interpreted as a denial of the sovereignty of God. In this regard, it is significant that Book IV of the Psalter begins with the only psalm attributed to Moses (Ps. 90); and it seems no mere coincidence that Ps. 99, the climactic enthronement psalm, also explicitly mentions Moses and Aaron (v. 6; additional references to Moses in Pss. 103:7; 105:26; 106:16, 23, 32; the only reference to Moses outside Book IV is Ps. 77:20) as well as Samuel, who explicitly opposed the formation of the monarchy on the ground that only God could properly be Israel's king (see 1 Sam. 8:1–18).

It is perhaps significant too that there are several verbal links between Ps. 99 and Ex. 15:1–18, the song that Moses and the Israelites sang after being delivered from Egypt. Both songs of praise celebrate Yahweh's reign (Ps. 99:1; Ex. 15:18). In both, God is to be extolled (Ps. 99:5, 9; compare "exalt" in Ex. 15:2), because God is "great" (Ps. 99:2–3; compare "might" in Ex. 15:16), "awesome" (Ps. 99:3; Ex. 15:11), "mighty" (Ps. 99:4; compare "strength," Ex. 15:2, 13), and "holy" (Ps. 99:3, 5, 9; compare Ex. 15:11, 13). In both songs, "the peoples tremble" (Ps. 99:1; compare Ex. 15:14); and in both, Yahweh is established in Yahweh's own place (Ps. 99:2–3, 5, 9;

compare Ex. 15:13, 17). It is as if Ps. 99 intentionally recalls Ex. 15:1–18 as a way of affirming for a later generation that God *still* reigns! Like the other enthronement psalms, Ps. 99 is eschatological, for the proclamation of God's reign always occurs in a context in which it appears that God does *not* reign.

Psalm 99 is unique among the enthronement psalms in highlighting Yahweh's holiness. The phrase "Holy is he!" in vs. 3 and 5 divides the psalm into three sections, each with a distinctive theme: vs. 1–3, 4–5, 6–9. Verses 5 and 9 are almost identical; and v. 9 provides two more occurrences of the key word "holy." Holiness in its fundamental sense designated the awesome presence of God that evoked fear and required humans to keep their distance or to approach God only after taking special precautions (see Ex. 19:7–25, especially v. 23; 20:18–21). This fundamental sense of holiness is reflected in Ps. 99:1–3; the presence of God causes people to "tremble" and the earth to "quake" (v. 1; see Ex. 19:16; 20:18, although the Hebrew words translated "trembled" are both different from the one in Ps. 99:1). As the psalm proceeds, however, holiness is defined in very different terms. Rather than keeping humans at a distance, God relates to them—doing justice, answering cries, and both forgiving and holding accountable.

In addition to reflecting the fundamental sense of holiness, vs. 1–3 introduce the startling claim that while God's sovereignty is universal, it is focused "in Zion" (v. 2). God's enthronement "upon the cherubim" (v. 1) also points to the centrality of Jerusalem as God's special place. The reference is apparently to the Ark of God, which was understood symbolically as God's throne (see Ps. 80:1). The particularity of v. 1 continues throughout the psalm. God's "footstool" is another reference to the Ark (v. 5; see Ps. 132:7; 1 Chron. 28:2), and God's "holy mountain" is Zion (v. 9; see "holy hill" in Ps. 2:6). In short, Jerusalem is the earthly locus of God's presence and power (see Ps. 48). The theology of Ps. 99 is *incarnational*. Christians affirm a scandalous particularity that is analogous: Jesus became the earthly locus of God's presence and power, the focus and revelation of God's glory (see John 1:14–18). The incarnation of Jesus is the ultimate redefinition of holiness: God resides in human flesh! Psalm 99, however, evidences already the redefinition of God's holiness, which culminates in the incarnation.

In vs. 4–5 the awesome, holy God is intimately involved in human relationships. The "mighty King" is not enthroned above it all, but rather is to be found in the midst of the struggle for God's rightly ordered human relatedness. Not only is God a "lover of justice" (see Pss. 33:5; 37:28), but also God "does" (NRSV "executed," 99:4) justice and righteousness. The shift to the second person reinforces God's intimate involvement, and the appearance of the personal pronoun is emphatic: "justice and righteousness in Jacob, *you* have done" (v. 4, author's translation; see Pss. 89:14; 97:2). As the prophetic books make especially clear, justice and righteousness have to do with the concrete, daily realities of human existence and relatedness (see Amos 5:7–13, 21–24; Micah 3; 6:6–8; see also Ps. 82:1–4). As the other enthronement psalms affirm, God's reign means that God is coming to "judge" (or better, "establish justice") with "righteousness" and "equity" (Pss. 96:10, 13; 98:9; see 9:7–8). Psalm 99:4–5 makes clear that God's holiness includes God's involvement with God's people.

God's involvement with humanity means God has a problem (vs. 6–9). The reason Moses, Aaron, and Samuel "called on" God's name was the people's sinfulness (see Ex. 32:7–14; Num. 16:20–22; 1 Sam. 7:5–11). The "pillar of cloud" (Ps. 99:7; see Ex. 13:21–22; 14:19, 24; 33:9–10; Num. 12:5; 14:14) represented God's presence with the people throughout the exodus and wilderness experience. Although Ps. 99:7 suggests that "they kept his decrees . . . and the statutes," the wilderness experience was actually characterized by distrust, complaining, and disobedience that necessitated intercession by Moses and Aaron. God's answer (vs. 6, 8; notice the shift from third to second person between vs. 6 and 8, and there is also another emphatic pronoun: "*you* answered them" [emphasis added]), inevitably involved forgiveness (v. 8). Only by God's grace did the people continue to exist, but God also continued to demand the people's obedience. Herein lies God's problem—how to be *both* a "forgiving God" and "an avenger of their wrongdoings" (v. 8; see the same tension in Ex. 34:6–9). God's holiness ultimately involves not God's avoidance of sin and sinners, but rather God's bearing the burden of sin (Ps. 99:8; the Hebrew translated "forgiving" means literally to bear, carry) and loving sinners. In the tension represented in v. 8, it is not difficult to discern the shape of a cross.

## 2 Corinthians 3:12–4:2

One of the difficulties of interpreting letters such as those written by Paul is the large amount of shared information between author and projected readers to which we, as modern readers, are not privy. We often come late into the conversation, and can only make educated guesses as to what has previously transpired or what may be going on currently in the lives of the readers that is not spelled out for us in the one side of the conversation we are privileged to overhear. It is dangerous to base a lot on what we do not know, and yet often we are forced to historical judgments in order to make sense of the text.

This is the case with 2 Cor. 3:12–4:2. From 2:14 through 6:12 Paul writes about the nature of the apostolic ministry in which he is engaged. Apparently (and here is what we do not know for sure) he is under suspicion, if not attack, from some in Corinth who question his ministry, and he himself appears not too happy with the ministry of his rivals. The situation is not so combative as the one reflected in 2 Cor. 10—13, but the text hardly makes sense apart from the acknowledgment that it is both apologetic (defense) and polemic (attack). It is impossible to identify with any certainty who these rivals are, but the conflict with them undoubtedly shapes what Paul writes in this section of the letter.

Second Corinthians 3:7–18 serves as an explanation of 3:6. God has made Paul and his colleagues ministers of a new covenant, marked by the presence and activity of the Spirit. A way of reflecting on the distinctiveness of the new covenant is to recall the event in Ex. 34:29–35, when the Israelites were overawed by the shining countenance of Moses after he had talked with God (see 2 Cor. 3:7–11). Moses took up the practice of putting a veil over his face to ease the fears of the people. The glory of the new covenant, however, is much greater than that experienced by Moses and the Israelites; it is a brilliant glory that will not fade away.

In 3:12–18, however, the veil shifts from being a covering of Moses' face to being a shroud over the minds of the Israelites, keeping them from understanding where the old covenant is leading them. They cannot grasp that the glory of Moses has faded and yielded to another glory, the glory seen in the face of Jesus Christ (4:6).

But the blindness is not limited to Israelites, Chapter 3:16, using the words of Ex. 34:34, seems to universalize the problem. "When one turns to the Lord, the veil is removed." The event recorded in Ex. 34 becomes only an illustration of a larger failure to discern the meaning of the ancient text and thus to remain in bondage (compare 4:3–4). Only the Spirit brings the unveiling that leads to freedom.

In theological language, what Paul argues for is a hermeneutic of the Spirit. Instead of trying to understand Christ, the new covenant, and the Spirit in light of the law (as perhaps the opposition in Corinth advocates). Paul demands that the law be understood in light of Christ, the new covenant, and the Spirit. There is simply no natural or logical progression that leads from the law to the new covenant. The law can be only a death-dealing letter—apart from the life-giving Spirit (3:6).

A sermon for Transfiguration Sunday might well arise from 3:18, with its repetition of the word "glory." Here we learn how critical the hermeneutic becomes. The activity of the Spirit frees "all of us" from the veils that blind us and effects a transformation "from one degree of glory to another" (a phrase no doubt intended to contrast the dynamic glory of the new covenant with the fading glory of Moses' face). A faithful and Spirit-directed reading of the text ("with unveiled faces") then turns out to be more than an intellectual exercise leading to a more correct theology. It is a conversion. It changes readers so that they conform to the glory found in the crucified Christ.

It is just this new discernment and freedom given by the Spirit that buoys Paul's ministry, keeps him from cheapening the gospel, and lifts him above the level of being a mere peddler of the divine message (2:17). As he repeatedly reminds us, his confidence and competence come not from himself but from the Lord (3:4–6). How much of Paul's argument represents a defense against accusers and how much conceals an attack on his rivals is a difficult question to decipher. But our inability to answer it need not keep us from the transformative, Spirit-given hermeneutic that characterizes the ministry of the new covenant.

## Luke 9:28–36 (37–43)

Earlier in this chapter of Luke's Gospel, King Herod hears about the marvelous deeds of Jesus. Rumors have reached him that some people believe Jesus to be John the Baptist risen from the dead and that others think Jesus is the promised return of Elijah. In consternation, Herod asks, "John I beheaded; but who is this about whom I hear such things?" (9:9). The question "Who is this?" runs throughout the Gospel, of course, but it is especially important in this section of Luke.

One answer to Herod's question comes in the form of Peter's confession in 9:20: "[You are] the Messiah of God." To identify Jesus as God's "Messiah," however, is to offer more questions than answers, for the word connoted many things to many different groups within early Judaism. Jesus' immediate response (9:21–22) indicates that the meaning of Messiahship may be more complicated than either the disciples or Luke's readers have yet anticipated.

The transfiguration account provides yet another way of answering Herod's question. By means of this elusive event, Luke identifies Jesus in terms of Israel's past (Moses and Elijah), foreshadows his upcoming death on the cross, and anticipates his resurrected glory. Luke also uses this story to teach about the nature of discipleship.

First, the transfiguration identifies Jesus with Moses and Elijah. The disciples recognize these two crucial figures from Israel's past, and Peter refers to each of them by name. They appear "in glory," confirming that they are heavenly beings, not conformed to earthly limitations. That they talk with Jesus might suggest a kind of peer relationship among the three figures, a conclusion that seems confirmed by Peter's proposal. However, the heavenly voice speaks only of Jesus, and only when the other two have disappeared from the scene. It is Jesus alone who is "my Son, my Chosen." If Jesus stands in the line of Moses and Elijah, he is nevertheless far superior to that line.

Second, the transfiguration foreshadows Jesus' death on the cross. When Moses and Elijah talk with Jesus, they discuss his *exodos*, which the NRSV translates as "departure" and which literally means exodus and figuratively refers to death or departure. Exactly what Luke intends by this term is unclear, but it at least includes Jesus' death, as is indicated by the connection of this impending departure of Jesus with Jerusalem. Jesus' earlier reference to the necessity of his suffering and death and the reference later in the chapter to his determination to go to Jerusalem (9:51) confirm this impression.

If the transfiguration anticipates the death of Jesus, it also hints that death will not be the final word in this story. The dominant motif of this account, after all, is one of glory, a glory that most appropriately anticipates the resurrected Jesus. Several elements in the passage draw attention to Jesus' glory. The change in his appearance recalls Daniel's description of the Ancient One (Dan. 7:9) and signals divine favor (Eccl. 9:8). The glory of Jesus is visible to Peter and the other disciples, even when he stands alongside Moses and Elijah, and even though they are themselves overwhelmed with sleep (v. 32)! The cloud, the arrival and movement of which Luke depicts in some detail, is associated elsewhere with the very presence of God (see, for example, Ex. 16:10; 19:9; 1 Kings 8:10–11; Ps. 18:11). That these features of the story anticipate Jesus' resurrection is clear when we recall that, at Jesus' ascension, it is a cloud that removes him from the sight of the disciples (Acts 1:9).

As fascinating as the transfiguration itself are the responses of Peter and John and James. Initially, Luke explains that they were "weighed down with sleep," a problem that will overtake them again at the time of Jesus' arrest (Luke 22:45). This odd little detail may serve to emphasize the utterly astonishing nature of the event, in that it serves to wake them from such a sleep. Another possibility is that their grogginess explains the inappropriateness of Peter's suggestion in 9:33.

The proposal of Peter, that dwellings be erected to honor each of the three men, Luke immediately interprets as something of a faux pas ("not knowing what he said," v. 33). Despite his own identification of Jesus as Messiah, Peter still does not understand *either* the vast superiority of Jesus to even these giants of Israel *or* the impossibility of locating any of them in a building (compare Acts 7:47–49).

The final response of the three is that of awe (Luke 9:34) and silence (v. 36). That seems to be the only possible response to what they have witnessed. Their silence acknowledges the mystery of this event and the magnitude of its implications. Their silence also signals their obedience to Jesus' earlier warning that they should not tell anyone Jesus' identity (9:21). Their silence also reflects their own lack of readiness for the task of witnessing that will later be theirs (Acts 1:8); it is not yet time for the disciples to speak.

The silence of the disciples does not mean that they fully comprehend what they have seen and heard, as is clear from the stories that immediately follow. They are unable to cast out a demon from a severely afflicted boy (9:37–42); they do not understand Jesus' comments about his upcoming death (9:43–45); worse yet, they quarrel over which of them is greatest (9:46–48). They still must learn to listen to the Chosen One (9:35), but that hearing has its rightful beginning in their awed silence.

# Ash Wednesday

In ancient Israel the symbolism of ashes was understood to be a forceful reminder of the pervasiveness of human sin and of the inevitability of human death. Ashes represented that which, in the human experience, was burned out and wasted, that which once was but is no more. This traditional emblem of grief and mourning has been adopted by the Christian church as a signal of our own sinful mortality; it has also been embraced as a muted trumpet to warn us of the coming dark days in Jesus' life: his passion and death.

The texts for this day are true to the ominous quality the observance is intended to convey. Yet they also point forward—again, in keeping with the character of Ash Wednesday—to the redemptive power of God's grace.

The Joel lection is an alarm bell in the darkness of the night. The crisis is not specified nor is it described in any type of detail, but there is no mistaking its urgency. Those who are caught in this terrible moment cannot hope to save themselves, for they are basically powerless to do anything on their own behalf. They are powerless to do anything, that is, except to repent and to open themselves to God's intervening mercy.

Psalm 51 is a classic (some might say *the* classic) piece of literature that captures the faithful man or woman of God in the act of throwing him- or herself open to God's mercy. The poet is convinced of the personal and profound manner in which he or she has offended God and shattered a relationship that God intended to be warmly intimate. In casting him- or herself on God's grace, the poet not only acknowledges God's role as the unique savior of faithful people, but acknowledges as well the inevitable result of God's intervention: a changed and redirected life.

Paul is acutely aware of the dark power of sin and mortality, as he writes to the Corinthian Christians. Yet the apostle understands that God shares the concern of faithful people over these issues, and he takes pains to point out that it is God, not we, who has taken the initiative to set matters right. Jesus Christ is the one who, by the mercy of God, has been appointed the agent of our reconciliation with God. This present moment is the *kairos* time. "Now is the day of salvation."

The lection from Matthew's record of the Sermon on the Mount is, on its surface, an extended warning against false and manipulative piety. But, at a deeper level, the passage is a declaration that God responds in mercy to the faithfulness of those who attempt to do God's will. Just how the faithful will "receive their reward" is not described, but the strong implication is that a large part of their fulfillment is bound up in their sense of engagement with the ongoing purposes of God.

## Joel 2:1–2, 12–17                                          (A B C)

This text plunges the listener into a crisis. We know almost nothing about the historical setting of Joel. For that reason, it is impossible to identify the historical allusions of the poetry. It is enough to see that this text is a *summons to emergency* that is visible, public, and close at hand. The text is organized around two summonses to "Blow the trumpet in Zion." The first of these identifies the crisis (v. 1). The second requires a response to the crisis (v. 15).

The crisis is announced as urgent (vs. 1–2). The imperative at the beginning invites the sentry to sound a general alarm in Jerusalem. Read theologically, the trouble approaching the city is the "day of Yahweh," which comes as awesome, dreadful, irresistible threat. The crisis is that God has become an enemy attacker against God's own city and God's own people. Read militarily, the attack is a "great and powerful army" (v. 2). That is, the poem describes a military invasion.

We are not told, on the one hand, why God is attacking. On the other hand, we are not told who this great and powerful people is, or why they come. What matters for our reading of the text is that the hostility of God and the reality of human threat are spoken of in the same breath, that is, they are identical. This is not mere human politics, and it is not supernaturalist "scare theology." It is a genuinely human and immediate threat, rooted in and authorized by the will of God.

The poem is an invitation to imagine the city under deep assault. The poem intends to awaken a complacent, unnoticing citizenry to its actual situation, to evoke in it an intentional and urgent response.

The poem drives the listener to ask, "What then shall we do?" (compare Luke 3:10; Acts 2:37). That is the central question of concerned people in the midst of a crisis.

The answer to this implicit question is given: "Blow the trumpet in Zion" (v. 15). This trumpet, unlike that of v. 1, is not a warning. It is, rather, the signal for a response of profound, serious religion: authorize a fast, provide a meeting. The response urged to the military crisis wrought by God is an act of deep religious intentionality, an act of disciplining what is left from a shattered complacency, an act of obedience that breaks off all easy indifference. The community must come to its senses and honestly embrace its true situation. And that can be done only in a meeting that counters all "business as usual."

The "revision of reality" (repentance) urged by the poem is not a set of religious exercises. It is, rather, a deliberate act of re-presenting one's self vis-à-vis God, the same God who is invading the city. The summons to "return" and to "rend" (vs. 12–13) suggests that Jerusalem has forgotten who God is. When God is forgotten or distorted, society is inevitably, commensurately distorted and disordered. Thus the beginning point for rescue is to rediscern God. The rediscernment of God in v. 13 quotes one of Israel's oldest creeds, which voices the distinctiveness of Israel's God (Ex. 34:6–7).

Clearly Jerusalem has forgotten God's utter fidelity. When God's fidelity is jettisoned, human relations become unfaithful and society disintegrates. Thus the purpose of religious discipline is to remember who God really is, what is promised by God, and what is required for God.

This is an odd and suggestive text for Lent. This text plunges Lent (and us) into dangerous public reality. The text does not require dramatic overstatement of crisis, nor "hellfire and damnation."

It is clear to any observer, nonetheless, that our old, trusted, known world is under deep assault. AIDS and "crack" are only surface symptoms of a deathly sickness common to us all. That deep illness may be our counterpart to the invasion pictured in the text.

The "returning" and "rending" to which we are invited is the hard work of rediscerning God, and then making the responses—theological, socioeconomic, political, and personal—that are congruent with God's character. Lent is the reflective occasion out of which fresh discernments of reality may come. When we do not emulate God's mercy and faithfulness in the world, we are invaded by the power of death, which may take many forms. Either we turn in order to live, or we resist the choice and we die. Ash Wednesday is for renoticing our true situation, in the world and before God.

## Psalm 51:1–17                                              (A B C)

Psalm 51 is the classic statement of repentance from the Old Testament Psalter, and so deeply has it shaped the language of confession in both Jewish and Christian communities that its very cadences often echo in synagogue and in church when worshipers address in a corporate fashion their sinfulness before God. The psalm is no less powerful a vehicle for expressing the individual's sense of sin as one makes private confession. Thus its inclusion as an Ash Wednesday lection seems almost mandatory.

The superscription relates the psalm to the terrible incident in which David seduces or rapes (the text is ambiguous) Bathsheba, the wife of Uriah the Hittite, only to be rebuked by the prophet Nathan (2 Sam. 11—12). Yet the text of the psalm itself is lacking any detail that would reinforce that claim. In fact, it is the very universality of the psalm's language about sin that has allowed it to speak to the widest possible variety of human experiences.

The language of the psalm suggests that its author was a priest, well rehearsed in the cultic vocabulary. For example, when the poet prays, "Cleanse me from my sin" (v. 2), the verb that is chosen (*tāhēr*) is one that frequently appears in the Priestly literature of the Old Testament to describe cultic or liturgical activity (Lev. 12:7, 8; 14:20). Another example: the reference to hyssop (v. 7) recalls other Old Testament texts in which this plant was used as a liturgical purgative (Lev. 14:4; Num. 19:6). Yet, amazingly, the cultic acts of confession and absolution do not lie at the core of the psalmist's concern, as Ps. 51:15–17 takes great pains to point out. What is of greatest importance is the transformation of the worshiper. A "clean heart," a "right spirit" (v. 10), and a "contrite heart" (v. 17) are qualities most closely associated with God's salvation. What happens to the person is infinitely more important than what happens in the cult.

Psalm 51:1–12 exhibits many of the characteristics common to psalms of individual lament. Verses 1–2 constitute a kind of salutation in which the object of the petition is named ("O God" of v. 1), yet the most urgent phrases are those in which the psalmist pleads for redemption. Notice the four imperatives: "Have mercy," "blot out," "wash me thoroughly," and "cleanse me" (vs. 1–2). The basis on which the psalmist is so bold as to claim God's forgiveness is specifically mentioned: God's "steadfast love" (*hesed*) and "mercy" (v. 1).

Having set the agenda, the psalmist lays bare his soul in the subsequent section (vs. 3–5), confessing his sin with profound honesty. Several characteristics of the poet's sinfulness are made evident: (1) The poet's sense of sin is haunting in that he cannot escape it (v. 3). (2) Whatever damage the author's sinful deeds may have done to other human beings, the primary offense is against God (v. 4). Although NRSV correctly reflects the Hebrew text here, "you alone" should not be read as intending to imply that humans do not sin against one another, for there are a number of Old Testament texts that state clearly that they do (see 1 Sam. 26:21). The statement apparently means that, even when other people suffer because of human wrongdoing, all sin is basically an affront to God. (3) Sin is a universal and deeply rooted part of human nature (Ps. 51:5).

In the third section (vs. 6–12), the psalmist returns to the plea for God's redeeming presence that characterized vs. 1–2. (Verse 6 offers special problems in translation and interpretation, for it is not entirely clear to what "inward being" [the Hebrew word is a very rare term—*tuhôt*—apparently related to a verb meaning "to spread over"] and "secret heart" [Hebrew, "that which has been closed"] refer.) Although, as mentioned above, some of the language here is cultic, the primary focus is on the change that takes place within the individual as a result of God's redemptive activity. "Joy and gladness" (vs. 8, 12) characterize the outlook of the forgiven sinner, as do a "clean heart" and a "willing spirit" (vs. 10, 12) and an awareness of God's immediacy (v. 11).

A final section (vs. 13–17) brings the sequence of confession and restoration to an important climax, in that here the promise is made that salvation results in a changed and renewed individual. The psalm is insistent that to be forgiven is not to return to some status quo ante, to some level of consciousness where we resided before our experience of grace. Rather, to be forgiven is to be changed. It is to slough off the old and put on the new—to exchange the heart of despair for a heart of service of God. The climax to our psalm is vs. 13–14, which proclaim, in so many words: "When you have come into my life, O God, that life will never again be the same."

The distinctive place that this psalm has found in the literature of confession is the result not only of its beauty, but also of the relevance of its language, which enables it to speak to and for all varieties of sin-oppressed persons. What is more, it has claimed a home in so many hearts because it recognizes a crucial reality about the task of coming to terms with our sin, and that is, that apart from the grace of God we are absolutely incapable of dealing with the pervasiveness of human evil. It is not until we recognize our own finitude and corruption before God (v. 17) that we receive empowerment from the One who forgives and redeems.

## 2 Corinthians 5:20b–6:10                                      (A B C)

Contemporary Christians sometimes look back to the early days in the church's life with rose-tinted glasses. That period seems to have been inhabited by believers who were filled with zeal, who knew the necessity of evangelism, who had the advantages of a new and innocent faith. Read with care, Paul's letters reveal another side to the story, one in which there are conflicts, struggles, and misunderstandings. In the present passage, Paul pleads with baptized Christians, people whom he elsewhere characterizes as being "in Christ" and belonging to the "body of Christ," to become reconciled to God. The need for reconciliation is inherent in the Christian faith—it is not a symptom of degeneracy in the latter days of the church's life.

Set against the other texts assigned for Ash Wednesday (for example, Ps. 51) and other reflections on the need for reconciliation between God and humankind, 2 Cor. 5 sounds a distinctive note. Here human beings do not cry out to God for forgiveness and reconciliation, for it is God who seeks reconciliation. In the sending of Jesus Christ, God acts to reconcile the world to God (5:20a). Paul characterizes the gospel itself as God's making an appeal to human beings to be reconciled to God (5:20; 6:1). Consistent with Paul's comments elsewhere (Rom. 1:18–32), the point he makes here is that it is not God who must be appeased because of human actions; but human beings, who have turned away from God in rebellion, must accept God's appeal and be reconciled. Even in the face of the intransigence of human sin, it is God who takes the initiative to correct the situation; human beings have only to receive God's appeal.

The urgency of the appeal for this reception comes to the fore in 6:1–2. Without accepting God's reconciliation, the Corinthians will have accepted "the grace of God in vain." Moreover, the right time for this reconciliation is now: "Now is the acceptable time; see, now is the day of salvation!" This comment about time lays before the Corinthians the eschatological claim of the gospel. As in 5:16 ("from now on"), Paul insists that the Christ-event makes this appeal urgent. There is also, however, a very specific urgency that affects the Corinthian community. It is time—or past time—for them to lay aside their differences and hear in full the reconciling plea of God made through the apostles. Time is "at hand" (NRSV, near), both for the created order as a whole and for the Corinthians in particular.

Throughout the text, Paul asserts that it is God who brings about this reconciliation, but he also points to the role of Christ. God reconciles the world "in Christ," that is, by means of Christ. Specifically, God "made him to be sin who knew no sin" (5:21). To say that

Christ "knew no sin," consistent with Paul's understanding of sin as a state of rebelliousness against God, means that Christ was obedient to God, that Christ submitted to God's will. That God "made him to be sin" suggests, in keeping with Rom. 8:3 and Gal. 3:13, that Christ's death on the cross had redemptive significance. Through it human beings are enabled to "become the righteousness of God" (2 Cor. 5:21b); in Christ's death the reconciling act of God becomes concrete.

Paul's eloquent plea for reconciliation stands connected to comments on the ministry that he and his co-workers are exercising among the Corinthians. Throughout this entire portion of the letter (1:1–7:16), in fact, the focus is on both the nature of the gospel and the nature of the Christian ministry. That dual focus exists not simply because Paul is once more defending himself against his critics (although he certainly is defending himself!), but because the ministry can only be understood rightly where the gospel itself is understood rightly. Paul's ministry, like his gospel, has to do with reconciling human beings to God. In 6:3–10 he expands on that role, insisting that he and his colleagues have taken every measure that might enhance the faith and growth of believers in Corinth. Ironically, he begins his itemization of the things that commend him with a list of things that would certainly not impress many readers of a résumé or letter of recommendation—afflictions, hardships, calamities, beatings, imprisonments. . . . For those who see the gospel as a means of being delivered *from* difficulties rather than *into* difficulties, Paul's commendation of the ministry will have a very negative sound. As earlier in the letter, he insists on the contrast between how the apostles are viewed by the world and how they stand before God. If the world, with its standards of measure, regards them as impostors, unknown, dying, punished, those assessments matter not at all. Before God, the apostles know that they are in fact true, well known, alive, and rejoicing.

This aspect of the passage makes powerful grist for reflection for those engaged in Christian ministry today, but it is equally relevant for all Christians, especially on Ash Wednesday. The reconciliation God brings about in Jesus Christ obliges not only ordained ministers but all Christians to proclaim the outrageous, universal, reconciling love of God.

## Matthew 6:1–6, 16–21                                            (A B C)

The Gospel text for Ash Wednesday provides a formidable context for the self-reflection and piety characteristic of the Lenten season. The text focuses not so much on what Christians should pray for or what acts of service they should perform, as on the manner in which they are to do them. The introductory verse (Matt. 6:1) in a sense says it all, and yet the repetitive parallelism of the three examples cited (almsgiving, prayer, and fasting) carries a powerful effect beyond what a single verse can convey. The language in which the examples are described serves not only to reinforce the point, but to jar the reader a bit, to open the possibility for self-reflection about a matter like hypocrisy, which otherwise could easily be dismissed.

The passage *warns against a manipulative piety that, in effect if not by conscious design, is carried out for an audience other than God.* No one in his or her right mind sets out to be a hypocrite. It is not a planned activity. People are simply drawn into situations or habits whereby their practice of religion is meant to have an impact on others—on children, on fellow church members, on the broader community—until the need for human approval subtly becomes the idol to which worship is offered. The practice often becomes so conventional that the guilty would be surprised by the charge of hypocrisy. Part of the difficulty is this blindness to what is taking place and the fact that the religious establishment tends to thrive on the social pressures that nurture such piety.

The literary structure of the passage and its hyperbolic language, as the commentators note, serve to get the reader's attention. The three examples are given in a parallel pattern, and in each case an antithesis is set up: either sounding a trumpet when giving alms or not letting the left hand know what the right hand is doing; either praying on the street corners or in the closet at home; either parading the fact that one is fasting or disguising it. No doubt most readers would judge their own intentions and actions to be somewhere in between the extremes, but the very sharply stated polarities serve as a lens through which to clarify the ambiguities. The obscure and provisional areas are brought into focus. The alternatives present the opportunity to view one's existence afresh and to detect the dangerous tendency toward hypocrisy.

It is critical that the interpreter recognize the hyperbolic character of the language and not turn the examples into new laws. The passages do not outlaw public prayer or pledging to congregational appeals. Neither do they sanction one's boasting about praying only in the closet. Instead, they function to warn Christians about the natural tendency to use religious exercises for ulterior purposes, to engage in a piety that for whatever reason seeks social approval.

But there is a positive side to the examples cited. They *speak of God's responsiveness to a single-minded piety.* It is intriguing how frequently the notion of "reward" appears in the text. In the introductory verse (6:1), those who practice their piety to be seen by others have no reward from the Father. In the description of the three examples of ostentatious piety, it is conceded that they have a kind of reward, perhaps just the reward they are looking for, namely, that they are seen by others. In the antitheses, however, those engaged in acts of piety with integrity and wholeheartedness, oriented completely to God, will encounter a responsive Father. Three times the statement occurs, ". . . and your Father who sees in secret will reward you" (vs. 4, 6, 18).

We are not told about the nature of the divine reward. From other passages in Matthew one could speculate that the reward is the joy of the presence of God (25:21, 23), but here the issue is simply that God sees the piety practiced "in secret" and responds, in contrast to ignoring the piety done for show. The desperate need for engagement with God is satisfied when God is sought in candor and simplicity.

The concluding verses of the lesson (6:19–21) in a sense initiate a new section of the Sermon on the Mount, a section dealing with one's attitude toward material possessions (vs. 19–34). The antithetical parallelism of vs. 19–20, however, prolongs the sharp either/or choice that so dominates the previous section (vs. 1–6, 16–18). What are we to make of this uncompromising attitude toward money, over against the importance of saving a little for the rainy days? The extreme character of the antithesis leaves the church feeling a bit disquieted with the usual ways wealth is valued and turns a searchlight on the practice of how people earn and spend their money. No concrete answers are offered. The text seems more interested in where the heart is: Is it bound up with a search for security vulnerable to various forms of decay, or is it engaged in a pursuit of God's will?

# First Sunday in Lent

What does it mean to call on God? Despite their diversity, each of the readings for the First Sunday in Lent touches on that theme of calling on God. In Deut. 26:1–11, Moses instructs Israel on commemorating its deliverance by God from the oppression of Egypt: "When the Egyptians treated us harshly . . . we cried to the LORD, the God of our ancestors" (vs. 6–7). That cry and the salvific response of God serve to define Israel; Israel exists because it cries to God out of its bondage and God delivers.

Psalm 91 generalizes on this theme: "When they call to me, I will answer them" (v. 15). The psalm depicts God's deliverance in terms that are all-encompassing. Some of the claims, taken at face value, are extravagant indeed (for example, "You will tread on the lion and the adder," v. 13). No longer is God called upon to rescue Israel collectively from a situation of oppression; here those who love God call on God and find that God answers them.

Do these readings suggest that God will allow nothing bad to happen to those Israelites who love God, or do they suggest that Israel is never without God, never finally alone? The New Testament readings insist that the latter is the case. First, Rom. 10:8b–13 provides a forceful reminder that human beings do not control the number or identity of those who may call on God. There "is no distinction between Jew and Greek" (v. 12), meaning that "Everyone who calls on the name of the Lord shall be saved" (v. 13). "Everyone" means just that, and prevents any human effort at definition or limitation.

The story of Jesus' temptation offers a powerful rejoinder to those who would claim that loving God and calling on God result in rescue in any and all circumstances. The devil quotes from Ps. 91 and is met with a fierce reminder: "Do not put the Lord your God to the test" (Luke 4:12). God's all-encompassing care is not a commodity to be gained by human beings through wheedling; it is, instead, a promise that no one ventures outside the realm of God's care. To call on God, then, is not to ask for power to be dispensed but to acknowledge human finitude and divine providence.

## Deuteronomy 26:1–11

It is interesting to scan the index of a standard book of quotations and to notice how differently various writers have responded to the idea of history. (The examples that follow are from *The Oxford Dictionary of Quotations*, 2d ed.; Oxford University Press, 1953.) Some believe that only by understanding the human past can a nation or a society come to terms with its own identity and its own future. Francis Bacon, for example, was of the opinion that "histories make men wise." While Samuel Taylor Coleridge appeared to agree, he seemed somewhat less optimistic about the matter, musing that "if men could learn from history, what lessons it might teach us!" One the other hand, the Victorian writer Charles Kingsley believed that "history is a pack of lies," at least if we are to believe what his contemporary William Stubbs says about him. And the celebrated philosopher Georg Wilhelm Hegel laid down this pessimistic axiom:

> What experience and history teach is this—that people and governments never have learned anything from history, or acted on principles deduced from it.

The Old Testament is rather clearheaded on this issue. That is especially true with respect to the book of Deuteronomy and that great history which Deuteronomy inspired, the books of Joshua through Second Kings (excluding Ruth). The basic assumption here is that the memory of the community of faith not only allows each generation of God's people to relive God's great deeds of redemption of the past, but opens them up to God's continuing activity in their own lives. What is more, it is through their common memory that the integrity, the wholeness, of the community is retained across the generations.

> Recite [the traditions of Israel] to your children and talk about them when you are at home and when you are away, when you lie down and when you rise. (Deut. 6:7)

Deuteronomy knows that when a people forgets its past, it loses both its present and its future.

It is no accident that Deuteronomy and the Deuteronomistic History contain three important passages that many scholars believe to have been creedal statements originally spoken in a context of public worship. As such, these texts provided the ancient Israelite with an opportunity to reimpress on himself or herself and on his or her family an awareness of the presence of God in their lives and an awareness of who they were as people. One of these important texts is the Old Testament lection for this day (notice also Deut. 6:20–25 and Josh. 24:1–28).

It is clear that the setting for Deut. 26:1–11 is a harvest festival, an occasion for celebrating God's gift of the fruitfulness of the earth. Although there were two major festivals of this kind in ancient Israel (not including Passover), the focus here seems to be on the Festival of Weeks in the spring, also known from the New Testament as Pentecost (Acts 2:1). Occurring seven weeks after Passover, this feast was held to observe the conclusion of the harvest of grains and cereal produce. (The Festival of Booths in the autumn celebrated the harvest of vines and fruit trees.) According to the instructions at the beginning of the passage, the worshiper is to come to the sanctuary bringing as a gift to God a basket containing a portion of the actual harvest, in effect returning to God a small part of that which God's grace has bestowed on the worshiper.

The heart of the passage is the confession that is to come from the lips of the worshiping Israelite (vs. 5–9). It is a recital of Israel's history, beginning from the time of Israel's earliest ancestors (Jacob is probably the "wandering Aramean" of v. 5) and continuing until the settlement in the Land of Promise. Throughout this brief but revealing text, emphasis is placed on the grace of God, who, in response to the cries of the people, saved them when they were unable to save themselves. From a situation of danger and oppression in an alien land, God brought them to safety in their own home. The basket of produce in the hands of the worshiper is itself evidence of God's continuing care of the people in their land.

Thus the moment celebrates the past. It also rejoices in the people's future under the benevolent rule of their God. Beyond that, however, the history that is recited here, and thus reimpressed on the memory, is the means by which the community of faith understands its own identity.

The Christian faith is also based on the collective memory of the people of Christ (1 Cor. 11:24), and it goes without saying that the church's memory—its creeds, if you will—celebrates God's saving deeds of the past and God's continuing promise to redeem now and in the future. The church's story is also the means by which Christian people identify themselves both individually and corporately. All of this is so axiomatic and self-evident that it would seem to need no repetition. Yet the matter is so foundational and crucial to the life and identity of the Christian community that it needs to be repeated over and again, especially in an age that, in some respects, has so little regard for history of any kind.

Yet a caveat is in order. A people's memory is a beneficial force in their lives and in the lives of others only to the extent that it reminds the owners of the memory that there are other stories and other memories. One of the challenges facing the twenty-first century is how humankind's many-splendored ethnic and religious memories may be used in the service of the whole human family. If the ancient hatreds are ever to be laid to rest, some selective forgetfulness must take place, or humans will continue to fight the old battles over and over. So George Santayana was only partly right. It may be true, as he wrote, that those who "cannot remember their past are doomed to repeat it," but it is also true that those who remember history too vividly are doomed to be enslaved by it.

## Psalm 91:1–2, 9–16

Psalm 91 is an eloquent affirmation that God can be trusted at all times, even or perhaps especially in the worst imaginable circumstances (see vs. 3–8, which are omitted by the lectionary). At the end of Ps. 90, the psalmist had prayed for God to "have compassion" (v. 13), "satisfy us" (v. 14), "make us glad" (v. 15), and "let your work be seen" (v. 16; NRSV "let your work be manifest"). Psalm 91 seems to provide an answer to this prayer. It even concludes uniquely, with God promising that "I will *satisfy* them" (v. 16, emphasis added; compare 90:14) and "cause them to *see* my salvation" (91:16, emphasis added; NRSV "show them my salvation"; compare 90:16).

The divine speech in Ps. 91:14–16 is preceded in vs. 1–13 by the psalmist's testimony, to an unidentified "you," that God can indeed be trusted. Verse 2 can be construed as an invitation. In any case, v. 2 is a summary of the psalmist's faith (the Hebrew actually reads, "I will say to the LORD"), and it represents what the psalmist wants others to profess as well. The words "refuge" and "fortress" (see Pss. 18:2; 31:2–3; 71:3; 144:2) in v. 2 are essentially synonymous with "shelter" (see Pss. 27:5; 31:20; 32:7; 61:4) and "shadow" (see Pss. 17:8; 36:7; 57:1; 63:7) in v. 1. The word "refuge" is repeated in vs. 4 and 9, thus becoming a key word in Ps. 91, as it is from the beginning and throughout the Psalter (see Pss. 2:12; 5:11; 11:1; 14:6; 16:1; 31:1, 19;

and twenty-five more times). To take refuge "under his wings" (v. 4; see Ruth 2:12; Pss. 17:8; 36:7; 57:1; 63:7) may originally have referred to the practice of seeking sanctuary in the Temple from persecutors (see 1 Kings 1:49–53) and/or to Israel's experience of finding security in worship. In the final form of the Psalter, the notion has been broadened. To take refuge in God means to entrust one's whole life to God in every circumstance. It means to approach God constantly as "my God, in whom I trust" (Ps. 91:2).

Verses 3–13 suggest the comprehensive effectiveness of trusting God. As Walter Brueggemann points out, God provides for the psalmist both a safe *place* (vs. 1–4, 9–10), and a safe *journey* (vs. 5–6, 11–13); that is, God's protection is effective everywhere (*The Message of the Psalms*; Minneapolis: Augsburg Publishing House, 1984, pp. 156–57). Verses 5–6 suggest that God's protection is also effective at all times—"night," "day," "in darkness," "at noonday." In addition, every manner of danger and difficulty is mentioned in vs. 3–13—surprise attack ("snare of the fowler," v. 3; see Pss. 124:7; 140:5; 141:9; 142:3), disease ("pestilence," vs. 3, 6), demonic powers (vs. 5–6 seem to refer to demons), war (v. 7), enemies (v. 8), wild animals (v. 13). In short, no place, no time, no circumstance is beyond God's ability to protect. God's angels or messengers will "guard you in *all* your ways" (v. 11, emphasis added).

The eloquence and comprehensiveness of the psalmist's affirmation of trust make Ps. 91 not only a "remarkable psalm" (Brueggemann, p. 156) but also a possible source of misunderstanding. For instance, Jews and Christians have sometimes worn written portions of Ps. 91 in amulets in attempts to ward off danger magically, and Ps. 91:11–13 has supported the notion of guardian angels who are believed to provide personal protection from harm (see James L. Mays, *Psalms*, Interpretation series; Louisville, Ky.: John Knox Press, 1994). Luke 4:9–12 (compare Matt. 4:5–7), in the Gospel lesson for the day, illustrates the possible misuse of Ps. 91. Here the devil quotes Ps. 91:11–12 to tempt Jesus to jump from the pinnacle of the Temple, but Jesus refuses to claim God's promise of protection for his own benefit. To do so, Jesus says, would be to test God rather than to trust God. In short, Ps. 91 is not to be cited as a guarantee against facing danger, threat, and difficulty. Rather, Ps. 91 is an affirmation that no danger, threat, or difficulty "will be able to separate us from the love of God" (Rom. 8:39). Neither Jesus nor the apostle Paul sought to avoid danger or difficulty. In fact, their faithfulness to God and God's purposes impelled them into the midst of danger (see 2 Cor. 6:4–10); and when Jesus claimed the assurance of the psalms, it was *from the cross* (see Luke 23:46, where Jesus quotes Ps. 31:5).

The comprehensiveness of the psalmist's profession of trust (vs. 1–13) is matched by a more compact but equally comprehensive divine promise of protection in vs. 14–16. The Hebrew contains seven first-person verbs (deliver . . . protect . . . answer . . . rescue . . . honor . . . satisfy . . . show—the number seven often represents completion or comprehensiveness) surrounding a verbless clause in the middle of v. 15. It contains an emphatic personal pronoun: "with them [am] *I* in trouble" (author's translation). The only other use of the emphatic pronoun in Ps. 91 is at the very heart of the psalm. In the Hebrew text, it too refers to God: "Indeed, *you*, O LORD, [are] my refuge" (v. 9a, author's translation). The effect of the two emphatic pronouns and the seven first-person verbs is to locate the psalmist's source of life in God alone. The Hebrew word translated "love" in v. 14 has the nuance of "be attached to, be connected with." Verse 14 does not suggest that God's deliverance and protection are a reward that is earned by loving God, but rather that relatedness to God *is* the essence of life. The verb "know" in v. 14 also connotes the intimacy of relatedness to God. This thoroughly God-centered perspective is especially appropriate for the beginning of Lent. It warns us not to allow our Lenten disciplines to become trivial, self-help schemes. Genuine self-denial begins with the kind of radical affirmation of trust that we find in Ps. 91.

## Romans 10:8b–13

The season of Lent always brings the church back to the basics, to issues that are bedrock and essential. It is no time for marginal matters that linger about the periphery, but is for those topics and experiences that lie close to the heartbeat of the faith. The texts of Lent force us to reflect on where we as communities and individuals stand in relation to the center, and then they invite a process of self-examination, repentance, forgiveness, and new life.

The Epistle reading for today (Rom. 10:8b–13) confronts us with some fundamental affirmations that define who we are and, by implication, who we are not. Identifying the lesson as fundamental, however, by no means implies that the passage is simple and without problems. Commentators enter the complex argument of Rom. 9—11 with care, because it concerns not only Christian basics but Israel's rejection of the gospel and Paul's agonizing but hopeful prophecy of Israel's destiny. Any comments about Israel must take into account the optimistic conclusion of this section (11:25–36).

Romans 10:1–17 focuses on Israel's predicament. Its rejection of the Messiah stems not from its lack of religious zeal but from its failure to grasp that the Torah points to Christ, the Torah's very goal and completion (10:4). Its ignorance of this peculiar expression of divine grace ("the righteousness that comes from God") leaves Israel futilely seeking to initiate a relationship with God on its own (10:3).

Then the text underscores the affirmation of 10:4 by declaring that the Torah (in this case Deut. 30:12–14) really witnesses to Christ (10:6–10). With a midrashic form of exegesis, the case is made that Christ's coming and his inclusion of non-Jews as well as Jews into the community of the "saved" does not represent a change in God's intentions, a plan B that goes into effect when plan A won't work. Rather, in Jesus, God is faithful to the original promise made to Israel. The message that is near to Israel in the Torah is the same as the message that is near now in the gospel. Deuteronomy 30:14 (cited in Rom. 10:8a) finds its fulfillment in the two confessions of Rom. 10:9—Jesus is Lord and God raised him from the dead. (Interestingly, the link is made by correlating three terms—"word," "lips," and "heart"). Whereas the Jews saw in the Torah an instrument by which to justify themselves before God, Paul sees in it a pointer to Christ, in whom God fulfills the promise.

Verses 11–13 draw out three further implications of God's action in Christ—believers can count on God ("No one . . . will be put to shame"); Jews and non-Jews are brought together in the community of the "saved" on the same footing; and the acceptance of both is rooted in the amazing generosity of God.

What does the preacher do with this passage? Its complexity threatens its use. There are at least three directions in which one might move with a sermon during Lent. First, there is the basic recitation of what we believe—Jesus is Lord, and God is the one who raised him from the dead. These two creeds fill out Israel's otherwise unfinished story (found in Deut. 26:1–11) and show God as faithful to the promises made. Both creeds also carry challenging overtones. Other pretenders to lordship are excluded; other answers to the riddle of death are rejected.

Second, the text provides an opportunity to reaffirm the basic Pauline message of grace, to say again that our relationship to God is rooted in the divine benevolence and not in our self-sufficiency. It is often here that the Jews are mistakenly used as a foil against which to contrast grace, as if they knew (and know) nothing of God's mercy. Such a notion grossly distorts the plight of the Jews and often leaves Christians somehow feeling superior simply because they are not Jews. Paul is sensitive to the temptation and later warns his Gentile readers about becoming proud in their situation vis-à-vis Israel (11:17–20). Grace is meant to evoke awe, not arrogance.

Third, the text invites us to reaffirm the breadth and inclusiveness of God's people (10:12–13). Throughout Romans, pride of place has gone to the Jew (1:16; 9:4–5), but ultimately grace makes all sinners equal: "There is no distinction," "the same Lord is Lord of all," "everyone who calls on the name of the Lord shall be saved." The chosen people are defined no longer in terms of the torah, but in terms of Christ.

On the one hand, we rejoice at such inclusiveness. As outsiders we are brought into God's family and made full participants. On the other hand, we sometimes wonder at God's decision to be gracious to so many. Like Jonah pouting over the inclusion of the Ninevites and the elder son offended at his father's generosity to his prodigal brother, we find grace puzzling, if not offensive. Our reaction unfortunately exposes our failure to comprehend the richness of God's mercy.

So in struggling in Rom. 9—11 with the situation of his kinfolk, Paul presents us with the ABCs of our faith, more than enough for our Lenten reflection.

## Luke 4:1–13

As provocative and uncomfortable as the notion may be to contemporary Christians, early Christian traditions maintain that Jesus was subject to temptation. Various strands within the New Testament reflect such awareness. Mark's Gospel contains only a brief note about Jesus being "tempted by Satan" (Mark 1:13), with Luke and Matthew expanding on that note from their common traditions (Matt. 4:1–11; Luke 4:1–13). The author of the Fourth Gospel does not include stories such as these, but even there we find some awareness of Jesus' temptation (see, for example, John 12:27–28). The author of Hebrews explicitly speaks of Jesus' temptation (2:14–18; 4:15). Where did such convictions about Jesus come from, and what prompted Christians to tell them again and again? These historical questions are fascinating, but they are nonetheless unanswerable. What is more significant, particularly for the task of proclamation, is how different writers make use of the temptation tradition.

Luke closely connects the temptation of Jesus with his identity as Son of God. From the beginning, Luke's Gospel has established that title for Jesus. Gabriel announces to Mary that her child will be called

"Son of God" (1:35). At Jesus' baptism, the heavenly voice announces, "You are my Son, the Beloved; with you I am well pleased"
(3:22). The genealogy, which immediately follows the baptism,
culminates with the disclosure that Jesus is "son of Adam, son of
God" (3:38). The temptation scene serves, then, to raise significant
questions about what it means to be called God's Son (4:3, 9). What
precisely is to be the nature of Jesus' Sonship?

Each of the three scenes in 4:1–13 suggests an interpretation of
Jesus' Sonship, and in each Jesus rejects that interpretation. While
the three temptations may also be said to have a kind of universal
pertinence (and, thus, they would make sense to a Gentile Christian
audience), each has a particular currency in the life of Israel.

First, the devil suggests to the famished Jesus that he make bread
from the stone around him. A private act, this would provide for
only Jesus' need and do no harm to anyone. Why not use his
considerable power in this way? The response ("One does not live
by bread alone," v. 4) makes little sense unless its biblical context is
recalled. In Deut. 8:3, from which this saying comes, Moses is
recalling for the people of Israel their sojourn in the wilderness and,
in particular, God's gift of manna. Moses explains that their hunger
and God's gift of manna took place because "one does not live by
bread alone, but by every word that comes from the mouth of the
LORD." Israel's need for bread was secondary to Israel's need to
understand that God alone gives bread. Jesus, because he understands that fact, can resist the temptation to take matters into his
own hands.

The second temptation, that to political power, is likewise one
that would make sense to any reader; who has not, at one time or
another, wished for some such might? In the context of Israel's
history, however, a particular set of concerns about power are
evoked by this scene. Israel's desire to be like its neighbors—to
worship their gods, to have a king such as their kings—lies close to
hand. Jesus replies to the devil by quoting Deut. 6:13 (see also Deut.
10:20), which not only rejects the devil's demand for worship of
himself, but simultaneously insists that the only real power comes
from God.

The temptations reach their peak in Luke 4:9–13. Here the pinnacle of the Jerusalem Temple serves as the locus of temptation. Given
the way in which Luke centers his story in Jerusalem, and Luke's
interest in the Temple, already we know that something especially
important is about to occur. This time, when the devil speaks, he
uses scripture itself to buttress his suggestion. If Jesus is God's Son,
then he can force God to prove it and protect him, just as Ps. 91

suggests will be the case. For the third time, Jesus responds with words of scripture taken from Deuteronomy. In this instance, Deut. 6:16 recalls Moses' warning that God should not be tested, as Israel had tested God in the past.

At the end of these three temptations, Luke explains that the devil "departed from him until an opportune time" (v. 13). Since neither Matthew nor Mark refers to "an opportune time," some interpreters argue that Luke sees Jesus' ministry as a time when the devil's work is suspended. The devil cannot operate in Jesus' presence. That surely reads too much into this comment, for Jesus' ministry continues to be marked by struggle with the devil, as manifested in disease and demonic possession.

What does it mean to say that Jesus is God's Son? Luke answers that question here in a negative way. Jesus is not the kind of child Israel proved to be. Israel thought it needed only bread; Israel succumbed to the temptation of idolatry; Israel indeed tested God. Jesus is not that kind of Son. Jesus understands that God alone is God.

What Jesus' Sonship means, put positively, will emerge in the second half of chapter 4 of Luke, as Jesus begins to preach and as Jesus begins to heal. For now, it is enough to understand that being God's Son does not mean seeking power for oneself. It means, by contrast, acknowledging the oneness and otherness of God.

# SECOND SUNDAY IN LENT

"Things are not always what they seem." That conventional wisdom, modified slightly to "things are *never* what they seem," characterizes much of the history of Israel. The impossibility of Israel's release from the overwhelming power of Egypt is only apparent, for the reality is that God will render Egypt powerless and Israel free. The apparent unsuitability of David, the youngest of Jesse's sons, yields to God's decision that he indeed is the one to rule over Israel. Jesus' apparently insignificant and, in fact, ignominious birth belies the reality that he is the true king of Israel.

That same contradiction between appearance and reality runs through three of the readings for this Sunday. Hearing God's assurance of protection, Abraham seizes the moment to remind God that he and Sarah are childless. They may have God as their "shield," but there is little evidence that they will have any posterity. Hearing God's promise once again, Abraham believes (Gen. 15:6), but he believes in the face of all the evidence.

Paul often struggles to articulate the difference between what can be seen with the eyes and the reality that can be seen only by faith. In Phil. 3:20, he employs the powerful language of citizenship to explain that Christians live as citizens of another realm. That notion has given rise to many problematic conclusions, but it acknowledges a fundamental truth, namely, that believers live out of an allegiance that cannot be witnessed with ordinary vision.

"Herod wants to kill you," Jesus is warned (Luke 13:31). Whether it is Herod or the Pharisees who want to kill Jesus remains a complicated question, but the contradiction here is that Jesus' death will not prove an end to the threat he poses to either Roman or religious authority. In addition, the Jerusalem that awaits Jesus (v. 35) will also become the Jerusalem that is determined to destroy him.

If Ps. 27 does not so clearly distinguish between appearance and reality, it is because the psalmist knows on whose side reality lies.

199

The psalmist celebrates even those who appear bent on his destruction, for he knows that God's protection will deliver him. He anticipates a time when things will appear the way they actually are, that is, when he will live in God's very presence.

## Genesis 15:1–12, 17–18

The frequently perceived distance between what God has promised and what human beings are experiencing lies at the heart of this text's concern. Although the passage as we have it is presumably the work of the Yahwist, there are elements within that point to the hoary antiquity of the story and that suggest a long period of transmission before reaching the hands of Israel's first great historian.

No sooner has the book of Genesis introduced the persons of Abraham and Sarah (Abram and Sarai, initially) than it records Yahweh's promise to this first family of Israel. "Go from your country . . ." (Gen. 12:1) is immediately followed by "I will make of you a great nation" (12:2), words by which the reader is clearly informed that this journey is to be like no other of the countless folk migrations of human history. Yahweh is summoning Abraham and Sarah to a new life, in order that all of humankind may experience renewal and deliverance from sin. "In you all the families . . . shall be blessed" (12:3) has in mind the depressing cycle of sin and suffering represented by the previous stories of Abel's murder (Gen. 4), of widespread sexual license (Gen. 6:1–4), and of the enormous hubris of the human family (Gen. 11:1–9). Things must change, or Yahweh will simply not be able to tolerate these miserable humans whom Yahweh has created.

The vehicle of this change is to be the family of Abraham and Sarah. They are to become a "great nation" not for purposes of grandeur or political power, but in order that they may "be a blessing" (Gen. 12:2). But, in the chronology of today's text, all of that was some time ago. Abraham and Sarah have not only traveled to Canaan, but have even spent some time in Egypt, where Sarah narrowly escapes with her virtue intact and where Abraham loses much of his (12:10–20). There is a quarrel within the extended family, which results in a separation between Abraham and his nephew Lot (13:2–18), after which Abraham is drawn into a bloody conflict involving major principalities of southern Palestine (ch. 14). Perhaps most threatening of all is the reality that Abraham and Sarah have no children. How can this family, which seems to be subject to all the perils of life in a dangerous age, become a "great nation" or a "blessing" to others when it does not appear that it will last into the next generation?

Thus, when the swords are laid down after the fighting of Gen. 14, and Yahweh renews his promise to the chosen family by recourse to a military metaphor ("I am your shield," 15:1), Abraham quite logically questions the sincerity of Yahweh's intentions and wants to know, "O [Yahweh] GOD, what will you give me?" in view of the fact that Sarah and he have no child (15:2).

Yahweh's response is the striking of a covenant by which Yahweh's very honor is pledged to the fulfillment of the divine vow. We do not know the meaning of the symbolism involving the split carcasses (even less why the birds are treated differently from the quadrupeds, v. 10, or why the flames are passed between the animal parts, v. 17), but scholars suspect that this liturgy enshrines a distant memory concerning the making of treaties and agreements among ancient Near Eastern peoples. Perhaps a threat was implied when this ritual was first devised that, should the weaker party violate the treaty, its people could expect to be carved up like the animals. Almost certainly the liturgy that is described here is somehow related to the fact that the Hebrew verb usually employed in the phrase "make a covenant" (see v. 18) literally means "cut a covenant."

In any event, Yahweh is here clearly pledging Yahweh's divine person to Abraham as a means of instilling confidence that Yahweh's promise will be fulfilled. (For another account of Yahweh's covenant with Abraham and Sarah, see Gen. 17.) Even before participating in the covenant ritual, however, Abraham expresses his trust in Yahweh, and Yahweh affirms that, come what may, there will always be a right relationship ("righteousness") between the two of them (15:6).

Ultimately, Yahweh will provide Abraham and Sarah with a son (Gen. 21:1–2), and the concern that Abraham expresses at the beginning of this text will be met. Before that time, however, Abraham and Sarah will undergo other adventures that will appear, at least, often to threaten Yahweh's promise. The faith of the first family will waver (Gen. 16:1–6), but the reader knows that Yahweh's commitment to them and to the promise will be as strong as ever. The reader will also know that the distance between what God has promised and the realities that human beings experience lies more in human perception than in fact.

This is not to belittle those genuine moments of terror when

women and men are so impressed with the absence of God that not
even their most sincere petitions bring any results (Ps. 22:1; Mark
15:34). Nevertheless, the witness of the scriptures is that the God of
mercy and grace will have the last word in our affairs. Our challenge, like that of Abraham and Sarah, is to believe that this will be
so, in spite of frequent and impressive evidence that would suggest
the contrary.

## Psalm 27

Like Ps. 91 for the First Sunday in Lent, Ps. 27 is a remarkable
affirmation of trust in Yahweh. It begins with an extended profession of faith in vs. 1–6, which speaks of Yahweh in the third person.
The shift to second-person references to Yahweh in v. 7 signals the
beginning of a prayer for help. Many commentators treat 27:1–6 and
27:7–14 as two separate psalms; however, the verbal links between
them suggest their unity (see "salvation" in vs. 1 and 9; "adversaries" in vs. 2 and 12; "heart" in vs. 3, 8, 14; "rise up"/"risen against"
in vs. 3 and 12; "seek" in vs. 4 and 8; "life"/"living" in vs. 1, 4, 13).
There is a conceptual unity as well. The profound profession of faith
serves as the basis for the prayer in vs. 7–12 and the concluding
testimony in vs. 13–14. The sequence is instructive. Faith in God does
not eliminate difficulties, but rather equips God's servants (see v. 9)
to live with courage and hope (see vs. 13–14) in the midst of
difficulties.

The familiar opening verse summarizes the message of the entire
psalm. The similarity between the Hebrew words translated "my
light" and "shall I fear" emphasizes the contrasting alternatives that
are open to the psalmist—fear or faith (see the same contrast in Mark
5:36). The psalmists elsewhere pray for or celebrate the light of God's
face or countenance (Pss. 4:6; 24:6; 31:16; 44:3; 67:1; 80:3, 7, 19; 89:15;
see Num. 6:25). When this psalmist begins the actual prayer, he or
she is determined to "seek [God's] face" (Ps. 27:8–9). In short, the
psalmist professes to others (v. 1) and to God (vs. 8–9) that his or her
life will be lived in God's presence. To profess Yahweh as "my
salvation" (see, for example, Ex. 15:2; Pss. 18:2; 24:5; 25:5; 95:1) and
"my stronghold" (see NRSV "refuge" in Pss. 28:8; 31:2, 4; 37:39; 43:2)
reinforces the conviction: the psalmist's life derives from and is
sustained by God.

It is this faith that casts out fear, even amid the kind of circumstances that are described in Ps. 27:2–3, which H.-J. Kraus suggests
"portray the worst threats to life" (*Psalms 1—59*, trans. H. C.

Oswald; Minneapolis: Augsburg, 1988, p. 334). The two alternatives are presented again in v. 3: the psalmist "shall not fear" but rather "will be confident" (this Hebrew root is often translated in NRSV as "trust"). The psalmist's single-mindedness is clear in v. 4: "one thing" does she or he "seek" (compare v. 8). Verses 4–6 may indicate that the psalm was originally used by someone seeking asylum in the Temple from persecutors (compare vs. 2–3, 12); however, the language need not be taken literally. What the psalmist fundamentally seeks is the experience of God's presence. That experience will be the psalmist's protection (vs. 5–6a; see also Pss. 23:6; 31:20), and the psalmist's response will be gratitude, joy, and praise (v. 6bc).

The occurrence of "my heart" and the twofold occurrence of "seek" in v. 8 links the prayer for help with the preceding profession of faith (see vs. 3–4). As suggested in vs. 4–6, the psalmist seeks God's presence, represented by the threefold occurrence of "face" in vs. 8–9. The psalmist's resolve to seek God's face is striking in view of the tradition that one could not see God's face and live (see Ex. 33:20), but it effectively expresses the intimacy of communion with God that the psalmist desires. Psalm 27:9 begins a series of seven imperatives, all of which ask God to be actively present. Verse 10 interrupts the series with another affirmation of trust. Even when forsaken by the closest of kin, a dire threat to life in ancient cultures, the psalmist can count on God to "take me up" (see Isa. 40:11, NRSV "gather"). The request in Ps. 27:11, "Teach me your way," is reminiscent of Ps. 1 and its claim that happiness belongs to those who are constantly open to God's instruction (1:2, NRSV "law"; "instruction" and "teach" are from the same Hebrew root). Such happiness involves not freedom from trouble and threat (see Ps. 27:12), but rather a solid foundation of faith to endure trouble and threat. As Kraus suggests, v. 11 "pleads for the opening of a new possibility for life" (Psalms 1—59, p. 336).

The psalmist's openness to God's teaching suggests that she or he lives by faith and by what is always inseparable from faith, hope (see Rom. 8:24–25; Heb. 11:1). Verses 13–14 of Ps. 27 effectively communicates the psalmist's faith ("I believe," v. 13) and hope ("Wait for the LORD," v. 14). Verse 13 recalls the profession of faith in vs. 1–6; the psalmist entrusts her or his life and future to God. The psalmist's witness is made publicly. The psalmist had earlier made it clear that "my heart shall not fear" (v. 3; compare v. 8). Now she or he exhorts others to "let your heart take courage" (v. 14). Verse 14 invites others to join the psalmist in a community of faith, hope, and courage. To live in God's presence means ultimately that we live also among God's people as an eschatological community. We "wait for the

LORD" (v. 14), but our waiting contains *already* (see "now" in v. 6) the possibility of strength and courage.

Psalm 27 is reminiscent of the concluding chapter of the book of Micah. The prophet is surrounded by violence and oppression, including the inability to trust the closest of kin (Micah 7:1–6; compare Ps. 27:10). His response is to "wait for the God of my salvation" (Micah 7:7; compare Ps. 27:9, 14), whom he describes as "a light to me" (Micah 7:8; compare Ps. 27:1). Amid the inhumaneness, brutality, and greed of our culture, Micah 7 joins Ps. 27 in inviting us to seek light, life, strength, courage, and direction in God.

## Philippians 3:17–4:1

In the spirit of Lent we continue this Sunday with an Epistle reading that is definitional in character. It offers an image of the people of God from early Christian days powerful enough to spark reflection about who we are today and what it means to live in a post-Constantinian age. The church in North America has certainly not thought of itself in a long time as a commonwealth of heaven, a community of resident aliens, but the disestablishment of Christianity in the late twentieth century makes such a reflection more urgent than it has been. The fundamental question is: What gives the Christian community its distinctiveness in relation to the broader culture?

The lesson (Phil. 3:17–4:1) begins with an unabashed invitation from Paul to the readers to join in imitating him and others like him. Before we too quickly accuse the apostle of arrogance, we need to keep in mind the historical and social circumstances of the early church, which demanded mentors and models as a means for discerning life's directions. Furthermore, before pointing to himself Paul has set before his readers three other such models—Jesus Christ (2:5–11), Timothy (2:19–24), and Epaphroditus (2:25–30). Each receives more detailed commendation and more explicit description than does Paul.

The group against which Paul sets himself (and later the readers) is identified as "enemies of the cross of Christ" (3:18). Their ideology and behavior have aligned them in opposition to the self-giving obedience (2:8) and sufferings (3:10) connected with the death of Jesus. We might be helped if we could make more of Paul's allusion to this group—what they were advocating and what made them tick—but 3:19 is too broad and vague to warrant specific description.

For example, does the statement "Their god is the belly" imply an antinomian hedonism or a scrupulous keeping of food laws? Are these people the same group earlier called "the dogs . . . the evil workers . . . those who mutilate the flesh" (3:2)? It is hard to tell. What matters most is that the cross of Christ, with its scandal and ignominy, is established as the decisive norm, a reality that people either embrace and live by or find offensive and reject (or ignore). The choice, then, is between the model established by Paul or that embodied by the "enemies of the cross."

The "but" (*gar*) in 3:20 also sets the Philippian readers in contrast to the "enemies of the cross." Though living on earth, they do not set their minds on "earthly things," as the "enemies of the cross" do, but take their marching orders from elsewhere. "Our citizenship is in heaven" (3:20). The imagery comes straight out of the ancient context. Citizens of Rome often went to live and work in far distant places in the empire, but they always kept their names on the registry of the capital city. No matter what their mailing address, their identity came from Rome.

The church, then, is to cherish an identity that comes from outside itself, from heaven. It lives by a vision and from a source that is unworldly. Inevitably its style of life will come across as strange, awkward, and at times even ludicrous. To some, the church may appear quaint, its language dated, its dreams unrealistic. To others, it may seem threatening, subversive, anti-American. The church marches to a different drumbeat. Its system of values appears alien and does not always add up.

To use the word "heaven" like this, however, makes some people nervous. They fear that the church will become so otherworldly that it will be of no earthly use. Whether this is a justifiable fear, or whether the greater danger lies in the church's absorption into the culture, is a matter of debate. In any case, the text gives no warrant for a pie-in-the-sky religiosity. There is no promised flight from this world and its dilemmas, no thought that death is an escape hatch from unsolvable problems. The hope rather lies in a Savior, who will come *from* heaven *to* earth, who will transform earthly existence and make it conform to the divine glory. Though its marching orders come from elsewhere, the church's life is clearly rooted in the soil and shifting sands of this world, with its social turmoil and personal anguish.

The text, no doubt ironically, declares that a thoroughly earthly preoccupation ends in destruction, whereas a heavenly identity anticipates a transformation of the world and results in a "stand[ing] firm in the Lord" (4:1).

## Luke 13:31–35

The familiar Lukan motif of necessity figures prominently in this brief and enigmatic passage. Jesus refers to the necessity of his own work with the phrase "I *must* be on my way" (*dei*, literally, "it is necessary," 13:33; emphasis added) that he elsewhere uses to characterize the divine plan (for example, Luke 24:7, 44; Acts 1:22). He speaks of the impossibility that a prophet of Israel should die outside of Jerusalem (v. 33), suggesting both the necessity of his own death and the necessity of Jerusalem's involvement in that death. The solemn character of v. 35 implies the further necessity of judgment on Jerusalem for its treatment of this prophet.

Exactly who initiates this episode remains somewhat unclear. The Pharisees warn Jesus to leave the area because Herod wants to kill him. Pointing to Luke's positive treatment of the Pharisees relative to that of Mark and Matthew, some interpreters conclude that this report by the Pharisees should be taken at face value; that is, the Pharisees are neutral concerning Jesus and make their report in order to protect him from the cruelty of Herod. Other interpreters, pointing to Herod's curiosity regarding Jesus and emphasizing the belligerent character of the Pharisees' encounters with Jesus, insist that the Pharisees' report is merely a strategy for ridding themselves of Jesus' troublesome presence.

For the purposes of preaching this passage, resolving this dispute is not particularly urgent, although it may be helpful to bear the two possibilities in mind. What is important is the phrase "at that very hour" at the beginning of v. 31 and its reference back to Jesus' sayings in vs. 22–30. Jesus' ministry signals the overthrow of those who are regarded as "first." Whether Herod or the Pharisees, the holders of the "first" seats will surely react vehemently to this word.

The warning of the Pharisees may be genuine or deceitful, but Jesus' response essentially dismisses it in any case. He announces that his work of casting out demons and healing people will continue "today and tomorrow," and then "on the third day" he will complete his work. Whatever the Pharisees or Herod might have planned for Jesus, those plans will fail because his own plans (or God's) have priority. The time references here suggest not specific amounts of time, but its shortness. It is only for a brief while that Jesus can continue with healing and exorcising. A Christian reader will surely hear in the reference to the third day the day of Jesus' resurrection, although here that third day probably refers more generally to both the death and resurrection of Jesus.

Not only does Jesus' work continue, but also the place and agent of successful opposition to Jesus will not be determined by Herod or by the Pharisees, but by Jerusalem itself. Jesus will not be overpowered in Herod's Galilee, but in Jerusalem. Here Jesus conjures up the history of Jerusalem and its treatment of the prophetic figures of Israel's past. For example, Jer. 26:20–23 recalls the fate of Uriah, who "prophesied against this city" and was put to death. Jeremiah himself is threatened for speaking prophetically in Jerusalem (Jer. 38:4–6). In addition to looking to the past, however, Jesus' words anticipate both his own rejection by Jerusalem and that which will await his witnesses. Stephen explicitly refers to Israel's treatment of its prophets (Acts 7:52), and later on Paul must defend himself in Jerusalem. Ironically, tragically, the city that houses God's Temple also houses a persistent refusal to hear God's word.

The word of judgment against that city and its people sounds clearly in this passage: "Your house is left to you" (Luke 13:35). Understated though this saying may be, its implications are chilling. Jerusalem is handed over to its own devices, which means that Jerusalem cannot stand. The "house" here may refer to the Temple itself or to the people of Jerusalem, but in either case the implication is clear. Similar sayings in the Hebrew Bible call to mind the desolation of the city without God's protection (see, for example, 1 Kings 9:7–8; Ps. 69:25–26; Jer. 12:7; 22:5).

Over against this word of judgment stands Jesus' poignant lament: "How often have I desired to gather your children together as a hen gathers her brood under her wings, and you were not willing!" Here Jesus applies to himself imagery of protection that the Hebrew Bible often applies to God. Deuteronomy 32:11 describes God's guidance as that which an eagle gives to its young (as it "hovers over its young; as it spreads its wings"; compare Ruth 2:12; Ps. 17:8; 36:7; 91:4; Isa. 31:5). Neither God nor God's Son may be likened to the fox that preys on the young of others, but rather to the hen who gently cares for her young.

The passage closes with the ironic note that Jerusalem will indeed see Jesus on the day "when you say, 'Blessed is the one who comes in the name of the Lord' " (Luke 13:35). This quote from Ps. 118:26 appears in slightly altered form again in Luke 19:38, when Jesus does enter Jerusalem to the accolades of the crowds. There also the Pharisees warn Jesus to stop the reaction of the crowd, and there Jesus weeps over Jerusalem and its fate.

In the early sermons of Acts, Christians proclaim *both* that those dwelling in Jerusalem were responsible for the death of Jesus *and* that even that action was part of God's plan (see Acts 3:14–15, 17–18). That theme is anticipated even here, for Jerusalem is responsible for its action against Jesus, and yet that action is part of the larger divine necessity that propels Jesus toward Jerusalem (Luke 13:32–33).

(For comments on the alternative reading for this Sunday, Luke 9:28–36, see earlier, under Transfiguration Sunday.)

# THIRD SUNDAY IN LENT

Lent is not concerned only with long faces. To be sure, the need for introspection and repentance looms large during this season of the church year, and should the community or the individual neglect that aspect of the gospel, a very significant omission would indeed occur. Yet there is also room for joy, as the Old Testament lection for this day, Isa. 55:1–9, reminds us. The joy that issues from this text is generated by the prophet's realization that God's mercy is close at hand, that it is freely available to any who will draw on it. The image of the banquet is raised, and God's mercy is compared to wine and milk that one may purchase "without money and without price" (55:1). Yet it will not be forced on the person or the community; one must come for it. The imperative "Seek the LORD" strikes a note of repentance and decision that provides a link with other passages for this day.

Psalm 63:1–8 is similar in mood to the Isaiah passage, although somewhat more restrained. Instead of a lavish banquet, the initial image is that of a traveler in a desert land who longs for a precious drink of water (v. 1). The implication is that the thirst will be slaked, and so the psalmist expresses a strong confidence in God, praising God for past outpourings of mercy. Then (v. 5) the longing for sustenance is transformed into a "rich feast," which satisfies the innermost being of the psalmist. So renewed is the psalmist by this encounter with God's grace that God's presence permeates even the night hours. Then exuberance gushes forth, and the psalmist lifts a note of praise: "I sing for joy" (v. 7).

The Lenten themes of self-examination and renewal are addressed quite directly in 1 Cor. 10:1–13. Paul views the lives of his fellow Christians in Corinth against the background of ancient Israel's experiences of exodus and wilderness wanderings. The element the apostle highlights is the continuing sinfulness of the people of old, even in the face of such a momentous outpouring of

God's grace. They engaged in idolatry, sexual immorality, putting Christ to the text, and complaining, and the Corinthian believers are exhorted to learn from the example of these Israelites, lest they too be judged by God. Paul balances the warning with a promise: God's grace is active, even in times of greatest pressure to forsake God's calling.

The series of Lukan readings continues with 13:1–9, the theme of which is the urgent need for repentance. In the first section, vs. 1–5, two negative examples of sudden death are drawn by Jesus from contemporary life as a way of stressing the precariousness of the human state. Because health and well-being may be ended in the twinkling of an eye, one needs to consider the state of one's relationship with God. In the second section, vs. 6–9, a parable concerning a fruitless fig tree becomes for Jesus another vehicle for stressing the need for repentance. Yet the cameo portrait of the patient, forbearing gardener stands as a reminder of the grace of God.

## Isaiah 55:1–9

For expressions of sheer, unmitigated joy there are few parts of the Old Testament that equal the "book" of the Second Isaiah (Isa. 40—55). Although the prophet recognizes that the people are in exile because of their sin, he (or perhaps she) insists that that sin is now a thing of the past (40:1–2) and that Yahweh, the God of Israel and of all creation, is about to do a new and liberating thing in the life of the people Israel and, indeed, in the life of the world (42:5–9). To obtain a model of Yahweh's impending work of salvation, one must go all the way back to the exodus from Egypt (43:2; 44:27), or perhaps even to creation itself (44:24). And because of the staggeringly good thing that is about to happen as a result of Yahweh's grace, the people and the very world of nature are to rejoice (40:4–5).

This mood of wonderment and ecstasy reaches a climax in chapter 55, vs. 1–9 of which constitute the Old Testament lection for this day. (For a discussion of 55:10–13, see the Eighth Sunday After Epiphany.) Throughout most of this passage the speaker is none other than Yahweh, although at one point (vs. 6–7) the prophet interjects himself to admonish the people on Yahweh's behalf. The reason for the joy that resonates through these lines is quite clear: Israel's God is a God of mercy and grace. "He's got the whole world in his hands," and the future of all humankind is one of justice and peace under Yahweh's sovereign rule.

Verses 1 and 2 are an invitation to feast on God's amazing love. It is possible that the prophet had Prov. 9:5–6 in mind, for this metaphor is strikingly similar to the one found there. (This text also calls to mind Jesus' parable of the banquet in Luke 14:15–24.) Why should one waste one's precious resources on things that do not satisfy or sustain life? Israel's gracious God has flung wide the door of the banquet hall and is insisting that all who eat at the tables there do so without cost to themselves. Not only this, but the food that stands waiting is "good" and "rich," in that it is capable of sustaining life and hope. If these verses sound as though they were written with today's homeless men and women in mind (and with the church's obligation to such people also in mind), that may not be coincidental. For the dispossessed Jewish exiles in Babylon there must have been many lean years (literally speaking), so that the metaphor of a banquet of free, wholesome food must have been particularly striking. God's unequivocal intention is that the people be fed, and that joy and hope flourish!

The attention given to the figure of David in vs. 3–5 is quite interesting, in light of the fact that the political power of the Davidic dynasty was now in shambles. Also, unlike the great Isaiah of Jerusalem, whose prophetic activity is central to the first part of the book that bears his name (Isa. 1—39), the Second Isaiah shows very little interest in a messianic future. Here, however, the person of David is used to define God's relationship to the people not only in the past, but also in the future. The "everlasting covenant" of 55:3, "my steadfast, sure love for David," resonates to 2 Sam. 7:1–17 and points to the reaffirmation of the Davidic family as the special vehicle through which God's grace will be bestowed on Israel and, as Isa. 55:5 makes clear, on all humankind.

In the days to come, both the prophet Haggai (Hag. 2:20–23) and the prophet Zechariah (Zech. 6:9–14) will reaffirm Israel's Davidic expectations, but those hopes seem to have something of a political cast to them, probably the yearning to set the Davidic crown on the head of the leader Zerubbabel. It is evident here that this is not a political statement, but a theological one. Yahweh will reaffirm the Davidic ruler as the special instrument of Yahweh's saving love, and that love will be invested not just in Israel, but in the "nations," even "nations that do not know" Israel. (One may wish to compare the universalism here with similar expressions in Isa. 42:6–7; 49:6.)

The prophet steps forward at this point, 55:6–7, to speak to the people (notice how Yahweh is referred to in the third person). The implication is that there is a crucial significance to the present moment in the life of the people, a moment that may not continue indefinitely. "Seek the LORD while he may be found" suggests urgency, suggests *carpe diem*. The time is ripe for repentance and for restoration; to delay would be a serious mistake. As for Yahweh, "he will abundantly pardon." There is no uncertainty here about Yahweh's openness; the only question concerns the people's readiness to be restored.

Yahweh's self-description finalizes the text (vs. 8–9). If women and men find the riddles of life not completely solvable, they should not be distracted from Yahweh's loving purposes. The plain truth of the matter is that God so transcends the normal patterns of human thought and understanding that an enormous gulf will always remain. The distance between God and humankind is not a matter of the heart, but only a matter of the intellect. We can never completely understand God or the ways of God, but in the end that does not matter. What we can understand and respond to is the love of God. What we can incorporate in our own lives is the compassion of the God who brought Israel out of Egypt and out of exile, the God whose Son died and rose again. That is the central message of this text.

## Psalm 63:1–8

Psalm 63 was used in the early church as a morning psalm, due in part to the references in v. 6, as well as to the fact that the verb translated "seek" in v. 1 seems to have meant originally "to look for dawn." Scholars offer a variety of proposals for categorizing Ps. 63: song of praise, song of thanksgiving, lament of the individual, psalm of trust, royal psalm (note the mention of "the king" in v. 11), and psalm for a night vigil (see v. 6). More important than categorization and possible original setting, however, is the psalmist's claim that his or her life depends on God. As in Ps. 27 for the Second Sunday in Lent, the psalmist seeks the experience of God's presence (Ps. 63:1; see 27:4, 8–9; the Hebrew verbs translated "seek" in Pss. 27 and 63 are different, but essentially synonymous); and this experience is described in terms of seeing God in God's sanctuary or Temple (see "beholding" in 63:2 and "behold" in 27:4).

That Ps. 63 is fundamentally about life and its true source is suggested by the fourfold occurrence of the Hebrew word *nepes*, which NRSV translates as "soul," in vs. 1, 5, and 8 and as "life" in v. 9. The word means fundamentally vitality, life, being. The psalmist's life is threatened (v. 9), but he or she finds sustenance, satisfaction, and security in the experience of God's presence. "Soul" or "life" is the key word in Ps. 63, and the occurrences in vs. 1, 5, and 9 mark the beginning of the three major sections of the psalm.

The psalmist's need is expressed in terms of thirst in v. 1, a need that he or she addresses by looking on God (v. 2; see Ps. 42:2, where also the psalmist's "soul thirsts," and where the expressed solution is to "behold the face of God"; compare Ps. 27:8–9) and beholding God's "power and glory." "Power" and "glory" are elsewhere associated with God's sovereignty (see Ps. 29:1 where the two also occur together, but where NRSV translates "strength" instead of "power"). In effect, the psalmist entrusts himself or herself to God's rule. This dependence on God is expressed in a remarkable way in 63:3. "Steadfast love" is at the heart of God's character as a forgiving and redeeming God (see Ex. 15:13; 34:6–7). God's "steadfast love is better than life" in the sense that human life depends on God's faithfulness. But perhaps even more is meant in Ps. 63:3. As James L. Mays suggests, "Trust becomes for a moment pure adoration that leaves the self behind as any participant in the reason for adoration. . . . This verse leads us in prayer to the point of devotion to God alone that must be the goal of all true faith" (*Psalms*, Interpretation series; Louisville, Ky.: John Knox Press, 1994). For the psalmist, praise becomes a way of life, a lifelong vocation (v. 4). The psalmist's "chief end is to glorify God" (see the first question and answer of the Westminster Shorter Catechism), in response to God's faithful love that makes life possible.

Whereas thirst symbolized the psalmist's need in v. 1, it is hunger in v. 5. The psalmist's being is "satisfied," and again the response is praise. "Mouth" and "lips," organs used in eating, become instruments of praise. This time the experience of God's presence is not linked directly with the Temple as in v. 2, but rather comes during the night as the psalmist thinks and meditates "on my bed" (v. 6; some scholars contend, however, that the psalmist is spending the night in the Temple to await an answer from God). Apparently, the psalmist remembers (the phrase "think of" in v. 6 means more literally to remember) past experiences of deliverance that demonstrated that God was "my help" (see Ps. 27:9). Again in 63:7, the response to God's presence ("shadow of your wings"; see Pss. 17:8; 36:7; 57:1) and activity involves an act of praise. Psalm 63:8 indicates the closeness and intimacy of the psalmist's relationship to God (see "clings" in Gen. 2:24), as well as reiterating the psalmist's dependence on God (see "uphold" in Isa. 42:1).

Although not a part of the lection, verses 9–11 of Ps. 63 provide closure for the psalm. It should be noted that as one whose life is sought by enemies (v. 9), the psalmist is in good company—Moses (Ex. 4:19), David (1 Sam. 20:1; 22:13; 23:15; 2 Sam. 4:8; 16:11), Elijah (1 Kings 19:10, 14), and Jeremiah (Jer. 11:21) in the Old Testament, and Jesus in the New Testament. The superscription of Ps. 63 even invites the hearing of the psalm in conjunction with the stories of David in the wilderness when he was in flight from either Saul or Absalom. In David's case and the others as well, the one threatened with death is given life. So also is the case in Ps. 63. The psalmist finds life by clinging to God (v. 8), while the enemies "go down" to a realm cut off from God's presence (v. 9). The psalmist is satisfied as if having eaten "a rich feast" (v. 5), whereas the enemies are eaten by jackals (v. 10).

The repetition of the word "mouth(s)" in vs. 5 and 11 is significant. The mouths of the enemies "will be stopped" (v. 11), whereas the "mouth" of the psalmist is open in joyful praise. The open mouth seems to summarize the psalmist's orientation throughout the psalm—thirsting for God, hungering for God, praising God, praying to God. The open mouth symbolizes openness to God. The psalmist seeks God and lives. In contrast, the enemies seek not God but the life of their neighbor (v. 9; compare v. 1). Their mouths are closed (v. 11). They are left unable to praise, incapable of being satisfied, unable to live. To be closed to God is death. Psalm 63 presents the psalmist as a model of those who, in Jesus' words, "strive first for the kingdom of God" and find that "all these things [food, water, clothing] will be given . . . as well" (Matt. 6:33; see Isa. 55:1–9).

## 1 Corinthians 10:1–13

The lesson from the Epistle for today presents the readers with an extended warning and a promise (1 Cor. 10:1–13). On the one hand, the Corinthians are faced with the failings of the Israelites of old, and thereby are called themselves to avoid the practice of idolatry (actually sharing in the cultic meals in the pagan temples). A confidence about their own status in no way guarantees immunity; idolatrous behavior will inevitably lead to disaster. On the other hand, the readers are reminded of the faithful God, who has not abandoned the chosen ones and who always provides a means to cope with the testing.

The structure of the passage is significant. The first paragraph (10:1–5) lists four miraculous events enjoyed by the Israelites at the time of the exodus: the leadership of the cloud, the crossing of the Red Sea, manna from heaven, and water from the rock. Together they function as something like "sacraments" for the Israelites—like baptism and the Eucharist. All the people (and the "all" is stressed) are distinguished by the special attention given by God. Yet their privileged position in no way assures them of automatic protection from the divine displeasure when their behavior warrants it. "They were struck down in the wilderness" (10:5). The paragraph reads like a Christian midrash on the story of the exodus.

The second paragraph details four particular occasions (10:6–12) when "some" of the people failed and were appropriately judged by God for their failings: idolatry (Ex. 32:1–6), sexual immorality (Num. 25:1–9), putting Christ to the test (Num. 21:4–7), and complaining (Num. 14:1–38; 16:41). The reports of these incidents serve as warnings for the readers that they not be caught in the same temptations and so be judged. They are to learn from the experience of Israel, especially if and when they think themselves "above" judgment and immune to the divine displeasure. The homily on Israel is meant to teach the readers a lesson.

The concluding verse (10:13) offers a word of comfort to those addressed by the warnings of the previous twelve verses. God has not forgotten people caught in intense testing (the Greek word can mean either "testing" or "temptation"). The divine provision is stated in three ways: a protection from its being too much, an escape from it (ekbasis), and the sustenance to endure it.

At the heart of the gospel lies an unconditional word of acceptance—God's love for the unlovely. It is a message needing to be heard time and again. Yet the repetition of the good news often breeds indifference, arrogance, and presumptuousness. In familiar categories, grace gets cheapened, and God gets treated like a doting parent who can never say no and can never resist indulging the weaknesses of the children. Israel at times thought like this. Apparently the Corinthians were in danger of the same delusion. Their privileged position and the fact that they enjoyed an active sacramental life dulled their sensitivities and led them to suppose that a little idolatry here and a little idolatry there would hardly bother God. A reminder of Israel's story is meant to get their attention and prod a reflection on their own present.

But the good news is not compromised by the warnings against false security. In fact, warnings can become good news when they shake us from a stupor and alert us to danger. A smoke alarm is good news when a fire breaks out. We can be grateful for the lessons drawn from Israel's story, and now from the Corinthians' story, that prod us to change.

In this light, the familiar 10:13 does not need to be taken as a caveat to the warnings, as if the warnings are only idle threats that a kindly God would never carry out. Rather, 10:13 can be taken as a promise. Testings are common to human experience, but because God is faithful, God can be counted on to keep the testings from exceeding our strength to bear them and to provide for us an escape hatch. Implicit in the verse is a recognition of humans' need for help from beyond themselves.

Though 10:14 is beyond the bounds of the passage, its presence is noteworthy ("Therefore, . . . flee from the worship of idols"). The reassurance about God's faithfulness and the news about God's providing a way out do not relieve individuals and communities from the imperative of the First Commandment. In fact, they become yet another reason to abandon our idols, to leave behind the alluring deities created by human hands, whether they be ancient or modern.

## Luke 13:1–9

As is the case with much in this section of Luke's Gospel, the city of Jerusalem and its rejection of Jesus overshadow this lectionary passage, a passage without parallel in the other Gospels. Pilate, governor of Judea, operated from headquarters situated in Jerusalem, and sacrifices could be offered only in the Jerusalem Temple. The tower of Siloam, a tower in the old wall around Jerusalem, likewise draws attention to that city. As disaster awaited these people in Jerusalem, so disaster awaits the innocent Jesus as he makes his way to that place (see 9:51).

The two incidents in vs. 1–5 differ markedly from each other. The Galileans die as a result of Pilate's willful action. Attempts to identify this reference with some particular event in the tenure of Pilate have been unsuccessful, but the notion that Pilate acted with cruelty is certainly consistent with the historian Josephus's account of Pilate's governorship. The poignant depiction of Pilate mingling the Galileans' blood with their sacrifices suggests that the Galileans traveled to Jerusalem for peaceful purposes, perhaps to observe the Passover. The collapse of the "tower of Siloam" is likewise undocumented outside this passage. Here, by contrast with the incident involving the Galileans, the deaths come entirely by accident. Eighteen people simply happen to be in the wrong place at the wrong time.

One feature that connects the two events is that both may be interpreted as punishment for sins: "Do you think that because these Galileans suffered in this way they were worse sinners than all other Galileans?" (v. 2). The notion that disaster comes as punishment for sin is found elsewhere in the Hebrew Bible, of course, especially in the blessings and warnings of Deut. 28—30. It also appears in John 9:2, with the question as to whether the man is blind because of his own sin or that of his parents (see also Luke 5:20–24).

Many contemporary readers may want to think of this connection between disaster and sin as a "primitive" notion they themselves have outgrown. It smells more than a little of what we customarily refer to as "blaming the victim." When tragedy strikes, however, in the form of a devastating illness or a natural catastrophe, such conclusions come to mind all too quickly. Recalling that tendency may generate some sympathy for a position that otherwise seems rigid and foreign.

Jesus does not dispute or affirm the connection between sin and disaster. Instead, he declares that those who died were not more sinful than other Galileans or other Jerusalemites. He then warns that "unless you repent, you will all perish as they did" (vs. 3, 5). What is meant by this declaration? How can those who hear Jesus anticipate death *like* that of the Galileans whom Pilate slaughtered or that of the Jerusalemites on whom the tower fell? Will Pilate kill them also? Will other towers collapse? What point of comparison supports such an analogy?

In addition to the fact that these two events can both be interpreted as punishment for sin, what they have in common is that they appear to happen quite suddenly, and the devastation is total. Without warning, worshipers in Jerusalem find themselves overcome by the power of Rome in the person of Pontius Pilate. Without warning, the tower collapses on people engaging in daily business near the old city wall. No chance of repentance remains for them. Here, apparently, is the force of the warning: repentance cannot be delayed, for death may come at any time. Repentance needs to be an ongoing attitude toward one's life, rather than an occasional act.

The chilling warning of vs. 1–5 is followed by a parable that concerns both the demand for repentance and renewal and the forbearance of God (vs. 6–9). A fig tree growing within a vineyard calls to mind scriptural passages in which the fig tree and the vine together signal the favor of God (see, for example, Joel 2:22; Micah 4:4). This particular fig tree, however, fails to produce fruit, and the owner's understandable response is that it should be cut down, as it takes up ground that might be used more productively (see Ps. 80:8–19; Isa. 5:1–7; Hos. 9:16). The gardener makes an alternate proposal, asking for one more year in which to nurture the tree. If it still fails to produce, then it should be destroyed.

Here the warning about the need for repentance is softened

somewhat by the forbearance of the gardener. Another year might
be all that is needed, especially if the tree receives just a little
additional care. The warning, however, still concludes the parable:
"You can cut it down" (v. 9). Repentance and productivity are
expected.

The temptation to allegorize this little parable is serious indeed,
but such interpretations will prove difficult. If the owner of the
vineyard represents God or Jesus, is the tree the church or the
individual believer? And what of the vineyard itself? Most perplexing, who is to be understood as the gardener?

The call for repentance, ever timely but particularly so during
Lent, plays a major role in both parts of this lection. What may give
courage to those of us who wonder whether our repentance is
adequate is the role of the gardener. The tree must bear fruit, but it
does not labor alone. The gardener promises to tend it and to watch
over it, reminding us that repentance and reformation do not occur
apart from the watchful care of God.

# FOURTH SUNDAY IN LENT

A number of themes may be identified in the lection for this Sunday, but the one that appears to be common to all or most of the texts is that of joy over the restorative love of God.

Joshua 5:9–12 describes in an almost understated manner the first celebration of Passover in the Land of Promise. This is an important moment of transition for the Israelites, in that the wilderness is now behind them ("The manna ceased . . .") and their new life is at hand. God's promise has been realized; the goal of their lengthy journey is beneath their feet. The people celebrate God's mercy in the manner appointed for them by remembering their liberation from Egypt and the beginning of that series of events which has now, by God's grace, brought them to this place.

Psalm 32 celebrates the forgiving love of Israel's God in a mood that is both realistic, and yet joyful. The psalmist is aware of the truly devastating nature of human sin, but nevertheless celebrates the reality that *confessed* sin is a means of reconnecting the relationship between him or herself and God. Over and again the lyric quality of this psalm surfaces in the poet's choice of words: "happy," "glad cries," "steadfast love," "be glad," "rejoice."

Paul celebrates the "new creation" that in Jesus Christ has come to pass, in the passage 2 Cor. 5:16–21. Because of Jesus' death, certain consequences emerge: (1) the cross opens up a new way of knowing, (2) to see with the eyes of the cross is to see a new world, (3) God's reconciling love is clearly revealed, and (4) Christ's women and men are commissioned to be engaged in the ministry of reconciliation.

The Gospel passage, Luke 15:1–3, 11b–32, is the familiar parable of the prodigal son, or, as it may also be called, the parable of the lost son, or the parable of the loving father. The parable is basically concerned with matters of recognition and nonrecognition. The younger son comes to his senses about his own situation, and his repentance is recognized by the father. The older son chafes under what he perceives as a lack of recognition by his father, while the father recognizes his older son's need and reaches out to him in a love that knows no limitations.

## Joshua 5:9–12

The words from an old spiritual might serve as a summary of this brief lectionary text: "There's a new day dawnin', yes, my Lord." These verses from Josh. 5 relate in terse, almost telegraphic language the story of Israel's first Passover celebration in the Land of Promise. Unlike the accounts of some later Passover celebrations (compare 2 Chron. 30), we are given so little detail in this passage that it is easy for the reader who is working through the book of Joshua in systematic fashion almost not to notice. However, one should not be misled by the understated character of the narrative, for this is a signal moment in the history of Israel's life in the land.

A few pages earlier, at the beginning of the book, we are reminded of Moses' death (Josh. 1:1; compare Deut. 34) and are informed that the nation is now under the leadership of his divinely appointed successor, Joshua. Immediately Joshua begins preparations for entering the land, directing the people to be ready (Josh. 1:11) and dispatching scouts to reconnoiter (ch. 2). Then as the people cross, led by the priests carrying the Ark of the Covenant, the waters of the Jordan are turned back so that the people cross over on dry land (ch. 3). At this point the text goes out of its way to emphasize the miraculous nature of the crossing, calling attention to the oversized condition of the river, swollen by spring floods (3:15). What is more, the geographical location, "opposite Jericho" (3:16), is near the mouth of the river, and thus the people confront the river at a spot where, under any circumstances, its expanse is the widest.

Thus, the crossing is clearly carried out under the direct intervention of Yahweh, a miracle of God. A passing reference by the writer(s) to the earlier crossing of the Red Sea is reserved for somewhat later in the narrative (4:23), but it would be abundantly evident to any devout reader of this text that the authority of Israel's God, previously exercised so decisively over the sea, is now on display again as the power of the surging Jordan is tamed for the benefit of the people. This would not be the last time that an ancient Hebrew writer would subtly invoke the images of the exodus as a model of God's saving activity in Israel's present (compare Isa. 43:16–21, the lection for the Fifth Sunday in Lent, this year).

A stone memorial is then erected on the spot of the crossing in order that all future generations might remember the greatness of Yahweh (Josh. 4; note especially vs. 21–24). Also, because the practice of circumcision had been discontinued in the wilderness, thus permitting an entire generation of Hebrew males to grow up without this ritual reminder of Yahweh's covenant (see Gen. 17:1–14), there is a mass circumcision (Josh. 5:2–9)—as with the about-to-be-celebrated Passover, the first observance of this important rite in the Land of Promise.

The text appointed by the lectionary begins at v. 9, but, because this verse forms the conclusion to the narrative of the circumcision of the nation, it does not make much sense unless v. 8 is included in the lectionary reading. The meaning of the phrase "the disgrace of Egypt" is not quite clear, but it almost certainly refers to the conditions of oppression forced upon the Israelites by their pharaonic masters. On one level, v. 9 is an attempt to provide a logical explanation for the name Gilgal, a word akin to the Hebrew verb meaning to roll. (Incidentally, this is one of our best clues to the location of the settlement of Gilgal, that is, that it is near Jericho. The exact site of this important town—see 1 Sam. 11:14–15; Amos 5:5—has never been identified.) But on a deeper level, Josh. 5:9 is a declaration of freedom, a manner of asserting that the old has passed away (the slavery of Egypt, the nomads' wanderings in the wilderness) and that the new is at hand (life in the Land of Promise). Perhaps this association between the new freedom of the people and the city of Gilgal accounts for the reference to this site in connection with the establishment of Israel's monarchy (1 Sam. 11:14–15).

Then the first-ever-in-the-land Passover is celebrated, just when it should be, that is, on the fourteenth of Abib (Josh. 5:10; compare Lev. 23:5; Deut. 16:1) This most important meal in the liturgical year of ancient Israel is on this occasion made up of foodstuffs produced in the land. (The text does not address the moral question of how the tribes obtained produce sown and raised by other people.) And immediately the manna ceases: "The Israelites no longer had manna; they ate the crops of the land of Canaan that year" (Josh. 5:12).

Thus an essential promise of Yahweh has been kept. To be sure, the nation will undergo many adventures before the land is their possession in anything approaching a complete sense. But they are here—now! The Land of Promise is not some distant goal, but is beneath their feet. And the tribes greet this "new day dawnin' " in the most appropriate manner possible: they give thanks to God for this present grace by recalling the grace of God of old. Red Sea and Jordan commingle. And the people praise the Lord!

## Psalm 32

Psalm 32 is one of the seven penitential psalms (see Pss. 6; 38; 51; 102; 130; 143), an ecclesiastical grouping that perhaps dates from Augustine. In fact, Augustine is said to have had the words of Ps. 32 written above his bed so that they would be the first thing he saw every morning (see Rowland Prothero, *The Psalms in Human Life and Experience*; New York: E. P. Dutton, 1903, p. 29; see also Lam. 3:22–23). The psalmist's penitential posture is obviously appropriate for the observance of the season of Lent, but her or his joyful celebration of forgiveness also anticipates Easter and is appropriate for all seasons. Psalm 32 is ultimately a proclamation of the gospel, and it is not surprising that the apostle Paul cites Ps. 32:1–2 in his exposition of justification by faith through grace alone (Rom. 4:6–8).

Psalm 32 begins with two beatitudes that recall the beginning of the Psalter (see 1:1; 2:12). In fact, several other items of the vocabulary of Ps. 32 recall Pss. 1 and 2—"sin" (32:1, 5; compare "sinners" in 1:1, 5), "day and night" (32:4; compare 1:2), "teach" (v. 8; the root is the same as "law" or "instruction" in 1:2), "way" (v. 8; compare 1:6; 2:12), "wicked" (v. 10; compare 1:1, 4, 5, 6), and "righteous" (v. 11; compare 1:6). By defining "happiness" in terms of forgiveness, Ps. 32 functions as a warning against any tendency to misunderstand Ps. 1. To be righteous is not a matter of being sinless, but rather a matter of being forgiven, of being open to God's instruction (Ps. 1:2; see Ps. 1, Sixth Sunday After Epiphany), of trusting God rather than trusting self (Ps. 2:12). In fact, as Ps. 32 suggests, sin and its effects are pervasive in the life of the righteous.

Words for sin in vs. 1–2, 5 surround the psalmist's self-description in vs. 3–4—"transgression" (vs. 1, 5), "sin" (vs. 1, 5), "iniquity"/ "guilt" (vs. 2, 5). The effects of sin are real, even physical— something to which contemporary persons can also attest. But the reality of forgiveness is even more encompassing than the reality of sin, an affirmation reinforced by the literary structure of the psalm. Whereas sin encompassed the psalmist's life, God's forgiveness encompasses sin (vs. 1a, 5c). Those who do "not hide [their] iniquity" (v. 5) will be the "happy" ones "whose sin is covered" (v. 1; "hide" and "cover" are from the same Hebrew root). Verse 5c is crucial. Its pronoun "you" (God) is emphatic, and it marks the turning point of the psalm. None of the words for sin recurs after v. 5. Things are different for those who acknowledge their sin in reliance on the grace of God.

The focus of the psalmist had been on herself or himself in vs. 3–5, but the reality of forgiveness apparently directs the psalmist outward. Attention now is focused on others, who are invited to share the psalmist's experience (v. 6). Attention is also directed to God, who is addressed in gratitude with a profession of faith (v. 7). The emphatic "you" that opens v. 7 recalls the "you" of v. 5c. The effect is to emphasize God's character and activity. As Robert Jenson suggests, "The psalmist's own stance is that of *witness*, to his experience and to the grace of God" ("Psalm 32," *Interpretation* 33 [1979]: 175). The substance of the psalmist's witness in v. 7c points forward to vs. 10–11, which also highlight God's character and activity. The word "surround" recurs in v. 10 in conjunction with God's "steadfast love," a fundamental attribute of God (see Ex. 34:6–7, where the issue is also forgiveness). The Hebrew root translated "glad cries" in Ps. 32:7c underlies "shout for joy" in v. 11. The psalmist can invite others to "shout for joy" because God has already acted to surround her or him with "glad cries." The link between vs. 6–7 and 10–11 is also structural—namely, the function of each verse forms a chiastic pattern as follows: invitation (v. 6) . . . profession of faith (v. 7) . . . profession of faith (v. 10) . . . invitation (v. 11).

The chiastic pattern of vs. 6–7, 10–11 focuses attention on vs. 8–9, which can be taken as a further instance of the psalmist's witness. It is possible to understand the "I" of v. 8 as God speaking to the psalmist; however, in view of the psalmist's witness in vs. 6–7 and 10–11, it is more likely that the psalmist is speaking in vs. 8–9. As in Ps. 51, another penitential psalm, the forgiven sinner teaches others God's "way(s)" (see 51:13). This teaching ministry is not presumptuous. The psalmist witnesses not to her or his own righteousness, but to God's grace. Thus, "the way you should go" points to the psalmist's example of confession of sin (v. 5) and profession of faith in God's willingness to forgive and restore (vs. 7, 10). The instruction is, in essence, another invitation—an invitation to others, including the readers of Ps. 32, to entrust their lives to God (v. 10) as the psalmist has done (v. 7).

Psalm 33:1 takes up the invitation with which Ps. 32 ends. A "new song" (33:3) is certainly the appropriate response to God's renewing grace. Psalm 33 also ends the same way as Ps. 32, except the witness is made in the plural. It seems that a whole congregation has heeded the psalmist's invitation and instruction (32:6–11). The whole congregation is "glad" (33:21; compare 32:11); they affirm their "trust" (33:21; compare 32:10) in God's "steadfast love" (33:18, 22; compare 32:10). Psalms 32 and 33 together demonstrate what always befits sinful human beings—confidence in and praise for God's "steadfast love" (32:10; 33:4–5), and prayer for God's "steadfast love" (33:22).

## 2 Corinthians 5:16–21

It is highly appropriate that this rich passage should appear in the lectionary cycle for a Sunday close to Good Friday. (The first two verses also occur in the reading for Proper 6, Year B.) Beginning with 2 Cor. 2:14, Paul argues the case for the ministry in which he is engaged, and theologically grounds his work in the death of Jesus (so 4:7–14). What "urges on" the apostle (the Greek verb in 5:14 might be translated "lays claim to") is nothing less than the love of Christ expressed in the cross, where God acts to shape a new creation out of the chaos of alienation and estrangement, a timely topic for the Fourth Sunday in Lent.

While the assigned lesson begins at 5:16, the dominating theme of the section is laid out in 5:14–15 and is returned to in 5:21. Christ has died for all, and thus all have died. Another way to put this is in the language of interchange; God made the one who did not know sin to be sin in our behalf, that we might become the righteousness of God. Something earth-changing (apocalyptic) has occurred in the cross, with sweeping implications for the rest of human history.

At least four consequences ("therefore") are drawn from this statement of the inclusive nature of Jesus' death. First, the cross opens up a new way of knowing. The NEB puts it sharply: "With us therefore worldly standards have ceased to count in our estimate of any[one]" (5:16). The old categories—race, gender, social status (used in Paul's day as well as our own)—have become obsolete as far as judging people is concerned. The cross has played havoc with these and other accepted norms for making decisions. They are components of the so-called "worldly wisdom," which finds the message of Christ crucified to be sheer folly but which in turn is shamed and exposed by persons categorized as weak, foolish, low, and despised (1 Cor. 1:18–31).

Nothing may be more difficult for Christians in North America than adopting the new way of discernment inherent in the gospel. The seductive voices from the culture condition us to value people and to make moral decisions according to a plausible logic of acquisitions and achievements. We even turn the gospel into a self-help message to enable us to acquire and achieve more. But the text affirms that the old standards of judgment and the rigid systems of perception are ephemeral and thus powerless. Not surprisingly, then, the consequence of Jesus' inclusive death that is listed first is a new way of knowing.

The second consequence broadens the first. To see with the eyes of the cross is to behold a brand-new world. It is critical that 5:17 not be reduced merely to a statement about the change within the individual—that in Christ a person becomes a new woman or a new man. The use of "all" in 5:14–15 and "world" in 5:19 demand the translation "new creation." If 5:16 affirms the transformed perception of Christians, then 5:17 announces and celebrates the advent of the new order, long promised and now inaugurated in the cross. To say that the old order is gone is not to deny that our lives must be lived in the midst of a broken, distorted world, but it is to say that the old order is ultimately powerless to effect changes and to provide meaning for human existence.

The third consequence of Jesus' death is God's reconciling activity. The stress falls on both the subject and the objects. On the one hand, God is clearly the actor, the one who has broken through the alienation and hostility to win over the enemy. It is a divine work that transforms and renews the divine-human relationship. At its heart lies a word of forgiveness (see Ps. 32:2), which melts the antagonism of a people that often does not even recognize its own antagonism.

On the other hand, the objects of God's reconciliation are "us" (2 Cor. 5:18) and "the world" (5:19). Both are helpless to deal with their own estrangement. Neither is any less dependent on the grace of God than the other. But since Paul is reflecting here on his own ministry, it is critical to note this connection he readily acknowledges with the world. A solidarity between "us" and "the world" protects "us" from assuming a superior stance, somehow better than "the world."

A fourth consequence of Jesus' death is the commission to be engaged in the ministry of reconciliation. The distinction made between "us" and "the world" becomes a dynamic for mission. The task is to declare to the world that God, unlike everyone else, keeps no account of their sins. God is no angry deity out to get even with a world that has rejected the divine presence. And thus the world need no longer live as God's enemies, but as friends. To be reconciled to God means to be an agent of reconciliation for the world.

## Luke 15:1–3, 11b–32

"There was a man who had two sons." Even in these days of rampant biblical illiteracy, many in the congregation will recognize the so-called "parable of the prodigal son" immediately from its opening sentence. The astonishing theological implications, the penetrating psychological insights, and centuries of representations

and retellings make this among the most familiar of biblical passages. That very familiarity may prompt preachers to turn to other
readings or to seek to wrench some new insight from the parable,
but this parable can stand on its own. Simply to tell it once more is to
preach the gospel afresh.

While the parable is commonly referred to as the "parable of the
prodigal son," some refer to it as the "parable of the lost son," in
keeping with the parables of the lost sheep (15:3–7) and the lost coin
(15:8–10) that precede it. Still others refer to it as the "parable of the
loving father," reflecting both the opening words of the parable itself
and the dominant motif of the father's generosity to his sons.
Whatever title we use, this parable concerns three people ("a man
who had two sons"), all of whom are involved in matters of
recognition and nonrecognition.

The younger son initiates the action in the parable. For reasons
that remain unstated, he asks that his father give him the property
that he stands to inherit on the father's death. Attempts to clarify the
legal details of this situation are not terribly successful, given our
limited knowledge of first-century Palestinian practice. Clearly the
younger son could expect to receive a fraction of what the elder son
would receive.

Heedless of the advice of Sir. 33:19–23, the father accedes to the
son's request. The son then leaves for a "distant country" and
squanders his inheritance. Because of the assumptions often made
about his behavior, it is worth noticing that Jesus says only that the
son was engaged in "dissolute [*asotos*] living," which simply refers
to inappropriate or undisciplined habits. Later on, the *elder* son
accuses him of spending the father's money "with prostitutes" (v.
30), but that charge should be read with some suspicion, since the
elder son is scarcely a neutral observer of his brother's habits! What
concerns Jesus is that the young man runs out of money and finds
himself in a position utterly abhorrent to Jews, that of tending pigs.

Verse 17 marks the turning point in the younger brother's story:
"He came to himself." The Greek expression has connotations very
like those in contemporary English. What prompts this recognition
is irrelevant, for what is important is that the son recognizes his
situation. As a hired hand in his father's household, he would be
better off than he is at present.

The younger son's recognition of his situation stems from a
perception about his own plight. It is crucial to see, however, that the
father's recognition stems, not from the son's recognition (or from
his repentance), but from the sheer joy of seeing his "lost" son once
more. The father, essentially absent from the story since v. 12,

suddenly becomes the primary actor; he sees, he is filled with compassion, he runs, he embraces, he kisses. Before the son can complete his own confession of recognition, he calls for the best clothing and the best food and initiates a magnificent celebration. Both father and son are found.

Contemporary readers enjoy this moment in the parable, for we identify with the relief of the son and the joy of the father. What that enjoyment overlooks is that the father has acted with an exuberance that would merit scorn from his neighbors. The wise and dignified patriarch ought not run to meet anyone. Certainly he ought to inquire about this son's behavior, to ascertain his intent, to hear his confession before extending forgiveness. At the very least, the neighbors will mutter about cheap grace.

The older son does more than mutter, of course. For him there is no recognition scene. He does not run to meet his brother or even assent to his father's generosity. Instead, this "loyal" son gives voice to the complaint of all "good" children everywhere. He has worked, not as a hired hand, but as a slave. Never has he received even a goat for celebrating with his friends. But the "bad" child has been rewarded simply for coming home, when no other option was left to him anyway.

How to respond to the older son, who has indeed done everything right and never been rewarded for his goodness? Two options come to mind. The father might agree with the son's assessment and offer him his own fatted calf and grand celebration, humoring him into acceptance. Or the father might defend himself and scold the son for his selfishness, enjoining him to put aside such legalistic measurements.

Perhaps the most poignant movement of the father in the story is in relation to this good, loyal older son. When the son refuses to enter the celebration, the father takes the initiative to find him and plead with him (v. 28). When the son makes his case, the father does not disagree or belittle. He restates his own recognition but with these words of introduction: "Son, you are always with me, and all that is mine is yours" (v. 31). The generosity lavished on the son who was lost outside the household is now extended also to the son who is lost within the household. The father's love knows no limitations.

# FIFTH SUNDAY IN LENT

The Old Testament lection, Isa. 43:16–21, reveals the anonymous Isaiah-prophet of the exile in one of his most profoundly creative moments. In attempting to portray the redemptive activity of God that is about to be introduced into Israel's life, the prophet draws on the images of the exodus from Egypt and the wandering in the wilderness. Yet, even as he lifts these memories of the long ago, he calls on the faith-community to forget them. Not even the great liberation from Egyptian bondage is an adequate model for the redemption God is about to bring now. All paradigms lie shattered before the enormity of God's grace!

Psalm 126 is one of the most unabashedly joyful statements in all of the Psalter. The joy is occasioned by the memory of God's great (but unspecified) act of redemption in the past, and also by the anticipation that a similar intervention is immanent now. Phrases like "mouth . . . filled with laughter" and "shouts of joy" (three times) catch the reader up in the mood of the psalm. But sandwiched between the memory and the anticipation is the people's prayer reflecting their own weakness and need for God's grace.

Paul's autobiographical sketch directed to the Philippians, Phil. 3:4b–14, is much more than just a sharing of data about the apostle's life. Paul wishes also to confess the fundamental change that has come into his life as a result of "knowing Christ Jesus my Lord," and to share with his friends his new perception concerning the purpose of his life. But this cameo autobiography proves to be much more than a statement about Paul. It, rather, becomes a paradigm of the gospel, a description of the work of the gospel in changing the lives of all who, in Paul's words, "know Christ."

The magnificent story in John 12:1–8 of Mary's anointing of Jesus' feet is the Gospel lection for this day. Occurring when it does ("six days before the Passover"), the incident must be read in the context of Jesus' looming passion. The reader is struck not only by the

228

extravagance of Mary's deed (one can almost smell the lavishly dispensed perfume), but also by Judas's mock concern for the poor. In the end, it is Jesus who sets Mary's actions in their proper perspective by linking them to his own death, even as he deflects Judas's counterfeit compassion.

## Isaiah 43:16–21

The themes of newness and joy, which characterize the Old Testament lections for the Third and Fourth Sundays in Lent of Year C, are continued in this text from Isa. 43. Perhaps the passage might be summarized: The Lord is on the verge of doing such a startlingly new thing that models for this impending act of grace are to be found almost nowhere, and even the one model that suggests itself has to be turned on its head in order to be applicable.

Water is the element that is common to the three sections of this brief lection. The first section (vs. 16–17) identifies the exodus from Egypt as a paradigm for what Yahweh is about to do in the life of the people. That the prophet is speaking (or writing) with divine authority is made clear by the opening cadences. "Thus says [Yahweh]." The Lord who now summons Israel to listen is the same Lord who called Israel out of Egypt and who, in advance of the liberated people, made "a way in the sea, a path in the mighty waters." There are several allusions in the Second Isaiah to Yahweh's mastery over the waters of the Red Sea at the time of the exodus (compare 43:2), but none is more forceful than this.

Yet it is not the waters only that are subject to Yahweh's mastery. In an ironic play on words, the prophet uses the same verb, "brings out" ($ys'$), to describe the activity of the Egyptian army that is used in other exodus narratives to describe Yahweh's "bringing out" of Israel from bondage (Ex. 3:10 and elsewhere). The enemies of human liberty are responding to the initiatives of the same sovereign Lord as were the liberated tribes. The forces of evil are summoned from their place of safety and are crushed ("extinguished, quenched like a wick") by the power of Israel's God.

(It goes without saying that, in dealing with this aspect of the text, the preacher will avoid interpretations that are racial, nationalistic, or ideological in character. The pursuing Egyptians should be understood to represent the reality of evil in human life, but should not be made into an embodiment of any specific group or class of human beings.)

The second section (vs. 18–19) gets to the heart of the matter: the same Lord who was present at the exodus is present in Israel's life now—yet there is a difference. After having anchored his proclamation in the past, the prophet now demands that the hearers (readers) of this text forget the past. "Do not remember the former things" is usually understood to be a reference to Israel's long history of sinfulness which, according to the prophetic interpretation (as in Jer. 37:6–10), was the cause of the Babylonian exile. That view is undoubtedly correct, as a reading of Isa. 40:1–2 will attest.

But something else seems to be going on here. The injunction to forgetfulness may also be understood to refer to that specific issue from the past that has just been raised: the exodus. The people are asked to forget the exodus not in the sense that it is insignificant or irrelevant, but because not even *that* model is an adequate portrayal of what Yahweh is about to do now! What Israel's God is on the verge of accomplishing breaks all the patterns of past behavior, including that preeminent pattern, the exodus.

That manner of understanding vs. 18–19 is emphasized by what the prophet does to the elemental image of water. In the past, the water was tamed, set aside, in order that the fleeing Israelites might pass over safely and in order that the vindictive Egyptians might be killed. The "way in the sea" of v. 16 was a dry route through the threatening waters created by a merciful Yahweh. But the "way" in v. 19 is a life-sustaining thread of water through an arid wasteland. It is "a way in the wilderness"; it is "rivers in the desert." The imagery has been turned 180 degrees!

One may argue, of course, that vs. 18–19 do not constitute a denial of the exodus motif, but merely an extension of it, by virtue of the fact that the prophet has simply moved us along from the Red Sea moment to the crisis at Massah and Meribah (Ex. 17:1–7). And that is undoubtedly so. But being the poet of genius that he is, the Second Isaiah is capable of describing more than one reality at the same time, and the admonition to forget the past that opens v. 18 cannot be confined to Israel's former sinfulness. It must also be understood as a manner of saying that Yahweh's saving grace so far outstrips human comprehension that only the language of negation is capable of describing it. To be sure, God's grace is like what Yahweh did at the Red Sea; but it may also be said that it is *not* like the Red Sea incident, in that it far surpasses that moment in time.

A final section (vs. 20–21) carries forward the sense of vs. 18–19, and reaches a climax by stating the reason for Yahweh's gracious protection of Israel. The people are saved not just for their own sake, but because that is simply the way God deals with people (compare Isa. 49:6). Grace is who Yahweh is.

The realization that this prophetic discourse moves on at least two different planes opens extensive interpretative possibilities in that the salvation that the Second Isaiah describes is both rooted in his concrete historical situation, and yet transcends it. Therefore, the text's joyful anticipation over God's impending grace is not confined to the sixth century B.C., but is relevant whenever and wherever women and men anticipate some new expression of the life and work of Jesus Christ.

## Psalm 126

Psalm 126 has been called "perhaps the most beautiful in the whole psalter, both in content and form" (Bernhard Duhm, quoted in W. Beyerlin, *We Are like Dreamers: Studies in Psalm 126*, trans. D. Livingston; Edinburgh: T. & T. Clark, 1982, p. 1). It is traditionally used during Advent and Lent, both of which are seasons of penitence that remind us that we always live as people of memory and people of hope. The structure of Ps. 126 is significant in this regard. Verses 1–3 look back to a past deliverance; v. 4 is a prayer for help in the present; and vs. 5–6 look forward to a joyous future that will match the past (note the repetition of "shouts of joy" (in vs. 2, 5, and 6).

As the NRSV footnote indicates, it is difficult to decide how to translate v. 1a. The more general phrase, "restored the fortunes," is to be preferred; but, as the footnote suggests, it is probable that v. 1a referred originally to the return of exiles from Babylon to Jerusalem (see Deut. 30:3; Jer. 30:3, 18; 32:44; Ezek. 39:25). This extraordinary event (see the "new thing" of Isa. 43:19, in the Old Testament lesson for the day) would have been enough to make the people think they were dreaming (see Acts 12:9, and see below).

Even though an event such as the return from exile may account for the origin of v. 1, it is not necessary to tie Ps. 126 to a specific historical occasion. As H.-J. Kraus recognizes, the phrase "restored the fortunes" (v. 1a; cf. v. 4) can properly be understood as "an expression for a historical change to a new state of affairs for all things" (*Psalms 60—150*, trans. H. C. Oswald; Minneapolis; Augsburg, 1989, p. 450). In short, Ps. 126:1 can function as a remembrance of any past deliverance that evokes laughter (see the similar vocabulary in Job 8:21) and joy among God's people. Similarly, the prayer in Ps. 126:4, "Restore our fortunes," is a prayer that is perpetually appropriate for faithful individuals and for the whole people of God. No matter how often we are able to say, "The LORD has done great things for us" (v. 3; compare v. 2), we will find ourselves in need of help and renewed deliverance. In other words, Ps. 126 reminds us that we live eschatologically, always remembering what God has done in the past (vs. 1–3) and always anticipating what God will do in the future (vs. 5–6)—including, we trust, the renewal of "all things" (see Rev. 21:5; compare Isa. 43:19; 65:17).

The mention of "the watercourses in the Negeb" in the prayer in Ps. 126:4 emphasizes both the people's neediness and their confidence in God. While often dry, the streambeds in the Negeb can suddenly become rushing torrents when it rains. So the simile functions to communicate the people's dryness as well as their expectation of the life-giving deliverance of God. In Ps. 42:1–2, the need for God is also represented in terms of the desire for "flowing streams," the same Hebrew word translated as "watercourses" here. A description of future deliverance in Joel 3:18 also uses the same vocabulary and image (see NRSV "stream beds").

The image shifts to sowing and reaping in Ps. 126:5–6 (see similar agricultural imagery in the description of future deliverance in Amos 9:13–15). That the people "sow in tears" and "go out weeping" need not be interpreted as the vestige of pagan rituals of mourning for a dead fertility god, as commentators often suggest. Sowing is always an act of anticipation and hope, and the mention of "tears" and "weeping" in this case simply emphasizes the urgency of the need already articulated in Ps. 126:4. Appeals for God's help are made elsewhere with "tears" (see 2 Kings 20:5; Ps. 39:12; 42:3; 56:8; Jer. 9:1, 18; 13:17; 31:16; Lam. 2:18) and weeping (Lam. 1:16; Joel 2:17). Whereas the people's neediness is very real, so is their hope. Like Ps. 126:6, v. 5 could also be translated with an indicative force: "those who sow in tears *will* reap with shouts of joy." The repetition of "shouts of joy" in v. 6 is emphatic; there will be a joyful harvest.

At several points, the vocabulary of Ps. 126 is similar to that of the book of Joel—"restore the fortunes" (Joel 3:1; compare Ps. 126:1, 4); "dream dreams" (Joel 2:28; compare Ps. 126:1); "the LORD has done great things" (Joel 2:21; compare Joel 2:20 and Ps. 126:2–3); "watercourses"/"stream beds" (Joel 1:20; 3:18, compare Ps. 126:4). Indeed, Beyerlin (*We Are like Dreamers*, pp. 41–58) suggests that the author(s) of Ps. 126 used the book of Joel as a source in attempting to address the disappointing circumstances that prevailed in Judah following the return from exile. While this historical connection may be questionable, it is instructive to read Ps. 126 alongside the book of Joel. Like Ps. 126, Joel moves from an articulation of need (1:2–2:17) to the promise of God's response (2:18–3:21). Regardless of the historical circumstances out of which they arose, Ps. 126 and Joel join in proclaiming the good news that God will ultimately provide for

God's people. Thus, even amid perpetual neediness of one sort or another, the people of God live by faith and hope, anticipating even the renewal of all things. This approach to Ps. 126 suggests the possibility that dreaming in v. 1 involves not simply the incredulous response to a divine act of deliverance. It suggests, rather, that every divine act of deliverance evokes a joyous vision of the future by which the people of God live (see Joel 2:28). The joyful tone of the gospel hymn based on Ps. 126, "Bringing in the Sheaves," suggests the effect of living as visionaries or of living eschatologically— namely, anticipated joy becomes a present reality even amid the pressing circumstances that lead us to pray, "Restore our fortunes, O LORD."

## Philippians 3:4b–14

The various autobiographical passages found in the undisputed Pauline letters are remarkable in many ways (for example, Phil. 3:4b–14; 2 Cor. 4:7–15; 6:3–10; or Gal. 1:13–24). The restraint (when compared with other ancient writers), the rhetorical power, the contextual appropriateness, and the author's vulnerability—all make them convincing statements. The most striking feature, how ever, is their theological character, the way the little story of Paul's life becomes meaningful by its relation to the big story of God's activity. Unlike many modern autobiographies, Paul's story does not invite readers to do their own thing, but asks them to see themselves in the light of the divine story, the center of which, of course, is the Christ-story.

Philippians, 3:4b–14 is an autobiography in three stages: a statement of Paul's heritage and religious achievements (3:4b–6); a reevaluation of Paul's life in light of knowing Christ (3:7–11); and a statement of his present intentions (3:12–14). The first stage essentially provides the background for the latter two stages.

About the critical second stage of the autobiography, two features of the passage stand out. First, the knowledge of Christ has forced a profound reevaluation of Paul's life and religious credentials. Note the use twice in 3:7–8 of the phrase "I regard." At the heart of Paul's witness to the gospel is a changed perspective about himself, what he is up to in life, and what he deems as important and unimportant. He has gained a new lens, through which to see life differently. The effective employment of the commercial terms "gain" and "loss" suggests (to mix the metaphor slightly) a rearrangement of the price tags of life in such a way that items previously thought of as valuable are recognized as worthless and items once regarded as having little import are cherished. In more theological terms, the text speaks of the new epistemology inherent in the gospel.

Second, the surpassing value of knowing Christ is spelled out in two particular ways. On the one hand, it entails having a relationship to God ("righteousness") based not on law, but on Christ. Often v. 9 is explained as an abandonment of justification by works (earning one's salvation) in favor of justification by faith (human acceptance of Christ). But since it is unclear that Paul, even as a Pharisee, ever thought he was saved by his own efforts, the verse more likely depicts the changed identity that comes with knowing Christ. No longer do religious credentials, both inherited and acquired (3:5–6), determine his status before God, but Christ alone. (The marginal reading of the NRSV in v. 9, "the faith of Christ," seems the more appropriate.) Christians ultimately are accepted by God not because of their works or their faith, but because of the faith and obedience of Christ (so 2:8).

On the other hand, knowing Christ is spelled out in terms of participation with Christ, of knowing the power of his resurrection and sharing his sufferings by being conformed to his death. The sequence of the phrases in v. 10 is arresting. One would expect another order—of suffering and then resurrection, of Good Friday and then Easter, of anguish endured and then resolution. Instead, the reversed sequence suggests that the power of Christ's resurrection leads to and is known in the obedience of faith and the inevitable strife it brings.

Resurrection power comes to expression, then, in the midst of tribulations, Karl Barth puts this sharply: "To know Easter means, for the person knowing it, as stringently as may be: to be implicated in the events of Good Friday. . . . The way in which the power of Christ's resurrection works powerfully in the apostle is, that he is clothed with the *shame of the Cross*" (*The Epistle to the Philippians*; Richmond: John Knox Press, 1962, p. 103).

The third stage of the autobiography (3:12–14) adds an essential component to the first two stages. The knowledge of Christ is not information one acquires that assures a privileged place in the resurrection of the dead, but rather is an experience that spurs the knower to an active life of anticipation. God's future beckons and evokes a "pressing on" and a "straining forward." Paul's story is unfinished; he has not yet arrived. His sense of acceptance by God energizes a continuous pursuit of the vocation to which he is set.

It is important to note that the language of the paragraph does not hint at a frantic striving, as if the final outcome were uncertain. Verses 12–14 provide no warrant for anxious, handwringing efforts, motivated more by fear than by grace. They seem directed to those among the initial readership who thought they were already perfect and thus could expect nothing new from the future.

Paul's telling of his own story thus provokes far more than historical interest. It provides a paradigm of the gospel, how the gospel works in producing a changed view of life and a renewed attitude toward the future.

## John 12:1–8

Both Matthew and Mark include in their Gospels stories that parallel this one (Matt. 26:6–13; Mark 14:3–9; compare also Luke 7:36–40), and for them also the event is closely connected with the impending passion and death of Jesus. With his customary eye for detail, John has taken particular care to locate the anointing of Jesus between the raising of Lazarus and the death of Jesus.

The story begins with the chronological note that this episode occurred "six days before the Passover" (v. 1). Since the narrator has just referred to the nearness of the Passover in the preceding scene (11:55–57), the time reference here seems superfluous. In that preceding scene, however, people are speculating as to whether Jesus will dare to go to Jerusalem for the festival, for the officials have arranged to arrest Jesus if he in fact comes for the Passover.

The story also begins by connecting this episode with the resurrection of Lazarus. It takes place in "Bethany, the home of Lazarus, whom he had raised from the dead" (v. 1). Verses 2–3 again refer to Lazarus and to the presence and activity of Mary and Martha. Neither Matthew nor Mark identifies the woman who anoints Jesus, and it can scarcely be accidental that John so carefully names the three individuals whose presence is significant in chapter 11. The raising of Lazarus is a pivotal event in John's Gospel, one to which it is impossible to remain neutral. It prompts belief on the part of some (11:45), but it also prompts the decision by others that Jesus must be put to death (11:46–57).

The response of Mary to the restoration of her brother's life can be gauged by the extravagance of her act in v. 3. She "took a pound of costly perfume made of pure nard, anointed Jesus' feet, and wiped them with her hair." Even before Judas' calculating remark about the value of this perfume, first-century readers would know that this large quantity of high-quality perfume was remarkably valuable. That its fragrance filled the entire house (v. 3b) further affirms its costliness and the luxuriousness of Mary's act.

What first-century readers would find extremely odd in this story is that Mary anoints the feet of Jesus rather than his head, as is the case in the Mark 14:3 and Matthew 26:7. She then wipes his feet with her hair, which results in the dissipation of the very costly perfume she has just poured out onto his feet! Two possibilities for interpreting this gesture both seem plausible. First, in John 13:1–20, Jesus washes the feet of the disciples, dries them, and then instructs them that they are to do the same for one another. Mary's gesture of anointing the feet of Jesus and wiping them with her hair may anticipate symbolically this act of service. Second, anointing the feet may also anticipate the anointing for burial that Jesus refers to in v. 7.

Judas's response, of course, addresses the money involved rather than the part anointed. In the parallels to this story, the question about the value of the ointment seems to reflect a straightforward concern about priorities. Here, by contrast, the question covers the sinister purposes of Judas. Had the perfume been sold, he was the one who stood to benefit from the money thus acquired. The narrator elsewhere explains that Judas's betrayal of Jesus comes about as a result of the devil's intervention, and this comment gives specificity to that claim (see 6:70–71; 13:2, 27).

Jesus' response comes on two fronts: first, a defense of the action of Mary, and second, a rebuttal to Judas's feigned concern for the poor. The claim that Mary bought the perfume "so that she might keep it for the day of my burial" is a little unclear. Had Mary consciously intended such usage for the perfume, she would not have used it at this dinner. Jesus probably refers to the unanticipated function of Mary's action. The day of his burial is now quite close, and Mary's action foreshadows the anointing needed then.

More familiar, of course, is the saying that concludes the lection: "You always have the poor with you, but you do not always have me." Removed from its narrative context, as it too often is, this saying seems almost callous. "You always have the poor" is not, however, a statement about the social attitudes that ought to govern the church's behavior. Instead, it contrasts the presence of the poor with the impending absence of Jesus. The Johannine Jesus frequently refers to his return to the Father, to the imminence of his departure, to conditions that will obtain in his absence. Given that feature of the Fourth Gospel, this statement is but a forceful reminder that Jesus will be present only for a brief time.

The irony within this passage is striking. Judas speaks for the poor, at least he does on the surface. We might even characterize his words as reflecting prophetic concern for the outcast and marginalized. Mary, by contrast, appears to engage in a frivolous, wasteful act. It is Mary, however, who is the real prophet in this story, for she is the one who knows what the hour is and where the crisis occurs.

# Sixth Sunday in Lent

## (PALM SUNDAY OR PASSION SUNDAY)

Palm/Passion Sunday confronts the church with strong crosscurrents of emotion. It is a time of celebration over the coming of the King, but it is also a time of foreboding because the celebrants know that the King is soon to die. It is a time of irony in that this King is a king like no other, yet he goes almost unrecognized by those over whom he rules. This Sunday is thus a moment of greatest joy (Hosanna!), but also an occasion of introspection and gloom.

The lectionary texts capture these contrasting, jolting energies. Isaiah 50:4–9a, the third so-called Servant Song from the Second Isaiah, portrays a servant of God who is aware of deep trouble yet faces it with bold confidence. The confidence emerges out of a sense that the servant is doing the will of God, but this does not diminish the hostility or render the servant less vulnerable to it. The servant's single purpose is to affirm the rule of God, and it is in submitting to this rule that the servant is sustained.

Psalm 118:1–2, 19–29 possesses obvious connections to Palm and Passion Sunday themes because of its references to the opening of the "gates of righteousness" (v. 19) and to the binding of "the festal procession with branches" (v. 27). Yet its relevance to the celebration of this day is much more profound than these superficial parallels, for the psalm also celebrates the reality that the rejected building stone "has become the chief cornerstone" (v. 22). Thus in Ps. 118 we identify the continuity between the Old and New Testament witnesses to the Christ-event and to the reality that God's "steadfast love endures forever" (vs. 2, 29).

The Epistle lection is the marvelous hymn in Phil. 2:5–11, which sings of Christ's humiliation and exaltation. Because its origin was probably liturgical, it is appropriate that it be used in the context of a modern worship service. This great hymn is not just about the Christ-event in and for itself, but also about those who commit themselves to the subject of this hymn. They are summoned to conform to Christ and adopt Christ's attitude of self-giving in their relationships with one another.

Luke 19:28–40 is the narrative from that Gospel of Jesus' entry into Jerusalem, and this passage captures the irony of the event. Jesus enters as King and his greeters extend to him a royal welcome. Yet missing is the extravagant opulence that characterized royal parades in the ancient world (and in our own!). To the naked eye, this King appears as an ordinary man astride an ordinary beast. To add to the element of irony, Luke quickly introduces the Pharisees, and the reader is at once reminded of the hostility to this king that will soon lead him to a cross.

## Isaiah 50:4–9a                                                         (A B C)

This text is the voice of God's servant, who acknowledges deep trouble and who confesses bold confidence. We are not told who the servant is, or why there is such trouble. It is clear that every faithful servant of God has life placed in jeopardy, because the truth of God does not easily mesh with our dominant illusions about reality. As this poem concerns the deep jeopardy of the servant, so the church knows that Jesus' conflict will lead to suffering and death. In that deep conflict, however, he continues to be God's trusting, faithful, obedient servant.

This text is dominated by the fourfold "the Lord GOD." Thus, the statement of the servant is passionately theocentric. The servant is focused utterly on God.

The servant acknowledges his particular ministry as given by God (Isa. 50:4). His ear must be receptive to a very odd message from God, and his tongue must be skillful in speaking that same oddity.

This ministry of hearing and speaking has a specific intention. His work is to "sustain the weary." The weary ones are the ones in exile, who have their life shaped and crushed by the power of the empire, and who daily live close to despair. To "sustain" does not mean simply to speak a gentle word of consolation. It means, so we gather from the context of the poetry, to speak a reality that counters the weariness, to mediate to the exhausted an alternative reality, which creates space, freedom, and energy. Thus, the speech that can sustain the weary in exile is the word that Yahweh has defeated the power of the empire, that it is Yahweh who governs and not the debilitating power and ideology of the empire (compare 40:9; 52:7). Thus, sustenance to the weary is the bold theological assertion that reshapes the world, that voices new possibilities outside the assumed realities that dominate, and that invites the weary to change their self-perception and therefore their action.

Such a daring theological assertion is sure to evoke resistance and hostility (vs. 5–6). Hostility to this prophetic message might come from the empire itself, which when threatened seeks to silence such a dangerous alternative. Or resistance might come from the religious community of exiles who have become acclimated to the empire and do not want such demanding good news (see 45:9–13).

The hostility enacted against the servant suggests physical abuse, social exclusion, and harassment (v. 6). This servant, however, neither breaks off nor strikes back. This servant is free to make a more effective and peaceable response of nonresistance, because "the Lord GOD has opened my ear." Perhaps this means that the Lord God has spoken to the servant assurances and consolation.

The theme of confidence in the face of hostility is explicated in vs. 7–9a. This language and tone of these verses is disputatious. Perhaps the servant has been called into court, accused of speaking treasonable words in asserting Yahweh's sovereignty over the empire. Or perhaps the courtroom language is only a metaphor for a messenger under social pressure. Either way, as a literal courtroom or as a metaphor for a trial, the servant is called to hostile account for his speech and for his faith.

The language of vs. 8–9 offers a courtroom scene. The brief unit is built around two contrasting figures, but the sharp contrast is lost in translation. At the beginning of v. 8, the vindicator is the *one who declares me innocent.* At the beginning of v. 9, the alternative is the *one who will declare me guilty.* The two words, to declare innocent and to declare guilty, make a perfect contrast in the two words ṣaddiq and rāšaʻ, which we usually translate "righteous" and "wicked." The servant is sure he will be declared innocent, and so has no fear of those who want to see him pronounced guilty. He has utter confidence in the outcome of the court proceeding, because his message is true.

There may be a temptation, because the text is elusive, to treat it on rather formal grounds concerning the office of the servant, without attending to the hard-nosed substance of the servant's claim. The servant's business is to assert that Yahweh is indeed the one who governs. The servant is sustained because he himself believes the message he asserts. That same message which puts the messenger in jeopardy is the one that will sustain. Opposition to the claim of this God does not detract from the truth of the claim, its validity for the weary, or its power to guard and keep the messenger.

## Psalm 118:1–2, 19–29                                          (A B C)

Psalm 118 has long occupied a special place in both Jewish and Christian liturgical traditions. This final psalm of the "Hallel" collection (Pss. 113—118) particularly recalls the exodus event (compare especially vs. 14–28 with Ex. 15:2; see below) and this is especially appropriate for Passover. The Christian tradition has long associated Ps. 118 with the resurrection of Jesus, which is celebrated on Easter and every Lord's Day (see v. 24; Ps. 118:1–2, 14–24 is also the Psalm lection for Easter Day, and vs. 14–29 are an alternative for the Second Sunday of Easter). Because of the use of Ps. 118 in Mark 11:1–9 and parallels, Ps. 118 is also the psalm for Palm/Passion Sunday. In short, Ps. 118 has traditionally been associated with the key saving events of the Old and New Testaments—the exodus and the cross/resurrection.

Contemporary interpreters usually identify Ps. 118 as an individual song of thanksgiving. Following the invitation in vs. 1–4, vs. 5–18 apparently offer the testimony of an individual who has been delivered from some dire distress (see vs. 5, 13–14, 17–18). Scholarly debate has often centered on the identity of the speaker: Is it an ordinary Israelite, or perhaps the king or some other leader? The answer is not clear. What is clear is that the testimony in vs 5–18 unambiguously recalls the exodus, a *communal* experience of deliverance. In addition to v. 14, which quotes Ex. 15:2a, vs. 5–18 contain key words from the summary of Ex. 14:30–31 (see "salvation" in Ps. 118:14 and "look" in v. 7, which correspond to "saved" and "saw" in Ex. 14:30–31) and the song of Ex. 15:1–18 (see "right hand" in Ps. 118:15–16 and Ex. 15:6, 12). The effect is to open the psalm for communal use, and it is not surprising that the psalm is framed by invitations for all to join in the thanksgiving for deliverance (vs. 1–4, 28–29). Like vs. 5–18, the invitations also recall the exodus (compare v. 28 with Ex. 15:2b, and see "steadfast love" in vs. 1–4, 29 and Ex. 15:13).

In conjunction with their interest in the identity of the speaker in Ps. 118:5–18, contemporary scholars also attempt to identify a precise liturgical setting for Ps. 118. That some kind of liturgical ceremony—seemingly a processional, perhaps culminating a thank-offering—originally lay behind vs. 19–29 seems clear (see especially vs. 19–20, 26–27), but the precise nature and setting of it remain elusive. Of more interest and theological significance is the juxtaposition of the psalmist's gratitude (vs. 19–24, 28–29) with the psalmist's petition for continuing help (vs. 25–27).

The one who has offered the testimony in vs. 5–18 requests in vs. 19–20 to enter the Temple area. The intent is to "give thanks to the LORD" (v. 19), which the psalmist does explicitly in v. 21 in a way that recalls vs. 1–18 (see "thanks" in vs. 1–4; "answered" in v. 5; "salvation"/"victory" in vs. 14–15). As Walter Brueggemann points out: "Thanks is no casual gesture. It is, rather, a dramatic, public assertion of the source, trust, and goal of one's life" ("Psalm 118:19–29—Psalm for Palm Sunday," *No Other Foundation* 10/2 [Winter 1989–90]: 13).

The psalmist's commitment in gratitude of his or her whole life to God is reinforced by the metaphor of v. 22 and the direct affirmation of God's initiative and activity in vs. 23–24. The neglected, needy one has become of primary importance (v. 22), and God is responsible (vs. 23–24). Like vs. 5–18, vs. 21–24 recall the exodus. The psalmist experiences "salvation" (v. 21; see Ex. 15:2) that is "marvelous" (Ps. 118:23; see "wonders" in Ex. 15:11); this deliverance marks "the day on which the LORD has acted" (Ps. 118:24a, NEB; compare Ex. 14:13). The verb "made" or "acted" is the same verb translated "do" in Ps. 118:6. The repetition suggests that oppressive human activity is ultimately inconsequential in comparison to the saving activity of God.

The affirmation of God's initiative and activity serves as the basis for the petition in v. 25. The plea "Save us, we beseech you" is represented in Mark 11:9–10 by "Hosanna," where it appears to have become a celebrative cry, but here it is a real and urgent petition. A shift to the first-person plural had occurred in Ps. 118:23, and v. 25 continues in the plural, indicating again a communal dimension to the psalm. The psalmist's testimony (vs. 5–18, 21–22), though voiced in the first-person singular, recalls a past communal deliverance (the exodus), and the testimony serves as the basis for prayer in the midst of present communal distress. As people and psalmist had been saved in the past (vs. 14–15, 21), so now the people need to be saved again. The plea for "success" involves not abundant material prosperity, but rather the request that God provide resources for life amid the current threat.

The blessing and affirmation of vs. 26–27 should be heard in the context of the petition of v. 25. Blessing is possible in the midst of the current need (v. 26), and the present threat does not diminish the people's trust that "the LORD is God" nor their memory of God's past faithfulness in giving light (v. 27). Indeed, v. 27 may express the people's confidence in God's illuminating presence in the midst of the current crisis. In any case, the people apparently are intent on celebrating during the moment of threat, although the precise nature and significance of the activity described in v. 27b are unclear.

Verse 28a returns to the first-person singular as the psalmist echoes in a very personal way the communal affirmation of v. 27a: "You are *my* God" (emphasis added). He or she also reaffirms the intent to give thanks (see vs. 1, 19, 21); recalls one more time the exodus (v. 28b; see Ex. 15:2b); and invites the community to participate (Ps. 118:29; see Pss. 100:5; 106:1; 107:1; 136:1).

The movement of Ps. 118:19–29—thanks (vs. 19–24) to petition (vs. 25–27) to thanks again (vs. 28–29)—suggests to Brueggemann that Ps. 118 "is a model for evangelical prayer" ("Psalm 118:19–29," p. 16). Praise and petition join in affirming God's sovereignty and the persistent reality of human neediness. That Ps. 118 can serve as a model for prayer suggests too that its subjects—human need and God's saving activity—"are not tied to a particular historical occasion or social setting or festival, but are read as functions of the canon" (James L. Mays, "Psalm 118 in the Light of Canonical Analysis," in *Canon, Theology, and OT Interpretation*, ed. Gene M. Tucker et al.; Philadelphia: Fortress Press, 1988, p. 310). To hear Ps. 118 in the context of the whole canon "opens the psalm to use and interpretation in later and other times by the community for whom the canon of scripture is the guide to faith and life" (ibid.). For instance, the Gospel writers used Ps. 118:25–26 in the account of Jesus' entry into Jerusalem; and vs. 22–23 become a testimony to Jesus' death and resurrection (see Matt. 21:42; Acts 4:11). In short, the Christian church affirms that "the day on which the Lord has acted" (v. 24, NEB) now includes not only exodus but also the cross and resurrection of Jesus. Thus, Ps. 118 can be seen as a focal point for discerning the continuity between the Old and New Testament witnesses that God is "for us" (see vs. 6–7; compare Rom. 8:31) and that God's "steadfast love endures forever" (vs. 1–4, 29; compare Rom. 8:38–39).

## Philippians 2:5–11                                                    (A B C)

While some of the assigned readings for Palm/Passion Sunday change in each of the three years of the lectionary cycle, the Old Testament and epistolary lessons remain the same. Furthermore, this is the only occasion in the cycle when the remarkable Christ-hymn from Philippians appears. Unfortunately, it is often bypassed as the choice for sermon texts because of the traditional observance on this Sunday of Jesus' triumphal entry into Jerusalem. Whether on Palm Sunday or on some other occasion within the season of Lent, Phil. 2:5–11 warrants attention because of its powerful narration of the Christ-event and its subtle manner of drawing implications from the story for the attitude and life of the community.

First of all, *the passage tells (sings?) the story of Christ's humiliation and exaltation.* In the initial movement (2:6–8) Christ is the decision maker, who chooses not to cling to his divine prerogative but enters into the enslaved human predicament. He never flinches, but obediently follows the divine will, even to his crucifixion. The second movement (2:9–11) relates God's responding activity, making Jesus' name exalted above all others and the confession of him as Lord a universal one.

It is not unimportant that the passage is a piece of liturgical poetry, perhaps a hymn or a creed. Scholars may debate its conceptual background, its authorship, and its exact metric flow, but there is no questioning its rhythmic quality. The NRSV helpfully prints the text in a plausible poetic structure. Its original context is that of worship, where all good theology ultimately belongs. The intent is to praise God, to invite the congregation to join in the genuflecting and in the confession of Jesus' Lordship.

The last two verses are, of course, a promise. A Philippian audience that was suffering for the sake of the gospel (1:29–30) knew only too well that all knees had not yet bent in obeisance nor had all lips yet confessed Jesus as Lord. They, like Jesus, were living in a violent world and were facing opposition without and tensions within. But liturgy shapes life and molds expectations. Sunday after Sunday the congregation could rehearse the promise and by it be nurtured in its vocation in the world. Jesus' scandalous death, which also characterized both Paul's life and the reader's lives, was not the end. The future was in the hands of the servant Lord.

But in context *the hymn also calls readers to conform to Christ and adopt the same self-giving attitude in their relations to one another.* However Phil. 2:5 is translated (and it is notoriously difficult), it exhorts a style of life patterned after the self-chosen humiliation of Jesus. (The NEB reads, "Let your bearing towards one another arise out of your life in Christ Jesus.") The direction of 2:1–4, with its insistence on a common mind and attention to the interests of others, makes sense in light of the example of Christ. Or to put it another way, the character of Jesus' life provides content for the obedience to which Jesus' followers are called.

The context emphasizes not so much specific actions as attitudes. The verb "think" (*phronein*) found in 2:5 appears an inordinate number of times in this letter (ten times). Its range of meanings includes not only the activity of the intellect, but the direction of the will—"to be intent on," "to be disposed toward," "to set the mind on." This or that kindly deed does not exhaust the obligation believers have to one another. Their entire identity—their intuitions, sensitivities, imaginations—is to be shaped by the self-giving activity of Christ.

Perhaps a word is needed on the way in which Jesus' so-called humiliation becomes a model for Christian thinking and action. Humility is often misinterpreted in our culture, leaving people with the notion that meekness equals weakness. Yet in this context humility differs radically from both self-depreciation and false modesty. Either putting oneself down or playing a charade that one is really not so gifted as others mocks the intent of the text. Readers are not invited to think ill of themselves or to engage in some self-degrading practice.

The model is Christ, whose self-emptying was in fact a fulfilling of his true vocation. He attended to the needs of an enslaved humanity. He "humbled himself" by resisting the temptation to follow an easier calling, which would have denied his authentic self. There is no hint at all of self-depreciation. In fact, the implication of Christ's self-giving, drawn prior to the citing of the hymn (2:3–4), does not forbid taking an interest in one's own affairs. It simply condemns a selfish preoccupation that ignores or prevents interest in the life of others. Readers are urged to rejoice in the good in fellow Christians.

## Luke 19:28–40

Inevitably Palm Sunday carries with it a strong note of irony. On the surface, the story depicts the welcome of Jesus into Jerusalem. Disciples and others who have witnessed Jesus' deeds and heard his teachings gladly (if not always with comprehension) somehow perceive that this is a momentous occasion, and they mark it as such. Readers who have followed the story from the beginning, however, know that those who fear Jesus and plot against him have not disappeared. Within a few days' time, those who now welcome him will flee or even join with Jesus' enemies. The "triumphant entry" lives but an instant.

Luke's version of this entry underscores the irony by emphasizing the power of Jesus and his royal welcome. As Jesus draws near, he sends two disciples with instructions about the colt they may expect to find. Here he knows where it will be tied, what will be asked them, and what they should say in return. Such prescience more often characterizes the Johannine Jesus than the Lukan one, but in the Passion narratives such demonstrations of Jesus' knowledge become more frequent (see Luke 22:7–13).

When he arrives, those gathered praise God "for all the deeds of power that they had seen" (v. 37). If we were reading Mark's Gospel, we might suspect that those words carry a kind of sneer at the people who follow Jesus only for his miracles. Luke, however, understands that Jesus has divine power from the beginning of his ministry (see 4:14), a power that marks him as God's Son (4:36; 5:37; 8:46; 10:13), a power that he imparts to his disciples (9:1). Those who come to welcome Jesus to Jerusalem because of his "deeds of power" respond rightly to his ministry.

In addition to underscoring Jesus' power, Luke in this passage emphasizes his kingship. Several times in the Hebrew Bible an animal that has not previously been worked is used for some special role in Israel's life (Num. 19:2; Deut. 21:3; 1 Sam. 6:7), although the use of such here does not necessarily convey royalty (contrast the quotation from Zech. 9:9 in Matt. 21:5). The spreading of the cloaks along the road does, however, recall the army's greeting of Jehu following his coronation (2 Kings 9:13).

The most direct association of Jesus' entry with kingship, of course, comes in v. 38, with the quotation from Ps. 118:26. Here Luke alone inserts the word "king." The whole of Luke 19:38 recalls the opening of Luke, with the annunciation to Mary concerning the kingship of her son (1:32) and with the heavenly chorus declaring glory in heaven and peace on earth (2:14). With Jesus' entry into Jerusalem, the disciples acknowledge that he indeed is the king whose coming has been awaited.

Lest the reader lose track of what inevitably awaits Jesus in Jerusalem, however, Luke immediately introduces the Pharisees: "Teacher, order your disciples to stop" (v. 39). In the Pharisees' ears, this exaltation of Jesus sounds perilously close to blasphemy, and they warn Jesus that it must be stopped. His response, that the stones themselves would cry out if the people were silent, not only invokes the inevitability of his own acclamation, but anticipates the comments he will soon make about the stones of the Temple area (19:44).

In fact, divine necessity has impelled the movement of Jesus toward Jerusalem since at least 9:51, and it impels this final stage as well. In 9:51, Luke explains that Jesus "set his face to go to Jerusalem." At several points along the way, the narrator reminds readers that Jesus continues his journey toward Jerusalem (see 13:22;

17:11; 18:31; 19:11). This lection itself opens with the comment that Jesus "went on ahead, going up to Jerusalem" (v. 28).

Lest readers misunderstand the journey to Jerusalem as a journey that will culminate with the establishment of a political kingdom, the last teaching of Jesus that precedes the triumphal entry is the parable of the pounds, which Jesus tells "because they supposed that the kingdom of God was to appear immediately" (19:11). Here the central question is what the slaves will do in the time when their master is away, whether they will be faithful, and how he will respond to their decisions. Whatever awaits Jesus in Jerusalem, it is not to be the immediate establishment of a political kingdom (see Acts 1:6–11).

One element of the triumphal entry in the other Gospels is missing, or at least muted, in Luke's Gospel. Here it is consistently the leaders of Israel who lead and carry out the conspiracy against Jesus. With the exception of the note in 23:5, Luke does not attribute to the people in general the desire to bring about Jesus' death. The division that Simeon anticipated at the Jerusalem Temple (2:34–35) now is enacted in Jerusalem itself, as the disciples greet him with joy and the Pharisees with suspicion and disingenuous warnings.

# Holy Thursday

With its multiple historical connections—the betrayal and arrest of Jesus, the Last Supper, the Passover—Maundy Thursday becomes an occasion on which Christians recall these important events in the life of Jesus and the history of Israel. But merely remembering does not do justice to these events, which have ongoing, present significance for believers. The passages assigned for Maundy Thursday press beyond recollection of what happened to re-presenting (in the sense of presenting again) them to Christians today.

The notion of re-presenting Passover comes to expression in the text's instructions to Israel. Elaborate instructions regarding the celebration of Passover serve not simply to remind Israel of a past event but to present, even to create, that event afresh in each generation. In that sense, the exodus is not a faint memory of something that happened to distant relations, but an experience that is shared by each new generation.

Paul's instructions regarding the Lord's Supper urge a similar connection between present community and past event. As Paul saw it, the Corinthians ate the Lord's Supper in a way that failed to acknowledge its connection with the death of Jesus, but the meal itself was a proclamation of that death. In the meal, believers stand between the death of Jesus and his parousia, living with the reality of both those events.

Although the Fourth Gospel's story of Jesus washing the feet of his disciples finds scant place in the church's liturgy, it too urges re-presentation rather than mere recollection. Not a simple tale about Jesus' humility and service, the story foreshadows the death of Jesus and thus represents his ultimate act of servanthood. By virtue of his service to his disciples and the service of his death, Jesus radically challenges conventional, hierarchical notions about leaders and followers. Small wonder that the story of Jesus' betrayal immediately follows this disturbing scene.

In one sense, the psalm stands apart from these stories or instructions about specific events in the life of Israel or the church. The psalmist's gratitude, however, expresses itself in a public way, "in the presence of all his people." By virtue of this public display of thanksgiving, and indeed by means of the psalm itself, the psalmist presents again to believers of every age the present need for thanksgiving and praise.

## Exodus 12:1–4 (5–10) 11–14                                         (A B C)

Jesus' last supper with his disciples before his death is linked to the celebration of the Passover. For that reason, the Old Testament reading concerns Israel's provision for Passover. The Passover regularly needs to be understood on its own terms as a commonality shared by Christians while a genuinely Jewish practice. When understood on its own Jewish terms, it is then possible, as a second interpretative move, to incorporate into this festival the story of Jesus. Obviously such a Christian appropriation of the story and the festival must take care not to intrude on the intrinsically Jewish character of the festival.

The larger part of this text is a Priestly instruction for the careful liturgical management of the festival (Ex. 12:1–10). Liturgical rites, especially those which are precious and crucial, take on a life of their own. As a result, some of the detailed observances continue to be honored and taken seriously even though the original reasons for them may have been lost. These verses may be understood as analogous to a manual of instruction for Christian priests in a high sacramental tradition, concerning the particular gestures of celebrating the Eucharist. Every gesture counts and must be performed with precision.

This festival marks a beginning point in Israel's life (v. 2). It is as though life begins again in this moment of remembering and reenactment. The focus is the lamb. The lamb is both good food and costly commodity. A whole lamb may be too much meat and too much expense for a small household (v. 4). Careful attention is paid to the economic factors in the festival requirement. The lamb must be a good one, not a cull, for it must be worthy of its holy function (v. 5). The lamb provides blood as a sign on the doorposts and roasted meat for the meal. Israel's religious act consists in replicating a memory of eating together.

After the actual guidelines for proper celebration, we are offered theological interpretation of the act (v. 11). The meal with the lamb could be simply a meal. In the community of memory, however, the meal takes on peculiar signification. This is not an ordinary meal, and it must not be eaten in an ordinary way. Israel is to dress for the occasion in its travel clothes, with shoes (sandals) and weapons on (girded loins), with a staff in the hand, ready for leave-taking. The meal must be eaten quickly, with a sense of urgency. This "street theater" will be reenacted as though it were the moment before the exodus departure. In each new generation, the boys and girls participate in the drama of leave-taking from Egypt. They gulp the food, lean toward the door, watch in eagerness, and wait in anxiety, for they are at the brink of dangerous freedom. At the edge of freedom, nobody wants to linger with Pharaoh. This is a quick meal, not fancy or decorous, just provision for the long, hard trek to newness.

The passage concludes with a more formidable connection to the exodus memory (vs. 12–14). The term "Passover" now becomes a routinized festival, originated (so Israel remembers) in an awesome, dread-filled political act of violence wrought by God. The meal refers, as Israel tells it, to a powerfully partisan act. God acts against the Egyptian empire, on behalf of the shamelessly abused slaves who became Israel.

The text is a liturgical memory, but it is cast as a present-tense happening. God is the key actor: "I will pass through. . . . I will strike down. . . . I will execute judgments." The act of justice (judgment) that God performs is to crush the oppressive power of the empire. In that act of justice, it is clear that "our story" revolves around Yahweh, the God of freedom and justice.

## Psalm 116:1–2, 12–19                                           (A B C)

Psalm 116 is, in its entirety, a song of thanksgiving on the part of one who has been delivered by God from some distress, probably physical illness. As is typical of both psalms of thanksgiving and psalms of lament, attention is here given to the psalmist's vow to Yahweh. While such an element may seem to modern readers an offensive sentiment, in that it smacks of an attempt to bribe God, the interest of the poet lay in quite a different direction. The vow was an effort to say, in essence, "In response to your saving love in my life, O Yahweh, I confess that I will never again be the same person that I was before." Psalm 51, a model psalm of confession, contains this realization by the psalmist:

> [In response to your love, O Yahweh,]
> . . . I will teach transgressors your ways,
>     and sinners will return to you.
> [When you have delivered me, O God,]
>     O God of my salvation,
>         . . . my tongue will sing aloud of your deliverance.
>                                                   (Ps. 51:13–14)

The Psalm lection for Holy Thursday, after an introduction that affirms the grace of Yahweh (Ps. 116:1–2), turns to that part of the psalm which comprises the vow. Having thanked Yahweh for saving him, the poet now describes the change this salvation has brought to his life.

Structurally, this passage is composed of two quite similar parts, vs. 12–14 and vs. 16–19, separated by a verse (15) which, because it seems to break the logical flow of the text, may be a later insertion.

The first section, and thus the entire lection, is introduced by a question in v. 12 that reminds one of Micah 6:6. Yet the concern here is not, "How may I please God?" but, "How may my life more adequately express the redemptive power of God within me?" The response (Ps. 116:13) is in terms of drinking the cup of salvation and of openness to the reality ("the name") of God. The brief section closes (v. 14) with a promise, the major theme of the passage: "I will pay my vows to Yahweh."

The second section (vs. 16–19) is closely parallel to the first except in two respects. In place of the question of v. 12, v. 16 insists on the low status of the pray-er. The description of the psalmist as the child of a serving girl may suggest to Christian readers the figure of Jesus Christ, son of Mary, but to ancient readers the phrase would have been evocative of Ishmael, the son of Abraham's (Sarah's) servant Hagar (Gen. 16). Although a son of the patriarch Abraham, Ishmael was cut off from the promise because of his mother's inferior status. And so the psalmist is calling attention to his own weakness and alienation at the same time that he celebrates God's intervention, which has overruled these realities. The force of Ps. 116:16 is strikingly captured by the REB:

> Indeed, LORD, I am your slave,
> I am your slave, your slave-girl's son;
> you have loosed my bonds.

The other important manner in which the second section differs from the first is in the substitution of v. 17a for 13a, identifying a "thanksgiving sacrifice" as an appropriate vehicle for expressing God's redemptive presence instead of "the cup of salvation."

The balance of the second section replicates the first, in that vs. 17b–18 are identical to vs. 13b–14. Verse 19, which has no precise equivalent in the first section, is merely a poetic extension of v. 18b (14b).

The result of viewing the lection as two parallel sections, divided by the "foreign" (?) v. 15, is that we may identify three specific acts as the psalmist's means of expressing the reality of what God has done in his life:

1. Because of the goodness of Yahweh (vs. 1–2), I will lift the cup of salvation (v. 13a).

2. [I will] call on the name of Yahweh (v. 13b).

3. I will offer to [Yahweh] a thanksgiving sacrifice (v. 17a).

The relevance of this lection to the Last Supper and to Maundy Thursday observances through the ages may be found in all three of the psalmist's affirmations. (It is not entirely clear what the psalmist had in mind by the phrase "the cup of salvation," although a liturgical setting is likely, as in Num. 28:7.) Not only are these themes present in the narrative descriptions of Jesus' final meal with the disciples before the crucifixion (see Mark 14:22–25), but they permeate all celebrations of the Christian Eucharist. And by one of those hermeneutical "leaps" that transform many Old Testament texts, the subject of the psalm, the one who prays it and who experiences that which the text describes, is not just any human being, but Jesus Christ, that quintessential human being who is also God's representative to humankind. It is Jesus Christ who both lifts the cup of salvation and, through his shed blood, fills that cup. It is Jesus Christ who not only calls on the name of the Lord, but provides us with that unique name by which we approach God. It is Jesus Christ who not only offers a thanksgiving sacrifice, but himself becomes that sacrifice.

Even the "intruding" (?) v. 15 of Ps. 116 assumes new meaning when this text is read christologically.

> Precious in the sight of the LORD
> is the death of his faithful ones.

Of all the Lord's faithful ones, who was more faithful than He? Of all the deaths, whose is more precious than His?

## 1 Corinthians 11:23–26                                    (A B C)

These lines concerning the sharing of bread and wine are so familiar to most Christian ministers that the act of reading the text may seem superfluous. As the "words of institution" they are known by heart and can be recited verbatim. And, indeed, that intimate knowledge of this passage is consistent with the way in which Paul introduces it. When he writes, "For I received from the Lord what I also handed on to you," he uses technical language for the transmission of tradition, and the church's intimate knowledge of this passage continues that understanding of it.

The tradition itself contains the simple and direct words that connect the ordinary sharing of bread and wine with the death of Jesus and its significance for humankind. The bread signifies the body of Jesus, broken in death. The cup signifies the blood of Jesus, poured out in death. Through that death comes a new covenant, and through participation in the meal comes the remembrance of Jesus. The word remembrance (*anamnēsis*) appears in both the statement regarding the bread and the statement regarding the wine, suggesting that the Lord's Supper is vitally connected with the church's memory of Jesus. What the exact nature of that remembrance is becomes clearer in 1 Cor. 11:26.

With v 26 Paul no longer cites the traditional words of Jesus, but offers his own interpretation of the Supper: "For as often as you eat this bread and drink the cup, you proclaim the Lord's death until he comes." Two crucial points emerge here. First, Paul asserts that the very act of the meal *is* an act of proclamation. In the celebration of the Lord's Supper itself, the church engages in the preaching of the gospel. Protestant exegetes, uncomfortable with the omission of the verbal act of proclamation in this passage, long rejected this point by attempting to argue that Paul means that preaching *accompanies* every celebration of the Supper. If understood that way, however, the verse simply tells the Corinthians what they already know (preaching accompanies the meal) and adds nothing at all to the passage. Verse 26, in fact, culminates Paul's discussion of the meal by explaining its significance. The Lord's Supper is not just another meal, the eating of which is a matter of indifference; this celebration is itself a proclamation of the gospel of Jesus Christ.

The second point Paul makes in this verse comes in the final words, "You proclaim the Lord's death until he comes." The Lord's Supper is a very particular kind of proclamation—a proclamation of

Jesus' death. A different kind of celebration, perhaps a celebration of Jesus' miracle of multiplying the bread and the fish, might proclaim Jesus' life and teaching. Even the Lord's Supper might be understood as a celebration of the person of Jesus as a divine messenger. Building on the words of institution with their emphasis on the coming death of Jesus, Paul forcefully articulates his view that the Lord's Supper proclaims Jesus' death. Unless the final phrase, "until he comes," merely denotes the time at which celebration of the Lord's Supper will come to an end ("you keep proclaiming in this way until Jesus returns"), what it does is to convey the eschatological context in which the church lives and works. The church proclaims Jesus' *death* within the context of a confident expectation that he will come again in God's final triumph.

In this passage Paul has a very sharp point to make with Christians at Corinth, who are preoccupied with factions, with competing claims about the gospel, and with what appear to be class struggles. Paul's comments about their celebration of the Lord's Supper do not make the situation entirely clear to us, but it appears that they have followed the customs of the day, according to which the hosts of the meal served the choicer foods to their social peers and the less desirable foods to Christians of lower social or economic status. The activity of eating and drinking, and the struggle over that activity, have dominated the celebration of the meal. Paul's response to that situation is to recall forcefully the nature of the Lord's Supper. This is not another social occasion. It is *in and of itself* the proclamation of Jesus' death. Because it is a proclamation, Christians must treat it as such. Whatever conflicts there are about eating and drinking, they belong outside and apart from this occasion.

As earlier in the letter, Paul emphasizes the proclamation of Jesus' death as central to the gospel itself (see 1 Cor. 1:18–25; 2:1–2). Over against the Corinthians' apparent conviction of their own triumph over death, their own accomplishments and spiritual power, Paul asserts the weakness of Jesus, whose faithfulness to God led to his death, and Paul insists that the church lives in the tension between that death and the ultimate triumph of the resurrection.

In the context of the church's observance of Maundy Thursday, this passage recalls again the death of Jesus. That recollection is no mere commemoration, as occurs with the recollection of an anniversary or a birthday. The remembrance, especially in the Lord's Supper, serves to proclaim the death of Jesus Christ once again, as the church continues to live between that death and God's final triumph.

## John 13:1–17, 31b–35                                                (A B C)

Thursday of Holy Week is often a time for congregations to celebrate the Lord's Supper. The four texts listed in the lectionary for the day in varying ways provide interpretations appropriate to the observance. Of the four, the reading from John's Gospel is unique. Jesus' washing of the disciples' feet is found in no other Gospel, and in the Johannine narrative it takes the place of the institution of the Supper. In doing so, it provides an interpretation of Jesus' death, just as the traditional words of institution in the Synoptic Gospels and in the Pauline letters do.

Before considering the foot washing as an example of service given to the disciples, we must first see it as *a dramatic commentary on Jesus' death*. The introductory verses (13:1–3) set an unusual context for the action Jesus performs—he knows that the time for departure has come; he loves his disciples to the uttermost; he anticipates a return to the Father. Before Jesus takes the towel and the basin, we the readers are reminded of what is to occur immediately beyond the incident. Further, the language that says he "took off his outer robe," "tied a towel around himself" (v. 4), and "put on his robe" again (v. 12) is reminiscent of the good shepherd who lays down his life in order to take it again (10:17–18).

The dialogue with Peter occupies most of the story and provides the essential explanation of Jesus' action (13:6–10). Peter is not chided for his misunderstanding, but is told, "You do not know now what I am doing, but later you will understand." After Jesus' death and resurrection, Peter will be in a position to grasp what has happened to him. When Peter vehemently resists, Jesus warns him, "Unless I wash you, you have no share with me." The only way to belong to Jesus is to receive his cleansing service, to let him do what he came to do. Peter apparently prefers a different kind of Savior, one whose journey to God takes him by another route than the cross. He might have been happier washing Jesus' feet than letting Jesus wash his. The thought of Jesus on his hands and knees at Peter's feet is too threatening. Only with great reluctance does he yield to a serving Lord.

The shorter reading of 13:10 (see the margins of RSV and NRSV) is probably to be preferred over the longer reading ("except for the feet"). "One who has bathed" *is* the one whose feet have been washed. Nothing further is needed. The humiliating death of Jesus is sufficient to provide thorough cleansing.

After seeing in Jesus' washing of feet an interpretation of his serving, saving death, the reader is in a position to view the washing as *a drama of what Jesus' followers are to be and do.* He has given "an example" which the disciples are to emulate, and what a radical example it is! More than simply kindly deeds to the neighbor, more than a cherry pie in a time of crisis, more than money donated to a worthy cause.

The precise wording of the challenge in vs. 13–14 is critical. It is "your Lord and Teacher" who washes feet. While it might not have been so unusual for the pupil to wash the feet of the teacher, in this incident the roles are reversed. The One who had come from God and was going to God performs the menial chore for reluctant disciples. The action of Jesus subverts the regular hierarchical structure. The accepted patterns of authority are undermined, or, better said, authority is redefined in new and vivid images—a towel and a basin.

Following Jesus' example ("You also ought to wash one another's feet") means creating a community of equals, where the status of superior/inferior is reversed in the act of service. The world demands a pecking order in which everyone knows his or her place and in which power is carefully protected. Jesus' deed and his subsequent challenge to the disciples reject such a structure in favor of a new kind of parity. The Lord takes on the role of the slave. When people have a share with Jesus and respond to his cleansing death, they constitute a community where such reversal of roles is the norm and not the exception. The church is "blessed" when it follows Jesus' example (v. 17).

It is instructive that at two points in the narrative there is mention of the presence among the disciples of one who will betray Jesus (vs. 10b–11, 18–19). The church should not be surprised that it is a mixed body, that it includes both the faithful and the unfaithful, both the washers of feet and the betrayers. Yet Judas is not mentioned by name. He is not singled out. The other disciples do not know who the guilty one is until after the fact. They are not told to wash only the feet of those they think are faithful and to ignore the rest. In fact, they expect to serve the betrayer in their midst—just as Jesus does.

The incident provides real depth for understanding the new commandment Jesus gives (vs. 34–35). Love is defined as more than feelings, more than liking, more than compassion-from-a-distance. "Just as I have loved you, you also should love one another."

# GOOD FRIDAY

The Gospel writers often frustrate modern readers, whose pre-occupation with human emotion wishes to know not just what happened and why, but how those involved *felt* about things. Readers of the stories of Jesus' passion and death may wonder why the Gospels give so little detail about the crucifixion itself, especially about the emotional state of those present. John, the only Gospel writer who includes Jesus' mother among those present at the cross, ascribes to her not a single thought or word. Perhaps the utter shame of crucifixion prompted the evangelists to move with some dispatch through this scene. More likely, the horrors of crucifixion were too well known to require rehearsal for a contemporary audience.

In the Synoptic Gospels, the dominant emotional tone of the story stems from the dying Jesus, who cries out his despair and forsaken-ness. This connection between Jesus' death and his sense of being abandoned by God probably stems from the reading of Ps. 22 and, in turn, prompts Christians to see in this psalm, as in Isa. 52:13–53:12, reflections of the abandonment of Jesus. The passage from Heb. 4 and 5 likewise emphasizes Jesus' suffering, a suffering that makes him fully human.

At the same time, it is not appropriate to conclude that God disappears at the cross and only emerges again in the event of Easter. Christian proclamation of the cross begins with the under-standing that *even* in Jesus' utter abandonment, God was neverthe-less present. John's narrative displays that presence through the sign that proclaims Jesus "King of the Jews" and through Jesus' own declaration that all is fulfilled (19:30). The revelation to Mark's centurion, who proclaims Jesus to be "God's Son" when Jesus breathes his last breath, likewise shows God's presence in and through the cross.

The passages from Isaiah and from the Psalms continue to aid Christians who struggle to articulate the profound mystery of this

257

event. It displays the profound despair of God's Son. It prompts human despair at the utterly corrupt ways of a world in which the innocent suffer, too often alone. And yet it simultaneously asserts God's presence, even within that final aloneness. If the promise of God's final triumph reveals itself only in Easter, it nevertheless presses to be seen even in the noon hour of Good Friday, for even there God does not abandon the world.

## Isaiah 52:13–53:12                                              (A B C)

This well-known text is notoriously elusive and elliptical. The text is far from clear, and the historical reference is completely obscure. Indeed, David Clines (*I, He, We, & They: A Literary Approach to Isaiah 53*; Sheffield: JSOT Press, 1976) has urged that the poem deliberately avoids concrete historical reference. That poetic strategy, among other things, has permitted the church to hear in "my servant" an allusion to the suffering and death of Jesus as a saving event willed by God.

The poem (the part chosen for today's lection) begins with a resounding, triumphant assertion (Isa. 52:13). This nearly defiant enunciation becomes more astonishing as we hear the subsequent poem, which reads like a contradiction of this buoyant verse. Thus, from the outset, the poem voices a remarkable dissonance. This one who "had no form or majesty," this one "despised and rejected . . . held [to be] of no account . . . struck down . . . wounded . . . oppressed . . . afflicted," this one will prosper. We know from the beginning what the abusers of the servant never discern. The servant will be "lifted up . . . very high."

The servant may prosper. For now, however, the servant is lowly, unattractive, and without commanding presence (52:14–53:3). We are not told his precise condition; it is enough that he is "marred." His condition "startles." He has the sort of defect that causes people to look away in repulsion and yet to look glancingly back in fascination. He is a loser, an outsider from whom no one expects anything. He reminds nobody of authority, or of the power to transform or save.

Nonetheless, the servant carries in his body the capacity to heal and restore (53:4–9)! Verses 4–6 make some of the most remarkable statements in all of scripture. These claims are so familiar to us that we almost miss their power and daring. This unattractive loser has embraced and appropriated "our" griefs, sorrows, transgressions, and iniquities. It is *his* suffering embrace that has caused *us* to be healed, forgiven, and restored.

We are here at the central mystery of the gospel, and the miracle voiced by this poem. We are face to face with the deepest issue of biblical faith: How can one in suffering appropriate the hurt and guilt of another? This is not a question that is ever resolved by conventional logic. It rests only on a poetic affirmation that lives very close to honest human experience. It is the case, for example, that the suffering of a parent does indeed transform a child. It is the case that a "wounded healer" can profoundly heal. Here that same inscrutable power of transformation (which defies conventional logic) is embraced by the servant with overwhelming force. This servant gives self over to the hurts and guilts that he could have shunned. He does not shun, but embraces. And "we" are made whole, that is, "given shalom."

The appropriation of hurt and guilt could not happen boisterously, aggressively, or violently. It is done, rather, silently, peacefully, with no violence, with not even an outcry (vs. 7–9). The servant acts vulnerably, in the only way hurt can be healed or sin assuaged. Thus the poem not only witnesses to the agent but also radically asserts the only kind of act that can heal and make whole. In his staggering appearance and in his more staggering action, the servant has indeed changed the world, tilting it (and us) toward wholeness and well-being.

Now the promise of 52:13 will be kept (53:10–12). We return to the word "prosper" (see 52:13). This utterly obedient one will have long life and prosperity. The one who gave his life will receive back an abundant life. He will be exalted and lifted up, because he carried the burdens that were unbearable for the others.

On this holy day, the poem helps the church in rediscerning what Jesus has done and is doing. Jesus' entry into the hurt and guilt of the world has indeed changed the world toward wholeness. We must not exult and expostulate too much. The poem, and its evangelical enactment in the cross, do not warrant loud claims. They call rather for stunned, awed silence in the face of a mystery too deep for speculation or explanation. The miracle here characterized calls for a long, quiet, grateful pause. We watch while God acts vulnerably to do what could only be done vulnerably, caringly, at enormous risk, hurt, and pain. We watch while a healed world is birthed out of the wretchedness.

## Psalm 22                                                    (A B C)

The power of Ps. 22 lies in the fact that it is a statement by one who has felt utterly cut off from both God and the human community, yet who, in the end, achieves a remarkable level of peace and lifts to God moving affirmations of thanksgiving and praise. The manner in which the poet initially (vs. 1–21) alternates between expressions of despair and self-reminders of God's goodness in the past strengthens the forcefulness of the text, as if to portray the emotions of one who is utterly at the end of life's rope. The text thus becomes the vehicle for expressing the hopelessness of anyone who feels cut off from all the sources of support so necessary for happiness and well-being. And because of later echoes of this psalm in the narratives of Jesus' passion (especially vs. 1, 7–8, 18), it has a particular relevance for the Good Friday observance.

The "movement" in vs. 1–21 is that of one who tries without success to raise his head, only to sink again into despair and frustration. After having complained to God that God is not to be found in spite of all the poet's efforts (vs. 1–2), the thought of the poor mortal turns to the history of God's people (vs. 3–5). Yet the promises of old,

> To you [our ancestors] cried, and were saved;
>   in you they trusted, and were not put to shame,

become a bitter mockery to the psalmist for the very reason that God's saving activity of yesteryear seems not to be available here and now.

Again the cycle is repeated, but this time the psalmist complains of total alienation from the human community. With the bitterness of one who has taken life's social relationships for granted, only to discover how vital they are now that they are gone, the poet laments the loneliness of isolation. Those other human beings who should be sources of comfort and strength have turned their backs, so that in v. 6 the very humanity of the psalmist is brought into question:

> I am a worm, and not human.

Once more a remembrance of the past goodness of God is raised by the poet (vs. 9–11), with special emphasis on one of the strongest of all human bonds, that of the mother and the child. But in despair, the poet must acknowledge that the God who created and sustained him is now nowhere to be found.

Having vainly tried twice to lift his spirits through references to the past goodness of God, the psalmist now attempts to describe his total desolation (vs. 12–21). Most of the metaphors employed here have counterparts elsewhere in the Psalter (compare Pss. 31:9–10;

32:3–4), but the manner in which they are piled on one another imparts an unusually heavy mood of melancholy and resignation.

In a general sense, vs. 1–21 give tongue to the unutterable despair felt by one whom circumstance has cast completely adrift from all the reference points of life and from all other persons who lend joy and hope. There is no glimmer of divine grace, except that which the memory can borrow from the past. Only the act of prayer itself, which implies that someone must be listening, betrays any hope on the part of the poet. God is gone, and God's only presence is a distant flame, whose glimmer can be seen faintly across the years. The entire substance of vs. 1–21 is summed up in v. 1.

Yet there are two features that prevent these stanzas from becoming, like Ps. 88, an almost completely negative statement. The first is that vs. 1–21 are balanced by vs. 22–31, where the saving deeds of God are celebrated with thanksgiving and joy. (For comments on vs. 22–31, see the Second Sunday in Lent, Year B.) The other—and far more important—feature of this text is to be found in its association with the sufferings of Jesus Christ. As noted above, this includes direct connections with the passion narratives in the New Testament, but it is an association that extends beyond these verbal links. For whoever the original psalmist may have been or whatever human figure that inspired writer may have had in mind, Christians have understood that this psalm describes in a special way that human being who, because of the weight of sin attached to his suffering and death, stood in greatest isolation from God—Jesus Christ!

Thus, one cannot read v. 1 as an expression of one's own sense of apartness from God without remembering the utter despair with which these same words fell from the lips of the Crucified (Mark 15:34). One cannot consider vs. 7–8 as relevant to whatever betrayal and isolation one has experienced from those who were supposed to be friends without remembering the betrayal and mockery of Jesus (John 18). And one cannot find in v. 18 a statement concerning injustice suffered at the hands of others without recalling the terrible miscarriage of justice at Calvary (John 19:23–24).

But if despair, betrayal, and injustice had been the only realities at Calvary, we would today remember the execution of the Galilean peasant in a very different way, if we remembered it at all. However, in the end, despair was overturned by hope, betrayal gave way to trust, and injustice was conquered by the righteousness of God. For Good Friday was subordinated to Easter, and joy returned: the God who seemed to have forsaken Jesus raised him from the dead. And in Jesus' place, God crucified the despair of those who were convinced that they could never find God again.

## Hebrews 4:14–16; 5:7–9                                    (A B C)

In its opening chapters, the Christology of Hebrews strikes a tone of exaltation. Jesus is the "heir of all things" (1:2), an agent of creation (v. 2), superior even to the angels (vs. 5–14). Even if the subjection of Jesus to the weakness of human life is mentioned (for example, 2:14–18), that subjection pales in comparison with the language that celebrates the "apostle and high priest of our confession" (3:1). In its characterization of Jesus as the "great high priest who has passed through the heavens" (4:14) and as "without sin" (v. 15), the passage assigned for Good Friday continues this theme of the exaltation of Jesus. Alongside the exaltation of Jesus, however, this passage sounds a different note. Jesus is able to "sympathize with our weaknesses" (4:15), and Jesus "offered up prayers and supplications, with loud cries and tears" (5:7). Like human beings who serve as priests, Jesus' priesthood results from God's will, rather than his own (5:1–6).

At the heart of the passage is a comparison of Jesus' priesthood with that of human beings. This comparison allows the author of Hebrews to say something important about Jesus and, at the same time, to offer comfort and encouragement to the audience. In 5:1–4, Hebrews describes three aspects of the priesthood of human beings. Human priests have a particular function (they are "put in charge of things pertaining to God"); they have certain personal characteristics (they are themselves "subject to weakness" and "must offer sacrifice" for their sins); and they are designated by God ("And one does not presume to take this honor, but takes it only when called by God").

Hebrews 5:5–10 demonstrates that the priesthood of Jesus shares in these same three aspects, taking the three in an order that is the reverse of vs. 1–4. First Jesus, like human priests, serves at the appointment of God (vs. 5–6). Second, again like human priests, Jesus has the characteristic of being subject to weakness. Jesus' weakness is not sin—a statement that seems unimaginable to Hebrews (4:15)—but nevertheless Jesus participates in the human vulnerability of feelings and needs. As evidence of Jesus' human feelings, the author refers to Jesus' act of offering "prayers and supplications, with loud cries and tears" (5:7). Read in the context of Good Friday, these "loud cries and tears" appear to refer to the agony of Jesus on the cross. In the context of Hebrews, however, where Jesus' supplication addresses "the one who was able to save him from death," Jesus' cries seem to be a plea for deliverance from *out of death.* That is, the author envisions the already crucified and dead Jesus calling to God for deliverance from death. The overarching point, however, remains that Jesus' priesthood is one characterized by sympathy with human anguish. Third, like human priests, Jesus' priesthood has a function. He learned obedience through his suffering (5:8), and he initiated not just forgiveness of sins but eternal salvation for humankind (vs. 8–9). In v. 10, the author places Jesus within the priestly order of Melchizedek, essentially repeating the opening verse of the passage with its designation of Jesus as the "great high priest."

In an attempt to make real the familiar story of Jesus' death as a criminal, Christian preachers and teachers sometimes emphasize the details of physical and emotional suffering produced by crucifixion. And, indeed, the cruelty and shame attached to this particular form of execution, reserved largely for the outcasts of society, can serve to counter the romanticism signified by the wearing of the cross as jewelry. Sometimes, however, rehearsal of the horrifying details of crucifixion has the effect of suggesting that the significance of Jesus' death arises from the extent of his suffering; that is, Jesus suffered extreme physical pain and, as a result, brought about a glorious form of salvation for humankind. The flaw in this way of thinking about the crucifixion can be seen when other deaths, arguably even more cruel and inhumane, enter the conversation. Many of those who died in the Holocaust, with no shred of human respect or decency, as a result of an unbelievable process of cruelty and torture, surely endured more sheer physical pain and emotional grief than did Jesus or other victims of crucifixion. Does that mean that their deaths are somehow salvific or that their pain purchased the eternal life of others? In common with other New Testament writers, the author of Hebrews would answer that question negatively. Hebrews does not elaborate the details of Jesus' pain because that pain is not itself salvific. Jesus' priesthood derives, not from the quantity of his suffering, but from God and from Jesus' own obedience. It is God's sacrifice of Jesus, God's Son, that makes Jesus appropriate as "great high priest."

This reflection on the priesthood of Jesus, here as elsewhere in Hebrews, has a pastoral thrust to it. *Because* of Jesus' priesthood, believers may and should "hold fast" to their confession (4:14), confident that what they say together about God is reliable. Believers may and should "approach the throne of grace with boldness" (4:16), for Jesus has taught them that God hears their prayers. Believers need not be afraid of God, who wants them to approach and who intends to help them.

## John 18:1–19:42                                              (A B C)

John's narrative of Jesus' arrest, trials, crucifixion, and burial is made up of numerous individual scenes, each of which is appropriate for a Good Friday sermon. And yet the two chapters are themselves a literary gem, relating the events with sophistication and subtlety. The preacher's task is to isolate a piece of the broader story for preaching, but at the same time (as with all the Johannine narratives) not to lose sight of the whole and the powerful impact it makes on the careful reader. The skillfully fashioned narrative presents a portrait of Jesus as King of the Jews, who is in complete charge of his own destiny, in the presence of religious authorities who lose faith and governmental officials who lose power.

In reading the narrative, it is critical to notice the strategy of staging that gives individual scenes enormous force. Two examples (though there are many): (a) Jesus is questioned before Annas and Caiaphas in scenes that in themselves carry little significance (18:12–14, 19–24, 28). The scenes serve, however, an important purpose in that the narrator interrupts the questioning to tell about the denials of Peter (vs. 15–18, 25–27) happening simultaneously. The readers are faced then with two trials, one in which Jesus affirms his consistent testimony and is punished with a slap on the face by a guard and another in which Peter rejects his real relationships and goes free. (b) When Jesus is brought to Pilate, we are told that the Jewish authorities do not enter the praetorium, so as to maintain their ritual purity (v. 28). Pilate moves back and forth from talking to the Jews on the outside to talking to Jesus on the inside. The careful staging highlights the ludicrous behavior of the religious people, preoccupied with eating the Passover lamb, but all the while preparing for the death of the Lamb of God. A universal hazard of religious people!

Almost every scene in the narrative exhibits at least some element of irony, incongruities that expose the true nature of Jesus and the feeble, often pretentious schemes of other characters. For example, before Jesus is sentenced Pilate has him flogged by the soldiers, who turn the scene into a mock coronation of the King of the Jews (19:1–3). Interestingly, the narrator never uses the word "mock" (as do the Synoptic accounts), nor is it suggested that this is a charade. The soldiers see and speak the truth when they say, "Hail, King of the Jews!" He is in fact a rejected, maligned King.

Perhaps the most telling irony in the story occurs when Pilate brings Jesus outside the praetorium face to face with the Jews and announces him as "your King." When the people persist in demanding that Jesus be crucified, they justify their actions to Pilate by declaring, "We have no king but the emperor" (19:13–15). Within hours they would recite in their Passover liturgy that their only king is God, but here, in order to reject Jesus, they have to reject God. They unwittingly testify to the fact that Jesus and the Father are one.

Pilate is a key player in the narrative, occupying center stage with Jesus from 18:28 to 19:22. From early on, the reader gets the clear impression that Pilate, representing the power of political authority, is on trial, not Jesus. Jesus asks the pertinent question (18:34) and points out that Pilate inadvertently acknowledges his kingship (v. 37). "Do you not know that I have power to release you, and power to crucify you?" Pilate asks rhetorically (19:10), but as the trial progresses it becomes increasingly clear that Pilate has no power at all. The religious authorities play the stronger hand. Where once Pilate offered the authorities the choice of Jesus or Barabbas, now the tables are turned, and the authorities offer Pilate the choice of Jesus or Caesar (v. 12). Inside the praetorium Pilate is impressed with Jesus, but outside he is at the mercy of his subjects.

But ultimately it is neither Pilate nor the religious authorities who hold the power at the trial and crucifixion. The narrator includes three fulfillment scenes (vs. 23–24, 28, 36–37), whereby details of the story are viewed in light of the Hebrew scriptures, as the fulfillment of divine predictions. The effect is to remind the reader that what is happening is part of the greater plan of God. Jesus confronts Pilate's pretense of power: "You would have no power over me unless it had been given you from above" (v. 11). At his death Jesus utters a word not of distress or God-forsakenness, but of completion: "It is finished" (v. 30). The purpose of God has been fulfilled.

# EASTER

Perhaps on no other Sunday of the Christian year are the lections so nicely focused as they are for Easter Day. The common themes of the reality of death, the powerful intrusion of the delivering God, and the manifold responses to resurrection run prominently through the texts—themes needing to be rehearsed in every congregation.

The readings from Ps. 118 and from John 20 honestly face *the reality of death*. In the former, as the psalmist rejoices at an occasion of divine deliverance, death is remembered as the threat, the power opposed to God, from whose clutches God has provided rescue. In the latter, Mary acknowledges the devastation of death and begins to come to grips in a reasonable way with her grief and consternation. In neither case is there any covering over of the fierce and destructive fashion in which death separates and threatens the vitality of life.

All four texts announce *God's deliverance from death*, the divine "power play" that brings life not only for "the one ordained by God as judge of the living and the dead" (Acts 10:42), but also for God's people (1 Cor. 15). The resurrection of Jesus is more than a miracle; it is an eschatological event that makes possible a radical style of new life. Closed worlds are broken open, and old perceptions of what is plausible and possible are shattered. The future becomes a promise of sharing in the resurrection (1 Cor. 15).

Finally, in varying ways, the Easter texts enumerate *several responses to God's deliverance*. The psalmist offers a prayer of thanksgiving for the Lord, "my strength and my might," who "has become my salvation" (118:14). Mary becomes a witness to declare, "I have seen the Lord" (John 20:18). The text of Peter's sermon alludes to eucharistic fellowship and puts the hearers under a mandate to preach and testify to the risen Jesus (Acts 10:41–42). First Corinthians 15 is a reminder that Jesus' resurrection is a critical chapter in a larger story, reaching back to Adam and forward to the Second

Advent. In the meantime, the call is to steadfastness and growth in
the work of the Lord. In both worship and everyday human
relationships, responses are made to the gracious word of the empty
tomb, the word of divine deliverance.

## Acts 10:34–43                                                      (A B C)

The Easter celebration is the central event of the Christian year,
the center around which all else revolves. In recognition of its special
character, the lectionary provides during the entire Easter season
(including Pentecost) a reading from Acts as a first lesson. The
emphasis in these texts is on the kerygmatic proclamation of the
early church and on the work of the Holy Spirit in the response of
women and men to that proclamation. The death and resurrection of
Christ are viewed by these texts as God's acts of grace, by which
women and men are saved and reconciled to God and to one
another. In certain respects, many of these texts are the gospel *in
nuce,* and that is certainly the case with the passage at hand.

Acts 10:34–43 is one of several sermons by Peter reported in Acts,
this one directed to a godly Roman centurion, Cornelius. It is evident
to the reader of this text that the presence of the Roman is not
incidental to the narrative, inasmuch as the author of Acts wishes to
use this occasion to stress the universality of the gospel. Not only has
the Spirit spoken to the Roman in a dream commanding him to seek
out the preached word (10:1–8, 30–33), but Peter has likewise
received a special visitation, which declares, in effect, God's inclusion of Gentiles in the church (vs. 9–16). Yet, even though we have
been prepared by these elements for the inclusive nature of Peter's
sermon, the force of Peter's universalism is as refreshing as it is
energetic. Twice in a single breath the inclusiveness of the gospel
is stressed: "In every nation anyone who fears [God] and does what
is right is acceptable to him" (v. 35) and "Jesus Christ—he is Lord of
all" (v. 36). No matter that the first of these assertions lays emphasis
on the oneness of the human family before God, while the second is
primarily focused on the unlimited nature of Christ's dominion. In
the final analysis, they boil down to a basic affirmation: neither race
nor any other quality that marks some as different from others may
separate a person from the love of Christ. Neither ought these
qualities to separate persons from one another.

Then Peter turns to the Word itself (notice how the declaration of
"the message"—or, "the word" [NRSV]—in v. 36 is repeated in v. 37
and made the focus of the balance of the passage). Verses 37–42

recount the events that, in greater detail, are recorded by the four evangelists. Jesus, who had been empowered by God from the beginning (v. 38a), lived a life of remarkable good works, which were intended to thwart the power of the devil (v. 38b) and which were experienced by many people (v. 39a). (Notice that no mention is here made of what Jesus taught.) The outcome of this good life was Jesus' execution (v. 39b). But God did not allow this evil to carry the day, for God both raised Jesus from the dead on the third day and demonstrated his resurrection to those whom God chose as witnesses (vs. 40–41a). These witnesses joined Jesus in eating and drinking—a remark (v. 41b) with clear eucharistic overtones—and they have been charged with the responsibility of spreading the word about the risen Christ (v. 42). Then, almost as an afterthought, the role of the Old Testament prophets is recalled (v. 43).

Two considerations. The first is that this passage, which began by striking such a strong chord of inclusiveness, defines the human family more narrowly only at one point: those who were/are witnesses to the resurrection of Jesus do not include everyone, only those "chosen by God" (v. 41). At first blush this seems a contradiction of the bright note of universalism with which the lection opens. If God "shows no partiality" (v. 34), why are only some chosen? If Jesus Christ is "Lord of all" (v. 36), why are not all persons his witnesses?

The text has, of course, confronted one of those imponderable paradoxes of the gospel. Although the arms of the risen Christ are stretched wide to receive all persons, only some exhibit evidence of the work of the Spirit within them. And since their testimony is that it is not they, but God, who has initiated this saving relationship, we cannot help but wonder about others. Yet of one thing we may be sure: God has not abandoned them or ceased to yearn for them. But the limits of human understanding prevent us from saying more.

A second consideration: the unambiguous turning point in the text is v. 40. All that goes before and all that comes after hinges on the resurrection of Christ. It is the resurrection that demonstrates in a unique manner God's vindication of Jesus and that overturns the work of those who plotted evil. (Notice how, in the text, the murderers of Jesus are not singled out for God's wrath. These people are simply referred to by the innocuous pronoun "they" in v. 39b.) It is also the resurrection that makes it possible for those "chosen by God" to be witnesses to the risen Christ, to eat and drink with him, and to preach and to testify that God raised him from the dead.

In its spare and economical language, Acts 10:34–43 reminds us of that central affirmation of the Christian faith that is repeated in

countless ways on Easter Day: "Jesus Christ is risen today. Alleluia!"
Let us keep the feast!

## Psalm 118:1–2, 14–24                                        (A B C)

(See Palm Sunday for vs. 1–2, 19–24.)

The speaker of these verses (14–24) has just been rescued by God
from the assaulting nations (vs. 10–13). A seemingly hopeless
situation has been transformed by the radical intrusion of God: "The
Lord helped me" (v. 13). For that reason, the speaker gives thanks to
God. In the context of Easter, the church reads this psalm as the voice
of Jesus, who has been beset by the powers of death. It is only by the
greater power of God that the life of Jesus is wrenched out of the grip
of death. For that reason, thanksgiving is an appropriate tone and
posture for Easter.

Our reading begins with a powerful assertion (v. 14). "[Yahweh]
is my strength . . . my might . . . my salvation." The psalm echoes the
language of Moses, who celebrates God's massive defeat of the
Egyptian empire (Ex. 15:1–3). This verdict is, on the one hand, a
conclusion in the psalm, derived from the recent rescue. On the other
hand, it is a premise for what follows in the psalm. God's recent
rescue of the speaker becomes the ground for the hope and buoy-
ancy that follow.

The voice of the psalm is one of grateful righteousness (Ps.
118:15–20). The "righteous" are not necessarily the good or the
obedient or the pious. They are, rather, the ones who are rescued and
vindicated by God. The text speaks of the "tents of the righteous,"
where the rescued live (v. 15), the "gates of righteousness" through
which the obedient enter to worship (v. 19), and the entry of the
righteous, the willingness of Yahweh's rescued to come to worship
(v. 20). This community consists of those who have known God's
massive action on their behalf and who live their lives in glad
response to that action. While there is a moral dimension to righteousness, this psalm concerns those who are glad benefactors of
God's powerful love. They are righteous not because of what they
have done, but because of what they have received from God.

The righteous are not self-congratulatory. Rather, they are exuberantly grateful. They shift all attention away from themselves to
the rescuing power of God. Thus the grateful rescued sing three
times, "The right hand . . . the right hand . . . the right hand"
(vs. 15–16), an allusion to God's powerful, continuing purpose and
presence. The church knows at Easter, as this psalm knows, that

Easter would not have happened, and new life would not have been given, except by God's powerful intrusion.

It is because of that "right hand" of power that the speaker draws the conclusion, "I shall not die" (vs. 17–19). I was about to; I could have, but I did not, because God moved against death. Death is a formidable power, which wants to take control; but God will not let it happen. Thus death is not simply a state of negativity, but is an active force for evil. Evil, however, is no match for the power and resolve of God, and so singing is appropriate. Note well that the entire structure of these verses depends on understanding death as an active force, which cannot withstand the authority of God. Neither this text nor the claim of Easter makes sense unless God and the power of death are seen to be in profound conflict.

The utterance of the word "death" is decisive for this psalm. In the world of modernity, it is exceedingly difficult to voice "death" as a hostile power that threatens to undo our lives. That, however, is what the psalm is about. And that is what Jesus knows between Friday and Sunday. Jesus is being undone by the power of death, and the world is being undone with him. But Yahweh "did not give me over to [the power of] death" (v. 18), because God has kept me for the power and prospect of life.

The reading ends in boundless gratitude (vs. 21–24). God has answered. God has heard the need. God has rushed to intervene. God has changed death to life. God has overpowered Friday for the sake of Sunday. The rejected one, left for dead, is the valued one (v. 22).

What a day (v. 24)! The day of rescue is a day for joy. What a day—Easter Day—life day—new day—beginning day. It is a special day. For those saturated with the claims of this psalm, every day is a day of new life. This is the day of God's power for life, and therefore our day of singing and gratitude. On this day, God's people are at a beginning, not an ending.

## 1 Corinthians 15:19–26

On Easter we want to hear and to tell the story once again. We gather to hear about women going to the tomb to anoint Jesus and finding an empty tomb (Mark 16:1–8). It may be the Johannine story of Mary Magdalene weeping (John 20:1–18) that moves us, or perhaps the Lukan account of the women's words being dismissed as an idle tale (Luke 24:1–12). In whatever version, we anticipate that the Easter proclamation involves the telling of a story.

Paul disappoints this expectation. Whatever his preaching and teaching may have included, his letters give us no story of Easter. To be sure, in 1 Cor. 15:3–11 he refers with great certainty to several traditions about Christ's appearances to a large number of persons. And he insists that the risen Lord appeared also to him (1 Cor. 15:8; compare 9:1–2). But he gives us no story about the disciples' discovery, their confusion, or even their joy.

In 1 Cor. 15, Paul's most sustained reflection on the resurrection of Christ, he does not tell a story in the customary sense of an Easter story. Yet, for Paul, the resurrection plays an essential role in a much larger story, a story that extends back at least to Adam and forward to the final triumph of God. Because the resurrection is crucial to that story, and because Paul believes that the Corinthians have misunderstood both the resurrection and the larger story, he works methodically (even a bit tediously, perhaps) through his argument.

The first part of the chapter recalls the resurrection traditions, which for Paul are absolutely nonnegotiable. Whoever preached in Corinth, whether Paul or any other apostle, the Corinthians would have heard exactly the same convictions (vs. 1–11). He then argues for the integral place of the resurrection in Christian faith; Christian preaching is pitiful and empty without the resurrection (vs. 12–19).

In vs. 20–28 (note that the boundaries of the lection do not exactly correspond to the stages of Paul's argument), Paul provides us with a glimpse of the larger story of God and the place of Christ's resurrection in that story. First, he insists that Christ is the "first fruits" of those who have died (v. 20). The resurrection of Christ is not significant as an isolated event, a kind of special trick performed by God solely for the benefit of Christ. Rather, this resurrection, like the first fruit on the tree, signals that the full harvest can be relied on to follow. Versus 21–22 amplify this central point by reference to Adam. Just as Adam introduced death into the world, and all human beings die because of Adam, so Christ introduced resurrection into the world. All will be made alive in Christ.

Verses 23–24 modify the harvest reference with the caution that these things happen in an order that is proper. The first resurrection is that of Christ, then comes the resurrection of those who belong to Christ. "Then comes the end" (v. 24) seems not quite to fit; the "end" is not something or someone who is being raised from the dead. Yet the move from Christ and Christ's own to "the end" is crucial, for it reveals that Christ's resurrection anticipates the end. Christ's resurrection inaugurates the end, the final triumph of God over "every ruler and every authority and power" (v. 24), even over death itself (v. 26).

At least two statements in this passage will have caused the Corinthians some discomfort. First, the Adam-Christ typology emphasizes that both death and resurrection come about "through a human being" (v. 21). That is not to say that Adam invented death or that Christ raised himself from the dead, but that Christ was really a human being. He was not a spirit somehow masquerading as a human being, who had only to will himself to be released from death. Just as he died as a human being (15:3–4), so resurrection came about through this human being.

Second, and perhaps more controversial at Corinth, Paul portrays the resurrection of believers as an event that takes place in the future: "so all *will be made alive* in Christ" (v. 22, emphasis added), "then at his coming those who belong to Christ" (v. 23). Whatever the nature of the social and theological conflicts at Corinth and between at least some of the Corinthians and Paul, clearly there were those who regarded themselves as having already moved into a kind of resurrection life. Because that resurrection had already been accomplished, they were free to do as they pleased with their bodies (see, for example, 1 Cor. 5:1–2; 6:12–13). Throughout the letter Paul battles this mentality, but here he makes the point explicitly: only Christ has already experienced the resurrection; that of believers comes with Christ's parousia, and not before.

The Corinthians probably were not provoked by Paul's use of battle imagery in this passage, but many contemporary Christians are. When Paul refers to Christ "destroy[ing] every ruler and every authority and power" (v. 24), and when he speaks of God's enemies and subjecting all things to God, it becomes clear that there are forces in the cosmos that compete with God. In fact, these forces have power with which God's forces must do battle. Although the final victory is assured, that final victory has not yet taken place. What Easter continues to promise is not that all battles have been fought and won, but that God's power has assured that the final victory will belong to God.

## John 20:1–18                                                    (A B C)

At the heart of the Gospel reading for Easter is the resurrection appearance of Jesus to Mary Magdalene, leading to her confession, "I have seen the Lord." The narrative tells a wonderful story of a seeking woman, who is surprised by what she finds, or better, by the One who finds her. Hearing her name spoken by Jesus' familiar voice brings a transformation of her grief and the opening of a new world. A number of exegetical puzzles in the text remain to be solved, but, fortunately, they do not hinder our grasp of the basic story.

The actual encounter between Mary and Jesus occupies only four of the eighteen verses. We need, therefore, to pay special attention to what occurs prior to the encounter, in order to be able to understand what is at stake in Jesus' disclosure to Mary, and we need to take note of the brief account of Mary's response to Jesus in the closing verse.

Mary's participation in the story is marked by three parallel statements she makes—to the two disciples (John 20:2), to the two angels at the tomb (v. 13), and to Jesus, alias the gardener (v. 15). Her preoccupation is with the body of Jesus. The empty tomb does not prod her to faith, but rather makes her worry about what has become of the corpse. Who might the "they" be who "have taken the Lord out of the tomb" (v. 2)? The Jews? Joseph of Arimathea and Nicodemus? Grave robbers? The gardener?

Mary's anxiety and consternation are natural. She comes to the tomb early, perhaps for a time of private grieving, for beginning the slow, painful process of coming to grips with the absence of one she deeply loves. Her tears are right on the surface. The cemetery is an appropriate place to grieve. But the removal of the stone and the empty tomb disrupt what she is about and only create fear and frustration. Her mind moves logically to the conclusion that someone has taken Jesus' body. What other possibility might there be?

When faced with the open tomb, Mary functions as a reasonable, sane character. Her grief does not cloud her rational faculties. She arrives at the only conclusion a person in her (and our) right mind can arrive at. Dead bodies do not simply "disappear." Someone has to move them. In a world of cause and effect, of established rules as to what can happen and how, in a closed structure that allows only for the old and familiar to recur, Mary's logic is right on target. Find the body, wherever it has been taken, and get on with grieving.

Apparently, the two disciples (at least, "the other disciple") share Mary's predicament. On hearing the news of the empty tomb, they go to the site and confirm things for themselves. The grave clothes are there, all neatly folded. The text reports that "the other disciple . . . saw and believed" (v. 8). But believed what? Clearly *not* that Jesus was risen from the dead, since the text goes on to explain that the disciples did not yet understand the scripture and that they "returned to their homes." Their experience of the resurrected Jesus comes later (vs. 19–29). For now, what "the other disciple" believed was evidently Mary's report that the tomb was empty. His investigations confirm her statement. He sees no more than she sees, but he is less inquisitive.

Mary's closed world (and ours) is broken open when Jesus calls her name. Something illogical, impossible, and unnatural takes place. The One who was certified as dead (19:33) greets Mary. The established rules as to what can happen and how are overthrown. The old plausibility structure is left in shambles. It is a new day.

The part of the dialogue between Mary and Jesus, though not entirely transparent, is critical. Mary says to the gardener, "Tell me where you have laid him, and *I will take him away*" (20:15, emphasis added). Mary wants the body of Jesus; she wants to do for him what is conventional and proper. She cannot accept the prospect that the corpse has been stolen or hidden. He deserves a decent burial. Jesus responds, *"Do not hold on to me,* because I have not yet ascended to the Father" (20:17, emphasis added). The risen Jesus cannot be controlled, even by Mary's loving concern for him. Her logical and kindly pursuit of his deceased body simply does not leave room for the miracle that has happened, for resurrection, for ascension. The voice of Jesus calling her name shatters her customary world, reasonable though it may be, and opens up a brand-new future. What she is to do is to grieve no longer, but to go to the disciples with the word of Jesus' impending ascension.

Mary's reaction includes an obedient response to Jesus' command and an amazing statement, "I have seen the Lord" (v. 18). Her preoccupation with the corpse is made irrelevant by her encounter with the risen Jesus. Her logical language of cause and effect is replaced by the language of confession. It is a confession to sustain her in the new era without the historical Jesus, an era, nonetheless, in which Jesus' God and Father is the God and Father of the church (the word "your," where used in v. 17, is plural).

# SECOND SUNDAY OF EASTER

The texts chosen for the Sunday following Easter converge in their common interest in the way believers respond to the resurrection of Jesus. Such a decisive happening (an eschatological event, we call it) is not so much to be analyzed and debated as to be witnessed to. The texts help us to grasp what it means to be "witnesses" of the resurrection.

The brief vignette from Acts 5 is a critical text in the way it depicts the apostles in Jerusalem announcing both the resurrection of Jesus to those who shared in his death and his exaltation as Leader and Savior. The apostles witness by means of a verbal proclamation, through which the Holy Spirit functions as divine authorization. Though their actions put them in sharp conflict with the religious authorities, they refuse to be silent about such earth-changing realities.

Revelation 1:4–8 continues the theme by declaring Jesus as "the faithful witness, the firstborn of the dead, and the ruler of the kings of the earth" (1:5) and by designating the community as "priests serving his God and Father" (1:6). Identification with Jesus produces a body of people, interceding before God in behalf of the world and standing before the world in behalf of God.

The encounters with the risen Jesus in John 20, in addition to being commissioning and empowering experiences, record the transformation of Thomas, for whom analysis and debate ultimately give way to confession: "My Lord and my God!" (20:28).

The Psalter reading, of course, cannot be construed as an explicit witness to Jesus' resurrection. Nevertheless, as a song of praise its language testifies to a God who does "mighty deeds" and whose greatness surpasses all others (Ps. 150:2). The call to praise becomes a summons to live one's life in the context of God's powerful rule.

Proclamation, priestly activity, confession, and praise—all rather risky endeavors—inform the vocation of God's people as witnesses to the resurrection.

## Acts 5:27–32

The joy of participating in the resurrection of Jesus Christ contains a darker side, and that consists in the clash between Christ's vision of what human life should be, on the one hand, and, on the other, the power of all those contrary visions that dominate the social and cultural (to say nothing of religious) milieu in which daily life is lived.

The brief text for this day is clear enough about this matter: when forced to choose, the people of Christ must be faithful to their Lord's calling, come what may. "We must obey God rather than any human authority" (Acts 5:29) resolves the issue for the disciples and—it is to be hoped—for the reader. But the larger literary context in which these six verses are placed (vs. 12–42) gives flesh and blood to this bare-bones text, and, as the lectionary nowhere else draws attention to Acts 5, some consideration of this larger context is perhaps in order.

The ministry of Peter and other disciples has begun to arouse sizable public interest, and, along with that interest, it has aroused the hostility of some of the same authorities who were culpable in Jesus' death. Already there has been trouble (Acts 4:1–12), but the disciples bravely press on. When Peter and others continue to preach and to perform acts of mercy, they are arrested again (5:12–18), only to be delivered from their dungeon by divine intervention (vs. 19–21). The authorities, frustrated both by their own apparent inability to stop this activity and by the disciples' boldness, bring them before the Sanhedrin. The charges: insubordination and slander (vs. 27–28).

This trial provides Peter and the others with an opportunity to deliver their message to some of the very people who need to hear it the most. After insisting that the will of God is of more binding authority than that of any human group, they once again affirm their central kerygmatic proclamation (vs. 29–32). First, the Jesus for whose death certain members of the council stand culpable is no longer dead, but alive, in that he has been raised by the very God of Israel. This affirmation of the resurrection lies at the core of what they, the disciples, are about.

Second, God has honored Jesus, "exalted him . . . as Leader and Savior," not just to vindicate a righteous person who has been unjustly executed, but as an act of mercy toward Israel. This is the Jesus who stands ready to "give repentance" and "forgiveness of sins." The contrast that is drawn by the disciples' words between

God's grace and the murderous actions of Jesus' enemies is stark and obvious.

Third, the disciples themselves are witnesses to the reality of the events their words describe. Because they have been empowered by the Holy Spirit, they possess a courage that is generated not simply from within. And the wonderful thing about this is that this Spirit is available not just to some inner and secret circle, but "to those who obey him."

Very helpful to modern preachers who address this text is the description of the Sanhedrin's reaction to the disciples' spirited defense (vs. 33–42). It is extremely important that any exposition of this text not be shaped so that it may be misunderstood as anti-Semitic in nature. The portrait of Gamaliel and the record of his advice to the Sanhedrin (vs. 33–39) is a valuable reminder that the issue here is not Christians versus Jews. Although there are significant historical forces that caused this text to be shaped in the manner in which we have received it, our own historical situation demands that the preacher be clear that the enemies of Jesus are not Jews, since both Jews and Gentiles participated in Jesus' death. Those who oppose the will of the Lord Jesus Christ are those who would posit other gods and those who would work against the presence of justice and compassion in human life—whatever branch of the human family tree they may represent.

Gamaliel deserves to be mentioned in any consideration of Acts 5:27–32 because his memory serves as an important corrective to a misunderstanding many modern Christians have of the biblical Pharisees. The description of this man is not that of a narrow and censorious legalist, but that of a warm and compassionate teacher who was quite aware that the God of Israel sometimes acted in benevolently surprising ways. According to rabbinic tradition, Gamaliel took pains to see that the provisions of the Torah were enforced in ways that were humane and just. He taught, for example, that the burden on a widowed woman should be eased by allowing her to remarry on the basis of only one witness (instead of the customary two) to the fact that her husband was dead. That portrait of a sensitive and open-minded sage is consistent with the record in Acts 5:33–39.

The central thrust of this text is the disciples' affirmation that the crucified Jesus is the living "Leader and Savior" whom God raised from the dead. Furthermore, this living Lord is at work, by the power of the Spirit, in the lives of "those who obey him." But if we read far enough the text goes forward to remind us that it is not always easy to categorize or to place under one roof those who live just and compassionate lives. "In my Father's house there are many dwelling places" (John 14:2), and one of those would seem to shelter the Gamaliels of the world.

## Psalm 150

The Hebrew title for the book of Psalms means "Praises." Even though the Psalter contains more prayers of lament or complaint than it does hymns or songs of praise, the designation "Praises" is an accurate one. The whole Psalter moves toward praise in two senses. First, almost all the prayers of lament or complaint end with an expression of or a vow to praise. Second, the laments are clustered in Books I–III of the Psalter (Ps. 1–89), whereas songs of praise are predominant in Books IV and V. Psalms 146—150, all of which begin and end with "Hallelujah" ("Praise Yah," a shortened form of the divine name "Yahweh"), represent the culmination of the Psalter's movement toward praise; and Ps. 150 is the final crescendo of praise.

Here every creature in heaven and on earth is invited to praise God, and every instrument is to be used. The effect is heightened by the uniqueness of Ps. 150. It departs from the usual structure of a song of praise—invitation to praise followed by reasons for praise. Rather, Ps. 150 is an extended, unbroken invitation to praise. Walter Brueggemann well describes the form and its effect ("Bounded by Obedience and Praise: The Psalms as Canon," *Journal for the Study of the Old Testament* 50 [1991]: 67):

> This psalm is a determined, enthusiastic, uninterrupted, relentless, unrelieved summons which will not be content until all creatures, all of life, are "ready and willing" to participate in an unending song of praise that is sung without reserve or qualification. The Psalm expresses a lyrical self-abandonment, an utter yielding of self, without vested interest, calculation, desire, or hidden agenda.

As an expression of "lyrical self-abandonment," Ps. 150 is an eminently appropriate conclusion to the Psalter, which from the beginning has commended openness to God's instruction (Ps. 1) and recognition of God's sovereignty (Ps. 2). Praise is the offering of one's whole life and self to God, and Ps. 150 is indeed an enthusiastic expression of yielding the self to God.

Every line of the psalm contains an imperative form of the verb *hll*, "praise," except v. 6 where a jussive form has the same effect. What sets vs. 1–2 apart from the rest of the unbroken summons to praise is that the summons here implies what is usually an explicit feature of a song of praise—that is, reasons for praise. The vocabulary of vs. 1–2 is associated elsewhere with Yahweh's kingship or sovereignty, a key theme throughout the Psalter and especially prominent in Pss. 145—149 (see 145:1, 11–13; 146:10; 149:2). For instance, "sanctuary" elsewhere is where God dwells as King. God's throne is there (Ps. 11:4), and God is explicitly greeted as King upon entry "into the sanctuary" (Ps. 68:24). It is not clear whether the sanctuary here should be understood as God's heavenly abode or the earthly Temple. Perhaps both senses are intended (compare Ps. 11:4 with 68:24). As H.-J. Kraus suggests, "At the holy place heaven and earth touch each other" (*Psalms 60—150,* trans. H. C. Oswald; Minneapolis: Augsburg, 1989, p. 570). "Firmament" in Ps. 150: 1b suggests heaven, but it is not clear whether v. 1a and v. 1b are synonymously parallel.

The Hebrew roots behind the words "mighty" (v. 1b) and "mighty deeds" (v. 2a) occur together in Ps. 24:8 to describe Yahweh, "King of glory." The word "mighty" is often used in the context of the proclamation of Yahweh's kingship (see 99:4; see also NRSV "strength" in 29:1; 93:1; 96:6), as is the root behind the word "greatness" (see "great" in 47:2; 95:3; 99:2). In short, the summons to praise is the invitation to yield the self to Yahweh's rule; it is the invitation to enter and to live in the reign of God.

Praise involves both life and liturgy. The praise of God in worship reinforces, renews, and reshapes the commitment of the whole of life to God. In vs. 3–5, the worship of God in the Temple is in view, especially music. Every section of the orchestra—horns, strings, winds, percussion—is invited to join in a symphony of praise. Elsewhere, the sound of the trumpet announce's Yahweh's kingship (Ps. 47:5–7); and several of the instruments in Ps. 150 are involved in the liturgy of 2 Sam. 6, where the Ark on which Yahweh "is enthroned" (v. 2) is brought to Jerusalem (see especially v. 5; see also 1 Chron. 13:8; 15:28; Neh. 12:27; Pss. 68:24–25; 149:3, among others). Liturgy involves the joyful enactment of the commitment of life to God.

The symphony of praise must ultimately involve all creatures and all creation (see Ps. 148). The songs of praise regularly push toward universality, inviting "all you nations" (117:1) and indeed "all the earth" (100:1) to praise God. Psalm 150:6 is the ultimate extension of that invitation. The word "breathes" recalls the creation of the world and human life (Gen. 2:7) as well as the Flood story, in which the destiny of human and animal life went awry (Gen. 7:22). Against this background, Ps. 150 proclaims that the proper goal of every creature is praise—that is, life shaped and lived under God's rule. It is this destiny that Jesus sought to enact by inviting persons to enter the realm of God (Mark 1:15). As the apostle Paul put it, for those who "live no longer for themselves" (2 Cor. 5:15), "there is a new creation" (2 Cor. 5:17).

## Revelation 1:4–8

Because of the narrative content of much of the Revelation to John, it is easy to overlook the fact that this apocalyptic work presents itself as a letter. The lection for this week is the salutation to that letter (see 22:21 for the letter closing) and, as is often the case with letter openings, it identifies several issues that are important for the work as a whole.

The passage opens with the letter greeting (vs. 4–5a), the doxology (vs. 5b–6), and two separate prophetic statements (vs. 7–8). Throughout the lection, the author amasses descriptions of both God and Jesus. These descriptions have parallels in a variety of Jewish and non-Jewish sources and, therefore, would have sounded familiar notes in the ears of John's audience. (This feature of the passage is discussed in more detail when it is assigned for Proper 29 of Year B.)

Read in connection with Eastertide, what emerges from this lection with particular clarity is the richness of its understanding of Jesus' role. Here Jesus is described in terms of the work of his ministry (especially his death), his role as God's witness, and the present and future accomplishments of his resurrection. What makes the depiction particularly forceful is that much of the imagery used to describe Jesus is probably better known to many of us from other early Christian writings, but here John brings that imagery together forcefully.

Jesus is the one "who loves us and freed us from our sins by his blood, and made us to be a kingdom" (vs. 5, 6). Despite the use of the present tense for the verb "love," this aspect of the description seems to refer back to the work of Jesus in his ministry, and especially in his death. That the Christ-event stems from love, God's love for humankind and also Christ's love, appears prominently in Paul (Rom. 8:37; Gal. 2:20) and in John (3:16). Reference to forgiveness through Jesus' blood similarly appears in Paul (Rom. 3:21–26) and in 1 John (1:7). First Peter speaks of the Christian community as a priesthood and a nation (2:5, 9), but the nuance here is somewhat different, for the kingdom John envisions is the one that is established over against the kingdom of Satan (see, for example, 2:13). What makes this description of the work of Jesus powerful, then, is the way it resonates with many other themes in early Christian Christology.

Just prior to this description in the doxology, John refers to Jesus as "the faithful witness" (v. 5). While the theme of witnessing is prominent in other New Testament works (for example, Acts 1:8; John 1:7–8), in Revelation the notion of witnessing becomes highly charged because of the references to the deaths of Christian witnesses. In Rev. 2:13, the letter to Pergamum singles out the witness of Antipas, who was killed. Chapter 6:9–11 speaks of the cry of the slaughtered witnesses, who seek vindication for their blood. Chapter 17:6 likewise refers to the "blood of the witnesses to Jesus."

These passages are commanding precisely because the slaughtered witnesses are connected with the witness to or about Jesus. As early as 1:2, the author speaks of John "who testified [literally, "witnessed"] to the word of God and to the testimony [literally, "witness"] of Jesus Christ." The witness or testimony of Jesus appears again in 1:9; 12:17; 19:10; and 20:4. Exactly what the phrase means is a bit unclear, the more so because the Greek may refer either to the testimony about Jesus (that is, witness to Jesus given by someone else) or to the testimony of Jesus (that is, testimony he gives). Probably the phrase encompasses the notion of Christian proclamation, particularly proclamation that is given despite a context of danger and persecution.

For John, the first such witness is Jesus himself, the "faithful witness" (compare 3:14). Because of the witness Jesus gives to God, because of the witness embodied in Jesus' ministry, believers know how to witness and what their witness should include.

What makes this reading particularly appropriate for Eastertide, of course, is its reference to the accomplishments of the resurrection. By virtue of the resurrection, Jesus is the "firstborn of the dead" (1:5). This recalls 1 Cor. 15:20–28, with its association of the resurrection with the "first fruits" of the harvest (see the discussion of this passage for Easter Day). As "firstborn," Jesus similarly becomes the promise, the absolute conviction that neither death nor Satan nor the powers of Satan have the final word. Resurrection here becomes the promise of the "new heaven" and "new earth," not a trick by which one individual is resuscitated but the renewal of creation itself.

Unlike 1 Cor. 15, however, Revelation identifies Jesus as the "ruler of the kings of the earth." Although the rulers of the earth are not yet aware of it, and many of the inhabitants of the earth fail to recognize it, Jesus *already* rules as the chief among the kings of earth.

The closing lines of this lection, words attributed to God, place all of it in context. "I am the Alpha and the Omega." The God who had the first word, the word by which creation came into being, will also have the last word, the word by which new creation will come into being. That is the promise of Easter.

## John 20:19–31

Two of the distinct sections of the Gospel lesson for this Sunday are tied together in a connected narrative, built on a clear time sequence; the third section is an appended conclusion to the whole Gospel.

First, Jesus, having previously appeared to Mary Magdalene, comes to a gathered company of disciples (20:19–23). They have heard Mary's testimony as to having met the risen Jesus, but the news results only in a fearful retreat, a clandestine meeting behind locked doors. The location speaks volumes about the disciples' confusion and their frantic efforts at self-protection.

Jesus' appearance carries the marks of revelation, commission, and empowerment. First come the words of reassurance ("Peace be with you") and then the distinctive signs. The wounds make it clear that he is no ghost, but the very one they knew as scarred and crucified. As it had been with Mary, so now it is with the disciples—a moment of disclosure that transforms their fear into joy.

The revelation immediately carries with it a commission. The One who is himself the agent of God deputizes the disciples. His mission from the Father becomes the paradigm for their mission to the world. The words of peace—Jesus' peculiar gift to the disciples, different from the world's gift (14:27)—are not for them alone, but are meant to be spoken through them to other groups crouched behind bolted doors, dismayed and upset, who have not yet heard or find it hard to believe that death is not the end. And the commission carries with it the empowerment. The strange expression "he breathed on them" (20:22) surely echoes Gen. 2:7. The giving of the Spirit signals a new creation, a new community that declares a gospel of forgiveness. The words "Receive the Holy Spirit" fulfill the various promises Jesus has spoken throughout the farewell discourses about the coming Paraclete, who will lead the disciples "into all the truth" (16:13). No doubt the church's responsibility in forgiving and retaining sins (20:23) has to do with the hearers' acceptance or rejection of the gospel of forgiveness. Those who hear are judged by how they respond to the offer of life (3:19–21).

The second section (20:24–29) recounts, first, the absence of Thomas when Jesus appeared to the disciples, his skepticism at their account of the incident, and finally his own encounter with Jesus a week later. The disciples had had their chance to see the scars on Jesus' hands and side, and Thomas needed such visible evidence himself. The disclosure evokes from him the remarkable confession, "My Lord and my God!"

Thomas joins the group of believing eyewitnesses, in effect becoming one of its most significant members. His doubt is dispelled only by seeing the same evidence the other disciples have seen. He stands as another in a series of figures (Mary, Peter, the beloved disciple, and the other disciples) whose experience of the risen Jesus becomes the witness for all the readers of this narrative. Jesus' response to Thomas in 20:29 is not meant to disparage his faith nor to undermine his confession, but rather to say that Thomas has no privileged place over those who come later, who are not eyewitnesses but who nevertheless believe.

It is clear in the Gospel of John that characters are led to faith with differing experiences and varying degrees of evidence. Not all are the same. But the Gospel has a special concern for its readers, for those removed in time and space from the originating events and whose faith is born and nurtured by means of the witness of the text.

The concluding statement of the assigned reading (20:30–31) appropriately follows Jesus' blessing of those who have not seen and yet believe. The Gospel, recording a selection of the signs Jesus did (including the sign of the resurrection), is intended to create and/or foster belief in Jesus. (It is impossible in 20:31 to determine for sure whether the verb in Greek is present or aorist, whether it should be rendered "you may continue to believe" or "you may come to believe." A consideration of the Gospel as a whole leads to the probable conclusion that it was written to nurture a Christian community in crisis rather than as an evangelistic tract for the unchurched.)

What may be more significant is the implication of 20:30–31. In a peculiar way the readers of this Gospel are being described as a textually constituted community, that is, a community whose faith is mediated by the recorded witness of others. Putting Jesus' deeds into writing enables "those who have not seen" to become and remain believers. The church then is depicted as a people of the book. It lives not by oral tradition nor by a continuum of mystical experiences but by encountering the signs of Jesus found in the text.

This familiar statement of the Gospel's purpose provides a powerful impetus to reflect on what it means for the church to be a

Bible-centered community. Why must preaching, teaching, church programs, and pastoral care be rooted in scripture? Why is biblical illiteracy such a serious threat to the health and vitality of faith? Why is the faithful interpretation of the text so critical to the life of the congregation?

# THIRD SUNDAY OF EASTER

Moments of disclosure—they happen all too rarely. Often after long periods of frustration and confusion, the light dawns, and what has been shrouded in darkness suddenly can be glimpsed—if only for an instant. But the momentary disclosure is liberating. It frees us to go on with life, with a new sense of enthusiasm. It is not a matter of new information that has made the difference; it is a revelation, a gift from beyond ourselves.

Such a disclosure happened to the disciples after a long night of unsuccessful fishing. When weary and ready finally to beach the boat, they hear a voice directing them to let down the nets on the right side. As they do so and find an enormous catch of fish, they wonder who has such insight about the waters. The beloved disciple voices the revelation, "It is the Lord!" (John 21:7).

Just so, the light that flashed on the Damascus road and the voice of identification constituted such a moment of disclosure for Paul (Acts 9:1–6). In reflection, the psalmist sings about such a moment for him- or herself, if not for the whole people of God:

> You have turned my mourning into dancing;
> you have taken off my sackcloth
> and clothed me with joy.
>
> (Ps. 30:11)

These are not merely moments when we finally find the right sentence with which to conclude the sermon or when it suddenly dawns on us why the session meeting went so badly. These texts relate revelations of the divine mystery, expressions of the transformative presence of God. The apocalyptic scene in Rev. 5 puts it most clearly. The scroll that not only explains the final events of human history but sets them in motion is to be opened, but who is worthy do it? "The Lion of the tribe of Judah, the Root of David," shouts one

285

of the elders—only John discovers that the Lion is really the Lamb, slaughtered (5:5–6).

The Lord on the beach, directing the disciples to better fishing; the Lord revealed as "Jesus, whom you are persecuting"; the Lord who grants the psalmist healing—is ultimately disclosed as the suffering, crucified One.

## Acts 9:1–6 (7–20)

This lection, one of the biblical texts that has influenced the church's understanding of the nature of the Christian life most profoundly, also plays a pivotal role in the literary structure of the book of Acts. The introduction of Saul/Paul into the story of the early Christian community redirects the attention of the reader of Acts so that, for most of the balance of the book, the work of other early preachers and teachers is subordinated to that of the converted Pharisee. The missionary activity of Paul now begins to unfold in the kind of detail that is missing from the narratives concerning Peter and others.

This account of Paul's violent reorientation of his life from the role of enemy of the church to that of evangelist is in some tension with Paul's own account of his conversion in Gal. 1:13–24, a reality that has resulted in considerable discussion among scholars over the years. Nevertheless, when most Christians, both laity and clergy, think about Paul's dramatic change of commitment, the "Damascus road experience" of Acts 9 is the one that usually comes to mind. That very three-word phrase, in fact, may be found in the inventory of speakers and writers who have never bothered to read the twenty verses that constitute the present lection.

Thus a large part of the challenge to the interpreter of this passage is that which faces the interpreter of any biblical text that has grown overly familiar through repeated reference, other prominent examples being Ps. 23 and John 3:16. How does one bring fresh insights to understanding a passage that either has been repeated so much that the mere words roll off inattentive ears, or—as in this case—is so straightforward that it appears to be completely understood already?

One possibility the use of a lectionary provides is for the interpreter to investigate possible lines of communication among the various texts appointed for a given day. Often the interaction of the lectionary passages provides insights that would not emerge from any of the individual texts standing alone. Thus the preacher on this text will wish to consider the other texts for this day in light of this one.

Another manner of bringing to life a text that, by its very familiarity, has become moribund to many is by permitting the text in question to challenge stereotypes that often arise out of a traditional misreading of the text itself. In the case of Acts 9:1–6 (7–20), one particular stereotype comes to mind.

This is the misunderstanding that the experience of Paul is normative and that it somehow represents what all or most Christians should undergo in their own appropriation of Christ into their lives. The reality would seem to be that Paul's Damascus road experience is noteworthy not just because the subject of this experience later became the early church's foremost missionary to the Gentiles, but because it was *atypical* and *extraordinary*. It simply was not the sort of thing that new converts to Christianity universally experienced.

Before his conversion Paul was not a run-of-the-mill Pharisee. His intense opposition to the "Way" (v. 2) may have found allies among some members of the Jewish community, but most of Paul's Jewish contemporaries seem to have been much less severe in their resistance to this new faith. The question has often been raised as to how Paul could have been so harsh in his attitude toward Christians (vs. 1, 13–14; compare Gal. 1:13), while his teacher Gamaliel (Acts 22:3) was relatively tolerant (see Second Sunday of Easter, Acts 5:27–32). It was Gamaliel's view, after all, that prevailed in the Sanhedrin, so the preconversion Saul stands out as a zealot who may have had sympathizers in the high-priestly party, but whose views were not shared by all Jewish leaders.

Thus, the very nature of his conversion is a reflection of his state of mind and heart in the period leading up to his changed life, and it perhaps demonstrates as remarkably as any other biblical text that God employs means of reaching an individual that are commensurate with that individual's needs.

Acts 9:1–20 stands not so much as a formulaic representation of what God would do with each individual as it stands as a reminder that God would deal with each of us according to who we are. In Paul's case his fierce energies, which had been expended in persecuting Christians, are now redirected so that they are employed in winning women and men to faith in Christ. There can be little doubt that his preaching was both authoritative and convincing (v. 20, compare vs. 21–22), and those qualities may be understood as derivative not only of his complete commitment, but also of his own intense personality.

However, different persons respond to different initiatives from God, and more subtle means of persuasion than the intense energies of the Damascus road can be just as effective in eliciting in response to Christ's grace. One may wish to note, as an example, John 21:5–7 (see commentary below)—or, more subtle still, that "other road," the one to Emmaus (Luke 24:13–35, especially v. 35).

The one reality about Paul's experience on the Damascus road that does seem to be universal is its declaration that God's love knows our personal needs and steps forth to meet them, even if it does not always knock us to the ground in the process.

## Psalm 30

Psalm 30 is one of the few psalms that are identified with a specific occasion, in this case "the dedication of the Temple." In rabbinic sources, Ps. 30 is associated with the Feast of Dedication (Hanukkah), which originated to celebrate the restoration of proper worship under the Maccabees in 165 B.C., after the desecration of the Temple by Antiochus (IV) Epiphanes. Most scholars think that the association of Ps. 30 with Hanukkah is secondary, since the psalm itself is likely to be much older than the second century B.C., since it appears to have no specific relationship to a dedication, and since the prayer is offered in the first-person singular. For these reasons as well, Ps. 30 has traditionally been identified as an individual song of thanksgiving. Even if it is an individual thanksgiving, however, it would not be entirely exceptional to associate an individual deliverance with a communal deliverance such as the triumph of the Maccabees (or perhaps even the return from exile that led to the construction and dedication of the second Temple in 515 B.C.). Psalm 118 (see the Sixth Sunday in Lent), for instance, apparently another individual thanksgiving, clearly recalls the exodus, a communal deliverance, and was used at Passover. In any case, whether individual or communal or both simultaneously, Ps. 30 "makes important points about the relation between prayer and praise" (James L. Mays, *Psalms*, Interpretation series; Louisville, Ky.: John Knox Press, 1994). For the most part, the psalmist addresses God, that is, he or she prays, but the substance of the prayer is praise.

The psalmist's praise in prayer is evident in the opening words of the psalm, "I will extol you, O LORD." The word used in v. 1b to indicate the reason for praise—God has "drawn me up"—is used elsewhere for drawing water out of a well (Ex. 2:16, 19). The image anticipates the mention of Sheol and "the Pit" in v. 3 (see Ps. 88:3–4;

Isa. 38:18, where both words also occur), two designations for the realm of the dead. The delivery from a life-threatening situation is described differently in v. 2, which is a summary of the whole psalm: the psalmist "cried" and God "healed." On the basis of v. 2, most scholars identify the delivery as a recovery from sickness, and this may well be correct (see Isa. 38:9–20, Hezekiah's prayer after recovery from sickness, and Ps. 6, which shares several words in common with Ps. 30). The verb "heal," however, can be used metaphorically (see Hos. 6:1; 11:3; 14:4; Jer. 3:22; 33:6; Ps. 147:3); and as Kraus suggests of vs. 2–3, "In this formulary, room could be found for many of the misfortunes of life" (H.-J. Kraus, *Psalms 1–59*, trans. H. C. Oswald; Minneapolis: Augsburg, 1988, p. 355).

The prayer is interrupted in vs. 4–5 as the psalmist invites the whole congregation to join in what he or she is committed to doing "forever" (v. 12)—praising and thanking God. The word "name" in v. 4 is more literally "remembrance" (see Ps. 97:12). As Ps. 6:5 suggests, there is no "remembrance" or praise of God in Sheol (see also 30:9). Praise and thanks are the vocation of the living. Indeed, as Kraus suggests, what the psalmist has learned from the experience is this: "The purpose of his existence is to praise God" (p. 356; see Ps. 150 for last week, the Second Sunday of Easter). This new under-standing of life motivates the psalmist to be a witness to others (v. 4), and it effects a reevaluation both of suffering (v. 5) and of his or her former approach to life (v. 6).

The prayer resumes in v. 6. Verses 6–12 are a sort of flashback in which the psalmist reviews the former distress and deliverance, even quoting a portion of his or her earlier prayer for help (vs. 9–10; compare Pss. 6:4–5; 88:11–12; Isa. 38:18–19). The psalmist's former approach to life involved *self*-confidence and *self*-sufficiency (v. 6). The word "never" in v. 6 is the same as "forever" in v. 12; that is, the whole experience of distress and deliverance has reoriented the psalmist's approach to life. Formerly "forever" self-confident (v. 6), the psalmist is now "forever" thankful (v. 12). To be sure, it seems that the psalmist's situation has improved (v. 11), but one has the impression that when the next round of distress arrives (as it always does!), the psalmist will remain "forever" thankful even as she or he voices a prayer for help.

Mays speaks of the psalmist's experience as "risky," since it is possible to hear Ps. 30 in a very simplistic way—that is, pray hard enough and God will make everything all right—but there is something deeply profound about relating every experience of life, even life's worst, to God. As Kraus suggests, the psalmist's new orientation to life means a reevaluation of suffering: "Suffering is fitted into the course of life in a comprehensive way. . . . The new reality of the nearness of God and the help of God fills life and determines the understanding of existence" (pp. 356–57). In short, suffering need not be an indication of the absence of God for those "who take refuge in" God (Ps. 2:12; see John 9:1–3; 11:4). The existence of suffering does not negate the good news that life is a gift from God.

Psalm 30 is appropriate for Easter, because it is finally an affirmation of life as a good gift of God. As such, Ps. 30 is of crucial contemporary importance. As Jürgen Moltmann puts it, "In this world, with its modern 'sickness unto death,' true spirituality will be the restoration of the love of life—that is to say, *vitality*. The full and unreserved 'yes' to life, and the full and unreserved love for the living are the first experiences of God's Spirit" (*The Spirit of Life: A Universal Affirmation;* Minneapolis: Fortress, 1992, p. 97). In a real sense, the psalmist's deliverance is not so much from physical sickness to physical health as it is from deadly self-centeredness to a lively awareness of God's presence. It is this awareness that engenders thanks, praise, dancing (vs. 4, 11–12)—a love for life. In this light, v. 9 need not be understood as an appeal to God's self-interest (as many scholars suggest), but rather may be heard as the psalmist's " 'yes' to life" and as an expression of "love for the living." The psalmist prays to live, and lives to praise.

## Revelation 5:11–14

This reading forms the culmination of the scene that begins in Rev. 4:1 with John's vision of the court of heaven, and the lection itself will scarcely make sense without attention to the preceding context. John witnesses the splendor of the divine throne itself, the glorious court that surrounds the throne, and the multitude that offers ceaseless praise to God (4:2–11; note the many references in Revelation to this heavenly throne; for example, 1:4; 3:21; 6:16; 7:9–11; 20:4). He then sees the scroll held by "the one seated on the throne" (5:1), a scroll that not only explains the final events of human history but whose opening will actually set those events in motion (see 6:1 and the following depiction of the opening of the seals).

Only one thing is lacking, and that is the agent who is worthy to open the scroll. One of the elders announces that there is one who can open the scroll: "the Lion of the tribe of Judah, the Root of David" (5:5). When John looks, however, he sees not a lion at all but a "Lamb standing as if it had been slaughtered" (v. 6). The Lamb receives the scroll from the hand of God, and then the heavenly court breaks forth in song, praising the Lamb and acknowledging its worthiness to open the scroll (vs. 7–10).

At this climactic point in the vision, the lection proper opens. Verses 11–14 can best be characterized as a great crescendo, for the crowd of singers swells throughout and the praise escalates in scope. In the first song to the Lamb, those who sing are the "four living creatures and the twenty-four elders" (v. 8). In v. 11, this throng has grown to include "many angels" and "the living creatures and the elders," so that the numbers are now "myriads of myriads and thousands of thousands." By the conclusion of the singing, however, "every creature in heaven and on earth and under the earth and in the sea" has joined in this majestic praise (v. 13).

This crescendo is no mere literary flourish, however. The vast numbers of singers in this passage recall the vast numbers of the heavenly court also imagined in Dan. 7:10; 1 Enoch 14:22; 40:1; and in Heb. 12:22. Moreover, the apocalyptist is surely aware that the court of the Roman emperor likewise comprised large numbers of people from an array of social classes, and that the emperors were often acknowledged with songs and chants. By ascribing those same features here to the God Christians worship rather than to the Roman emperor, the apocalyptist challenges the fundamental power assumptions of the state.

The intense crescendo of vs. 11–14 relies both on the singers and on the content of their hymns. The hymns of vs. 9–10 and 12 address the Lamb alone, as the hymns of 4:8 and 11 address God alone. With v. 13, however, the singers address their praise "to the one seated on the throne and to the Lamb." What belongs to God also belongs to the Lamb. It is anachronistic to read Trinitarian thought into this passage, as some interpreters have done, but the elevation of the Lamb is striking.

Here also the hymn concludes with the words "forever and ever" and is followed by the amen of the four living creatures (v. 14). The heavenly court, unlike those known on earth, will have no end.

Central to the passage is its praise of the "Lamb that was slaughtered" (v. 12). Here we encounter both a central figure in Revelation (for example, see 6:1, 16; 7:9, 10, 14, 17; 12:11; 13:8; 14:1, 4, 10; 15:3; 21:9, 14, 22, 23, 27) and a much-disputed historical problem. Does the presentation of Jesus as a lamb stem from the paschal imagery of Ex. 12 (see 1 Cor. 5:7; 1 Peter 1:19) or perhaps from the "lamb . . . led to the slaughter" of Isa. 53:7, or even the apocalyptic image of the sheep or ram in 1 Enoch 89:42; 90:9 (compare Dan. 8:20–21)?

Whatever the origin of the imagery, its ironic thrust in this passage is clear. The Messianic figure (the "Lion of the tribe of Judah," the "Root of David") is none other than a lamb, and a lamb who has been slaughtered. It is that Lamb who is worthy, not only to open the seals of the scroll (v. 9), but to receive "power and wealth and wisdom and might and honor and glory and blessing" (v. 12). The sheer diversity of the gifts ascribed to the Lamb is astonishing. They include the political and economic realms and form a profound challenge to the authorities that suppose themselves to be rulers of the world.

Elisabeth Schüssler Fiorenza has rightly observed that a question fundamental to the book of Revelation is, "Who is the true Lord of this world?" (*Revelation: Vision of a Just World*; Minneapolis: Fortress, 1991, p. 58). That question is not only important for understanding the seemingly bizarre visions of Revelation, but for understanding their appropriateness for the Easter season. Employing a variety of forms and drawing on a large array of sources, early Christians consistently asserted that the resurrection confirmed irrefutably the power of God over all creation and in every time and place. The implication of that power for the supposed power of Rome emerges more clearly in Revelation than elsewhere in the New Testament, as the apocalyptist unabashedly declares that God's sovereignty means the end of human power.

## John 21:1–19

The final chapter of the Gospel of John in many ways appears to be an appendage to the previous chapters, perhaps the contribution of a redactor of the narrative. The apparent conclusion of 20:30–31, the numerous discontinuities introduced in chapter 21, and the preoccupation with the relationship between the beloved disciple and Peter suggest that it is an epilogue intended to address live issues in the community of the initial readers. The critical commentaries on John provide a fuller discussion than can be offered here.

The fact that the chapter may have come from a different hand than the one responsible for the previous twenty chapters, however, in no way lessens its potential for preaching. Despite its complexities, the story unfolds in a powerful way, providing us with further appearances of the risen Christ recommissioning the disciples and challenging them to become servant leaders.

The assigned reading (21:1–19) includes three scenes. The first revolves around the decision of Peter and the disciples to go fishing, their failure to catch anything, and Jesus, at first an unrecognized figure on the shore, directing the disciples to a remarkable haul (21:1–8). In line with the earlier appearances to Mary Magdalene (20:14–16), to the disciples gathered behind bolted doors (20:19–22), and to Thomas (20:26–28), there is in the scene a moment of disclosure when an unrecognized Jesus who engages the disciples is finally identified ("It is the Lord!"). The beloved disciple's confession is appropriately responded to by Peter, who eagerly plunges into the water, leaves behind the boat and the full net of fish, and makes for the shore.

What distinguishes this disclosure scene from the earlier ones is the disciples' response to Jesus before they know who he is. His directions about where to cast the net are explicitly followed. Obedience precedes recognition, and in the obedience the disciples discover that it is the Lord—a point Albert Schweitzer so eloquently makes in the conclusion to *The Quest of the Historical Jesus* (1910; New York: Macmillan Co., 1961, p. 403):

> He comes to us as one unknown, without a name, as of old, by the lake-side, he came to those men who knew him not. He speaks to us the same word: "Follow thou me!" and sets us to the tasks which he has to fulfill for our time. He commands. And to those who obey him, whether they be wise or simple, he will reveal himself in the toils, the conflicts, the sufferings which they will pass through in his fellowship, and, as an ineffable mystery, they shall learn in their own experience who he is.

This initial scene can also be read symbolically as a statement about the mission of the community, its broad and diverse scope. Disciples, whose efforts at fishing are without success, obey the voice of Jesus, and their nets overflow with a huge catch of fish. It is intriguing that the Greek word translated here as "haul" (21:6, 11) appears twice earlier in the Gospel to denote the divine movement in "drawing" people to Jesus and to the community of salvation (6:44; 12:32). The detail mentioned later, that the net was not torn despite the vast number of fish (21:11), may suggest that the unity of the church is maintained even in the face of a diverse and growing company of people.

The second scene finds Jesus on the shore welcoming the disciples and providing them a breakfast of fish and bread (21:9–14). Whether or not the author intended the incident to be a post-resurrection eucharist, the passage is certainly open to such an interpretation. It parallels the feeding scene alongside the Sea of Galilee in John 6 (compare especially 6:11 and 21:13).

In the midst of images that speak of the length and breadth of the Christian mission, we discover the image of support and sustenance, provided by Jesus for disciples weary with a night of fishing. Even before Peter finally draws the full net ashore, Jesus as host has prepared the meal, and later serves it to his hungry guests. It turns out to be a time of renewal for the disciples, who are confirmed in their knowledge of Jesus as Lord (21:12).

The third scene is more familiar than the previous two and depicts the reinstatement of Peter as both leader and follower (21:15–19). Three times Peter failed Jesus precisely at the time of his trial before the high priest (18:12–27). Now three times he is queried by Jesus about his devotion and three times commissioned to be a shepherd with responsibility for the flock. The variation in the use of two Greek verbs for "love" often noted in this passage does not seem to carry any theological significance, as if two degrees or types of love are implied. Instead, the impact of the story lies in the threefold questioning and commissioning, heightened by the narrator's comment that Peter was hurt because Jesus repeated the query a third time (21:17).

Two further dimensions of Peter's reinstatement are critical. First, Peter is commissioned not only as a leader, a shepherd charged with feeding the sheep, but also as a follower (21:19). Leadership in the Christian community is destined to misuse its prerogatives and fail unless at the same time it is embraced as discipleship.

Second, Peter's decision to feed the flock and to follow Jesus results in his seizure and death. His story parallels Jesus' story in that his end is not one he would choose for himself, but an end that nevertheless glorifies God. It is not a Horatio Alger story, alive with the overcoming of obstacles and the achievement of great successes. It is marked by danger, risk, and the loss of control, features of the life of faithful disciples.

# FOURTH SUNDAY OF EASTER

The four readings for this Sunday offer distinctive themes for preaching, each rooted in its own context—Peter's raising of Dorcas, the Twenty-third Psalm, Jesus' engagement with the Jews at the Feast of Dedication, and the apocalyptic scene of Rev. 7. Each one of the texts offers a fertile field for homiletical grazing. (After all, the sheep metaphor *is* prominent!)

And yet all four passages eloquently voice the providential care of a loving God, whose concern reaches out to needy folk, many of whom have no other arm to lean on. The widows in the Acts 9 account are saintly, known for their acts of charity, but widows were also vulnerable in the broader society and subject to being manipulated by ruthless and aggressive scoundrels. They find in Peter an instrument of divine mercy to bring life out of death for their leader, Dorcas.

In the vision in Revelation, the great, diverse host of people, gathered before the throne to sing in various languages praises to the Lamb, "have come out of the great ordeal" (Rev. 7:14). They have known hunger and thirst, exposure and weeping (7:16–17), but they now experience a deliverance, a shelter, and a way to the "springs of the water of life" (7:17).

Both Ps. 23 and John 10 relate God's providential care in the familiar picture of the good shepherd, who provides every want the sheep may have. The passages abound with images of guidance, protection, presence, and assurance. To be a part of the shepherd's flock means to be watched carefully so that no foe can snatch the sheep from the hands of the divine caretaker.

Together, the texts give ample reason for living without fear; with trust in the vigilant, loving God.

## Acts 9:36–43

The book of Acts, after relating the events surrounding the conversion of Paul (Acts 9:1–20; see last week, the Third Sunday of Easter), returns to the subject of Peter's work as evangelist. Soon, of course, the focus will be on Paul again, beginning with his famous "first missionary journey" (Acts 13:1–15:35), but for now Peter stands at center stage, as he did in those passages dealing with Pentecost and its immediate aftermath (Acts 2—4). The result of these shifts of attention—note the passages dealing with the martyrdom of Stephen (Acts 7) and with the witness of Philip (Acts 8:26–40; the Fifth Sunday of Easter, Year B)—is that the reader is impressed that many faithful witnesses were carrying on the church's work in many different quarters. As the text frequently points out, the work of these disciples is in reality the work of the Spirit, who initiates and guides these early followers of Christ (note, for example, Acts 8:29). But while the impulses originate with the Spirit, the sharing of the great good news about Jesus is also accomplished by the willingness and obedience of these selfless women and men who "belonged to the Way" (Acts 9:2).

The context for the present lection is set by the brief introduction in 9:32–35 (which is not, of course, a part of the lection itself). The vagueness of the statement in v. 32 that Peter was "here and there" is doubtless meant to convey a sense of constant activity, as if to say, "Peter was constantly on the go for the Lord." It is striking that the subject of the miracle attributed to Peter in Lydda is almost certainly a Gentile, in that the paralyzed man bore the name Aeneas, the name of the central character in Virgil's great epic poem, *Aeneid*. In this, the greatest example of poetry written in the Latin language, the original Aeneas is portrayed as a great hero who survives the Trojan War and, after many adventures, becomes the father of the Roman people. This epic, written between 30 and 19 B.C., was so widely read and loved by Peter's day (as well as Luke's) that the appearance here of the name Aeneas cannot be accidental, but is to be understood as the text's way of preparing the reader for that critical moment in Peter's life related in Acts 10 (see Easter Day, Years A, B, C, and the Sixth Sunday of Easter, Year B), the mission to the Gentiles.

The passage appointed by the lectionary, Acts 9:36–43, is another, very straightforward account of a miraculous act performed by Peter in the name of the Lord Jesus Christ. This story is rendered all the more poignant because of the character of the deceased, in that Gazelle (which is what both the Aramaic term Tabitha and the Greek

Dorcas mean) was a woman of exemplary faith and compassion. It is not essential to Peter's act of restoration that she was "a disciple" who was "devoted to good works and acts of charity," for those who receive the Spirit's miraculous gifts of health and life have not always themselves led lives of faith. Often, it is the faith of those who bring the crisis moment to the attention of a person of God that seems to be the channel through which the grace of the Spirit flows, as in the case of the four friends who brought the paralytic on his pallet to Jesus (Luke 5:18–26). But the simple fact that Gazelle was such a good and faithful person adds an element of human urgency to the narrative: "Please come to us without delay" (Acts 9:38).

Her devotion to the cause of helping other people, to say nothing of her discipleship, had apparently won for her a leadership role in a circle of friends who had been the beneficiaries of her generosity and who, in turn, had begun to reach out to assist others. These "widows" of v. 39 almost surely constituted what amounted to a guild of persons who provided charity (note the "widows" of 1 Tim. 5:3–16) to needy individuals in the name of Christ (compare the interesting phrase "saints and widows" in v. 41). That their sister was dead brought forth genuine tears, not, as has sometimes been suggested, the tears of hired mourners (v. 39). The sorrow of these faithful women, again, heightens the sense of urgency surrounding the crisis.

Peter's prayer of v. 40 is to be understood as an act by which Peter opens himself to the powers of the Spirit, and when he addresses the body of the dead woman he speaks only two words (in the Greek): one is her name, the other the command to "arise," or, as NRSV has it, "get up." There is no elaboration, no conjuring, no pleading. The Spirit, having responded to Peter's prayer, now works God's gracious will on the lifeless corpse. It is of enormous significance that the Greek verb used here, *anistēmi*, meaning "arise," is the identical verb used elsewhere to refer to Jesus' resurrection. That it is found on Peter's lips in this sense is especially significant: "This Jesus God raised up," Peter proclaimed at the Pentecost festival (Acts 2:32), and he is now invoking the Spirit to perform the same miracle on Gazelle.

Yet there is an important difference: Jesus' resurrection was dependent only on God's power, whereas Gazelle's resurrection is clearly done in the light of and as a consequence of Jesus' resurrection. The raising of Gazelle stands as a witness to the power of the resurrection of Christ over all persons—not in the sense that our flesh and bones will be reconstituted before the eyes of our weeping friends, but in the sense that the resurrected Christ possesses the power to bring new life to all persons, and that that power flows directly out of the new life God gave to him on the first Easter Day.

The wider implications of Gazelle's resurrection are noted in v. 42, while v. 43 prepares the reader for Acts 10. Tanners were suspect, under Jewish law, because they engaged in unclean work. It is clear that the mission of Peter and that of the church as a whole is looking to more and more distant horizons.

## Psalm 23

A friend told me recently that when Ps. 23 was read aloud during Sunday morning worship, she could see in people's faces the powerful effect of the psalm. Another friend, a hospital chaplain, once remarked concerning the use of Ps. 23 in pastoral situations: "I mean there is *power* in the Twenty-third Psalm!" Indeed there is—a power matched only, perhaps, by the simple beauty of the psalm.

The psalm begins with a simple profession, "The LORD is my shepherd," which has radical implications: "I shall not want." The sense of this statement is probably best captured by the translation, "I shall lack nothing" (see Deut. 2:7). I prefer to retain the NRSV, however, because we live in a culture that teaches us to *want* everything. It is particularly radical in our setting to say, "I shall not want"; that is, God is the only real necessity of life! The rest of the psalm explicates this fundamental profession of trust.

In the ancient world, kings were known as the shepherds of their people. Their job was to provide for and protect the people, but they often failed to do so (see Jer. 23:1–4; Ezek. 34:1–10). In contrast to the failure of earthly kings, God will be what a shepherd/ruler is supposed to be (see Ezek. 34:11–16). God will provide for every need, and the rest of Ps. 23 tells how.

Verses 2 and 3 are usually understood to offer images of peace and tranquillity, suggesting security and rest. They do, but they also relate how God provides all the basic necessities of life. For a sheep, "green pastures" mean food, and "still waters" mean drink (v. 2). In short, God "keeps me alive," as v. 3a could be translated (see Pss. 30:3; 116:8). For a sheep, to be led in "right paths" means that danger is averted and proper shelter is attained (see Pss. 5:8; 27:11). Thus, the shepherd provides food, drink, shelter—the basic necessities of life. The psalmist professes that life depends solely on God, and that God makes provision for the psalmist "for his name's sake" (Ps. 23:3b)—that is, in keeping with God's fundamental character.

By alluding to God's character, v. 3b anticipates the mention of "goodness" and "mercy" (v. 6), two fundamental attributes of God. Not surprisingly, the vocabulary of vs. 2–3 occurs elsewhere in relation to key events that reveal God's character. For instance, the two Hebrew verbs translated "leads" in vs. 2 and 3 occur together in Ex. 15:13 in a song that celebrates the exodus. The verb in Ps. 23:2 also occurs in Isa. 40:11, where God is also portrayed as a shepherd who leads the people home from exile (see also Isa. 49:10–11, and the following texts where God's role is shepherd: Gen. 49:24; Pss. 28:9; 74:1; 95:7; 100:3; Jer. 31:10; Micah 7:14). God keeps the people alive.

Verse 4 of Ps. 23 is the structural and theological center of the psalm. At the moment of greatest threat, God still provides. Thus, the psalmist can "fear no evil." This affirmation recalls the prophetic salvation oracle, "Do not fear," which occurs frequently in Isa. 40—55 (see 41:11–13, 14–16; 43:1–7; 44:6–8; 54:4–8). The word "comfort" is also a key theme in Isa. 40—55 (see 40:1–2; 49:13; 51:3, 12, 19; 52:9), in which the prophet proclaims deliverance from exile, Israel's "darkest valley." The echoes of exodus and deliverance from exile in Ps. 23:2–4 provide a corporate dimension to what is usually and legitimately understood as individual assurance.

The shift to the second person as the psalmist addresses God reinforces the closeness of God and God's help: "You are with me," an affirmation that again belongs to the salvation oracle (see Isa. 41:10, 13; 43:5; Gen. 15:1; 26:24; compare Ps. 118:6). The "rod" may be understood as a shepherd's tool of trade, but the word more often means "scepter" and connotes royal authority (Gen. 49:10; Judg. 5:14; Ps. 45:6; Isa. 14:5). God's provision is reliable, because God is sovereign. Not even the darkest, most deadly threat can separate the psalmist from God (see Rom. 8:31–39).

It appears that the metaphor shifts in Ps. 23:5 and 6, from God as shepherd to God as a gracious host who welcomes the psalmist into "the house of the Lord." Verse 6b may refer to the Temple and suggest an original cultic setting for the psalm, perhaps as part of a thank-offering ritual; however, it is more likely that the "stay in the sanctuary is . . . metaphorical for keeping close contact with the personal God" (Erhard Gerstenberger, *Psalms, Part 1, with an Introduction to Cultic Poetry*, Forms of the OT Literature 14; Grand Rapids: Wm. B. Eerdmans Publishing Co., 1988, p. 115). In this case. v. 6b reinforces the central affirmation, "You are with me" (see Pss. 27:4–6; 36:7–9; 52:8–9; 61:4). Indeed, the psalmist cannot get away from God, for God's "goodness and steadfast love will *pursue* me all the days of my life" (Ps. 23:6a; author's translation). God's active pursuit of the psalmist is striking in relation to the mention of "enemies" in v. 5. Usually it is the enemies who pursue the psalmist (see 7:5; 69:26; 71:11; 109:16, for example), but there they are harmless.

In Ps. 23:5–6, the gracious host does for the guest what the shepherd does for the sheep—that is, provides the necessities of food ("a table"), drink ("my cup"), and shelter or protection ("in the presence of my enemies"/"the house of the LORD"). Both metaphors proclaim the same radical message—life depends solely on God (see Matt. 6:25–34). This message is reinforced by Isaac Watts's beautiful metrical paraphrase of Ps. 23:6 (1719; alt. 1972, in *Hymns, Psalms, and Spiritual Songs;* Louisville, Ky.: Westminster/John Knox Press, 1990, no. 172):

> The sure provisions of my God
>   Attend me all my days;
> O may Your House be my abode,
>   And all my work be praise.
> There would I find a settled rest,
>   While others go and come;
> No more a stranger, or a guest,
>   But like a child at home.

The childlike trust articulated in Ps. 23 recalls Jesus' words about entering the realm of God "as a little child" (Mark 10:15). It is appropriate finally that Christians hear Ps. 23 in relation to Jesus, who said, "I am the good shepherd" (John 10:11, 14); who as gracious host invites persons to eat and drink at his table (1 Cor. 11:23–26); and whose name Emmanuel means "God is with us" (Matt. 1:23).

## Revelation 7:9–17

The "great day of their wrath has come, and who is able to stand?" (Rev. 6:17). This stark question culminates the opening of the sixth of the seven seals on the eschatological scroll, an opening that has displayed events of majestic and terrifying proportions. Earthquake, blackening of the sun and falling of the stars, disappearance of sky, mountain, and island, fleeing of king and slave—who could witness this vision and not wonder whether deliverance was possible?

At just this point, when readers anticipate the opening of the seventh seal, the apocalyptist pauses, building into the narrative itself the silence described in 8:1 with the opening of the seventh and final seal. In the interlude of chapter 7, the question of 6:17 finds an answer: God's people will indeed be rescued from the wrath, and they alone will have no need to be hidden from God's face (see 6:16).

The answer to the question comes in the form of two complementary visions, 7:1–8 and 7:9–12, with vs. 13–17 providing an interpretation for the second vision. Chapter 7:1–8 depicts the sealing of a large but finite number of those from within Israel, the infamous 144,000. Exactly how this number relates to the more inclusive vision of vs. 9–12 remains a matter of great debate. Sometimes interpreters suggest that the 144,000 may consist of those who display some particular loyalty, or who come from within Jewish Christianity, or who remain alive at the day of wrath. Whatever is intended by this number, the second vision makes it emphatically clear that these are not the only persons to be rescued from the eschatological wrath.

In fact, v. 9 deliberately emphasizes the vast, almost unimaginable scope of God's people. They are innumerable, as were the children promised by God to Abraham and Sarah (Gen. 15:5). They come from every place and people and speak with every tongue, a gathering that the great multitude at Pentecost could only anticipate (Acts 2:1–13). Any sense of limitation or conformity derived from the image of the 144,000 shatters here on this graphic depiction of the diversity of God's people. Together with the heavenly host already depicted in Rev. 4, they join in ceaseless praise of God.

Perhaps the most striking thing about this multitude is that its amazing diversity yields to an equally amazing unity. All are robed in white, all stand with the palm branches of victory in their hands, all cry out together to God.

Like the heavenly host in chapters 4 and 5, this throng also addresses God and the Lamb. Here the first word is "Salvation," for salvation "belongs to" God and to the Lamb. Because we sometimes reduce the English word "salvation" (Greek *sōtēria*) to a personal relationship with God or to personal vindication before God, it is important to remember that the Greek word has somewhat larger connotations, several of which are described in 7:15–17. Certainly in this context salvation includes rescue from devastation, victory over the powers of the world, deliverance from danger. All these features of the word come into play, and each stems directly from God and the Lamb.

Precisely because this vision occupies a significant place in Revelation as a whole, the apocalyptist does not permit it to stand uninterpreted (as does 7:1–8, for example). In what appears to contemporary readers an amusing exchange, one of the elders (see

4:4) asks John to identify the vast multitude of people, and then proceeds to tell him who they are. The question itself is a literary device that simply enables the interpretation to be inserted (compare 5:2).

The multitude consists of those "who have come out of the great ordeal" (7:14). Since apocalyptic writings frequently anticipate a period of anguish or tribulation (see Dan. 12:1; Mark 13:19), identifying some specific experience here is probably unwise, beyond understanding the multitude to consist of those who have remained faithful.

More important than looking for clues by which to identify the multitude is noting the way in which the apocalyptist anticipates their future. They will have "washed their robes and made them white in the blood of the Lamb" (Rev. 7:14). New Testament writers elsewhere speak of Jesus' blood and its power (1 John 1:7; Heb. 9:14), even its power to cleanse, but here that imagery is intensified to a degree that makes it startling. To whiten something by washing it in blood is, by any customary standard, absurd.

As a result of this cleansing, the multitude stands before God's throne day and night (Rev. 9:15). Chief among the blessings granted them is to live in the very presence of God. Reference to God's Temple completes the parallel to the throne and ought not to prompt confusion over whether or not the new Jerusalem contains a temple (see 21:22). The thrust of both passages is that God dwells among God's people. The blessings depicted here are truly comprehensive. Physical needs will be no concern (7:16), and personal pain will cease to exist (v. 17). The Lamb, itself slaughtered and yet victorious, here becomes the shepherd who know where to find water.

The question of 6:17 has been answered, but perhaps the more important question has also been answered. Chapter 6:17 asks *who* can withstand the day of wrath, and the answer is that uncounted multitudes of God's faithful will do just that. The more significant question, however, is *how* they will stand. Here the answer is implicit, but no less certain: the faithful stand because God and God's Lamb sustain them.

## John 10:22–30

Questions and requests are always important. Who makes them, how and when they are made, and what response is sought often tell us a great deal about the seeker. Certainly in the narratives of the

Gospels the nature of both the questions and requests put to Jesus and the character of the ones making them determine the responses given. Some are sincerely posed, some seek to entrap Jesus, whereas others, whether honest or devious, expose mistaken assumptions that make a straightforward response impossible.

The request of the Jews, "How long will you keep us in suspense? If you are the Messiah, tell us plainly" (John 10:24), is hard to categorize. A literal translation of the initial question ("How long are you taking away our life?") could suggest a threatened, defensive posture of the Jews. Is it sincere or hostile? While readers of John's narrative have come to recognize "the Jews" not as a designation for the Jewish people as a whole but only for religious leaders who oppose Jesus and regularly provoke antagonistic debate, the previous passage relates a division among this group in which some predictably react negatively to Jesus and others at least are curious (10:19–21). From which group do the question and request come?

Whether the questioners are genuine or adversarial, in either case the request demands an unambiguous answer to a straightforward question ("If you are the Messiah, tell us plainly"). Jesus is asked to declare himself in categories that are firmly in place in the ideology of those making the request. "Do you or do you not fit our criteria for messiahship? Tell us without equivocation."

Jesus' reply reminds us that an understanding of who he is cannot be simply a matter of deciding whether Jesus measures up to some preconceived notion of how a divine figure *ought* to act. Jesus eludes prior categories, totally redefines even those cherished titles drawn from Israel's past (for example, Messiah, Son of man, Son of God). It is no different with our contemporary categories—superstar, healer, guarantor of happiness, peace-giver. Jesus transcends and transforms them all.

There is another problem with the Jews' request. They seem to assume that a decision about the Messiah is merely a matter of processing information. If Jesus will provide the data, they can arrive at a reasoned conclusion. Jesus' response throws that sort of logic into a cocked hat ("You do not believe, because you do not belong to my sheep," v. 26).

Knowledge of the Messiah has to do with a reorientation of the knower, a change of location from one community to another—a persistent theme of John's Gospel. Nicodemus came with his knowledge, and it was not all bad ("We know that you are a teacher who has come from God"), only to be told that he had to be born from above (3:2–3). Knowing the Messiah involves a radical conversion, a movement from one fold to another. The Jews, for whatever reason, demand a straightforward answer, but they discover the issue is far more complex and demanding than that.

Reorientation and relocation are not all. There are promises made, tender promises of protection and security (10:27–29). Referring back to the earlier section of the chapter (10:1–18), believers are called "my sheep" and receive a divine commitment that they cannot be separated from the care of the Shepherd. The threat of those who might seek to "snatch" them from Jesus'/the Father's hand apparently also follows from references earlier in the chapter to thieves, bandits, and wolves (10:8–10, 11–12). Such preservation comes at the cost of the Shepherd's life. (Interpreters will note the very ambiguous textual problem in 10:29, which leads to differing translations and varying nuanced readings. A critical commentary can shed light on the textual problem.)

Jesus' focus on the works that he does must not be misunderstood (10:25). The works testify to Jesus not because they are extraordinary and attention-getting—which of course they *are* (changing water to wine, healing the official's son, feeding the multitudes)—and not because they offer conclusive proof of his Messiahship, but because they are the Father's works. Jesus' hand protecting the sheep is no less than the Father's hand (10:28–29). As the following section explains, the works are critical "so that you may know and understand that the Father is in me and I am in the Father" (10:38). The works witness to the coincidence of the activity of Father and Son, taking us close to the heart of John's Christology.

The concluding verse of the lection (10:30), which has led to much speculation through the centuries (some of it idle and highly conjectural), spells out the implication of Jesus' works. In context, it is not a statement about the metaphysical connection between two persons of the Trinity, but an affirmation about the functional unity between Jesus and the Father. Moreover, in the narrative the urgency of the confession is highlighted, since it proves highly offensive to the audience and places Jesus at great risk (10:31, 39).

# FIFTH SUNDAY OF EASTER

With differing emphases, the New Testament witnesses affirm the radically new era ushered in with the advent, death, and resurrection of Jesus Christ. The community related to Christ finds itself in an old, familiar ballpark but playing a new and different game. Some of the players have changed, making for a new team. The game demands changes and a fresh set of strategies. It is a time of excitement and expectation.

None of the witnesses emphasizes the newness of the game any more strongly than the Gospel of John. Perplexed disciples are instructed by Jesus before his departure; they are given their game plans for the time after he has gone. The words are familiar (compare Lev. 19:18), but they are called "a new commandment" (John 13:34), because Jesus' presence and action give them a fresh intensity and sharpness.

The expansion of the team to include new players does not come without struggle. Peter learns about it in a dream, and then has to go and explain his dream to the old players, who are understandably reluctant to welcome the newcomers (Acts 11:1–18). In fact, the playing of a new game in an old park is filled with all sorts of tension and at times frustration. The contention between the old and the new sometimes reaches a fever pitch.

Nevertheless, the players caught up in the game continue to play it with persistence and commitment. In part they do so because of the promise of a new ballpark, a time when the conflicts between old and new will have completely faded (Rev. 21:1–6).

In the light of Easter and the anticipation of a new heaven and a new earth, Ps. 148 becomes a marvelous expression of praise to God. Voices from heaven and from earth, voices of angels, animals, and humans, voices of women and men, young and old join in a splendid harmony to the One who makes all things new (Rev. 21:5).

(Since Ps. 143 is listed as a reading also for the First Sunday After Christmas, a commentary on the psalm can be found there.)

## Acts 11:1–18

The passage from Acts for this day is a continuation of the incident involving Peter and the Roman centurion Cornelius (Acts 10; compare Easter, Years A, B, C, and the Sixth Sunday of Easter, Year B). The question of the propriety of extending the gospel to the Gentiles was a burning one among the very earliest Christian disciples, and Acts emphatically sides with those who understand the Gentile mission to be not only acceptable, but essential to the nature of Christian evangelism. Although Peter has previously healed a Gentile paralytic and proclaimed the gospel to him (Acts 9:32–35; see the Fourth Sunday of Easter), it is not until his vision of the "four-footed creatures and reptiles and birds of the air" (10:12; 11:6) that he is given an understanding concerning the universal nature of the gospel.

Peter's sermon to the Gentiles at Caesarea results in a Spirit-endowed response on the part of the Gentiles, but astonishment on the part of Peter's fellow Jewish Christians who are traveling with him (10:44–48). They are not prepared to accept this unexpected outpouring of God's grace until Peter directs that the new Gentile converts should be baptized, and perhaps they do not accept this astonishing new turn of events even then. The text is not totally clear in the matter. In any event, the resistance of the Jewish-Christian community to Gentile evangelism is continued in 11:1–18, where we read that in Jerusalem, to which Peter has now returned, "circumcised believers criticized him" for his fellowship with Gentiles (vs. 2–3).

Peter demonstrates what is perhaps uncharacteristic patience by explaining "step by step" (v. 4) the events that led him to Cornelius's home in Caesarea and to his moving sermon to the Gentiles there. Verses 5–17 are basically a replication of chapter 10, but cast in abbreviated form. As in the prior text, Acts 11:5–17 places great importance on the work of the Spirit. The voice that speaks to Peter following his vision (v. 7; compare 10:13) is unquestionably that of the Spirit of God, a fact confirmed by the mention of the Spirit in 11:12 (compare 10:19). The Spirit is again brought into the narrative in 11:15, which makes abundantly evident that the response among Peter's Gentile audience at Caesarea was not occasioned by Peter's oratorical skills, but by the work of the Holy Spirit of God (compare 10:44, 45). Near the end of Peter's remarks to the Jewish Christians of

Jerusalem, the text refers back not to Acts 10, but to a statement recorded, in slightly different ways, in all four Gospels (Matt. 3:11; Mark 1:8; Luke 3:16; John 1:33). Baptism by the Spirit has been conferred upon the Gentile Christians of Caesarea (Acts 11:16). What has happened to these sisters and brothers is not Peter's doing, but God's!

At the conclusion of our lection, the Jewish Christians of Jerusalem are first silenced into submission by the power of Peter's statement, then they find their voices in praise to God, whom they now credit with offering "even to the Gentiles the repentance that leads to life" (v. 18).

The "decision" by God (if one may call it that) to extend the good news concerning Jesus Christ to all humankind was nothing new, of course, as a text such as Gen. 12:3 clearly indicates. However, one may only speculate concerning the subsequent course of human history if the Christian faith had remained one of the several sects within first-century Judaism. Perhaps, like the Sadducees, Christians would not have survived the destruction of Jerusalem in A.D. 70. Or had they survived to become important rivals of the Pharisees within Judaism after 70, or imaginations conjure up several different scenarios as to how that competition would have played itself out. But such speculation is simply that, speculation, for the Holy Spirit willed otherwise. That is where our attention is directed by the text of Acts 11.1–18, to the work of God's Spirit!

There is a sense in which this text generates a certain kind of terror in the heart of the reader, for it makes clear the fact that it is the nature of the Spirit to remain free, bringing to bear the intention of God in the most unlooked-for ways. If those early disciples who stood much nearer the Christ-event than we were not prepared for the Spirit's fresh initiatives, how much less prepared are we? If Peter's generation of Christians could be astounded, what might the Spirit have in store for us?

There is also a sense in which the text liberates us and banishes terror from our minds. For this seemingly unpredictable Spirit is in very important ways quite predictable. Although we may not be prepared for the Spirit's every expression, we may count on the Spirit to be motivated by no other concern than love for that humankind for which Christ died. So the Spirit's seemingly astonishing movements are all quite consistent, expressing God's love for this world in ways that we, limited by our own frail powers, could never do.

Thus, our astonishment at the Spirit's power is accompanied by our joy over the Spirit's love.

## Revelation 21:1–6

The epistolary readings for Eastertide in Year C affirm again and again that the resurrection of Jesus Christ signals in a decisive way the lordship of God over all creation and all time. This particular lection reinforces that theme through its striking and beautiful depiction of the aftermath of God's final victory, the blessing that enables God's people to live in God's very presence.

In a vision that draws heavily on earlier prophetic and apocalyptic imagery, the apocalyptist sees the coming of a "new heaven and a new earth." Isaiah 65:17–25 anticipates the creation of "new heavens and a new earth" and looks forward to a Jerusalem that will give joy and delight. Second Esdras 7:26 speaks of the revealing of a city that is now unseen and connects that with the reign of a Messiah figure (see also 2 Esd. 10:41–44). In the New Testament, Heb. 11:16 speaks of the city God has prepared for the faithful (see also Heb. 12:22).

Clearly, the author of Revelation draws on traditional imagery in this passage, but this is more than the simple reassertion of tradition for tradition's sake. The identity of the writer of this apocalypse is unknown to us, but the extent and manner of his use of scripture make it virtually certain that he is a Jewish Christian. Some interpreters hypothesize that he may have been among those who fled Palestine following the Jewish war against Rome in A.D. 66–70. If that is the case, the reference to "a new heaven and a new earth" and particularly the reference to the "new Jerusalem" take on a highly charged meaning. For this writer may have no city in which he is truly at home. If that is true both for the apocalyptist and for his congregation, this evocation of a new Jerusalem would touch the deepest yearnings of human beings for a sense of place, for sheer physical security.

The security invoked in this vision is comprehensive. It begins with the notion of a new dwelling place that encompasses all the cosmos. "A new heaven and a new earth" includes all of creation, all of which is now restored. The vision also begins with the curious comment that "the sea was no more" (Rev. 21:1). For Revelation, as for Old Testament writers (see, for example, Ps. 74:13), the sea itself is a threatening chaos, the location of powerful opposition to God (see Rev. 13:1). Here it becomes the final enemy of God to be defeated (see 19:20; 20:10, 14), so that the new Jerusalem can descend from heaven in an atmosphere of peace.

Later the apocalyptist depicts the new Jerusalem in careful detail

(21:9–27), but here the most important identification is that in v. 3: "See, the home of God is among mortals. He will dwell with them as their God." The earlier Jerusalem, now in ruins as a result of the ravages of the Roman army, derived its glory from the fact that the Temple was located there, the locus of the worship of Israel's God. In this Jerusalem, by contrast, there will be no temple (see v. 22), for here God lives among God's own people.

That presence guarantees the end of all the "first things" (v. 4). When the apocalyptist speaks of these "first things," they are confined to death and the pain associated with it. Earlier visions referred to the distress of hunger and thirst, the discomfort of excessive heat (see 7:16), but this vision restricts itself to the fundamental human pain of separation. That shift may result from the contrast with God's presence; in God's presence, that is, all separation is finally over. It may also reflect the profound losses and griefs of the apocalyptist and his community, who longed for an end to those separations.

Revelation 21:5–6 emphatically underscores both the vision of vs. 1–4 and the dramatic pronouncement of v. 6. The vision is indeed the making new of all things. The vision is "trustworthy and true." Its guarantee comes from "the Alpha and the Omega, the beginning and the end" (see 1:8; 22:13). Employing language that would have been familiar from Hellenistic religious life, "the Alpha and the Omega" signals the one who reigns over all parts of life. In the context of Israel's history, the phrase alludes to both the God of creation and the God of the eschaton; God is one and the same in the beginning and at the end.

The lection ends with 21:6, and that for obvious reasons. The warnings of v. 8 sound an ominous note in an otherwise joyous passage. More important, they have often been taken literally, so that hell is pictured as an ever-burning lake and as the punishment for those who miss the mark in any respect whatever. If every liar may anticipate burning eternally (v. 8), then there is little hope for any of us.

Omitting vs. 7–8 constitutes a serious problem, however, despite the admitted difficulties with the way in which the warnings of v. 8 have been interpreted. At its most fundamental level, the book of Revelation intends to encourage and exhort God's people to faithfulness and endurance. Reading vs. 1–6 alone offers comfort, but without vs. 7–8, the goal of exhortation may fall by the wayside.

(See the additional commentary on this passage for All Saints, Year B.)

## John 13:31–35

It may seem a bit strange to be directed during the Easter season to texts that are set in the last few moments of Jesus' life. One would think them more appropriate for Lent than for Easter. In John's Gospel, however, Jesus' farewell conversations with the disciples immediately before the crucifixion regularly speak of his "departure," a term that includes his death, resurrection, and return to the Father. The language is typical of John's Gospel, where the incarnation is depicted as a journey from the Father to the world and back to the Father (for example, 13:1). Thus today's selection (John 13:31–35) is particularly apt for the season between Easter and Pentecost.

First, we must observe the context. The verses preceding the assigned lesson recount Jesus' prediction of Judas's betrayal, concluding with his departure from the group and the poignant observation, "And it was night." The verses following the lesson relate Jesus' prediction about Peter's denials. Between these two dark and foreboding brackets comes the declaration of Jesus' glorification (13:31).

The irony should not be lost. At the darkest moment in the narrative, when the anticipation of human failure seems certain because colleagues are conspiring to undermine their leader, the announcement is made of Jesus' glorification. His moment of exaltation, honor, and praise is set against the backdrop of betrayal and denials.

But the prominent "now" of 13:31 has a double reference. On the one hand, Jesus' glorification comes at a time of incredible disloyalty and faithlessness. On the other hand, it is the right moment, the moment of fulfillment, the time for returning to the Father (13:1). Nothing has been left undone or incomplete; as Jesus' last words from the cross will put it, "It is finished" (19:30). The betrayal and denials do not deter or thwart the divine intention.

Second, we observe the mutuality between God and the Son of man in the moment of glorification. The language of 13:31b–32, in fact, is awkward in its effort to draw the two together in this climactic event. God's glory is made known as the Father is glorified in the Son and as the Son is glorified in the Father. John's characteristic Christology emerges here (as in the Gospel lesson for last Sunday: "The Father and I are one," 10:30), a functional unity in which the actions of the Son are no less than the actions of God, and vice versa.

The awkwardness underscores that Jesus is the full revelation of God, particularly at this moment of death and departure. The

anticipated actions of Judas, Peter, the religious authorities, Caiaphas, Pilate, and the soldiers only serve as a foil for the *real* action,
namely, the reciprocal disclosure of the identity of Son and Father.

Third, there is an appropriate word for the disciples who are faced
with the impossibility of following Jesus at his departure: "I give you
a new commandment, that you love one another" (13:34). The pain
of separation is addressed with a reminder about their mutual
relationships in the community of faith. But if the commandment is a
reminder (see Lev. 19:18), then why is it called "new"? What
distinguishes it from the many other places in the Bible where
people are told to love one another?

Two features of the commandment make it "new." (1) A new and
unparalleled model for love has been given the disciples. "Just as I
have loved you, you also should love one another." Jesus, who had
loved his own in the world and was returning to the Father, "loved
them to the end" (John 13:1), or, as it might be translated, "loved
them to the uttermost" (see 15:13). In Jesus the disciples have a
concrete, living expression of what love is. Love can no longer be
trivialized or reduced to an emotion or debated over as if it were a
philosophical virtue under scrutiny. Jesus now becomes the distinctive definition of love.

(2) Jesus' love for the disciples not only provides a new paradigm;
it also inaugurates a new era. The Johannine eschatology is tilted
heavily in a "realized" rather than a futuristic direction. While one
can speak of continuity with the past and hope for the future, the
present moment is the decisive one. Jesus' coming opens up a
radically new and different situation, in which the life of the age to
come ("eternal life") is no longer only to be awaited as a future
possibility (for example, 17:3). As the writer of 1 John put it, "I am
writing you a new commandment that is true in him and in you,
because the darkness is passing away and the true light is already
shining" (1 John 2:8).

At the center of the new era is the community established by
Jesus, the intimate (though at times unfaithful) family, whom he
affectionately addresses as "little children" (John 13:33). What holds
the family together and makes it stand out above all the rest is the
love members have for one another—dramatic, persistent love like
the love Jesus has for them.

It troubles interpreters sometimes that the command Jesus left is
not a command to love the world or to love one's enemies, but to
love one another. In other places the Johannine narrative expresses
the divine concern for the world (3:16) and directs the disciples to

engage it (20:21), but here Jesus' concern is for the community itself. He makes love the distinguishing mark of the church, that characteristic of its life by which even outsiders can discern its authenticity.

Needless to say, this text lays a heavy challenge before the contemporary church to evidence in the world a unique quality of life and action. Lest that become too burdensome a challenge, the church needs also to be reminded that it is itself the object of unconditional love ("Just as I have loved you . . .").

# SIXTH SUNDAY OF EASTER

The heart of the gospel is that God so loved *the world*, and the Easter proclamation is that Jesus Christ died and rose for the sins of *the world*. In three of the four lessons for today, all the peoples and nations of the world are in view. The texts remind us that from the beginning God's love has been cosmic in scope. They thus warn us against the persistent temptation to make our God too small.

In Acts 16:9–15, Paul takes the gospel to Macedonia. This is a crucial step in the spread of the gospel beyond "Judea and Samaria . . . to the ends of the earth" (Acts 1:8). Lydia becomes, as far as we know, the first European convert to Christianity. It is a fulfillment of Jesus' commission to the disciples "that repentance and forgiveness of sins . . . be proclaimed in his name to all nations" (Luke 24:47).

That the wideness of God's mercy is not a New Testament innovation is indicated by Ps. 67, in which "all nations" (v. 2; see v. 4) and "all the peoples" (vs. 3, 5) are to experience God's "saving power" (v. 2) and are to participate in praising God. The repeated mention of "earth" (vs. 2, 4, 6, 7) and "bless" (vs. 1, 6, 7) recalls the opening chapters of Genesis. The story of God and the world begins with Creation, an expression of the cosmic extent of God's love and involvement. Even when the story narrows to Abraham, Sarah, and their family, it is clear that God still intends to bless "all the families of the earth" (Gen. 12:1–3).

The same concern on God's part is manifest in Revelation. The immediacy of God's presence will be recognized by "the kings of the earth" (21:24). The presence is described in imagery that recalls Creation. The "tree of life" (22:2; see Gen. 2:9) is present, and its "leaves . . . are for the healing of the nations" (22:2). God so loves *the world!*

The peoples and nations are not explicitly in view in John 5, but the unsolicited and undeserved healing is expressive of the "unprovoked grace" (see the commentary on the Gospel lection for today) that flows from God's limitless love for the world and all its people.

## Acts 16:9–15

This text celebrates one of the memorable events in the life of the young church, the bringing of the gospel to Europe. And so it is fitting that the impetus for so significant a development should be cloaked by a certain numinous quality, in this case a vision (Acts 16:9–10). The identity of the "man of Macedonia" who appears in Paul's vision has been the subject of unceasing speculation. Who was he? (Luke himself is one answer that has been given.) How did Paul know that he was a Macedonian? (Perhaps by his accent, or by the very nature of the invitation.) Whatever may be the answers to these questions, one thing is clear: Paul regarded the voice of the man as the voice of God and, without delay, began preparations to sail (v. 10).

(The use of the plural pronouns "we" and "us" in v. 10—and "us" in v. 17—has given rise to considerable speculation as to who "we" might be.)

Ancient readers of this passage, at least those with some sense of history, would probably have been struck by the irony that Macedonia was the first known toehold of the gospel on the soil of Europe. For Macedonia, which had been a cultural backwater during the great golden days of Greek art, philosophy, and literature, had become prominent on the world's stage when Alexander the Great, king of Macedonia, conquered the known world. In one of the most celebrated decades in ancient history (332–323 B.C.), Macedonian and Greek armies under Alexander slashed their way through the old Persian Empire and carried not only Greek arms but Greek culture and language as far as Afghanistan and Egypt. The very city that is Paul's destination, Philippi ("a leading city of the district of Macedonia," v. 12), bore the name of Alexander's father, Philip of Macedon, who shortly before his death in 336 B.C. had forcibly united the city-states of mainland Greece.

Paul is Alexander in reverse! The "commodity" that this foreigner brings is not warfare, but the good news about Jesus Christ. In a certain sense, therefore, the bringing of the gospel to Macedonia parallels Paul's later trip to Rome (Acts 28:14–31).

After Paul and Silas (and Luke himself?) had reached Philippi, they waited until the Sabbath Day, when they went in search of devout Jews. The reference to a "place of prayer" by the river (v. 13) seems to suggest that there was no organized synagogue in Philippi, as that phrase is not the usual designation for a synagogue (compare Acts 17:1). Yet that seems unlikely in view of the fact that, by his time, the Diaspora had embraced most major cities in the Roman Empire. Thus, it is virtually certain that the first recorded Christian sermon in Europe was delivered in a synagogue, in light of the fact that Paul, as a visiting rabbi, would have the right of speaking to those who had come together to study the Torah. (Compare Paul's posture of sitting to interpret the scripture to that of Jesus in the synagogue, Luke 4:20.) The one local person named in the text, Lydia, responds warmly to Paul's message about the Lord Jesus Christ, and both she and her family (including her servants?) were baptized. Whether Lydia was the woman's given name or a reference to the fact that she was born a Lydian (Thyatira was in Lydia) is of small import. The text has memorialized her as Lydia, the first convert to the Christian faith on European soil.

It is not accidental that both here and elsewhere those who prove to be Paul's most receptive listeners are Jews, in that they are most aware of God's nature as a Being of compassion and justice, and they are most aware of God's gracious expectations for humankind. That aspect of the text is so obvious that it almost needs no comment, but it does provide important instruction for preachers/teachers of the gospel in any age. Rarely does a new sense of commitment to Christ come "out of the blue"; almost always the soil of the heart has been prepared in some manner beforehand.

Lydia is so warm in her acceptance of Paul and Silas and their message that she insists that they accompany her to her home. In fact, the manner in which she extends the invitation makes of their response a test of their confidence in her. "If you have judged me to be faithful to the Lord, come and stay at my home" (v. 15). It is a way of saying, "I have believed what you have said to me; now show me that you believe my response!" Under such circumstances, the disciples have little choice but to accept Lydia's hospitality. That she is still willing to receive them later, as former prisoners (v. 40), is a further example of her faith.

In some ways Acts 16:9–15 is but one of many stories in this book that relate the power of God's Spirit in the life of Paul, especially in Paul's role as missionary to the Gentiles (note the unusual reference to "the Spirit of Jesus" in 16:7). Still, this text is important not only in its narrative of the first recorded preaching of the gospel in Europe, but also because of the prominent place given to a woman. Lydia is not the first woman to become a Christian (compare Acts 8:3), but she is the first known European Christian. Those who would attempt to deny to women full and equal participation in the church—and many of these people are themselves of European extraction—must stand reminded that the pilgrimage in which they are engaged was pioneered by a woman!

## Psalm 67

Psalm 67 has traditionally been interpreted either as a psalm of thanksgiving, possibly associated with a harvest festival (see v. 6), or as a prayer for God's blessing (vs. 1, 7). Perhaps it is both. In any case, it is clear that a major theme of the psalm is blessing (vs. 1, 6, 7), which is directed toward Israel (the object of "bless" in each case is "us") but which ultimately involves the whole earth and its peoples.

The psalm is usually divided into three parts (vs. 1–3, 4–5, 6–7), the first two of which end with an identical refrain (vs. 3 and 5) and the last with what can be understood as a variation of the refrain (v. 7b). As an alternative, I would suggest a chiastic structure (emphasis added):

(a)  vs. 1–2       blessing and the knowledge of God among "*all* nations"
  (b)  v. 3           refrain
    (c)  v. 4              central profession of God's sovereignty
  (b')  v. 5          refrain
(a')  vs. 6–7      blessing and the reverence of God by "*all* the ends of the earth"

A chiastic arrangement highlights v. 4, which lies at the heart of the psalm and which also stands out as the only three-part line in the psalm. This central structural feature of the psalm makes a profession of faith that represents the theological heart of the Psalter—namely, God rules the world. The profession that "you judge the peoples with equity" occurs elsewhere in contexts that explicitly affirm that the "LORD" reigns (see 9:7–8; 96:10; 98:6–9; compare 99:4). Only a sovereign God can "guide the nations upon earth" (see Ex. 15:13, 18, where the celebration of God's guidance of Israel culminates in a proclamation of God's reign). It is this central profession of God's sovereignty that underlies the request for a blessing that will have worldwide effects.

The central profession is surrounded and set off by the refrain in Ps. 67:3 and 5. The verb translated "praise" is usually translated "give thanks"; that is, the psalmist's wish is that "all the peoples" acknowledge with gratitude God's sovereignty as well as God's "way" and "saving power" (v. 2). The word "all" emphasizes the psalm's universal perspective, as does the sevenfold occurrence of "peoples"/"nations," one occurrence for each poetic line in vs. 3–5.

The opening and closing verses correspond both in terms of the request for blessing (vs. 1, 7) and the placement of blessing in a universal perspective. Twice more the word "all" occurs (vs. 2, 7), and the final occurrence is the most comprehensive—"all the ends of the earth" are to "revere" God. This phrase occurs also in Pss. 2:8 and 72:8 (see also Isa. 52:7–10), both of which assert the sovereignty of God through God's chosen agent, the king (messiah). Psalm 72 in particular portrays what blessing involves—"prosperity"/"peace" (Heb. *shalom*, vs. 3, 7; and compare Ps. 67:6 with Lev. 26:4) accompanied by "justice" and "righteousness" (Ps. 72:1–2, 6–7; compare "judge," which could be translated "establish justice," in 67:4). As in Ps. 67, the blessings experienced by the king and his people (72:15) are to involve ultimately "all nations" (72:17).

Psalm 67:1 clearly recalls the so-called Aaronic or priestly benediction in Num. 6:22–27. God's blessing is inseparable from God's presence or "face" (Ps. 67:1; Num. 6:25–26, NRSV "countenance" in 6:26; see also Pss. 4:6; 31:16; 80:3, 7, 19; 119:135) and ultimately from a knowledge of God's "way" (67:2; see Ps. 119:135, where the request for God's "face" to "shine" is accompanied by the request for God to "teach me") and God's "saving power" (67:2; see Pss. 80:3, 7, 19, where "let your face shine" is to result in being "saved"). The appropriateness of Ps. 67 as a benediction may be reflected in the traditional Jewish practice of reciting it at the end of the Sabbath (see Marvin E. Tate, *Psalms 51—100*, Word Biblical Commentary, 20; Dallas: Word, 1990, p. 155).

The theme of blessing and the universalistic perspective of Ps. 67 recall Gen. 12:1–3, the promise of blessing to Abraham and Sarah and their descendants, a blessing that will somehow involve "all the families of the earth" (Gen. 12:3). The promise is echoed throughout the Old and New Testaments (see Ex. 9:16; Ps. 22:27–28; Isa. 2:2–4; 19:23–24; 49:5–7; Gal. 3:6–8, 28; Rev. 22:1–5), including Ps. 67. As H.-J. Kraus suggests concerning the message of Ps. 67, "The community of God here learns how to break away from all narrowness in the reception of salvation" (*Psalms 60—150*, trans. H. C. Oswald; Minneapolis: Augsburg Publishing House, 1989, p. 42). In our contemporary world, torn by racial and ethnic exclusivism and strife, it is crucial that we hear the message of Ps. 67: God rules the world and intends blessing for all the world's peoples. In short, Ps. 67 can assist us as, in the words of Cain Hope Felder, "we . . . engage the new challenge to recapture the ancient biblical vision of racial and ethnic pluralism as shaped by the Bible's own universalism" (Preface, *Stony the Road We Trod: African American Biblical Interpretation*, ed. Cain Hope Felder; Minneapolis: Fortress, 1991, p. ix).

## Revelation 21:10; 21:22–22:5

In the final vision of Revelation (21:9–22:5), John sees in great detail the new Jerusalem that has already been mentioned briefly in 21:2. The lection omits the lengthy description of the physical substance of the city (including its dimensions, the gates, the materials used), but it would be well simply to read that section in worship should time permit. Those details contribute to the overall sense of unbelievable extravagance that is at the heart of this passage: what awaits God's people includes every hope imagined and many that are beyond human conception.

As is the case throughout Revelation, the apocalyptist draws heavily on Hebrew scripture, and on apocalyptic traditions in particular, so that the narrative is literally dense with those allusions. Especially significant for this passage are the Genesis traditions about Eden (Gen. 2:4–14) and its restoration (*1 Enoch* 25:1–7; *2 Enoch* 8:1–8), and prophetic traditions about the restoration of Jerusalem (Zech. 14:11; Tobit 14:4–7; *4 Ezra* 8:52; *1 Enoch* 90:28–42). Disagreements abound over the influence of any of these traditions and the extent of Revelation's conformity or innovation. What is more significant for preaching than those historical questions is the awareness that, however strange the language of Revelation is for modern readers, the apocalyptist is speaking language that had currency for his audience. If he and his audience are indeed Jewish Christians living in exile following the destruction of the Jerusalem Temple, the appeal to these well-established traditions would yield comfort and hope.

The specific portion of the vision assigned for the lectionary reading underscores the all-inclusive nature of the blessings afforded by the new Jerusalem. In Rev. 21:22–27, several of those blessings are couched in terms of the safety or security of the people. This city needs no sun or moon, for "the glory of God is its light, and its lamp is the Lamb" (v. 23). The same promise is reiterated in 22:5. Whether God and the Lamb replace the sun and moon or outshine them is a question quite beside the point. The inhabitants of this city need no longer be concerned about whether there is sufficient light by which to conduct their affairs—there will always be light.

Perhaps the most striking promise regarding security comes in

21:25: the gates of this city "will never be shut by day—and there will be no night there." Anyone can come and go at any time, and no one need feel threatened or insecure. Indeed, people from the nations *will* come in, and they will be welcome (v. 26). To inhabitants of the ancient Mediterranean world, as to modern urban dwellers, this word about safety in the city would be unbelievably welcome. Not even a thought needs to be given to security.

Within this setting of light and safety, people from every nation will live in harmony. Only in 22:2 is the "healing of the nations" spoken of directly, but the references to the "nations" and "kings" in 21:24 already indicate that the community envisaged is all-encompassing. People from all over will bring to it "the glory and the honor of the nations" (v. 26). Asking about the diversity of this population is introducing an admittedly very contemporary concern, but implicit in the picture here is a city in which diversity and unity have found balance.

Beyond even these physical characteristics of the city, however, lies the promise of God's presence. Several times in Revelation the apocalyptist has anticipated the presence of God with God's people (see, for example, 7:15–17; 21:3–4). Here that note is sounded once again, and with great force. The new Jerusalem needs no temple, not because Christians reject the Jerusalem Temple, but because the city itself has become the dwelling place of God. Revelation 22:3–4 reflects the earlier claims that God has made priests of all believers (see 1:6; 5:10). With every Christian a priest and every place sacred, there is no need for a temple.

Most important, God's presence with God's people here becomes not only continual worship (22:3) but the very gift of actually seeing the face of God. Biblical tradition knows well that no human being may look at God's face (Ex. 33:12–23; John 1:18). It also knows that being in God's presence, seeing God's face, is among the hopes of God's people (see Ps. 17:15; Matt. 5:8). Here the apocalyptist anticipates the fulfillment of that deepest longing, the gift of seeing God's face, living in God's presence, and thriving on that presence.

The passage concludes with a reference to power. God and God's people "will reign forever and ever" (Rev. 22:5). Given the destructive power of Rome that would have been all too familiar to the audience of Revelation, it may seem surprising that the author concludes with reference to God's power, especially since the opposing powers have all been destroyed. The power envisaged here, however, like the power inherent in the "river of the water of life" (22:1) and in the "tree of life" (v. 2), is the power to give and sustain life.

Extravagant passages such as this one have given rise to much bad interpretation, as people scramble to identify each item in the text with some concrete expectation about life in a heavenly city. That sort of reading actually destroys the passage itself, for fundamentally the vision promises that Easter finally results in gifts that are beyond calculating, imagining, or describing.

## John 5:1–9

The lectionary offers a choice for the Gospel reading for this Sunday—either John 14:23–29 or 5:1–9. Since this is the only reading from John 5 in the three-year cycle, and since there are three other selections from John 14 in the cycle, the commentary will deal with the story of Jesus' healing of the man beside the pool of Beth-zatha. Though the limits of the lection include only the miracle itself, it is difficult to understand the story and its significance in the Johannine narrative without giving attention to the broader context (at least 5:1–18).

There are many features of the healing that remain unclear, and it is best to acknowledge them up front. What precisely was the man's physical ailment? It was something that had persisted for thirty-eight years and apparently kept him from moving promptly into the pool, but beyond this we are told little.

What is the narrator's attitude toward the superstition that the troubled waters of the pool offered healing? Since 5:3b–4, omitted in the better manuscripts, represents a scribal explanation of the pool's supposed healing powers, it offers no help. Could Jesus' later words to the man, "Do not sin any more" (5:14), be a charge to him not to return to the idolatrous fascination with the pool? Possibly, but the words are general and more likely refer to his lack of gratitude for the cure. If the interpreter is looking for a condemnation of the superstition, it might best be found in the fact that Jesus did not help the afflicted man to get to the edge of the pool to benefit from its curative powers, but performed the healing another way.

The lack of any request to Jesus for healing, or any hint of faith on the part of the sick man prior to the cure, emerges as the most prominent feature of this incident. Particularly when this story is compared with the preceding one, about the healing of the son of the official who begs Jesus for help and demonstrates profound faith (4:46–54), the feature stands out even more.

The healing by the pool is a demonstration of unprovoked grace. Nothing in the man's conduct or disposition accounts for the cure that brought to an end nearly four decades of affliction. He becomes a passive recipient of a remarkable gift. But the incident raises all sorts of questions about the indiscriminate character of God's goodness and the fact that God (at least on occasion) helps those who do not even ask for it. It threatens a theology that would carefully control God's activities by the faith (or lack of it) of humans. The old slogan that faith works miracles utterly breaks down with this story. It is *God* who works miracles, and not even faith is a precondition.

Jesus does, however, ask the man, "Do you want to be made well?" The man's reply may not be very satisfactory (it is more an explanation of why he has not been healed than an expression of confidence in Jesus), but it does remind us that, though it may be unprovoked, grace is not mechanical. The healing is not a transaction that happens somehow apart from the man, who at least *implies* that he wants to be cured. God's kindly intrusiveness into human lives may not be dependent on prior faith, but it can be thwarted.

The section that follows the miracle itself (5:9b–18) indicates two further features about the incident. First, the healed man apparently exhibits no gratitude to Jesus for his healing. (The statement in 5:9 that "he took up his mat and began to walk" indicates not so much the man's obedience as a confirmation that the healing had really occurred.) When queried by the authorities about why he carries his pallet on the Sabbath, he swiftly passes the buck to Jesus, whom the text tells us he does not know (5:13). Then when Jesus meets him later in the Temple, he goes back to the authorities, not skipping and jumping in delight because he has been made whole, but clearly to report on Jesus. The narrator appears miffed at the healed man by holding him directly responsible for the persecution of Jesus ("Therefore," 5:16). The story, which no doubt is a part of John's struggle with the relation of signs to faith, states not only that miracles can be performed independently of faith but that miracles do not always produce faith.

Second, the opposition of the authorities to Jesus in the narrative takes on a new dimension with this incident—they plot to kill him (5:18). It is not simply his breaking of the Sabbath code but Jesus' identification of himself with God that angers them ("My Father is still working, and I also am working"). Ironically, they perceive precisely the Christology that this gospel advocates and just how offensive it can be. Thus the healing of the man by the pool triggers a conflict that leads to the crucifixion.

# ASCENSION

The festival of the Ascension is endlessly problematic and admits of no simple or single "explanation." It is clear in these texts that the church struggled to voice a reality that ran beyond all its explanatory categories. We must take care that we do not engage in domestication that curbs the wonder and wildness of these texts.

The presenting problem is, on the one hand, the disposal of the body of Jesus, what happened to Jesus after Easter. That, however, is a small agenda. On the other hand, the continuation of the church when Jesus is no longer present is an acute issue. Thus the issue in the narrative is much more a church question than it is a Jesus question. That presenting problem, however, only provides "cover" for the larger story. That story is that this fearful, waiting community, which is anxious and bewildered, has no power of its own. It possesses none and it can generate none for itself. It has no claim and no cause for self-congratulation. And yet, oddly, power is given that causes this fragile little community to have energy, courage, imagination, and resources completely disproportionate to its size. How can one speak about this changed situation that can only be attributed to the inscrutable generosity of God? How is it that this church with no claim becomes a powerful force in the larger scheme of public life?

The church has no special language of its own through which to utter the unutterable. For that reason, it must rely on its ancient doxological tradition (in the Psalms), which breaks out beyond reasoned explanation into wonder, awe, amazement, and gratitude. Worship is the arena in which the new power given the church by God is voiced. And that lyrical worship leads to glad witness, asserting that the world is oddly open to new governance.

The preacher will profit from noticing that these stories are cast in odd modes of discourse. There is nothing here that is conventional, controlled, or predictable. The nature of the story requires a peculiar mode of utterance. The narrative lets us see in wonderment glimpses and hints, but not more. God's new rule is beyond our logic. We see only its residue and effect in a transformed community. That community is not certain what has happened, but is sure enough to affirm its identity and embrace its proper work.

## Acts 1:1–11                                                        (A B C)

In the Lukan narrative of God's saving activity in Jesus Christ (the Gospel) and in the Holy Spirit (Acts), the story of Jesus' ascension marks the end of Jesus' postresurrection appearances to his disciples and the prelude to the sending of the Spirit, thereby marking a transition point from Easter to Pentecost. In the liturgical tradition of the church, Ascension is all of that and more, for it also has become a festival of the exaltation of the risen Christ.

The Acts lection for this day consists of two main components. The first (Acts 1:1–5) serves not only as an introduction to the entire book of Acts and thus to the work of the Holy Spirit in the life of the young church, but also—in a more immediate sense—as an introduction to the Ascension miracle. The second part (vs. 6–11) is the account of the miracle itself. In both these sections, however, the primary emphasis is on the coming of the Holy Spirit.

Verses 1–5, after a brief statement of purpose (vs. 1–2) which parallels Luke 1:1–4, set forth a terse summary of the events of the forty days following Easter, a time when Jesus "presented himself alive to [the disciples] by many convincing proofs" (v. 3). It is perhaps assumed by Luke that "Theophilus" has heard of these appearances of the risen Christ, since no effort is expended to provide the details of these encounters, other than what is offered in Luke 24. Following Jesus' order to the band of his faithful followers to remain in Jerusalem (Acts 1:4), he delivers the promise of God, namely, that God's Spirit is soon to be made evident in fresh ways. This coming of the Spirit is explained in baptismal terms: whereas water was the baptismal medium of old, "you will be baptized with the Holy Spirit not many days from now" (v. 5).

The second part of our text (vs. 6–11) repeats this emphasis on the coming of the Spirit, but in a different context. Here this gracious and decisive gift of God's Spirit is compared to the political hopes the disciples had vested in the Messiah. Their question about the restoration of the kingdom to Israel (v. 6) betrays that not even the events of Easter and the succeeding forty days had disabused them of a comfortable stereotype, that is, that God's Messiah would reinstitute the political fortunes of the old Davidic monarchy. Jesus deflects their question (v. 7) and refocuses their attention on the marvelous display of God's power and love that they are soon to see. It is not the restoration of the kingdom of Israel that will energize you, Jesus says in effect. Rather, "You will receive power when the Holy Spirit has come upon you" (v. 8a). Thus vs. 5 and 8 lift before the reader an announcement from God that is not to be overlooked: the age of the Spirit is about to dawn.

Then Jesus is elevated beyond the limits of their physical senses, and "two men in white robes" (compare Luke 24:4) gently chide the disciples for vacant gazing, even as they promise Jesus' Second Coming (Acts 1:9–11).

While the liturgical tradition of the church has tended to make the ascension of Jesus into a festival to his glory and power, the emphasis in the biblical tradition is elsewhere. Not only is the ascension rarely mentioned in the New Testament (compare Luke 24:51 and Mark 16:19), but the interest in Acts 1 appears to be less in what is happening to Jesus than in what is about to happen in the lives of the earliest Christians. Twice in this brief passage the declaration is made that the Holy Spirit is about to infuse the life of the church in new ways. Not that the Spirit was unknown before this. The "Spirit of God" was the phrase that from very early times had been applied to special expressions of God's guiding and redemptive presence in human life (note, for example, 1 Sam. 11:6, and compare it to 1 Sam. 16:14). But the import of Acts 1:5 and 8 is that a new dimension to the Spirit's work is about to become evident. It is as different from what has gone before as the Spirit is different from the ordinary water of baptism. It is as different from what has gone before as the transcendent kingdom of God (v. 3) is different from the political kingdom of David and his descendants.

Just how the Spirit finds expression the disciples are not told. That is a matter of suspense, which will not be resolved until Pentecost (Acts 2). In the interim, they (and the disciples in every age) are to "be my witnesses in Jerusalem, in all Judea and Samaria, and to the ends of the earth" (1:8). It will become clear only later that in this very activity of witnessing they will provide the channels for the Spirit's power and grace.

So in the New Testament perspective, Ascension is an interim time, a period—not unlike Advent—between promise and fulfillment. The disciples of Christ are called to live faithful and obedient lives and to remember that the wonder of God's love and presence revealed so radically in the cross and the open tomb still has in store fresh surprises of joy. The disciples of Christ are called to witness, little realizing how the Spirit lurks to transform all that they do into magnificent occasions for the outpouring of God's love. In this manner Ascension points to Pentecost and to all the marvelous ways of the Holy Spirit of God.

## Psalm 47                                                    (A B C)

The festival of Ascension is not about the physical ascent of a body (the body of Jesus) into heaven. It is, rather, a liturgical celebration whereby Jesus "ascends to the throne," that is, is dramatically elevated to a position of sovereign authority. In enacting this ritual of enthronement, the church's liturgy draws heavily on the liturgy of ancient Israel, whereby Yahweh was elevated and enthroned as a powerful sovereign. Our psalm reflects such a liturgical enactment.

The initial hymnic unit celebrates the power, authority, and sovereignty of Yahweh (Ps. 47:1–4). The hymnic summons is addressed to "all you peoples" (v. 1). The liturgy of the Jerusalem Temple dares to imagine that its worship is an act concerning all nations and peoples. This inclusive horizon is advanced by reference to Yahweh as "Most High" ('Elyôn, v. 2). The title is not an Israelite name for God, but is a generic name for the great god, a name to which all peoples could subscribe.

The reason for such praise is the kingship of Yahweh, the establishment of Yahweh's sovereign rule (vs. 2–4). The ground of praise is twofold. On the one hand, this God is "Elyon," the God of all peoples, who presides over all the earth, who has subdued peoples and nations and drawn them under a new aegis. On the other hand, the actual speakers in the liturgy and in the psalm are Israelites, who know this universal God by the exodus name of Yahweh, and who confess that God chose land "for us" and loves us (v. 4). Thus the hymn holds together the sweeping notion of universal sovereignty and the concreteness of the experience of the Israelite community.

The first characterization of enthronement in this psalm is a splendid liturgical act (v. 5). "God has gone up"! The language portrays an act of coronation or enthronement whereby the candidate (like the winner of the Miss America contest) ceremoniously, magnificently, and ostentatiously ascends the throne and dramatically claims power and receives obeisance. The kingship of Yahweh is enacted and implemented liturgically, as is every political ascent to power. When we say of Jesus in the creed, "He ascended into

heaven," in the first instance this is the language of ritual enthronement and coronation. What is claimed substantively, politically, and
theologically is first asserted dramatically and liturgically.

The second hymnic element reiterates the main themes of the initial
verses (vs. 6–7). Four times the congregation is urged to "sing praises"
(zāmar, v. 6). The identity of Yahweh in this summons is "God," a
universal title, which is matched by "our King," the governor and
guarantor of the Jerusalem political-religious establishment.

The second reflective statement describes the new world situation
in light of this act of coronation (vs. 8–9). We are taken into the
throne room. Around the throne sit all the obedient, glad subjects
(v. 9). There is among them no conflict, dispute, or challenge to the
authority of Yahweh. "The princes of the peoples," that is, all the
other kings and rulers whose gods have been defeated by Yahweh
and who now submit to Yahweh, all are present. The wonder of our
phrasing is that they are gathered together "as the people of the God
of Abraham" (v. 9). This does not say that they have entered into the
Mosaic covenant and have become adherents to the Torah. It is
affirmed, however, that they have embraced the promises God has
made to Abraham and Sarah, and have agreed to live under the
power of God's promise.

This psalm invites us to understand the festival of Ascension
anew. The festival is not about getting the body of Jesus off the earth,
and it is therefore not marginal and incidental to the life of the
church. The festival is a dramatic moment whereby the presence of
Jesus in the church is converted into a large, cosmic rule. Rooted in
liturgical rhetoric, this claim for God (and subsequently for Jesus)
envisions important political spin-offs. All kings are indeed under
God's feet (see Eph. 1:22). God's promise, we know very well, is a
rule of mercy, compassion, forgiveness, and caring. The new enthronement changes the climate of the earth and the modes of power
now permitted in the affairs of princes and kings. The kingship of
God revamps all other forms of governance.

## Ephesians 1:15–23                                              (A B C)

Since it separates him from his followers—at least in a physical,
visible sense—the ascension of Jesus might have been recalled by the
church as a time of grief and confusion. How would the straggly
group of Jesus' followers continue in his absence? What meaning
could his absence from them have, other than their own isolation
and aimlessness?

Luke, alone among the Gospels, not only describes the ascension but portrays it as a time of empowerment. Both in the Gospel and in Acts, Jesus tells his disciples to wait for the Spirit, a Spirit that comes only after Jesus himself has departed. At the ascension itself (Luke 24:44–53; Acts 1:1–11) Jesus' final instructions immediately precede his ascension and the repeated instructions of two men in white robes. By this means, and by virtue of the narrative connection, Luke depicts the ascension of Jesus as the empowerment of the church itself.

The brief reference to the ascension in Eph. 1:15–23 stands out in contrast to the accounts in Luke and in Acts. Here we find no references to Jesus' postresurrection stay with his disciples, to his mysterious ascension, to the return to Jerusalem. Instead, the ascension functions as part of the author's general doxology about God's actions in Christ on behalf of humankind. A closer examination, however, will show that in Eph. 1, as in Luke-Acts, the ascension of Jesus signals the empowerment of the church.

While the passage is a single unit, the content of which is a prayer, it moves from thanksgiving to intercession to doxology. Verses 15–16 first recall the faith of the Ephesians and their love toward all believers. This faithfulness on their part prompts the writer to an exuberance of thanksgiving. As elsewhere in New Testament letters, the response to the gospel in itself provides a reason for gratitude to God.

That thanksgiving does not mean that the church now stands alone or can operate autonomously. The intercession of vs. 17–19 specifies that the church needs wisdom, revelation, and hope. Believers need to know God's power "for us who believe, according to the working of his great power."

At first glance, the remaining verses of the prayer appear to be only a kind of christological footnote. The content is familiar, perhaps so familiar that it slips out of the reader's awareness, dismissed as so much theological "filler" without any substantive connection to the issue at hand, the needs of the community. Several aspects of the passage, however, connect it firmly with the intercessory prayer of vs. 17–19.

Most clearly, both the intercession and the doxology revolve around the writer's confidence in the power of God. Verse 19 refers to the "immeasurable greatness" of God's power and the working of God's "great power." Verse 20, which begins the section on the ascension, begins with "God put this power to work in Christ." In Greek, vs. 19 and 20 are connected by the repetition of "working" (*energeia*) at the end of v. 19 and "put to work" (*energeō*) at the beginning of v. 20. The power already at work in the community and invoked by the author for "wisdom and revelation" is none other than the power that raised Jesus from the dead and exalted him to heavenly places.

What follows in vs. 20–23, then, serves to tie the empowerment of the community to the power of God more than it does to describe in precise detail the present whereabouts and activity of the risen Lord. The statements about Christ's ascension are nevertheless important, particularly for the way in which they underscore this notion of God's power. For the writer of Ephesians, reference to the resurrection alone does not suffice, but must be expanded by a glimpse of the further exaltation of Christ in the ascension. Christ sits at the right hand (v. 20), above every form of "rule and authority and power and dominion," and "above every name" of every age. All things are already subjected to him (v. 21).

These same motifs occur elsewhere in the New Testament, of course, but here Christ's complete triumph has already taken place. The Philippians hymn *anticipates* the exaltation of Christ above every name, but that event has not yet occurred (Phil. 2:5–11). In 1 Cor. 15, Paul confidently asserts that God will finally triumph over "every ruler and every authority and power" (15:24), but that triumph also lies in the future. The apparent conflict among these texts perhaps arises because the author of Ephesians wants to ground the power of the church in this overwhelming demonstration of the power of God. That Christ has already triumphed means that the church itself will surely be sustained by God's power.

The connection between the ascended Christ and the church becomes explicit, of course, in Eph. 1:22–23. Here the metaphor of the church as a body *in Christ,* found already in 1 Corinthians, changes so that the church itself *is the body of Christ.* In 1 Corinthians, that metaphor serves to underscore the unity necessary for the church, even within its diversity. In Ephesians, the transformed metaphor serves to ground the church itself in the power of God. The church may act with confidence, because it knows itself to *be* Christ's own body, the body of the one whose exaltation derives directly from God's own power.

## Luke 24:44–53                                                    (A B C)

In the conclusion of Luke's Gospel, the narrator draws the story to a close by sounding again several notes that the careful reader has heard in earlier chapters. They come appropriately now as the final message of the risen Jesus to his disciples and, together with the account of Jesus' departure, serve as the connecting link to the beginning of the book of Acts, Luke's second volume.

What are those repeated themes? First, the Jewish scriptures provide an understanding of the Messiah and his destiny. This concern emerges early in the chapter, as Jesus walks with the two travelers to Emmaus (Luke 24:25–27, 32). Now, as he meets with a group of disciples, he again speaks of the scriptures and their witness to him, to the gospel, and to the mission to the nations. It is not important what specific passages Jesus (or the narrator) might have had in mind. The point to be made is that what happens to Jesus and what the disciples are to do in the days ahead are consistent with God's intentions from the beginning. The suffering and resurrection of the Messiah and the mission to the nations are not accidents of history, but fulfill the divine plan. One has to look to the scriptures to discern God's strategy in inaugurating the anticipated reign of justice and peace.

While the Jewish scriptures provide an understanding of the risen Jesus, it is the risen Jesus who rightly interprets the scriptures. A veil of mystery hangs over the text, leaving it enigmatic and inscrutable, until the resurrection. "Then he opened their minds to understand the scriptures" (v. 45). Neither the intellectual acumen of the scholars nor the spiritual capacity of the mystics grasps the intent of God in the ancient writings, apart from the presence of the one to whom the writings point.

Second, the declaration is made, "You are witnesses of these things" (v. 48). What (or who) is the antecedent of "you"? At the historical level, the answer is presumably "the disciples," though one has to go all the way back to v. 33 to find a specific referent. At another level, one might answer "the Jewish community," since this commission reconstitutes the people of God and gives them the particular responsibility to begin at Jerusalem and proclaim the gospel to the non-Jewish world (see Isa. 49:6). Not surprisingly, the group returns to the Temple as the place of worship and waiting.

At still another level, the "you" is directed to a broader company of readers, ancient and modern, who at the end of the narrative are drawn in as participants in the story. They (we) are witnesses, who are not allowed to put the book down like a good novel and return to business as usual, but are mandated to proclaim the story, to call for repentance, to declare divine forgiveness. They (we), like the original hearers, are to be recipients of the power that the Father promises, an indication that God intends for the plans to be completed and the divine strategy to work.

Third, the narrative ends in a remarkable outburst of worship. Rather than being depressed that Jesus has withdrawn and left them with a heavy responsibility, the disciples are ecstatic and worship Jesus. And their joy seems more than a temporary high, since they are "continually in the temple blessing God" (Luke 24:53). Just as Jesus' entry into the world evoked songs of praise from Mary, Zechariah, Simeon, Anna, and the angelic choir, so Jesus' departure to the Father sets the community again to singing.

Worship and witness belong together. Like the bud that will not bloom without regular watering, the church's mission dries up without the renewal of worship. The singing of hymns, the prayers of thanksgiving and intercession, the reading and exposition of scripture, and the breaking of bread keep the church in touch with the promised power of the Father and make possible the glorifying and enjoying of God that is done outside the sanctuary. Worship becomes the occasion when the story that must be told and retold among the nations is heard afresh, when the witness to the world is reenvisioned. At the same time, worship divorced from witness is empty. The church merely turns in on itself, loses its reason for being, and finds its singing, praying, and reading of scripture bland and impotent.

Ascension Day is an appropriate time to reflect on the church's mission in the world, on the importance of worship as a partner to mission, and on the critical role of the scriptures in providing direction.

# SEVENTH SUNDAY OF EASTER

The lessons for this Sunday offer the preacher an opportunity to reflect on and affirm the enduring foundation of the church's unity and hope. This opportunity may be especially important in this era of divisiveness and even "panic about current ecclesial problems" (see commentary below on John 17:20–26).

The unity for which Jesus prays in John 17 involves a communion of the Father, Son, and believers in every generation. This communion of saints, grounded in the unity of Father and Son, is a reminder that the church and its future are larger than any one generation can experience or perceive. The "glory" that Jesus has given to the church (v. 22) involves a participation in Jesus' crucifixion as well as his resurrection. A church that loves as God loves (see v. 26) can expect opposition and suffering, as Jesus' life and death reveal.

The Revelation to John originated in a situation where the church and its future were direly threatened by the power of Rome. The urgency of the threat is reflected in the urgency of the expectation of Jesus' coming again (Rev. 22:12, 20). The early church may have been mistaken in its understanding of the timing of God's work, but the certainty that underlay the church's expectation is forever timely— namely, that God rules the world (see Rev. 7:15) and that God guarantees the future of God's people and of the cosmos.

Psalm 97 is a rousing affirmation of God's cosmic reign. God's rule is recognized by earth (v. 1) and heaven (v. 6) as well as by God's people (v. 8). The wicked may have their day, as Rome had its day (v. 10), but it is the reality of God's reign that, even amid opposition, gives hope to God's people and makes joy possible (vs. 10–12).

In a real sense Paul and Silas do exactly what the concluding verse of Ps. 97 invites. Though locked in jail, they rejoice (Acts 16:25). What makes their singing possible is their trust that God's rule is more powerful than the rule of their opponents. They know, and the story shows, that God "rescues them from the hand of the wicked" (Ps. 97:10). It is God's reign that grounds the church's unity and its hope.


## Acts 16:16–34

This narrative of the imprisonment of Paul and Silas is a continuation of the story of the disciples' work at Philippi, the first recorded Christian missionary activity on European soil (Acts 16:9–15; see the Sixth Sunday of Easter). Yet the present lection is a self-contained theological unit, and thus may be allowed to speak for itself without dependence on that larger narrative of which it is a part.

The initial section of the text (vs. 16–18) describes the "offense" for which the disciples run afoul of the authorities. The issue of demon possession is a difficult one for preachers and interpreters of the text in our time, because the topic has become so "loaded" by Hollywood portrayals of demon possession (the movie *The Exorcist*, for example) and by contemporary cultic behavior on the part of persons who at least appear to many to be of questionable emotional balance. Nevertheless, the New Testament takes demons and demon possession quite seriously, and regardless of how the interpreter may feel about a demonic presence in our own world, the New Testament view must be respected and not simply dismissed out of hand.

The demon in possession of the slave girl in this narrative (actually referred to as a "spirit," vs. 16, 18) reveals at least two characteristics that are also true of the demons that Jesus subdues. It so controls a person that the person says and does things that would otherwise be out of character. In addition, when the demon speaks (through the possessed human) it recognizes the power of God for what it is and, in the end, obeys that power. The girl's declaration, "These men are slaves of the Most High God, who proclaim to you a way of salvation" (v. 17), is directly on target, as was, for example, the confession of the demoniacs in Matt. 8:29 in recognizing Jesus as the "Son of God." The evil, then, consists in the enslaving power the demon exercises over the person. That slavery, in fact, is made quite clear in Acts 16:16–18 in that it says the possessed girl was being used by her owners for financial profit. These unnamed persons were manipulating her and her "spirit" to their own advantage, and they perceived the power of God—vested in Paul and Silas—as a threat to their power over the girl.

This brief text, then, becomes an interesting study in slavery. Paul and Silas are accused by the "spirit" of being "slaves of . . . God," a true enough charge when slavery is understood in the sense of committed service. But the real slaves, in the pejorative sense of the term, are the girl and, in a secondary sense, the "spirit" itself. When Paul delivers the girl from her spirit, he not only demonstrates the power of God over evil, but he liberates both her and, interestingly, her "spirit" from the power of the wicked handlers.

The second section of the text (vs. 19–24) tells of the arrest and beating of the disciples. It is not clear what law the disciples had violated in their restoration of the girl. They are not accused of being Christians, and in any event such an accusation would have been meaningless at this time, since Christians were as yet virtually unknown in Greece. Perhaps the disciples violated a law directed at Jewish proselytizing, although such a charge does not square with the actions of Paul and Silas. The whole affair smacks of the proceedings of a kangaroo court, and that is undoubtedly what it was. The authorities, wishing to keep public order and perhaps to mollify influential business interests, arrest Paul and Silas simply because it is more convenient than not arresting them. The step was obviously a popular one to take (v. 22).

The third section (vs. 25–34) provides a narration of the disciples' miraculous deliverance from prison and of the conversion of the jailer and his family. Some commentators have taken note of the fact that the earthquake (v. 26) was a natural phenomenon and that therefore the release of the disciples should not be thought of as a miracle. But clearly the text (note the jailer's response to the event in v. 30) regards this occurrence as an example of God's gracious power, no matter what adjectives one chooses to characterize it. No less exemplary of God's power is the conversion of the man "and his entire family" (v. 33). Their baptism parallels that of Lydia "and her household" in v. 15, and their hospitality (v. 34) is quite similar to hers.

We are reading here of one further demonstration, among many, of the power of the Spirit of God in the life of the young church, a theme that dominates the entire book of Acts. The key to the Spirit's redemptive energies is contained in v. 31 where, in response to the jailer's urgent question, Paul and Silas reply, "Believe on the Lord Jesus, and you will be saved." This is the kerygma in its most straightforward, unadorned essence. It was in Paul's day. It is in our own.

## Psalm 97

Like Pss. 96 and 99 (see Christmas, Proper 1, the Last Sunday After Epiphany, and Proper 4), Ps. 97 belongs to a group of psalms that explicitly proclaim, "The LORD is king" (97:1; see also 93:1; 96:10; 99:1; compare Pss. 29; 47; 95; 98), and that form the theological "heart" of the Psalter (see above on Pss. 96; 99). While sharing much of the vocabulary and conceptuality of the other so-called enthronement psalms, Ps. 97 is also unique. The first section (vs. 1–5) features the language of theophany (an "appearance of God"), to which the heavens respond (v. 6), as do "all the peoples" (v. 6), the gods (v. 7), and Yahweh's people (vs. 8–9). The final section (vs. 10–12) extends to the readers of the psalm in every generation the invitation to respond.

In vs. 1–5, it is immediately evident that Yahweh's reign has cosmic significance, for "the earth" and "the many coastlands" (see Isa. 41:5; 42:4, 10; 49:1; 51:5; and NRSV "isles" in Ps. 72:10) are the first invited to respond to the initial proclamation. Two more occurrences of "earth" (Ps. 99:4, 5) provide a frame for the first section. As is appropriate for one who is "Lord of all the earth" (v. 5), Yahweh's appearance is surrounded by manifestations of the natural order—"clouds and thick darkness" (v. 2), "fire" (v. 3), "lightnings" and thunder that shakes the earth (v. 4). Other Old Testament passages use the same "high poetic fashion" (Marvin E. Tate, *Psalms 51—100*, Word Biblical Commentary 20; Dallas: Word, 1990, p. 519) to describe Yahweh's appearing, including Ex. 13:21–22; 19:16–20; 20:18–21; 24:16–17; Pss. 18:7–15; 50:3; Micah 1:4; Hab. 3:3–12. The passages from Exodus are particularly noteworthy, because there God's appearing is associated with God's gracious leading of the people (13:21–22), God's instructing of the people (chs. 19—20), and God's making a covenant with the people (ch. 24; see 19:5–6). The dimension of relatedness is also present in Ps. 97, as suggested by the mention of "righteousness and justice" as foundational principles of God's rule (see Ps. 89:14). The crucial and remarkable affirmation is that God's will for the right ordering of human relationships is built into the very structure of the cosmos (see Ps. 82:5, which suggests that in the presence of injustice the very existence of the earth is threatened). Nor surprisingly, the response to the theophany involves the celebration of God's will for righteousness and justice, beginning in Ps. 97 with v. 6.

As "the earth" was called on to respond to v. 1, so v. 6 begins with a description of the response of "the heavens" to God's presence. As a pair, "the heavens and the earth" designate the whole cosmos (see Gen. 1:1). In short, the whole universe responds to God's reign. Interestingly, it is the heavens that "proclaim . . . righteousness" (v. 6a; compare Ps. 19:1 where the heavens proclaim God's glory), a term for describing God's will for human relatedness. Again, the effect is to link inextricably God's rule of the universe with the right ordering of the human family. Appropriately, the human family is in view in 97:6b. To behold God's "glory" is to confront God's presence (Ex. 16:7, 10; 24:16–17; 33:18, 22; and others) and acknowledge Yahweh's sovereignty (Pss. 24:7–10; 29:1–3, 9; 96:3, 7–8; and others).

Psalm 97:7 recognizes the existence of persons who do not acknowledge Yahweh's sovereignty, but they "are put to shame" as their so-called gods "bow down" before Yahweh. In contrast to the idol worshipers, Yahweh's people—Zion and Judah—celebrate Yahweh's "acts of justice" (v. 8; NRSV "judgments"). Thus, they are in tune with the cosmos, with "the heavens," which proclaim God's righteousness (v. 6), and with "the earth" and "coastlands," which are also called to "rejoice" and "be glad" (v. 1). As the focus narrows to Yahweh's own people, the form of address becomes more intimate. Verse 8 shifts to direct address, which continues in v. 9. Like v. 5, which ends the first section, v. 9 ends the second section by asserting God's sovereignty over "all the earth." The word "exalted" in the final line of v. 9 also occurs in the climatic concluding line of Ps. 47 (v. 9), another enthronement psalm.

In Ps. 97:10, the NRSV note should be followed. Here Yahweh's own people in every generation are addressed directly with a call to decision. They are to conform their lives to God's will for righteousness and justice by hating evil (see Amos 5.15, Prov. 8:13; compare Micah 3:2). In all times, hating evil out of allegiance to God's rule arouses opposition from those whose loyalties differ—"the wicked" (Ps. 67:10; note the contrast between "the wicked" and "the righteous" in Ps. 1, Sixth Sunday After Epiphany, and throughout the Psalter). The mention of "the wicked" reminds us that, like Pss. 96 and 99, Ps. 97 is eschatological; it asserts God's rule in circumstances where it appears that God does *not* rule. The "faithful" (v. 10) and the "righteous" (vs. 11–12) will not go unopposed, but they will be guarded and ultimately rescued from the power of the wicked. That is, Yahweh's will and power are finally determinative; Yahweh rules, not the wicked. Thus, light—another cosmic element (see vs. 1–5) and symbolic elsewhere of God's presence and protection (see Pss. 4:6; 27:1; 43:3; Micah 7:8)—"dawns for the righteous" (v. 11). In short, the righteous by their lives are in harmony with the universe as God intends it; they contribute to the arrangement of the cosmos by living as God intends. Thus, even amid the reality of "the wicked," "joy" is possible (v. 11); and the righteous can be invited to "rejoice in the LORD" (v. 12). The closing invitation to the righteous is essentially the same as the opening invitation to the earth and the coastlands. Again, those who live under God's rule will be in tune with the cosmos. They will also be in harmony with Jesus, who invited people amid opposition and persecution to "rejoice and be glad" (Matt. 5:12), an invitation that makes sense only for those who live in the new world of God's reign (see "kingdom of heaven" in Matt. 4:17; 5:3, 10, 19–20, for example).

## Revelation 22:12–14, 16–17, 20–21

The concluding lines of Revelation consist of a string of several independent sayings that reiterate some major emphases of the book as a whole and formally close the work. Beginning with Rev. 22:12, the risen Jesus speaks, first and last, about the imminence of his return (vs. 12–13, 20), about the judgment his return will necessitate (vs. 14–15), about the testimony for the churches in the words of Revelation (v. 16), the call to salvation (v. 17), and the warnings about tampering with the book (vs. 18–19). While it is difficult to discern any organized movement through the passage, the general themes are evident.

Preeminent in this passage is the promise that Jesus will soon return. The notion of the imminence of the Parousia appears earlier in the book (1:1; 2:16, 25; 3:11), but here references come often and with urgency (22:6, 7, 12, 20). The return of Jesus poses a threat for some, those who persist in sin and in opposition to Jesus himself. But for the church, that promise is hope itself. Both urgency and perhaps a note of poignancy sound at the book's close, as the community responds to "Surely I am coming soon," with "Amen. Come, Lord Jesus!" First Corinthians closes with the same cry (16:22; there in Aramaic rather than Greek), suggesting that this urgent hope for Jesus' return was shared across several Christian communities; the cry itself may have a fixed place in the eucharistic liturgy (see 1 Cor. 11:26).

In Rev. 22:12, Jesus announces what will be one result of his coming: "My reward is with me, to repay according to everyone's work." The lectionary omits vs. 15 and 18–19, presumably because of their harsh statements concerning the judgment that will constitute Jesus' repayment for the works of some. Understandably, the preacher needs to approach these verses with particular care, so that the sermon does not serve only to engender fear or worsen guilt. Deleting these verses, however, deletes a crucial piece of the apocalyptist's worldview, namely, dualism.

Throughout Revelation, as is the case with most apocalyptic writings, the author clearly divides the inhabitants of the world (indeed, of the cosmos) into the good and the bad. There can be no confusion about who sides with Babylon and who sides with the Lamb. Explaining this dualistic mentality is notoriously difficult, especially since it appears in so much ancient literature (and in many contemporary controversies as well!). In the context of a writing like Revelation, it functions to reinforce the community's boundaries and to encourage faithful behavior. Such dualism also reinforces Revelation's insistence that God will finally triumph, for those who are aligned with the Lamb will both persevere and be rescued from the trials ahead.

For those who are aligned with the Lamb, the words of v. 17 form a call to perseverance, patience, and also hope and joy: "Come." It is not simply that Jesus must come for his own, but his own must be ready for his coming. Let "everyone who is thirsty come" and "take the water of life as a gift" (see 22:1). Those who stand with the enemies of the Lamb may yet cross over, although the overwhelming evidence of Revelation is that the apocalyptist holds out little hope for such conversion (see, for example, 22:11).

In part because of this impending judgment, Revelation concludes with an insistence on its own reliability. Throughout the book, assertions such as "I am the Alpha and the Omega, the first and the last, the beginning and the end" (v. 13; see 1:8; 1:17; 21:6) have served to guarantee the trustworthiness of the visions and their interpretation. Here that reliability extends to the book itself, which is to be made available rather than sealed up (22:10), and which is not to be altered in any way (vs. 18–19). Particularly the warnings about altering the words of the book would be well known to John's audience, for various sorts of ancient writings carried warnings about their completeness and integrity.

Understanding the apocalyptist's work in this concluding section is one thing; preaching it is quite another matter. The urgency that pervades Revelation here comes to a head, and as it does contemporary preachers and teachers inevitably face the question of how to interpret such urgency some two thousand years later. Especially in those Christian communities that live under oppression, the cry of v. 20 may be vivid and heartfelt, but what do we say in light of the delay? And what do we say to those (perhaps including some of us) who find the language of Revelation too wild even to consider?

When all is said and done, apocalyptic literature is not about predictions of time and events, but about the certainty that the God who stands before the beginning of history also stands beyond its ending. The evil that torments the cosmos, whether in human or metahuman form, may rule for a while, as Rome did and as other empires of varying sorts have since that time. But evil will not finally win, and God's people will finally be vindicated.

In the context of Eastertide, this distinction between urgency and certainty becomes especially important. The power of God evident in the risen Lord guarantees the future and total reign of God. Varying strands of the New Testament verbalize that certainty in different ways. Paul logically deduces the connection between the two and then envisages God's final triumph (1 Cor. 15). Mark depicts it in terms of the traditional hope for the return of the Son of man (for example, Mark 8:38–9:1). Revelation imagines the future in terms both vivid and foreign, but the underlying certainty remains the same.

## John 17:20–26

It is intriguing to reflect on Jesus' prayer for the unity of his followers (John 17:20–26) at a time when ecumenical concerns are clearly on the wane. For a variety of reasons, enthusiasm for formal ecumenical projects has dissipated. National and international conferences come and go without much effect on the life of local congregations. The continued struggle with internal uncertainties has made it difficult for institutional churches to become very excited about suggested moves toward fully unity. What does unity entail in a day like this? Can a fresh look at Jesus' high-priestly prayer point us in some new directions?

For one thing, the unity proposed in the prayer transcends generations. The immediate followers of Jesus are sent into the world (17:18), and Jesus prays for those who will respond to their message and become believers (17:20). The concern reaches out to another generation of believers, to yet unknown disciples beyond the present circle. The prayer in fact envisions a long line of followers, stretching all the way to the eschaton, who will share in a profound fellowship not only with each other, but with Jesus and the Father (17:24).

The scope of Jesus' petition for unity makes it, then, an affirmation of the communion of the saints. It encompasses past and future believers in an almost unimaginable circle of unity that culminates in a heavenly reunion. The prayer serves as a healthy reminder that the church is bigger than any one generation and prevents a paralyzing preoccupation with the present. It helps to alleviate our panic about current ecclesial problems and informs us that we and our grandchildren are the objects of Jesus' praying.

Second, the nature of the unity prayed for reflects the mutuality of the Father and the Son (17:21–23). We here run head-on into John's Christology, which repeatedly affirms a functional unity between Father and Son (for example, 10:30). All Jesus' works are in sync with the Father's works. The Christology is then extended to the character of the Christian life: genuine human relationships mirror divine relationships. But what in the world does this mean?

Two terms provide a handle with which to understand the mirroring of divine relationships: glory and love. Think of glory as powerful presence. The presence given Jesus by the Father is now bestowed on the church and becomes a sign of the church's oneness (17:22). Jesus is the revealer of God's presence, and the church becomes a special vehicle in the communication of the divine presence to the world. The church is given a unique place. But remember that Jesus' hour of glorification includes not only moments of exaltation—resurrection and return to the Father—but also the crucifixion (12:23–33; 21:19). Thus the reflecting of divine glory is no cause for triumphalism, but for sober, wide-eyed mission.

Love is a more manageable notion. The love of a parent for a child (though with us humans a fallible, distorted love) serves as the analogy for God's relation to Jesus. It is a love reaching back prior to the incarnation (17:24), but made known and available to the human community in the revelation of Jesus (17:26). In fact, it is a love that gets redefined by Jesus' act of self-giving (13:34). As the community of believers demonstrates the love with which it has been loved, it exhibits the mutuality between the Father and the Son and the unity for which Jesus prayed.

Third, the concern for unity serves a greater end: as a witness to the world. It never becomes unity for its own sake—"The more we get together, the happier we'll be"—but "so that the world may believe that you have sent me" (17:21). This means that while there is much in the text to suggest that Jesus prays for a spiritual or invisible unity, it clearly must be at the same time a visible unity, a reality that can bring the world to faith.

What does visible unity entail? An earlier, parallel statement of Jesus provides help: "By this everyone will know that you are my disciples, if you have love for one another" (13:35). Bureaucratic mergers and institutional unions have rarely made the witness of the church more effective, but instead the quality of its life, the intensity of its expression of love for the world, and the depth of caring between members have been essential to its proclamation. They have been means whereby the experience of having been loved becomes obvious to those needing to be loved.

There is in the original setting of this Gospel as well as in the modern world a concern for the oneness of the church. It clearly lies in something beyond doctrinal agreement and institutional related-ness (neither of which is unimportant)—in their experienced love of the Father that keeps believers together in spite of their multiple differences and links them with disciples past and future.

# PENTECOST

The lessons for the Day of Pentecost virtually force the preacher to consider and address a subject that we often prefer to avoid—the Spirit of God. As the commentary this week on Rom. 8:14–17 suggests, the goal should not be to explain the Spirit. The very nature of the Spirit defies our attempts to explain or control. A further complexity is that different biblical texts offer different perspectives on the Spirit; there are, however, some common affirmations we can make without pretending to exhaust the mystery of the Spirit.

The Spirit gives life! In the account of the Day of Pentecost in Acts 2, the Holy Spirit gives new life to a dispirited band of disciples. The church is born. Birth imagery is present too in Rom. 8 where "all who are led by the Spirit of God are children of God" (v. 14). Our very lives derive from and depend on God, whom we properly address as "Abba! Father!" (v. 15; see "life"/"live" in vs. 6, 10, 11, 12, 13). In John, it is the Spirit or Advocate whose presence will continue to make life possible for the disciples in the absence of Jesus' physical presence. These New Testament views of the Spirit are congruent with that of Ps. 104. Here it is not just God's people who are enlivened by the Spirit. Rather, the Spirit of God is responsible for the origin and sustenance of all creation (Ps. 104:27–30; see Gen. 1:2).

The life-giving power and presence of the Spirit is a gift—unsolicited, unexpected, undeserved. The exuberant account in Acts 2 makes it clear that the gift of the Spirit shatters all reasonable expectations. Only God could be responsible for such marvels. In John, it is stated repeatedly that the Spirit is given or sent, either by the Father (John 14:16, 26) or by Jesus himself (15:26; 16:7). The people of God and the whole creation live by grace.

To be sure, not everyone will acknowledge God's grace. To live by the Spirit is to live in some sense at odds with "the world" (John 14:17); the sneers from the crowd in Acts 2:13, the presence of "the

341

wicked" in Ps. 104:35, and Paul's mention of suffering in Rom. 8:17 serve to instruct us that life in the Spirit will mean opposition. But life in the Spirit is life as God intends. It is to know a peace that the world cannot give (John 14:27). In our world that so desperately seeks peace in self-help and the ability to manipulate and control, it is crucial that we wrestle with these texts and their claim. In a world devoid of wonder, they may begin to open us to experience the presence of mystery and the mystery of Presence.

## Acts 2:1–21                                                          (A B C)

New life—sudden, unmerited, irresistible new life! That is the reality the Pentecost narrative in Acts 2 broadcasts, and the text transmits the story in the most expansive way imaginable. All the stops on this great literary organ are employed: a heavenly sound like a rushing wind, descending fire, patterns of transformed speech, and the like. It is as if not even the most lavish use of human language is capable of capturing the experiences of the day, and that is undoubtedly one of the emotions the text wishes to convey.

It is not accidental, of course, that the birth of the church, this great "harvest" of souls, should occur on this important festival. The Feast of Pentecost, or Weeks, as it is known in the Old Testament, marked the end of the celebration of the spring harvest, a liturgical cycle that began at Passover and during which devout Israelite families praised God for God's grace and bounty. It also was the beginning of a period, lasting until the autumnal Festival of Booths (or Tabernacles), in which the firstfruits of the field were sacrificed to Yahweh. And among at least some Jews the Feast of Weeks was a time of covenant renewal, as the following text from the Book of Jubilees (c. 150 B.C.) makes clear:

> Therefore, it is ordained and written in the heavenly tablets that they should observe the feast of Shebuot (Weeks) in this month, once per year, in order to renew the covenant in all (respects), year by year. (*Jub.* 1:17; trans. O. S. Wintermute in James H. Charlesworth, ed., *The Old Testament Pseudepigrapha;* Garden City, N.Y.: Doubleday & Co., 1985, vol. 2, p. 67)

Pentecost/Weeks is thus a pregnant moment in the life of the people of God and in the relationship between that people and God. Or to put the matter more graphically, but also more accurately, Pentecost is the moment when gestation ceases and birthing occurs.

Thus, it is both an end and a beginning, the leaving behind of that which is past, the launching forth into that which is only now beginning to be. Pentecost therefore is not a time of completion. It is moving forward into new dimensions of being, whose basic forms are clear, but whose fulfillment has yet to be realized.

Those who follow the cycle of lectionary texts (or, for that matter, those who simply read the book of Acts) have been prepared for this moment. Twice, in connection with Jesus' ascension, the coming of the Spirit has been promised: "You will receive power when the Holy Spirit has come upon you" (Acts 1:8; compare 1:5). That promise is now realized in a manner far surpassing the expectations of even the most faithful disciples. New life for the church! New life for individuals within the church! New life through the Spirit of God! That is the meaning of Pentecost.

No one present is excluded from this display of God's grace. Unlike other important moments in the history of God's mighty acts of salvation—the transfiguration (Mark 9:2–13), for example, where only the inner few are witnesses to the work of God's Spirit—everyone is included at Pentecost. The tongues of fire rest upon "each" (Acts 2:3) of the disciples, and a moment later the crowd comes surging forward because "each one" (v. 6) has heard the disciples speaking in his or her native tongue. In order that not even the least astute reader may miss the inclusiveness of the moment, the list of place names that begins in v. 9 traces a wide sweep through the world of the Greco-Roman Diaspora. That which happens at Pentecost is thus no inner mystical experience, but an outpouring of God's energy that touches every life present.

Yet not everyone responded to the winds and fires of new life, at least not in positive ways. Some mocked (v. 13) and, in their unwillingness to believe the freshness of God's initiatives, reacted with stale words (compare 1 Sam. 1:14) as they confused Spirit-induced joy with alcohol-induced inebriation. Perhaps it was the very extravagant expression of the Spirit's presence that drove them to conclude: "This cannot be what it seems to be!" Yet what it seemed to be is precisely what it was. God's Spirit unleashed! New life—sudden, unmerited, irresistible new life! We may hope that those who mocked were among those who, on hearing Peter's sermon, were "cut to the heart" (v. 37).

Peter's sermon begins—and this day's lection ends—with a quotation (vs. 17–21) from the prophet Joel (Joel 2:28–32a), and nothing could be more symptomatic of the nature of Pentecost than the transmutation of this text. That which in the prophet's discourse appears prominently as a forecast of destruction and death has become on Peter's tongue a declaration of new life. For Joel the signs of the outpouring of the Spirit are a prelude to disaster (see especially Joel 2:32b, c), but for Peter these wonders have been fulfilled in Jesus Christ, himself the greatest of God's wonders (Acts 2:22), and their purpose, *Christ's* purpose, is nothing less than the redemption of humankind. Again the Spirit has invaded human life in ways that shatter old expectations. It is not death that is the aim of the Spirit's visitation, but new life—sudden, unmerited, irresistible new life! "Everyone who calls on the name of the Lord shall be saved" (v. 21).

## Psalm 104:24–34, 35b                                                   (A B C)

Psalm 104 has been called "one of the crown jewels of the Psalter" (H. Darrell Lance, "Psalm 104:24–34," *No Other Foundation* 7 [winter 1986]: 42). Along with Ps. 103, to which it is bound by the repetition of "Bless the LORD, O my soul" (103:1, 22; 104:1, 35), Ps. 104 provides eloquent testimony to the inseparable unity of God's saving and creating work on behalf of humanity and of the entire universe. Unique in its sustained attention to creation (see also Pss. 8; 19:1–6; Gen. 1:1–2:4), Ps. 104 is a song of praise which can be divided as follows:

vs. 1–4     God and the heavens
vs. 5–13    God and the earth (note "earth" in vs. 5, 13)
vs. 14–23   God and people (note "people" in vs. 14, 23)
vs. 24–30   "all" (vs. 24, 27) God's works and creatures
vs. 31–35   conclusion: divine joy (v. 31) and human joy (v. 34)

The lection consists of the final two sections, which do serve to emphasize what has been clear all along: God rules the universe! As H.-J. Kraus puts it, "The conception of the heavenly king stands behind the whole psalm" (*Psalms 60—150*, trans. H. C. Oswald; Minneapolis: Augsburg, 1989, p. 304).

(Also see Last Sunday After Epiphany regarding Ps. 99, the Seventh Sunday of Easter regarding Ps. 97, and Proper 4 regarding Ps. 96.)

The opening and closing invitation is unique to Pss. 103—104. The word "bless" seems to have meant originally "to bend the knee." Thus, to bless the Lord is an act of homage in recognition of God's rule. The phrase "my soul" could also be translated "my whole self." It is an especially appropriate invitation for a psalm that affirms that all life derives from God, is sustained by God, and finds its destiny in God (see Ps. 104:14–15, 27–30, 33–34).

Verse 24 is a sort of summary exclamation that looks back over vs. 1–23. It contains two of the six occurrences of the key word 'šh, "do, make" (see "make"/"made" in vs. 4, 19, 24; "work(s)" in vs. 13, 24, 31). *Everything* derives from God. The heavens, the earth, animals, and people—God "made them all" (to quote Cecil Frances Alexander's hymn "All Things Bright and Beautiful"); and the whole creation is a witness to God's wisdom (see Prov. 3:19; 8:22–31; Jer. 10:12; Rom. 1:20). This verse expresses the same evaluation of creation that is expressed in Gen. 1 by the affirmation, "It was good."

In Ps. 104:25, not coincidentally perhaps, the sea is called "great" just as the Lord was called "great" in v. 1. In Canaanite religion, the sea was considered a god that represented chaos and that was defeated by Baal. Psalm 104 has already suggested that God has ordered the chaotic waters into life-giving springs and rivers (vs. 6–13). As vs. 25–26 suggest, even the mighty and mysterious oceans are subject to God (see Ps. 29:10; Isa. 51:9–10). The most fearsome creature of the sea, Leviathan—a version of the chaos monster known in other sources—is here but a mere creature, and a harmless one at that (see Job 41:1–11; Ps. 74:12–14).

The "all" in Ps. 104:27 apparently refers to more than just the sea creatures mentioned in vs. 25–26; it recalls the "all" of v. 24. Every creature, human and otherwise, depends on God for life. God's "hand" continually feeds them; all creatures gather food as Israel gathered manna in the wilderness (see Ex. 16:16). God's "breath" or "spirit" (Ps. 104:29–30; the Hebrew word is *rûaḥ* in each case) keeps all creatures alive (see Job 34:14–15). Psalm 104:29 and 30 suggest a continuing creation empowered by God's Spirit. God's *"face"* or presence serves to "renew the *face* of the ground" (emphasis added). Because God rules the world, new things are always possible. The life-giving and life-renewing power of God's breath/Spirit is an appropriate theme for the Day of Pentecost, which celebrates the gift of God's Spirit, who gave new life to a discouraged and dispirited band of disciples (Acts 2), who then went about "turning the world upside down" (Acts 17:6). Like all God's creations, the church lives by the power of God's Spirit, not by its own ability, merit, or ingenuity.

Just as Ps. 8 affirms that the majesty of God *includes* the earth and its creatures (Ps. 8:1, 9), so Ps. 104 suggests that God's "glory" is all bound up with the "works" in which God rejoices. Elsewhere, "glory" is associated with God's sovereign rule (see Pss. 24:7–10;

29:1–3, 9–11; 145:1, 5, 12; Isa. 6:1–5). The appropriate response to God's rule and God's rejoicing in God's works is praise. Praise is the recognition that God—not humans—rules the world (see Ps. 100:3); and praise involves the yielding of the whole self to God in liturgy and in life (Ps. 104:33–34). Verse 35 begins by recognizing the reality that not all humans submit themselves to God's rule, and it concludes with the psalmist's reaffirmation of allegiance to God's rule.

In an increasingly secular, human-centered world that is dominated by the conviction that "nature" exists to serve people, Ps. 104 offers a vitally different view of the world—a thoroughly God-centered view. "Nature" is not God, but neither does it exist apart from God's creative and sustaining breath/Spirit. Everything we humans do has an effect on God's world and thus on God. Ultimately, ecology, economy, and theology are inseparable. Life belongs to God. Human fulfillment consists not of self-actualization, but rather begins with the simple invitation: "Bless the LORD, O my soul."

## Romans 8:14–17

Perhaps nowhere in the New Testament does the human need to explain, and therefore to establish a sense of control, falter more convincingly than when it encounters references to the Spirit. As the notes in the NRSV indicate, we sometimes do not even know whether the word refers to the wind, to God's Spirit, or to a human or some other spirit (thus confusion over whether the English word should appear in uppercase or lowercase). The early church's dealings with the Spirit prove extremely difficult to understand (for example, the baptism of the Spirit in Acts). What we repeatedly fail to acknowledge is that the desire to explain is antithetical to the Spirit itself, precisely because the Spirit does blow where the Spirit wills and not where exegetes and preachers might like. The celebration of Pentecost ought to remind us of that important fact.

Even in Rom. 8, in the middle of the letter so often understood to be Paul's most mature and refined theological statement, a clear grasp of the notion of the Spirit eludes us. Instead, Paul refers to the Spirit's work with a variety of expressions. The "law of the Spirit of life" sets believers free (8:2); believers then live "according to the Spirit" and have their minds set "on the things of the Spirit" (vs. 4–6). The Spirit lives in believers (v. 9) and is life itself (v. 10). Through the Spirit believers "put to death the deeds of the body" and cry to God as Father (vs. 13–16). The Spirit intercedes for humankind and is known by God (vs. 26–27). Not only do these varying expressions frustrate logical explanation; but they also demonstrate that Ernst Käsemann was surely right to observe that, when it comes to talk about the Spirit, "Paul was not so timid as his expositors" (*Commentary on Romans*; Grand Rapids: Wm. B. Eerdmans Publishing Co., 1980, p. 226).

The lection assigned for this Sunday opens with the assertion: "For all who are led by the Spirit of God are children of God" (v. 14). As often in Paul, the "for" connects this statement with the preceding verse, but does it refer to all of the verse, so that the statement highlights the exclusion of some? Or, on the other hand, does the "for" refer to the second half of the verse, so that v. 14 simply amplifies what it means to live "by the Spirit"? The Greek does not allow for a precise decision of this question, but the tenor of the passage as a whole suggests that the "for" refers to the second half of v. 13. That is, "all who . . ." is a positive statement about those who are led by the Spirit, not an attempt to restrict the number or to define out certain other people.

Verses 15–17 serve to explain what it means to be "children of God." A child does not have a "spirit of slavery," but a "spirit of adoption." Whether Paul imagines an actual state that can be characterized as a "spirit of slavery," or whether this is a rhetorical expression to contrast sharply with a "spirit of adoption," is unclear. The contrast itself would have great currency in a world so dominated by the slave system as was the Greco-Roman world of the first century.

The "spirit of adoption" that results from being children of God yields certain specific results. God's children freely cry to him as "Father" (v. 15). They are both God's children and, thereby, "heirs of God and joint heirs with Christ" (v. 17). Paul's language escalates as he struggles to depict what it means to be "led by the Spirit."

In the closing phrase of the passage, the NRSV lends itself to a misimpression. We are heirs with Christ, the NRSV reads, "if, in fact, we suffer with him so that we may also be glorified with him" (v. 17). The word *eiper*, here translated "if, in fact" does sometimes have the connotation of "if" or "if indeed," as in 1 Cor. 15:15 ("if it is true"). It may also be translated as "since," as it is in Rom. 3:30 ("since God is one") and 8:9 ("since the Spirit of God dwells in you"), where there is no question about something having happened. Here, where following verses make it quite clear that Paul knows that believers are suffering as they await the concluding stages of God's triumph, there is no question whether believers are suffering. The point is that they are, and that their suffering is actually a suffering "with" Christ.

This small point of translation touches on a much larger issue, of course. With the universal human anxiety about safety and security, readers of this passage may find themselves asking *whether* they are among the "children of God" in 8:14 and *whether* they indeed are suffering with Christ. The focal point of the reading then becomes essentially anthropological: "Am I among those who are led by the Spirit?"

For Paul, by contrast, the focal point is not anthropological but christological and pneumatological. He is not concerned to predict or decide or verify who is within the circle and who is outside the circle. Rather, he struggles to articulate the gracious, unmerited, sustaining work of the Spirit in human lives. For him, the Spirit is a sign of the new age that is breaking in and that cannot be overturned (vs. 31–39).

(For further commentary, particularly on the phrase "children of God," see the discussion of Rom. 8:12–17 for Trinity Sunday, Year B.)

## John 14:8–17 (25–27)

The liturgical calendar during this season is organized according to the sequence of events in the two New Testament books of Luke and Acts. Thus Good Friday, Easter, several Sundays in the Easter season, Ascension, and Pentecost follow one another in an orderly fashion. The fact that the term "Pentecost" is used at all and that Acts 2 is a suggested reading for each of the years of the lectionary cycle indicates the dependency on the schema of Luke-Acts.

The primary theme for this Sunday—the Holy Spirit—is, however, treated differently in other New Testament writings, less dramatically perhaps than the mysterious happenings of Acts 2, but no less profoundly. "Gospel of the Spirit," a label often put on John, is symptomatic of an extensive consideration of the Spirit in that Gospel, and particularly as a topic of Jesus' teaching throughout his ministry. "Pentecost" happens not after a period of fifty days after Easter, but on Easter evening. John helps us to think of the Spirit in ways other than sheer excitement or emotional agitation.

In John, especially instructive are the five passages found in the farewell discourses where the terms "Advocate" and "Spirit of truth" are used, and where Jesus anticipates the coming of the Spirit immediately following his departure (John 14:16–17, 25–26; 15:26–27; 16:7–11, 13–15). Two of those passages are included in the Gospel lesson for today, and another is recommended for next Sunday (Trinity Sunday).

Four features of the Spirit stand out in the selection from John 14. First is the term *paraklētos*, rendered by the NRSV as "Advocate." This represents a perhaps unfortunate change from the RSV "Counselor," since "Advocate" highlights the legal overtones of the term (as in 1 John 2:1), prominent only in John 16:7–11. The text itself defines *paraklētos* by adding "to be with you forever" (14:16). The Spirit as *paraklētos* is God's powerful and nurturing presence, given to the disciples in the wake of Jesus' departure.

Specifically, the disciples are faced with Jesus' words, "If you love me, you will keep my commandments" (14:15). How are they to live in such a way that their affection for Jesus does not degenerate into sentimentality, but expresses itself in concrete deeds of mercy and in faithful obedience? Without his physical presence, how are they to cope with the forces arraigned against them, and not regress to what they were before he entered their lives? The answer is the Counselor, whose sustaining influence has no termination.

Second, we encounter in 14:17 the term "Spirit of truth," which recurs later in 15:26 and 16:13. The Spirit teaches. The Spirit enables the community to remember its link with Jesus.

The phrase is a promise that embodies both a threat and a hope. On the one hand, the Spirit will keep the church's feet to the fire when it wanders into accommodating paths in search of an easier way. The "Spirit of *truth*" (emphasis added) forces a reality check, prodding, needling, cajoling the community to embrace its distinctiveness as the people of God. The Spirit does not make things easier, only harder. On the other hand, the words Jesus taught contain commitments about resurrection, life, a secure dwelling place, a meaningful present, and a hopeful tomorrow. The Spirit prevents the church from forgetting that it has a future and helps it translate the message of Jesus so that the future is not simply endless time but rich with promise.

Third, the Spirit is sent by the Father—a divine gift. Twice in these five passages in John, the Father is specified as the sender (14:16, 26), and twice Jesus is the sender (15:26; 16:7). The stress is not coincidental. All the stratagems in the world cannot entice or force the Spirit's hand. No manipulation of a group, no set form of prayer, no upstretched hands. The promise to the church of God's presence always remains at God's initiative, and yet it is a promise of *God*, and one on which the church can rely.

Finally, the Spirit distinguishes the disciples from the world. The church becomes a peculiar community, set apart by being indwelt by the Spirit. That carries some interesting implications. For one thing, the church cannot take its cues for its life and mission from the culture, as if the culture posed all the right questions. As the text puts it, "the world cannot receive" the Spirit, "because it neither sees him nor knows him" (14:17). Without taking a superior stance toward the world (after all, the Spirit is a gift), the church follows a script that seems to the world no more than an impossible jumble of letters.

For another thing, the peace that the church seeks and receives is distinctive (14:27). All those "peaceful" scenes thrust at us by Madison Avenue, enticing as they may be, turn out to be mirages, false promises that haunt us in the seeking. The peace given the church is nothing other than the promise of the divine presence, the assurance of people not orphaned and destitute.

The Gospel of John confronts us with sobering and penetrating words for Pentecost.

# TRINITY SUNDAY

The lessons for Trinity Sunday offer an additional opportunity to consider the work of the Holy Spirit. For instance, Rom. 5:1–5 makes reference to God, Jesus Christ, and the Holy Spirit. Paul obviously does not have a detailed doctrine of the Trinity, but the three "Persons" are present, and it is through their mutual work that the believer experiences peace. In particular, it is through the Holy Spirit that the love of God "has been poured into our hearts" (Rom. 5:5). As the lessons for last week also suggested, this peace does not preclude suffering.

The lesson from John is another passage in Jesus' "farewell discourse" that mentions the Spirit. The Spirit's role in this case is teacher. The Spirit "will guide you into all the truth," including "things that are to come" (16:13). An exploration of this remarkable claim will involve the preacher in a consideration of the relationship between the Spirit and Jesus. What the Spirit teaches will be in continuity with what Jesus has already made known (vs. 14–15).

Even the lesson from Prov. 8 may be pursued in a direction appropriate to Trinity Sunday. It is likely that the figure of personified Wisdom lies behind the Logos Christology of John 1. Thus, the text opens the way to consider the feminine dimension of the Godhead.

The mention of "glory" in Ps. 8:5 and Rom. 5:2 offers another possible theme for preaching. The juxtaposition of Pss. 3—7 with Ps. 8 suggests that the God-given "glory" of humanity is not incompatible with suffering. This conclusion is reinforced by Rom. 5:1–5. To "boast in our hope of sharing the glory of God" (Rom. 5:2) means to "boast in our sufferings" (v. 3). As the Romans lesson from last week suggested of the relationship between the believer and Christ: "We suffer with him so that we may also be glorified with him" (8:17).

351

## Proverbs 8:1–4, 22–31

A reasonable God has created a rational world. Such a declaration might be suggested as containing the essence of this day's Old Testament lection. Yet this affirmation of rightness and order is expressed not in a logically structured argument—such as an ancient Greek philosopher might have made—but in an arresting poem impregnated with metaphor and personification, the language of the wisdom schools of the ancient Near East. Behind the poetry is a statement about the majesty and creative control of Israel's God, one that finds resonance with other parts of the Old Testament, of which Ps. 8, this Sunday's Psalm lection, is an outstanding example.

The initial section of our text (Prov. 8:1–4) introduces the figure of Wisdom, a personification that is feminine not only in the Hebrew Bible (compare Job 28, and note Sir. 24), but in much of the literature of ancient Israel's neighbors. In the characterization here, Wisdom stands in the most populated, high-profile spaces of life ("the heights," "the crossroads," "the gates," "the entrance of the portals") to broadcast her message. It is a message intended for every woman and man, and it is one that contains the gift of life (v. 4; compare vs. 35–36). (Although they are not part of the lection, vs. 6–21 amplify the themes of vs. 1–4, in that they describe how Wisdom's message is both true and good and how human life is enriched by embracing it.)

The heart of the text (vs. 22–31) declares that the rationality of Israel's God expressed itself at the beginning of creation and—for those who are willing to see it—this rationality, this wisdom, has been in evidence ever since. Order, structure, sanity are not Yahweh's afterthought; they are part of the very fabric of creation in that they are a reflection of Yahweh's own nature. Verse 24 is interesting in that it seems to resonate to both Old Testament "accounts" of the Creation, that of P (compare the "depths" with Gen. 1:2) and that of E (compare the "springs" with Gen. 2:6). The fact that this Wisdom poem thus seems to have been composed after the book of Genesis had reached its present shape is one of many evidences scholars cite for regarding Prov. 8 as a relatively late literary creation—although one that contains very ancient conceptual roots.

Other Creation motifs follow that find parallels in various parts of the Hebrew Bible (compare v. 25 with Ps. 90:2; v. 27 with Job 26:10; and so on). All these citations of Yahweh's creative skill and power converge in v. 30, which insists not only that Wisdom was present at Creation, but that she played an important role at the world's beginning. Wisdom was, in effect, Yahweh's "assistant creator."

A technical discussion is in order here. NRSV probably has it right when it translates the first line of v. 30 "I was beside him, like a master worker." This clearly makes Wisdom and Wisdom's attributes of rightness and order part of the very constitution of the world (or, as modern people would say, "of nature"). But as the NRSV marginal note points out, there is some doubt about the Hebrew word ('āmôn) translated "master worker," because by reading the vowels differently, the word means something like "little child" or "nursling" (and one remembers that the vowels were not supplied in early Hebrew manuscripts). At least one important ancient Greek translation, that of Aquila, has it as "child." Thus other renderings of this verse must be taken seriously, such as the Revised English Bible:

> Then I was at his side each day,
> his darling and delight,
> playing in his presence continually. . . .

or the New Jerusalem Bible:

> I was beside the master craftsman,
> delighting him day after day,
> ever at play in his presence. . . .

It is frustrating to the interpreter when ambiguity or uncertainty clouds a key term, but in this case the weight of the textual evidence is on the side of NRSV, and the preacher may feel on solid ground in drawing theological conclusions from this way of understanding the text.

The sum of our passage, then, would appear to go like this: Yahweh has fashioned an ordered and good world, a reasoned shape that is evident for all to see. When women and men allow this Wisdom to govern their lives, the result is wealth (v. 18), justice (v. 20), happiness (v. 32), and life itself (vs. 4, 35–36). The experience of a truly wise person begins with a fear of Yahweh (v. 13; compare Prov. 1:7) and is consummated in joy and prosperity.

The strength of such a proposition lies in its obvious appeal, not just to the human mind, but to the emotions as well. Life *is* under control. Given the presuppositions of Wisdom, truth may be known and one's day-to-day living adjusted accordingly. Evil is banished; randomness and chance are kept at a safe distance. "God's in his heaven: All's right with the world," as Robert Browning put it.

Yet those who live in the "real" world know that this declaration, while genuine, is only partial. Evil is not so easily dispelled. Chance and chaos lurk on every hand. Job knew that well, and complains against all tidy rationality, such as that expressed in Prov. 8:

> The earth is given into the hand of the wicked;
>   [God] covers the eyes of its judges—
>   if it is not he, who then is it?
>
>                                         (Job 9:24)

Yet while evil and chance must be dealt with day by day, beyond the apparent randomness of things is the compassion of a rational God. Perhaps when all has been said, that is the real value of Prov. 8.

## Psalm 8

The psalms preceding Ps. 8 have depicted human beings who are beset by "many . . . foes" (3:1); who are "in distress" (4:1); whose "honor suffer[s] shame" (4:2); who are "sighing" (5:1); who are "languishing," "struck with terror," "weary," and "weeping" (6:2–7); who are pursued and threatened (7:1–2). Even so, Ps. 7 ends with the psalmist's promise to "sing praise to the name of the LORD" (v. 17), and Ps. 8 is a song of praise that fulfills that promise. In so doing, it offers a remarkably exalted view of the human being that must be heard alongside Pss. 3—7.

The most obvious feature of Ps. 8 is the refrain that frames the psalm (vs. 1, 9) and draws attention to Yahweh's sovereignty (see Ps. 93:4 where "majestic" occurs in the context of the affirmation that "the LORD is king"). Whereas the boundaries of Ps. 8 focus on God, the center of the psalm focuses directly on humanity: "What are human beings . . .?" (v. 4). The words "how" (vs. 1, 9) and "what" (v. 4) are the same in Hebrew, so the reader is encouraged to hear the boundaries and the center together. Indeed, according to Walter Brueggemann, the key interpretative question for Ps. 8 is how to hold the boundaries and the center together. In short, structural observations lead toward theological conclusions (*The Message of the Psalms*; Minneapolis: Augsburg Publishing House, 1984, pp. 37–38).

The structure of Ps. 8 affirms the central importance of humanity (v. 4). The human, seemingly a mere speck in a vast universe (v. 3), is "a little lower than God" and has been "crowned . . . with glory and honor" (v. 5). The language is used elsewhere of human kings and of Yahweh as king (see "crown" in 2 Sam. 12:30; Ps. 21:3; Jer. 13:18; "glory" in Pss. 21:5; 24:7–10; 29:1–3, 9; 145:5, 12, NRSV "glorious"; and "honor" in Pss. 21:5, NRSV "majesty," and 145:5, 12, NRSV "splendor"). In short, the sovereign God bestows sovereignty on the human creature. The human has "dominion" over "all things" (Ps. 8:6). The occurrences of "all" in vs. 1 and 9 as well as vs. 6–7 suggest that God's majestic sovereignty *includes* the dominion of humanity (see Robert Alter, *The Art of Biblical Poetry*; New York: Basic Books, 1985, p. 119). God has chosen to share God's power! To fail to recognize the remarkable vocation of humanity in the created order would be to risk shirking the God-given responsibility to be partners with God in the care of creation.

It is just as important to recognize, however, that human honor, glory, and dominion are God-given gifts, not inherent qualities or inalienable rights. Again, the structure of Ps. 8 is the clue to this theological conclusion. Both structurally and theologically, human centrality and dominion (vs. 4–8) are bounded by God's sovereign majesty (vs. 1, 9). Human dominion is *derivative*. If the centrality of the human is not understood as bounded by God's sovereignty, then the exercise of dominion becomes simply autonomy, self-rule. In the psalms, the assertion of the human self apart from the claim of God is the essence of wickedness, and it invites disaster, ecological and otherwise (see James Limburg, "Who Cares for the Earth? Psalm Eight and the Environment," *Word and World* Supplement Series 1 [1992]: 43–52).

The foregoing discussion of the boundaries and center of Ps. 8 may shed light on v. 2, which is notoriously difficult to translate and understand (compare the RSV and NRSV translations). As the NRSV renders it, v. 2 seems to suggest that God uses the speech of helpless infants as a first line of defense against God's "enemy"—perhaps the chaotic forces represented by the "formless void" and "darkness . . . of the deep" in Gen. 1:2. This may anticipate the affirmation of vs. 3–8 that God uses the weak and seemingly insignificant human creature as a partner in the task of caring for a creation that is persistently threatened by its enemy, chaos (see Gen. 1:1–2:4, to which Ps. 8:6–8 is clearly related; compare also Job 38:8–11; Pss. 74:12–17; 104:5–9).

In any case, the remarkable affirmation of the human creature in Ps. 8 should be heard, as we stated, alongside Pss. 3—7. The movement from Pss. 3—7 to Ps. 8 raises a crucial theological question: How do we understand a creature who both suffers miserably (Pss. 3—7) and yet is "little lower than God" and "crowned . . . with glory and honor" (8:5)? In a word, the juxtaposition of Pss. 3—7 and Ps. 8 suggests that the "glory and honor" of humanity are not obliterated by suffering. In other words, to be in the "image of God" inevitably involves suffering. It is to this conclusion that the book of Job also points, and, not surprisingly, Ps. 8 figures prominently in Job. For instance, Job in his suffering specifically denies the affirmation of humanity found in Ps. 8:4–5 (compare Job 7:17 with Ps. 8:4, and Job 19:9 with Ps. 8:5). Eventually, however, God challenges Job to accept the vocation articulated in Ps. 8 (see Job 40:10); and Job says finally, "I . . . change my mind about dust and ashes [=humanity]" (Job 42:6; for this translation as opposed to NRSV, see J. Gerald Janzen, *Job,* Interpretation series; Atlanta: John Knox Press, 1985, pp. 254–56). In short, Job understands that being human inevitably involves both suffering and glory, and furthermore that the human experience of suffering is ultimately a participation in God's suffering with and for creation!

Thus, the juxtaposition of Pss. 3—7 and Ps. 8, along with the book of Job, articulates the understanding of God and humankind found in the New Testament. In Heb. 2, which quotes Ps. 8:5 (Heb. 2:9), it is Jesus—"the reflection of God's glory" (Heb. 1:3) and the full embodiment of authentic humanity (see Heb. 2:14, 17; 4:15)—who demonstrates that God's glory is not incompatible with suffering and thus that the suffering of humanity does not prevent humans from sharing in the glory of God (Heb. 2:10–18; see "glory" in 1:3 and 2:10). Finally, therefore, when heard in its larger literary and canonical context, Ps. 8 calls humanity to live under God's rule and to exercise "dominion over . . . all things" as a suffering servant (see Mark 10:41–45; Phil. 2:5–11).

## Romans 5:1–5

In Rom. 5, Paul begins to explore the nature of the new life of those who have been "justified by faith." The letter earlier affirms with relentless power the sinfulness of all human beings (1:18–3:20) and then the radical intervention of God in the event of Jesus Christ (3:21–31). Now the topic shifts to the consequences of that event for human beings: "We have peace with God through our Lord Jesus Christ" (v. 1); "we boast in our hope" (v. 2); and "God's love has been poured into our hearts" (v. 5).

In contemporary English, the word "peace" is used in a variety of ways, some of which are quite subjective and individualistic, such as "being at peace" with oneself or feeling "peaceful." In its biblical context, however, "peace with God" primarily connotes an objective sense of peace, the peace that comes when conflict is at an end (see, for example, Ps. 72:7; 147:14). Given Paul's earlier portrayal of sin as the entrenched human denial of God or rebellion against God (Rom.

1:18–32), peace with God connotes recognition that such rebellion is at an end.

In addition to peace, justification produces the "hope of sharing the glory of God" (v. 2). Paul traces the birth of hope ("suffering produces endurance, and endurance produces character, and character produces hope," vs. 3–4); as he does so it becomes clear that he uses hope in a sense far different from the flabby and trivial hopes for pleasant weather or a hearty supper. "Hope" for Paul is not the equivalent of desire or wish. To the contrary, hope refers to confidence, trust, conviction. The "hope of sharing the glory of God" is Christian certainty that God's glory will be shared with all.

Hope "does not disappoint" because "God's love has been poured into our hearts" (v. 5). Although grammatically the phrase "God's love" may refer either to human love of God or to God's love of humankind, in this passage Paul almost certainly has the second meaning in mind, as is clear from his comment on God's love in 5:8. In fact, Paul does not often use the vocabulary of "love," apart from references to the beloved in the churches (see, for example, Rom. 1:7; 16:5; 1 Cor. 4:14; Phil. 2:12). When he does speak of God's love, it is, as here, in connection with the action of sending Jesus Christ on behalf of humankind (as in Gal. 2:20).

Those who are justified, then, have peace, hope, and love. For these gifts and in these gifts they may boast. That may seem an odd assertion from the man who elsewhere writes that "boasting is excluded" (Rom. 3:27; compare Rom. 2:17; 1 Cor. 1:29; 5:6). But here Paul does not contradict himself, for the problem is not boasting in and of itself, as if boasting were simply a matter of bad taste or flawed manners. The criterion for discerning whether boasting is or is not acceptable is the basis on which it is done. People who boast in their own accomplishments (or what they believe to be their own accomplishments) stand condemned, but those who boast in God or in the things made possible by God are praised.

It is important to notice that peace, hope, and love are already, even now, present within the community: "We *have* peace with God" (Rom. 5:1, emphasis added). Given Paul's experience with the Corinthians, who mistakenly assumed that the gifts of resurrection were already theirs, he was wary of asserting too much about the present (as in Rom. 6:5: "We *will* certainly be united with him in a resurrection like his," emphasis added). Does 5:1–5 assign too much to the present possession of believers?

We might answer that question in the affirmative, except for the powerful statements of agency that drive this passage and ground them firmly in God's action rather than in human accomplishment.

To begin with, the peace that believers have with God comes "through our Lord Jesus Christ, through whom we have obtained access to this grace in which we stand" (vs. 1–2). Later, it is God's glory that enables Christian hope (v. 2). Finally, God's love comes into the human heart "through the Holy Spirit that has been given to us." If believers have peace, hope, and love, it is because and only because of the action of God in Jesus Christ and the sustaining power of the Holy Spirit.

Read in connection with Trinity Sunday, these references to God, Christ, and the Spirit take on a particular significance. In common with other New Testament writers, Paul does not talk about the Trinity as such. The later christological controversies that prompted sustained reflection on the Trinity lay far ahead. Instead, Paul and other New Testament writers search for language with which to express the experience and convictions of early Christians. As a result, their comments do not always yield themselves to a systematic framework.

In this passage as elsewhere, the members of what would later be called the Trinity provide the basis for Christian existence. Christians live in peace with God because of Jesus Christ. Christians know the love of God because the Holy Spirit has poured out that love to them. Christians boast in God's glory, which they know through Christ and the Spirit. If Christians today find talk about the Trinity abstract and remote, for Paul it is as close as life itself.

(For additional commentary on this passage, see the Third Sunday in Lent and Proper 6 for Year A.)

## John 16:12–15

The Gospel lesson today includes the final Paraclete saying embedded in the farewell discourse of John's Gospel. Last Sunday, with the celebration of Pentecost, the focus was on the first two of the sayings (14:8–17, 25–27), and the Day of Pentecost in Year B of the lectionary cycle highlights the third, fourth, and fifth sayings (15:26–27; 16:4b–15). Since each of the passages uses common terms for the Spirit and all are set in a common context, there is a natural overlapping in the interpretations. Clearly the focus of the final saying is the role of the Spirit as ongoing teacher in the life of the church.

So much to say and so little time in which to say it is the universal problem when goodbyes are exchanged. A particular problem arises for Jesus in the farewell to his friends. He is the revelation of God,

and the events immediately on the horizon—crucifixion, resurrection, and departure—cannot possibly be grasped by the disciples
ahead of time. The incidents are not just ordinary occurrences, but
fundamental to who Jesus is and what he has come to do.

There are implications to be faced about what Jesus has already
said and done. The book of Acts recites the story of the growing
comprehension of the believing community about the reception of
Gentiles into the church, including even the "conversion" of Peter as
he encounters the centurion Cornelius (Acts 10—11). The church has
much to learn. "I still have many things to say to you" (John 16:12)
puts the Christian community in a learning mode, and the Spirit is
the divinely appointed teacher.

"He will guide you into all the truth; . . . he will declare to you the
things that are to come" (16:13). Those are rather extravagant claims,
but claims for a community that has extravagant needs. While the
inclusive scope of the text ("all the truth," "the things that are to
come") may be open to being misconstrued, it should certainly not
be underestimated. "The things that are to come" no doubt includes
both eschatological events and the immediate circumstances the
community faces as it seeks to live out its calling. If what the church
needs is not new information but fresh discernment, better focused
eyes with which to read the signs of the times and the relevance of its
message, then the Spirit is a timely gift.

In technical language, the Spirit is the critical hermeneutic for the
church. The Spirit is the indispensable reality for the community as it
seeks to interpret its tradition and its context. The Spirit enables the
church to be a community of both memory and hope. The Spirit
"brings forth fresh light from the Word" and enlivens it for its
readers. If the Spirit is not operative in its vision, to enable the
understanding of its sacred text and to expose the true situation of
the world, then the church is left to its own distorted sight.

How can the church be sure? How can it discern what is right and
what is wrong? How can it determine which of the many voices
speaking is the voice of the Spirit? Does it go with every new fad?
The Johannine community itself had problems with contesting
claims that finally resulted in schism. The warning is appropriate:
"Beloved, do not believe every spirit, but test the spirits to see
whether they are from God; for many false prophets have gone out
into the world" (1 John 4:1). Not every new burst of energy, not
every spurt of growth, not every surge in attendance is necessarily to
be identified with the Spirit's activity, and not every speaker mouthing biblical phrases represents the voice of God.

The text offers something of a test in depicting a decisive characteristic of the Spirit: "He will glorify me, because he will take what is mine and declare it to you" (16:14). No new revelation is offered as an addenda to Christ. As one commentator puts it, "Pneumatology is subordinated to christology" (Charles H. Talbert, *Reading John: A Literary and Theological Commentary on the Fourth Gospel and the Johannine Epistles;* New York: Crossroad, 1992, p. 219). The Spirit quickens the community's sensitivity to the revelation already given in Jesus rather than uncovering unheard-of data. What does not cohere with what Jesus taught and did cannot have come from the Spirit of truth.

The Spirit's role, then, is self-effacing, in that the attention falls somewhere else—on a deepened appreciation of the Christ-event. Maybe this explains the difficulty the church often has had in talking about the Spirit. To discern the Spirit rightly pushes one inevitably to reflect on the One about whom the Spirit bears witness.

For Trinity Sunday, this fifth Paraclete saying speaks primarily to the relationship between Son and Spirit. The final verse mentions also the Father (16:15), and in the broader perspective of John's Gospel refers to the mutuality shared in the godhead.

# PROPER 4

Ordinary Time 9

*Sunday between May 29
and June 4 inclusive
(if after Trinity Sunday)*

The question that lies just beneath the surface of the Gospel lection for this Sunday serves as a telling introduction to all the readings: Who has power?

Elijah has no power. He is but a "troubler of Israel," as Ahab calls him in 1 Kings 18:17. Yet Elijah knows that the prophets of Baal, who seem to have power by virtue of their numbers and their influence with the people, are the ones who truly stand powerless. Elijah's prayers summon the power of God, while the prayers of the apparently powerful prophets of Baal summon only judgment (see 1 Kings 18:40).

Paul has no power. The churches in Galatia have learned that the gospel he proclaimed to them was derivative and, indeed, defective, for he neglected to teach them to observe the law of Moses. He has no authority with which to enforce his understanding of the gospel. He can only insist, as he does in this lection, that there is one and only one gospel, no matter who preaches it. And he can and does, in the remainder of the letter, explain the character of that gospel in his own life, in their experience, and in the language of scripture.

The centurion of Luke 7 does have power. The citizens of Capernaum know that, and they urge Jesus to heal the servant of this powerful man. He has used his power well among the people, even to the extent of building them a synagogue. And the centurion himself knows his power, but he also knows its limitations. He is not worthy to have Jesus, the powerless one, enter his home. For this acknowledgment of where real power lies, Jesus praises the man's faith and demonstrates once again the power of God.

The question of who has power finds its most direct answer in Ps. 96: "For great is the LORD, and greatly to be praised" (v. 4). Not only must the peoples of the earth recognize this power, but so must their gods, and the heavens and earth themselves. The coming judgment will provide final confirmation of this power over all the earth.

361

# 1 Kings 18:20–21 (22–29) 30–39

For the remainder of Year C, the Common Lectionary draws on the prophetic corpus for readings from the Old Testament, beginning with a series of narratives about Elijah and Elisha (Proper 4 through Proper 9). The initial story, this day's text, is from the passage that describes Elijah's encounter with the prophets of Baal at Mount Carmel. The larger context of this passage is, of course, the account of Elijah's opposition to the policies of King Ahab (reigned 869–850 B.C.), who, as the strongest member of the Omri dynasty to rule over the Northern Kingdom, proved to be a tough adversary for all who yearned for simple justice and for all who wished to remain faithful to Yahweh, Israel's God.

In reading the texts about Elijah and Elisha, one is impressed over and again that these are, indeed, two issues that deeply concern the prophets of Yahweh—faithfulness and justice. In 1 Kings 18, the struggle is over loyalty to Yahweh, while in 1 Kings 21 Ahab's (and Jezebel's) injustice is the flash point of controversy (see Proper 6). Some scholars have drawn these two issues together and, relying on both biblical and nonbiblical sources (the latter including certain archaeological discoveries), have attempted to reconstruct the social-political environment in the Northern Kingdom of Ahab's day. According to this reconstruction, an aristocratic mercantile group, with close commercial ties to the powerful Phoenician coastal centers of Tyre and Sidon (Jezebel was a princess of Sidon, 1 Kings 16:31), enriched itself off the produce of the land, often at the expense of the northern Israelite peasantry. Not surprisingly, this ruling class tended to ape their Phoenician neighbors in cultural and religious matters, and promoted the worship of Baal, a Canaanite/Phoenician god, over the worship of the God of Israel, Yahweh. Thus (according to this reconstruction), in struggling for justice and faithfulness to Yahweh, Elijah and Elisha were working for the interests of the oppressed "common" men and women against powerful predators with strong non-Israelite ties.

Such a reconstruction has been criticized for being simplistic and for not considering all the evidence (for example, how is it that Baal, an agricultural/fertility god, was so popular in the urban centers of Tyre and Sidon and in the "ivory house"—1 Kings 22:39—of Samaria?). Yet, while many questions remain to be answered, this larger social, political, and economic portrait appears to be basically correct, and its implications are absolutely critical to an appreciation of these important Elijah-Elisha texts to which the lectionary directs us over the next few weeks.

Perhaps the first thing to strike the reader of 1 Kings 18:20–39 is the element of the miraculous. Indeed, this is one of the prominent features of this entire cycle of stories, and those writers who are responsible for them wished to impress the reader with the fact that power over what we would call the world of nature was an important sign of God's presence in the work of Elijah and Elisha. Some of these miracles strike a responsive chord in modern hearts, such as the feeding of the widow and the raising of her son (1 Kings 17:8–24; Proper 5), deeds that seem very much like certain of the miracles of Jesus. But a few of the miracles border on the magical, such as the floating axhead (2 Kings 6:6–7), or are downright reprehensible, such as the killing of the small boys (2 Kings 2:23–25). (There is, in fact, a great deal of bloodletting in some of these stories, not all of it of a miraculous nature; note 1 Kings 18:40.) All of this is to say that, while the miraculous element in these stories must be acknowledged, it would be a serious mistake to see it as containing the essence of the meaning of the text.

That essence lies elsewhere, and is to be found in the prophets' commitment to the God of Israel as the true Lord of life, in their dedication to justice, and in their compassion and intention to help people who did not have the means to help themselves.

In 1 Kings 18:20–39, the sheer courage and faithfulness of Elijah stand forth in bold relief. In contrast to the multitude of Baal prophets (18:19) Elijah is alone, a reality that weighs heavily on him. "I, even I only, am left a prophet of the LORD" (v. 22), he laments. It was an experience he apparently suffered on many occasions (compare 19:10, 14), and which, indeed, was all too common to the role of being Yahweh's prophet (note, for example, Jer. 15:17 and, most poignant of all, Mark 15:34). It makes little difference that there is a larger prophetic band (1 Kings: 18:4), for they are not with Elijah now. There is only Elijah and the mob of Baal prophets, with the militia of King Ahab lurking somewhere in the unspecified background.

In addition to Elijah's loneliness, a second important reality in this narrative is the presence of the God of Israel. In spite of Elijah's complaint concerning his loneliness (a complaint that despite his understanding is all too real), Elijah has confidence that Yahweh will not abandon him. Or to be more precise, Elijah is confident that Yahweh, the God of Israel, will not abandon those realities for which this God stands. Elijah may genuinely fear for his own life (again, note 19:10), but in his heart of hearts he knows that God will be true to God's own commitments: in this case, a saving presence in the life of the people. Elijah risks everything, and God responds to that risk.

To be sure, there is little personal reward for Elijah, for he must now flee for his life. But the God in whom he has trusted has acted in ways that affirm his trust.

## Psalm 96

Psalm 96 culminates in the conviction that forms, as suggested earlier (see Ps. 99, the Last Sunday After Epiphany), the theological heart of the Psalter: namely, "The LORD is king" (96:10)! Psalms 93 and 95—99 appear to be strategically placed in Book IV (Pss. 90—106) to address the apparent failure of the Davidic covenant and dynasty that is documented by the end of Book III (Ps. 89:38–51). David and his descendants may no longer reign, but all is not lost because Yahweh reigns (see Ps. 99 for the Last Sunday After Epiphany)!

Psalm 96 doubly illustrates the typical structure of a song of praise. Invitations to praise in vs. 1–3 and 7–10a are followed by reasons for praise in vs. 4–6 and 10b–13. The scholarly debate concerning the setting, use, and meaning of Ps. 96 can be approached by considering the three basic options for identifying the "new song" in the opening imperative (v. 1a):

1. The "new song" may be Ps. 96 itself, as it was perhaps sung in the Temple on the occasion of the celebration of the enthronement, or reenthronement, of Yahweh at the beginning of each new year (see 1 Chron. 16:23–33). In this case, the liturgical ceremony would serve to recall Yahweh's past deeds (Ps. 96:2–3) and profess the ongoing reality on which Israel based its existence—that is, that Yahweh, not any of the "gods of the peoples" (v. 5a), had created the world (v. 5b) and rules the world. "Honor and majesty" in v. 6 are kingly attributes (see Ps. 21:5), as are "strength" (vs. 6–7; see Pss. 93:1; 99:4, NRSV margin) and "glory" (Ps. 96:3, 7; see Pss. 24:7–10; 29:1–3, 9; 145:11). Thus, to sing a "new song" for the reasons stated in 96:4–6 would be to profess and embody the reality that God rules the world.

2. The "new song" may be understood not so much as part of a liturgical ceremony, but rather as the response to a historical event, such as the return of the exiles from Babylonian captivity. In this regard, it is significant that Deutero-Isaiah (Isa. 40—55) also invites the people to "sing to the LORD a new song" (Isa. 42:10) in response to the "new thing" (Isa. 43:19; see 42:9) that God is doing in returning captives to their land. The relationship between Ps. 96 and Isa. 40—55 is reinforced by several other parallels. Both texts are

concerned with the proclamation of "good news" (Isa. 40:9; 41:27; 52:7; NRSV "tell" in Ps. 96:2) involving the reign of God (Isa. 52:7; Ps. 96:10), the proper response to which is singing for joy (Isa. 52:8; Ps. 96:12). And in both texts, Yahweh's purpose is justice (Isa. 42:1, 3–4; Ps. 96:10, 13) for the earth and its peoples (Isa. 42:1; 45:22–23; 49:1–6; 52:10; 55:4–5; Ps. 96:7, 10, 13).

3. The "new song" may be sung not so much in celebration of what God has done, but rather in anticipation of what God will do. In Ps. 96:13, in particular, it seems that God's coming is still in the future as is God's establishment of justice and righteousness. In short, the psalm is eschatological in orientation.

In actuality, the above three options are not mutually exclusive. The liturgical celebration of God's reign in the present is related to experiences of God in the past, and both the past and present dimension lead to the anticipation of God's presence and activity in the future. It seems that a liturgical or historical reading of Ps. 96 will inevitably be also eschatological. The proclamation of God's reign, whether in liturgy or in response to historical circumstance, always occurs in a context in which it appears that God does *not* reign. Our proclamation of the reign of God is always made before all the evidence is in. The justice and righteousness that God wills have not been fully established, and our world often seems to be falling apart rather than "firmly established" (v. 10). To join in singing Ps. 96 is to affirm that we have made a crucial decision. We have decided that even amid the same discouraging realities we confront every day, new things are possible and "a new song" can be sung. We affirm that even when the force of evil seems overpowering, God rules the world and God will ultimately enact God's will for the world and its peoples.

It is significant that "all the earth" (vs. 1, 9) and the "families of the peoples" (v. 7) are invited to sing and praise and worship. Because Yahweh rules the world, it is not sufficient to gather a congregation less than "all the earth." This includes humans, to be sure (v. 7), but it also includes "the heavens," "the earth," "the sea," "the field," and "all the trees of the forest" (vs. 11–12). The ecumenical implications are profound; we are partners with all the "families of the peoples." The ecological implications are staggering: we humans are partners with oceans and trees and soil and air in glorifying God. The future of humankind and the future of the earth are inseparable. We—people, plants, and even inanimate entities— are all in this together (see Hos. 4:1–3; Pss. 148; 150:6).

It is noteworthy that the invitation in Ps. 96:7–9 is essentially identical to that in Ps. 29:1–2, with the exception that the invitation in

96:7 is extended to the "families of the peoples" rather than to "heavenly beings," as in 29:1. This difference suggests that Yahweh's sovereignty is to be effective on earth as well as in heaven. To hear Ps. 96, especially in conjunction with Ps. 29 (see the First Sunday After Epiphany), is to pray in effect: "Thy kingdom come, thy will be done on earth as it is in heaven." The message of Ps. 96 is essentially the same as the message of Jesus (see Mark 1:14–15); it proclaims the reign of God and invites people to enter it.

(For additional commentary on Ps. 96, see Christmas, Proper 1.)


## Galatians 1:1–12

The first of six epistolary lessons drawn from Galatians, Gal. 1:1–12 immediately reveals that something has gone seriously awry between Paul and his correspondents. The details of scholarly reconstructions vary enormously, for here as elsewhere we overhear one side of a conversation and must tease from it a more detailed picture. Clearly some Christians have entered the Galatian congregations with a very different version of the gospel, one that insists on observance of the Mosaic law (or at least the practice of circumcision) as a means of becoming part of Abraham's family. Perhaps these same teachers or evangelists have attempted to bolster their argument by attacking Paul himself.

He responds with vehemence. At first glance, it appears that he couches his response in only the most personal and defensive terms. He identifies himself in the salutation as an apostle "sent neither by human commission nor from human authorities" (v. 1). The lection closes with a similar reminder that he did not preach a gospel with a "human origin" or receive it from a "human source" (vs. 11–12). While he insists that he is not trying to "please people" (v. 10), he does seem intent on pleasing—or at least persuading—the Galatians. (Surely some parts of this letter did not please the Galatians!)

If these assertions about Paul's apostleship and its origins seem exceptionally fervent, the center of the passage is also surprising. Where we conventionally find the thanksgiving of the letter, with its praise of the correspondents (as, for example, in 1 Thess. 1:2–10 or Rom. 1:8–15), in Gal. 1 we find instead an angry outburst. Verses 6–9 contemplate the possibility that what the Galatians have done is to adopt "a different gospel," one contrary to Paul's preaching. His insistence that there can be no such thing, that only his preaching is the gospel, sounds frighteningly narrow and self-righteous to the ears of Christians who know all too well the dangers of such rigidity.

Before we dismiss this passage as mere self-serving apologetic, however, another look is warranted. Alongside Paul's insistence on his divine commission (vs. 1–2), he provides in vs. 1–4 a virtual summary of the gospel. First, the gospel comes into being by the power and the will of God, in that it is God who raised Jesus from the dead (v. 1), God through whose will Jesus acted (v. 4).

Second, Jesus Christ "gave himself for our sins." The use of the plural "sins" rather than Paul's more customary singular (see, for example, Rom. 7:7–25) may well indicate that he is quoting early Christian tradition here (as in 1 Cor. 15:3), a tradition that epitomizes the Christ-event in his death on behalf of human sins.

Third, Jesus acted in order "to set us free from the present evil age." Here we glimpse the apocalyptic framework within which Paul operated. Sin is not merely a bad deed that can be avoided and for which a punishment might be calculated (as with a small child who sits in the corner for breaking a house rule). Instead, the presence of sin offers evidence that human beings live in some kind of slavery (see Gal. 4:8–11), slavery to an "evil age," the power of which has been broken by Jesus Christ.

The plan of God, the self-giving death of Jesus Christ, the freedom from the sinful present age—with these three elements Paul encapsulates the gospel of Jesus Christ. He then moves in 1:6–9 to the assertion that there is no gospel other than this one. More stridently still, he pronounces a curse on anyone who might offer another gospel (vs. 8–9).

This insistence that the gospel must be understood in the way Paul understands it sounds a harsh note for those of us accustomed to respecting the views of others, to tolerant discussions with other positions, to exploring the advantages of alternative arguments. Before writing off Paul's comments as sheer intolerance, however, we need to recall the instances in which he does model compromise and toleration. He urges Christians in Rome to make room for other viewpoints and practices and to welcome those of differing judgments (Rom. 14:1–15:3). In 1 Corinthians he similarly implores Christians not to offend other believers (10:23–11:1) and boasts of his own ability to adapt ("I have become all things to all people," 1 Cor. 9:22).

Perhaps the reason such adaptability does not appear in Galatians is that what is at stake, as Paul sees it, is nothing less than the gospel itself. Here the quarrel concerns something far more vital than what food is consumed; it concerns what belongs at the center of the gospel itself. As the letter later makes clear, the new teaching among the Galatians is that both the law and Christ are needed for an adequate understanding of the gospel. However much Paul perceives the law as a gift of God, Paul can hear in that insistence on the law only a compromise of the gospel's centrality in Jesus Christ. There can be no such compromise.

The letter opens, then, with two foci. It addresses both the legitimacy of Paul as an apostle *and* the content of the gospel. If Paul here insists on his own apostolic role, that is because the proclamation of the gospel depends on the apostle just as the apostle's preaching role derives from the gospel. The two cannot be separated, however uncomfortable and dangerous the connection.

## Luke 7:1–10

The issue of authority is a thorny problem for most people. Some hanker after a structured existence, where order prevails and where the lines of authority are clearly drawn. They respect those who occupy places of power and who in reasonable ways maintain peace and stability. They may even willingly forfeit personal rights to established authorities for the sake of harmony. Others, however, are suspicious of any exercise of authority. Experience has taught them that authority figures, however well-meaning, will inevitably dominate and manipulate those over whom they have power.

The complexity of the experiences and opinions of listeners needs to be taken into account when one talks about the story of Jesus' healing of the centurion's slave (Luke 7:1–10), because the focus is clearly Jesus' authority. The way the centurion acknowledges Jesus' authority and in turn is commended for his faith comprises the heart of this vignette.

Notice how little attention is given to the act of healing itself. We are told that the valued slave is near death, but we learn nothing about this person, about the nature of the illness, or why the slave is so respected by the centurion. The concluding verse relates simply that the slave regains health (7:10). In a sense, the one healed becomes no more than a detail in the telling of the story.

The focus falls, rather, on the centurion, about whom we learn a great deal. He is obviously held in high regard by the Jewish leaders, since not only do the elders willingly become his emissaries to Jesus, they also offer extravagant commendation of him and what he has done for the Jews. "He is worthy of having you do this for him, for he loves our people, and it is he who built our synagogue for us" (7:4–5). We get a picture of a highly respected foreign dignitary, whose authenticity is unquestioned. Jesus without comment responds to the elders' request by immediately going with them to the centurion's house.

Then comes the surprising feature of the story. The centurion sends a second delegation to Jesus, with the message that he is really not worthy to entertain Jesus. He does not even presume to make a personal approach himself. All he asks for is the divine word that will restore his servant. Jesus is deeply moved at his expression of faith.

As several commentators note, undoubtedly what lies behind the story is the system of patronage in the Greco-Roman world. The centurion is a powerful person, with access to immense resources that he can deploy for the benefit of the Jewish people of Capernaum. He is their patron, and they in turn become his clients, dependent on his support and offering their loyalty. As recipients of his generosity, they gladly honor his request to appeal to Jesus on behalf of his sick servant. The scenario reflects an ancient pattern of social reciprocity in which lower-class people gain benefits (here, a synagogue) from a more powerful patron in exchange for their allegiance (petitioning Jesus for help). Emperors function this way with public leaders, and the latter in like manner relate to their subordinates. (See Bruce Malina and Richard L. Rohrbaugh, *Social-Science Commentary on the Synoptic Gospels*; Minneapolis: Fortress Press, 1992, pp. 326–29.)

The virtue of the centurion is that he does not treat Jesus like a client. The message of the second group of emissaries makes this clear (7:6–8). Though a person in authority, able to order soldiers and servants, the centurion acknowledges that Jesus is his superior. He steps out of his position as benefactor and declares himself a client of the divine patronage that Jesus brokers. It is this remarkable reversal of roles that evokes the amazement and commendation from Jesus.

Critical, however, is the recognition that the authority Jesus exercises markedly differs from the patron and military roles of the centurion. Jesus is not depicted as a powerful figure who cultivates clients and has servants at his beck and call. His authority, already documented in the narrative (for example, 4:31–37), is the power to push back the forces of darkness, to bring healing, to teach convincingly, to fulfill the mission of the divine prophet (7:16).

The centurion's authority sits well with the Jewish leaders. They benefit from it. No doubt there are others in Capernaum who are suspicious and would welcome a complete overthrow of the patronage system, even when personified in such a benevolent figure as the centurion. Jesus' authority, however, is not regulative and controlling, but expansive and empowering. It authorizes health for sick people, liberation for enslaved people, forgiveness for sinful people, and good news for the poor and depressed. There is no question that it poses a threat to those who prefer the status quo, as the crucifixion confirms.

It is to the credit of the centurion that he not only recognizes Jesus' authority but puts his trust in it. Jesus is not a rival; he is the ultimate source of healing power.

# PROPER 5

## Ordinary Time 10

*Sunday between
June 5 and 11 inclusive
(if after Trinity Sunday)*

Three of the readings for this Sunday concern the ways in which God intercedes powerfully for God's people. The reading from 1 Kings 17 continues the story of God's protection of Elijah from the wrath of Ahab, but God's protection here extends beyond his prophetic messenger to a non-Israelite widow. As one who lives not only outside Israel but outside the male-dominated economic structures, she personifies powerlessness. When she accedes to Elijah's request, whether out of faith or from desperation, she places herself and her child under God's own protection and learns that that protection may be trusted.

Psalm 116 reminds us that God's action in the instance of Elijah and the widow is typical, rather than unusual. God alone may be trusted, for God is the one who cares for the outsider and the powerless, those rejected by human society and neglected by the "normal" standards of the world. The princes of the world (Ps. 146:3) cannot be trusted, both because of their own mortality and because they care only for their own strength.

In the Gospel lesson, Jesus encounters a woman whose position closely parallels that of the widow of Zarephath. This woman also lives outside the protective sphere of a husband's household and has lost the protection of her son as well. For her also God intercedes, this time in the person of Jesus, whose own power restores the life of her son.

The Epistle lesson touches on none of these themes. Here, God does not intercede to rescue or restore life. In fact, God's intervention in the life of Paul overturns a life that would have moved along a predictable and even comfortable course. The gospel disrupts Paul's good life within the traditions of his ancestors and thrusts on him instead a call that will be anything but comfortable. Placed alongside the other readings, Gal. 1:11–24 reminds us that God's intercessions

371

do not always supply the pleasant fulfillments of our needs; sometimes they lead us where we would be happier not to go.

## 1 Kings 17:8–16 (17–24)

The series of Old Testament lections drawn from the cycle of Elijah-Elisha stories in 1 and 2 Kings continues with this account of a widow's hospitality to Elijah and of his subsequent demonstration of God's power and concern. For anyone who has been reading 1 Kings chapter by chapter, the present pericope comes as a breath of fresh air. Chapter 16 is a dreary account, perhaps based on Israelite royal archives, of the succession of rulers of the Northern Kingdom from the time of King Baasha (c. 900–877 B.C.). Politically undistinguished except in terms of their ability to employ terror as an instrument of statecraft, these monarchs earned the scorn of the Deuteronomistic historians not only for their inhumanity, but also for embracing the heresies of Jeroboam I, founder of the Israelite state (note, for example, 16:2). The series of sad, brief mini-biographies appears to end with a reference to the accession of Ahab (c. 869), the most evil of all Northern rulers to date (16:29–34, note especially v. 33).

The opening lines of chapter 17 introduce the reader to Elijah from Tishbe (in Gilead), who enters the story as the bearer of Yahweh's word and, therefore, as Yahweh's champion who stands against Ahab and against the moral and spiritual corruption of Israelite life. It is clear from the manner in which the text has been structured that the writers wished to convey their understanding that, in raising Elijah to the office of prophet, it is Yahweh's intention to break the cycle of violence, oppression, and apostasy that has characterized the life of the North since the establishment of the kingdom under Jeroboam. Some commentators have suggested that, since Elijah is introduced into the narrative in a somewhat abrupt manner, an earlier, more detailed account of the call of Elijah—originally a part of an independent cycle of Elijah stories—has been dropped by the Deuteronomistic historians. Perhaps so, but the very direct manner in which Elijah is brought to our notice (17:1) contributes to the reader's realization of the distinctive mission of this distinctive personality.

Chapter 17, vs. 1–7, provides the context for this day's lectionary text. In response to the enormous evil of Ahab, Yahweh is sending a drought. No sooner has the prophet announced this terrible intervention of Israel's God (question: How did Elijah gain access to Ahab's court?) than Yahweh directs him to flee for his life beyond the Jordan and, it would seem, beyond the reach of Ahab's vengeance. The text implies here what it elsewhere makes explicit (18:17), that Ahab takes Elijah's proclamations quite personally and intends to silence the voice of Yahweh by silencing Elijah. In the desert Elijah is fed by ravens and he drinks from the Wadi Cherith. But eventually even that stream dries up and, driven by thirst, Elijah seeks another sanctuary.

The first and principal (that is, unbracketed) part of the lection concerns the widow's kindness to Elijah (17:8–16). Notice should be given to the fact that the widow is not an Israelite, but a Sidonian. (Elijah still does not dare to venture into the territory of Ahab.) The assumption that she, as a Canaanite/Phoenician woman, does not worship Israel's God is confirmed by her reference to "[Yahweh] your God" in v. 12 (emphasis added). In this regard, vs. 8–24 call attention to Mark 7:24–30 (parallel Matt. 15:21–28), the incident regarding the so-called "Syrophoenician" woman (or "Canaanite woman," as Matt. 15:22 has it). There are important lessons to be drawn here concerning the universal love of God, a love that reaches beyond the narrow confines of Israel or Judah. There is also an implied statement here concerning the kindness of a stranger, as in Luke 10:29–37. The text does not draw these implications out, but it does not place undue strain on the text for the preacher to call attention to them.

Also unemphasized by the text, yet clearly present, is the contrast between the widow and Queen Jezebel, who has already been introduced in 16:31. Both women are Sidonians, presumably both are worshipers of Baal. The vast difference between them thus lies not in their nationality/ethnicity, or even in the nature of their religious beliefs, but in their levels of compassion—or lack of it, in the case of Jezebel.

The widow supplied Elijah with water willingly enough, although, as the drought had also affected the region of Zarephath, the water that she possessed was probably just enough for her own needs and that of her son (note 17:14). When the prophet asks for food, her pitiful response proves to be the occasion of Elijah's first recorded miracle. The text makes evident that the miracle of the meal and oil is not some kind of magic, or a strange wonder based on Elijah's power over the world of the supernatural. The miraculous food is the gift of God. As Yahweh had fed Elijah in the wilderness, so Yahweh now feeds both Elijah and the poor widow who has showed such kindness to Yahweh's prophet.

Although the second section of this day's Old Testament lection (vs. 17–24) is listed in parentheses, the preacher may wish to use the

longer reading, for the reason that vs. 17–24, more than vs. 8–16, find
several parallels in this day's Gospel lection, Luke 7:11–17. In both
instances, a widow's son is brought from death to life by the power
of God, a power that is made active by God's special servant. While
many of the lessons of the Lukan text (see comments on the Gospel
lection) are applicable here, vs. 17–24 are distinctive in that they
describe a life-restoring miracle of God, which occurs against the
background of a God-sent drought. Under the governance of God,
faithlessness invites desiccation and death, while compassion, even
when exercised by a nonbelieving Gentile, opens up the possibilities
of life. Deuteronomistic theology, with both its strengths and its
weaknesses, in the very place one would expect to find it!

## Psalm 146

Psalm 146 is the first in a series of hymns (Pss. 146—150), all
beginning and ending with "Praise the LORD!" (hallĕlû-yāh), that
bring the book of Psalms to a conclusion with a crescendo of praise.
Quite appropriately for a psalm that initiates this concluding collection, Ps. 146 is reminiscent of both the beginning of the Psalter (Pss.
1—2) and the theological "heart" of the Psalter (Pss. 93; 95—99). In
particular, Ps. 146 is explicitly instructional (vs. 3–5), recalling Ps. 1,
which orients the reader to hear the entire collection as torah,
"instruction" (1:2, NRSV "law"). The content of the instruction in Ps.
146 is essentially the same as that of Ps. 2—namely, trust God, not
human rulers. Because human rulers and their plans "perish" (146:4;
compare 1:6; 2:12), "happy" are those who entrust their lives to God
(146:5; compare 1:1; 2:12). The message of Ps. 2 anticipates the
theological heart of the Psalter: "The LORD reigns" or "The LORD is
king" (see the Last Sunday After Epiphany, on Ps. 99). It is not
surprising that this message is echoed clearly at the conclusion of the
Psalter, including Ps. 146:10 (see also 145:1, 12–13; 149:2).

As is typical for a song of praise, Ps. 146:1 begins with an
invitation in the imperative, although it is unusual that the invitation
is addressed to "my soul." This happens elsewhere only in Pss.
103:1, 22 and 104:1, 35. Psalm 146:2 is also reminiscent of Ps. 104:33.
Praise—the offering of the whole self to God in worship and
work—is the lifelong vocation of the human creature (see the Second
Sunday of Easter, on Ps. 150).

While all the songs of praise are instructional, Ps. 146 is very
explicitly so (see also Ps. 100:3, which immediately follows the group
of psalms that proclaim the Lord's reign). The antithesis of praising

God "all . . . life long" (146:2) is to trust oneself or trust human
agencies and institutions in place of God. It is precisely this that the
psalmist warns against (v. 3; see also Ps. 118:8–9; Jer. 17:5–7). The
Hebrew play on words emphasizes the transience of human life and
human help: "mortals" ('ādām, v. 3) soon return to the "earth"
('ădāmāh, v. 4). As suggested above, the word "perish" recalls
Pss. 1:6 and 2:12, where the "way of the wicked" (1:6) and the way of
those who refuse to "serve the LORD" (2:11) will "perish." In the
psalms and the Bible as a whole, wickedness is essentially the
decision to trust oneself rather than to trust God. To trust in
"princes" and "mortals" is a perennial and pervasive temptation,
especially in a thoroughly secularized society like ours. Now, as
then, to succumb to this temptation invites destructive consequences
(see 146:9). As Claus Westermann suggests, "The praise of God
occupied for Israel actually the place where 'faith [i.e., trust] in God'
stands for us. . . . The directing of this praise to a [hu]man, an idea, or
an institution must disturb and finally destroy life itself" (*Praise and
Lament in the Psalms*, trans. Keith R. Crim and R. N. Soulen; Atlanta:
John Knox Press, 1981, pp. 159, 160–61).

In contrast to human rulers, who can provide "no help" (v. 3),
God offers a source of "help" and "hope" (v. 5; two different
Hebrew words underlie the English "help" in vs. 3 and 5). The word
"happy" again recalls Pss. 1—2 (see 1:2, 2.12), and the focus on the
concept of help recalls Ps. 3, where against the claims of his or her
foes (3:1–2), the psalmist concludes, "Help [NRSV "Deliverance"]
belongs to the LORD" (3:8). In short, as the sweep of the Psalter
makes clear, happiness is not the absence of pain and trouble, but
rather the presence of a God who cares about human hurt and acts
on behalf of the needy.

A series of participial phrases in Ps. 146:6–9a affirms Yahweh's
creative and redemptive power on behalf of the needy. Verse 6 cites
Israel's two basic traditions—God is creator (v. 6a; see Gen. 1—2)
and God is redeemer (v. 6b; see "faithfulness" in Ex. 34:6, the
self-revelation of God that forms the real culmination of the exodus
story). In the rest of the series, God's creative and redemptive
activity has as its object persons in need—"the oppressed" (see Pss.
76:9; 99:4; 103:6), "the hungry" (see Ps. 107:9; Isa. 58:7), the imprisoned (see Isa. 61:1), "the blind" (see Isa. 42:7), the "bowed down"
(see Ps. 145:14), "the strangers" (see Ex. 23:9, NRSV "resident alien";
Ps. 94:6; Jer. 7:6, NRSV "alien")—with the possible exception of v. 8c
(although "the righteous" in the psalms are generally needy and
afflicted; see Ps. 34:19). Psalm 146 returns to the use of finite verbs in
v. 9bc, but again the affirmation is that God helps the needy (see Jer.

7:6; 22:3; etc.) and opposes "the way of the wicked" (see Pss. 1:6; 145:20; 147:6).

In light of Ps. 146:10, which explicitly affirms the eternal reign of Yahweh (see Ex. 15:18; Pss. 29:10; 145:13; for example), 146:6–9 may be understood as a policy statement for the kingdom of God. What God wills and works to enact includes justice, provision for basic human needs, freedom, and empowerment. Psalm 146 anticipates Jesus' proclamation of the reign of God (Mark 1:14–15), as well as Jesus' enactment of God's will in a ministry of justice, feeding, liberation, healing, and compassion (see, for example, Luke 4:16–21; Matt. 11:2–6). Psalm 146 offers encouragement to God's people to continue to pray as Jesus taught:

> Your kingdom come.
> Your will be done,
>     on earth as it is in heaven.
>                 (Matt. 6:10)

## Galatians 1:11–24

The character of this passage may incline preachers to select another lection, assuming that this reading is more autobiographical than theological. A review of some of the standard commentaries on Galatians would confirm that preliminary judgment, as they often divide Galatians into three parts: autobiographical (chs. 1—2), theological (chs. 3—4), and ethical (chs. 5—6). Among the problems with that schema is that it overlooks the way in which theological concerns pervade the whole of the letter. Specifically, when Paul speaks of himself and his own experiences, he usually has some larger theological point in view. In this instance, he refers to his own experience as an instance of the working of the gospel.

The opening lines of the passage (which overlap with the conclusion of Proper 4) assert emphatically that Paul's gospel came to him through "a revelation of Jesus Christ," and not through a human being (vs. 11–12). Paul's sharp denial that he received a gospel "of human origin" or "from a human source" has prompted the assumption that he is here on the defensive, and that he may well be. Nevertheless, the statements made here are not simply defensive; instead, they point to Jesus Christ as source of the gospel itself.

In vs. 13–14, Paul abruptly takes up the character of the life he led prior to the invasion of the gospel. Few modern readers will understand the particular connotation attached to Paul's claim that his was a life in "Judaism" (vs. 13–14), but the word itself is quite rare in this period. Indeed, it occurs nowhere else in the New Testament and only a few times in the Septuagint, where it is associated with those whose zeal for the ways of Israel prompted them to revolt against the Maccabees (see, for example, 2 Macc. 2:21; 8:1; 14:38; 4 Macc. 4:26). In other words, this word in itself carries expectations about loyalty and fervor.

Paul specifies that his own zeal consisted of "persecuting the church of God" and "trying to destroy it" (Gal. 1:13). Immediately, the dramatic stories of the Acts of the Apostles spring to mind (Acts 8:1–3; 9:1–2; 22:4–5; 26:9–11), but Paul himself never says of what this persecution consists. Given his penchant for hyperbole (as in 1 Cor. 4:21, where he threatens to visit Corinth with a stick!), as well as the historical difficulties of understanding how such a physical persecution might have been legal, his persecution may well have consisted of social and economic pressure rather than more concrete physical measures.

Whatever the nature of Paul's persecution, he offers it as an instance of his allegiance to things Jewish. By this and other means he "advanced in Judaism beyond many" of his peers, for he was zealous "for the traditions" (Gal. 1:14). In an age that prized ancient customs and values, Paul signals that he played by the expected rules. The whole of vs. 13–14 underscores this point: Paul lived a good life by the best standards of his people.

Verse 15 abruptly marks the end of that good life: "But when God . . ." The contrast between vs. 13–14 and the section that follows is striking. "But" at the beginning of v. 15 marks this shift (although the Greek word, *de*, is not always disjunctive). More telling, however, is the shift in agency. Verses 13–14 have Paul as their subject: "I was violently persecuting . . . I advanced . . . I was far more zealous . . ." Verses 15–16, by sharp contrast, begin with the action of God: God "who had set me apart before I was born and called me through his grace, was pleased to reveal his Son to me. . . ." When Paul's own action reappears in v. 16, it clearly returns as a response to God's initiative.

Paul's description of God's initiative borrows from the language of the prophetic call. God speaks to Jeremiah with the words: "Before I formed you in the womb I knew you, and before you were born I consecrated you" (Jer. 1:5); Isaiah claims that "the LORD called me before I was born, while I was in my mother's womb he named me" (Isa. 49:1). Paul's application of these words to himself serves to reinforce the claim that his apostolic vocation is God's idea (not

Paul's), and that it is part of God's larger plan. When God reveals Jesus Christ to Paul (Gal. 1:16), God does so, not to glorify Paul or allow Paul to wallow in that exalted experience, but to lay before Paul a commission.

The remainder of the passage details Paul's initial actions. Reinforcing his insistence that he was not taught about the gospel (v. 12), he reports that his journey did not lead him to Jerusalem (where he might have been instructed by others). When he did eventually visit Jerusalem, it was three years later and then only to speak with Cephas and James.

The amazed response of the Judean churches in vs. 23–24 sums up the dynamic of passage: " 'The one who formerly was persecuting us is now proclaiming the faith he once tried to destroy.' And they glorified God because of me." In the gospel of Jesus Christ, God has brought about an astonishing change in Paul's life. Not a change from bad to good—for Paul already lived an exemplary life—this change embodies the overwhelming power of the gospel by which all other allegiances, good, bad, or indifferent, are simply eclipsed. The same dynamic will persist when Paul maintains that all believers find their previous allegiances and categories overturned by the gospel (see 3:28).

## Luke 7:11–17

This remarkable story of the raising of the son of the widow in Nain presents Lukan scholars with a lot to write about. The fact that the account is found only in Luke, its close association with Elijah's raising of the son of the widow in Zarephath (1 Kings 17), and the responses of the people (Luke 7:16), all are grist for the scholar's mill in showing how Luke depicts Jesus as "a prophet mighty in deed and word before God and all the people" (24:19), but also as a prophet to be rejected.

We offer three observations about the story. First, the account is astonishingly detailed. Many reports of healing miracles are terse, with only extended comments about the nature of the illness or the response of the crowd. This story, however, is full of information, crafted in an artistic fashion, making a profound impact on the reader.

Three lengthy verses precede the miracle itself (7:11–13), relating the setting at the gate of Nain, the crowd with Jesus and the crowd of mourners with the widow, and the fact that the dead man's mother was a widow and that he was her only son. Jesus' feelings and actions are spelled out in detail (his compassion, his coming forward to touch the coffin, his addressing the man, his giving the restored man to his mother). Finally, the response of the crowds and the resulting widespread report of the incident are given full play (7:16–17).

From the outset, it becomes clear that the narrator's interest is not primarily in the deceased, but in the deceased's mother. She is immediately placed center stage as Jesus approaches her with the words, "Do not weep" (7:13). The reader is alerted to the fact that this is a story about the restoration of a vulnerable woman.

Second, what also becomes immediately obvious is Jesus' compassion for the woman. The pathos of the scene is gripping. A widow left in a man's world without her only son is a vivid picture of destitution. Her future without his support and protection is bound to be grim. The narrator stirs not only interest in but deep feelings of sympathy for the widow as the reader is left to ponder her dire circumstances. Her grief for her son is compounded by the dim prospect of what lies ahead.

Jesus sees the woman, has compassion for her, acts in raising her son, and then gives her son back to her. The latter statement underscores her restoration, her return to a place of protection and security, the renewal of her future as a time of opportunity and not misfortune. As one who identifies with and has compassion for a marginalized person, Jesus also acts to remedy her situation. There is more than an understanding look and a sympathetic word. There is a resurrection that reclaims the future. In a sense, then, the raising of the widow's son foreshadows the raising of God's Son, where the power of death is defeated once and for all.

Third, the story (the event as well as how it is told) recalls the story in 1 Kings 17 of Elijah's raising of the widow's son in Zarephath. There are both details and phrases parallel in the two stories (see the commentaries for particulars), which provoke an even more careful search for clues to the meaning of Luke 7:11–17. (The story of the Elijah healing is explicitly cited in Luke 4:25–26.)

For Luke, Jesus is a prophet fulfilling and exceeding the role of Elijah. At times he is compared to Moses and at times to Elijah (and Elisha), but these are miracle-working prophets. Jesus is a prophet of action, who not only has eyes to see the present and discern the future but in whose presence are healing powers, effective for the least and most exposed of society. Just as the widow of Zarephath on receiving back her son said to Elijah, "I know that you are a man of God" (1 Kings 17:24), so Jesus is acknowledged as "a great prophet . . . risen among us" (Luke 7:16).

The NRSV translation of one of the comments of the people, "God has looked favorably on his people!" is rendered in the RSV as "God has visited his people!" The notion of "visitation" is used at critical points in the Luke-Acts narrative to indicate God's action with compassion and power to redeem the divine people (Luke 1:68, 78; 19:44; Acts 15:14). So here in Jesus' action with the widow and her son, the people recognize not only a prophet with power, but also the presence of God working redemptively.

# PROPER 6

Ordinary Time 11

*Sunday between
June 12 and 18 inclusive
(if after Trinity Sunday)*

The readings from 1 Kings and from Ps. 5 nicely complement each other. In the familiar story of Naboth's vineyard, Ahab and Jezebel act with unbelievable treachery against an innocent man. Ahab's desire for a particular plot of land blinds him to the rightful concern of Naboth for the protection of his family's property, and Jezebel's desire to see Ahab's wishes fulfilled similarly makes her impervious to the concerns of others. It is only when Elijah confronts Ahab that Ahab recognizes what he has done for what it actually is—a sin against God.

Read together with the story of Ahab and Jezebel's action against Naboth, Ps. 5 powerfully recalls that only God may truly be called king (v. 2), and that the true king will not finally tolerate the wickedness of humankind (vs. 4 6). On the other hand, God enables those who are faithful to enter into God's own presence (vs. 7–8). Both these passages serve to remind us that the relationship between an individual and others reveals something powerful about the individual's relationship with God.

The Gospel and epistolary readings for this week might be said to argue for the corollary, namely, that an individual's relationship with God reveals something powerful about that individual's relationships with human beings. The mystical overtones of Paul's statement that "it is no longer I who live, but it is Christ who lives in me" (Gal. 2:20) might be heard as a call for retreat from the realities of the world. Paul, however, introduces the statement in order to deal with the boundaries some have attempted to reinforce between Jews and Gentiles. To say that "Christ lives in me," then, has powerful implications for behavior within the human community.

Similarly, the Lukan version of the woman who anoints Jesus with oil presents us with a Pharisee who does not understand that relationship to God involves social relationships as well. Perceiving in the sinful woman who comes to Jesus a threat to his own orderly sense of who is acceptable and who is not, the Pharisee protests her presence. Jesus responds with a story linking divine forgiveness with human love of God, but in the very act of telling the story to the Pharisee, Jesus also insists that the love of God requires loving generosity among human beings.

## 1 Kings 21:1–10 (11–14) 15–21a

The narrative of the criminal confiscation of Naboth's vineyard by Jezebel and Ahab is one of the more important texts in the cycle of stories concerning Elijah and Elisha. These tales, although originally woven together by Northern Israelite writers, have been incorporated into the great Deuteronomistic History fashioned by sages of the court of Judean king Josiah (640–609 B.C.). Their presence, together with stories of other prophetic personalities, helps to explain why, in the rabbinic tradition, the books of Joshua through Kings (minus Ruth) have been considered to be part of the prophetic corpus. (In the Jewish manner of structuring the scriptures, Joshua, Judges, Samuel, and Kings—the four "former" prophetic books— are balanced by Isaiah, Jeremiah, Ezekiel, and the Book of the Twelve, or the Christian "Minor Prophets"—the four "latter" prophets.) Thus, to understand this literature as theological reflection on Israel's history and not just as a record of that history is an important key to understanding its function and purpose.

The prophetic nature of the Deuteronomistic History is nowhere more apparent than in the present lection. Notice has previously been made of the socioeconomic and theological atmosphere in which Elijah, Elisha, and their prophetic contemporaries worked (see comments on 1 Kings 18:20–39, Proper 4). According to the view of many scholars, the figures of Ahab and Jezebel represent more than just wicked persons, even wicked persons in high office; they are emblematic of an oppressive social order in which the structures of power, fortified by cultural and financial interests from abroad, deprive ordinary citizens of their wealth and their happiness. Faithfulness to the God of Israel and simple justice in dealing with one another appear to be the two issues that drive the prophets of Yahweh in their confrontation with the Baal-worshiping royal house. If such a text as that in 1 Kings 18 emphasizes the importance of fidelity to the religious traditions of Israel, the present text stresses the crucial role of social and personal justice in Yahweh's land.

The intensely personal nature of the Elijah-Elisha stories is evident in the first part of the present lection (1 Kings 21:1–4). Just as we are frequently admitted to the inner heart of the prophet (especially Elijah; note 1 Kings 19:4, for example), in this case we are admitted to the gloomy mood of the king. "Resentful and sullen" (v. 4), Ahab pouted on his bed, refusing even to eat, when informed of Naboth's decision not to sell his land. Ahab's self-imposed fast is a harbinger of the even larger fast that Jezebel will soon proclaim for Naboth's fellow citizens. In both instances, that which the traditions of Israel intended for good (note 1 Sam. 7:6) becomes a tool of manipulative evil.

For his part, Naboth is the quintessentially faithful Israelite. As he himself makes clearer (v. 3), his decision is not an economic one, for he cannot sell his property to someone outside his family—not even the king—without violating ancient God-given principles concerning the relationship between Israelites and their land (note Lev. 25:1–34). Even in the face of a disaster as ruinous as the Babylonian invasion of the early sixth century, a hard-pressed but faithful Jew of Jerusalem would sell his land only to a relative (see Jer. 32:6–12). Naboth's faithfulness to the land is understood for what it is: faithfulness to the God of Israel, who has entrusted this land to the people of Israel. Naboth's faithfulness demands to be noticed as the bold contrast it is to the egregious *un*faithfulness of Ahab and Jezebel.

There is also a subtle note struck here for democracy. We often assume, quite rightly, that the ancient roots of modern democracy are to be found among the Greeks, whose tenacious opposition to tyrants made them noteworthy among peoples in the classical age. But Naboth, while not a democrat in the ultimate sense of that word, is aware that all persons have rights, even persons who till the land, and not even the kings of the earth may deprive these persons of those rights without violating God's intention for human life.

When Jezebel learns what has happened, she does what absolute rulers have done since the beginning of time: she acts with unbridled self-interest. Naboth is killed on trumped-up charges, whereupon Jezebel presents the land to a delighted Ahab (vs. 5–16). Jezebel, the actual murderer of Naboth, is not more evil than Ahab. She is simply less troubled by the humanitarian aspects of Israelite faith and tradition.

However, as Ahab goes to claim his prize, he is intercepted by Elijah, who has been directed by Yahweh to confront the king (vs. 17–21a). Notice that in Elijah's condemnation of Ahab there is no apparent need to explain why what he and the queen have done is so evil. The first part of v. 19 appears in NRSV and in some other English translations as a rhetorical question, but it is better read as a declaration: "You have committed murder and now you usurp as well" (Jerusalem Bible). Elijah does not have to explain what Ahab already comprehends: that Israel's basic covenant with God has been violated ("You shall not murder . . . ," "You shall not covet . . . ," Ex. 20:13, 17). The irony in v. 20 is profound. Ahab has sold himself to gain an advantage over faithful Naboth, who would not sell his patrimony. The king may consider Elijah his enemy, but his real enemy is himself, and his ultimate destruction is self-engineered.

## Psalm 5:1–8

The book of Psalms begins by affirming that "happy" are those whose "delight is in the instruction [NRSV "law"] of the LORD" and "who take refuge in" the Lord (1:1–2; 2:12). Psalms 3 and 4 make it clear that this happiness does not guarantee an easy, carefree life. The psalmists, surrounded by "foes" (3:1–2) and "in distress" (4:1), "cry" (3:4) and "call" (4:1) to God for help. In Ps. 5 also, the psalmist is not unopposed (see "enemies" in v. 8), and so must "cry" and "pray" and "plead" and "watch" (5:2–3). As is usually the case, the precise nature of the opposition and the identity of the enemies are unclear, but the psalmist seems to be the victim of some sort of false testimony (5:6, 9–10). His or her plight is reminiscent of the kind of opposition experienced by Jeremiah and Jesus, as well as by Naboth in the Old Testament lesson for the day.

The psalm falls most naturally into five sections, as follows:

vs. 1–3    Petition and affirmation: the "I" and God
vs. 4–6    Affirmation: God and wickedness
vs. 7–8    Affirmation and petition: the "I" and God
vs. 9–10   Affirmation and petition: God and the wicked
vs. 11–12  Petition and affirmation: "all" the "righteous" and God

As the above outline suggests, the psalmist's attention alternates between his or her own situation (vs. 1–3, 7–8) and the plight of the wicked (vs. 4–6, 9–10; note that both of these sections begin with "For"). A final section broadens the focus beyond the psalmist to "all who take refuge in" God, and a final "For" (v. 12) introduces an affirmation concerning God's treatment of the righteous that contrasts explicitly with the way God treats wickedness (vs. 4–6; see also v. 10). The alternation of sections dealing with the "I"/"righteous" and the wicked has the effect of focusing attention on vs. 7–8 as the center of the psalm. It is thus somewhat fitting that the lection concludes with v. 8; however, the whole psalm should be kept in view.

In language typical of the prayers for help, the psalmist asks in vs. 1–3 to be heard (see, for example, "give ear" in Pss. 17:1; 55:1; "listen" in 61:1; 86:6; "cry" in 28:2; 31:22). The addressing of God as "my King" is significant, since this is the first occurrence of the Hebrew root *mlk* (to reign, be king) in the Psalter (see also 10:16; 24:7–10; 29:10; 44:4; 47:2, 8; 93:1; 95:3; 96:10; 97:1; 98:6; 99:1; among others). This title for God relates Ps. 5 and other prayers for help to what has been identified as the theological "heart" of the Psalter— God rules the world. (See the Last Sunday After Epiphany regarding Ps. 99.) In Ps. 5, as is always the case, this fundamental affirmation is made amid opposition. Indeed, the affirmation of God's sovereignty has the effect of *inviting* opposition, as the life and death of Jesus illustrates. In other words, to call God "my King" is eschatological. It articulates the present reality that our lives belong to God, but it also anticipates a future when God's sovereignty will be fully manifest. The psalmist's posture is the persistent posture of the people of God; that is, it is always necessary to "watch" (v. 3). This posture also explains how the psalmist—beset by opposition, "sighing" (v. 1), and crying out for help (v. 2)—can call for rejoicing and singing (v. 11). Because the sovereign God is a "refuge" (v. 11; see 2:12 and others), the people of God will always be able to proclaim joyfully, "Thine is the kingdom," even as we pray, "Thy kingdom come."

Verses 4–6 of Ps. 5 elaborate on the character of the one addressed as "my King and my God," and explain why it makes sense to "plead my case" (v. 3) to God. The rationale is simple: as ruler of the world, God opposes wickedness and the wicked. Seven words or phrases describe wickedness, perhaps suggesting God's complete opposition. The word "destroy" in v. 6 is, more literally, "cause to perish," recalling the word "perish" in Pss. 1:6; 2:12. Wickedness will finally lead to its own destruction, because the wicked cut themselves off from God, who is the source of all life.

In contrast to "the boastful" (Ps. 5:5), the psalmist humbly attributes the opportunity to "enter your [God's] house" to "the abundance of your steadfast love" (v. 7). Verse 7 represents the first occurrence in the Psalter of the crucial word *hesed*, "steadfast love" (see also Pss. 23:6, NRSV " mercy"; 31:7, 16, 21; 32:10; 33:5, 18, 22; 100:5; 103:4, 8, 11, 17; 130:7; and others). The meaning of this Hebrew word is difficult to capture fully in English; it includes God's graceful and faithful dealing with sinful people (see especially Ex. 34:6–7). The appropriate human response is gratitude and service, which the psalmist displays as he or she states the intention to "bow down" (see Ex. 34:8, NRSV "worshiped"; Pss. 95:6; 138:2; and others) "in awe of you" (see Ps. 2:11, NRSV "with fear"). The central petition also bespeaks humble gratitude and openness to God's help rather than a reliance on the self (see Ps. 23:2). In effect, the psalmist prays what Jesus taught disciples to pray: "Lead us not into temptation, but deliver us from evil."

Psalm 5:9 is quoted by Paul in Rom. 3:13 to support his argument that all people "are under the power of sin" (Rom. 3:9). In a sense, Paul ignores the fact that Ps. 5:9 originally served to indict particular enemies (see v. 8) rather than to characterize all humanity; however, Paul's use of Ps. 5 and the psalmist's example of humble reliance on God challenge us to make a decision. Are we the "boastful," or do we "take refuge in" God? In other words, do our words and actions enhance our own selves and further our own agendas, or do we live humbly by God's grace and guidance? As Peter Craigie suggests, Ps. 5 can be "a prayer of self-examination and a request for forgiveness and deliverance" (*Psalms 1—50*, Word Biblical Commentary, 19; Waco, Tex.: Word, 1983, p. 89). It reminds us too of the tremendous power of speech (see James 3:5–12) and of the enduring importance of the Ninth Commandment, "You shall not bear false witness against your neighbor" (Ex. 20:16).

## Galatians 2:15–21

Numerous debates plague the interpretation of this passage, making it easy to lose track of the importance of Paul's point in the midst of sorting through a morass of exegetical views. Does Gal. 2:15 belong with the direct quotation of v. 14 (see the NRSV note) and, if so, where does that quotation end? What is to be understood by what some have referred to as the "Christ-mysticism" of vs. 19–21? Most important, is the NRSV translation "faith in Jesus Christ" correct, or should the phrase be translated "faith [or faithfulness] of Jesus Christ"? The Greek can be translated either subjectively or objectively, and a number of recent studies argue for the subjective reading ("faith of Jesus Christ"). Here we will focus on the general development of Paul's argument, attending to these questions only in passing.

Whether vs. 15 and 16 are to be understood as a continuation of Paul's response to Cephas or not, they clearly posit a fundamental contradiction between "works of the law" and "faith in [or of] Jesus Christ." One may not be justified by both. As often in this letter and elsewhere, Paul thinks in terms of opposites.

Crucial to understanding this passage is that the opposition Paul addresses does not concern "law" and "faith," two contradictory principles that are somehow abstracted from concrete situations. The question is not whether one achieves justification by following the law or by believing. Instead, the question is "works of the law" versus "faith in *Jesus Christ*" (emphasis added). Does justification come by means of the law of Moses or by means of Jesus Christ? Throughout this letter, the pivot remains the action of God in Jesus Christ, not the superiority of believing over doing, the principle of faith.

For Protestants, accustomed to characterizing this letter as concerning the controversy of "faith versus works," this point may be exceedingly difficult to understand. To say that Galatians concerns "faith versus works," however, suggests that one achieves justification either by believing or by doing. Ironically, either way of putting it grossly distorts Paul's point, which is that justification comes by means of Jesus Christ, the one who "gave himself for our sins" (1:4) and who "loved me and gave himself for me" (2:20). In this fundamental sense, then, it matters little whether the Greek expression *pistis christou* (literally, faith of Christ) refers to faith "in" Christ (that is, human belief) or faith "of" Christ (that is, Christ's own faithful obedience), since even faith "in" Christ comes about solely on the basis of God's intervention.

The logic of the opposition Paul establishes in 2:15–16 means that "works of the law" can no longer exist. For that reason he insists that "if I build up again the very things that I once tore down, then I demonstrate that I am a transgressor" (v. 18). This statement recalls his earlier retrospective account of his conversion, in which he sharply contrasts his "earlier life in Judaism" with the call to apostleship. What Paul "tore down" was not a bad or wicked life, but one that the gospel has rendered passé.

The language of vs. 19–20 depicts this same point in dramatic terms: "I died to the law, so that I might live to God.... It is no longer I who live, but it is Christ who lives in me." Whether or not this relationship is rightly characterized by the slippery term "mystical," what Paul again labors to express is the sense that the gospel overwhelms, eclipses, renders nil all previous values and commitments. Indeed, the allusion to the crucifixion prohibits us from understanding this solely in mystical or quasi-Gnostic terms. The "Son of God, who loved me and gave himself for me" recalls a concrete, historical act of self-denial by a human being, not union with some ethereal being.

Verse 21 completes the passage by returning to the point at issue between Paul and Peter and revealing what Paul understands to be at stake in that debate: living according to the law nullifies God's grace and suggests that Christ "died for nothing." The details of the controversy at Antioch are much disputed and will probably remain hidden from us. Something prompted Peter (Cephas) to withdraw from fellowship with Gentile Christians, returning to familiar patterns. Paul saw this as nothing less than a denial of the gospel itself.

Attending to the end of this passage and the section that precedes it (2:1–14) is absolutely essential if we are not to misunderstand it utterly. Despite the personal language of vs. 15–21 ("we" and especially "I") and the deeply personal involvement Paul's words reflect, he does not address a matter that is only private or individual. His concerns are profoundly social, addressing the possibility that Jew and Gentile may together inhabit the same church.

For the one who asserts that Christ "lives in me," the previous standards of the law—of ethnic pride, of personal accomplishment, whatever those standards might be—have been swept away. If Christ "lives in me," then, Christ may also live in all other human beings, regardless of their origin or viewpoints or behavior. To withdraw from fellowship with any of those human beings on the basis of my own individual judgment is fundamentally to misunderstand the gospel of Jesus Christ.

## Luke 7:36–8:3

The version of this beautiful story found in Luke has two foci. On the one hand, two sinners, coming from different circumstances, meet Jesus, and their responses stand in sharp contrast to each other. On the other hand, Jesus is depicted as a unique prophet who is able to see below the surface of things, who teaches, and who forgives sins. No sermon faithful to the text can avoid either focus, and yet particular attention to one or the other may be appropriate.

First, there are the two sinners. One is a nameless woman, who did not accidentally wander in from the streets and happen upon Jesus but who came prepared, with her alabaster jar of ointment. She is identified by the narrator, by Simon, and by Jesus as a sinner, but we are not told what qualified her for such a label. To speak of her as a prostitute is to engage in useless speculation.

The woman says nothing but does plenty—weeping, bathing, kissing, and anointing Jesus' feet and wiping them with her hair. Her action fulfills the hospitality neglected by the host, but much more. The parable of Luke 7:41–42 and verse 47 suggest that her lavish display of affection is the result of her having already been forgiven. At some point she has heard a word of divine pardon, and her deep sense of gratitude prompts an extravagant response, in spite of the hostile, critical context. Jesus' statement to her in 7:48 is a necessary (in light of the skepticism of Simon) confirmation of her forgiveness. She has returned like the Samaritan leper to give thanks for her newfound life (see 17:11–19).

The other sinner is Simon the Pharisee. We should anticipate his negative reaction to the woman's extravagance, since the narrator has already made the telling comment that while tax collectors in receiving John's baptism acknowledge the justice of God, the Pharisees by refusing John's baptism reject God's purpose for themselves (7:29–30). The woman has accepted the divine verdict on her life and has received divine pardon. Simon, on the other hand, simply finds such grace offensive and takes the woman's presence at the dinner to be a scandalous intrusion.

Simon's criticism is not spoken aloud, and in fact is aimed more at Jesus' acceptance of the woman's behavior than at the woman herself (7:39). If Jesus is a prophet, surely he should know about the woman and not let her carry on so shamefully. But then follows Simon's exposure—a simple parable that functions like a trap to snare the unsuspecting predator (7:41–43). Whether Simon failed to get the point of the parable or not, we are not told, but Jesus offers an explanation contrasting the lavish behavior of the woman with Simon's failure to provide even the basic elements of hospitality (7:44–47).

The two sinners provide a striking contrast. It may be difficult for contemporary audiences to identify fully with either character. The woman is so stigmatized by her sins as to be a public figure, and Simon comes across as a blind, smug religionist, who cannot perceive the genuine gratitude of a forgiven woman. Yet the two figures retain their cutting edge. Like the parable Jesus tells, they serve to expose our modern moralisms and dramatize for us an authentic response to divine grace.

The story of the two sinners makes sense only in light of the words and actions of Jesus, who throughout the whole of Luke 7 functions as a prophet (7:39). Three features of his prophetic role are highlighted here: his discernment of Simon's unspoken criticism (7:40), his teaching the truth about the current predicament (7:40–47), and his pronouncement of divine forgiveness (7:48–49).

Even so, to depict Jesus as a prophet is not somehow to reduce his authority to the level of other prophets and to minimize his uniqueness. Jesus fulfills the promise given to Moses about the raising up of a prophet (Deut. 18:15, 18), and his words become decisive for the destiny of the people of God (see Acts 3:22–23). The rhetorical question of those at table, "Who is this who even forgives sins?" (Luke 7:49), hangs in the air for the reader to decide.

It is intriguing in the parable Jesus tells to find forgiveness of sins depicted by forgiveness of debts, an experience no doubt well known to Galilean peasants. Their whole lives as well as their futures were bound up with their fiscal obligations. Pardon of debts, then, has nothing to do with guilt but rather with the restoration of life and the renewal of hope.

The suggested reading for this Sunday goes on to include 8:1–3, one of Luke's typical summaries. In many ways it serves to introduce a new section more than it does to conclude chapter 7. It includes among Jesus' followers not only the Twelve, but also three women by name and "many others" who serve as benefactors to the group. There is no historical or literary reason to connect the nameless woman of 7:36–50 whose sins are forgiven with Mary Magdalene, "from whom seven demons had gone out" (8:2).

# PROPER 7

Ordinary Time 12

*Sunday between
June 19 and 25 inclusive
(if after Trinity Sunday)*

Over and over, biblical writers remind us that it is only in the acknowledgment and service of God that human beings find their rightful place in the order of creation. Yet those same writers also recognize that the acknowledgment and service of God brings with it powerful threats to the way in which the world generally does its business.

Precisely because he has done the Lord's bidding in killing all the prophets of Baal, Elijah must flee from Jezebel's wrath (1 Kings 19:1–3). Utterly discouraged by the limitations of his own resources, Elijah proposes that he be allowed to die. God's response comes, not in the form of words of encouragement, but in the form of nurture (vs. 4–9), God's own presence (vs. 11–13), and finally in the form of yet another summons to work (vs. 15–18).

Psalms 42 and 43 might well be read as Elijah's own thoughts during this period of dismay. The psalmist portrays the human need of God's presence, as real as the need for food and water, and the human cry in the face of God's apparent absence. The reading ends with the assurance that God will again be present for those who praise him.

The words of Gal. 3:23–29 have become exceedingly familiar because of their implicit call to liberation from anthropological boundaries of race, class, and gender. We rightly hear in them the assurance that the reign of the gospel of Jesus Christ brings with it freedom. That freedom is threatening and costly, however, since the freedom of the gospel is freedom to be in Christ, to belong utterly to him and to his cross.

The Gospel lection provides yet another instance in which the liberating gospel poses a threat to the status quo. For the man possessed of demons, the arrival of Jesus Christ means freedom and the opportunity to serve. For those standing by, however, this man's freedom brings with it an economic threat: the destruction of an

391

entire herd of pigs will not be perceived by everyone as liberating! Jesus' power to do good carries with it a threat to those for whom possession is all.

## 1 Kings 19:1-4 (5-7) 8-15a

The Old Testament lection for this day is to be read in the light of the contest between Elijah and the prophets of Baal on Mount Carmel (1 Kings 18:17-46; note Proper 4). In that celebrated episode, Elijah not only cuts down the flower of the Baal "clergy" (18:40), but does so in a manner that attacks the hubris of the royal house of Israel. Elijah's declaration to Ahab that the drought that Yahweh has sent is a personal matter between the king and the God of Israel is sufficient to make of the prophet an enemy of the court in Samaria (18:1, 17). Thus when the Baal prophets are killed, the reader is not surprised to learn that Jezebel has put a price on Elijah's head (19:1-2). The fact that it is now the queen rather than the king who asserts the royal power seems consistent with the personality of this Phoenician princess (compare Jezebel's and Ahab's response to Naboth's refusal to sell his vineyard in 21:5-14; see Proper 6). She appears at this distance as a person who brooked no opposition and, what is more, as a Phoenician she was perhaps more personally attached to the prophets of Baal than was Ahab.

Elijah's terrified response (19:3) is understandable, and the prophet flees to a spot that is as remote from Samaria as it is possible to be and still be in the land of Yahweh: Beer-sheba, in the far south of Judah. (A note about versification: in spite of the paragraph division in NRSV, v. 3 is best seen as a part of the section vs. 3–9a. The decision of the lectionary to place vs. 5–7 in brackets is not a fortunate one, in that these verses provide part of the reason for the prophet's extended journey down to Mount Horeb/Sinai. And as these verses are quite brief, the parentheses may be ignored when reading the text aloud in public worship.)

In the section vs. 3–9a, Mosaic covenant theology begins to emerge as the pattern for Elijah's own prophetic role. Verse 4 may best be understood as "I am not as good as my ancestors," the "ancestors" in mind being Moses and Joshua and their generations. It is clear from other texts of a north Israelite provenance, notably the books of Deuteronomy (1:1) and Hosea (12:13), that Moses and the Mosaic covenant occupied a central place in the faith of true Yahwists in the north, similar to that which David and the Davidic covenant occupied in the hearts of loyal Yahwists in the south (2 Sam. 7:1–17). The fact that Mount Horeb (the name used in north Israelite circles for the site where Moses received the commandments) is Elijah's ultimate destination (1 Kings 19:4–8) leaves little doubt as to who the "ancestors" of v. 4 are. In v. 4, then, Elijah is confessing, in effect, "I have failed to provide the kind of leadership for the people of Yahweh that Moses provided in an earlier day."

The reader will not wish to accept such an evaluation from this selfless man of God, however, and apparently Yahweh does not accept it either. For instead of permitting Elijah to die, Yahweh sends an angel who, as the ravens had done earlier (17:1–7), provides the prophet with nourishment and who, in addition, urges Elijah to continue his journey (19:5–7). The prophet does so, and after an extended time ("forty days and forty nights") the prophet arrives at "Horeb the mount of God," where he beds down in a cave (vs. 8–9a).

The climax of this lection is achieved in vs. 9b–15a, in which Yahweh reveals Yahweh's self to Elijah. As has often been pointed out, the parallels between this passage and Ex. 33:17–23 are striking, once more revealing that the figure of Moses is in the mind of the writer(s) and thus, one may suppose, in the mind of Elijah himself. The similarities between these texts are not limited to the details of the theophany (the location at Sinai/Horeb, the cleft in the rock/cave, the unseen face of the Deity, and the like), but extend to the purpose of Yahweh's self-revelation. In both instances the prophet is reequipped and remotivated to do Yahweh's will. In Moses' case this is to return to the people with new tablets of the law. In Elijah's case it is to return to the struggle with Ahab. To be more specific, Elijah is directed to set in motion that series of events which will bring about the downfall of Ahab's family (19:15b–18; compare 2 Kings 9).

Great interest has been expressed by interpreters over the years in the manner in which Yahweh ultimately speaks to Elijah. It is not in a great wind, or in an earthquake, or in fire that Yahweh speaks. It is in, as the King James has it, "a still small voice" (v. 12, as also the RSV). The literal Hebrew means something like "a thin whisper," so REB and JB are probably near the mark with "a faint murmuring sound" and "a light murmuring sound," respectively. NRSV is decidedly incorrect in its "sound of sheer silence." The contrast is between the violence of the wind, quake, and fire, on the one hand, and, on the other, the gentle cadences of Yahweh's whisper. (One may—or may not—wish to reflect on the fact that the contrast presented to Moses in Ex. 33:17–23 was between the dazzling glory of Yahweh's face and the more subdued effect of Yahweh's backside.)

The result of the theophany at Horeb is to reenergize a downcast Elijah and to place him again in the role of the leader of those who are attempting—against great odds—to be faithful to Yahweh. Elijah is a new Moses, raised up by God to lead the people in the time of their peril.

## Psalms 42 and 43

The early Christians found in Ps. 42—43 a symbol for baptism: "The hart [42:1, NRSV "deer"] . . . was the emblem of those thirsting souls who, in the cooling streams of the baptismal font, drank freely of the fountain of eternal life" (Rowland E. Prothero, *The Psalms in Human Life and Experience;* New York: E. P. Dutton, 1903, pp. 9–10). When Augustine was baptized on Easter Sunday in 387, Ps. 43 was sung (Prothero, p. 29). The symbolism is appropriate, for Pss. 42—43 affirm what we Christians profess in the sacrament—that each human life derives from and belongs to God and is lived authentically only in relationship to God. In other words, human life depends on God; we need God.

This need is expressed poetically in the opening simile and then more directly: "My soul thirsts for God" (Ps. 42:2; see Pss. 63:1; 143:6). Thirst is not simply a desire; the human body cannot survive without water. For the psalmist, God is not an option; God is a necessity. The question in 42:2 may suggest that the psalmist is exiled and cannot make a pilgrimage to the Temple to "behold the face of God" (v. 2). In any case, the psalmist desires a depth of communion with God that does not seem available. The mention of the "face of God" in v. 2 and "bread" (NRSV "food") in v. 3 suggests again that the desire for communion with God is expressed in terms of a wish to visit the Temple, which housed the "bread of the face" (NRSV "bread of the Presence"; see Ex. 25:30; 1 Sam. 21:6; 1 Kings 7:48). Denied this opportunity, the psalmist's "bread" has been his or her own tears; and the grief has been exacerbated by the question of others, "Where is your God?" (Pss. 42:3, 10; 79:10; 115:2; Joel 2:17; Micah 7:10).

Apparently, the only thing the psalmist can do is to "remember" (v. 4), and so he or she recalls the joy of past visits to "the house of God" (v. 4). This memory leads to the first occurrence of the refrain (v. 5; see v. 11; 43:5), which seems to be a sort of inner dialogue that expresses both the temptation to despair as well as the possibility of help and hope.

The beginning of the second section (42:6–11) emphasizes the note of despair as it echoes the first line of the refrain. Again, all the psalmist can do is to "remember you" (v. 6; compare v. 4). The geographical references in v. 6 may be understood literally, in which case they would locate the psalmist outside of the homeland, or they may be understood as an imaginative way to introduce the metaphors of v. 7. In contrast to the scarcity of water in vs. 1–2, there is too much water in v. 7; the "deep" represents the chaotic forces that are overwhelming the psalmist (see Ps. 69:1–3). Verse 8 seems surprisingly hopeful, but it may refer to an aspect of a bygone era that the psalmist is remembering. In any case, it leads to further complaint in vs. 9–10. The psalmist's remembering leads to the conclusion that God has forgotten (v. 9), a situation that does not escape the notice of the enemies (v. 10), who repeat the haunting question of v. 3. The juxtaposition of this question with the second occurrence of the refrain again emphasizes the note of despair.

Psalm 43:1–5, the third section of Pss. 42—43, moves beyond complaint to petition. "Vindicate me" in v. 1 could also be translated "establish justice for me"; and "defend my cause" could be paraphrased in the contemporary idiom "get on their case." While questions still remain (v. 2; compare 42:9), the psalmist's tone is more hopeful. He or she can envision being led by God's "light" (see, for example, Pss. 27:1; 44:3; 89:15) and "truth" (or "faithfulness"; see, for example, Ex. 34:6; Pss. 40:10–11; 54:5; 71:22) to the temple to "praise" God (v. 4). The word "praise" anticipates the final occurrence of the refrain, and serves to emphasize this time the hopeful aspect—"I shall again praise."

The powerful refrain of Pss. 42—43, while it appears intensely personal, may actually be more liturgical than autobiographical, as James L. Mays suggests: "In it the ego who speaks to the downcast soul is the liturgical and confessional ego speaking to the consciousness shaped by a society and circumstances that do not support faith" (Psalms, Interpretation series; Louisville, Ky.: John Knox Press, 1994). In other words, the refrain professes the faith of the whole people of God, the church. That it does so in a hostile environment makes Pss. 42—43 very timely, for, as Stanley Hauerwas and William H. Willimon have recently reminded us, the church is in a sort of permanent exile. Christians now live as "resident aliens" in a culture that clearly does not support faith. Instead of affirming that human life derives from and depends on God, our culture teaches us that "it is all up to us" (Resident Aliens: Life in the Christian Colony; Nashville: Abingdon Press, 1989, p. 36). In this cultural context, Pss. 42—43 suggest that the most important thing we can do is to "hope in God" (42:5, 11; 43:5), that is, to claim the baptism that marks us as children of God, whose souls will not rest until they rest in God. The spirit of Pss. 42—43 pervades the opening paragraph of Augustine's *Confessions:* "The thought of you stirs him [the human being] so deeply that he cannot be content unless he praises you, because you made us for yourself and our hearts find no peace until they rest in you" (Book I, 1; trans. R. S. Pine-Coffin; New York: Penguin Books, 1961, p. 21). As children of God, we shall understand what the world cannot begin to fathom: "Blessed are those who hunger and thirst for righteousness, for they will be filled" (Matt. 5:6; see also John 4:14; 6:35; Rev. 21:6).

## Galatians 3:23–29

This lection forms the climax of the argument that began in Gal. 3:1 (or even in 2:15!) opposing the law with faith in Jesus Christ. Over against those in the Galatian churches who affirm that Christians must obey the law of Moses in order to participate fully in the Christian life, Paul insists that the two, the law and Christ, are incompatible. In 3:1–5, Paul argues his case on the basis of experience, and in 3:6–18, on the basis of exegesis.

With 3:19, Paul takes up the purpose of the law. It was given "because of transgressions" (3:19), but it could not "make alive" (3:21). With our passage, Paul continues this line of argument. The law held people "imprisoned and guarded" (3:23). It was a "disciplinarian until Christ came" (3:24). "Disciplinarian" translates the Greek word *paidagōgos,* which refers to a particular kind of household slave, one who was charged with overseeing the behavior of a boy on his way to school and back. The *paidagōgos* had a largely protective role and his services were temporary, no longer needed when the boy attained manhood. Elsewhere Paul suggests a more positive interpretation of the law (for example, Rom. 7:14–21; 9:4), but here the law's role is essentially negative and temporal. It served to protect from harm until "faith would be revealed" (v. 23).

Does that last phrase suggest that there is no faith under the law, that belief itself is only possible in the Christian era? The example of Abraham in vs. 6–9 argues against that view. Instead, the faith that Paul speaks of in v. 23 abbreviates the phrase of v. 22—"faith in Jesus Christ." Thus, v. 24 identifies Christ as the one who arrived. What has changed is not that people who were previously unable to believe are now able to do so, but that Christ arrived and rendered futile all previous allegiances and commitments.

Not only did Christ appear on the scene, but also believers are profoundly connected with him. The spatial imagery of the passage vividly makes this point. Before the arrival of Christ, "we were imprisoned and guarded *under* [*hypo*] the law" (v. 23, emphasis added), but now "we are no longer subject to a disciplinarian" (literally, under [*hypo*] a disciplinarian). Believers have moved away from the sphere in which the law is in charge.

They have moved into (or they have been moved into) the sphere of Christ Jesus. They are *"in* Christ Jesus" and have been *"baptized into* Christ" (emphases added). They have even "clothed" themselves "with Christ." Here it becomes clear that the language Paul applies to himself at the end of chapter 2 applies equally well to all believers. Christ lives in and through them, and they live in Christ. What this means for the law, as for any other loyalty, is that its role has been displaced by the centrality of Jesus Christ.

With 3:28, Paul states in extremely forceful terms (terms that may be drawn from an early Christian baptismal formula) the implications of this exclusive relationship: "There is no longer Jew or Greek, there is no longer slave or free, there is no longer male and female; for all of you are one in Christ Jesus." With these three brief phrases, Paul encompasses the three fundamental anthropological divisions known to his world. "Jew or Greek," the Jew's version of "Greeks and . . . barbarians" (see Rom. 1:14), identified the world along ethnic-religious lines, dividing those who were within one's circle from the outsider, the other. "Slave or free" identified the world along socioeconomic lines, dividing those who possessed a measure of freedom from those who possessed very little. (The nature of slavery in the Greco-Roman world is far more complicated than was previously understood.) "Male and female," which follows Gen. 1:27 and therefore does not exactly conform to the other divisions, identified the world along gender lines determined at birth.

"For all of you are one in Christ Jesus" (v. 28). These previous identifications and divisions, the most powerful known in the ancient world (or in the present), have ceased to exist because of the single identity "in Christ Jesus." Verse 29 applies this general statement to the specific issue at hand: Who can rightfully be called a child of Abraham? Those who are "in Christ" are the children of Abraham, whether Jew or Greek, slave or free, male or female. The only identification that counts is that of baptism in Christ.

Since this passage has become a hallmark of the church's discussion of the limits and responsibilities of women, it may seem superfluous to discuss it yet once again. What often is overlooked in those discussions, however, is that this passage operates something like a two-edged sword. On the one hand, it profoundly undercuts the way in which we persist in distinguishing among human beings on the basis of gender, race, class, or any other anthropological identification. In the sphere of Jesus Christ, these distinctions have no place.

On the other hand, this passage confronts us with the claim that Christians are *one in Christ Jesus*, insisting that we are radically united on the basis of Christ Jesus. The solipsism that allows others to divide up again on the basis of ethnic or gender experience cannot be countenanced in the Christian community. Here, identity in Christ Jesus is the only identity that matters. As so often, Paul manages to offend virtually everyone with his insistence on the prior and exclusive claims of the gospel of Jesus Christ.

## Luke 8:26–39

It may be appropriate from time to time in preaching on texts from the Gospels to deal with the phenomenon of demon possession. The so-called scientific mind today often finds the stories in which Jesus exorcizes an evil spirit to be primitive and unsophisticated. One can always offer a brief explanation by pointing to the common experience shared by ancients and moderns of unexplained terrors that create enormous emotional, if not physical, havoc in the lives of individuals and communities. But most of the exorcism stories found in the Gospels really need little explanation. They make themselves remarkably immediate to modern audiences without extended clarification of the first-century worldview.

Such is the case with the longest of the exorcism stories, the healing of the Gerasene demoniac. The vivid narrative relates powerful conflicts, transformations, rejections, and resolutions, and leaves the interpreter with more than enough relevant material to deal with.

Right away the reader encounters *the conflict of authority between Jesus and the demons* (Luke 8:26–31). It is not surprising, since this is the second of four vignettes in which Jesus' authority is displayed (calming the storm, exorcizing the demons, healing the woman with the hemorrhages, and raising Jairus's daughter), culminating in his delegating authority to the Twelve as they begin their mission (9:1–6). Despite their number, the demons here are no match for Jesus. They fall before him and beg that he not send them back to the abyss. Their end comes, rather ironically, in the sea, since demons assiduously avoid the water (compare 11:24).

We dare not downplay the element of conflict. At Jesus' command that the unclean spirit leave, the demon-speaking man replies, "Do not torment me" (8:28–29). He rightly perceives Jesus as a menace who will engage destructive forces and destroy them. It is the nature of Jesus' authority that he threatens inhumane and oppressive powers, sometimes directly, sometimes subversively. Not every individual or institution is ready for the overhaul that Jesus always brings.

Jesus' authority effects *an amazing transformation from terror to wholeness.* The details of the "before" and "after" are stunning. Once naked, banished from the city, living in the caves, convulsive, kept unsuccessfully under guard, totally uncontrollable, he becomes a disciple of Jesus, sane and appropriately clothed. The Greek participle translated "in his right mind" (8:35) is the same characteristic Paul urges for all Christians ("sober judgment," Rom. 12:3). It is hard to improve on the pictures of transformation painted in the narrative itself.

It is critical that this transformation occurs in the country of the Gerasenes (Luke 8:26). Considerable textual and geographical confusion prevents a certainty of the location on a map, but the presence of the pigs feeding on the hillside assures us that we are talking about a predominantly Gentile territory and the restoration of a non-Jewish person. Here Jesus' saving arm reaches beyond the national bounds of Judaism, anticipating the broader mission to the Gentiles so prominent in the book of Acts.

The transformation of the demoniac leads to *discipleship.* Luke alone describes the healed man as "sitting at the feet of Jesus" (8:35). At Jesus' departure, the man begs that he might accompany Jesus, as other disciples have done. Instead, he is sent home (that is, back into the city) to "declare how much God has done for you" (8:39). He is commissioned to bear his personal witness in the Gentile area, and does so in response to Jesus' direction.

The movement from the exertion of Jesus' authority to the transformation of the Gerasene demoniac results in a new disciple, who becomes a model for mission. But the story also has its down side. There is *the fearful rejection of Jesus* by the people of the area. The "happy ending" of the eager evangelist is countered by the pressure of his peers, who force Jesus to leave the area.

It is striking that the folks who come from the city and the country around to see the restored demoniac exhibit no sense of amazement or awe, much less belief. They are overcome with fear (8:35, 37). The transformation leaves them terribly afraid. Why? We are not told explicitly what caused their fear and why they wanted Jesus to leave, but one cannot help drawing a connection between Jesus' act of healing and the destruction of a herd of pigs. Someone's assets are sharply reduced by the action of Jesus, and it may be that other acts of kindness will further threaten economic stability. It often happens.

Whatever the reason for their rejection of Jesus, the Gerasene people represent a tough mission field for the healed demoniac to tackle.

# PROPER 8

## Ordinary Time 13

*Sunday between June 26
and July 2 inclusive*

The sequence of lections from the Elijah-Elisha cycle continues with the account in 2 Kings 2:1–2, 6–14 of the transition of leadership from master to chief disciple, a theme prominent in other parts of the Bible. This (quite literal!) assumption of the mantle of Elijah's prophetic authority by Elisha finds its closest parallel in the Moses-Joshua relationship. However, echoes of the account in Acts 1 of the ascension of Jesus will not escape the reader. The passing of a great leader of God's people is necessarily the occasion of a crisis of sorts, for only the work of the Spirit of God can supply a newly empowered person around whom the people may rally. That God does not abandon the people and the fruit of the work of the Spirit may be seen in the authorization of Elisha to fill the void left by the passing of Elijah.

Psalm 77 is a cry of distress from one in trouble, but the bulk of the verses chosen, 77:1–2, 11–20, have to do with the psalmist's meditation on the goodness of God, especially on God's saving deeds in the past. References to God's mastery over the waters in vs. 16–20 make this psalm an appropriate companion piece to the passage from 2 Kings 2, where the parting of the waters of the Jordan occupies a climactic moment in the narrative (2 Kings 2:14). The memory of God's saving deeds in the past makes it possible for women and men of faith to embody the reign of God even in the midst of circumstances that suggest that God does not reign. Out of the memory of the community of faith emerges hope.

Galatians 5:1, 13–25, an important statement on Christian freedom, is also an important statement on the work of the Spirit. Freedom in Christ must not be confused with irresponsible license, basically for the reason that it is a freedom grounded in Christ and it therefore involves obligations to Christ and to others. In what manner, then, is this freedom to be lived? Through reliance on the Spirit, for the "fruit of the Spirit is love, joy, peace, patience, kindness, gene.osity, faithfulness, gentleness, and self-control" (vs. 22–23).

The memory of Elijah is raised in the Gospel lection, Luke 9:51–62, for in the spirit of that prophet Jesus' disciples consider calling down fire on those who have rejected their Master (v. 54; compare 2 Kings 1:9–14). However, unlike Elijah, Jesus will hear of no such talk and rebukes his followers. Moreover, instead of calling down destruction on those who resist him, Jesus invites further resistance by a series of statements concerning the nature of discipleship, which are so sweeping in their demands that they seem all but impossible. What Jesus requires of those who would be his followers is nothing other than a single-minded faithfulness.

## 2 Kings 2:1–2, 6–14

The issue of succession in the leadership of God's people is addressed in several biblical texts. Most extensively, the question is highlighted in 2 Sam. 11–1 Kings 2, where trouble in King David's own household clouds the peaceful transition of authority. But the pair of biblical figures whom this day's Old Testament lection brings to mind more than any other are Moses and Joshua. For reasons discussed previously (see 1 Kings 19:1–15a; Proper 7), the inspired leadership of Moses appears to be the pattern in the mind of the writer(s) of the Elijah narratives in their description of the role of this important ninth-century prophet. In significant respects Elijah is portrayed as a new Moses, who has been designated by Yahweh to call the people of Israel back to their traditions of faithfulness and justice, traditions closely linked to God's self-revelation at Mount Sinai (or Horeb, as it was known in northern Israelite circles). As the people of Israel once had to face the bitter reality that Moses must be taken from them (Deut. 31:1–13), so the faithful worshipers of Yahweh in the kingdom of Ahab's son Jehoram are forced to confront the reality of Elijah's end.

Elijah's bitter enemy, King Ahab, is now dead, as is his son and successor, Ahaziah. A second son, Jehoram (also called Joram), now occupies the throne of the Omri dynasty (2 Kings 1:17), and it will be he who will feel the wrath of the revolt instigated by Elisha and led by Jehu, which ultimately decimates this family and removes them from power in Israel (2 Kings 9). This situation is made somewhat confusing for modern students of the period by the fact that there is also a King Jehoram, a member of the Davidic family, who rules over Judah at this time (2 Kings 8:16).

The text, in describing the events surrounding Elijah's ascension, admits the reader to the innermost emotions of Elijah's friends as the moment of his leaving draws near. Although 2:3–5 is not included in the lectionary passage, it is here that we are twice informed that those near the prophet, including his closest friend, Elisha, know what is about to happen. Elisha's simple, "Yes, I know," when forewarned by members of "the company of prophets" (Elijah's band of followers) helps the reader understand Elisha's reluctance to leave Elijah's side in vs. 2 and 6. Yahweh is about to call Elijah up on the whirlwind and, although we are not told how Elijah's friends are privy to Yahweh's counsel, it is obvious that they are. Yet Elisha does not speak the obvious. (One assumes that Elijah understands what is about to happen also, although the text does not say so directly.) Elisha simply refuses to leave the master's side. Partly this is in hope of receiving Elijah's blessing and authority (v. 9). But it is also an effort to savor every last minute of fellowship with the great prophet of God. Elijah may be so faithful that he will not taste death, but that will not overrule the sense of loss on the part of those who have known and loved him. And so Elisha clings to the prophet.

One remembers the sense of loss and bewilderment—mingled with their great joy—that struck Jesus' disciples at the moment of his ascension (Acts 1:6–11). In a similar manner, those who are with Elijah know that the moment of his leaving will come, but their mood appears to be more one of resignation than of celebration. (Note in 2 Kings 2:16–17 how Elijah's followers appear to be unwilling to accept the reality of his absence.)

The itinerary of the band moves from Gilgal to Jericho to the Jordan and then (for Elijah and Elisha only) just beyond, and it is now that the parallels to the narratives about Moses and Joshua become most evident. First, there is geography. As Elijah, like Moses, experienced an important theophany at Mount Horeb/Sinai (1 Kings 19:1–15), so Elisha, like Joshua, becomes God's leader for the people just beyond the Jordan. Second, as Joshua's new leadership received divine confirmation by means of a miraculous crossing of the Jordan (Josh. 3:14–17), in a similar manner Elisha's first act as Elijah's successor is the use of his departed master's cloak to divide the waters of the river (2 Kings 2:13–14).

Before we reach this point in the narrative, however, we encounter the description of Elijah's ascension into heaven. (Enoch is the only other person accorded this distinction in the Old Testament, Gen. 5:24.) Interestingly, there is no charge delivered to Elisha, as there is to Joshua (Deut. 31:23; Josh. 1:1–9), Solomon (1 Kings 2:1–9; 1 Chron. 28:9–21), and Jesus' disciples (Matt. 28:16–20 and elsewhere). There is, in fact, some doubt expressed by the departing prophet that Elisha will inherit his (Elijah's) divine powers (2 Kings 2:10). However, it soon becomes clear that Elisha's petition has been answered in the affirmative (v. 15). The meaning of the curious phrase in 2:12, "the chariots of Israel and its horsemen," is unclear, but it is viewed by many interpreters as a manner of comparing human with divine power (the "horses . . . and chariots of fire"; note 2 Kings 6:17; 13:14).

A great and godly leader is gone, but in his place God has raised another great and godly leader. Thus the faithfulness of those who yearn to be true to the God of Israel is affirmed and given direction by the very God whom the faithful seek to follow. The manner in which this motif recurs in the Bible underscores the continuing promise of God not to abandon God's people in the times of their need.

## Psalm 77:1–2, 11–20

Psalm 77 deals with a familiar pastoral, theological issue—unanswered prayer. The urgency and intensity of the psalmist's prayer is expressed by the repetition in v. 1. The psalmist has prayed tirelessly "day" and "night" without "comfort" (v. 2). Indeed, in the verses omitted from our lection (vs. 3–10), the thought of God has become a source of weakness rather than strength (v. 3). The psalmist cannot sleep; and having run out of words (v. 4), the "cry aloud" of v. 1 becomes anguished meditation (v. 6) on a series of questions that strike at the very heart of faith in God (vs. 7–9). Of particular significance in vs. 7–9 are several words that occur in God's self-revelation to Moses in Ex. 34:6—"steadfast love," "gracious," "compassion" (NRSV "merciful" in Ex. 34:6). In short, the current trouble—whether it be personal or the corporate experience of exile—causes the psalmist to doubt God's fundamental character. Verse 10 climactically summarizes this crisis of faith; the psalmist is "sick" (a more literal translation than "my grief") that God "has changed."

Verse 11 marks a transition so abrupt that many commentators have suggested that vs. 1–10 and vs. 11–20 are separate psalms. However, a common vocabulary unifies the two sections. For instance, the psalmist in vs. 11–20 continues to "remember" (the Hebrew root zkr, "to remember," occurs twice in v. 11, as well as in vs. 3 and 6, where NRSV translates it "think of" and "commune") and to "muse" (v. 12; see the same Hebrew word in vs. 3, 6, NRSV "meditate"). But the content and result of the psalmist's remembrance is quite different. Whereas his or her previous meditation had led to moaning and troubling doubt (vs. 3–10), now the meditation focuses on God's "wonders of old" and "mighty deeds" (vs. 11–12). The psalmist apparently reaches a new understanding of God's character and mode of activity—God's "way" (vs. 13, 19). Between the two references to God's "way" lies a hymnic celebration that is rich in allusion to the exodus, especially the song in Ex. 15:1–18 that celebrated the sea crossing (see, for instance, "wonders" in Ps. 77:11, 14 and Ex. 15:11; "holy"/"holiness" in Ps. 77:13 and Ex. 15:11; "might"/"strength" in Ps. 77:14 and Ex. 15:2, 13; "redeemed" in Ps. 77:15 and Ex. 15:13; "trembled" in Ps. 77:16, 18 and Ex. 15:14, as examples).

Of particular interest and significance are the affirmations about God's "way" that frame the recollection of the exodus; it is "holy" (Ps. 77:13), and it occurs in such a way that God's "footprints were unseen" (v. 19). Both these affirmations suggest the otherness and mystery of God's character and activity. What the psalmist apparently realizes in the process of recalling the exodus is that God's way is not always clearly comprehensible in terms of human ways (see Isa. 55:8–9). Or, as Marvin Tate suggests, the psalmist learns that God has God's "own schedule and often the faithful must endure the anguish of waiting" (*Psalms 51—100*, Word Biblical Commentary 20; Dallas: Word, 1990, p. 276).

Even so, this suggestion does not account for the suddenness of the transition between vs. 10 and 11 of Ps. 77, nor for the psalmist's remarkable change from seemingly hopeless despair (v. 10) to expectant waiting (see v. 20). Walter Brueggemann has suggested that the transition marked by vs. 11–12 involves "a shift from 'I' to 'Thou' " (*Israel's Praise;* Philadelphia: Fortress Press, 1988, p. 138). Verse 11b shifts to direct address of God, and the answer to the question in v. 13b begins with an emphatic pronoun: "*You* are the God who works wonders." This affirmation begins the explicit remembrance of the exodus that effectively "takes the mind off the hopelessness of self" (Brueggemann, p. 138). This transition is not an achievement of the individual psalmist. Rather, he or she articulates and participates in a communal process of remembering. As Brueggemann concludes, "Everything depends on having the public, canonical memory available which becomes in this moment of pain a quite powerful, personal hope" (p. 140).

This canonical memory would have been available and recited in worship; and, as James L. Mays points out, the recital itself is evocative of God's presence (*Psalms,* Interpretation series; Louisville, Ky.: John Knox Press, 1994):

The LORD is there in the recital as the God whose right hand has not changed. The hymn [vs. 13–19] does what praise and confession are meant to do—to represent the God of revelation as the reality and subject of truth in the face of all circumstances and contrary experience.

It is clear that Mays, like Brueggemann, assumes that the psalmist is still left in the midst of "the day of my trouble" (v. 2). What *has* changed is the psalmist himself or herself. No longer an isolated self, the psalmist is part of "your people" (vs. 15, 20). Previously hopeless, he or she now lives with the faith and the hope that God still "works wonders" (v. 14a).

Brueggemann, Mays, and most other commentators clearly interpret vs. 13–19 as genuine praise. Tate is not so sure; he hears these verses as a continuation of the psalmist's "distressed meditation" (p. 275). This means that the questions of vs. 7–9 are "left open," and that the "reader must answer" (p. 275). According to Tate, while vs. 11–20 give a solid basis for answering no to the questions of vs. 7–9, "the decision is ours" (p. 276). Thus, Ps. 77 is finally a call to decision (see Luke 9:51–62, the Gospel lesson). In every age, the people of God are called on to proclaim and embody the reign of God in circumstances that make it appear that God does *not* reign. In short, Ps. 77 reminds us that we live inevitably and simultaneously as people of memory and people of hope.

## Galatians 5:1, 13–25

"For freedom Christ has set us free. Stand firm, therefore, and do not submit again to a yoke of slavery." Paul's stirring words in Gal. 5:1 culminate his long argument about the incompatibility of faith in Jesus Christ and works of the law, and open a discussion about the particular freedom initiated by Christ.

Here the preacher and teacher need to move with great care, for the word "freedom" has connotations in contemporary North America that it surely did not have for Paul. The thesaurus identifies freedom with autonomy, independence, and sovereignty—in other words, with freedom to "do as I please." But such concepts Paul would not include in freedom, at least not in Christian freedom.

First, Christian freedom is just that: freedom *in Christ*, not freedom in and of itself. Because it is Christ who has set human beings free, they are obligated to him, bound to his service. Similarly, when he writes in v. 13 that "you were called to freedom," both parts of the

statement deserve attention. The freedom Paul envisions here is
freedom from the law, but equally important is his insistence on the
One who does the calling. For the third time in this letter (see 1:6 and
5:8), Paul urges the Galatians to remember their calling, a calling that
carries with it both freedom and obligation.

Second, the obligation of those who live in freedom is both an
obligation to Christ and an obligation to one another: "Through love
become slaves to one another" (v. 13). The imagery of slavery
startles and perhaps even offends, for it seems (in fact, it is!)
incompatible with our notions of freedom. Here as elsewhere (see
especially Rom. 6), however, Paul understands that all human
beings are free in some sense and enslaved in some sense. The
question is from what or whom they are free and to what or whom
they are enslaved. In Galatians, he urges freedom from the law, but
that same freedom carries with it enslavement to Christ as liberator
and also to others who belong to Christ. For Jews, of course, that
obligation to others was well known in the law, "You shall love your
neighbor as yourself."

Precisely because freedom can be misunderstood and abused,
Paul turns to the question of how one lives in this space *between* the
law and license (that is, freedom understood as autonomy). What
does freedom in Christ look like? The answer Paul gives to this
question is both profound and exceedingly difficult: "Live by the
Spirit" (Gal. 5:16). He introduces the contrast between flesh and
Spirit, a contrast that often proves confusing when "flesh" is heard
as a reference to some part of an individual (that is, to the flesh or
body as opposed to the spirit or soul).

Paul employs the word "flesh" in a variety of ways. "Flesh" can
refer in a neutral way to the fact of physical existence, as in the
phrase "flesh and blood" (see, for example, 1:16, which the NRSV
translates "any human being"). "Flesh" can also refer to natural
biological processes, as when Paul refers to Jesus as Israel's Messiah
"according to the flesh" (Rom. 9:5). In this lection, however, flesh
refers to a way of thinking or behaving that is confined to the human
sphere, that operates without the guidance of the Spirit of God.

Life in the sphere of the flesh, as Paul understands it, is characterized by a variety of evils: fornication, impurity, licentiousness,
idolatry, and so forth. While some of these might be characterized as
stemming from the limitations of physicality, others have nothing to
do with the human body as such and everything to do with the
orientation of the human being as a whole: quarrels, dissensions,
envy, and so forth.

By contrast, the "fruit of the Spirit," according to Paul, is "love, joy, peace, patience, kindness, generosity, faithfulness, gentleness, and self-control" (vs. 22–23). These gifts of the Spirit likewise have few intrinsic connections with a disciplining of the flesh. They reflect instead a mind-set that is informed by the Spirit of God and the real freedom that comes in Jesus Christ.

As commentaries on this passage will explain, much work on these passages in recent years has demonstrated that the lists of the "works of the flesh" and the "fruit of the Spirit" resemble some lists of virtues and vices that appear also in the writings of the moral philosophers of Paul's era. Such similarities should not surprise us, for they only mean that Paul attempted to state his case in terms that people could understand. More important, these similarities should not prevent our seeing the difference between the two. For the philosophers, knowledge of the virtues and vices provided a means for living the virtuous life. Paul, by contrast, holds that the virtues ("the fruit of the Spirit") come about, not as the accomplishments of human knowledge or wisdom, but as gifts of the Spirit for those who have been freed from the power of sin.

How is it possible to live as one ought without the security of the law? Paul's answer to this question is maddening: believers are to "live by the Spirit," which has certain recognizable characteristics (not rules). In a sense, the answer is tautologous: to live in Christ is to live in the Spirit, the gift of Christ. Behind such logic is, however, the radical insight that those who "belong to Christ Jesus" belong to him completely and can no longer belong to the law or to sin.

## Luke 9:51–62

Today's Gospel reading is the fifth in a series of twenty-seven from the Gospel of Luke, running from the week after Trinity Sunday until the end of liturgical Year C and All Saints. Today's reading is also the first in a series of nineteen to come from the lengthy travel narrative of Luke's Gospel (9:51–19:27), actually a literary unit in which there are repeated references to journeying and, specifically, to movement toward Jerusalem.

The primary thematic stress of the travel section has to do with the coming rejection, death, and resurrection of Jesus to happen at Jerusalem, and instruction to those who accompany Jesus regarding the demands of discipleship. Since the instruction includes a variety of material (short vignettes, a mission sermon, the commandments to love God and neighbor, parables, teaching on prayer, eschatological instruction, healings, and more), and since "Ordinary Time" in the liturgical calendar makes few seasonal demands, this may be a good time for a series of sermons from Luke on discipleship or "the way of the Lord." With the notion of life as a pilgrimage with Jesus as a thematic backdrop, there are texts here that are insightful about the common tasks and trials of being a faithful follower in a hostile world.

Luke 9:51 sets the stage and hints at what is coming. Two points are made: it is the determined intent of Jesus to get to Jerusalem, and the trip will conclude with his exaltation, the completion of the divine purpose. (The Greek literally reads, "As the days for his being taken up were coming to fulfillment . . .")

The persistence that pushes Jesus to the final events of his ministry is not to be equated with fate or some unavoidable social force, but the fulfillment of a divine plan for the salvation of God's people. Furthermore, Jesus' single-mindedness in finishing his task paves the way for the later word to the disciples that they too must not let even plausible distractions deter them from persistent discipleship (9:57–62).

Some of those accompanying Jesus are given a specific task—to go ahead of the group into a Samaritan village and make preparations for a visit. Immediately they meet rejection. We are not told clearly why the Samaritans are so inhospitable ("because his face was set toward Jerusalem"). Perhaps it is because they are offended that his destination is Mount Zion and not Mount Gerizim. In any case, the reader is alerted not to be surprised if the missions authorized by Jesus are met with formidable opposition.

In retaliation for the rejection, James and John, using words reminiscent of Elijah's deeds (2 Kings 1:10–14), propose consuming the Samaritans with fire from heaven—only to be rebuked by Jesus. Now is not the time for judgment on Samaria, a territory specifically designated for mission (Acts 1:8). Furthermore, Jesus' response to repeated rejection is not a macho display of violence (see Luke 23:34). Judgment is real, but it belongs to God and happens according to God's timetable (see 10:10–12).

Then come the encounters with the three would-be disciples (9:57–62). The first seems determined enough, but Jesus confronts him with the insecurity and homelessness of life with the Son of man. With the second, Jesus takes the initiative and sharply responds to his excuse about family obligations. The third professes commitment but couples it with a delaying tactic. Jesus' words with all three are unambiguous. Discipleship places heavy demands on followers. The way Jesus takes involves an unprotected mission, a clear choice about priorities, and a clean break with the past.

The engagement with each of the followers in a sense involves matters of home and its social responsibilities. Homelessness, for example, is a condition that involves not only physical but social dislocation. One is no longer related to the family of origin, but becomes a member of a community of wanderers. Rejecting the sacred obligations to bury one's parent in order to serve under the reign of God entails a separation from the structure of the biological family. Not saying goodbyes and not even looking back vividly depict the stark choices to be made. Though not stated, implied here may be the new, reconfigured family of those "who hear the word of God and do it" (8:21; compare 14:26).

While there is a metaphorical quality about Luke's language (for example, "Let the dead bury their own dead"), it nevertheless sharply confronts the family-oriented social system of the Jewish and Hellenistic worlds with the critical nature of discipleship. The translation to the contemporary setting must somehow not water down the rigor and severity of Jesus' demands. Accommodation to social structures rather than separation from them, divided loyalties rather than single-mindedness, are more likely to characterize modern Christians, and Jesus' words can continue to challenge, prod, and even anger today's followers and would-be followers.

# PROPER 9

The last in the series of texts relating to the prophetic ministries of Elijah and Elisha is the narrative of the healing of the Aramean general Naaman, 2 Kings 5:1–14. The passage is a study in contrasts, portraying the arrogance of the leprous Naaman, on the one hand, and the faithfulness of Naaman's anonymous servants, on the other. Because of the trust expressed by these unnamed menials and because of the power vested in Yahweh's prophet, Elisha, Naaman's body is renewed. But much of the theological force of the narrative is found in vs. 15–19, a section not included in the day's Old Testament lection. Because these verses describe the renewal of Naaman's innermost being, his "soul," the preacher will wish to bring them under consideration. Today's psalm, Ps. 30 (see the Third Sunday of Easter), expresses God's help in suffering.

The Epistle lection, Gal. 6:(1–6) 7–16, is composed of two quite different sections. The first section, vs. 1–10, concludes the consideration of the nature of the Christian life begun at 5:1 (see Proper 8). Here emphasis is placed on the responsibilities that Christians have for one another, a responsibility founded in the "law of Christ" (6:2) and one for which Christians are to be held accountable at the last judgment. The second section (vs. 11–16) recapitulates the entire Galatian letter, especially Paul's exclamation: "A new creation is everything!" (v. 15). The gospel's radical invasion of human life is linked to nothing less than a cosmic change, initiated by God.

Luke 10:1–11, 16–20 is so difficult a text that modern readers are tempted to dismiss it as irrelevant or nonsensical. To embark on a mission with no provision made for one's well-being and to assume absolute power over "snakes and scorpions," either real or figurative, would seem the height of folly. Yet the authority of this passage lies not in its details, but in its larger declarations. Crucial in this regard is Jesus' call for prayer on the part of those who undertake his mission. The Lord who sends out the laborers is also the Lord who is in charge of the harvest. The mission is tough, but the fact that it is also of absolute importance motivates those who are sent. Their joy flows not from their success, but from their identification with Jesus and with Jesus' people.

## 2 Kings 5:1–14

The stories concerning Elisha have a certain legendary cast in that many of them rely heavily on the element of the miraculous, a quality missing from literature associated with Amos, Hosea, and other "canonical" prophets. In many cases the miracles of Elisha are calculated to relieve human suffering (for example, 2 Kings 4:1–7), but others appear to serve human need only in an oblique manner, if at all (2:23–25). The present lection, an account of Elisha's restoration of a leprous man, is certainly among those miracle narratives that point to the prophet's concern for human suffering. Yet from the standpoint of the theology of the passage, much of the weight of the text lies in 5:15–19, verses the lectionary has omitted. Without vs. 15–19 the passage seems to be just "another" miracle story, as the reader is deprived of a report of the effect that Elisha's powers have on Naaman. Therefore, the preacher will probably wish to consider 5:1–19, as a primary theological unit.

We are not told the identity of the "king of Aram," but it is presumably Ben-hadad (note 8:7–10). (The NRSV has wisely transliterated the name of the Semitic kingdom centered in Damascus as "Aram," since the term "Syria," used in other translations, invites confusion with the modern nation of that name.) Joram, also called Jehoram (2 Kings 3:1), is probably the "king of Israel" who is so disturbed by Naaman's request (5:7). It is somewhat unusual that only the names of Elisha and Naaman are cited in this passage and that other persons remain anonymous, but that technique serves to heighten the roles of the two principals. Yet some of the unnamed individuals play significant parts in the unfolding drama: the "young girl captive" who tells Naaman's wife of Elisha's powers (vs. 2–3) and the "servants" of Naaman who persuade their master to follow the prophet's advice (v. 13). Sadly, the identity of these persons of debased social standing had been forgotten even by the time this story reached the final editors of 2 Kings, although without their trust in Elisha—and presumably in Elisha's God—the cure of Naaman would not have taken place.

One of the issues that the text addresses is the arrogance that results from great power, in this case political and military, and the hollowness of such arrogance. On the one hand is Naaman the great soldier, who disdains the simple instructions of the prophet because they appear to him to be too humdrum. He was expecting thunder and lightning—a theophany! If Yahweh, Israel's God, would not appear, at least Yahweh's representative could make sounds and gestures appropriate to Yahweh's greatness and suitable to his, Naaman's, elevated social standing (v. 11). (The marginal note in NRSV correctly points to the fact that "leprosy" in ancient Israel referred not necessarily to Hansen's disease, but to a wide variety of disorders of the skin [note Lev. 13]. In fact, in the public reading of Old Testament texts that contain the word "leprosy," the term "skin disease" is a helpful substitute.)

On the other hand is Naaman the wretched sufferer, whose condition of the skin is not only uncomfortable (presumably) and unsightly, but socially humiliating. For all his power and wealth, he cannot heal himself. His arrogance almost prevents the restoration of his health, as he considers it beneath his dignity to wash in the Jordan (note the last sentence in v. 12). But his folly is balanced by the wisdom of his servants (who, as menials, were uncontaminated by hubris), who talk him out of his rash disdain of Elisha's instructions. The one who commands armies but who cannot command the powers of his disease is saved, in part, by the humility of his slaves.

Another and more significant issue is the effect that Elisha's miracle has on Naaman. A frequent theme in the scriptures is the change in a person's attitude and orientation that the saving presence of God brings about. The psalms frequently express this reality, especially psalms of distress. In Ps. 51, for example, the psalmist promises that, on the forgiveness of his or her sin "I will teach transgressors your ways, and sinners will return to you" (Ps. 51:13). Psalm 30, also one of this day's lections, sings exuberantly:

> You have turned my mourning into dancing. . .
> so that my soul may praise you and not be silent.
> (Vs. 11–12)

The point is clear: when the redeeming grace of God is given an opportunity to enter the life of a person, that life can never, ever remain the same! It is a new life, reoriented, redirected.

The specific nature of Naaman's response may seem absurd to us, even comical. Because he assumes that all deities are territorial, his affirmation is that the only true God resides "in Israel" (v. 15). In gratitude and devotion to this God who has saved him, he requests that he be permitted to take part of Israel home with him, in the form of "two mule-loads of earth" (v. 17). He will then be able to worship the God of Israel on Israelite soil, a daring thing to do in light of the traditional enmity between his and Elisha's nation.

His change of heart is so thorough and sincere that his request for absolution in future instances of politically motivated idolatry is indulged by Elisha, who simply says, "Go in peace" (v. 19).

## Psalm 30

See the discussion of this passage under the Third Sunday of Easter.

## Galatians 6:(1–6) 7–16

Two distinct sections comprise this lection. The first (6:1–10) concludes the discussion of the Christian life begun in 5:1. The second (6:11–16) contains the postscript of the letter, in which Paul restates the fundamental claims of the whole of Galatians.

At first glance, vs. 1–10 appears somewhat disjointed, with its admonitions about restoring those who transgress (v. 1), sharing with those who teach (v. 6), and not growing weary (v. 9). What all the first six verses have in common, however, is the importance of mutual responsibility within the Christian community. The importance of restoring the transgressor "in a spirit of gentleness" derives from the importance of that person within the larger community (v. 1). Bearing "one another's burdens" (v. 2), of course, involves the understanding that Christians have a connection between them that requires mutual responsibility. To say that "all must carry their own loads" (v. 5) does not contradict this overriding theme, since carrying one's own load is a way of lessening the responsibility of others. Similarly, sharing with the teachers in the community comes about because of the community's cohesiveness.

For those who have experienced the church as a meddlesome place, a place for the invasion of privacy and the purveying of gossip, these words will be most unwelcome. And for those who experience the church as a disparate gathering of folk who seem to have little or nothing in common, these admonitions sound like a foreign tongue. They fundamentally challenge the isolation that runs through much of our church life. While Paul surely does not envision the church as a collection of intruders, he does understand

Christians to be profoundly connected with one another in ways that require mutual admonition and responsibility.

By caring for one another, Paul writes, Christians "fulfill the law of Christ" (v. 2). In a letter so concerned to counter the notion that Gentiles must adhere to the Mosaic law, this phrase comes as a shock. Interpreters disagree vehemently over Paul's meaning here, with proposals that include: Christ as an example ("law" here as principle), a new Messianic law, the love command of Jesus, and the Mosaic law reinterpreted. The issues are complicated, but the phrase itself reveals that Paul understands the primary norm of the Christian life to be Christ himself.

In the concluding verses of this discussion of ethics (vs. 7–10), Paul connects Christian behavior with eschatological judgment. A review of his other letters will demonstrate that this is typical of his reasoning (see, for example, Rom. 13:11–14; 1 Thess. 5:1–11). Unlike the moral philosophers of his day, who extolled good behavior as a means to the improvement of the individual's character, Paul places good behavior in an eschatological context. Simply put, the time has grown short, and how one lives is a matter of urgency.

The personal exclamation of v. 11 clearly identifies the transition to the letter's conclusion: "See what large letters I make when I am writing in my own hand!" Presumably, Paul dictated the bulk of this letter to a secretary but reserves the final lines for his own hand, drawing further attention to the importance of what he is about to say.

We may hope (and probably assume) that the initial hearers of this letter understood vs. 12–13 better than we do. Reconstructing the historical situation that causes Paul to charge those who teach the necessity of circumcising Gentiles with the motive of avoiding persecution has proved awkward, at best. And it is perhaps impossible to know how seriously to take his charge that these people do not themselves keep the law. The point he quickly reaches, however, is a contrast between the boasting of these teachers, which is a boasting in the flesh, and his own boasting, a boasting in the cross (vs. 13–14).

Verse 14 may sound a sweet, pious tone in our ears, until we recall the reality surrounding crucifixion in the ancient world. Death on the cross carried with it the kind of shame we might associate with death in the electric chair. To boast in nothing "except the cross" literally makes no sense. It makes sense only because God has used the cross itself to reveal God's Son, God's wisdom, God's power (see 1 Cor. 1:18–25).

With v. 15 Paul restates the letter as a whole, but with an astonishing twist: "neither circumcision *nor uncircumcision* is anything" (emphasis added). The words "nor uncircumcision" threaten to undo Paul's arduous argument that Gentiles must not be circumcised. If uncircumcision and circumcision alike count for nothing, then why has Paul so strenuously resisted the notion of circumcision?

The answer shortly follows: "A new creation is everything!" Here the NRSV enlarges on Paul's frustratingly brief Greek. Literally, what he writes is simply "new creation"—no verb, no predicate nominative. However, the NRSV rightly captures Paul's outburst. All that counts is this "new creation," in which neither circumcision nor uncircumcision commends persons to God.

At the beginning of Galatians, Paul speaks of the gospel's radical invasion of his own life, an invasion that resulted in the overthrow of the life he had regarded as exemplary (1:11–17). In the center of Galatians, it becomes clear that this radical invasion applies not to apostles alone but to all believers (3:27–29), for whom the customary divisions between human beings are no longer acceptable. As the letter concludes, the final card is revealed: the gospel is nothing less than a cosmic change, a "new creation" indeed!

## Luke 10:1–11, 16–20

When we come upon passages like Luke's report of Jesus' commission of the Seventy (10:1–11, 16–20), we are reminded of the need for a historical respect for the narrative, a willingness to let it be an account of the first-century community. The drive for "instant relevance" becomes a ludicrous, if not dangerous, inclination with a text like this. The directions to "carry no purse, no bag, no sandals," even when translated as "no wallet, no suitcase, no change of clothes," can be a counsel of irresponsibility if taken literally—not to mention the authority given to the Seventy to tread on snakes and scorpions and not be hurt.

Yet we dare not ignore Jesus' words of commission as if they were a modern embarrassment, merely an outmoded bit of advice for ancient times. The stress on the difficulty of the mission and the need for a spartan style, in fact, seem surprisingly immediate to contemporary disciples, who are called to bear witness in the post-Constantinian world. The increasing experience of the disestablishment of the church makes Jesus' directions amazingly up-to-date.

The mission of the Seventy (note the confusion in the manuscripts as to whether the number should be seventy or seventy-two) parallels the mission of the Twelve in 9:1–6, but expands the words of commission and elaborates on the success of the venture. We shall highlight three dimensions of Jesus' speech, and then look at his conversation with the Seventy when they return.

What is initially striking is *the subtle but critical call for prayer*. The sequence of a plentiful harvest and a slim work force would suggest a direct appeal for laborers, but instead the text reads, "Ask the Lord of the harvest to send out laborers into his harvest" (10:2). Later in the narrative, Luke provides more extended instructions about prayer (11:1–13), but here at the outset of the mission the Seventy are told to beseech the Lord of the harvest for a sufficient number of reapers.

The wording of 10:2 underscores the fact the Lord is not only in charge of the harvest but also in charge of sending the laborers. The authentic workers, those who will get the job done and reap what has been grown, are only those specifically sent by the Lord. This is not a place for self-appointed entrepreneurs, who chart their own course and work as if the outcome depended entirely on themselves. Petitionary prayer clarifies who is in charge and under whose authority one works. The Seventy are obviously part of the chosen work force, because they are immediately told to get on with the job ("Go on your way").

Prayer and a sense of being under commission are important because *the mission is tough*. "I am sending you out like lambs into the midst of wolves" (10:3). One could hardly have a more vivid picture of the precarious plight of the laborers. No mention here of a shepherd to protect the lambs—only their vulnerability to the wild animals. The declaration of the nearness of God's reign (10:9, 11) is simply not a popular theme everywhere, especially not among those in power, who find its coming a threat to their own stability. They are inclined to react with violence and brutality, because it is the only kind of response they know.

The difficulty of the mission accounts for the detailed instructions about traveling light. When one enters an environment likely to be hostile, one does not want to be encumbered with extra baggage or to risk too much with strangers met on the road. In so many ways "things" become a hindrance and not a help. Furthermore, one is not to make unnecessary trouble: Declare a "peace" on every house you enter; don't move from house to house as if searching for a more comfortable spot; eat what is put before you, whether kosher or not. In a word, keep yourself focused on what is really important, and don't be distracted by issues of little consequence.

The warning about the difficulty of the task is in no way meant to detract from *the absolutely critical importance of the mission*. Both to the towns that welcome the Seventy and to the towns that reject them, they are to announce, "The kingdom of God has come near" (10:9, 11). To one it comes as a word of salvation: the inbreaking of God's rule means deliverance and hope. To the other it comes as a word of judgment, a destiny comparable to Sodom. The stakes are high for those who receive or don't receive the laborers sent into the harvest.

The importance of the mission appears again in 10:16, when through a form of juridical identification both Jesus and God become linked with the laborers. The acceptance or rejection of the laborers becomes an acceptance or rejection of Jesus and God. In declaring God's rule, the Seventy are engaged in a life-or-death business.

According to Luke, the Seventy report a joyous and profitable mission (10:17). Their announcement that even the demons are subject to them evokes from Jesus a theological interpretation and a word of warning. On the one hand, Jesus sees that the exorcisms performed by the Seventy constitute an assault on the heart of the opposition, Satan himself. The rule of the enemy is being overcome. The conflict between the lambs and the wolves is a critical stage in the larger war between God and Satan. On the other hand, Jesus warns that they not become too preoccupied with their successes, but instead be content to be numbered among God's people. Their identity comes from their inclusion among a great and honored group.

# PROPER 10

Amos 7:7–17 introduces a series of lectionary readings from the prophets. The initial section of the passage is the third in a series of four visions experienced by Amos concerning God's judgment on Israel. Amos appears to have lost all hope that the people would realize the serious nature of their sin and renounce it. Because Amos has now come to terms with this melancholy reality, he also understands that God's judgment must inevitably come. The second section records negative reaction to Amos's preaching on the part of the nation's officials; yet Amos refuses to soften his words in spite of the ominous threats that are implied against him.

Psalm 82 is saturated with the mythological imagery of the world of ancient Israel's neighbors, and because of this feature it may sound strange to modern ears. Yet in its proclamation of the supreme rule of the God of Israel, the psalm delivers a quite contemporary message: those who forfeit loyalty to the true God will only have their lives dominated by false and destructive gods of their own creation.

The Epistle lection, Col. 1:1–14, is the first of several readings from Colossians. After a somewhat typical salutation (vs. 1–2), the text includes a remarkable statement of thanksgiving (vs. 3–8), which emphasizes the crucial place within the Christian life of the qualities of faith, love, and hope. Then the author discusses his prayers on behalf of his readers, prayers that center on their need for the "knowledge of God's will in all spiritual wisdom and understanding." Images of light, power, and redemption conclude the passage, perhaps reflections of a baptism formula.

The parable of the good Samaritan, Luke 10:25–37, is rendered extremely difficult for the preacher because of its familiarity to modern women and men, both those inside the church and those outside. At the same time, the secularization of the parable has resulted in important distortions of Jesus' message in delivering it.

The Samaritan was an outsider, a person looked down on by "good" Jewish society. Yet in an ironic twist the one who is "good" is this very outsider. The power of the parable does not end there, for as one begins to imagine its larger meanings, one places oneself in the ditch as the victim who is at the mercy of the very outsider who has been rejected. Thus the parable points to the role of Christ himself.

## Amos 7:7–17

With this text from Amos the lectionary begins a series of readings from the prophetic books (in the sense of books associated with individual prophetic figures), which continues for the balance of the liturgical year, the only quasi-exception being Proper 22 (Lamentations is associated with Jeremiah, but is no longer believed to have been written by him). The order is chronological, the first six texts (Proper 10 through Proper 15) being from preexilic prophets.

The passages appointed for this day and for Proper 11 both come from a section of the book of Amos in which four, or possibly five (depending on how one classifies them) related visions are recorded. The sequence of these visions is important and helps to set the theological outlook of the lectionary passages. The first two visions (7:1–3 and 7:4–6) are identical in form. The prophet sees images of destruction (locusts, fire) which indicate God's impending judgment on the people. In each case the prophet successfully intervenes, and Yahweh decides not to pursue the divine purpose. The second set of visions (7:7–9; 8:1–3) is similar in structure to the first pair, in that each begins with a vision of destruction. (The plumb line is obviously Yahweh's standard by which the people's justice and faithfulness are determined. For the reasons why the basket of summer fruit is a sign of judgment, see Proper 11.) But the second set of visions takes an ominous turn in that, following each vision, there is no attempt by the prophet to intervene on the people's behalf. What is more, there is no change in Yahweh's intentions: judgment appears inevitable; the people will be destroyed.

(A fifth vision is found in 9:1–4, but its form is considerably different from any of the visions in chaps. 7 and 8.)

Amos 7:7–9, which constitutes the beginning of the present lection, is thus a sharp turning point in the series of visions. One suggestion is that the prophet has become so discouraged about the possibility that the people will ever pull back from their sinful ways that he makes no effort to dissuade Yahweh from Yahweh's purpose, as he had in 7:2, 5. Amos's complaint is twofold: the people have turned their worship into a meaningless exercise (4:4–5) and they have replaced compassion with cruelty and greed in their dealings with one another (2:6–7). Those who possess power and wealth are especially condemned (6:4–7), and they and the nation will be forced into exile (note 3:2, Amos's message in a nutshell). The prophet's memorable appeal in 5:21–24, perhaps the most-often-quoted passage from Amos, seems to imply that he still has hope that the nation can be saved. But it lies beside another text, 5:18–20, which suggests that even Amos has lost hope for a reconciliation between the people and their God. Perhaps, then, 7:7–9 marks that moment in time when the prophet surrenders in anger and disgust over the people's ways. It appears to be Amos's way of saying, "You have been patient long enough, O Yahweh. I can no longer ask you to delay the inevitable consequences of the nation's sinfulness."

The balance of our passage, 7:10–17, contains one of the few biographical references to the prophet. (The book of Amos, it will be remembered, is a watershed in the writing of the Bible. Whereas earlier prophets had been remembered anecdotally—the stories about Elijah and Elisha are examples—Israel now begins to collect anthologies of what its prophets have *said*. The book of Amos thus helps give shape to the books of Hosea, Isaiah, Jeremiah, and the like.)

Amos's preaching (see 1:3–2:16, where we may have an entire sermon by the prophet) had reached the ears of those in high places, and the results were predictable. The prophet's attacks on social predators and on false worship threatened the political-religious establishment, because their interests were vested in precisely those abuses which Amos exposed. Because the temple at Bethel, like the Temple at Jerusalem, was under the protection of the king, the priest Amaziah had no trouble receiving royal sanction for his order to Amos to leave the land. This is a pattern that would be repeated again and again, involving such persons as Jeremiah, John the Baptist, and—of course—Jesus himself. (Also note 1 Kings 22:1–28, which records a similar incident a century before Amos.)

At first glance, Amos's reply in Amos 7:14–15 seems puzzling. How is it that this man could claim to be "no prophet . . ."? When one remembers, however, that much early Israelite prophetic activity was carried on by groups like the "company of prophets" of Elijah and Elisha (see 2 Kings 2:7; note also 1 Sam. 10:5), it becomes evident that Amos is saying that he belongs to no prophetic band, but has been designated by Yahweh to be a solitary bearer of the divine word. How much lonelier this would have made Amos's task! Amos had obeyed the command of God to assume the pro-

phetic role, not because he cherished it, but because, like Jeremiah
(Jer. 20:7–9), he had no alternative. He could not be Yahweh's person
and say no to the terrible task to which Yahweh called him. And so
he answers Amaziah's demand with a further promise of Yahweh's
judgment to come (vs. 16–17). Whether he was punished by the
authorities for this faithfulness we can only guess.

## Psalm 82

Psalm 82 may sound strange to many people, since more than any
other psalm it gives us a view of the ancient Near Eastern polytheism
that formed Israel's religious background. In Canaanite religion, it
was the high God El who convened the council of the gods. (For
other Old Testament views of this concept, see, for example, Ps.
58:1–2; 1 Kings 22:19–23; and Job 1:6–12.) In Ps. 82:1, it is Israel's God
who has displaced El and who convenes what proves to be an
extraordinary meeting. Israel's God proceeds to put the other gods
on trial. After the gods are indicted (vs. 2–4), the case is summarized
(v. 5), and the sentence is announced (vs. 6–7). Verse 8 is the
psalmist's plea for God to claim the dominion that the gods had
formerly held, and to rule justly. In essence, then, Ps. 82 affirms
again what we have identified as the theological "heart" of the
Psalter: the Lord reigns (see especially Pss. 96, 97, and 99).

The key issue in the trial of the gods is how they "judge" (v. 2) or
administer "justice" (v. 3; note too the two other occurrences of the
root špṭ—"holds judgment" in v. 1 and "judge" in v. 8). In a role that
combines the functions of prosecutor and judge, God accuses the
gods of judging "unjustly" ('āwel) and showing partiality (v. 2). The
inadequacy of such behavior is also clear in another context, where
God commands the people of Israel to "do no injustice ['āwel] in
judgment [mišpāṭ]" and "not be partial" (Lev. 19:15). The rationale
for these commandments involves the nature of divinity. Leviticus
19, part of the Holiness Code, is governed by the opening exhortation, "You shall be holy, for I the LORD your God am holy" (19:2). In
short, injustice among humans and certainly injustice among the
gods violates the very nature of divinity and the divine will for the
world.

The importance of justice in the human realm is emphasized in Ps.
82:3–4. The series of imperatives does not really function to exhort
the gods, but rather to indict them. The gods have failed to "give
justice" and "maintain the right" (v. 3). The roots of these two verbs
often appear in noun forms as the parallel pair "justice" and

"righteousness," especially in the prophets (see Amos 5:7, 24; 6:12; and the Old Testament lesson for the day). Justice and righteousness exist where human relationships are ordered properly; the criterion is what is done for the categories of people mentioned in vs. 3–4—the weak, the orphaned, the lowly, the destitute, and the needy. Not surprisingly, another place that justice and righteousness appear as parallels is in the psalms that proclaim the Lord's reign (see Pss. 97:2; 99:4; compare 96:10, 13; 98:9). Again the establishment of justice and righteousness is the measure both of divinity and of human life as God intends it. God intends all persons, especially the powerless, to have access to the resources that make life possible.

The speaker in 82:5 could be the psalmist as narrator, but it seems more likely that God continues to speak. The case against the gods is summarized, and the result of their failure is stated. The shaking of "all the foundations of the earth" represents a worst-case scenario. According to the ancient view of the world, the mountains were the foundations that held the sky up and held the waters back from flooding dry land. For the foundations to be shaken meant that the whole creation was threatened by chaotic collapse (see Isa. 24:18–19; Ps. 46:1–3). In other words, v. 5 suggests that injustice destroys the world! Because the gods have failed to do justice, they are guilty of destroying human life as God intends it, and thus they deserve to die (vs. 6–7). The death of the gods opens the way for Yahweh's reign of justice (v. 8).

How do we hear such an overtly mythological text in our very different world? Needless to say, Ps. 82 is a poetic profession of faith, not a literal description of a trial in heaven. In other words, without adopting the ancient Near Eastern worldview, we can still appreciate the conviction that injustice destroys the world. In fact, we can see it happening around us in the chaotic conditions that exist in our world, in our cities and neighborhoods, in our schools and churches and homes. The fact that the foundations of the earth are still shaking in our day suggests again that Ps. 82 does not literally describe the death of the gods, but rather denies them ultimacy. As the apostle Paul put it in 1 Cor. 8:5–6: "Indeed, even though there may be so-called gods in heaven or on earth—as in fact there are many gods and many lords—yet for us there is one God, the Father, from whom are all things and for whom we exist, and one Lord, Jesus Christ, through whom are all things and through whom we exist." Paul elsewhere refers to these "so-called gods" as "the rulers and authorities" (Col. 2:15; compare RSV "the principalities and powers"; see also Eph. 3:10); and they are still with us in many forms—wherever and whenever some persons benefit by denying the God-given humanity of other persons. As James L. Mays suggests, "As long as nations and their peoples do not see the reign of God as the reality that determines their way and destiny, there will be other gods who play that role" (*Psalms*, Interpretation series; Louisville, Ky.: John Knox Press, 1994).

For followers of Jesus Christ, the gods are dead; all "rulers and authorities" other than the Lord have been dethroned. We profess to live solely under the reign of God that Jesus announced and embodied, in a ministry of justice and righteousness that was especially directed to the weak and the needy. Thus we cannot help hearing the plea of Ps. 82:8 in terms of the prayer Jesus taught: "Your kingdom come. Your will be done, *on earth* as it is in heaven" (Matt. 6:10, emphasis added).

## Colossians 1:1–14

This lection opens in a familiar way, both for its initial recipients and for contemporary readers. Whether or not the original audience had previously received letters from a Christian apostle, they certainly knew what to expect from the beginning of a letter. Even the thanksgivings of early Christian letters, which may sound odd to modern ears, were standard fare. "I thank the lord Serapis [that is, the god] that when I was in peril on the sea he saved me immediately," writes one young man to his father. Another writes to his mother: "And continually I pray that you may be in health. I make intercession for you day by day to the lord Serapis." (These letters may be found in Howard Clark Kee, *The Origins of Christianity*; Englewood Cliffs, N.J.: Prentice-Hall, 1973, pp. 264–65.)

For contemporary readers, the familiarity stems from our knowledge of the Pauline letters as a whole. In this particular instance, of course, there has been considerable debate regarding the authorship of Colossians. While the details of that debate have no place in the pulpit, the discussion itself does illuminate certain aspects of this letter (for example, the very high Christology of Col. 1:15–20 and the identification of the church with Christ's body in 1:24). Suggesting that the letter could have been written by a student or disciple of Paul may also be a way of highlighting the impact of Paul and the collegial nature of his ministry.

The thanksgiving of this letter (1:3–8) consists of one long Greek sentence, although English translations will not reflect that fact. It moves almost in a circle, from thankfulness for the faith, love, and hope of the Colossians to the growth of the gospel, and back to the love of the Colossians (as reported by Epaphras). To put it somewhat differently, the thanksgiving begins locally and specifically, with its focus on the Christian life and experience of this particular audience. Then it moves in a more general direction, toward the "bearing fruit and growing" of the gospel in the whole world (v. 6). Finally, it returns to the specific experience of this local group with the ministry of Epaphras.

With vs. 9–14, the author takes up his prayers of intercession on behalf of this congregation. He prays that they will have knowledge and strength. In light of the remainder of the letter, with its concerns about some false teachers who might mislead the Colossians, this prayer for knowledge and strength has a very special force to it. Although the problem at Colossae cannot be reconstructed precisely, glimpses through the letter suggest that the deceivers (2:4) who threaten have emphasized their own knowledge and their own strength. They introduce "plausible arguments" (2:4) and parade their own "philosophy and empty deceit, according to human tradition" (2:8). They encourage some teachings with "an appearance of wisdom" (2:23).

The intercessory prayer that begins in 1:9 ably responds to this emphasis on human wisdom, a temptation in every age. The writer prays for knowledge, but knowledge of a particular sort: "knowledge of God's will in all spiritual wisdom and understanding" (v. 9). This knowledge does not exist for its own sake or as an end in itself, but "so that you may lead lives worthy of the Lord" (v. 10). Likewise, the strength the writer seeks on behalf of the Colossians is a strength that comes from God and enables its recipients to endure and give thanks to God (vs. 11–12). Only such knowledge and strength genuinely deserve to be called by those names.

The prayer concludes with traditional language that may have been drawn from a baptismal liturgy. Three powerful images about God's action on behalf of humankind come together here. First, God "has enabled you to share in the inheritance of the saints in the light" (v. 12). We find this imagery of light not only in Judaism and Christianity, but in many other religious traditions. It stems from the experience, universal in a world without artificial illumination, of stumbling in the dark of night versus walking with confidence in the light of day.

Second, God has "rescued us from the power of darkness and transferred us into the kingdom of his beloved Son" (v. 13). The contrast between two realms of power strongly suggests that the "power of darkness" here is not simply the darkness of night but the realm of Satan, who takes advantage of the night (compare Luke 22:53). God has literally moved people from one region to another.

Third, by means of this movement "we have redemption, the forgiveness of sins." Elsewhere, outside the New Testament, redemption refers to release from imprisonment or slavery. In the Pauline letters, however, it takes on an eschatological flavor, as in Rom. 8:23 and Eph. 4:30. The fact that Colossians refers to redemption as a present state may weigh against its having been written by Paul.

Surely the joy and confidence of this letter prompted a joyous and confident response on the part of its first audience. From the vantage point of the church at the end of the twentieth century, however, an element of irony intrudes when Col. 1:6 refers to the gospel's growth "in the whole world." By the time this letter was written, of course, the gospel was spreading rapidly, but a generous amount of hyperbole is involved in the phrase "the whole world." By contrast with our crisis of confidence over the future of the church, the author of this letter knew that the gospel could not ultimately be defeated.

## Luke 10:25–37

What possibly new and fresh word can one say about the parable of the good Samaritan? No portion of scripture is so widely known and quoted as this story of Jesus. What makes preaching on it so difficult is the fact that the good Samaritan has become a secularized saint. Hospitals, helping groups, and civic awards are named after him, without much attention to who he is or who introduced him into the literary world in the first place. To be a good Samaritan is shorthand for helping once a week at the local soup kitchen, going out of one's way at the Christmas season to see that the food baskets get delivered to the neediest people, sacrificing five Saturdays in a row to work on a Habitat for Humanity project.

There is nothing wrong with lending a helping hand, mind you. It is just that our secularized saint has little resemblance to the character in Jesus' story. Wrenching him out of his context and making him a symbol for do-goodism (usually the favored fortunate doing good to the unattractive, less fortunate) misses the sharp bite of the parable and helps us avoid its shocking and threatening challenge. The task the preacher faces is to find a means to displace the distorted image of popular piety (Christian and non-Christian) and invite the congregation to hear the disturbing tale afresh. Maybe a paraphrase like that of the *Cotton Patch Version* would help.

It is essential to begin with the lawyer's initial interchange with Jesus (Luke 10:25–29). While his question about inheriting eternal life is raised "to test Jesus," the mood of the scene does not seem peculiarly combative. When directed by Jesus to the Torah, this expert in the Torah provides the right answer. He is commended by Jesus, but then, lest he think this a purely academic debate, he is also told, "Do this, and you will live" (10:28).

"Wanting to justify himself," the lawyer poses the question, "And who is my neighbor?" Does this mean that he is a bit embarrassed by his previous question about eternal life, which Jesus made him answer for himself? Does he want to "justify himself" by raising another, more complex issue? Or is his counterquestion a way of avoiding the personal directness of Jesus' response ("Do this, and you will live")? It is hard to tell. In either case, his second question is a legitimate one, debated often by the scribes, especially since the original command to love the neighbor specifies "your kin" and "any of your people" (Lev. 19:17–18; compare Matt. 5:43).

Instead of a direct answer, the lawyer gets a parable—maybe a more direct answer than he bargained for. Four features of the story need to be underscored. First, the priest and the Levite ought not to be immediately turned into bad guys—either hardhearted and calloused or too prissy to get their hands dirty. Their decision to pass by on the other side would not have been a surprise to, nor would it likely have been condemned by, Jesus' hearers. The victim in the ditch no doubt seemed to be dead ("half dead"), and priests were forbidden from going where there was a dead body, even when the dead body was a parent (Lev. 21:10–11). The priest and Levite simply represent the traditional way religious figures would deal with a situation like this.

Second, the Samaritan really was a despised person. Adding the adjective "good" (not in the parable) to Samaritan has tended to reduce the element of racial tension that underlies the story and gives it its force. To the lawyer, to the Jews in Jesus' audience, and to Luke's readers, there was no misunderstanding about Samaritans. (After all, in the narrative a Samaritan village had just denied welcome to Jesus and the disciples, and James and John wanted to call down fire to consume it, Luke 9:52–54.) They were half-breeds, who had refused to participate in the restoration of Jerusalem and had aided the Syrian leaders in their wars against the Jews. Their temple had been destroyed by a Jewish high priest. Anyone else might have been the third character coming along the road to Jericho, but Jesus' choice of the Samaritan, the ultimate outsider, to help the victim, was (and is) a stunner. To miss this is to miss a major feature of the story.

Third, the question "Who is my neighbor?" gets asked again, this time by Jesus, and answered by the lawyer (10:36–37). He, a Jew, has to acknowledge that the despised Samaritan plays out the role of neighborliness by all he does for the victim. He becomes then the object of the command of Lev. 19:17–18, not just "your kin" and "any of your people." The result is to destroy any parochial understandings of God that presume God's interest is limited to "me and my family" and to expose deep-seated hatreds between individuals, races, and nations that have become an accepted way of life.

Finally, a parable is meant to arouse the imagination in ways that cannot always be anticipated or, as C. H. Dodd said in his classic definition, it leaves "the mind in sufficient doubt about its precise application to tease it into active thought" (C. H. Dodd, *The Parables of the Kingdom*; New York: Charles Scribner's Sons, 1961, p. 5). One way the imagination is stirred is by the invitation the parable makes to the hearer to identify with the victim in the ditch. Instead of being the favored fortunate who helps the less fortunate, the hearer begins to sense himself or herself as the needy at the mercy of the outsider, who is otherwise thought of as the enemy. It is certainly not the way the lawyer expected things to turn out.

Another way the imagination has been stirred by interpreters all the way back to patristic times is to recognize the Samaritan as Christ, the ultimate helper, who sees, has compassion for, and restores the beaten, naked figure whom religious figures have ignored. Rather than being a secularized saint, the Samaritan symbolizes the divine Prophet.

# PROPER 11

Amos 8:1–12 is, in certain respects, a companion piece to 7:1–17 (see Proper 10), in that both texts record visionary experiences of the prophet which become vehicles for delivering words of profound judgment. In the present Old Testament lection, the vision of judgment (vs. 1–3) is followed by a statement of God's impending justice, which forms an important bridge between Old Testament prophecy and apocalyptic.

Psalm 52 is quite curious in that it is addressed to some anonymous tyrant who, out of love for evil, has worked against God. But God will not allow such tyranny to go unchecked (v. 5) and will ultimately vindicate those who have lived faithful lives. Such faithful persons are compared to "a green olive tree" (v. 8), their sustenance coming from the permanent, enduring love of a God who will never tolerate tyrants or their ways.

It is probably a pupil of Paul, rather than the apostle himself, who is responsible for reinterpreting an existing hymn in Col. 1:15–28. The purpose of the hymn (vs. 15–20) is to praise a cosmic Christ, but the author of the letter has reshaped the hymn so as to heighten the connection between the cosmic Christ and the church, his earthly body. Verses 21–27 form a kind of commentary on the reshaped hymn and reinforce the images of a transcendent, yet indwelling Christ.

The familiar complaint of Martha directed against her sister, Mary, constitutes the Gospel lection for this day, Luke 10:38–42. It is easy to misunderstand this incident and see it as the result of Martha's whining nature. On the other hand, if placed in its larger context, the pericope is seen as balanced by 10:25–37 (see Proper 10). The parable of the good Samaritan suggests that listening without doing is an empty exercise. The story of Martha and Mary maintains that doing without listening is equally futile.

## Amos 8:1–12

This lection begins with the fourth in a series of four visions (8:1–3) in the book of Amos and, like the third vision, this one carries a message of unrelieved judgment (see the discussion of 7:7–9, Proper 10). It is almost impossible to reproduce in English translation the Hebrew wordplay on which the vision is based (NRSV marginal notes for 8:2 point to the homophonic quality of the Hebrew terms: *qayis,* meaning "summer fruit," and *qēs,* "end"). The Revised English Bible catches the flavor of the passage, if not its precise meaning, with this rendering of v. 2:

> "What is it that you are looking at, Amos?" he said. I answered, "A basket of ripe summer fruit." Then the LORD said to me, "The time is ripe for my people Israel. Never again shall I pardon them."

(Comparison may be made with a similar translation in the Jerusalem Bible.)

There is no effort on the part of the prophet to dissuade Yahweh from the terrible tragedy to come, as there was in 7:1–3 and 7:4–6. It is as if the prophet has lost all hope that the people will turn from their wickedness; Amos has become resigned to the self-destruction of Yahweh's beloved nation (compare 3:2). The use of the phrase "songs of the temple" (v. 3) reminds one of 5:23, part of what is probably the most-often-cited passage from the book of Amos (5:21–24). In that verse, "noise" (*hāmôn*) in the phrase "noise of your songs" is sometimes used in the sense of "great racket" or "cacophony." Amos thus already has a negative opinion of the liturgical music used in the royal sanctuary at Bethel (see 7:10), and he here declares that it will be transformed into "wailing" in the coming Day of Yahweh (see Amos's seminal description of the Day of Yahweh in 5:18–20). Death and destruction will be on every hand.

The relationship between 8:1–3 and the balance of the passage appointed by the lectionary is not altogether clear, but vs. 4–12 should probably be viewed as being a commentary on the vision, or perhaps a sermon inspired by the vision, and not part of the vision itself. The reason for arriving at this conclusion goes something like this:

The first two visions are positive in tone: the nation will be allowed to live. It is not until the third vision with its damning indictment ("the sanctuaries of Israel shall be laid waste," 7:9) that the authorities protest. Thus, according to this manner of looking at the text, 7:10–17 is not just an autobiographical digression, but is organically related to the third vision. In other words, Amos's declaration of the vision precipitates the enraged response of Amaziah. Following this line of reasoning farther, 8:4–12 may be viewed as the prophet's own expansion of Yahweh's message in 8:2b–3. Just as 7:7–9 led to the events/words of 7:10–17, so 8:1–3 inspired the prophet's message in 8:4–12.

Amos 8:4–12 contains some of the most terrifying words of judgment in all of the Old Testament, and it is in passages such as this that one senses that prophecy is being transformed into apocalyptic. The passage begins in a concrete enough setting: the contemporaries of Jeroboam II live lives characterized by such greed and oppression that Yahweh simply will not delay imposing judgment. Merchants fret that the arrival of a holy day ("new moon," "sabbath" of v. 5) closes their markets, and they can hardly contain themselves until the resumption of their crooked trades ("ephah" of v. 5 is a measure of quantity, "shekel," of course, a monetary unit). The language of v. 6 seems, at first glance, to suggest slavery, a terrible reality in the nations of the ancient world, including Israel. But the slave images here are probably metaphors for economic conditions, generally, that dehumanize women and men.

Verses 7 and 8 spell out the consequences of such immoral activity. Yahweh is a God of justice, and will brook no violation of that basic principle by which both Yahweh and Yahweh's people are to live. (Notice that Amos, like other prophets, feels no need to argue for the basic justice in Yahweh's nature. That reality is assumed, because it was made quite clear when the nation was [re-]constituted on Mount Sinai.) The "pride of Jacob" in v. 7 might also be translated (as in REB) the "arrogance of Jacob." In other words, the false pride of the nation is bringing about its downfall. But the phrase may also be understood positively: the "majesty" or "wealth of Jacob," in which case it becomes a euphemism for Yahweh. Read in this manner, the passage is stating that, because of the kind of being Yahweh is, judgment will surely transpire.

In vs. 9–12 the language begins to hint at apocalyptic. The text is moving us beyond a specific point in time, c. 750 B.C., and is beginning to view a cosmic judgment. This is especially so in vs. 9 and 12. Cosmic portents of God's final judgment are often cited in apocalyptic literature (compare Joel 2:30–31). As for the quality of God's judgment, v. 12 indicates that this is to be more than the violent intrusion of a foreign army. It will be nothing other than alienation from God, the most dreadful judgment of all.

## Psalm 52

Unlike most other psalms, Ps. 52 is neither prayer nor praise directed to God. Rather, vs. 1–5 are addressed to a "mighty one"— apparently a wicked, powerful person who intends to do violence to the psalmist and perhaps others of "the righteous" (v. 6) or "the faithful" (v. 9). Verse 6 is an affirmation about the righteous, who are then quoted in v. 7. Verse 8 is the psalmist's profession of faith. Only in v. 9 is God addressed directly. The uniqueness of Ps. 52 means that it "resists form-critical analysis"; it is sometimes categorized as a prophetic exhortation or "communal instruction" (see Erhard Gerstenberger, *Psalms, Part 1*; Grand Rapids: Wm. B. Eerdmans Publishing Co., 1988, p. 216). The content of this exhortation or instruction focuses on the nature of true security, wealth, and power.

The alternatives for seeking security are clearly contrasted in v. 1, although the NRSV obscures the matter. Marvin Tate (*Psalms 51—100*, Word Biblical Commentary 20; Dallas: Word, 1990, p. 32) translates v. 1 as follows:

> Why brag about evil, you hero!
> —God's loyal-love [*ḥesed*] does not cease.

As this translation and the subsequent verses suggest, security may be sought in self-assertion at the expense of others. This is what the "mighty one" does; he has no qualms about lying, cheating, and stealing in order to get ahead (see the description of the perpetrators of evil in Amos 8:4–6, part of the Old Testament lesson for the day). In Tate's translation, "hero" is used sarcastically; others suggest the derisive term "big shot." In any case, this person *loves* (vs. 3, 4) "evil" (v. 3; the word "mischief" in v. 1 is the same Hebrew root) and is willing to use any means to get his or her own way, regardless of how destructive (v. 2; the same Hebrew word "destruction" appears in v. 7, where NRSV translates it as "wealth") or manipulative (see "treachery" in v. 2 and "deceitful" in v. 4; these words are from the same Hebrew root). The "mighty one" shows no concern for doing what is "good" (v. 3; see also v. 9 and Pss. 34:15; 37:3, 27; Amos 5:14–15; and Micah 3:2) or speaking what is "right" (Ps. 52:3; NRSV "the truth"). As James L. Mays puts it, "The portrait is that of a person who turns human capacities and possession into the basis of his existence" (*Psalms*, Interpretation series; Louisville, Ky.: John Knox Press, 1994). In short, the "mighty one" embodies what is the essence of wickedness in the Psalms—autonomy, "self-rule" (see Ps. 1, Sixth Sunday After Epiphany).

The alternative to autonomy is dependence on God and God's *hesed* (v. 1; "steadfast love," "loyal love"). Verse 1 already suggests that this alternative is the only true and enduring one, and v. 5 tells why (see Ps. 73:18–20). The affirmation that God "will uproot" the wicked anticipates the image of the psalmist as a stable, fruitful tree in 52:8, which also contains the psalmist's explicit assertion that she or he has chosen the proper alternative—"I trust in the steadfast love of God forever and ever." The psalmist knows the secret of life that has eluded the wicked: life depends ultimately on God, not on ourselves and our possessions (see Luke 12:13–21, especially v. 15).

The judgment announced in Ps. 52:5 will be witnessed by "the righteous" (v. 6), who will take it as confirmation of their choice of dependence on God. Their laughter will echo God's laughter at those who oppose the divine will (see Pss. 2:4; 37:13; 59:8; see Prov. 1:26). To "take refuge" (Ps. 52:7) or seek security in "riches" or in self-assertive attempts to destroy others (NRSV "wealth") or in anything less than God is finally futile (compare Pss. 37:1–11, 37–40; 49:5–6). Psalm 52:5–7 does not describe a reward/punishment scheme that operates in an overtly tangible way. The punishment of the wicked is that they cut themselves off from God, who is the source of life, and the reward of the righteous is that they are grounded in God and thus connected to life's source and destiny (see above-mentioned commentary on Ps. 1).

Verse 8 of Ps. 52 articulates the psalmist's connection to the source of life. Like a tree growing on the Temple grounds, the psalmist is rooted in God (see Pss. 1:3; 92:12–15; Jer. 17:5–8). In explicit contrast to the "mighty one," the psalmist's trust is placed not in the self or in riches, but in God's *hesed*, which is "forever and ever" (52:8; see v. 1; and note "forever" in v. 5). Consequently, while the existence of the wicked is characterized by greed (vs. 2–4, 7), the life of the psalmist is characterized by gratitude to God (v. 9). His or her life becomes a witness to others—"the faithful" (v. 9)—of God's "name" or character. Thus, he or she promotes the "good" that the wicked spurn (vs. 3, 9). The NRSV's "proclaim" is literally "wait for," "hope." The psalmist is an example of those who, surrounded by opposition, live by faith and hope.

The title of the psalm attributes it to David at a point when Saul was seeking to kill him and when Doeg, one of Saul's servants, informed Saul of David's locale (see 1 Sam. 21:1–22:19; 22:9 is quoted in the title). This attribution should be taken illustratively rather than historically. Other servants of God were also threatened by rich and powerful enemies—for instance, Amos (see Amos 7:10–17), Jeremiah (see Jer. 26:10–19 and 38:1–13), Jesus. For those of us called to follow Jesus, the alternatives presented in Ps. 52 are still very real. We can live for ourselves, or we can live for God. "In the midst of the growing secularism of North American society, and the culture's increased hostility to the gospel," the choice to trust God will be both increasingly difficult and increasingly important (quoted from "The Report of the Special Committee to Study Theological Institutions to the 205th General Assembly of the Presbyterian Church (U.S.A.)").

## Colossians 1:15–28

One particularly sensitive focal point for the church's quarrels regarding the use of inclusive language has been the hymnal. Some Christians press for editing traditional hymns so that they will reflect the presence of both genders among the children of God and the presence of both maternal and paternal characteristics in God, while others resist any alteration to familiar wording. The importance of the hymns used in corporate worship may be gauged by the intensity of this debate, as both sides understand the ability of words sung as proclamation and confession to shape developing faith.

Both sides in the debate might be surprised to realize how early in the church's life theological debate was carried on through hymns, for there is evidence of such debate even in the New Testament itself. In Col. 1, the writer (probably a student of Paul's) employs what may well have been a familiar hymn, but he edits and interprets the hymn so as to make a particular point for this congregation.

Despite many careful scholarly attempts at historical reconstruction, the situation at Colossae remains very much an enigma. Some comments in the letter suggest that the writer's opponents insist on various ascetic practices (2:16–19), and others seem to assume highly abstract philosophical speculation that would be compatible with Gnosticlike thinking (2:8). *Perhaps* some at Colossae advocate a mystical approach to Christianity, with asceticism as a means of enhancing one's mystical access to God. Read in that context, the hymn of Col. 1 grants some of what the opponents are arguing but also provides a serious challenge to their presuppositions.

The hymn, which constitutes 1:15–20, interprets Christ in exalted and cosmic language. He is "the image of the invisible God, the firstborn of all creation" (v. 15). "All things have been created through him and for him" (v. 16), and "in him all the fullness of God was pleased to dwell" (v. 19). If this sort of thinking sounds foreign to the ears of contemporary Christians, it would not have seemed odd in the first century. Already Proverbs speaks of the figure of

Wisdom as the first of God's creatures (Prov. 8:22–31) and the means by which God founded the earth (Prov. 3:19); rabbinic tradition will later refer to Torah as God's instrument of creation. By referring to Christ in this way, then, early Christians confess that they cannot imagine a time, even the time of creation, without Christ.

The writer of Colossians endorses this viewpoint, but he also edits the hymn. Scholars differ in their analyses of the redaction, although they generally agree on at least two additions: "the church" in v. 18 and "through the blood of his cross" in v. 20. Importantly, each of these additions has the effect of connecting the "cosmic Christ" firmly with earthly existence.

The statement that Christ is "the head of the body, the church" (v. 18) has received much attention because the genuine Pauline letters speak of the church as Christ's body (for example, 1 Cor. 12:12–31) but not of Christ as its head. What may be more important for understanding the passage than this variation, however, is the fact that the reference to the church firmly connects Christ with earthly existence. Christ is not a cosmic presence, abstracted from the level of everyday life and accessible only to the spiritually elite; he is present in the church, which is nothing less than his own body.

Similarly, the addition of the phrase "through the blood of his cross" (Col. 1:20) recalls the fact that the human existence of Jesus Christ culminated in a violent, physical death. Blunt as the language is, it has the effect of pulling the Colossians back down to earth. The Christ-event has its origin before Creation and it has cosmic implications, but its intersection with human history was real, concrete, and brutal.

Verses 21–23 reinforce this general direction in the interpretation of the hymn. Here the reconciliation of "all things" (v. 20) becomes concretized in the reconciliation of "estranged and hostile" humanity through the death of Jesus Christ. Moreover, that reconciliation has ethical consequences. Those who have been reconciled must "continue securely established and steadfast in the faith" (v. 23). The exaltation of the cosmic Christ is not some grand and glorious scene to be witnessed by a passive, unchanged humanity, but an exaltation that manifests itself in a reconciled and faithful humankind. Here the writer resumes the language of rescue and transfer that introduced the hymn in vs. 12–14.

The lection continues through 1:24, but v. 24 actually introduces a new section that continues through 2:5, as the NRSV paragraphing indicates. Here the writer turns to Paul's ministry as a concrete instance of the reconciliation brought about by Christ. The perplexing statement that Paul's ministry involves "completing what is lacking in Christ's afflictions for the sake of his body" (v. 24) has raised a number of questions. Since the word the NRSV translates as "affliction" (*thlipsis*) elsewhere has strong apocalyptic connections (see, for example, "suffering" in Mark 13:19 and "the great ordeal" in Rev. 7:14), the "afflictions" may refer less to physical suffering than to the turmoil that accompanies the apocalyptic events. That is, Paul's ministry is part of the final revelation of God's ultimate mysteries.

## Luke 10:38–42

The Gospel readings for the past three Sundays have come from the beginning of Luke's travel narrative (9:51–19:27) and have concerned the theme of discipleship—the sharpness of the call, the vulnerability of those sent, and the practicality of helping and being helped. At a first reading of the story of Martha and Mary (10:38–42), one might reasonably ask what this incident has to do with discipleship? It seems more like a typical family squabble that Jesus settles by giving each participant the right to do her own thing. A careful examination not only of the story but of its location following the parable of the despised Samaritan, however, yields a different conclusion.

Martha comes on the scene first, as a woman who welcomes Jesus into her home. Though the phrase "her home" can be questioned on textual grounds, Martha's action establishes her as the leader of the household. She is clearly in charge, as women in the first century usually were in the limited world of the home. But the *responsibilities* of the household also fall on Martha. We are not specifically told that a meal is being prepared, but it is not hard to imagine, since the words behind "many tasks" and "to do all the work" (*diakonia, diakoneō*) are commonly used for "waiting tables."

Martha very naturally becomes upset that her sister, Mary, spends all her time with Jesus and does not help with the family chores. We miss the point if we caricature Martha as an obsessive type who gets angry because she wants to be sure that everyone works as hard as she does. For the narrator, there clearly are many chores to be done, and Martha seems more distracted by the work that has piled up, with guests in the house, than by some inner need to see to it that if she is working, then, by golly, Mary is going to work too. There are apparently no servants to help, as Martha is working by herself.

Why does Martha go to Jesus with her complaint rather than to

Mary? Who knows? Maybe there is a history of Mary's not helping with the housework. Maybe there has been a family rift. Maybe it is simply the narrator's way of having Jesus confirm Mary's choice. In any case, Martha's preoccupations with the household responsibilities are given secondary priority by Jesus' statement that "Mary has chosen the better part" (10:42).

What is "the better part" Mary has chosen? Interestingly, the narrator tells us only two things about Mary. She "sat at the Lord's feet and listened to what he was saying" (10:39). Her posture is a way of declaring her a disciple (see Acts 22:3). She has made herself a learner of Jesus. Hearing what he says means that she has received Jesus as a prophet. She is doing what loyal disciples should do—she is listening.

It is hard to overemphasize the importance of "hearing and doing the word" in the Lukan narrative. It is the decisive activity in building on a solid foundation (Luke 6:46–49), in maturing as in good soil (8:15), in being a member of Jesus' family (8:21), in being truly blessed (11:27–28). Mary, in listening to Jesus' word, has at least begun where faithfulness begins, and this warrants the commendation of Jesus in the face of Martha's complaint.

But what does this suggest? That the life of contemplation is preferred over the life of action? Hardly. The literary context here becomes critical. At 10:25 we encounter the lawyer who ultimately answers his own question to Jesus about eternal life by citing the two commands to love God and to love one's neighbor. Then follows the parable highlighting the action of the Samaritan, who assists the victim left in the ditch by tending to his wounds, carrying him on his donkey to an inn, and paying the costs incurred (10:29–37). He is a model for loving one's neighbor (as well as identifying who the neighbor is).

Then comes Mary, who is distinguished not for her action, but for her attentive listening to the word of Jesus. Her place alongside the Samaritan affirms that discipleship has to do not only with love of neighbor but also with love of God, not only with active service but also with a silent and patient waiting upon God's supreme prophet. The Samaritan and Mary belong together. Doing without listening can easily degenerate into busyness that loses its purpose. Listening without doing soon becomes no more than a mockery of the words.

Consider a footnote that perhaps should be a prelude: The story of Martha and Mary is one in which a stereotypical role of a woman (Martha's concern for the household tasks) is given secondary status. Many women in the congregation can identify with Martha and feel put down by the way she is treated, as if her complaint is only neurotic whining. The critical point is that the text does not so much "put down" Martha (who certainly is not a neurotic whiner) as it honors Mary's ministry of the word, a ministry Luke consistently elevates to a place of priority and sets alongside the ministry of the Samaritan. It is proper for a woman to leave the stereotypical role for that of a full and faithful disciple.

## Ordinary Time 17

*Sunday between*
*July 24 and 30 inclusive*

The series of texts from the preexilic prophets continues with Hos. 1:2–10, a passage that has intrigued and—in certain respects— baffled interpreters over the years. Although specific details are unclear, the larger import of the lection is quite evident: the relationship between God and Israel is similar to a marriage that has been ruined by an unfaithful spouse. Yahweh, who has patiently wooed, has been scorned by the object of the divine love, and the pain of judgment is at hand. Yet even in announcing this terrible verdict the prophet implants a reminder that Yahweh's final word is not destruction, but redemption.

Psalm 85 reveals a community of God's people who are suspended between the "already" and the "not yet." On the one hand, God's people are deeply aware of God's mercies in the past— mercies that have transformed the life of the community. On the other hand, there is a pressing need for some new outpouring of God's grace, some intervention in the lives of the people that will rescue them from their present peril. Precisely because of their experience of God's love in the past, they are now motivated to pray urgently for a fresh infusion of it. Their anxiety and concern are evident, yet even their very expectation of God's mercy results in peace.

The sequence of readings from Colossians moves to 2:6–15 (16– 19). The passage begins by reminding the readers of this letter of the tradition concerning Christ in which they live. In remembering this tradition they are moved to thanksgiving, the appropriate response to their reception of Christ. After warning the readers against some unspecified danger, the author of Colossians returns to the nature of the relationship Christians have with Christ. There is no other force or personality that may compete with Christ, for Christ, and only Christ, embodies "the whole fullness of deity." Baptism is the means by which Christians are joined to Christ, and the evidence of this union is the life of faith lived by Christ's persons. For Christians, faith and action are one.

Luke's interest in prayer is nowhere more evident than in the Gospel lection for this day, Luke 11:1–13. In response to the disciples' request, Jesus offers them a model prayer. The exclusively petitionary nature of this prayer becomes a vehicle for directing the attention of the disciples to their real needs, as well as reminding them of the only one ("Our Father") who may fulfill those needs. A parable and a brief observation on human nature contrast it with the nature of God. If those who are evil know how to do good things, just imagine what your heavenly Father is like!

## Hosea 1:2–10

Sin, judgment, restoration. The full panoply of the divine-human drama is etched out in the lines of this brief passage, which continues the cycle of Old Testament readings from preexilic prophets.

The sin of the nation is characterized in vs. 2–3, a celebrated text which, although it presents formidable problems for the interpreter, is clear in its larger import. The reader feels an urge to protest God's command to the prophet that he marry a prostitute, even if—as is commonly assumed—Gomer is no common "lady of the night" but a cultic prostitute attached to a local Baal shrine. How could God order so repulsive a thing? How could any self-respecting worshiper of Yahweh comply? Some have suggested that Hosea married Gomer only *later* to discover that she was engaged in sacral or some other kind of prostitution. Another possibility is that "whoredom" is not a literal description of Gomer's activities but is, rather, a metaphor for idolatrous worship, as in 2 Kings 9:22. (Second Kings 9—10 contain another important parallel to Hos. 1; see below.) But the likely interpretation is that it was the very reprehensible nature of Hosea's action that caused it to be such an object lesson to the prophet's contemporaries. Hosea seems to have married Gomer knowing the full measure of her character, and this union is then transformed into a paradigm of God's relationship with Israel, a relationship that the nation has corrupted almost beyond recognition (compare Hos. 2:1–15).

The relation between 1:2–3 and 3:1–3 raises intriguing questions. Are Gomer and the unnamed woman of chapter 3 the same person? Some interpreters have understood that these are the same woman and that 3:1–3 is an autobiographical account of the same events that were described by a third party (a follower of Hosea?) in 1:2–3. But if that is so, how can the sexual abstinence of 3:3 be reconciled with the three children born, according to 1:4–9, to Hosea and Gomer?

God's word of judgment on the nation (vs. 2–9) is vested in the names of the three children who are born to this scarred marriage: Jezreel (God Sows), Lo-ruhamah (Not Pitied), and Lo-ammi (Not My People). Of these three, Jezreel is the most intriguing, as it recalls the bloody events recounted in 2 Kings 9:1–10:11. A curious thing is that the prophet Elisha is portrayed in this latter text as condoning, in Yahweh's name, the massacre at Jezreel of the royal house of Israel (note 10:10), but Hosea cites these same events as evidence of the nation's sin (Hos. 1:4–5). Not only so, but the carnage inflicted by Jehu on Ahab's family will soon be imposed by Yahweh on the nation itself, a kingdom presently ruled by Jehu's descendant, Jeroboam II.

Not Pitied (v. 6) and Not My People (v. 9) are names of a different order from Jezreel in that, instead of pointing to the past, they indicate Yahweh's present activity: "I will no longer have pity . . ."; "You are not my people and I am not your God." Yahweh's patience is at an end and—not because Yahweh wishes it to be that way, but because there is now no alternative—the special ties binding this people to their God are about to be broken once and forever.

And yet . . . And yet . . .

Hosea understands as few do the essential nature of the God of Israel. This is a God whose very nature demands justice and fidelity, and who cannot tolerate a relationship from which these qualities are absent.

And yet . . . And yet . . .

These sinful people are Yahweh's people. They are persons of Yahweh's own choosing, connected by ties that can never be totally dissolved. Elsewhere (11:8; see Proper 13) Hosea expresses the anguish of a God who cannot ultimately let go even of those who repudiate God:

> How can I give you up, Ephraim?
>   How can I hand you over, O Israel?
> . . . . . . . . . . . . . . . . . . . . . . . . . . . . . . .
> My heart recoils within me;
>   my compassion grows warm and tender.

And so, even when it appears that the final word of God's judgment has been spoken, there is still a further word of restoration (1:10): "In the place where it was said to them, 'You are not my people,' it shall be said to them, 'Children of the living God.' "

Now the full power of the family metaphor is felt. Like a spouse whose life has been turned to shambles by an unfaithful partner, Yahweh has grieved. Like a parent who cannot love his or her children into being the kind of persons they are capable of being, Yahweh recognizes a relationship of brokenness. But in the end, Yahweh—loving spouse, loving parent—will never turn loose. In the end, Yahweh—loving Creator, loving God—will finally redeem.

## Psalm 85

It is a revealing observation about Ps. 85 that it was a major inspiration to both the contemplative Thomas à Kempis, who relied on it heavily in the third book of *The Imitation of Christ*, and the militant activist Oliver Cromwell, who found it "instructive and significant" as he proclaimed his intent that seventeenth-century England embody the reign of God on earth (see Rowland Prothero, *The Psalms in Human Life and Experience*; New York: E. P. Dutton, 1903, pp. 76–77, 190, 196). The impact of Ps. 85 is due in large part to vs. 8–13 and its striking portrayal of God's promise of peace to God's people, which, as James L. Mays suggests, is "an Old Testament form of the announcement 'on earth peace among those with whom God is well pleased' (Luke 2:14)" (*Psalms*, Interpretation series; Louisville, Ky.: John Knox Press, 1994).

The promise is delivered in the midst of current distress. Verse 1 looks back to a more "favorable" time when God "restored the fortunes of Jacob." This latter phrase elsewhere is used to describe Israel's return from the Babylonian exile (see, for example, Jer. 30:3, 18; 31:23; 33:7, 11; and Ezek. 39:25), and some would prefer to translate it here as "you returned Jacob from captivity." Indeed, Ps. 85 makes very good sense as a corporate prayer for help in the early postexilic era. God had forgiven the people (vs. 2–3; see Isa. 40:1–2) and brought them home, but the glorious vision of Isa. 40—55 had not materialized. The prophet Haggai laments the people's failure to rebuild the Temple; and using the same verb translated as "favorable" in Ps. 85:1, he suggests that this failure accounts for the lack of Yahweh's favor in the early restoration era (520 B.C.; see Hag. 1:8, NRSV "take pleasure in"). Perhaps not coincidentally, the deficiencies Haggai detects are the very things promised in Ps. 85:8–13. The "glory" of God does not dwell in the Temple (Hag. 2:7, 9, NRSV "splendor"; compare Ps. 85:9). The land yields no "produce" (Hag. 1:10; compare Ps. 85:12, NRSV "increase"). There is no *shalom* (Hag.

2:9, NRSV "prosperity"; compare Ps. 85:8, 10, NRSV "peace"). In short, Ps. 85 could well have originated as a prayer of the people amid the disappointing circumstances of the early postexilic era (see also Zech. 1:12–17). The people had recently been restored (Ps. 85:1), but soon found themselves again in need of restoration (v. 4).

In terms of the above scenario, the relatively rapid change of fortune that necessitated the petitions of vs. 4–7 is not really surprising in light of Israel's history. For instance, shortly after the deliverance from Egypt, the people's idolatry necessitates Moses' prayer that God "turn from your fierce wrath" (Ex. 32:12; compare Ps. 85:3, 5). Moses' petition is accompanied by his reminder to God of the promise of land (Ex. 32:13; compare the promise in Ps. 85:8–13, noting especially the mention of "land"/"ground" in vs. 9, 11, and 12). God does indeed "turn," allowing the people to live and finally revealing the divine character to consist of "steadfast love and faithfulness" (Ex. 34:6; compare Ps. 85:7, 10, 11).

The affinities between Ex. 32—34 and Ps. 85 are not intended to suggest another historical setting for the origin of the psalm, but rather to demonstrate that Ps. 85 is an appropriate prayer in a variety of circumstances. While the phrase "restored the fortunes of Jacob" suggests the likelihood of a postexilic prayer, the phrase can indicate more generally any "reversal of Yahweh's judgment" (John Bracke, "*šûb šebût*: A Reappraisal," *Zeitschrift für die alttestamentliche Wissenschaft* 97 [1985]: 242). Like Ps. 126 (see the Fifth Sunday in Lent), which also contains the phrase "restored the fortunes" in its first verse and then petitions for further restoration (v. 4; compare Ps. 85:4), Ps. 85 is perpetually appropriate for the people of God. Our own sinfulness and shortsightedness, as well as the difficulties of living faithfully in a world pervaded by the results of faithlessness, mean that it will always be necessary for us, like Israel, to pray, "Restore us again" (v. 4; see Mark 9:24).

The gifts prayed for in vs. 4–7—"steadfast love" and "salvation"—are promised in vs. 8–13. God's "salvation is at hand" (v. 9), and "steadfast love" is one of the four personified attributes in v. 10. In a sense, the gifts are conditional; God's "salvation is at hand for those who fear" God (v. 9). But in another sense, the remarkable description in vs. 10–13 exceeds any possibility of human merit or accomplishment. The focus is clearly on God's character and activity. "Steadfast love" and "faithfulness" are at the heart of God's character (Ex. 34:6–7); "righteousness" is the fundamental policy God enacts as sovereign of the universe (Pss. 96:13; 97:2; 98:9); and the result is "peace" (Ps. 29:11; see Isa. 60:17). God's character and activity will fill the universe—from "ground" to "sky" (v. 11). The word "righteousness" occurs three times (vs. 10, 11, 13), and the effect is to affirm that God *will* set things right.

Like Ps. 77 (see Proper 8), Ps. 85 left Israel and leaves us waiting expectantly, but the waiting itself affords us peace, albeit "not . . . as the world gives" (John 14:27). As we wait, we pray with the psalmist, "Restore us again" (v. 4). And we pray as Jesus taught us, "Your kingdom come" (Luke 11:2). Our waiting is not passive but active, for also like Ps. 77, Ps. 85 calls us to a decision. As Mays suggests (*Psalms*), Ps. 85 finally "is a judgment on any easy satisfaction with life under the conditions created by human character and a summons to look for and pray for the time and life created by the character of God."

## Colossians 2:6–15 (16–19)

This lection opens with what appears to be an innocuous statement that Christians "have received Christ Jesus the Lord" (v. 6), but the Greek verb translated "received" (*paralambanein*) elsewhere refers to the reception of tradition (see, for example, 1 Cor. 11:2, 23; 15:1). Since the section that precedes this reading concerns the ministry of Paul and his continued presence with the community, the reception of Christ Jesus probably refers specifically to the reception of tradition *about* him.

Far from a static understanding of tradition as a collection of historical particulars and constraints, however, the tradition of Christ is something in which Christians live: "Continue to live your lives in him, rooted and built up in him and established in the faith, just as you were taught, abounding in thanksgiving" (vs. 6–7). The multiplication of images here reveals something of the importance the writer attaches to being "in him." Believers are rooted in Christ, suggesting their origin and the source of their nurture. They are also "built up" in Christ, suggesting their continued growth and development. To be "established" in the faith connotes their security, as "established" or "confirmed" derives from legal language about certainty or security. All of this imagery gives way to thanksgiving, which is the sole proper response to the reception of Christ Jesus in one's life.

From this opening reminder of the many ways in which believers are connected with Jesus Christ, the writer issues a warning in v. 8. Exactly who or what threatens to take the Colossians "captive through philosophy and empty deceit" remains a much-disputed question, and the commentaries can provide an introduction to that discussion. Perhaps speculation about the nature of the universe, such as is found in later Gnostic writings, already has emerged in this area, accompanied by claims that self-denial enhances knowledge (see 2:16–19). Whatever the precise nature of the threat, for the writer of Colossians it constitutes "human tradition" as against the Christian tradition alluded to in v. 6. Moreover, it is associated with the "elemental spirits of the universe," those powerful beings who battle with God for mastery over the created order.

The remainder of the reading returns to the relationship between Christians and Christ, emphasizing first of all the excellence of the Christ as distinct from other rulers and authorities. The "whole fullness of deity dwells bodily" in him (v. 9). Whatever the relationship between this assertion and later christological formulations, here the assertion appears to distinguish Christ from any competing figures. Unlike the rulers and authorities of v. 10, or the elemental spirits and human tradition of v. 8, Christ partakes of God fully rather than partially.

In addition, as v. 10 indicates, Christians "have come to fullness in him." What the writer means by this unusual expression becomes clearer in vs. 11–14, which detail the identification between Christ and believers.

First, believers "were circumcised with a spiritual circumcision" (v. 11). Perhaps as much as any other line in Colossians, this one raises questions about Pauline authorship, for it is difficult to imagine that the Paul who argues against the necessity of circumcision would assert the imperative of spiritual circumcision (note especially the language of v. 13: "the uncircumcision of your flesh"). Whatever the judgment about that question, here spiritual circumcision means "putting off the body of the flesh in the circumcision of Christ." That is, as circumcision serves as the primary identity marker of Jewish males, so spiritual circumcision identifies Christians as belonging to Christ.

Verses 12–14 amplify this claim by detailing the ways in which Christians are joined with Christ. They are "buried with him in baptism" and "raised with him through faith." This resurrection consists of forgiveness, which Colossians describes as a clearing of the record. The graphic language of v. 14 makes the point well: the record is erased, set aside, nailed to the cross.

Verse 15 takes the action of the crucifixion and resurrection a step farther. Here it concerns, not forgiveness of the individual, but the disarming of "the rulers and authorities," of whom God made a "public example" and over whom he has triumphed. At first this statement seems a digression, but in two ways it provides a fitting conclusion to the thought of this lection. First, the disarming of "the rulers and authorities" means that Christians may live without fear of once again being captured by sin, so this final stage in the action of the cross secures the present and future for believers. Second, reference here to the "rulers and authorities" recalls v. 10 and its insistence that Christ is the one—the only one—in whom God fully dwells.

Perhaps the most important feature of this passage derives from its understanding of the relationship between Christ and the believer. Despite a rich theological heritage that teaches otherwise, Christians persist in understanding behavior as a means to a final reward (or as a means of warding off judgment!). Clearly reflecting earlier Pauline tradition, the writer of Colossians articulates an almost organic relationship between faith and action: faith and action are one. They are so precisely because believers are united in and with Christ, whose own experience shapes their lives. It is not incidental that the phrases "in him" and "with him" occur several times in this passage (vs. 9, 10, 11, 12, 13), for that identification in and with him forms the basis for Christian life.

## Luke 11:1–13

The thematic thrust of Luke's travel narrative concerns Jesus' destiny at Jerusalem and his instruction to his followers in the meaning of discipleship. It is not surprising that a crucial piece of the instruction has to do with prayer, since Luke of all the Gospels has the most extensive material and vocabulary on prayer. Jesus prays regularly and at critical moments in his ministry (for example, 3:21; 6:12; 9:18, 28; 10:21; 11:1; 22:32, 41; 23:34, 46). Prayer also becomes a mark of true discipleship, something that distinguishes the followers of Jesus from others. At the outset of their mission, the Seventy are told to petition the Lord of the harvest for divinely sent workers (10:2).

According to the texts assigned for this Sunday, the indispensability of prayer emerges from the fact that it puts those who pray in touch with the incredible generosity of God. "Successful prayer" depends not on the methods or strategies of the disciples (what time of day one prays or the posture one assumes), but on a listening Father, to whom petitioners are constantly referred.

It all begins with Jesus at prayer—something that prompts the disciples to ask for instruction, no doubt with the implication that Jesus' teaching will differ from John's teaching (11:1). What the

disciples receive is first a model prayer (11.2–4), then a parable that
by contrast stresses the character of God (vs. 5–8), and finally
reassurance that, as their heavenly Father, God will answer the
petitions of God's children and grant the Holy Spirit (vs. 9–13).

Little needs to be said here about the model prayer, since books
and books have been written about its meaning and implications.
Two observations, however, are important for the understanding of
the rest of the passage. First, God is addressed as "Father," and thus
the disciples are invited to pray with the same familiarity that Jesus
prayed (10:21). The fact that the one to whom they pray can be
thought of in such an intimate way markedly affects the confidence
with which they offer their prayers (see 11:13).

Second, the model prayer is exclusively petitionary. It contains no
adoration, thanksgiving, or confession, only five requests for God to
do something. The disciples are being taught what their real needs
are and to whom they need to go for satisfaction. God in turn is being
asked to fulfill the promises previously made regarding God's name
and reign and regarding the care and protection of God's people.

The parable that follows (vs. 5–8) makes sense only in light of the
high value placed on hospitality in the Middle Eastern culture. Many
people traveled, but most of the inns were disreputable, often
brothels or places where magic was practiced. Travelers had to
depend on friends or friends of friends for lodging along the way.
The parable itself may well be in the form of a question, paraphrased
like this: "Which of you will go to your next-door neighbor at
midnight and ask to borrow bread for an unexpected guest and be
turned down?" The anticipated answer would be, "Why, none of us.
We don't have unresponsive neighbors. It is unthinkable that a
request like that would be denied."

But the neighbor has excuses. In unbolting the door, he is bound
to wake up the children, and there goes his rest. The narrator adds,
"I tell you, even though he will not get up and give him anything
because he is his friend, at least because of his persistence [*anaideia*]
he will get up and give him whatever he needs" (v. 8).

The problem is that there is no hint in the parable that the one who
had the unexpected guest arrive pestered his neighbor into providing bread (as the persistent widow did in the parable in 18:1–8). We
are not told that he pounded on the door or called repeatedly. He
made a reasonable, not-out-of-the-ordinary request. Thus the Greek
word *anaideia* (not found anywhere else in the New Testament)
should probably be given its other meaning "shamelessness" or
"avoidance of shame." The neighbor finally responded, not because
he was badgered, but because he feared the shame that would

accompany his refusal. People in the community would talk if he denied a plea for help regarding hospitality. Better to risk waking the children than to have to face the reproaches of the villagers when they heard he had refused a request.

God, then, is contrasted with the unfriendly neighbor. If the neighbor who is initially prone to refuse requests finally responds to avoid shame, how much more will God respond to the pleas of the people of God? God can be trusted. Ask, search, knock, for God is not reluctant or hesitant. "If you then, who are evil, know how to give good gifts to your children, how much more will the heavenly Father give the Holy Spirit to those who ask him!" (11:13).

Prayer is rooted in the kindliness and generosity of God, thus making it possible for even unworthy, stumbling disciples to offer petitions for their journey. What they receive is the Spirit, the ultimate resource for mission.

# PROPER 13

## Ordinary Time 18

*Sunday between July 31
and August 6 inclusive*

Those who are tempted to believe that the Old Testament is concerned primarily with judgment (while the New Testament is about grace) will be disabused of such illusions by today's Old Testament lection, Hos. 11:1–11. There is no more poignant portrayal of the agony of God, who is torn between the demands of judgment and of grace. The images of both parent and spouse are used to emphasize the love of God, a love that is continually spurned by a sinful people. Yet the God of Israel cannot come to the point of destroying finally and irredeemably, for such a step would violate God's essential nature. When justice and grace are weighed in God's balances, grace always prevails.

Psalm 107:1–9, 43 is a song of thanksgiving over the *hesed* of Yahweh, God's "steadfast love." As such it forms an appropriate companion to the Hosea lection. Israel's experience of exile seems presupposed by this psalm, yet the language is such as to apply to many experiences of alienation. Lostness, hunger, thirst, and weariness characterize the condition of those cut off from God, yet if they seem abandoned, they are not. For God has guided them out of the desert and back to their homes once again. Their praise becomes an important climax in this paradigm of all human redemption.

The freedom to live in goodness might be characterized as the subject of the Epistle text, Col. 3:1–11. Even among the earliest Christians there were those who understood their faithfulness to Christ chiefly in terms of what they should not do. The author of Colossians (probably a pupil of Paul) seeks to correct this, however, by demonstrating the liberty of the baptized life. Although rejecting a pie-in-the-sky mentality, the passage points readers beyond "things that are on earth" to "things that are above." And it is in this spiritual freedom that they are to reject such things as fornication, impurity, and the like, and be clothed with a new self—renewal in the image of the Creator! In this way, all artificial distinctions among persons will cease to exist.

Freedom from greed is the focus of Luke 12:13–21, a text that addresses the difficult issue of how the Christian is to deny the temptations of materialism while living in a very material world. The parable is so transparent as to need almost no comment, for it basically points to the error of falsely trusting in material possessions to provide human security. The farmer is not condemned because he worked to produce a bumper crop, but his demise is viewed as tragic because he wrongly believed that his bulging barns would be his salvation.

## Hosea 11:1–11

It is tempting to caricature the prophets of ancient Israel as individuals of enormous anger. Because they are so often associated with words of judgment and destruction, a superficial reading of the prophets' message may lead one to the unfortunate conclusion that these spokespersons for God were motivated primarily by rage against those to whom they preached. Yet if one is enticed into such a misconception, the declarations of Hosea serve to dispel it, for Hosea agonized over the fate of his nation and suffered enormous pain as he described Israel's destructive waywardness before God. As one reads the text, it becomes clear that Hosea's pain is nothing other than the pain of God.

If the lection for this day says anything (and it says much!), it brings the prophet's agony, and that of Yahweh, into sharpest focus.

The image of Yahweh's love for Israel as that of a parent for a child (Hos. 11:1–4) strikes familial chords similar to those struck by Hosea's image of marital love (1:2–10, Proper 12). Yet the tone is different here, for while both images stress the faithlessness of the one who breaks the relationship, 11:1–4 emphasizes the helplessness of the beloved. If Yahweh had not loved Israel and nurtured it, Israel would not even have survived. Yet the tragic irony is that

> The more I called them,
> the more they went from me.
> (V. 2)

There are few scenes of tenderness in the Bible that match vs. 3–4. The rearing of infants has many aspects that are universally the same, regardless of temporal or cultural circumstances, and the parental love demonstrated in these lines can be understood with empathy by readers everywhere. Yet the beloved child is ultimately to repudiate the parent who has lavished such enormous affection.

(It is important in interpreting both this text and the Hosea passage from Proper 12 that one not overemphasize the element of gender. Just as it is possible for husbands as well as wives to prostitute themselves, so fathers, like mothers, are capable of nurturing love for their children. Yet the unspoken implication in 11:1–4 is that Yahweh is like a *mother* in her devotion to her child, and thus this passage stands as a fine corrective to the frequent tendency of interpreters to portray God in exclusively masculine terms.)

Verses 5–7 describe the inevitable consequence of the nation's faithlessness. "They shall return to the land of Egypt" of v. 5 refers back to "out of Egypt I called my son" of v. 1, and thus is to be understood as a symbolic (Egypt = bondage) rather than a descriptive statement. The descriptive declaration follows in the reference to Assyria, for in 722 B.C., not many years after Hosea was active in the Northern Kingdom, that nation fell to the advancing Assyrian armies. The reason for the destruction is clear: "They have refused to return to me."

(Verse 7 is typical of much of the Hebrew text of Hosea, in that part of it is so garbled as to defy logical translation. "To the Most High they call . . ." does not make much sense in the present context, and one may wish to consult other translations to note how very differently the text of this verse is reconstructed. If one has a translation with marginal notations, one may also note the frequency with which acknowledgment is made that a given translation is conjectural. Scholars have ventured many explanations for the difficult state of the Hebrew text of Hosea, but no completely satisfactory answers have been put forward.)

More moving than vs. 1–4 (if that is possible) are the emotions expressed in vs. 8–9. Perhaps the parental (maternal) image of vs. 1–4 is still operative here, although that is not stated. What is clear is that Yahweh, a God of compassion and mercy, cannot come to the point of completely destroying Israel. The lover, the parent, draws back from the horror of it all and, having placed judgment and mercy in the balance, decides in favor of mercy. And why is it that Yahweh's compassion ultimately wins out over Yahweh's justice? The answer defies all logic: that's just the way Yahweh is.

> I am God and no mortal,
> the Holy One in your midst.
> and I will not come in wrath.
> (V. 9)

And so God's people will be spared in spite of the judgment to come, a judgment they deserve very much.

(Admah and Zeboiim of v. 8 are cities that shared the fate of Sodom and Gomorrah, Deut. 29:23.)

A final section, vs. 10–11, is unclear in many of its details. (Why is it that "his children shall come trembling from the west," since neither Egypt nor Assyria lay in a westerly direction from Israel?) But its focal point is the final line. Those whom Yahweh has exiled shall finally return to their homes, and (so the implication is) to their God. Thus mercy has prevailed, although the sinfulness of the people has brought needless suffering and destruction into their lives.

Hosea stands as a reminder that judgment exacts a price from the one who is judged as well as from the one who does the judging. The sin of the people has brought suffering on them, but Yahweh suffers too! So all mistaken images of the prophet motivated by rage, all mistaken images of a God whose basic emotion is anger (à la Marcion), are cast aside by Hosea. The suffering God of Hosea anticipates the suffering Christ of Gethsemane and of Calvary's cross.

## Psalm 107:1–9, 43

Psalm 107 features in a particularly impressive way the word *hesed*, "steadfast love," which is a central theological concept in the book of Psalms and throughout the Old Testament. Psalm 107 begins and ends with the mention of "steadfast love," and one of the psalm's two refrains highlights it as well (vs. 8, 15, 21, 31). In a sense, it may be helpful to think about Ps. 107 as a sermon on God's "steadfast love," beginning with an invitation for congregational participation (vs. 1–3), followed by four narrative illustrations (vs. 4–9, 10–16, 17–22, 23–32), and concluding with hymnlike praise based on the four illustrations (vs. 33–42) and an admonition to continue to pay attention to the message of God's "steadfast love" (v. 43). As a whole, Ps. 107 effectively conveys what God's "steadfast love" is all about—compassion for people in need, including forgiveness, because the distress is sometimes the result of human sinfulness (see vs. 11, 17).

Most scholars categorize Ps. 107 as a song of thanksgiving and suggest that an original version of it (vs. 1, 4–32) may have been sung as persons offered thanksgiving sacrifices in the Temple (v. 22). These scholars further propose that Ps. 107 was expanded by the addition of vs. 2–3, 33–43 in order to be more immediately relevant to the postexilic generations who actually had been "redeemed from trouble and gathered in from the lands" (vs. 2–3), and were even known as "The Redeemed of the LORD" (Isa. 62:12). Support for this proposal is found in the placement of Ps. 107, which opens Book V of the Psalter. Not only does Ps. 107 appear to respond directly to Ps. 106:47, which presupposes an exilic situation, but it also appears to respond to the concluding psalm of Book III, especially its question, "Lord, where is your steadfast love of old . . . ?" (Ps. 89:49). If, as Gerald Wilson suggests, Books I—III document the failure of the Davidic covenant (see above on Ps. 99, Last Sunday After Epiphany, and Ps. 96, Proper 4), then it is particularly significant that the heart of Book IV affirms the reign of God (Ps. 93—99) and that Book V begins by defining God's sovereignty in terms of compassion and forgiveness—in a word, *hesed*. (See "The Use of Royal Psalms at the 'Seams' of the Psalter," *Journal for the Study of the Old Testament* 35 [1986]: 92.)

The lection includes only the first of the four narrative illustrations of God's "steadfast love" (Ps. 107:4–9), but these verses are sufficient to demonstrate the possibilities for hearing Ps. 107 and for discerning its theological significance. Verses 4–5 could refer to any experience of being lost in a desert and confronted with life-threatening hunger and thirst. When those in this situation "cried to the LORD" (v. 6a), the Lord "delivered them" (v. 6b) by leading them back to civilization (v. 7). The experience is cause for gratitude and celebration of God's "steadfast love" (v. 8), and it illustrates how God's "steadfast love" takes concrete form in provision for the needy (v. 9).

While it is possible to hear vs. 4–9 as the experience of any person or group, it is also difficult not to hear allusions to Israel's experiences of exodus and return from exile. Both involved wandering (Ps. 95:10; Isa. 35:8; NRSV "go astray") in a "desert" (Ex. 15:22; 16:1; Isa. 40:3) or in a "waste" (Deut. 32:10; Ps. 78:40; Isa. 43:19–20). Both involved hunger (Ex. 16:3; Isa. 49:10) and thirst (Ex. 17:3; Isa. 41:17) that was filled or satisfied by God (Ex. 16:12; Isa. 55:2). Both involved God's leading in God's way (Ex. 3:18; 5:3, NRSV "journey"; Isa. 11:15; 48:17), and both could be described or anticipated as "wonderful works" (Ex. 3:20, NRSV "wonders"; Micah 7:15, NRSV "marvelous things"). In short, even if Ps. 107:4–9 originated in the experience of "some" people (v. 4), these verses were easily adaptable to corporate experiences of deliverance such as exodus and return from exile.

The possibility that vs. 4–9 originated in the experience of "some" and were claimed by the whole people (or simply the fact that vs. 4–9 are applicable to a variety of experiences) is itself theologically significant, for it suggests that scripture is a "living word that is not exhausted in an ancient setting nor does it require the repetition of history to become valid again, but runs freely, challenging a new generation of believers to see a fresh correspondence between word and experience" (Leslie Allen, *Psalms 101—150*, Word Biblical Commentary 21; Waco, Tex.: Word, 1983, p. 65). Psalm 107 suggests that there are certain "typical" things we can count on as we look for fresh correspondence between our experience and God's word and work. In conjunction with the other three narrative illustrations, vs. 4–9 suggest the essential weakness, neediness, and sinfulness of humanity. Those who are "wise" and "give heed to these things" (v. 43)—that is, to the message of the four narrative illustrations—will realize that there is never a time when they are not in "trouble" (vs. 2, 6, 13, 19, 28). In contrast to what our culture teaches us, Ps. 107 teaches us that there is finally no such thing as self-sufficiency (see Luke 12:13–21, the Gospel lesson for the day). Human life depends on God; and the good news is, God can be depended on. God is "good" (v. 1), and God shares God's goodness (v. 9). It is God's character to love humankind steadfastly. We Christians profess that the steadfast love of God was revealed most clearly in the cross of Jesus Christ, who for us is "the power of God and the wisdom of God" (1 Cor. 1:24; see Ps. 107:43). The cross makes it clear that God chooses the weak and the foolish and the low, which means that no one should "boast in the presence of God" (1 Cor. 1:26–29). Rather, the fundamental attitude and activity of the faithful will be gratitude, to which Ps. 107 repeatedly invites us: "O give thanks to the LORD" (v. 1; see vs. 8, 15, 21, 31).

## Colossians 3:1–11

By some peculiar chemistry, religious conviction regularly finds itself reduced to a constrictive way of life, so that some religious folk give the impression that to be Christian is to be dour, moralistic, and generally unhappy. The historical circumstances that gave rise to Colossians are much disputed, but it seems clear in Col. 2:20–23 that already in the first century some people understood their faith in just such a confined way. The writer of the letter (probably a student of Paul's rather than Paul himself) warns about regulations that *appear* to promote wisdom, but whose piety and self-abasement actually contradict the gospel (see 2:18 with its reference to self-abasement). By way of introduction he asks, "Why do you live as if you still belonged to the world?" (v. 20). Colossians 3:1–11 offers an alternative to the narrow, self-promoting piety that masquerades as faithfulness but actually conforms to a worldly standard. Here the author sketches out an understanding of the new life that follows baptism, offering specifics, to be sure, but grounding those in a central affirmation about the Christian's liberating relationship to Jesus Christ.

The lection opens by recalling the earlier comments about baptism in 2:12: in baptism believers are both buried with Christ and raised with him. Here what comes into focus are the consequences of that resurrected life. If readers of Colossians recall the difficulties that arose at Corinth precisely *because* believers understood themselves to be living out the resurrection (see Paul's careful wording in Rom. 6), they will rightly wonder whether we have here an overly optimistic understanding of the nature of Christian life. Colossians 3:3b–4, however, protects against such a conclusion, for the true life of a Christian is "hidden with Christ in God," and its glory will be revealed with his in the last day. If the resurrection of Christians is real in the present, it is not yet complete.

Those raised with Christ will "seek the things that are above" and not "things that are on earth" (vs. 1 2). Statements like this one sometimes elicit concerns that the New Testament is otherworldly in its preoccupations, to the exclusion of any concern for what happens here and now. To put it bluntly, does Colossians advocate a kind of pie-in-the-sky mentality, in which all that matters is the future heavenly life of the believer?

The specifics of vs. 5–11 indicate that the answer to that question is firmly negative. "Things that are on earth" (v. 2) and the putting to death of "earthly" things (v. 5) have to do with some particular and distorted attitudes of human beings, attitudes controlled and governed by a perverted set of values, not with human life in general.

In vs. 5–11 two specific kinds of instructions are offered. First, in v. 5, the writer warns against "fornication, impurity, passion, evil desire, and greed (which is idolatry)." The physical—and indeed, sexual—nature of several of these prohibitions is noteworthy. It may stretch the warning just a bit to say that the concern here is with behavior that is overt, behavior that others might witness. Even evil desire and greed sometimes manifest themselves in actions that are visible. The equation of greed with idolatry merits notice, for it astutely assumes that greed exists where God has been replaced by other "deities" such as possessions, power, or one's own pleasure.

If the specific instructions of v. 5 generally address external, observable behavior, those of vs. 8–9 might be said to address behavior that is less available for others to observe: "anger, wrath, malice, slander, and abusive language" (v. 8) and lying (v. 9). As the heirs of Freud and Jung, we recognize that hostile emotions and attitudes often exist in ways of which we are unaware ourselves, which of course makes controlling them exceedingly difficult. Because the exhortation against lying in v. 9 specifically refers to the way in which Christians treat one another, what the writer has in view here may be the impact of such attitudes within the Christian community. Disputes and conflicts that fester produce just such behavior, which is highly destructive of community life.

Along with these ethical instructions, the author includes a warning (v. 6) and a reminder (vs. 9b–11). The warning about the "wrath of God" that is coming anticipates a final judgment, when all are held accountable for their practices. The reminder, however, suggests that Christians have already been changed in ways that should remove them from the fear of God's final wrath.

Believers have already "stripped off the old self" and have been clothed with the "new self" (vs. 9b–10). As the commentaries will explain, this passage probably draws on an early Christian baptismal liturgy, with its notion of putting off the old clothing and taking on new clothing, the new self that is nothing less than "the image of its creator" (v. 10).

The final verse, which of course recalls Gal. 3:28 and 1 Cor. 12:13, conjures up the many divisions human beings create among themselves, only to dismiss them. Whether ethnic (Greek and Jew), religious (circumcised and uncircumcised), cultural (barbarian, Scythian), or economic (slave and free), the walls that divide humankind have no place in the renewed humanity that follows from the resurrection. (Importantly, the author of Colossians does not include gender divisions here.) If "Christ is all and in all," then such subsidiary and competing identifications can only be rejected.

## Luke 12:13–21

There are few areas in the lives of modern Christians where help is needed more than in the matter of material possessions. Members of congregations may be familiar with stewardship appeals during the particular season of the year when pledges are solicited, but they very rarely find themselves confronted with the other passages in the Bible that speak to the threat and temptation that material possessions pose. The fact that many North American congregations have greatly benefited from the gifts of the wealthy makes ministers a bit reluctant to tackle the ominous texts that raise serious questions about the amassing of riches. What if the big givers are offended by what the Bible says?

Yet it is also true that many church members want help in discerning how they earn, invest, and spend their money. They live in a capitalistic culture that thrives on the profit motive and puts a high premium on expansion and growth. At the same time, they read in their Bibles about the condemnation of avarice, one of the seven deadly sins. How does one distinguish the profit motive from greed? Or how does one function (that is, earn a living, raise a family, live responsibly) in a society that values people in terms of what they possess, and where the accumulation of money is the quickest access to power? The latter question becomes a particularly urgent issue when one is faced with the loss of a job and the accompanying sense of failure and valuelessness.

Both this Sunday and next, the assigned Gospel lessons provide occasions for reflection on the meaning of possessions, and it is particularly appropriate to do so in the context of thinking about the larger issue of discipleship (one of the thematic foci of Luke's travel narrative). The Gospel texts are not immediately addressed to the broader culture, to provide a blueprint for an economic system that is peculiarly Christian. They in fact are addressed to disciples and would-be disciples, who have little or no leverage to change economic patterns but who want to live faithfully to their calling as believers. Jesus' words make sense only in the circle of faith where the intrusion of God into the lives of people (as with the rich man in the parable) is taken seriously.

The manner in which the nameless person in the crowd interrupts Jesus to ask that he adjudicate a family dispute over inheritance is abrupt (Luke 12:13). In an instant the topic changes from solemn encouragement to disciples to remain steadfast in their confessions of faith (12:4–12) to what seems like a trivial concern—except that Jesus makes it more than trivial. Though he refuses to be the arbitrator, Jesus warns the person who made the request of two things (constantly be on guard against all kinds of greed and know that your life does not consist of what you possess), and then tells a forceful parable.

The initial warnings are indirect. The person asking for arbitration is not immediately condemned for being greedy, nor is he chided for having abruptly changed the subject. Instead, he is instructed to set up a perpetual watch against the variety of ways greed operates in human life. (The imperative "Be on guard" is a present tense.) Greed (*pleonexia*, literally "the yearning to have more") is insidious and results in idolatry (see Col. 3:5). Furthermore, life is more than possessions. As a divine gift, it is valued in other ways than by the size of bank accounts and stock portfolios.

The parable is powerful and needs little explanation. It pushes the whole issue of possessions a step farther by depicting the tragedy of trusting in false security. The rich fool is not guilty of greed; his acreage simply produces a bumper crop. His problem is the misguided illusion that his prosperity has secured the future. He feels amply supplied "for many years." But then in the midst of a conversation he is having with himself, God interrupts to inform him that death is on its way. One whose whole speech has been delivered in the first person ("I will do this and that") is left with the rhetorical question, "And the things you have prepared, whose will they be?"

Now the text does not prescribe specific answers to our questions about possessions. It does not provide rules that define how much is "enough" and what people should do with their wealth if they have some. The reader hunts in vain for a guideline, a principle, a quantifiable definition of greed that will tell one whether he or she has stepped over the line. The text does not offer a new law, but it does confront the reader with eloquent language and powerful symbols that continue to prod the imagination. To be constantly on guard against greed, to be reminded that life is a gift of God and not a hard-earned acquisition, to be warned vividly against the presumption that affluence can secure the future—these are more than rules.

# PROPER 14

## Ordinary Time 19

*Sunday between*
*August 7 and 13 inclusive*

Both the lesson from Isa. 1 and the selection from Ps. 50 call the people of God to "Hear!" (Isa. 1:10; Ps. 50:7). In each case, the message has to do with sacrifices and burnt offerings: God does not want them! This apparent rejection of one of the hallmarks of Israel's liturgical life should not be interpreted as an outright rejection of worship. Rather, it seems that the sacrificial system had come to be understood as a means of attempting to manipulate God for self-centered purposes, and the texts therefore call for worship that is God-centered (Ps. 50:14–15, 23) and prepares the worshiper to enact God's will (Isa. 1:16–17). Both texts conclude with a promise and a warning, thus emphasizing the importance of the decision involved to honor God and God's purposes rather than self (Isa. 1:18–20; Ps. 50:22–23).

The Gospel lesson also calls the people of God to decision. As in Isa. 1 and Ps. 50, this call to decision is based on the good news that God rules the world and offers people a share in this reign (Luke 12:32; see Isa. 1:2–3; Ps. 50:1–6). Unlike the rich man who trusts only himself and acts only in his own self-interest (Luke 12:16–21), the people of God are invited to "sell . . . and give" as a sign of their trust in God and God's reign (Luke 12:33–34). The juxtaposition of vs. 32–34 with the call to "be dressed . . . be ready" (vs. 35, 40) suggests that our use of financial resources is inextricably related to our conviction that the future and our destiny lie ultimately with God. What we believe about the future affects how we live in the present.

This affirmation is precisely the message of Heb. 11. The entrusting of one's life and future to God is "the reality of things hoped for, the proof of things not seen" (Heb. 11:1; for this translation, see the commentary on the Epistle lection for this Sunday). There is no better example of this affirmation than the story of Abraham and Sarah (Heb. 11:8–16). The message of the four lessons may be

459

summed up by Heb. 11:16: For those whose trust in God's reign
'makes possible lives lived for God and for others, "God is not
ashamed to be called their God."

## Isaiah 1:1, 10–20

Important passages from Israel's preexilic prophets constitute the
Old Testament lections for this period of Year C, a series that now
turns its attention for two Sundays to Isaiah of Jerusalem. A number
of scholars hold the view that the material in Isa. 1—39 has been
grouped in a roughly chronological fashion (Isa. 40—66 is considered to reflect the activity of later prophets in the Isaian tradition). If
that is so, the present text may date from near the beginning of
Isaiah's ministry, or about 742 B.C. (see Isa. 6:1). Many texts attributed both to "early" Isaiah and "early" Jeremiah have close parallels
with the work of Amos and Hosea, their Northern predecessors, and
Isa. 1:10–20 is no exception. (Isaiah 1:1 is included in this day's
lection as a means of introducing vs. 10–20.) It does not strain the
imagination to assume that just as, let us say, young Beethoven
relied heavily on Mozart for models in musical composition, young
(if young they were) Isaiah and Jeremiah looked in similar fashion to
Amos and Hosea. (And for Jeremiah, Isaiah would have been a
model.) Isaiah 1:10–20 has especially close affinities to Amos 5:21–24
and Hos. 6:6 (compare Micah 6:6–8).

Each of these texts contains the same basic message: worship is an
idle exercise unless it brings about a changed heart within the
worshiper. Burnt offerings (v. 11) and special high holy days (v. 13)
mean nothing unless the worshiper lives a life of goodness and
justice (v. 17). That much seems clear, but what is less clear is the
prophet's basic attitude toward worship as such. It is one thing to
say that worship finds its ultimate meaning in the changed lives of
the worshipers, but quite another to say that worship, instead of
offering assistance in a life-changing experience, actually acts as an
impediment. Yet one can read this text from Isa. 1, as well as similar
texts from Amos and Hosea, in such a manner that this is precisely
what they seem to say. Thus it may be that, instead of calling for a
renewed worship, one that brings about reoriented hearts, the
prophets (some of them, at least) are calling for the abolition of
worship altogether. Their reason: formal worship prevents the
people of God from achieving their true calling—lives of justice and
compassion.

> Bringing offerings is futile.
> ......................
> Even though you make many prayers,
> I will not listen. (Isa. 1:13, 15)

Instead of worship, the people must

> learn to do good;
> seek justice,
> rescue the oppressed (v. 17)

and so on.

Now if this was indeed the prophetic attitude toward worship, the Old Testament as a whole does not share it. Nor can the modern preacher. The simple reason is that, in the experience of the community of faith, worship, when rightly engaged, elevates the spirits of the faithful and reinvigorates women and men to pursue fresh acts of justice and compassion. Both Old and New Testaments affirm this reality (Ps. 150; Acts 16:25), as do the traditions of synagogue and church.

The challenge for the interpreter of this text is permit it to speak, not as a denial of worship, but as an affirmation of worship, worship that leads men and women of faith to lives characterized by those qualities enumerated in Isa 1·17.

It goes without saying that this text is not a condemnation of Israelite or Jewish worship ("the blood of bulls," v. 11) in favor of Christian worship. While it is true that Christians would deny the value of certain acts of worship referred to here (as would devout Jews—although for different reasons), this passage should not be twisted so as to permit anti-Semitic innuendos.

Verses 18–20 offer words of hope in what seems an otherwise hopeless situation. The theological movement within the text is from outright condemnation (v. 10) to an offer of restoration (v. 18). The verb in "let us argue it out" comes from the language of the law court, and it refers to the kind of discourse that results in the disclosure of the truth (compare Job 23:7, where the same verb is used). That truth is this: Change is possible in the lives of women and men, change so complete that it may be compared to the transformation of red (a reference back to the blood of the sacrificed animals in v. 11?) into white. "If you are willing . . . ; but if you refuse . . . " set the options before each person. The choice of the one is life, of the other is death.

So the text, far from bringing us to a denial of worship altogether, reminds us of the urgency of *right* worship, a worship that understands that beauty and pageantry, loud noises, and good feelings are not of value in themselves. They are of value only as they help us to

> cease to do evil,
>     learn to do good;
> seek justice,
>     rescue the oppressed,
> defend the orphan,
>     plead for the widow.
>                         (Vs. 16–17)

## Psalm 50:1–8, 22–23

Most psalms are songs or prayers, but Ps. 50 is neither. Many scholars label it "a prophetic exhortation," but Erhard Gerstenberger more plainly calls it a "liturgical sermon" (*Psalms, Part 1;* Grand Rapids : Wm. B. Eerdmans Publishing Co., 1988, p. 210). To be sure, its accusatory tone does not accord very well with contemporary homiletical guidelines and techniques, but as Gerstenberger points out, "Accusatory and threatening rhetoric still today is part and parcel of many a Christian sermon" (p. 209). And, besides, Ps. 50 has much to commend it homiletically. For instance, the preacher—perhaps originally addressing a congregation in a postexilic synagogue—has exegeted the congregation well. Two problems are detected and then addressed in the two parts of the sermon: (1) a misunderstanding of sacrifice (vs. 7–15); and (2) the failure of congregational members to practice what they preach (vs. 16–22). In short, the problem involves the congregation's worship and its work. The two parts of the sermon are introduced by vs. 1–6, and v. 23 is a summary and conclusion.

As is fitting for an introduction, God is named three times in v. 1, starting with the old Canaanite name for the supreme deity and concluding with Israel's personal name for God: "El, Elohim, Yahweh." Verse 1 also introduces what Ps. 50 will predominantly involve—Yahweh's speaking. In this case, Yahweh speaks to summon the earth; in v. 4, Yahweh will call to the heavens and the earth. They are to serve as bailiffs and perhaps witnesses as Yahweh puts the people on trial (see Deut. 32:1; Isa. 1:2; Micah 6:1–2, where the heavens and earth also serve as witnesses to God's speaking or acting). Heaven and earth summon the people to court (v. 5). The mention of "covenant . . . by sacrifice" recalls Ex. 24:1–8, where sacrifice accompanied the reading of "the book of the covenant" (24:7) following the giving of the Decalogue. At that point, the people promised, "We will be obedient." But Ps. 50 suggests that God's people have not been obedient, and so Yahweh is coming to "judge" (vs. 4, 6; the Hebrew words here differ but are essentially synonymous). Yahweh may "have been silent" in the past (v. 21), but will "not keep silence" any longer (v. 3).

As James L. Mays suggests, the "trial . . . proceedings can be seen only by the eye of faith" (*Psalms*, Interpretation series; Louisville, Ky.: John Knox Press, 1994). In other words, the trial scenario is the preacher's rhetorical device for bringing the word of God to bear upon the congregation. The language of theophany in vs. 2–3 serves to assert Yahweh's authority to speak and to judge. As in Deut. 33:2, Yahweh "comes" from a mountain residence and "shines forth" (see also Ps. 18:7–15). The storm imagery in Ps. 50:3 is reminiscent of God's appearing on Sinai to establish the covenant and give the commandments to Moses and the people (Ex. 19, especially vs. 5–6, 8, 16, 18). The participation of heaven and earth also effectively points to Yahweh's authority—Yahweh rules all things as well as all people. Not coincidentally, in another psalm where the heavens "declare . . . [God's] righteousness" (97:6, NRSV "proclaim"), the context also contains the language of theophany (vs. 2–5) and the explicit affirmation, "The LORD is king!" (v. 1). In short, as sovereign of the universe, Yahweh has the authority to speak and act; and it is Yahweh's intention to set things right.

The beginning of Yahweh's direct address to the people in Ps. 50:7–15 is reminiscent of a key text from the book of Deuteronomy—the Shema, "Hear, O Israel" (Deut. 6:4). The Shema follows immediately upon Moses' rehearsal of the Decalogue, and indeed the whole book of Deuteronomy has the purpose of covenant renewal as the people prepare to enter the land. Psalm 50 is also, in effect, a call for renewal of commitment. The particular issue involved in the first part of the sermon is raised in v. 8—the sacrificial system. Verses 8–15 should not be heard as a call to abolish the system, but rather to put sacrifice in proper perspective. The people were bringing their sacrificial offerings not out of gratitude to God, but rather as a means of asserting their own merit and self-sufficiency. It seems that they thought God needed them instead of their needing God. In response to this misunderstanding, God through the preacher proclaims that the proper sacrifice is "thanksgiving" (v. 14; see NRSV note). The proper approach to God begins with gratitude. Verse 15 reinforces the message. The people have been using worship as a means of glorifying themselves. In vs. 8–15, God calls the people instead to "glorify me" (v. 15).

In spite of the NRSV translation of v. 16a, the "wicked" should not be understood as a different group. That is, vs. 16–22 are still addressed to the same congregation. The focus is now on the people's work or behavior, and the problem is hypocrisy. They say the right things (v. 16), but they do not act in accordance with their covenant identity (v. 17). Verses 18–21 illustrate how the people break the commandments—stealing, adultery, bearing false witness (see Ex. 20:14–16; Jer. 7:9–10; Hos. 4:1–3). As Ps. 50:3 has already suggested, God breaks the divine silence and indicts the people for their faithlessness (v. 21). The fundamental problem is that they have forgotten God. Unless they "understand this" (NRSV "mark this"), the results will certainly be destructive.

Verse 23 summarizes the two sections and declares the good news. God's will is to save, and God will "show . . . salvation" to those who can forget themselves long enough to understand their neediness and insufficiency. Verse 23a summarizes the message of vs. 7–15 (see especially vs. 14–15), and v. 23b summarizes vs. 16–22 ("way" suggests behavior or lifestyle).

Like all good sermons, Ps. 50 challenges the hearers to decide. Jesus' Sermon on the Mount presented the same call to decision: "Not everyone who says to me, 'Lord, Lord,' will enter the kingdom of heaven, but only the one who does the will of my Father in heaven" (Matt. 7:21). So did the apostle Paul; his dual appeal to the Romans corresponds to the two parts of the sermon in Ps. 50: (1) "Present your bodies as a living sacrifice, holy and acceptable to God, which is your spiritual worship" (12:1); and (2) "Do not be conformed to this world, but be transformed by the renewing of your minds, so that you may discern what is the will of God" (12:2). The decision is ours as well: Will we live to gratify ourselves? Or will we live in gratitude to God?

## Hebrews 11:1–3, 8–16

This lection consists of the familiar opening lines from the recital in Hebrews of the faith of Israel's ancestors, together with a significant sample from that recital, namely, the section regarding Abraham and Sarah. If time permits reading the chapter as a whole in the context of worship, the full impact of this history of faithfulness will be heightened.

That Heb. 11 is a single and coherent unit is clear. Chapter 10 concludes with a reminder that believers are "among those who have faith and so are saved," providing a smooth transition into this discussion of the faith of Israel. The chapter itself both begins by looking back to "our ancestors" and concludes by connecting their experience to that of Christians. Rhetorically, the chapter serves two purposes: as encomium it praises the faithfulness of the past generations (see the more extended account in Sir. 44:1–50:21), and as exhortation it implicitly urges that same faith on present believers.

The NRSV's translation of Heb. 11:1 is familiar but highly problematic, because two of the crucial words in this verse are exceedingly difficult to translate in this context. The writer defines faith as the *"hypostasis* of things hoped for," which NRSV translates as "assurance," giving the word something of a psychological connotation. Whatever *hypostasis* means, however, it almost certainly does not refer to an individual's certainty or assurance. Ascertaining what is conveyed here is complicated by the fact that Hebrews uses it in different ways earlier in the book. In Heb. 1:3, the same word appears with its customary philosophical overtones ("He is the reflection of God's glory and the exact imprint of God's very being [*hypostasis*]"). In 3:14 it appears to have ethical connotations, specifically regarding steadfast Christian behavior ("For we have become partners of Christ, if only we hold our first confidence [*hypostasis*] firm to the end").

Harold Attridge persuasively argues that the best translation of *hypostasis* in 11:1 is the philosophical one: faith is the "reality" of things hoped for (*The Epistle to the Hebrews*, Hermeneia; Philadelphia: Fortress Press, 1989, pp. 308–10). By striking contrast with the customary understanding of this verse, in which it asserts the obvious truth that faith involves confidence about things that cannot presently be verified, what Hebrews actually asserts is that in faith the believer already anticipates the final outcome (the reality) of what is believed. That is not to say that believing makes something true or that whatever one actually believes will happen, but that faith itself has a kind of eschatological power.

Consistent with this translation, v. 1 goes on to affirm that faith is the *"elegchos* of things not seen." Here again the NRSV is somewhat misleading, for *elegchos* does not mean conviction in the sense of personal, internal belief that something will happen. Instead, it normally refers to proof; faith is the *"proof* of things not seen" (emphasis added). What emerges from v. 1, then, is not a platitude about belief but a highly provocative claim that faith itself moves in the direction of the realization of those things that are presently beyond demonstration.

That astonishing claim begins to make sense in the recital of Israel's history that follows. Verse 2 anticipates that recital by introducing the "ancestors" whose stories will unfold in the chapter ahead. Verse 3 does not fit easily in the context, although it may connect to the issue of things that are presently not visible and those that will later become visible or known.

The discussion of Abraham's faithfulness has two foci: his obedience to the call to go to a new land and his confidence in God's promise of his own progeny. In verses 8–10, Abraham's (along with Isaac's and Jacob's) unsettled life in tents in land that had been promised to him is contrasted with the city he anticipated receiving. Earlier in Hebrews, the notion of "resting" in a settled place serves as a way of symbolizing the eschatological security and blessing anticipated by Christians (see 4:1–11). In 12:18–24, the "city of the living God, the heavenly Jerusalem" also appears in a context that looks forward to the eschatological future.

In 11:11–12, Hebrews recalls Abraham's faith in God's promise regarding the children that would be born to him and Sarah. As the note on v. 11 in the NRSV indicates, some manuscripts identify Sarah as the subject of v. 11, which is surprising on two counts. First, that Sarah "received power to conceive," translated literally, imagines Sarah as the one responsible for conception, a notion that would be highly unusual in the ancient world. Second, the Hebrew Bible does not interpret Sarah as responding in faith but in amused skepticism. However this complex knot is unraveled, the presence of Sarah in the passage is consistent with later references to women in this chapter (see vs. 31, 35).

The point toward which this reminder about Abraham moves become clear in vs. 13–16. Like many others, Abraham died without having either of these promises realized. He did not inhabit the land promised him, and he did not live to see the large family promised him. Because he trusted God and looked forward to the fulfillment of God's promises, however, "God is not ashamed to be called their God" (v. 16). This is no grudging concession, but a strident affirmation: God is proud of Abraham and others who trust in God!

## Luke 12:32–40

The Gospel lesson for last Sunday (Proper 13) came from a critical chapter in Luke's narrative, dealing with the devastating effects of wealth. It issued pointed warnings against greed and the presumption that by material possessions one can secure the future. The lection for Proper 14 continues the instruction about possessions, this time setting the issue in an eschatological context and offering more specific guidance about how one can act responsibly.

First, a word about the literary structure of the section. Following the parable of the rich fool (Luke 12:16–21), Jesus tells the disciples not to become preoccupied with even the basic necessities of life— food and clothing. Their one concern is to pursue zealously God's rule and to be assured that God will care for them. If God can feed the ravens and clothe the fields with lovely lilies, then God will not ignore their need for life's essentials. These are words of comfort for disciples who will be called to risk a lot for the kingdom (12:22–34).

The concluding paragraph of this counsel to avoid anxiety (vs. 32–34) is assigned as the starting point for today's lesson and is coupled with the next section, including Jesus' words about being prepared for the coming Son of man (vs. 35–40). The linkage between directions about possessions and calls for preparedness for the return of Jesus at an unexpected time presents a dynamic context for reflection.

Three dimensions of the text can guide our considerations about possessions. First, the presupposition for any talk about what to do with wealth is the reality of God's reign. Paradoxically, disciples are told to *strive* for the divine kingdom (v. 31) and at the same time to be comforted that God is delighted to *give* them the kingdom (v. 32). The striving is set over against the temptation to strive for food and clothes. The giving reassures them that the world is controlled not by fate or by the demonic forces of disorder and confusion, but by a caring parent ("your Father"), whose kindly gift is to the "little flock."

Whose rule prevails in the world makes a great difference when one begins to think about possessions. If one believes that the divine reign has begun with the advent of Jesus, and the present is oriented to the completion of that reign in Jesus' return, then one has reason to bring God into any discussion about money. If, however, what makes the world go round is chance or human aggressiveness or a demonic force, then Jesus' words make little sense. The presence of God's rule is the only justifiable reason for a carefree attitude toward life's necessities and a willingness to share one's possessions with the poor.

Second, in light of God's gift of the divine rule, disciples are told to sell their possessions and give to the poor. They are beginning to discover what the rich fool should have done with his abundant crops. Instead of deluding himself into thinking that his prosperity guaranteed his future, he could have eased the immediate burdens of those whose crops had been devastated by drought.

Furthermore, there is a clear affirmation that taking a carefree stance toward one's personal needs and giving alms to the poor result in heavenly treasure. A reward is promised, but one that demands rejection of the strategy of the rich fool and his ilk, "who store up treasures for themselves" (12:21). To be sure, the pursuit of wealth has its rewards, but they are ephemeral, fleeting, and at the mercy of the acquisitiveness of others more greedy, in contrast to purses "that do not wear out" and treasures "unfailing."

The theme of almsgiving is, of course, persistent in Luke (14:33; 18:22) and paves the way for the picture of the ideal community in Acts 2:45; 4:34–37, where a regularized program of caring for the needy is instituted. The Christian community cannot contemplate the meaning of discipleship apart from considering how it will serve the poor and less fortunate. It lies at the heart of faithfulness.

Third, the section Luke 12:35–40 talks about perpetual readiness for the Son of man, adding a new dimension to the importance of almsgiving. The initial vignette depicts a master returning from a wedding feast and finding alert servants, immediately opening the door on his arrival. The master is so delighted at their watchfulness that he exchanges roles with them and, like another master (kyrios) we know, becomes their servant (see 22:27). The second vignette describes an unfortunate homeowner whose house has been broken into. Had he known when the thief was coming, he would certainly have been prepared for him.

All life is lived in expectation of the Son of man's return. The time of the arrival is unknown, but the coming is sure. This eschatological anticipation sets the talk about possessions in a new context. One's attitude toward wealth and its enticements and one's actions with the money he or she has are not trivial matters. They are part of the disciple's readiness and watchfulness.

# PROPER 15

## Ordinary Time 20

*Sunday between
August 14 and 20 inclusive*

Isaiah 5:1–7 and Ps. 80:8–19 employ similar images to represent the
people of God—a vine or a vineyard. The image clearly communicates the careful commitment that God shows to God's people.
Unfortunately, the people do not respond in kind (see Isa. 5:7), so
God must destroy the vineyard (Isa. 5:5–6; Ps. 80:12–13). In Isa. 5:1–7,
the judgment is announced. In Ps. 80, it has already occurred, and
the people plead for restoration (vs. 1, 3, 7, 14, 19). As suggested in
this Sunday's Psalm comments, on the basis of Ps. 80:14 the future
life of God's people will depend not on their repentance, but rather
on *God's* repentance!

An important canonical insight is achieved when this remarkable
conclusion is heard in juxtaposition with Jesus' radical call for
human repentance in Luke 12:49–56—namely, while God demands
obedience and calls humanity to repentance, it is ultimately God
who will bear the burden of human disobedience and whose
gracious turning to humankind makes life possible. The clearest sign
of God's gracious turning is the cross of Jesus Christ. It is also the
cross that indicates the radical demand that repentance and discipleship involve, suggesting why repentance is so difficult and why
faithfulness so rarely characterizes the life of God's people (see Luke
12:51–53).

Nevertheless, Heb. 11 demonstrates that the story of God's people
does contain outstanding episodes and exemplars of faith, and Heb.
12:1–2 suggests that God never gives up on calling us to follow, to
run the difficult race that leads to life. There is nothing easy about the
course we are called to follow, and great perseverance is required
(12:1). The good news, however, is that God does not ask us to go
anywhere that God has not already gone in Jesus Christ, "the
pioneer and perfecter of our faith" (12:2).

## Isaiah 5:1–7

One of the most intriguing prophetic statements concerning the Lord's judgment on Israel is made so, not because its theological force is significantly different from other such statements in this section of the lectionary (note, for example, Amos 8:1–12, Proper 11), but because of its literary character. The central image of Israel as the unproductive vine and Yahweh as the disappointed vintager is enhanced by a literary structure characterized by frequent and surprising shifts, so that the attention of the reader is over and over again renewed.

It is often observed that Isa. 5:1–7 may have originally been inspired by a peasant song sung at the time of the autumn harvest (also the time of the Festival of Booths), in which the powers of the vine and of the grape were celebrated. While that is quite possibly true, the very first words suggest the beginning of a love song. "Let me sing for my beloved" invites the listener to (or reader of) the song to expect a statement of amorous intent (compare S. of Sol. 4:1–8). But in the first of several surprises, we are quickly informed that the song is really about the loved one's vineyard. In the balance of the initial section (v. 2) we are told that the beloved vintager did everything possible to ensure a sweet crop, but was rewarded with the failure of the vineyard:

> He expected it to yield *'ănābîm* (edible grapes),
> but it yielded *bĕ'ušîm* (stinkers).

The Hebrew term used to characterize the rotten fruit is also, for example, used in Isa. 50:2 to describe decayed fish (compare Ex. 7:18, 21).

A second section (stanza ?), vs. 3–4, contains the next important surprise, for the voice we hear is no longer that of the vintager's lover, as in vs. 1–2, but that of the vintager himself. What is more, the immediate hearers of the song are for the first time identified as the people of Jerusalem and of all Judah. They are asked to stand in judgment on the unproductive vineyard, and to them is put an inescapable conclusion: there is no more that can be done other than to tear out the vineyard root and branch. Yet the mood of the owner of the vines is less one of anger than of pained puzzlement, for the statement that concludes the first section is recast in the form of a plaintive inquiry:

> When I expected it to yield *'ănābîm*,
> why did it yield *bĕ'ušîm*?

This is perhaps not quite the broken heart of Yahweh so movingly described by Hosea (Hos. 11:1–11, Proper 13), but the words may certainly be understood to imply Yahweh's despondency.

In the third section (or stanza), vs. 5–6, the immediate impression is that the vintager is still speaking and is now promising to carry out the sentence demanded in vs. 3–4. The "hedge" and the "wall" of v. 5 make it clear that the vineyard owes its very existence to the protective care of the vintager and that, once that care is withdrawn, the vineyard will cease to exist. In the place of an ordered garden there will be "briers and thorns."

Yet it ultimately becomes apparent that this voice in vs. 5–6 is not that of a human farmer, but the voice of none other than Yahweh, for only Yahweh can command the clouds "that they rain no rain upon it." And so all of vs. 5–6 is suddenly cast into a new perspective, for this is no Judean landowner planning to reshape his acreage; this is Israel's God about to bring terrible justice to the nation.

In the final section (v. 7), the song of the vineyard—now a song of judgment—achieves its climax. The allusions of vs. 1–6 are now fully revealed: the vintager is Yahweh, the vineyard is Israel/Judah. The judgment that the nation was asked in v. 3 to render is really a judgment on itself. (Compare the manner in which Nathan manages to elicit from David a judgment on himself, 2 Sam. 12:1–12.)

Notice that the speaker of v. 7 is different from the vintager of vs. 3–4 and Yahweh of vs. 5–6. Perhaps the voice we hear is that of the female lover of the vintager, whom we heard in vs. 1–2, but more likely it is that of the prophet who now steps forward—in the manner of the chorus in a Greek tragedy—to pronounce Yahweh's judgment.

Yet it is still more in sorrow than in anger that Yahweh stands as judge over this sinful people, for the "refrain" that closed the first and second sections (vs. 2, 4) is now recast (v. 7). A disappointed Yahweh had "expected" (NRSV reflects the fact that the Hebrew verb —*qāwāh*—is the same in all three verses) one thing, but had experienced another. Notice the powerful wordplay.

> He expected *mišpāṭ* (justice),
>     but saw *miśpāḥ* (bloodshed);
> *sĕdāqāh* (righteousness),
>     but heard *sĕ'āqāh* (a cry)!

One cannot help being struck by the dramatic quality of this passage. Isaiah of Jerusalem lived three hundred years before the golden age of Greek drama, yet Isa. 5:1–7 could be easily and powerfully staged, with four speakers delivering their lines:

The female lover of the vintager: vs. 1–2
The vintager: vs. 3–4
Yahweh: vs. 5–6
Yahweh's prophet: v. 7

Perhaps this setting would be an effective manner of introducing this lection to a worshiping congregation.

## Psalm 80:1–2, 8–19

Psalm 80:1–7 was the reading for the Fourth Sunday of Advent. After repeating vs. 1–2, today's lesson resumes following the second occurrence of the refrain (vs. 3, 7, 19) and includes the remainder of the psalm. After the opening plea (Ps. 80:1–2) and initial complaint (vs. 4–6), each of which is followed by the refrain (vs. 3, 7), vs. 8–13 contain a historical allegory or parable. Verses 14–18 then return to petition and complaint before the final occurrence of the refrain.

The allegory of the vine in vs. 8–11 serves to remind Yahweh of past actions on behalf of Israel, and such recollections are typical in communal prayers of complaint and petition (see Pss. 44:1–8; 74:2, 12–17; compare Ex. 32:11–12). Verses 8–11 of Ps. 80 offer a brief overview of Israel's history from the exodus (the verb "ordered . . . to set out" in Ex. 15:22 is the same as "brought . . . out" in Ps. 80:8a), to the conquest (v. 8b; see "drove out" in Josh. 24:12, 18; Ps. 78:55), to the growth and culmination of the Davidic empire that stretched from the Mediterranean Sea to the Euphrates River (Ps. 80:9–11).

The Old Testament lesson for the day (Isa. 5:1–7) is a reminder that Ps. 80 is not the only text that likens Israel to a vine or vineyard. The image suggests careful planning, preparation, and patient nurture that make growth and fruitfulness possible. Thus, it is an appropriate one for representing the commitment that God shows to God's people (see the vine metaphor also in Jer. 2:21; 6:9; Ezek. 17:1–10; 19:10–14; Hos. 10:1; 14:7; John 15:1–11; and note the use of the verb "plant" even where the vine imagery is absent, as in Ex. 15:17 and Ps. 44:2, for example).

The allegory continues in Ps. 80:12–13. In view of God's careful planting and nurture, the question is, "Why . . . ?" (v. 12), recalling the question in v. 4, "How long . . . ?" After all God had done, why would God break down the walls around the vineyard (see Isa. 5:5; Ps. 89:40), and allow the vine to be devoured (see Ps. 89:41; and note "How long . . ." in 89:46)? The word "feed" in Ps. 80:13 is particularly poignant in light of v. 1, where "Shepherd" is literally

"Feeder." The one who is supposed to feed Israel is allowing Israel to be fed upon.

The question raised in v. 12 receives no answer. Rather, vs. 12–13 are followed by renewed petition, "Turn again," or as the imperative phrase could be translated, "Repent, O God of hosts" (v. 14). The sequence is reminiscent of Ex. 32:11–12, where two questions (see "why" in v. 11 and v. 12) lead immediately to Moses' request that God "turn" (v. 12). The request in Ps. 80:14 at least implies an answer to the question in v. 12, especially when Ps. 80 is heard in conjunction with Isa. 5:1–7 and Ex. 32:11–12; that is, God is punishing Israel for its sin. The people's promise that "we will never turn back" (Ps. 80:18a) also implies that the people have sinned previously, but there is no direct confession of sin.

This fact, plus the placement and construction of v. 14, places the initiative for restoration exclusively on God. Verse 14 occurs at a point where one might expect the refrain again (and indeed, some older commentaries actually amend the text to make v. 14 consistent with vs. 3, 7, 19); and the word "Turn" is a different form of the *same* Hebrew verb as "Restore" in vs. 3, 7, 19. This seemingly intentional variation in construction has the effect of emphasizing v. 14. Coupled with the absence of any confession of sin by the people, the message is clear: If there is to be life (v. 18) and a future for the people of God, it will result from *God's* repentance rather than the people's repentance. The fourfold imperative in v. 14 also has an emphatic effect. Not only does "Turn" recall the earlier exodus event, but so do "see" (Ex. 3:7, NRSV "observed"; 4:31) and "have regard for" (Ex. 3:16; 4:31, NRSV "given heed"). As in both major episodes of the exodus event—the deliverance from Egypt and the forgiveness following the construction of the golden calf—God's activity is determinative.

The petition in Ps. 80:17 reinforces v. 14. To have God's hand upon one is to experience protection and deliverance (see Ezra 8:31). The "one at your right hand" and "the one whom you made strong" are sometimes understood as references to a king or future king; however, these phrases probably refer to Israel. The Hebrew underlying "one whom" in the second phrase is literally "son of a human," and Israel is elsewhere referred to as God's son (see Hos. 11:1; see also Gen. 49:22, where Joseph, represented by a plant, is called a "son of a fruit-bearer"; in the NRSV "fruitful bough"). The final petition is the refrain in v. 19, which is slightly different from vs. 3, 7, by inclusion of the more personal divine name, Yahweh.

Psalm 80 provides a helpful perspective in relation to the Gospel lesson. Luke 12:49–56 is a radical call to repentance. More troublesome, perhaps, than the "family values" implications is the danger that repentance will be perceived as a meritorious work. Of course, the Gospels ultimately demonstrate what Israel's history demonstrates again and again—namely, humanity's failure to repent and be faithful as well as God's willingness to bear the pain of loving wayward children. Psalm 80 and the cross proclaim that our lives ultimately depend on God's willingness to repent (v. 14). What human repentance amounts to, at best, is turning to accept the loving embrace of God, which gives us life (see Luke 15:11–32). As Jesus suggested in extending the vine image, "Apart from me you can do nothing" (John 15:5).

## Hebrews 11:29–12:2

The elaborate praise of the faith of Israel's past generations in Heb. 11 does not lend itself readily to the needs of the lectionary for readings that are succinct and manageable. The sheer power and familiarity of the passage, however, make it difficult to omit altogether. Presumably it is as a result of these conflicting needs that the editors of the lectionary have decided to incorporate part of the opening of Heb. 11 in one reading (Proper 14) and part of the closing of Heb. 11 in this reading. Although that decision nicely presents the context of the athletic image of Heb. 12:1–2, the end of Heb. 11 becomes somewhat disjointed.

Hebrews 11:29–31 belongs with the preceding section about Moses (vs. 23–28), as is clear not only from the content but from the change from "by faith" (see vs. 23, 24, 27, 28, 29, 30, 31) to "through faith" in v. 33. The crossing of the Red Sea and the defeat of Jericho both belong, at least in a general sense, to the period associated with Moses.

With v. 32, the pace changes, as is clear from the conventional question and explanation that introduce this section ("And what more should I say? For time would fail me . . ."). Instead of detailing the faithful deeds of individuals, the author lists them and refers more generally to their accomplishments. Initially, in vs. 32–34, these are military or political deeds born of faithfulness: conquering of other nations, ruling with justice, triumph in war.

At v. 35 the subject changes. Instead of celebrating the triumphs of Israel, vs. 35–38 recount the faithfulness of the martyrs during the Maccabean period. Because no specific names are mentioned and this history is less familiar than that of earlier periods, the allusions may be missed, but the events depicted here may be found in the

Maccabean writings, especially 1 Macc. 1:60–63 and 2 Macc. 6:18–31, 7:1–42. The general point is clear, however, and prepares the way for the reference to Jesus in Heb. 12:2; faithfulness consists not only of triumphal behavior in battle and conquest but also of the faithful endurance of persecution.

With 11:39–40, Hebrews begins the transition to the hortatory section of chapter 12. Even these heroes and heroines of Israel's past did not attain the full victory for their faith, because "something better" had been promised them. That "something" now appears in the person of Jesus Christ.

The use of athletic imagery is a rhetorical convention (compare its use in the Pauline letters: 1 Cor. 9:24–29; Gal. 2:2; Phil. 2:16) that the author of Hebrews plays with effectively in Heb. 12:1–2. All the necessary elements of a race are included: the spectators, possible encumbrances, the trials involved in running a marathon, the lead runner, and the finish line. Together these features summon Christians to their own life of faithfulness.

The reference to the "cloud of witnesses" works on two levels. First, taking "witness" in its simplest sense, these are onlookers, presumably those invoked in chapter 11 who serve largely as spectators of the race. They stand along the route to encourage the efforts of the runners. Second, however, the "witnesses" are those approved by God. The Greek noun *murtys* used here is anticipated in Heb. 11 when the writer describes the forerunners of Christian faith as "approved" or "commended" (see 11:2, 4, 5, 39). In other words, this "cloud of witnesses" is not an indifferent gang of spectators who turn out on a pretty day to see who might win the race. On the contrary, this particular group of observers is anything but neutral; having already won God's commendation, they line the roadway to encourage those who follow.

The precise meaning of "every weight and the sin that clings so closely" is a little unclear, as the footnote in the NRSV indicates. Given the use of the race image, probably what is envisioned here is anything that might hamper the runners in their course. What is clear, at the end of 12:1, is that the race is a long one, for it calls for "perseverance."

Hebrews is throughout concerned with articulating the role of Jesus Christ, so it comes as little surprise that the lead runner in this race is Jesus himself. He is the "pioneer" or leader of the race. Already in 2:10, Hebrews has designated Jesus as the pioneer, and there also he is said to have become such through his sufferings. And he is the "perfecter of our faith," the one who so well embodies faithfulness that believers learn its meaning from observing him.

With the remainder of 12:2, Hebrews summarizes the way in which Jesus became "pioneer and perfecter." His own "race" consisted of enduring the cross and its shame. Because we have become accustomed to the cross as a rather innocuous piece of religious symbolism, contemporary Christians may too quickly read over this phrase, but the stigma attached to death on a cross was severe. Even this brief reference to the shame of the cross would not have been overlooked by a first-century audience.

By virtue of this endurance, however, Jesus has crossed the finish line. He has "taken his seat at the right hand of the throne of God." Once again the author of Hebrews draws on Ps. 110:1 (see Heb. 1:3; 8:1; 10:12) to refer to the triumph of Jesus.

The race image here drops out of sight, so that the finish line that awaits Christians is unnamed. In the conclusion to the book, of course, the "finish line" does emerge in terms of the new city that awaits (12:22; 13:14). In the meantime, what matters is that Christians understand that they are not alone; the heritage of Israel lines up along their course and the Son himself runs on ahead.

## Luke 12:49–56

If one were to list ten of the hardest sayings in the Gospels, the first portion of the selection for Proper 15 would undoubtedly be on the list (Luke 12:49–53). The statements that Jesus came to bring fire, a distressful baptism, and division, even among families, are hardly welcome words for any congregation. We are happier with Jesus as a peacemaker than as a home breaker.

The passage comes in a larger section where the talk becomes sober and the reality of judgment is clear. Following the admonitions to readiness in preparation for the advent of the Son of man (12:35–48) come these forceful words about Jesus' destiny and the implications for others (vs. 49–53), and then a chiding of the crowds for their failure to discern the times (vs. 54–56). Defendants are enjoined to settle out of court with their accusers (vs. 57–59). Two recent tragedies are recounted in order to urge those who have escaped them to repent (13:1–5). A bit more time has been granted the barren fig tree in hopes that it will finally bring forth fruit (13:6–9). The present is depicted as a time of crisis, demanding repentance and changed lives.

One immediately senses the passion and drama of 12:49–53. The first-person language, the anguished wish that the fire were already kindled, the admission of distress, the question posed in such a way that every single reader wants a yes answer, only to find it a no, the vivid description of the divided families (three against two and two against three, parents against children, children against parents)—it all adds up to an ominous scene, pictured in evocative terms. Appropriately, the translators punctuate each sentence with an exclamation point.

What is the fire Jesus wishes were already kindled and the baptism that causes such anxiety? Fire occurs repeatedly in Luke as an image for judgment (3:9, 16; 17:29), the flames that destroy and refine. Baptism is best understood in light of Mark 10:38, where it is associated with the cup and symbolizes Jesus' coming death. The two belong together. The days ahead are fraught with peril and judgment. Such a prophetic mission as Jesus has embarked on provokes sharp division—acceptance by some and rejection by others. It is a moment of painful crisis.

At the time of Jesus' presentation in the Temple, readers learn that he is "destined for the falling and rising of many in Israel, and to be a sign that will be opposed" (2:34). The very presence of Jesus precipitates a crisis, a division among people in terms of how they respond to him. His death epitomizes the crisis, but the crisis continues in the families and communities that are torn by conflict and disagreement. What is more, the way the text puts it, the divisions are not merely an unhappy consequence of human resistance, but a piece of Jesus' vocation. Robert Tannehill comments, "This extreme language emphasizes the inescapability of these experiences if God's plan is to be realized" (*The Narrative Unity of Luke-Acts: A Literary Interpretation*; Philadelphia: Fortress Press, 1986, vol. 1, p. 252).

From the beginning of Luke's story, promises of peace have been central to the presence of Jesus (1:79; 2:14; 8:48; 19:38), and peace is the message the Seventy are commissioned to preach (10:5–6). But disciples, both ancient and modern, are eager for an instant peace, a trouble-free fulfillment of the promised salvation. Jesus' words are jolting because they make it plain that there is no peace without conflict, no salvation without rejection. Jesus himself faces that at Jerusalem, and the disciples need expect nothing different. But rather than being signs of defeat, rejection and conflict are incorporated into the divine plan.

The concluding paragraph serves as a wake-up call to prod the readers into a sensitivity to the various expressions of God's rule in human life (12:54–56). If they (people somewhere on their way from Galilee to Jerusalem) are smart enough to know that a heavy cloud in the west (from the Mediterranean) means rain is on the way and that

a strong south wind (from the desert in the Negev) portends a heat
spell, then why are they not able to discern the present as a time of
crisis? Why do they remain blind to what is happening in their
midst? Common sense says to settle with your accuser before you
get to court and risk being thrown into jail (vs. 57–59). Common
sense also says to repent in face of the coming judgment.

While the words of the text are not very palatable to those seeking
safety and security, calls to change are reminders that judgment
need not be the last word, that destruction is not inevitable.

# PROPER 16

In Luke 13:15, Jesus addresses his opponents as he had addressed the crowds in 12:56, "You hypocrites!" The effect is to portray the healing that Jesus has just performed as a call to decision, a call to "repentance and changed lives," as suggested in the commentary on the Gospel lection.

The lesson from Heb. 12 also contains a summons to response (see v. 25). The call to repentance—to a transformed existence—makes sense only in the presence of a transforming power that is accessible to those called. Thus, the author of Hebrews proclaims to the readers that they "have come . . . to the city of the living God, the heavenly Jerusalem, . . . and to Jesus, the mediator of a new covenant" (vs. 22, 24). For Luke, it is precisely Jesus and his wonderful works that signal the accessibility of God's transforming power, and thus that signal also the time for repentance.

The accessibility of God's transforming power is evident in the lessons from Jeremiah and the Psalms, although these lessons do not involve a call to decision. In fact, in Jeremiah's case, Jeremiah has no choice! The decision about Jeremiah's vocation was made by God before Jeremiah was born (Jer. 1:5). Like it or not, Jeremiah will be transformed from an inexperienced boy into "a prophet to the nations" (1:5; see v. 10). The transformation has to do with the accessibility of God's power—" I am with you . . . , says the LORD." Like Jesus and like the Hebrews, Jeremiah will experience severe opposition; but he will be able to endure it, because he belongs to God.

The same is true of the psalmist. In fact, it is easy to imagine Ps. 71 as a prayer of Jeremiah. Amid opposition from the wicked, the psalmist affirms what Jeremiah had been told by God—that his life from its very beginnings has belonged to God.

## Jeremiah 1:4–10

This day's Old Testament lection is the first in a series of nine consecutive Old Testament passages associated with Jeremiah (the book of Lamentations, which provides the lection for Proper 22, was once thought to have been composed by Jeremiah). In addition to being the longest book in the Bible, the book of Jeremiah provides more insights of a personal nature into the life of the prophet who stands behind the literature than does any other book in the prophetic corpus of the Old Testament. Therefore, an expansive range of human emotions is laid before the reader, alongside Yahweh's word to the people, as that word is mediated through the heart and mind of the prophet.

The three sections of the passage (Jer. 1:4–5, 6–8, 9–10) stand out clearly in the NRSV text. Verses 4–5 appear abruptly, without attempting to provide any context in the life of the prophet. (If one momentarily sets aside the editorial introduction to the book, vs. 1–3, these lines form the beginning of the book proper.)

This quality of suddenness is quite different from the accounts of call experiences of some other major Old Testament figures (Ex. 3:1; Isa. 6:1–2), but we may assume that the year is 627 B.C. (the thirteenth year of Josiah's reign, Jer. 1:2) and that Jeremiah is either a ''boy'' (v. 7) like Samuel (1 Sam. 3:2–9) or a young man at the home of his priestly father, Hilkiah (Jer. 1:1; the name of Jeremiah's mother is unfortunately never provided) in Anathoth, a village quite near Jerusalem. What external stimulus, if any, ignited Jeremiah's sense of call is not clear, but 1:11–13 suggests that he was responsive to such things. One interesting suggestion is that, as this date is near that of the death of Ashurbanipal, the last strong ruler of the dominant Assyrian Empire, the passing of that monarch, with its portents for fundamental changes in the lives of the nations of the Near East, may have been the spark that ignited Jeremiah's sense of Yahweh's involvement in his life (compare Isa. 6:1).

In any event, the thrust of v. 5 is enormously sobering. That Jeremiah is to be the mouth of Yahweh during the last decades of the life of the Judean monarchy and on into a future that many could hardly imagine would be a difficult enough reality in itself. But the word of Yahweh is clear that this is no recent decision on Yahweh's part. To be Yahweh's prophet at this juncture in history is the very reason for which Jeremiah has been born. It is his very purpose for being! This startling declaration underscores the fact that, without Jeremiah's interpretation of the destruction of the nation and his words concerning Judah's future (texts explored in coming weeks), the Judeans of the sixth century might not have had the conceptual and theological tools with which to comprehend their monumental tragedy and to move beyond it. In a very real sense, therefore, it may be said that Jeremiah is the (human) savior of the people of God.

The final phrase of v. 5, "prophet to the nations," is probably a reference to Judah and its principal neighbors, Egypt, Assyria, and Babylonia (note 25:1–29). But the larger meaning of these words is obviously a reference to their role in lives of people far removed from that small arena of human history.

In this connection it is puzzling that, given the monumental role of Jeremiah in Judah's life, this prophet is never mentioned in 2 Kings. (Nor, for that matter, are Amos and Hosea.) This is in spite of Jeremiah's life are closely scrutinized in this part of the Deuteronomistic History (2 Kings 22—25), and in spite of the fact that the Deuteronomistic History places great value on the office of the prophet, as the stories about Nathan, Elijah, and Elisha attest.

It is small wonder, then, that young Jeremiah repudiates Yahweh's call (vs. 6–8). One is reminded of Moses' reluctance to lead the people of God (Ex. 4:10) and of Isaiah's efforts to spurn Yahweh's initiatives (Isa. 6:5). But Yahweh will not take no for an answer. Instead, Yahweh promises not only to strengthen the prophet but to provide the message that Jeremiah is to deliver. The assurance that "I am with you to deliver you" is recalled over and again, as Jeremiah is rescued from life-threatening situations (as, for example, Jer. 26:16–19). Yet the prophet often must have doubted the sincerity of Yahweh's intentions, for he was frequently in anguish over the prophetic role (Jer. 15:15–18; compare 8:18–9:1, Proper 20).

Jeremiah is "ordained" as Yahweh's prophet with the touch on his lips of Yahweh's hand (1:9–10). This symbolic internalizing of the word of Yahweh reminds the reader of similar "ordinations" of Isaiah (Isa. 6:7) and Ezekiel (Ezek. 3:1–3). The role of Jeremiah is to assist Yahweh in the twin tasks of destruction and reconstruction:

> to pluck up and to pull down,
> to destroy and to overthrow,
> to build and to plant.

That four verbs are devoted to judgment and only two to redemption may be interpreted as a reference to the immediacy of the fall of the nation. But the last, and thus the enduring, words are of restoration!

Jeremiah's work as a prophet is thus inaugurated. He is to suffer greatly in the years ahead, and the nation is to suffer even more. Yet out of their suffering will emerge a new day in the life of the Jews and in the life of humankind. God's acts of judgment always are intended to redeem.

## Psalm 71:1–6

See the discussion of this passage under the Fourth Sunday After Epiphany.

## Hebrews 12:18–29

A question about eschatology in the New Testament would probably send most preachers and teachers to consult with the apostle Paul, or the author of the Apocalypse, or perhaps the evangelists (as in Mark 13 and its parallels). The author of Hebrews would not readily come to mind, for much of Hebrews seems to have a timeless quality that runs against the grain of early Christian eschatology. Even the frequent contrasts between things earthly and things heavenly (such as sacrifice and temple) have more in common with platonic contrasts between temporal appearance and eternal reality than with the urgency of eschatological writings.

The lectionary reading from Heb. 12:18–29 makes it clear that Hebrews is anything but noneschatological, however. Here, as often in the New Testament, eschatology provides a context within which to discuss ethical behavior. That context serves to warn against the dire consequences of failure to follow through with a Christian life; it also holds out hope of blessings to come for those who endure. In this passage, the two are closely intertwined.

Consistent with the style of argumentation throughout Hebrews, the passage makes use of an a fortiori argument. What was true of an earlier generation will be *even more true* of this last generation (see especially v. 25). The author contrasts the generation of the exodus with that of the Christian community; both the challenges and the blessings of the Christian community are greater than those of their predecessors in the time of Moses.

The multitude of images that open the passage creates temporary confusion, for no reference in the preceding lines provides a hint as to what follows. The sudden introduction of "something that can be touched, a blazing fire, and darkness, and gloom, and a tempest, and the sound of a trumpet, and a voice" (vs. 18–19) will bewilder the reader who is not as immersed in biblical tradition as is our author. What this profusion conjures up, of course, is the experience of God's presence by the exodus generation, as Ex. 19 and Deut. 4:11–12 and 5:22–25 depict the giving of the law with just this imagery.

Verses 20 and 21 of Heb. 12 amplify the point in a way that is unmistakable: the presence of God was for that generation a fearsome thing. Even an innocent animal that unknowingly touched the mountain would be put to death (see Ex. 19:12–13). And Moses himself, God's chosen, is said to have been terrified by God's presence (see the earlier discussion of Moses in Heb. 3:1–6).

Until this point in the reading, it remains unclear what exactly the writer intends by recalling this experience of Sinai. Only with v. 22 do we understand that a contrast is under way here. "But" (alla in Greek) indicates a sharp disjuncture between vs. 18–21 and what follows. In addition, the words "you have come" (or, more literally, "you have approached") parallel the opening words of v. 18. Both the exodus generation and the Christian generation approach God, but their situations differ dramatically.

Unlike the exodus generation—which could not draw near to God's place, which experienced God's presence only through the darkness and gloom that accompanied that presence, which still had no place of its own—the addresses of Hebrews can expect to enjoy all these blessings of the divine presence. First, they "come to Mount Zion and to the city of the living God, the heavenly Jerusalem" (v. 22). Second, they enjoy the presence of "innumerable angels" and the "assembly of the firstborn" (see 1:6, which suggests that this is the assembly of those who believe in Jesus), God, and the "spirits of the righteous." Finally, they enjoy the presence of Jesus, "the mediator of a new covenant." Here the contrast with the generation of Moses culminates, for this covenant will not be broken.

In light of this contrast between the experience of the exodus and the experience that awaits Christians, the author moves to a warning: "See that you do not refuse the one who is speaking" (12:25). The Israelites disregarded the warning of Moses "on earth," and the consequences were dire. God now warns from heaven, and God's warning threatens to shake both earth and heaven itself.

This final "shaking" will destroy creation, but "what cannot be shaken" will remain. A review of the content of Hebrews will clarify this comment. Melchizedek "remains a priest forever" (7:3), and Jesus Christ is "the same yesterday and today and forever" (13:8). Christians themselves are in possession of "something better and more lasting" (10:34), anticipating a lasting home in the "city that is to come" (13:14).

The contrast with the exodus generation comes to an end with 12:27: Christians will enter into the place of God, the very presence of God, and that presence cannot be destroyed. "Therefore," v. 28 exhorts, "let us give thanks."

A list of specific instructions both precedes (12:14–17) and follows this reading (13:1–19), but the first instruction sets the tone for all the rest. The primary duty of the Christian is to acknowledge God's hand in all things. Only in that way is "acceptable worship" possible.

The reading ends with a reminder that "our God is a consuming fire," a clear reference to Deut. 4:24, which brings us back to the "blazing fire" in the opening of the passage. If the experience Hebrews anticipates for Christians differs dramatically from that of the exodus generation, the God they worship remains the same.

## Luke 13:10–17

Stories of Jesus' healing carry differing meanings depending on how an incident is related and in what context it appears. Some highlight Jesus' capacity to accomplish remarkable deeds; others precipitate controversies with the religious authorities; still others take on a didactic function as Jesus instructs about the way of discipleship.

Luke 13:10–17 is one of those accounts which reflect at least two "interests." On the one hand, since the healing occurs on the Sabbath it becomes the occasion for a sharp exchange between Jesus and the leader of the synagogue, which puts the latter to shame. It becomes a controversy story and ultimately a judgment on the Jewish authorities. On the other hand, it is the story of Jesus' authority over the forces of Satan that have left this woman badly crippled for eighteen years. It demonstrates the inbreaking of God's rule in human life. The two "interests" of the story, of course, belong together and mesh with the thematic thrust of the context.

First, we look at the conflict between Jesus and the leader of the synagogue. The account begins with the observation that Jesus "was teaching in one of the synagogues on the sabbath" (13:10). He was doing what a prophet should be doing on the Sabbath. While we are not told from what text Jesus was teaching, his healing of the crippled woman may have been no more than a carrying out of the implications of the text.

The indignant and persistent protest of the leader of the synagogue ("kept saying to the crowd") was based on a reading of Ex. 20:9 and Deut. 5:13 that categorized Jesus' actions as work that should have been done on a weekday. Challenged, Jesus responds with a sharp criticism of the synagogue leader's reading of the Fourth Commandment. He uses a clear and homely example to expose the fallacy of ignoring the woman's infirmity on the Sabbath. The crowds immediately get the point, and the leader of the synagogue and his cohorts are "put to shame."

But Jesus' retort indicates that the issue is more than an academic difference of opinion about the interpretation of texts. "You hypocrites!" raises the moral issue of interpretation. The charge is leveled in Luke at those who are blind to the real meaning of things, those who cannot perceive their own weakness (6:42) and cannot discern the present evidence of God's rule (12:56).

One of the things to which the leader of the synagogue is blind is the remarkable restoration of a "daughter of Abraham" (13:16). The illness this woman had had meant the disruption and loss of social relationships, exclusion, and therefore loneliness. What Jesus' action did was not only to bring physical wholeness to the crippled woman, but also to reinstate her to legitimate membership in the community of Israel, a fitting behavior for the Sabbath.

A second aspect of the account leads to the other major "interest" of the story. A teaching of Jesus in chapter 12 chided the people for their failure to discern the significance of the present. They knew that a cloud in the west meant rain and a strong wind from the south suggested a heat spell, but they could not perceive the clear signs of God's rule, nor did they realize that the present was a time of crisis, a time for repentance and changed lives (12:54–13:9).

The leader of the synagogue and his colleagues fail to see that Jesus has taken the initiative in releasing the woman from the bondage of Satan. By forbidding such conduct on the Sabbath, they put themselves on Satan's side in the struggle for human lives, and they become enemies of Jesus. They badly misjudge the conflict taking place between the rule of God and the rule of Satan (see 11:20). Not surprisingly, the thirteenth chapter concludes with Jesus' anguish over Jerusalem, "the city that kills the prophets and stones those who are sent to it!" (13:34). The authorities' blindness leads to their final rejection of the prophet who could save them.

It is important that the story leave us with a vivid picture of a divided Israel. The religious leaders are shamed. Their failure to detect the signs of God's presence condemns them. Homiletically, it is easy to let the leader of the synagogue symbolize Israel and stoke the fires of anti-Judaism. At the same time, the text says that the woman ("a daughter of Abraham") praises God for her healing (13:13) and the crowds rejoice at the wonderful things Jesus is doing (13:17). Rather than a judgment on Israel, the story becomes a fulfillment of the prediction that Jesus brings division (12:49–53), a phenomenon all too modern, when the present is discerned as a time for repentance.

# PROPER 17

Ordinary Time 22

*Sunday between August 28
and September 3 inclusive*

The admonition in Heb. 13:2 "to show hospitality to strangers" is vividly illustrated by the advice that Jesus gives to guests and hosts in Luke 14:7–14. The advice to guests leads up to the revolutionary saying in v. 11. As the commentary on today's Gospel suggests, the saying is a summary of the way God works; the effects are profound—"a world is overturned."

In the topsy-turvy world of divine hospitality, everybody is family. The strangers whom Jesus tells us to invite to our parties are not just any strangers; they are those who in Jesus' day were considered unclean and undesirable, and they will never be able to reciprocate. This kind of radical hospitality makes sense only in light of the conviction that God rules the world and therefore that adequate repayment for our efforts is simply our relatedness to God and our conformity to what God intends (Luke 14:14; Heb. 13:5–6). Both Heb. 13 and Luke 14:7–14 are calls to commitment to God's reign rather than to the ways of the world.

Both Jer. 2:4–13 and Ps. 81 also call the people of God back to commitment to God alone, rather than to the gods of the nations and their values (see Ps. 81:8–9; Jer. 2:11). Both texts portray God recalling God's gracious guidance of the people in the past and lamenting their present unfaithfulness. The call to commitment that is implicit in Jer. 2:4–13 is explicit in Ps. 81:8, "O Israel, if you would but listen to me!"

In our day, God is no doubt still lamenting our failure to listen, but is also, no doubt, still inviting us to take our humble place at a table that promises exaltation on a scale that the world cannot even imagine.

## Jeremiah 2:4–13

God's people, having been the recipients of a unique relationship with their Creator, have rejected both the relationship and the One

487

who extended it to them. Such is the thrust of the present text, in which the Lord is portrayed as not only deeply pained over the defection of Israel, but at something of a loss to understand it. The setting is a court of law (compare, for example, Micah 6:1–5), a place which with Jeremiah, as a member of a priestly family, was perhaps familiar, since the role of the priests was sometimes judicial as well as liturgical. The sum of the passage, therefore, is an indictment of Israel before the bar of justice.

After an introductory sentence (v. 4) the text proper begins with a haunting question put by Yahweh: "What wrong did your ancestors find in me, that they went far from me?" Just as Yahweh's love of the people has an ancient history, so has the people's rejection, for it is not just the present generation that will have nothing to do with Yahweh, but "your ancestors," as well. In a manner similar to that of Hosea (Hos. 11:1–4), Jeremiah regards the period of the exodus from Egypt and the wanderings in the wilderness as a time of Yahweh's greatest intimacy with the nation. Yet not even the One who "brought us up from the land of Egypt" is the object of the people's devotion. Emphasis in the text is on the terrors from which Yahweh has saved Israel, "deserts and pits," "drought and deep darkness" (Jer. 2:6), and on their opposites, those creature comforts which possession of the Land of Yahweh's Promise has yielded: "a plentiful land," "its fruits and its good things" (v. 7).

Yet not even this land, the object of their wanderings, has prompted the people to an appreciation of Yahweh's grace: for "when you entered you defiled my land."

In v. 8 the focus of attention shifts from the past to the present, and the failure of the ancestors is repeated by those in authority in that they too neglect to search out Yahweh and Yahweh's ways. (Notice how the question that the ancestors should have asked, but did not, is also missing from the lips of the leaders of the people: "Where is the LORD?" vs. 6, 8.) Four categories of leaders are identified: priests, law handlers (that is, interpreters of Torah), rulers, and prophets, and in its own way each group has prostituted its office. (The wordplay that NRSV produces in v. 8, "prophets . . . profit," is clever, but does not reflect a similar wordplay in the Hebrew.) It would doubtless be incorrect to conclude that Jeremiah sees evil only in the nation's leaders, for the people as a whole have sinned ("your children's children" of v. 9). Rather, the leaders of the people are singled out for dishonorable mention because they, above all, should know better.

The accusation is formalized in v. 9 with the use (twice) of the Hebrew word *rîb*, meaning "to file a lawsuit." Witnesses are summoned (v. 10) and urged to search from west to east ("Cyprus" to

"Kedar") for precedents: nations simply do not change their gods. Yet Israel has done this unheard-of thing. The "glory" (v. 11) that Israel has exchanged for "something that does not profit" (an echo of v. 8) is a reference to the active, gracious presence of Yahweh. For it was the "glory" of Yahweh that guided the people through the dangers of the wilderness and that appeared to the children of Israel as a pillar of fire by night and a pillar of cloud by day (note Ex. 40:34–38). The created order itself stands amazed at the magnitude of Israel's folly, for while creation knows its master, Israel apparently does not.

The error of the people is twofold, in that they have turned their backs on Yahweh, the God who has loved and called them in special ways, while they have lavished their affection on gods who are not God. They have substituted flawed cisterns for "living water" (Jer. 2:13).

A number of scholars maintain that there is a rough chronological sequence to the passages in the book of Jeremiah and, if that is so, it is quite likely that this passage comes from the early days of Jeremiah's active ministry, and therefore reflects those conditions of spiritual syncretism which Josiah inherited from his predecessor and father, Amon (2 Kings 21:19–26). It was this participation in the worship of alien deities that Josiah targeted in his reforms. It is interesting to speculate that Jeremiah's preaching may have helped to stiffen Josiah's backbone in this regard, but as Josiah seems to have taken no notice of Jeremiah—at least as far as 2 Kings is aware (note 2 Kings 22:14–20)—that possibility is remote.

Yet these words served notice on all who would listen that Yahweh, God of Israel, would brook no competition in the loyalty of the people. While the culture of ancient Israel is light years away from that of our own time, it is still a reality that God demands loyalty and love from the people of God (note Mark 12:30 and parallels). And it is still a reality, in this age when some people, at least, clamor that all the visible, public symbols of religion should stay in place, that justice and compassion still constitute the true worship of the God of Israel, the God and Father of Jesus Christ. Justice and compassion, more than prayers in visible places, constitute the calling of Israel and of the church (compare Hos. 6:6; Amos 5:21–24; Micah 6:6–8).

## Psalm 81:1, 10–16

Like Ps. 50 for Proper 14, Ps. 81 can be considered an example of a "liturgical sermon," in which the preacher speaks on behalf of God (compare vs. 6–16 with Ps. 50:7–23). Like that in Ps. 50, the sermon in Ps. 81 has two parts (vs. 6–10 and 11–16), preceded by an introduction. Whereas the introduction in Ps. 50 imaginatively portrayed the convening of a court with Yahweh as judge, the introduction in Ps. 81 involves the beginning of a festal celebration. Indeed, it is possible that the sermon was preached originally on one of Israel's holy days. Joyous praise accompanies the beginning of the festival (vs. 1–2), which is marked by blowing "the trumpet at the new moon" (v. 3). This practice accords with the description in Lev. 23:23–24 and Num. 29:1–6 of the observance of the first day of the seventh month (sometimes called the Festival of Trumpets). The conviction of the people for their faithlessness would also be appropriate for the Day of Atonement (see 81:11), and the recollection of the Decalogue (see especially 81:10ab) and the harvest theme (81:10c, 16) would be appropriate for the Festival of Booths or Tabernacles. Both of these observances were also in the seventh month (see Lev. 23:26–36; Num. 29:7–39), so perhaps Ps. 81 was originally related to this festal season. Regardless of its original setting, however, Ps. 81 functions as a call to commitment in all times and places. Although the lection omits most of the introduction and first section of the sermon, we shall examine them in order to set the context for hearing vs. 10–16.

Psalm 81 begins like a song of praise. People are invited to "sing aloud" (see Pss. 145:7; 5:11; 67:4; 96:12; 149:5, NRSV "sing for joy"; 95:1; 98:4, NRSV "joyous song"), "shout for joy" (see Pss. 95:1–2; 98:4, 6; 100:1, NRSV "make a joyful noise"), and "raise a song" (the Hebrew root occurs in Ex. 15:2; Pss. 33:2; 47:6–7; 95:2; 98:4–5, for example), with a variety of instrumental accompaniment (see Ex. 15:20; 2 Sam. 6:5; Pss. 149:3; 150:3–5). Beyond the fact that such joyous praise is appropriate for a festival, it should be noted that the same invitations occur frequently in contexts that make explicit what is really being celebrated—the reign of God over all peoples and things. For instance, of the psalms cited above, Pss. 5, 47, 95, 96, 98, 145, and 149 either contain the exclamation "The LORD is King!" (Ps. 96:10) or otherwise address the Lord as "king" (Pss. 5:2; 47:2, 7, 8; 95:3; 98:6; 145:1; 149:2). Furthermore, the song of praise in Ex. 15 culminates in the affirmation that "the LORD will *reign* forever and ever" (emphasis added), and 2 Sam. 6:2 suggests that God is "*enthroned* on the cherubim" (emphasis added). The invitations in Ps. 81:1–2 to celebrate Yahweh's sovereignty anticipate what will be the main theme of the sermon that follows—namely, only Yahweh is God (see especially vs. 9–10).

Verse 5c is problematic, but it should probably be understood as the preacher's claim that he or she will be delivering *God's* word rather than his or her own words. It may be similar to the contemporary "Listen for the Word of God." In any case, it is God who speaks in the first person in the remainder of the psalm, first reminding the people of the gracious deliverance from the burden of bondage in Egypt (vs. 6–7a; the word translated "burden" occurs in Ex. 1:11; 2:11; 5:4–5; 6:6), and then perhaps of further gracious dealings in the wilderness (Ps. 81:7c; God seems here to be giving Israel the benefit of the doubt, for Meribah is remembered elsewhere as a place where *Israel tested God:* see Ex. 17:7; Ps. 95:8). Psalm 81:7b may be an allusion to Sinai, if the phrase "secret place of thunder" is meant to refer to a cloud (see Ex. 19:16). In any case, an allusion to Sinai would be an appropriate anticipation of the clear recollection of the Decalogue in Ps. 81:9–10. Verse 10 is almost identical to the prologue of the Decalogue (Ex. 20:2; Deut. 5:6), and Ps. 81:9 is another way of formulating the First Commandment—"no other gods" (Ex. 20:3; Deut. 5:7; see also Jer. 2:4–13, the Old Testament lesson for the day).

At the heart of the first section of the sermon is the expression of God's desire that the people "Hear"—"listen to me!" (Ps. 81:8; the same Hebrew word lies behind both "hear" and "listen"). God had "heard" the people in Egypt (Ex. 3:7), and it seems only reasonable that they now "hear" God. Abundance awaits their hearing (Ps. 81:10c). The choice is theirs.

The second part of the sermon (vs. 11–16) begins by stating the people's choice (v. 11) and its consequence (v. 12). They "did not listen." God's response is to let the people have exactly what they chose—their own "stubborn hearts" and "their own counsels" (see Jer. 7:24, where both words also occur in the context of the prophet's accusation that the people "go after other gods" and "did not listen to me"; see vs. 6, 26). In effect, God's will to "fill" (Ps. 81:10c) and "satisfy" (v. 16) is thwarted by the people's refusal to "open" (v. 10c) themselves to God's gracious presence and action (see Rom. 1:24–25). Like a rejected lover, God's pain is evident. Verse 13 of Ps. 81 urgently repeats the desire God expressed in v. 8; the word "hear"/ "listen" occurs for the fourth time in the sermon. The setbacks the people have apparently experienced (note "enemies" and "foes" in v. 14) are not the result of God's will, but rather a result of the people's own choice. God wills abundant life—not just manna as in the wilderness, but the "finest of the wheat" (v. 16; see Ps. 147:14; see also the hymn "You Satisfy the Hungry Heart," by Omer Westendorf, in *The Presbyterian Hymnal;* Louisville, Ky: Westminster/John Knox Press, 1990, no. 521), and not just water from the rock as at Meribah (Ex. 17:6–7), but honey (see Deut. 32:13–14). O that the people would listen!

The admonition to "listen" to God calls to mind the story of Jesus' transfiguration (Mark 9:1–8). In a context that, like Ps. 81, recalls Sinai (note the "mountain" in v. 2, the presence of Moses, the cloud in v. 7), the divine voice identifies Jesus as "my Son," the bearer of the divine will, and says, "*Listen* to him!" (v. 7, emphasis added). What Jesus proclaimed was the reign of God, and he invited people to enter it (Mark 1:14–15). In our time and place, we are perhaps more bombarded by competing voices than any generation in the history of the world—newspapers, radio, TV, all vying for our attention and allegiance. In this din of competing voices, Ps. 81 calls us to discern the pained but persistent voice of the One who says simply, "Follow me" (Mark 1:17; compare Ps. 81:13b, John 10:4).

## Hebrews 13:1–8, 15–16

This lection opens with a series of traditional ethical admonitions (Heb. 13:1–7) that would have been equally at home in the moral writings of Hellenistic Judaism or the larger Greco-Roman world. It is difficult to detect an order to the admonitions or any overarching theme, although perhaps vs. 15–16 provide that theme (see the discussion below). Several of the admonitions are followed by statements of justification drawn either from experience or from the divine will (for example, v. 4b).

Although 13:1 appears to follow abruptly on 12:29, two features of the verse connect it closely to the preceding section. First, the verb "continue" translates the same Greek verb that appears in v. 27 as "remain" (*menein*). Among the things that must continue or remain is "mutual love" (*philadelphia*). Second, this admonition to mutual love recalls the earlier admonition to "pursue peace with everyone" (12:14). The expectation that love should characterize life within the Christian community appears in several strands of New Testament writings (for example, Rom. 12:10; 1 Thess. 4:9; 1 Peter 1:22; 2 Peter 1:7), but the admonition that follows in Heb. 13:2 may caution against understanding this circle of love too narrowly. If Christians love one another, surely that love spills over into their treatment of others.

The admonition "not [to] neglect to show hospitality to strangers" sounds a bit grudging to modern ears, in which a more positive formulation would be welcome. Rhetorically, however, the saying functions to emphasize the importance of hospitality. In other words, not to neglect hospitality is to make certain that it is carried out. Here a justification accompanies the admonition: "for by doing

that some have entertained angels without knowing it." This allusion to the scriptural stories of Abraham, Lot, and Gideon serves to
remind readers of the importance of welcoming those beyond the
confines of the community.

The next admonition, that concerning those who are imprisoned
or undergoing torture, recalls 10:32–36. Hebrews' own audience has
experienced such persecution and has already participated in ministry with those who are in prison. As the recipients of persecution,
Christians have a heightened sensitivity to the situation of others.

The reminder about the importance of faithfulness in marriage
(13:4) is accompanied by another statement of justification, this time
framed as a warning about divine judgment. The admonition to be
on guard about the love of money is likewise accompanied by a
statement about God's will, although here it is stated positively.
Human beings have no need to rely on money as a means of security,
for God "will never leave you or forsake you." Verse 6 amplifies this
assurance about divine protection, an assurance that may reach back
to include all the preceding admonitions.

The demand for remembering leaders of the Christian community in v. 7 continues this list of ethical demands, but here the
discourse shifts. Following v. 7, a long section of theological justification ties warnings about behavior to the sacrifice of Jesus himself.
This culminates in v. 17, with its renewed demand that Christians
obey the leaders of the church.

Verse 8, one of the most familiar lines of Hebrews, stands out
from its context. Literally, nothing connects it with what precedes or
follows. Theologically, however, this claim is very much at the heart
of Hebrews' understanding of Christology. The book opens with the
assertion that "you are the same, and your years will never end"
(1:12). More important in this context, the claim about the unchang
ing nature of Jesus Christ grounds the surrounding ethical instruction, for it is Christ who enables and demands responsible Christian
living.

The author returns to this point, although indirectly, in 13:15–16:
"Through him, then, let us continually offer a sacrifice of praise."
The sacrificial language here draws directly on the preceding verses,
in which Hebrews makes a final appeal to the sacrifice of Jesus
himself.

This "sacrifice of praise" recalls what Leviticus refers to as the
"sacrifice of the offering of well-being" (Lev. 7:11–18). In the psalms,
this sacrifice serves as a figurative reference to prayer or other
liturgical statements of praise (Pss. 50:14, 23; 107:22). Hebrews
includes this element of verbal praise ("the fruit of lips that confess

his name"), but clearly the "sacrifice of praise" includes one's behavior. As for Paul in Rom. 12:1–2, Hebrews applies this liturgical language to human life, all of which should be understood as a "sacrifice of praise." The end of Heb. 12 again enters into view, with its assumption that acceptable worship includes acceptable living.

Much in the vocabulary and style of Hebrews seems alien to contemporary Christians. Perhaps at this point as much as anywhere else, the distance that separates Hebrews from us is profoundly substantive rather than stylistic, however. Here Hebrews challenges our understanding of Christian life, for much within contemporary Christianity wishes to divide ethics from worship and worship from ethics. Congregations and individuals implicitly, sometimes explicitly, identify themselves with one emphasis or the other, as if they were alternative approaches to being Christian. The author of Hebrews radically connects the two, however, understanding that behavior does (or does not) reflect praise of God, and praise of God requires behavior consistent with that praise.

## Luke 14:1, 7–14

The Gospel readings from Luke for today and next Sunday come from the critical fourteenth chapter, where much of the action and teaching is set on the Sabbath in the house of a leader of the Pharisees. As if that setting were not enough to make readers anticipate conflict, the narrator adds that the Pharisees were watching Jesus closely (14:1). As the various incidents unfold, it turns out, however, that Jesus is really the aggressor—the one who challenges the lawyers and Pharisees (v. 3), who repudiates the guests who jockey for the "first couches" at the meal (v. 7), who instructs the host whom to invite to his next meals (vs. 12–14). By both ancient and modern standards, Jesus might be called a rude guest. The wary Pharisees are reduced to silence.

One can hardly overstate the importance of the meal as the setting for this section. Eating is essential for life; no one can manage for very long without it. But a dinner with guests is an occasion of social importance, to which people of one's class are invited and where there is an implied sharing of values and ideas. The status and rank of individuals are legitimated by their inclusion in the guest list and their location on the seating chart. For readers of Luke's narrative, meals are also symbols for the inbreaking and anticipated rule of God. In 13:29 we hear of people coming from east and west, north and south, to "eat in the kingdom of God." The Lord's table becomes a foretaste of the eschatological banquet (22:14–20).

There are four incidents that occur at this particular meal in the house of the leader of the Pharisees: Jesus' healing of the man with dropsy (14:2–6), his counsel about finding a place at the table (vs. 7–11), his instructions about what guests to invite (vs. 12–14), and the parable of the great dinner (vs. 15–24). The assigned lection focuses only on the two middle sections.

Jesus' warning about striving for a prominent seat and risking humiliation by being sent to a lower seat seems at first blush like no more than a piece of common sense, down-home wisdom. In fact, it can be paralleled by a variety of texts in both Jewish and Greco-Roman literature. There is nothing particularly distinctive about Jesus' counsel—until one reaches 14:11: "For all who exalt themselves will be humbled, and those who humble themselves will be exalted."

The saying is what the literary critics call a polar reversal. It is not just that the exalted will be humbled; we know about that from the story of Job. Nor is it simply that the humble will be exalted; we know about that from the story of Joseph. This is a complete reversal in which those who exalt themselves will be humbled and those who humble themselves will be exalted. When the north pole becomes the south pole and the south pole becomes the north pole, a world is overturned.

What starts out in the narrative as a breach of etiquette for a number of guests ends up with a prediction about a radical change. The passive voice of the two main verbs in v. 11 suggests that God is the real actor, the one who humbles the pretentious and exalts the humble. God is at the root of this polar reversal, a theme Luke will not let the readers forget (for example, 1:51–53; 6:20–26; 13:30).

The second section (14:12–14) spells out one of the revolutionary features of God's polar reversal. A guest list is usually composed of those closest to the host or hostess—relatives, friends, and rich neighbors—and it tends to foster a cycle of reciprocity. Hospitality takes on a self-serving purpose. Jesus abruptly proposes inviting a different group to the next "power lunch"—the poor, the crippled, the lame, and the blind. These are not only beyond the usual categories of family, friends, and rich neighbors; they are by Jewish law unclean.

The host is being urged to cross a big boundary and offer hospitality that cannot be repaid, at least in this life. As one writer puts it, "Jesus urges a social system without reciprocity" (Halvor

Moxnes, *The Economy of the Kingdom: Social Conflict and Economic Relations in Luke's Gospel*; Philadelphia: Fortress Press, 1988, p. 132). Through such activity these marginalized people become members of the group. Symbolically they are no longer outside the circle of power.

But why the poor, the crippled, the lame, and the blind? In the upcoming parable, they are the outsiders who end up being the insiders at the great dinner (14:21). They seem to be Jesus' favorites, his kind of people. They are those for whom he came (4:18–19). Because he likes them, his disciples cannot ignore them.

There is no doubt that Jesus is a disturbing, even rude, guest at this dinner party, upsetting standard protocol, but his presence and his words open the way for the transformed structures of the kingdom of God.

# PROPER 18

## Ordinary Time 23

*Sunday between*
*September 4 and 10 inclusive*

While each of the lessons has its own distinctive emphases, there are some common threads among them. Most prominent in the Gospel lesson is the theme of the cost of discipleship. One of the costs involves family, but the implication is that there are compensations as well as costs—in this case, the promise of a "new surrogate family" (see commentary on the Gospel lesson). In short, belonging to God affects the way in which one belongs to others. Traditional patterns, kinship and otherwise, are transformed.

It is this insight that lies at the heart of Paul's letter to Philemon concerning Philemon's slave, Onesimus. Without directly requesting that Philemon set Onesimus free, Paul clearly suggests that the ties that bind persons as brothers and sisters in Christ transform traditional social patterns, including slavery (see vs. 15–16). In short, belonging to God affects the way in which we belong to others.

While family or social patterns are not as clearly in view in Jer. 18 and Ps. 139, both texts do affirm our belongingness to God, individually and corporately. Psalm 139 is a marvelous affirmation that we are known by God. Such knowledge connotes intimate and inextricable relationship—we belong to God. While Ps. 139 speaks in terms of individuals, Jer. 18:1–11 has the whole people in view. As clay in the hands of the divine potter, we may be reshaped by God but never simply abandoned. We belong to God, and as both Jer. 18:11 and the New Testament lessons remind us, it is precisely this good news that calls us to a repentance that affects our relatedness to others in every sphere of life—familial, social, political, economic, and otherwise.

## Jeremiah 18:1–11

It is clear from the biblical record that the prophets of ancient Israel often responded to the sights and sounds of the world around

497

them. A basket of summer fruit (Amos 8:1–3, Proper 11), the invasion of a locust plague (Amos 7:1; Joel 1:4; 2:1–14), the chants of Temple priests (Isa. 6:1–3), a pot of boiling water (Jer. 1:13–14)— these and other ordinary realities became for the prophets emblems of the presence of God in Israel's life. They also sometimes became, as in the case of the present text concerning the potter and the clay, metaphors for God's judgment and/or redemption. When Jesus was later to draw on the realities of his world for the raw material of his parables, he was utilizing—very creatively!—an ancient prophetic tradition. (Note, for example, Mark 4:1–9.)

A large part of the power of the allegory of the potter and the clay lies in the fact that, although the form of the vessel on the potter's wheel may be "spoiled" (Jer. 18:4), its substance, its clayness (as Aristotle might have put it), is undisturbed. And so the potter simply begins again and refashions the vessel, this time to the proper shape and size. So it is with Yahweh and Israel. The sin of the people may distort the "shape" of their relationship to Yahweh, but they remain Yahweh's people still, to be remolded and repatterned according to the divine will. As the potter collapses the flawed vessel in order to begin again, so Yahweh judges in order to save.

(This passage offers considerable solace to the preacher who, in crafting sermons, has attempted to create illustrations in order to teach his or her congregation, only to discover that when pushed too far a given metaphor begins to say something unintended. So with this allegory of the potter and the clay. One might argue that, if the potter had been more competent, the pot would not have been spoiled in the first place. That is, it is the potter's fault, not that of the clay, that the vessel is ruined. But that is obviously not what the prophet intended to say! No metaphor, no allegory, no parable can be perfect.)

The language of vs. 7–10 reminds one of 1:10, part of the account of Jeremiah's call to the prophetic office (see Proper 16):

See, today I appoint you over nations and over kingdoms,
to pluck up and to pull down,
to destroy and to overthrow,
to build and to plant.

In both passages the vision of the prophet is not confined to Israel, but extends to the larger reaches of humankind. Jeremiah is, indeed, "a prophet to the nations" (1:4). Also in both passages the theology of the prophet is balanced between judgment and redemption. Yahweh's intention is that nations reflect the will of their Creator, and if they do not, Yahweh is quite likely to destroy them, but only in order to *remake* them. It is redemption that speaks the final word over judgment!

Thus this theology is strongly characterized by hope. Not only is there Jeremiah's confidence in Yahweh's gracious designs for human life, but there is also the prophet's understanding of the importance of human repentance and of Yahweh's forgiveness. Even that nation which Yahweh would "pluck up and break down and destroy" (18:7) may reshape itself and thereby escape the impending judgment. Ultimately Jeremiah, like Amos, seems to have concluded that the people would never repent, and thus that the destruction of the nation was inevitable (Jer. 27:1–11; compare Amos 7:1–9; 8:1–3). However, even then, late in his public life, Jeremiah knew that Yahweh would never completely renounce the people (Jer. 31:1–14). But at the time of his vision of the potter and the clay, perhaps during the encouraging years of Josiah's reformation (622–609 B.C.), the prophet's fear of judgment and his expectation of renewal were evenly balanced.

While Jeremiah may be "a prophet to the nations," he is primarily a prophet to Judah, and the final verse of our passage is directed specifically to that nation. There is still time to repent! There is still time for Yahweh's saving impulses to overrule Yahweh's administration of justice!

The phrase in 18:11 "amend your ways and your doings" recalls a similar phrase from Jeremiah's great "Temple sermon" of 609 B.C. (Jer. 7:1–20, especially vs. 3, 5; compare Jer. 26:1–6). This important declaration, perhaps preached at the time of the coronation of King Jehoiakim—a pivotal moment in the nation's life—reminds the people that the basis of a right relationship with God lies not in the correct liturgies of worship, but in justice and compassion:

> If you truly amend your ways and your doings, if you truly act justly with one another, if you do not oppress the alien, the orphan, and the widow, or shed innocent blood . . . (7:5–6)

The potter may yet find the clay to be an acceptable vessel, thus doing away with the need to reshape it. But only if the vessel can be used for that for which it was created in the first place.

## Psalm 139:1–6, 13–18

The key word of Ps. 139 is "know"/"knowledge" (vs. 1, 2, 4, 6, 14, and twice in v. 23). It may be purely coincidental that it occurs seven times—the number indicating fullness or completion—but such a pattern appropriately reinforces the message that the psalmist is fully known by God. This message is especially clear in vs. 1–6, 13–18, but it pervades the whole psalm, including the sections omitted from the lection. Verses 7–12 suggest that God's knowing presence reaches even to Sheol, the realm of the dead, which is ordinarily viewed as entirely cut off from God (see Pss. 6:5; 88:3–5; but compare Amos 9:2–4). Psalm 139:19–24, which expresses the psalmist's desire for vengeance against "the wicked" and "the bloodthirsty" (v. 19), may offer a clue to the origin of the psalm. It is possible that the psalmist had been accused of idolatry, and the appeal to God to "search me, . . . and know my heart" (v. 23) is the psalmist's affirmation of his or her innocence (compare Pss. 7; 17; 26). The expression of hatred for God's enemies, while unsettling in view of the call to "love your enemies" (Matt. 5:44), should be heard in this context as a confession of loyalty to God and God's way (Ps. 139:24). In any case, the psalmist's assurance of belonging inseparably to God transcends the particularities of the psalm's origin. It has communicated good news to persons in all places and times.

The very first word of Ps. 139 is "Yahweh," and the first word of v. 2 is the emphatic Hebrew pronoun "You." While vs. 1–6 are often interpreted as a statement of God's omniscience (all-knowingness), what really matters about God to the psalmist is this: *"You know me."* The vocabulary of v. 1 recurs in v. 23; the psalmist desires to be and is fully known by God. As Patrick D. Miller puts it, "From beginning to end it is 'I' and 'you' " (*Interpreting the Psalms;* Philadelphia: Fortress Press, 1986, p. 144).

God knows the psalmist's behavior (vs. 2a, 3), thoughts (v. 2b), and words before they are even spoken (v. 4). "Such knowledge," which the psalmist describes as "wonderful" (v. 6), could easily be perceived as threatening; and indeed, there seems to be a sort of ambivalence in the psalmist's mind. For instance, the verb in the phrase "hem me in" (v. 5) usually has the sense of "confine, besiege" (see, for example, 2 Sam. 11:1 and 1 Kings 15:27). Ambivalence would be understandable, for after all it is risky to "dismiss the deceptive coverings under which most men take refuge," as John Calvin describes the psalmist's posture (*Commentary on the Book of Psalms,* vol. 5; Grand Rapids: Baker Book House, 1949, p. 206). To be fully known is to be completely vulnerable; but on the whole, the psalmist certainly celebrates as good news the marvelous and mysterious reality that his or her life belongs to God in every aspect.

Psalm 139:13–18 constitutes an eloquent statement of the biblical view that human life is not simply a natural occurrence, but rather is the result of the will and work of a benevolent Creator. Like v. 2, v. 13 begins with the emphatic Hebrew pronoun: *"You . . . formed my inward parts"* (emphasis added). The verb "formed" is used elsewhere for God's gracious activity of constituting the whole people (Ex. 15:16; Ps. 74:2, NRSV "acquired"; Deut. 32:6, NRSV "created"). God's activity of creating Israel is also proclaimed elsewhere as one of God's "wonderful . . . works" (v. 14; see, for example, Ex. 3:20; 15:11; Judg. 6:13; and Jer. 21:2). That the same language is used here to describe God's creation of an individual human being affirms God's loving care for every person (see Matt. 6:26).

As for the actual activity of creating, the psalmist uses not the more familiar image of God as potter (see Gen. 2:7; Jer. 18:1–11, the Old Testament lesson for the day), but rather God as weaver. The psalmist has been "knit . . . together" (v. 13; see Job 10:11) and "intricately woven" (v. 15; see Ex. 38:23, NRSV "embroiderer"). James Limburg comments (*Psalms for Sojourners;* Minneapolis: Augsburg Publishing House, 1986, p. 108):

> This is a most unusual picture: God the knitter! I have a mother-in-law who has knit Norwegian sweaters. . . .
>
> "You knit me together" says this psalm. It is complicated to knit a Norwegian sweater. But it is much more complicated to knit a Norwegian! Or an African, or an American.

Quite properly, the psalmist concludes that he or she is "fearfully and wonderfully made" (v. 14); and he or she shows the appropriate response—gratitude: "I praise you" (v. 14). The psalmist knows (v. 14; compare RSV, which reads v. 14c as another statement that God knows the psalmist) that each human life belongs to God in every aspect—past (vs. 13–16a; see Jer. 1:5) and future (vs. 16bc, 24b; on God's "book," see Ex. 32:32–33; Ps. 69:28; Mal. 3:16), as well as present (vs. 23–24a).

The concept of predestination is sometimes used in relation to vs. 13–18 (see Miller, pp. 147–48), and it is appropriate if understood to mean fundamentally that our lives derive from God, belong to God, and find their destination in God's purposes. In Romans, the apostle Paul suggests that to be "predestined" (Rom. 8:29) means essentially that nothing "in all creation, will be able to separate us from the love of God in Christ Jesus our Lord" (8:39). The psalmist knew essentially the same good news. Although unable to comprehend God's thoughts (Ps. 139:17–18), the psalmist is sure of one thing, no matter what: "I am still with you" (v. 18). This assurance that God is

Emmanuel ("God with us"; see Matt. 1:23; 28:20) enables the
psalmist to entrust his or her whole life to God, inviting God's
searching gaze (Ps. 139:23) in openness to God's "way everlasting"
(v. 24). In effect, the psalmist displays what Ps. 1 calls "happy"—an
openness to God's instruction that derives from the assurance that
God "*knows* the way of the righteous" (Ps. 1:6, RSV, emphasis added;
see above on Ps. 1, Sixth Sunday After Epiphany).

## Philemon 1–21

This lection offers the rare opportunity to deal with virtually an
entire Pauline letter. Since the letters are occasional writings, written
as part of the ongoing conversation between Paul and other early
Christians, reading them "whole" brings us at least a step closer to
the experience of Paul's correspondents. It also decreases the danger
that we will read a passage out of context or overemphasize a
particular theme.

Even if we read the entire letter, however, we still have only half
of the conversation. Whether or not Paul accurately portrays the
situation, what Philemon's attitude was toward Onesimus prior to
the letter, what Onesimus's own attitude and actions were, and what
response Philemon made to the letter—all these factors remain
securely hidden away. Indeed, even what Paul says remains somewhat hidden, since he writes with such diplomacy that he does not
plainly state his own hopes for Philemon's action.

These are not observations born of scholarly timidity and concerning small details in the letter. Essential dimensions of
Onesimus's story are unknown. Traditionally, we refer to Onesimus
as a slave who has run away from Philemon's household in search of
his freedom. Somehow he has encountered Paul, who is coincidentally the "father" of Philemon's own faith, and has become a
Christian. The letter does not identify Onesimus as a fugitive,
however, and contemporary investigations of ancient slavery suggest that Onesimus may have fled because he had a significant
problem in Philemon's household. In that circumstance, a slave
would normally go to a trusted third party to appeal for intervention. Such a slave was not legally regarded as a runaway.

The more difficult question regarding the letter has to do with the
nature of Paul's request. Does he anticipate that Philemon will free
Onesimus? Does he want Onesimus assigned to himself as a helper?
Or is Onesimus simply to be restored to his position without
punishment? Given that slaves in the Roman Empire were very

often set free by the time they were thirty, some suggest that Paul has in mind early manumission.

Despite these serious unclarities in the letter, several features of it are both clear and significant. First, only here among the letters generally regarded as authentically Pauline does Paul write a personal letter. Even if Apphia, Archippus, and the church are addressed, the letter is nevertheless personal. It concerns the affairs of a single individual, Philemon, with regard to his slave, Onesimus, which explains why Paul moves so delicately through his appeal.

In this sense, the letter contrasts sharply with 1 Cor. 5:1–8, where Paul addresses the sin of an individual but does so in the context of addressing the larger congregation. Paul castigates what he takes to be the gross immorality of a man who is living with his father's wife, but he employs equally harsh language for the congregation and its failure to discipline this individual. In Philemon, perhaps because of local circumstances or perhaps because Paul does not see the same risk of "infecting" the larger congregation, he addresses an individual.

At the very same time that Philemon is a personal letter, it is also profoundly ecclesiastical. The slender references to the church in v. 2 and to other Christian workers in vs. 23–24 open this possibility, but the ecclesiastical dimension of Philemon enters primarily through Paul's own mission. Philemon's previous faithfulness has given refreshment to "the hearts of the saints" (v. 7). Onesimus has now become an embodiment of his own name, useful to Paul in the service of the gospel (vs. 11, 13). Because he is a new brother in Christ to Philemon, Onesimus should be received and treated as such. The church forms the horizon within which this personal matter must be addressed and settled.

Philemon also provides us with a glimpse of the way in which Paul's pastoral sensitivity intertwines with his theological convictions. Even if theological argumentation is largely absent from the letter, what permeates the letter is the knowledge that the Christian lives in profound connection to Jesus Christ and that Christian behavior must reflect that connection. Paul's imprisonment belongs to Jesus Christ (v. 1). Philemon's faith will be effective as he "perceive[s] all the good" he may do for Christ. By virtue of his conversion, Onesimus has become a brother in Christ, which necessitates that he be treated as brother. Paul concludes his request: "Yes, brother, let me have this benefit from you in the Lord! Refresh my heart in Christ" (v. 20).

Contemporary Christians can scarcely read this letter without longing for Paul to take the argument yet another step. Why not assert the profound immorality—the impossibility—of one human being owning another? Why not demand the release of Onesimus, the release of all slaves everywhere? With Paul's own convictions that the eschaton was imminent, such demands may have seemed unnecessary. In light of the pervasiveness of slavery in the Roman Empire, such demands may have been unthinkable for a single, obscure individual. The implications of vs. 15–16, however, should not be overlooked. One who is a brother in the Lord can scarcely be a slave in the flesh.

## Luke 14:25–33

The assigned lection for this Sunday from the travel section of Luke's Gospel specifically reminds us of the theme of discipleship that pervades the section. It is not an easy passage, because of the rash and exclusive way statements are made, but just for this reason it is important for contemporary audiences. It confronts us with hard choices and jars any notion that being a Christian leads to social enhancement or personal betterment. While there are texts that comfort the disturbed, this one disturbs the comfortable.

The location of the passage in the narrative is critical. The preceding parable of the great banquet (Luke 14:15–24) depicts previously invited guests who offer excuses for their refusal to attend the party and then relates the host's persistence in seeing that his dining hall is filled and his meal eaten. Two groups are recruited: (1) the poor, the crippled, the blind, and the lame, and (2) those in the countryside. It is a remarkable story of the divine grace, which reaches beyond traditional bounds to include those otherwise excluded.

But it is easy to be presumptuous about grace. The three who send excuses for their absence illustrate just how easy it can be to take lightly God's gracious invitations, and there is no reason to think that the outsiders brought in at the last minute are going to be any less vulnerable to such presumptuousness. Therefore, to the "large crowds" who "were traveling with him," Jesus delivers these sharp words about the demands and priorities of discipleship. If they are contemplating being more than hangers-on and intend to be regular diners at Jesus' table, they need to know what they are getting into and to decide whether they can sign on for the long haul.

The passage is cleanly structured. The introductory verse (14:25) is followed by three parallel statements about the nature of discipleship (vs. 26, 27, and 33). The middle one provides the clue for understanding the first and last. In between the second and third statements are two analogies (building a tower, waging a war) that raise the question whether would-be disciples can follow through on their initial commitments (vs. 28–32). The final words about salt and the potential loss of its usefulness, while outside the lection, provide a fitting conclusion to the chapter (vs. 34–35).

How are we to understand 14:26? It includes a piece of Semitic hyperbole that Matthew has softened a bit ("Whoever loves father or mother more than me . . . and whoever loves son or daughter more than me is not worthy of me," Matt. 10:37). Jesus is clearly not telling the crowds to hate their parents and abandon their children. He is sharply confronting them with the priority of their commitments and implicitly pointing them to the new surrogate family they join as they become disciples. It is a note repeatedly sounded in Luke's narrative (Luke 8:19–21; 12:52–53; 21:16) and needing to be heard in a society that talks much about family values.

The second statement about discipleship is the familiar word about cross-bearing (14:27). By putting the verb "carry" in the present tense, Luke tends to stress the everydayness of this identification with Jesus (compare 9:23). By including "one's own cross" (not clearly rendered in the NRSV), Luke underscores the need for a personal acknowledgment of such an identification.

The third statement about discipleship, with its inclusive "all," reiterates another Luke theme (14:33). Material possessions have a seductive appeal that can turn them quickly from being servants to being masters (12:13–34; 18:18–25; 19:8). They become excess baggage that makes the journey with Jesus difficult to negotiate. Thus, at the outset, choices have to be made. "You cannot serve God and wealth" (16:13).

The intervening analogies of assessing resources before building a tower and doing feasibility studies before going to war vividly argue the case for a commitment that is made with eyes wide open to the cost (14:28–32). A hasty or casual decision leaves one vulnerable to ridicule and defeat. The warning is not meant to encourage a calculating wariness about discipleship (which would certainly seem incongruous with the daring, risk-laden calls to follow Jesus), but a sober realism about what it entails.

In light of the hardness of the text and the overwhelming demands made, one is tempted to give the two analogies a further twist. In answer to the questions, "Which of you would fail to make an assessment before building a tower? Which of you would bypass reconnaissance before starting a war?" the responder of course says, "None of us." But then neither would God! God has counted the cost. God knows what it takes to build a tower. God knows how strong the enemy's forces are. The rule God has inaugurated will not be left unfinished. It may have a rather unpromising beginning, but do not be deceived: God means to win. It is just this certain and conclusive cause we are called to join.

# PROPER 19

Ordinary Time 24

*Sunday between*
*September 11 and 17 inclusive*

The Old Testament commentary summarizes the apparent message of Jer. 4:11–12, 22–28 in two words: "total despair." But then it observes that there is a "soft note of grace" in 4:27. In other words, while Israel's foolishness, stupidity, and skill in doing evil are very real (v. 22), God's redemptive purposes for the people will not ultimately be thwarted.

The first three verses of Ps. 14 suggest that the same sort of foolishness and perversity characterizes all humanity—"there is no one who does good" (vs. 1, 3). But in an apparent contradiction to vs. 1–3, vs. 4–6 give testimony to God's ability to gather from among sinful humankind a community of people who will find their refuge in God. Verse 7 suggests again that God's redemptive purposes will not ultimately be thwarted.

In 1 Tim. 1:12–17, Paul points to his own life as an example (v. 16) of God's ability to reclaim and redeem persons. Formerly immersed in ignorance and evil, Paul has now been appointed to Christ's service (vs. 12–14). This transformation is not testimony to Paul's own sufficiency or merit. Rather, he has "received mercy" (vs. 13, 16). His story is evidence of God's gracious will and ability to redeem (v. 14), and it gives reason to glorify God (v. 17).

Luke 15:1–10 suggests just how far God is willing to go to reclaim the lost. In the parables of the lost sheep and the lost coin, God is portrayed as remarkably and even recklessly active in pursuit of wayward persons. God does not just wait for people to return. Rather, God goes after them. In a striking way, Luke 15 reinforces the good news of the preceding lections: God's redemptive purposes will not ultimately be thwarted.

## Jeremiah 4:11–12, 22–28

Two words appear to characterize the Old Testament lection for this day: total despair. Although the text is set in a larger context that

507

finds the prophet still believing that the people may repent and that Yahweh's judgment may be averted (4:1–4; 5:1), the mood of the verses appointed for this lectionary passage seems completely negative. But are they?

The theme of the Day of Yahweh is in the prophet's mind in vs. 11–12, which serve as an introduction to the larger lection. As best we know, it was Amos who, among the prophets, first described this day (Amos 5:18–20), and in doing so he warned the people to prepare themselves for a terrible surprise. The implication of Amos's words is that the Day of Yahweh was an occasion to which his contemporaries looked forward with great anticipation, perhaps expecting a stunning military victory or some new outpouring of the grace of Israel's God. But it would be just the opposite, said Amos, a time of unimagined terror sent by Yahweh.

Jeremiah knows the lessons of Amos. "On that day" of Jer. 4:9 clearly has Amos's preaching in mind, and the horror described there will be so great that even those closest to Yahweh will not be prepared: "the priests shall be appalled and the prophets astounded." "At that time," the words with which the present lectionary passage begins (v. 11), stands in direct reference to "On that day" of 4:9, the Day of Yahweh. The metaphor of judgment here is that of the hot east wind, which on occasion blew off of the high Transjordanian plateau, searing everything in its path. The Day of Yahweh will be like that terrible wind in its ferocity.

The lectionary passage now skips to v. 22, a brief statement that, as the arrangement of lines in NRSV indicates, is more closely linked to vs. 13–21 than it is to vs. 23–28. The prophet enters the thought-world of the wisdom philosophers and borrows their terminology and conceptualization to make an important statement about the state of the people's relationship to Yahweh. They are "foolish," "stupid," without "understanding." They are like those described in the second line of Prov. 1:7 (compare Ps. 111:10):

> The fear of the LORD is the beginning of knowledge;
> fools despise wisdom and instruction.

"They do not know me," complains Yahweh. "[They] do not know how to do good." Then, in a fine use of irony, Jeremiah employs the adjectival form of the very word that means wisdom, *ḥākmāh*, to describe the inventiveness of the people's evil. NRSV's "They are *skilled* in doing evil" (emphasis added) does not catch this play on words as does Jerusalem Bible's "they are *clever* enough at doing wrong" (emphasis added).

Jeremiah 4:23–26 is composed of four sentences, each of which begins with a single Hebrew word meaning "I looked." (We are reminded again of how many of those in Israel's prophetic tradition responded to the sights and sounds of the surrounding world; see the discussion of Jer. 18:1–11, Proper 18.) The reader is signaled straightaway that what Jeremiah is witnessing is nothing other than the undoing of the created order. "I looked on the earth, and lo, it was waste and void" (v. 4:23). This is the only other place in the Hebrew Bible where there occurs the phrase of Gen. 1:2 that describes the chaotic state that prevailed before God began to create the world: *tōhû wābōhû*. (The Septuagint renders Jer. 4:23 even more bluntly: "I looked upon the earth and, behold, it was not.") The earth before creation is the spectacle that terrorizes Jeremiah's vision, as does the sight of the heavens with no light (Gen. 1:3, 14), an earth with no living creatures (Gen. 1:20, 24, 26), a desert instead of fruitful land (Gen. 1:11). All of creation must suffer because of the sinfulness of Yahweh's people. (Compare similar treatments of this theme in Gen. 6:5–8; Zeph. 1:2–3.)

Jeremiah 4:27–28 completes the passage. The desolation is to be total. There is no changing Yahweh's mind! To paraphrase Eccl. 1:2: "Despair of despair, says the prophet. All is despair."

But in the midst of this terrible clamor over Yahweh's anger, there is one soft note of grace. It is so inconspicuous as to be easily unnoticed, yet it is there, crouching in Jer. 4:27: "The whole land shall be a desolation; yet *I will not make a full end*" (emphasis added). So astonishing is this note of mercy, so out of character with the rest of the passage, that the editors of the standard critical edition of the Hebrew Bible, usually so insightful in their suggestions, propose that the Hebrew text is defective here and that it should read "The whole land shall be a desolation, and I will make *of it a full end*" (substituting *lāh* ["of it"] for *lō'* ["not"]). (*Biblia Hebraica Stuttgartensia*, p. 789. Note "a" in the critical apparatus to Jer. 4:22.)

Perhaps they are right. Perhaps this passage does reflect a time when Jeremiah had grown so weary with the waywardness of the people and so despondent over their deafness to his message that he saw no hope that things would ever be right again (compare Jer. 20:14–18).

But as the record of this prophet's oracles has come down to us (through who knows how many editorial hands) the very idea of the Day of Yahweh, linked so fundamentally to Yahweh's coming judgment, is transformed into a message of redemption. "The days are surely coming, . . . " says the prophet over and again (Jer. 31:27, 31, 38), when judgment will be overcome by restoration.

The days are surely coming . . . when . . . just as I have watched over them to pluck up and break down, to overthrow, destroy, and bring evil, so I will watch over them to build and to plant, says the LORD. (Jer. 31:27–28)

(Compare Jer. 1:10, Proper 16.)

Total despair? It is understandable that Jeremiah would sink into such desperate moods. Yet Jeremiah knew Israel's God as have few mortals, and Jeremiah knew that Yahweh's final word is not judgment, but redemption.


## Psalm 14

The first verse of Ps. 14 is one of the most memorable in the book of Psalms, and it is probably also one of the most misunderstood. Contrary to popular opinion, the issue is not atheism, in the sense of the denial of God's existence on philosophical grounds. There were very few, if any, of that sort of atheists in ancient Israel; and there are still relatively few today. The issue is what is often called "practical atheism"—that is, *acting* as if there is no God. And when atheism is so defined, then *all of us* are "fools." Indeed, vs. 2–3 suggest this conclusion rather explicitly. When God "looks down from heaven *on humankind,* . . . there is *no one* who does good, *no, not one.*" As H.-J. Kraus says in regard to this conclusion: "Finally, one must come to realize how shocking the assertions of Psalm 14 actually are" (*Psalms 1—59,* trans. H. C. Oswald; Minneapolis: Augsburg Publishing House, 1988, pp. 223–24).

What is so shocking and disturbing about Ps. 14:1–3 is that foolishness amounts to what the psalms elsewhere call "wickedness," which is to be understood essentially as autonomy—literally, to be a law unto oneself. The dimensions of the problem become clear when we consider that our culture considers autonomy one of the highest virtues. To be a functioning adult, one must be self-sufficient, self-directed; and the goal of life is often understood to be self-fulfillment or self-actualization (see the commentary on Ps. 1, Sixth Sunday After Epiphany). To be sure, all this makes some sense on the psychological level, but often our psychological formulations translate subtly into a theological conclusion—namely, we don't need other people, and we don't need God! Such a conclusion does not deny the existence of God, but it does effectively eliminate God as an essential, functioning aspect of our daily reality. For us, *in effect,* "there is no God" (see Ps. 10:4).

The assertion "There is no God" has behavioral consequences: "There is no one who does good" (Ps. 14:1, 3). The repetition is emphatic, as is the final phrase of v. 3, "no, not one." The verbs in vs. 1 and 3 recall two crucial episodes in the Pentateuch—the beginning of the Flood story (see "corrupt"/"corrupted" in Gen. 6:12) and Israel's worship of the golden calf (see Ex. 32:7, where the verb here translated "corrupt" appears as "acted perversely," and Ex. 32:8, where the verb here translated "gone astray" appears as "turn aside"). Both these episodes culminate in the establishment of a covenant (Gen. 9:8–17; Ex. 34:10–28), based on God's willingness to forgive and restore. And both these episodes prove paradigmatic; that is, the history of Israel and history in general reveal a remarkably persistent perversity on the part of God's people and humanity as a whole. In looking back over Israel's history, for instance, the book of Isaiah also uses the vocabulary of Ps. 14:1–3. The people "deal corruptly" (Isa. 1:4; compare Ps. 14:1) and "continue to rebel" (Isa. 1:5; compare "gone astray" in Ps. 14:3). Like the two key episodes in the Pentateuch, the book of Isaiah also culminates in the restoration of relationship (see "covenant" in Isa. 54:10, where it is linked to the Flood story, as well as in 55:3; 56:4; 59:21; 61:8), based not on the people's willingness to obey, but rather on God's willingness to forgive (see Isa. 40:1–2).

It is this message of universal human perversity that Paul utilizes in Rom. 3:10–18, quoting portions of Ps. 14:1, 3 and several additional verses of a longer version of Ps. 14 that is found in the Greek Old Testament. Paul's initial point that all people "are under the power of sin" (Rom. 3:9) is followed by the good news that "all . . . are now justified by his grace as a gift, through the redemption that is in Christ Jesus" (Rom. 3:23–24). As in the Old Testament, relationship is restored by God's gracious action. Salvation is not and can never be a human achievement, despite our persistent attempts to make it so. We contemporary, sophisticated human beings do not like to think about such "foolishness"; but then again, we do not like to think of ourselves as sinners either. Psalm 14 tells us that we are. Lest we think our enlightened era has left perversity behind, all we need to do is read the headlines of recent years or days—hunger, homelessness, political corruption, interminable warfare in our inner cities as well as around the world. Although our rugged individualism (that is, autonomy) usually leads us to deny it, there is not one of us who remains uninvolved in or unaffected by these realities—"no, not one."

Verses 4–6 offer a perspective that seems to contradict that of vs. 1–3, since these verses distinguish between "all the evildoers" (v. 4) and those called "my people" (v. 4), "the company of the righteous" (v. 5), and "the poor" (v. 6). Verses 4–6 may reflect a divided society in which a strong elite fed upon the oppressed (see Micah 3:1–4); however, as James L. Mays suggests, "theologically we would do well to let the tensions stand unresolved" (*Psalms*, Interpretation series; Louisville, Ky.: John Knox Press, 1994). On the one hand, it would be dangerous to ignore vs. 1–3 and thus to assume that we are not sinners (see Luke 18:9–14). On the other hand, it would be a denial of the biblical good news to conclude that God cannot gather sinners into "the company of the righteous"—Israel, the church. To be sure, our righteousness is not an achievement, but a gift. We remain sinners and victims of sin; we know, however, that our own insufficiency and destructive acts are not the final word. There is a source of life beyond ourselves; in short, the Lord is our "refuge" (v. 6; see Ps. 2:12). This is true "knowledge" (14:4), the wisdom for which God is looking (v. 2; see Ps. 2:10, where the admonition to be wise means to acknowledge God's rule rather than one's own power). To be sure, it is this very wisdom that appears foolish to the world. For us Christians, this wisdom takes finally the shape of a cross, which reveals clearly the two realities with which Ps. 14 confronts us—the reality of human sin and the reality of God's grace. To live among "the company of the righteous" is to trust that the reality of God's grace is the ultimate reality. Thus, we live not by what we see so pervasive around us, but rather by what we believe and what we hope for (see v. 7).

## 1 Timothy 1:12–17

Most letters in the New Testament throw us immediately into a conversation among early Christians. Even if only one partner in the conversation is speaking, we hear something of the faith and struggle of a congregation of real people. By contrast, the body of 1 Timothy opens with a set of general warnings that offer modern readers little opportunity to hear from or about a group of believers. Vague warnings about "certain people" and "endless genealogies" and "meaningless talk" scarcely allow us an avenue into identification.

With 1:12–17, we suddenly feel at home. Here is Paul (or, more likely, a follower of Paul's who speaks with Paul's voice to a later generation) talking about his conversion. Having read the accounts in Acts 9, 22, and 26, and the brief references in his other letters (for example, Gal. 1:11–17; Phil. 3:2–11), we know what to expect. Paul is "telling his story," to use the contemporary parlance.

To "tell one's story" in the church of our time is to focus on our experience. One's own life, or some aspect of it, becomes the beginning point for reflection on what it means to live faithfully in the world. Because of our capacity to identify with the experiences of others, "telling one's story" can serve to forge a crucial connection among individuals.

Despite our interest in this mode of reflection, the notion of having individuals narrate their own stories (in the sense of autobiographical accounts) is largely absent from the New Testament. Paul has very little to say about his own conversion. Even in the passages where he does touch on it, few details permit us access to the event. That has not prevented, but rather has encouraged, endless speculation on the cause and nature of Paul's conversion.

Here in 1 Timothy, by contrast, the conversion seems to come front and center. The Paul of 1 Timothy is not only not reticent, but seems to exaggerate: "I was formerly a blasphemer, a persecutor, and a man of violence" (1:13). Nothing in Paul's letters supports the claim that he blasphemed, and the claim to ignorance later in the verse contradicts this assertion. Perhaps it appears here largely to anticipate the situation of Hymenaeus and Alexander (1:20). That he was a violent persecutor the letters attest, but they do not draw such attention to "violence" as is the case here.

Not only did Paul persecute the church but he was, according to vs. 15–16, the "foremost" among sinners. This assertion contradicts Phil. 3:6, where Paul claims that he was "blameless" with respect to the law. The exaggeration of Paul's standing as persecutor prepares for this claim that he is the "foremost" among sinners.

In just this way, Paul now becomes the leading example for others. He received mercy so that Jesus Christ might make him "an example to those who would come to believe in him for eternal life" (v. 16). If Christ showed mercy on Paul, then Christ might show mercy on anyone, no matter what sins have been committed.

Looked at in this way, this passage is primarily about Paul. Paul (or his interpreter) tells the story of Paul in order to assist others. That way of looking at the passage, however, omits certain crucial elements. The passage begins, after all, with a statement of thanksgiving: "I am grateful to Christ Jesus our Lord, who has strengthened me, because he judged me faithful and appointed me to his service" (v. 12). And the passage ends with a doxological assertion (v. 17).

The opening and closing might be regarded as merely matters of form, less significant than Paul's own remarks about himself, but v. 15 indicates otherwise. Here, in the middle of the passage, we find the dramatic claim: "The saying is sure and worthy of full acceptance, that Christ Jesus came into the world to save sinners." Four other times, the author of the pastoral epistles uses such a declaration (that is, "the saying is sure"), in 1 Tim. 3:1; 4:9; 2 Tim. 2:11; and Titus 3:8. In every case the assertion being underscored has to do with salvation (even in the case of 1 Tim. 3:1, which probably belongs with the end of chapter 2 rather than the beginning of chapter 3, as the NRSV note indicates).

What primarily concerns the author is the salvation brought about by God in the gospel of Jesus Christ. Paul is but an example of the workings of that gospel, not a hero figure whose behavior must be emulated. After all, Paul did not bring about his own conversion. He was "judged . . . faithful and appointed" (v. 12), he "received mercy" (v. 13), and he was made an example (v. 16). Truly it is God who deserves the honor and glory, as the passage concludes.

With this lection, as with others from the pastorals, the preacher will have to determine how to refer to the author. Many factors, including the nature of the congregation and its readiness to venture into what may be unfamiliar territory, need to be taken into consideration. Although differences of opinion remain, many scholars regard the case against Pauline authorship of the pastorals to be strong (as the commentaries will indicate). As noted above, the author may well have been a student of Paul who believed himself capable of faithfully addressing new situations with Paul's voice. In the first century, such practice would not have occasioned the outrage that it would in our own time. When preachers explain the undertaking of the author in this positive light (and with humility and brevity), their congregations often respond in kind.

## Luke 15:1–10

Luke 15, with its moving parables of the lost sheep, the lost coin, and the two lost sons, comes in an interesting location in the Gospel narrative. For at least three chapters, the themes developed have been the demand for repentance (13:1–9) and the costliness of following Jesus (12:49–53; 14:25–33). Even when healings have been recounted, they have become the occasion for conflict with the religious authorities, who are adamantly opposed to deeds of mercy on the Sabbath (13:10–17; 14:1–6). Jesus the prophet joins the dinner party given by a prominent Pharisee and confronts the guests and the host with their need for humility and their failure to attend to the weak and marginalized people of the town (14:1–24). The tone of the narrative has been one of unrelenting warning and critique in an effort to redirect the focus of the disciples and the crowds.

But in Luke 15, in response to the persistent grumbling of the Pharisees and scribes, Jesus offers these memorable stories of divine mercy, of the unbounded joy of God when the lost are found. The stories are not without their subversive word of judgment to the grumblers, but before they are judgment they are good news. Whatever warning they contain is bounded by the gentle and unforgettable figures of the shepherd/woman/father searching for their lost treasures. (The third story, of the loving father and his two sons, is the assigned lection for the Fourth Sunday in Lent.)

What do these two stories, of the last sheep and the lost coin, depict for us? The first and most obvious element common to both parables is *the compassionate concern of a searching God.* The details heighten the importance and intensity of the protagonists' efforts. The shepherd risks temporarily abandoning the ninety-nine sheep in the wilderness (a decision many would no doubt question), and when he finds the straying sheep "he lays it on his shoulders and rejoices" (15:5). The woman is described as lighting a lamp and taking broom in hand in her attempt to recover her missing coin. Neither the shepherd nor the woman has a moment's hesitation as to what to do; neither forsakes the search until the sheep/coin is found.

God is like that, the stories say, meticulously pursuing confused and rebellious creatures. Such searching gives value to those being sought. They become treasured and significant because they are not left for lost, but are made the objects of divine concern.

The second striking image is that of *heaven's delight in the recovery of the lost.* So overcome are the shepherd and the woman with the success of their search that they call their friends and neighbors to come for a party. Neither wants to celebrate alone. As commentators note, the expense of the entertainment may have been more than the value of either the sheep or the coin, but that possibility only adds to the extravagance and joy of the occasion.

It is an unusual picture of God—throwing a celestial party, which the angels dare not miss. It may be an arresting depiction of God for those who imagine a stern taskmaster or a vindictive judge or a divine scorekeeper who is bound to pull for the other side.

It is true that the narrator makes a point of speaking of heaven's joy "over one sinner who repents" (15:7, 10). But the stories are not primarily calls to repentance. Sheep and coins can't repent. The image of a merciful and joyful God completely overshadows any interest in the behavior or remorse of the lost creatures.

Having seen the good news in these stories, with their vivid characters and powerful plots, we must not ignore their immediate context. They function as *a disturbing response to the complaints of the Pharisees and scribes*. Both the shepherd and the woman connote figures from the underside of Jewish society. Shepherds had notorious reputations and were generally avoided as outcasts. Women were treated as second-class citizens. The mere choice of the two as images for God must have caused a shock among the listeners, and especially among those who grumbled because Jesus was welcoming (the Greek verb suggests the offering of hospitality) and eating with tax collectors and sinners.

The listeners are immediately thrust into the middle of the parables: "Which one of you, having a hundred sheep . . . ?" (15:4). They are asked to reflect on their own experiences of losing a valuable article, of the search, and of the delight in finding it. By association they are invited to share with God and the angelic host in the celebration over the reclaiming of a lost sinner.

In answer to the complaint that Jesus has overstepped the boundaries in having table fellowship with sinners, the parables implicitly beckon the Pharisees and the scribes to join him, to be a part of the searching, because God is a searching God. Jesus' subtle response coheres with his earlier answer to similar charges: "I have come to call not the righteous but sinners to repentance" (5:32).

As with most parables, the text is open to multiple meanings. It offers good news to those who feel themselves unredeemably lost and who can delight in a God who patiently searches, not only for them, but also for others like them. It subverts and disorients, however, those offended by the remarkable generosity of God, especially when it reaches out to tax collectors and sinners.

# PROPER 20

Intercessory prayer is a difficult task for most Christians. Sometimes we simply do not know what to ask for and feel helpless in presenting to God a troubled friend or family member whose need baffles us. At other times we become fearful of asking for too much, lest our very prayers begin to make sharp demands on us to supply the needs of those for whom we pray (like food to the hungry and companionship to the lonely). Three of the texts for this Sunday deal with intercession, and although they certainly will not make praying any easier, they may make it more hopeful.

The readings from both Jeremiah and the Psalms depict the anguish of one who identifies with the pain of God's faithless people. Israel has created a situation of alienation and isolation. There appears no relief in sight for its hurt as it mourns the absence of God. Prophet and psalmist grieve with and for the people and join in the persistent and impatient plea for health and renewal. Only God's return can restore joy.

In the text from Jeremiah, however, we are surprised to discover that God is not absent at all, but in fact is also grieving over the plight of the people. The words that convey the prophet's hurt convey also God's pain over Israel's disobedience. God turns out to be, not an impassive or distant deity, but one bound up with the anguish of the prophet and the anguish of the people. Likewise, the psalmist discovers that the God who refuses to tolerate Israel's faithlessness nevertheless cannot finally abandon the chosen community.

First Timothy also challenges readers to offer prayers of intercession and specifies that they be made for those in positions of political leadership (without indicating their party affiliation). Lest this seem a hopeless venture, the text nudges our self-righteousness by reminding us that God's intent is that all should be saved—both pray-ers and politicians.

All three texts invite us to root our requests in the character of a gracious, involved, and passionate God.

## Jeremiah 8:18–9:1

It has often been observed by commentators that Jeremiah is the most personally visible of the Old Testament prophets. In other words, the literature that bears Jeremiah's name contains a record not only of what he said and did, but of how he felt about his prophetic vocation, and this expression of his emotional life is virtually unique among the ancient Israelite prophets. Jeremiah's so-called "confessions" (Jer. 11:18–12:6; 15:10–21; 17:14–18; 18:18–23; 20:7–12 and 14–18) are the most obvious examples of the prophet's personal struggles of faith, but the present lection could be included among them as well.

It should be observed that not all scholars consent to the view that these seemingly personal statements are a reflection of Jeremiah's own emotions. One view is that they are liturgical statements of the community's grief, similar to other literature of lament in the Old Testament (compare, for example, Ps. 31 or Joel 1:1–20), which in this case happened to be included in the book of Jeremiah in the course of its very complex literary history. While that issue cannot be debated here, it should be observed that the "confessional" literature in the book of Jeremiah presents itself to us as if it were, indeed, reflective of the prophet's own emotional life. Thus the interpreter has warrant to treat it as such, even as she or he bears in mind that a given piece of ancient Israelite literature may have served more than one function during the centuries before the standardization of the biblical text.

We do not do the text an injustice if we view it as being a response, initially, at least, to a drought that has descended on the land (compare Jer. 14:1–7). The end of the summer (v. 20) was, under normal conditions, the time when the rains returned. The harvest of grapes, olives, and other fruits was completed by late September or early October, the occasion for celebration of the Festival of Booths (Sukkot) and the observance of the New Year (Rosh Hashanah). Then the rains could be expected to begin, providing sustenance for the newly sown cereal crops (chiefly barley), which would be harvested in the spring. But this year the drought seems to have continued on into the winter, parching the newly sprouted grain into useless stubble:

> The harvest is past, the summer is ended,
> and we are not saved.

That motif is continued, and indeed consummated, by the final verse of our lection (9:1; in the Hebrew text this verse is included in ch. 8 as v. 23, a more logical manner of dividing the text). If this literature had its origin as a prayer in time of public distress, the petitioner would certainly have included in his or her plea to God an urgent request for the lifting of the drought. This might be paraphrased: "If my tears could be turned into springs and fountains, the suffering of my drought-stricken people would be ended."

In the mind of the prophet, however, the drought stands as metaphor for the larger alienation of the people from Yahweh. The opening lament (v. 18) is not over the drought, but over the apparent absence of Yahweh from the land and from the lives of the people. Their perception is that Yahweh is "not in Zion" (v. 19); thus the lament of the men and women of Judah gives rise to the prophet's lament. The people mourn because Yahweh seems absent. The prophet mourns because the people have brought about their own isolation from Yahweh and Yahweh's saving initiatives:

> For the hurt of my poor people I am hurt,
> I mourn, and dismay has taken hold of me.
> (V. 21)

(The final two lines of v. 19 are, in a helpful manner, set in parentheses by the NRSV translators. That is because, while the "my" and "me" of v. 18 may refer to the prophet, the "me" of v. 19c surely refers to Yahweh. Verse 19c reads as if some later scribe inserted it in order to ensure that the reader understood that Yahweh had been "provoked" into causing the drought/alienation. But there is another way of reading the text which brings the first person pronouns of vs. 18 and 19c into agreement. See below.)

The sickness of the people is beyond all known conventional cures (v. 22). Not even the renowned herbal remedies of Gilead, applied by those practitioners who utilize them to their best advantage, are potent enough to dispel the people's illness. Only the return of Yahweh can restore the people. Only the resumption of the life-sustaining waters, which symbolize Yahweh's presence, can heal.

Much of the power of this text lies in the fact that, as we read the words that convey the prophet's hurt, we suddenly realize that these same words are describing the hurt of Israel's God. There is ample precedent for this, especially in the recorded oracles of Hosea.

> My heart recoils within me;
> my compassion grows warm and tender.
> (Hos. 11:8; see Proper 13)

This is surely an expression of the anguish that Hosea felt over the waywardness of Gomer and of Israel. But it clearly is also the anguish of Yahweh over a sinful and faithless people. So, in Jer. 8:18, it is not just Jeremiah's joy that "is gone," but Yahweh's joy as well. "My heart is sick" because "they provoked me . . . with their images, with their . . . idols."

Thus, in a manner that quite awes us, the text, which began by speaking of the people's anguish over the drought, has now spoken of Yahweh's anguish over the sin of the people, Yahweh's pain over the faithlessness of that one family whose distinction from all other families is their tradition of faith.


## Psalm 79:1–9

Psalm 79 is a communal lament or prayer for help that is very similar to Pss. 44 and 74. Most scholars relate the catastrophe described in Ps. 79 to the events of 587 B.C., the destruction of Jerusalem by the Babylonians and the beginning of the exile. Several scholars, however, suggest that some other destruction of Jerusalem may account for the origin of the psalm, perhaps even the desecration of the Temple of Antiochus IV Epiphanes in the second century B.C. In fact, portions of Ps. 79:2–3 appear in the second-century First Book of the Maccabees as a comment on the murder of sixty faithful Jews by members of an unfaithful group (1 Macc. 7:17). In this case, however, Ps. 79 is cited as "the word which was written" (1 Macc. 7:16), suggesting a much earlier origin for Ps. 79. Thus, it is most likely that Ps. 79 originated in response to the destruction of Jerusalem in 587 and that it received several "contemporizations" (H.-J. Kraus, *Psalms 60—150*, trans. H. C. Oswald; Minneapolis: Augsburg Publishing House, 1989, p. 134), including that reflected in 1 Maccabees. Indeed, the "contemporizations" did not stop with the Old Testament period. Psalm 79 is alluded to in Rev. 16:6; it was cited by Jerome in response to the invasion of Rome by the Visigoths; it was frequently on the lips of persons as they died in the religious conflicts in sixteenth- and seventeenth-century Europe; and it was and is used by Jews on the 9th of Ab, which commemorates the destruction of Jerusalem, and in weekly services as well (see Rowland Prothero, *The Psalms in Human Life;* New York: E. P. Dutton, 1903, pp. 31, 146–47). As James L. Mays suggests, "In all these ways the psalm continues to voice the prayer of those who raise the question, 'Why should the nations say, Where is your God?' " (*Psalms*, Interpretation series; Louisville, Ky.: John Knox Press, 1994).

Verses 1–5 of Ps. 79 constitute the complaint by describing in graphic detail the desecration and destruction suffered by Jerusalem and its people. The focus shifts from the enemy (the "they" in vs. 1–3) to the people ("we," v. 4) to God ("you," v. 5). The mention of "your inheritance" (v. 1), apparently a reference to the Temple, recalls Ex. 15:17, which says the people have been "planted . . . on the mountain of your own inheritance" (NRSV "possession"). Exodus 15:18 then affirms that Yahweh "will reign forever and ever." When Ps. 79:1 is read in light of Ex. 15:17–18, the theological issue becomes clearer—namely, the destruction of Jerusalem calls God's sovereignty into question. In short, the nations are not the only ones asking the question, "Where is . . . God?" (v. 10; see Pss. 42:3, 10; 115:2). As Marvin Tate suggests, Ps. 79 echoes Israel's "deepest doubts and fears" (*Psalms 51—100,* Word Biblical Commentary 20; Dallas: Word, 1990, p. 301).

The language of v. 4 appears frequently in other complaints. The individual psalmist sometimes is "a taunt" (see Pss. 22:6, 31.11, NRSV "scorn"/"scorned"; 69:7, NRSV "reproach"; 69:20–21, NRSV "insults"), and so are the people (Pss. 44:13) or their representative, the king (Ps. 89:41, NRSV "scorn"; 89:50). The words "mocked" and "derided" also occur in Ps. 44:13 (NRSV, "derision" and "scorn"). What is particularly interesting in Ps. 79 is that v. 4 anticipates v. 12, which suggests that the taunts of the neighbors are really taunts *against God.* As v. 9 will make clear, what is really at stake is God's "name"—that is, God's reputation or character.

One side of God's character is mentioned in v. 5—God's anger and "jealous wrath." God's "jealous wrath" is mentioned elsewhere in the context of covenant-making, where it is clear that Yahweh wants Israel's exclusive allegiance (Ex. 20:5; 34:14; Deut. 4:24; 5:9; 6:15; Josh. 24:19). God the lover wants Israel to love no other gods. In short, God's "jealous wrath" is a manifestation of God's love. It is to God's love or "compassion" (Ps. 79:8) that the people finally appeal.

If God is going to be angry, God should be angry at the nations for their treatment of Israel (vs. 6–7; see Jer. 10:25). The people do not pretend to be innocent (see "iniquities" in Ps. 79:8 and "forgive our sins" in v. 9). Rather, having been "brought very low" (v. 8), they appeal to God's historically proven care for the lowly. God's "compassion" includes the willingness to forgive sinners, as evidenced in Ex. 34:6, where God describes God's character as "gracious" (the same Hebrew root as "compassion" in Ps. 79:8) after forgiving the people, even after they had built and worshiped another god (see Ex. 32:1–14). In essence, the people suggest that the opportunity for God to "deliver" them from their distress is an opportunity for God to prove God's character before the nations as God had done previously (Ps. 79:9; see Ex. 9:16). The nations who do not know God (Ps. 79:6) will come to know God if God acts to avenge (v. 10; see Ps. 115:1–2; Ex. 9:29).

The request for revenge (Ps. 79:10, 12) expresses Israel's desire that God set the things right that are so obviously wrong (vs. 1–3). When the lowly are liberated, then oppressors must be judged. In essence, then, the prayer for revenge is a request that God enact God's will: "Your will be done, on earth as it is in heaven" (Matt. 6:10).

The word "then" at the beginning of Ps. 79:13 is misleading; it sounds too much as if Israel is cutting a bargain. The Hebrew could better be translated simply as "and." Verse 13 is thus the people's affirmation that they will always respond with gratitude for God's compassion and that they will witness to God's praiseworthy deeds. It is a remarkable promise in light of vs. 1–3! But the biblical faith *is* remarkable! It is about a God whose fierce love for the people will not tolerate unfaithfulness, but whose deep compassion will not let unfaithful people go. And it is about a people who suffer miserably, due to their own unfaithfulness (vs. 8–9), but who continue to pray to live (v. 9) and live to praise (v. 13). They never lose sight of reality, yet they never lose hope. As Walter Brueggemann concludes (*The Message of the Psalms*; Minneapolis: Augsburg Publishing House, 1984, p. 74):

> Biblical faith is not romantic. It reckons with evil, and it knows that evil strikes at all that is crucial and most precious. Nonetheless, it does affirm.

## 1 Timothy 2:1–7

First Timothy sets out to offer instructions about the Christian life (see 1:18). Those instructions begin in today's passage with a plea for prayer: "I urge that supplications, prayers, intercessions, and thanksgivings be made" (2:1). The importance of this admonition is indicated both by the fact that the writer places it first and by the multiple ways in which prayer is named. Prayers should be offered "for everyone" (v. 1). The specific instructions that follow make the understanding inescapable that prayer is not limited to the circle of believers. It extends to all people, as does God's own salvation (see v. 6).

Verse 2 singles out one group in particular, "kings and all who are in high positions." Scriptural precedent for this practice may be found in Jer. 29:7, where Israel is admonished to pray for the places of their exile, and in Bar. 1:11–12, where the residents of Jerusalem are asked to pray for the life of Nebuchadnezzar. The reasons given in those instances are echoed here, for the well-being of the rulers may result in the opportunity for Christians to live "a quiet and peaceable life."

First Timothy 2:2–3, with its elevation of the quiet life of dignity and piety, and its insistence that this life is God's will, perhaps reveals something of the time in which 1 Timothy was written. The first Christian communities, convinced as they were that Christ would return even during the lifetimes of some within their own circles (see, for example, 1 Cor. 15:51; 1 Thess. 4:15), were less concerned with living quietly and peaceably than is the author of 1 Timothy. Given later instructions about the need for behavior that will commend believers to those on the outside (3:7, for example), some commentators have concluded that the pastoral epistles reflect an accommodation to societal expectations in order to win approval (and perhaps even conversion).

With the reference to God's approval in 2:3, the writer elaborates on the desire of God in the next verse; God "desires everyone to be saved and to come to the knowledge of the truth." Because of the various teachings that the author of 1 Timothy regards as unacceptable (see 1:3–6; 4:1–5), he connects salvation closely with accurate knowledge of the gospel.

The liturgical fragment in 2:5–6 anchors this claim about salvation and truth. God desires the salvation of all because God is one, God's mediator is one, and that mediator died for all people. These lines open up a number of questions about the relationship between God and Christ and between Christ and humankind. In the context, however, their function seems quite clear. They insist that the oneness of God and the oneness of Christ are substantially connected with the salvation of all humankind as one collective group. In other words, if God may not be divided, then neither may the people whom God has acted to save.

Once again the author points to the role of Paul in this salvation (v. 7). Here Paul is described, not simply as "apostle," but also as "herald" and as "a teacher of the Gentiles in faith and truth." Consistent with v. 4, the emphasis here falls on learning the gospel in truth, or accurately.

Three issues come to the foreground in this passage. First, God's desire is for universal salvation. The repetition of the words "all" and "everyone" points to this concern. God desires that all human beings be saved, and Christ's own death has that salvation as its goal. It is for this reason that Christians are urged to pray on behalf of all people. While the other theological and ethical concerns of 1 Timothy preclude labeling this theme as "universal*ism*," the concern of the author for all people runs against the grain of some exclusivist themes elsewhere in late New Testament writings.

Second, faith requires knowledge of the truth. Given the tendentious edge of 1 Timothy, with its rejection of what other Christians surely understood to be the truth, we are rightly suspicious of the narrowness that has sometimes plagued theological debates. For contemporary Christians, however, who have too often yielded to the temptation to baptize any sort of profession under the virtue of tolerance, the insistence of 1 Timothy on understanding the truth of the gospel may sound an important warning. Not every assertion that claims to be the gospel does so rightly.

The third issue in this passage is perhaps the one that makes late-twentieth-century Christians most uncomfortable, and that is the admonition to pray for "kings and all who are in high positions" (v. 2). Looking back on twenty centuries of the church's history, we fear coziness with the "powers that be." Perhaps if other groups were identified in addition to these political rulers, the sense of discomfort would be lessened. To be asked to pray for one group, and that group consisting of secular authorities, seems to misconstrue where real power lies.

The cure for this discomfort stems also from the passage, however. Any understanding of v. 2 as an endorsement of human power must fall before the simple reminder that "there is one God" and "there is also one mediator between God and humankind" (v. 5). Whatever the rulers and their supporters may think, they are not God. They do not mediate between human beings and God. Their power, such as it is, exists only within a tiny and frail human sphere.

## Luke 16:1–13

The parable of the unjust steward has baffled interpreters since the beginning of time. The simple fact of Jesus' commendation of a dishonest person seems puzzling enough, but then we discover he may not have been dishonest after all, or maybe we should be paying attention to the master and not the manager. We shall comment on a few of the problems below, and though many of the smaller ones can be finessed, preachers are urged to consult the critical commentaries. Be forewarned that they do not agree among themselves how the passage is to be read, but most commentaries at least surface and explore the problems and discuss possible solutions.

Problem 1: What is the manager up to? Does "squandering his property" mean he has embezzled some of the rich man's estate, or simply mismanaged it? The former makes him a criminal, the latter just a poor manager. When he calls in the master's debtors and reduces the amount of their debt, is he (further) cheating the master, or is this reduction to come out of the commission that was rightly his, thus making him worthy of the master's praise?

Problem 2: Does the parable primarily focus on the manager, whose shrewdness is held up for praise, or is it really about an incredibly generous master/rich man who, like the father of the prodigal son (15:11–32), does not exact retribution for "squandering property," but surprises everyone by his commendation of the manager?

Problem 3: How is 16:9 to be understood? Could it be an ironic, caustic end to the story? "If you are so impressed by the street-smartness of the manager, the expert in shrewd manipulation, then go ahead and make a bundle of friends as he did with his dishonest wealth, and see what they can do for you when you reach those 'pearly gates'!" Or should the "make friends" of 16:9 be taken as a symbol for almsgiving and the establishment of a new relationship with recipients? "Give your wealth to the poor, and do so in such a way that they are not your debtors but your peers. You will be welcomed (by God) into the eternal homes."

Even these problems cannot be solved here, but a reading of the parable is offered in light of the problems. Whether the manager has been previously dishonest or only incompetent is really not critical to the story. In either case, he is dismissed by the master and is asked as his final duty to provide an audit of his work. In view of the master's praise of the manager, his reduction of the debts most likely comes from the interest on the loans he himself would otherwise have received.

There is no question that the manager's action is motivated by self-preservation. He has put the debtors in *his* debt by lowering their loans and has created a network of clients who owe him favors.

He is struggling to avoid being a ditchdigger or a beggar. Though apparently he is not rehired as manager, he is commended for his shrewdness. According to 16:8b, he seems to be a model of "the children of this age," who are "more shrewd in dealing with their own generation than are the children of light." His shrewdness is shown by the fact that a group of (supposedly) farmers are now in his debt and under some obligation to reciprocate.

But, then, how does 16:9 relate to the story? It draws from the story (use your wealth), but it counters the story (make friends for yourself). Instead of employing your money to create a group that owe you favors, make friends with your money. Friendship involves commonality and equality, not indebtedness. Halvor Moxnes comments, "To 'make friends' by 'unrighteous mammon,' therefore, was the opposite of enslaving people in need. To 'make friends' by giving to those in need had a liberating effect. It meant to put people on the same footing" (Halvor Moxnes, *The Economy of the Kingdom: Social Conflict and Economic Relations in Luke's Gospel;* Philadelphia: Fortress Press, 1988, pp. 142–43).

The message is parallel to that given to the Pharisee who hosted Jesus for dinner (14:12–14). Instead of inviting only friends, relatives, and rich neighbors, who can and will repay their obligation, invite the poor, the crippled, the lame, and the blind, who have no possibility of reciprocating.

The concluding sayings of Jesus in 16:10–13 underscore an essential relation between material possessions and the person who has them. As 16:11 puts it (paraphrased), "If you can't be responsible and reliable with your money, how can you expect to be made a steward of things that really matter?" Furthermore, responsibility and reliability include more than honesty in accounting procedures. Wealth can easily become an idol to which one bows and scrapes, and such devotion leads to a despising of God, who always remains a threat to a confidence in riches (12:16–21).

The lection raises serious questions both about our attitude toward money, our subtle (and sometimes not so subtle) attachments, and also about the manner in which we give alms. Does our stewardship create communities of indebtedness, or does it "make friends"?

# PROPER 21

Ordinary Time 26

*Sunday between September 25
and October 1 inclusive*

It is amazing the amount of attention the Bible gives to material possessions. In parables and oracles it warns about the delusions that wealth brings, and turns iconoclastic about the way we humans make idols of our dollars. It repeatedly directs readers' attention to the poor and the destitute. It constantly asks impertinent questions about how we earn and spend our income. So brash is the Bible about material possessions that the preacher who tries to reflect the biblical accent is likely to be accused of "talking too much about money." Three of the texts for this Sunday offer a variety of angles on this most urgent issue.

A string of comments in Luke's Gospel culminates in Jesus' story of the rich man and Lazarus (Luke 16:19–31). The tale is spun around the curtains that wealth has drawn on the windows of the rich man so that he is unable to see the beggar at his gate. His flaw is not that he is mean or abusive or arrogant. He is simply blind. Only in the next life, when he is rid of his riches, is he able to see Lazarus, now secure at Abraham's side. The parable finally directs its hearers to the scriptures, where insight is available and where an option is offered to the blindness of the rich man.

The passage from 1 Timothy contains a series of warnings to prosperous readers that having the basic necessities of life should be enough. Greed has the devastating effects of leading people away from the faith and of causing grievous pain. It ironically diverts attention away from the God "who richly provides us with everything for our enjoyment" (6:17).

None of the biblical discussions about material possessions provides us with an economic blueprint or a Christian's guide to spending money. The beautiful story in Jer. 32, however, offers a powerful model. Against the best wisdom of all the financial planners of Judah, Jeremiah purchases the field at Anathoth. The

527

prophet invests his money in the divine promise, in the outlandish conviction that God is faithful.

## Jeremiah 32:1–3a, 6–15

Jeremiah's reputation as a bringer of words of doom is not without foundation. Time and again the prophet heralded God's intention to judge sinful Judah and, although Jeremiah himself often paid a heavy price for his forthrightness (Jer. 32:2), he did not soften the effect of his message (27:1–11). Thus, when we hear from the lips of this outspoken individual words not of gloom, but of hope, we have all the more reason to be attentive.

Two bits of data must stand in the background of any successful understanding of this lection. The first is historical. In 588 B.C. the armies of Nebuchadnezzar (or Nebuchadrezzar, as in Jer. 32:1) surrounded the city of Jerusalem for the purpose of reducing its inhabitants to starvation and its government to oblivion. For the second time in a decade a Davidic monarch had revolted against Babylonian authority—in this case Zedekiah, son of the renowned Josiah. As his brother Jehoiakim had done earlier, Zedekiah anticipated that help would soon arrive from Babylon's perennial foe, Egypt, and that Judean independence would quickly ensue. It was a false hope, as it turned out, and the same army that had forced the submission of Jerusalem in 597 had ringed the city once again. But this time there was blood in their eyes! Whereas the first capitulation of the city had been followed by a relatively mild treatment of the rebels on the part of Nebuchadnezzar, all realized that the punishment this time would be extremely severe. Judah must be taught a lesson!

The second bit of data is cultural and theological, and it has to do with the law of redemption. Leviticus 25:25–55 spells out the basic provisions of this legislation, which is based on the ancient Israelite understanding of the solidarity of the nation and of the nation's subdivisions, clan and family. Like all the laws of ancient Israel enumerated in the Old Testament, those having to do with redemption were more observed at some periods of time than at others. But the concept of redemption served a larger than legal purpose, in that it became for many biblical writers a model for understanding God's activity in the life of Israel and/or in the life of the world. In its simplest formulation it went something like this: Should anything or any person that belongs to a family fall into jeopardy of being lost, it is the duty of the most senior male family member to do what is necessary to claim for the family that person or thing. Ruth 4:4–6 is one example of the application of the law of redemption; Jer. 32:6–15 is another.

In the midst of conditions briefly described in vs. 1–3a, Jeremiah's cousin Hanamel visits the imprisoned prophet one day. It may be assumed that the "field at Anathoth" (vs. 7, 9) was now occupied by the Babylonian army, in that Anathoth, Jeremiah's ancestral home, lay just beyond Jerusalem's northeast wall. Being unable to work his land, Hanamel is destitute, and, invoking the law of redemption, the poor man asks Jeremiah to buy the plot. It will bring no benefit whatsoever to the prophet. Even if he were not in prison, Jeremiah could not work the land any more than could Hanamel. What is more, Jeremiah could not even sell the land, unless he could find someone else in the family to take it off his hands—a highly unlikely prospect! (Compare 1 Kings 21 for the unwillingness of a devout Israelite to sell his land to someone outside his family.)

So Jeremiah does what many would have considered unthinkable: he gives good money for worthless land! Seventeen shekels of silver for the Brooklyn Bridge!

The real beauty in this passage lies in what happens next. Summoning his trusted companion Baruch to his place of confinement, along with a number of other friends (the "witnesses" of vs. 10, 12), Jeremiah conducts the transfer of ownership in very conspicuous fashion. Elaborate steps are taken to render highly visible the exchange of money and the execution of the necessary legal documents. Then in a voice that is now familiar to many in Jerusalem, the prophet orders Baruch to store the documents in a place where they will be safe indefinitely. (Jeremiah's reference to "an earthenware jar" in v. 14 reminds one of the conditions under which many of the so-called Dead Sea Scrolls were discovered.)

> For thus says the LORD of hosts, the God of Israel: Houses and fields and vineyards shall again be bought in this land. (V. 15)

The city is soon to fall; Jeremiah himself has said so on the authority of Israel's God. But judgment is not the final word. Beyond judgment, beyond destruction, beyond the justice of God there is restoration, mercy, salvation! The sinfulness of the people and God's just response to that sin will not prevail. The one thing that will prevail is God's compassion.

Jeremiah has conducted a little drama in which he has played the role of God, performing the same task in a small way that Israel's God would perform on a larger stage. It was to be left to a later prophet to elaborate on the implications of what Jeremiah had done:

> Do not fear, you worm Jacob,
>    you insect Israel!
> I will help you, says the LORD;
>    your Redeemer is the Holy One of Israel.
>                                        (Isa. 41:14)

The Second Isaiah was explicating that which Jeremiah had already implied: when Israel was about to be lost, who should step forward as Redeemer but Yahweh, Israel's God!

## Psalm 91:1–6, 14–16

See the discussion of this passage under the First Sunday in Lent.

## 1 Timothy 6:6–19

Throughout 1 Timothy, the author is at work constructing a boundary around the Christian faith, so that those who spout "any different doctrine" (1:3) will not succeed with "Timothy" or others who may read this letter. In 6:1–5, the attack on false teachers culminates in a characterization of them as "conceited, understanding nothing" and having "a morbid craving for controversy and for disputes about words." Somehow they anticipate financial gain from their teaching, or so the author charges (v. 5), as many philosopher-teachers of the day accused other teachers of engaging in philosophy for profit.

However valid or invalid the accusation about money, it provides the transition into the lection, 1 Tim. 6:6–19, much of which addresses the problem of wealth. The first section of the lection (vs. 6–10) explores the folly of those who desire wealth; the second (vs. 11–16) presents a positive challenge to Timothy in contrast to the warning about wealth; and the final section (vs. 17–19) returns to the topic of wealth, this time to address the way in which the wealthy need to live so as not to be corrupted by their wealth.

The first section opens with the assertion that "there is great gain in godliness combined with contentment." The catchword "gain" connects this verse closely with v. 5: there *is* gain in religion, although it is not the monetary gain that some false teachers anticipate. The notion of "contentment" then moves to the center of the discussion, for Christians are to be content with the basic necessities of life.

The teachings regarding contentment are stock features of Greco-Roman moral philosophy, particularly of the Cynics and Stoics, for whom being "content" with as little as possible was regarded as a virtue. In fact, virtually every line in this discussion about wealth (vs. 6–10) may be found in the moral writings of the day. Many moral and religious traditions recognize the destructive force of the pursuit of money, even if they are less successful in actually helping people to control that force! For the author of the pastorals, of course, there is a particular danger to Christians, since the pursuit of wealth leads some to fall "away from the faith" (v. 10).

The direct address to Timothy in vs. 11–16 leaves this topic behind completely. It also seems to be a self-contained unit, as is indicated by the formal beginning in v. 11 and the concluding "amen" in v. 16. Were it removed from the context, the move from v. 10 to v. 17 would be quite natural. These observations have prompted some to suggest that vs. 11–16 may actually have been written for another setting (for example, a baptism or an ordination) and do not really belong here.

Even if this segment interrupts the discussion on wealth, however, it does make sense in the present context. By contrast with the warnings of vs. 6–10 (or better, vs. 2b–10), here the challenge to Christians is stated positively. "But as for you" turns Timothy from the preceding negative assertions to the positive virtues of faith. Christians are enabled to resist greed because of their grounding in the faith.

Certainly the stance of this direct address is positive, even aggressive. As a "man of God" (note that the Greek is *anthrōpos* or "person," as distinct from "male"), Timothy is one commissioned to a specific task (see, for example, Deut. 33:1; 1 Sam. 9:6–10; 1 Kings 17:18). In the performance of that task, he is to "pursue," to "fight," to "take hold of." The language here represents the life of faithfulness as a forceful and vigorous engagement in the pursuit of the good.

This active language does not permit the conclusion that Christians somehow secure their own salvation, however, as the end of v. 12 makes clear. Timothy is admonished to "take hold of the eternal life, to which you were called." Pursuit of the good *follows on* God's own initiatory action, rather than serving to obtain God's favor.

Because of the calling, Timothy "made the good confession in the presence of many witnesses" (v. 12). The exact referent of this "good confession" is unclear, much as we might like to know its context and content, although it presumably is a confession of Christian faith.

Verse 13 serves as a solemn introduction to the charge of vs. 14–16, but the connection between the confession of Christians and that of Jesus himself is intriguing. The charge takes place in the presence of God the life giver and in the presence of "Christ Jesus, who in his testimony before Pontius Pilate made the good confession." Rather than the witness of Christ's powerful words or deeds, his death or his resurrection, the author chooses the trial as the primary locus of Christ's testimony, presumably because it involves not only a hostile audience but a very powerful audience. The charge in vs. 14–16 anticipates the future "manifestation" of Jesus. By contrast with Pontius Pilate or any other human ruler, he alone is truly "Sovereign, the King of kings and Lord of lords."

The lection concludes by returning to the question of wealth, this time not in a general sense but with particular attention to wealthy Christians. Other passages in the pastorals assume that the community includes at least some who have resources sufficient for the purchase of fine jewelry and of slaves (see, for example, 1 Tim. 2:9; 6:2; Titus 2:9–10). Here they are admonished to be careful with their wealth, and especially with their attitudes toward it. Not riches but God alone should provide the basis for human hope.

## Luke 16:19–31

The issue of material possessions appears and reappears in the section of Luke's Gospel called the travel narrative (12:13–34; 14:12–24; ch. 16). Four of the lections in recent Sundays have focused on the deceptiveness of wealth (enticing the rich to presume they can ensure a secure future), the potential idolatry of possessions, the importance of attending to the poor, and the critical importance of the manner in which one gives alms (Propers 13, 14, 17, 20). The climax of this Lukan interest comes in the lesson for this Sunday, the dramatic story of the rich man and Lazarus (16:19–31).

Why is so much attention given to material possessions? Some commentators would argue that the narrative is directly aimed at Luke's community, which either is composed of predominantly rich people needing to be reminded of their obligations to the poor or is a community in tension between rich and poor. This may or may not be true. More evident than the sociological contours of Luke's community, however, are the sociological implications of the Christian message. At the heart of the gospel is the great reversal in which the rich and powerful, who in this life perceive no need for divine grace, are cut off from the people of God, while the poor, the lowly, and the outcasts are given a proper place in the community of faith. In any and all communities, the promise is that God reverses the social and economic scale in surprising ways. (This, of course, is a Lukan theme not limited to the travel narrative. See, for example, Mary's Magnificat, 1:46–55.)

Nowhere is this reversal more vividly put than in the story of the rich man and Lazarus. While there are at least two themes developed in the plot, the changed circumstances of the primary characters dominate the story. Right at the beginning we are faced with a sharp contrast—rich man, poor man. What is mentioned about the rich man are the signs of his lavish wealth, his well-stocked wardrobe and his sumptuous diet ("every day"). Lazarus is depicted in gross terms that we would rather not hear. The mention of dogs licking his sores identifies him as not only poor but also unclean, and thus an outcast.

It is only after the death of both characters and their reversed positions in the afterlife that we begin to discover the real problem with the rich man. He is not harshly condemned. He is not indicted because he is rich, as if there were something inherently evil about money. We are not told that he persecuted Lazarus or deliberately refused him food or sponsored legislation to rid his gates of beggars.

Perhaps the clue, as John R. Donahue notes, is the fact that now he *sees* Lazarus for the first time (16:23). The difficulty with their relationship all those years on earth is that the rich man never sees Lazarus. "One of the prime dangers of wealth is that it causes 'blindness' " (John R. Donahue, *The Gospel in Parable: Metaphor, Narrative, and Theology in the Synoptic Gospels;* Philadelphia: Fortress Press, 1988, p. 171). The rich man's wealth has so distorted his vision that he is unable to perceive the plight of the beggar at his gate, to identify with his predicament, and to ease his suffering. Unfortunately, prosperity has a way of limiting our perspective, of closing down the shades on the distasteful so as not to disturb our enjoyment. It is an age-old story.

And so the reversal occurs. The rich man's plea from Hades to "Father Abraham" recalls John the Baptist's warning to the crowds that they not glibly claim Abraham as their father. They are, rather, to bear fruits worthy of repentance (3:8). But all the entreaties of the rich man now are resisted. He can think of Lazarus only as an errand boy to assuage his thirst or to warn his brothers. Tragically, he seems beyond the time for repentance. In sharp contrast, Lazarus is sitting by Abraham's side.

The other theme of this parable, often overshadowed, comes at the conclusion. The rich man's request to send Lazarus, a person from the dead, to alert his brothers is denied on the ground that they already have Moses and the prophets. The scriptures are important to Luke (see, for example, 24:25–27, 32, 44–49). What is happening in the advent of Jesus is the fulfillment of prophecies contained in the holy writings. There are a host of texts in those writings that remind Israel of its covenant responsibility to the poor in the land. If the brothers pay no heed to them, then they will pay no heed to one from the dead. The continuity is affirmed between the scriptures and the witness of the community of the resurrection.

One of the dilemmas in preaching this passage is that it is hard to identify with either the rich man or Lazarus. It is difficult to picture oneself as affluent as the rich man in all his opulence or to imagine oneself as catastrophically devastated as Lazarus. They both represent people other than us. It may be, then, that contemporary audiences can most easily associate with the five brothers, those of us who still have an opportunity to be instructed by the scriptures and to see the beggar at our gates. If so, then the parable itself becomes a word to the rich man's siblings to "warn them, so that they will not also come into this place of torment" (16:28).

# PROPER 22

## Ordinary Time 27

*Sunday between*
*October 2 and 8 inclusive*

It is difficult to find a common thread woven through the four passages assigned for this Sunday. To move from the sadness of Lamentations 1 to the thanksgiving prayer of 2 Tim. 1 is to move from total darkness to "the appearing of our Savior Christ Jesus, who abolished death and brought life and immortality to light through the gospel" (1:10). Nevertheless, among the four readings there exists a remarkable similarity in the two Old Testament texts and in the two New Testament texts.

Lamentations 1 and Ps. 137 are both painful laments from the vantage of the exile. The former bemoans the tragic situation of Jerusalem, ravaged by the Babylonians. In image after vivid image, the poet depicts the havoc and destruction of the lonely city, whose friends have turned on her and whose children have been snatched away. It is a poem of unrelieved grief.

Psalm 137 emerges also from the exilic community, cut off from the symbols of faith and unable to sing the Lord's song in a strange land. The psalmist is forced to remember the holy city, but the remembrance brings only rage and feelings of revenge. Both laments dramatize the expression of honest pain, which offers to God anger as well as grief.

In contrast, the New Testament texts speak of faith. The writer of the epistle delights in Timothy's heritage of faith, nurtured by mother and grandmother and empowered by divine gifts of love and self-discipline. But it is a heritage that must put itself at risk for the sake of the gospel and not flinch in the face of inevitable suffering.

The disciples ask Jesus for "more" faith, only to be told that faith cannot be quantified. Faith the size of a mustard seed does great things, because faith is no more than an openness to God's power, a trust in God's faithfulness.

## Lamentations 1:1–6

Lamentations is a collection of five poems (most, including ch. 1, arranged as alphabetic acrostics), which deplore the condition of Jerusalem as a consequence of its destruction by the Babylonians in 587 B.C.. Once thought to be the literary creation of the prophet Jeremiah (note 2 Chron. 35:25—although that reputed dirge is over the fate of King Josiah), the book is placed next to Jeremiah in most canonical arrangements of the Christian Old Testament. In the Hebrew Bible, however, Lamentations is included in the third section of the canon, the Writings. By a remarkable coincidence—according to Josephus—the Temple built by Herod the Great was destroyed by a Roman army in A.D. 70 on the very same day that the Babylonian army had destroyed Solomon's Temple, the ninth day of the Jewish month Av (late July). Thus the Fast of Tisha B'Av (Ninth of Av) became a moment of sorrowful commemoration in the calendar of Judaism, a mood enhanced by the public recitation of passages from Lamentations.

Every linguistic feature of these Hebrew poems emphasizes the tragic nature of the situation. The metrical pattern is typically three beats followed by two, a characteristic rhythm of sadness which, in modern terms, may be compared to music written in a minor key and annotated with the direction "Largo." The key word of this anthology of sorrowful songs is 'êkāh, a Hebrew word that is both an interrogative adverb ("How?") and an exclamation ("How!"). It is the initial word in the first (Lam. 1:1), second (2:1), and fourth (4:1; also 4:2) poems, and also serves as the title of the entire book as it appears in the Hebrew Bible. The dual nature of 'êkāh is apparent in v. 1 of our lection, in that "How lonely sits the city . . . " is both a heart-searching question and an outpouring of immeasurable grief.

The overwhelming image of the first lament (ch. 1), as well as of other sections of the book, is that of the violated woman (compare 5:11). In most parts of the ancient Near East, as well as in many parts of the world today, a woman bereft of a man enjoyed virtually no rights at all—and virtually no protection! People in our own time are all too sickeningly familiar with the television images of widows and mothers, their men taken from them by war or repression, forced to fend for themselves in a society ruled by their oppressors and by the murderers of their husbands and sons. They wear faces grown old beyond their years, faces lined with wrinkles etched by terror, faces that tell tales words cannot bear to say or ears to hear.

> How like a widow she has become,
> she that was great among the nations!

The lovely young princess is now a faded slave (v. 1:1).

Yet the poet knows that Jerusalem/Judah is not without fault (note v. 5; compare v. 8). Behind v. 2 may lie imagery similar to that of Ezek. 23, in which Jerusalem and Samaria are portrayed as individuals who have engaged in prostitution, only to be attacked by their lovers (compare Lam. 1:9). The reason that "she has no one to comfort her" is that she has relied on false lovers, "friends who have dealt treacherously with her." Those who she thought were her friends have become her enemies.

The theme of the nation's loneliness is raised again in v. 3. Judah has no true friends, for in her condition of weakness her erstwhile friends have viciously attacked her. It is a cycle of vulnerability and exhaustion in that the more she is assaulted, the weaker she becomes, leading to more assaults.

> Judah has wasted away through affliction
> and endless servitude.
> Living among the nations,
> she has found no resting-place;
> her persecutors all fell on her
> in her sore distress
>
>                                      (V. 3, REB)

Verse 4 remembers the great, glad days when Jerusalem was the center of the nation's religious life, the focal point to which pilgrim bands came from all the tribes to worship Yahweh at festival time. Psalm 122 was then a happy song, which the people sang as they approached the Holy City:

> To [Jerusalem] the tribes go up,
>    the tribes of the LORD,
> as was decreed for Israel,
>    to give thanks to the name of the LORD.
>                                      (Ps. 122:4)

But no more such joy, for now the "roads to Zion mourn."

Verse 5 of Lam. 1 makes quite explicit the complicity of the nation in its suffering, a reality alluded to in v. 2. It is "for the multitude of her transgressions" that Yahweh has brought exile (note v. 3) on

Judah. The enemies of God's people were also considered to be God's enemies (note Ps. 74:4, 23), and a large part of the tragedy of the nation's sinfulness consists in the fact that those who have set themselves against Israel's God have prevailed. The exiled people are like helpless children, victims of the sins of the whole community.

The royal character of the suffering woman, the "princess" of Lam. 1:1, is revisited in v. 6. Her regal splendor has been dissipated, her princely sons have become like so many hunted animals (the "princess" of v. 1 now seems more like a queen). Notice may be made of the recurrent motif of the plight of the offspring of Jerusalem, the fallen queen mother: "her young girls" (v. 4, assuming the NRSV's reconstruction of a difficult Hebrew text), "her children" (v. 5), and "her princes" of v. 6—all are lost!

## Psalm 137

Perhaps because it is a psalm about singing (see "songs"/"sing" five times in vs. 3–4), Ps. 137 has frequently been set to music and used in worship services; however, its use has almost always been after the expurgation of vs. 7–9, or at least v. 9. The lection for today includes the whole psalm. A confrontation with the whole psalm, including its shocking conclusion, has much to teach us about prayer, ourselves, and God.

As H.-J. Kraus states, "Psalm 137 is the only psalm in the Psalter that can be dated reliably" (*Psalms 60—150*, trans. H. C. Oswald; Minneapolis: Augsburg Publishing House, 1989, p. 501). If it did not actually originate in Babylon during the exile (587–539 B.C.), then it must have been written shortly after the return to Judah, when the pain of exile was still fresh in the minds and hearts of God's people.

The pain of exile is expressed in vs. 1–4 in the form of grief. The "rivers of Babylon," including its system of canals between the Tigris and the Euphrates, must have been a prominent feature to people from Palestine (see Ezek. 1:1; 3:15). It was nothing like home, and the geographical disparity may have exacerbated the grief that came when "we remembered Zion." There was nothing to do but weep (see Lam. 1:2, 16, where the personified Jerusalem weeps at the devastation of exile). There was no need for musical instruments (v. 2), for singing "the LORD's song in a foreign land" was out of the question (v. 4). The "LORD's song" would be one of the joyful "songs of Zion" (v. 3). They can be sung in Jerusalem, the Lord's place, but not "there" (vs. 1, 3) in Babylon.

The people cannot sing in Babylon, but they can remember. Verses 5–6, which are central structurally, also highlight a central theological concept—remembrance. The chiastic structure (a,b,b,a pattern) of vs. 5–6ab emphasizes the importance of remembering. As painful as it is to remember Jerusalem (v. 1), it would be more painful not to. Indeed, it would be debilitating, deadly. If Jerusalem is forgotten, joyful praise will never again be possible, for there will be no hands for playing the harp and no voice for singing the Lord's song. It is remembering Jerusalem that offers hope, and indeed life, amid the grief (vs. 1–4) and devastation of exile (vs. 7–9).

The request for God to "remember" (v. 7) is an invitation to God to share the people's pain. Whereas the pain was expressed as grief in vs. 1–4, here it is expressed as anger, outrage; and this is more difficult for us to deal with. What Ps. 137 teaches us, however, is that in situations of extremity grief and anger are both inevitable and inseparable. The worst possible response to victimization would be to feel nothing. If there is to be hope and life beyond devastation, death, and despair, then grief and anger must be felt and expressed. And this the psalmist does.

From this perspective, the psalmist's outburst in vs. 8–9 is a psychological necessity. As Leslie Allen suggests, "Perhaps the citizen of a European country who has experienced its invasion and destruction would be the best exegete of such a psalm" (*Psalms 101—150*, Word Biblical Commentary 21; Waco, Tex.: Word, 1983, p. 242). But there is a theological dimension to vs. 8–9 as well. The psalmist's desire for revenge is motivated by his or her loyalty to Jerusalem, indeed, loyalty to God! As John Bright suggests of the psalmist, "it would not be too much to say that he [or she] hated so because he [or she] loved so" (*The Authority of the Old Testament*; New York: Abingdon Press, 1967, p. 237). Furthermore, there is no evidence that the psalmist acted out of the expressed desire for revenge. Rather, it is offered to God (the address is to God in v. 7) and apparently left with God. The cycle of actual violence is broken by the psalmist's brutally honest prayer (see Ps. 109).

Thus, Ps. 137 as a whole becomes an "invitation to a kind of prayer that is passionate in its utter honesty" (James S. Lowery, "By the Waters of Babylon," *Journal for Preachers* 15/3 [1992]: 29). To pray is to offer our whole selves to God—anger and vengefulness as well as grief—and to know that God loves us as we are. As Bright suggests, this aspect of Ps. 137 represents "a drive toward incarnation"; that is, God chooses to reveal God's self through people "of like passions with ourselves" (p. 236).

If we are honest, we shall have to admit that we are no less vengeful than the psalmist. After all, as Kraus suggests, v. 9 should be understood not only as the expression of a particular individual but also as "a reference to the cruelty of ancient warfare generally" (*Psalms 60—150*, p. 504), the typical practices of which are reflected in Hos. 10:14; 13:16; Nahum 3:10; Isa. 13:16; and 2 Kings 8:12 (see also Rev. 18, especially vs. 6, 20–24, for another expression of the desire for revenge against "Babylon"). In view of the cultural context, the psalmist's wish in Ps. 137:8–9 represents a principle that most Americans routinely espouse—that is, the punishment should fit the crime. We are no less vengeful than the psalmist.

The good news is that God loves us and chooses to use us anyway. Psalm 137 ultimately points toward God's forgiveness. It is even possible that the psalmist's cathartic expression of desire for revenge represented a first step toward his or her forgiving the victimizers. In the book of Isaiah, after proclaiming God's forgiveness of the sins that led to the exile (Isa. 40:1–2), the prophet proclaims that the mission of exilic and postexilic Israel is to be "a light to the nations, that my salvation may reach to the end of the earth" (Isa. 49:6). The desire for revenge has given way to a desire to save. Hate has been replaced by hope.

A psalm about a remembrance that both expresses pain and harbors hope cannot help reminding Christians of the Lord's Supper and Jesus' words, "Do this in remembrance of me" (Luke 22:19). The remembrance is painful, for it re-presents Jesus' death. But the remembrance is also hopeful—"You proclaim the Lord's death until he comes" (1 Cor. 11:26). The final verse of Ewald Bash's metrical paraphrase of Ps. 137 captures its theological trajectory ("By the Babylonian Rivers," *The Worshipbook*; Philadelphia: Westminster Press, 1972, no. 321):

> Let thy cross be benediction
>    For [those] bound in tyranny;
> By the power of resurrection
>    Loose them from captivity.

## 2 Timothy 1:1–14

This is the first of four consecutive Sundays when the epistolary reading comes from 2 Timothy, a letter that is much more personal in tone and content than either of the other pastoral epistles. Where the preceding readings from 1 Timothy address matters of church governance (for example, what qualifies a person as a bishop or a deacon), 2 Timothy addresses the faithful life of an individual Christian. The letter assumes that Paul writes from prison, probably toward the end of his life, to encourage Timothy as one who will carry on his work. While the personal details lead some interpreters to argue for the Pauline authorship of this letter, many others see them as a means of securing the empathy and attention of the intended audience and conclude that 2 Timothy was written by a member of the Pauline circle after Paul's death.

Already in the salutation of the letter (1:1–2) one of the major concerns of the pastorals appears: Paul's apostleship is "for the sake of the promise of life that is in Christ Jesus." This promise of life appears elsewhere both in 2 Timothy (for example, 1:10; 2:11) and in the other letters (for example, 1 Tim. 1:16; 4:8; Titus 1:2; 3:7). The pastorals exhibit great concern with the gospel as a means of salvation, and references to life or eternal life clearly play a role in that larger theme.

The thanksgiving (2 Tim. 1:3–5) brings the personal appeal of this letter to the foreground. In addition to the reference to constant prayer, a feature found in other Pauline letters (Phil. 1:4; 1 Thess. 1:2–3), the thanksgiving appeals to Paul's own family and its faith, the grief of Timothy (presumably at their parting), and the influential faith of Timothy's own mother and grandmother. Lois and Eunice have attracted considerable attention from scholars interested in integrating this bit of information with the reference to Timothy in Acts 16:1–3; they also figure prominently in discussions of authorship, for if the author is implying that Timothy has grown up in the faith, then the letter would probably date from after the time of Paul's death.

Of more significance for the preacher, however, is the way both this reference to Timothy's family and the prior reference to Paul's ancestors (2 Tim. 1:3) reflect the assumption that faith thrives in the family. Paul worships as did his own ancestors, and Timothy's faith "lived first" in these two women. These references to the antiquity of the faith, at least in the case of Paul, also serve to counter any Roman suspicions about Christianity as a new (and therefore suspicious) religion.

With v. 6, the immediate concern for Timothy emerges, namely, that he should "rekindle the gift of God" that he received with the laying on of hands. Because Acts associates the laying on of hands with particular tasks within the Christian community (for example, in 1:12–26; 6:1–6), interpreters refer to this as Timothy's ordination. So long as we do not read into this term later and more systematic understandings of ordination, and so long as we understand that what is said to Timothy pertains not just to the ordained, the term is a useful one.

Second Timothy 1:6–8 recalls for Timothy the nature of the gift he received from God at his ordination. Negatively stated, the gift he received was *not* cowardice; positively put, the gift is one of "power and of love and of self-discipline." In the context of Paul's imprisonment, then, this gift must be interpreted as pride and a willingness to share in suffering "for the gospel" (v. 8).

Verses 9–10 provide a brief summary of the author's understanding of the gospel. Perhaps a fragment from a confession of faith, this statement celebrates God's gifts of salvation and vocation and grace (v. 9b). It then characterizes the grace of the gospel in terms both of its eternal character ("before the ages began," v. 9b) and its eschatological manifestation. This grace "has now been revealed through the appearing of our Savior Christ Jesus" (v. 10) and his gifts of life and light.

Verses 11–14 return to Paul's own ministry and offer it as a model for Timothy. Paul's "appointment" to his apostolic task enables him to endure suffering with utter confidence that he will not be disappointed by the God in whom he trusts. The author urges Timothy to emulate this example, to follow the "sound teaching" he learned from Paul, and to guard the faith as a rare treasure.

What follows in vs. 15–18, although beyond the limits of this lection, serves to reinforce the picture of Paul's suffering. He has been deserted by "all who are in Asia." Onesiphorus alone searched him out in Rome, unwilling to be ashamed of Paul's imprisonment.

One of the questions that drive this passage is how Christians are to regard the sufferings of the apostles. For contemporary believers, accustomed to the stories of earlier generations, the sufferings are read through somewhat romantic lenses. Paul's letter to Philippi suggests, however, that some early Christians saw imprisonment as a sign of weakness and failure (see Phil. 1:12–18). Paul, of course, does not, appealing to the crucifixion of Christ as a precedent for his own suffering. Second Timothy, perhaps written a generation later, takes the argument a step farther by insisting that Paul's suffering provides an example for all who serve in Christ's name.

## Luke 17:5–10

The Gospel lesson assigned for this Sunday may at first blush scare the preacher off. It is composed of two sections (17:5–6 and

7–10), and while the former section is clear enough and offers a positive word of encouragement, the latter section is threatening. It seems to present an unfeeling master and a slave who is not sufficiently acknowledged for his faithful service. After laboring all day in the fields and preparing and serving dinner for his master, he is to think of himself as a worthless slave who has only done what he is supposed to do.

Though we may not like all those crassly commercial books in the stores on self-affirmation, with their "You're Number One!" theme, we nevertheless sense their appeal. Who doesn't want to feel worthwhile? Who doesn't like to be properly acknowledged for what he or she accomplishes? We go to great pains to see that no one in the congregation (or ourselves, for that matter) feels put down or put upon in his or her church activity, but that everyone is duly recognized and appreciated. But do Jesus' words in the latter section of the lection militate against that?

A closer look at the text shows us that the first section conveys an understandable and appropriate request from the apostles: "Increase our faith!" In the previous paragraph, they have had two heavy demands laid on them. They have been warned not to be a stumbling block to the "little ones" (17:1–3a) and to rebuke and forgive sins wherever among their own number they are to be found. Even if culprits ask seven times a day for pardon, they are to be forgiven (17:3b–4). How can the apostles live up to this? They sense their need for greater resources, and thus make their request to Jesus.

The response the apostles receive is reassuring. They are not to think of faith in quantitative terms, as if it were a commodity doled out in stingy or generous amounts. When faith is reduced to a positive attitude about life or a sense of self-confidence, then maybe "more" and "less" would be appropriate categories. An athletic team that performs badly can admit after the game, "We didn't believe hard enough." But in Luke's Gospel, faith is always related to God and God's actions in Jesus (for example, 5:20; 7:9). It is not so much what humans do or do not do, but what the limitless power of God does. Faith is the openness to God's power.

This is why faith can be compared with something so minute as a mustard seed, and yet can accomplish astonishing things. The analogy is not to meager beginnings and immense conclusions (as in 13:18–19), but to the necessary presence of a receptive and trusting faith. (The contrary-to-fact clause—"If you had . . ."—in the Greek of 17:6 may suggest that the apostles do not yet have this faith.)

The second section of the lesson (17:7–10) seems to point the reader in a different direction. But be forewarned: the parable sneaks up on you. The hearer is initially invited to identify with the slave owner ("Who among you would say to your slave . . . ") and to contemplate what would be the normal attitude toward one's slave when he comes in from working the fields. The rhetorical questions asked ("Would you not rather say . . . ? Do you thank the slave . . . ?") imply that the slave would not in any way be sidetracked from the usual responsibilities of fixing and serving the master's meal first and then his own. (The question of 17:9 in the Greek text is asked in such a way as to expect a negative response.)

But 17:10 switches the hearer from identification with the slave owner to identification with the slave. The real issue is not how the boss treats the servant, but how the servant understands his role.

Despite its problems, this parable remains remarkably relevant. The story (granted, in a sneaky fashion) reminds us of our place and shows how easy it is to exchange roles. God is God; we are God's creatures—no more, no less. But subtly the order can get reversed, as Adam and Eve discovered. Dominion over the earth is a heady challenge. "Why stop there?" the serpent asks. "You will be like God!" (Gen. 3:5).

Or we think of Jesus as the one who washes feet, forgives sins, hears prayers, supplies needs. Jesus gives; we receive. Pretty soon we come to expect it. And the old catechism question slowly but surely gets a skewed answer: Jesus' chief end is to glorify and enjoy us forever. But the parable pushes to keep the roles of master and servant in the proper order.

For many (women, minorities, third-world people) the language of servanthood may only conjure up the specter of another tyranny. When told to say, "We are worthless slaves," their response is likely to be "Not again!" (The NEB for Luke 17:10 may be preferred: "We are servants and deserve no credit; we have only done our duty"). In this light, it is important to recall that the teller of the parable himself identifies with the one who fixes meals and waits tables. "But I am among you as one who serves" (22:27). His mission leads him to the cross. Furthermore, the authority he exercises is not like "the kings of the Gentiles" (22:25), who lord it over others, and the leadership he proposes is that of service. Or as Martin Luther put it, only as we discover ourselves as the dutiful servant of all do we also discover ourselves truly free.

It is clear that the narrator sees something positive in the figure of the dutiful servant. Life is really impoverished when we think God is indebted to us. We lose the joy and spontaneity of those surprised by divine gifts, those overwhelmed by unmerited grace. We cannot whoop and holler the way the lone Samaritan does when he is healed by Jesus. The text says he came away not only free of his leprosy, but with a new kind of wholeness (17:11–19). In his own way, the faithful servant by quietly doing his duty is pointing us in the direction of that new wholeness.

# PROPER 23

Ordinary Time 28

*Sunday between
October 9 and 15 inclusive*

Biblical texts are full of surprises. Sometimes they become so familiar that we miss the arresting word they speak, a word that jolted original readers and made them aware of just how unpredictable God can be.

Take the counsel Jeremiah gives the exiles (29:4–7). One might have expected him to advise them to maintain their independence and to be constantly prepared to return at any moment to Judah, to the land God had given them. Instead, they are told to settle in, to build and plant, to seek the welfare of Babylon, even to pray for its prosperity. The judging purposes of God call for extended exile and not impatient rebellion.

Or take the story of the ten lepers in Luke 17:11–19. We are delighted to learn that one returns to praise and thank Jesus for giving him health. Only then we are stunned to learn that he was a Samaritan. The ultimate outsider becomes the model of faith.

Or take the testimony of 2 Timothy. It is not bad theology to reason that when the people of God are unfaithful, they will be punished. The consequences of disobedience mean judgment. Yes, up to a point. Then grace surprises us. It disrupts the expected pattern. "If we deny him, he will also deny us; if we are faithless, he remains faithful—for he cannot deny himself" (2:12b–13).

It is just this awesome character of God, always honoring divine commitments but thereby appearing to humans full of surprises, that the psalmist praises. God turns the sea into dry lands, keeps a watchful eye on the nations, leads the chosen people into hard circumstances, through fire and water, but brings them beyond into a safe and spacious place. This God merits the worship of all the earth.

## Jeremiah 29:1, 4–7

There is one very interesting historical phenomenon that is profoundly important to the history of humankind: the Jewish

546

people survived the Babylonian exile. If this fact does not appear particularly impressive on its face, one need only remember that Judah's twin, the Northern Kingdom of Israel, had been carried off in substantial numbers into captivity by the Assyrians in 722 B.C. Except for those people left in the land (who later came to be called Samaritans), the so-called "lost tribes" of Israel disappeared from history. (Claims that they were ancestors of Native American peoples are without foundation.)

However, by the mercy of God, the Jews survived their ordeal in Babylon. Many Jews, descendants of the original exiles of 597 and 587 B.C., would ultimately find their way back to Judea in the years following their release from captivity in 538 B.C. Others would elect to stay in Babylon and perpetuate a vital Jewish presence there, a presence that continued unbroken until anti-Jewish sentiment virtually destroyed the Jewish community in the Mesopotamian valley a few years ago.

In a sense, it is idle to raise the question of why the Jews survived, while the community of Samaritan exiles vanished. The short answer, of course, is that such was the will of God. But in human terms, much of the credit for the survival of the Jewish exiles may be laid at the feet of Jeremiah. For it was Jeremiah who, more than any other contemporary spokesperson for God, provided those words by which the people could come to terms with the tragedy of their nation and, thus, could rise above it. If Jeremiah's enemies had succeeded in any of their several attempts to kill him (Jer. 26:11, for example), one might argue that God would have raised another to take Jeremiah's place. Yet while God's mercy restored the nation (note Jer. 31:27–34, Proper 24), Jeremiah was an essential tool by which that restoration took place.

At some time after the initial capitulation of Jerusalem in 597 B.C., but before the terrible destruction of the city in 587 B.C. which marked the end of King Zedekiah's fruitless revolt, Jeremiah wrote a letter to those Jews who had been forced to go to Babylon in the company of King Jehoiachin (Jeconiah of 29:2). The questions with which those captives wrestled were haunting. Many in Jerusalem, who had heard the prophetic promise of judgment from Jeremiah and others, announced with satisfaction that the exiles of 597 had been chosen to receive God's wrath because they were more evil than those who had been spared (note the account of the vision of the figs in Jer. 24:1–10). Could that possibly be true? the exiles wondered.

What should be their attitude toward their present confinement? Should they resist, hoping that if they rebelled, God would send a deliverer to save them? It seems evident from the record in the book of Jeremiah that some Jews in Babylon actually tried to revolt, only to be condemned to a horrible death by the government of King Nebuchadnezzar (29:21–23).

Into their confusion Jeremiah injects his coolly reasoned advice (29:4–7). The captivity of the people is from Yahweh of hosts, the God of Israel, and, as such, should not be resisted by God's people (v. 4, compare 27:5–11). It will not end soon, and any who promise that it will are deluding the people. Instead, the people should "build" and "plant," two verbs that form part of Yahweh's original commission to Jeremiah (1:10, see Proper 16). They must expand their families, so as to ensure the survival—indeed, the expansion—of the people in this hostile land (29:6).

Perhaps most surprising of all, the exiles should so identify themselves with their captors' community that they look upon themselves as its citizens (v. 7). "In its welfare you will find your welfare" is the climax of this astonishing advice.

It is not difficult to comprehend why many of Jeremiah's Jewish contemporaries considered him a traitor to the cause of his nation and imprisoned him as a subversive (37:11–15). Even the Babylonians thought of him as their ally and offered him asylum after the destruction of Jerusalem (39:11–14).

But Jeremiah was no traitor, because his only motivation was to do and speak the will of Yahweh. Because Yahweh had designated Nebuchadnezzar as the divine agent of judgment, any resistance to the Babylonian king was resistance to Yahweh. In due time Yahweh would restore the people (29:10), but until then the people must make their peace with their situation. If that meant cooperation with the Babylonians, so be it. The will of Yahweh must be fulfilled.

This text raises fundamental questions, not all of which it answers. Perhaps the most important is: When should the people of God resist tyranny? Universal statements will not stand, for each tyrannical situation must be evaluated on its own. The Jews of Nazi Germany were forced to confront that question, as were many Christians. The Jews of the Warsaw ghetto and Dietrich Bonhoeffer, to name but two examples, decided that resistance to tyranny was the godly thing to do. No one may judge them to have been in error. But the testimony of Jeremiah is that sometimes resistance is not the will of God. Sometimes passiveness is God's will (compare 1 Tim. 6:1).

Each person must decide the issue for herself or himself—sometimes, again and again—relying on scripture, prayer, and the traditions of the church (or synagogue) as guides.

## Psalm 66:1–12

In *The Psalms in Human Life*, Rowland Prothero reports the following about John Bunyan, author of *Pilgrim's Progress*, and his use of Ps. 66: "In his *Grace Abounding to the Chief of Sinners*, which bears the motto, 'Come and hear all ye that fear God, and I will declare what he hath done for my soul' [Ps. 66:16], he has recorded, with a pen of iron and letters of fire, his own passage from death to life" (New York: E. P. Dutton, 1903, p. 185). In a real sense, Ps. 66 is about the "passage from death to life." The Septuagint and Vulgate versions even provide Ps. 66 with the title "Psalm of the Resurrection." This passage from death to life is presented in two parts—vs. 1–12, which feature a communal voice, and vs. 13–20, which feature an individual voice. Scholars have sometimes treated vs. 1–12 and vs. 13–20 as separate psalms, and, indeed, the lection consists of only vs. 1–12. As suggested below, however, there are parallels between the two sections, and it is important to hear them together.

The psalm begins by inviting "all the earth" to praise God (v. 1), and then reports that this praise actually happens (v. 4). God's "name," suggestive of God's character, is mentioned in vs. 2 and 4. God is worshiped because of who God is, and God's character is revealed by what God does (v. 3, God's "awesome . . . deeds"). In short, God rules the world. Not surprisingly, the invitations to praise in Ps. 66 occur frequently elsewhere in contexts that explicitly affirm Yahweh's reign (see "make a joyful noise" in Pss. 95:1; 98:4, 6; "glory" in Pss. 24:7–10; 29:1–3, 9; 96:3, 7–8; 145:5, 11–12; "power" in Pss. 29:1, 11; 93:1; 96:6–7; Ex. 15:2, 13, NRSV "strength"; "worship(s)" in Pss. 95:6; 99:5; "sing praises" in Pss. 47:6–7; 98:4–5; and so on). Because God rules the world, "all the earth" constitutes God's congregation.

Like the previous section, Ps. 66:5–7 begins with a plural imperative. The focus returns to God's activity (see "done" and "deeds" in v. 5), which is described a second time as "awesome" (vs. 3, 5). Not coincidentally, the adjective "awesome" also describes God's activity in delivering Israel from Egypt (Ex. 15:11); and the exodus comes into even sharper focus in v. 6 (see "dry land" in Ex. 14:16, 22, 29, NRSV "dry ground"). The exodus represented Israel's passage from death to life, but the exodus was not just for Israel's benefit. Israel's passage from death to life ultimately represents an enactment of God's will for "all the earth." As Terence Fretheim suggests (*Exodus*, Interpretation series; Louisville, Ky.: John Knox Press, 1991, p. 13):

While the liberation of Israel is the focus of God's activity, it is not the ultimate purpose. The deliverance of Israel is ultimately for the sake of all creation (see [Ex.] 9:16). The issue for God is finally not that God's name be made known in Israel but that it be declared to the entire earth. God's purpose in these events is creation-wide. What is at stake is God's mission for the world, for as 9:29 and 19:5 put it, "All the earth is God's" (cf. 8:22; 9:14). Hence the *public character* of these events is an important theme throughout.

What is true for the book of Exodus is also true for Ps. 66. Thus, "all the earth" is summoned to "Come and see" (v. 5). God's activity is for all people! God wills and works toward the end that "the nations" (v. 7) pass from death to life. Those who "see" God's sovereign purposes will no longer "exalt themselves" (v. 7), but rather will join Moses and the Israelites in their resolve to "exalt" Yahweh (Ex. 15:2).

In vs. 8–12 of Ps. 66, as in vs. 5–7, the focus of God's activity is on Israel, but the deliverance related in vs. 9–12 is again paradigmatic. Thus, in keeping with the creation-wide purposes of God, the "peoples" are invited to "Bless our God" (v. 8). The deliverance again involves the passage from death to life (v. 9; on not slipping or being "moved," see Pss. 38:16; 55:22; 94:18; 121:3). The specific distress involved is not clear (compare Ps. 66:12b with Isa. 43:2), but whatever it is, Israel is not so sure of God's sovereignty that the trouble cannot be experienced apart from God. Thus, the community professes that God has "tested us" and "tried us" (v. 10). Tests and trial need not be understood as punishment; in fact, they most frequently suggest an examination for the purpose of vindication (see Job 23:10; Pss. 11:4–5; 17:3; 26:2; 139:23; Jer. 12:3; Zech. 13:9). In any case, the emphasis in Ps. 66:9–12 is on God's deliverance of the people, as suggested literarily by the fact that vs. 9 and 12c surround the description of distress (see John Bracke, "Psalm 66:8–20," *No Other Foundation* 13/2 [winter 1992–93]: 42).

Although the lection ends at v. 12, it is important to note that in vs. 13–20 the psalmist presents his or her own life as a witness to God's ongoing activity of delivering persons from death to life. As above, the exact nature of the "trouble" (v. 14) is unclear, but the deliverance is given a public character. As the whole people had done (v. 5), the psalmist invites others to "Come and hear" (v. 16) that "God has listened" (v. 19; compare Ex. 3:7) and not removed "steadfast love from me" (v. 20; see Ex. 15:13). For the psalmist, the old, old story has become the new, new song. He or she joins Moses and all Israel in exalting God (see "extolled" in v. 17, which is the same as "exalt" in

Ex. 15:2). Thus, his or her life is an example to the nations "not [to] exalt themselves" (v. 7). And as the "peoples" have been invited to do (v. 8), the psalmist declares God "blessed" on account of who and how God is—steadfastly loving (see Ex. 34:6–7) in fulfilling God's creational purpose of life for people and nations. When taken as a whole, as Walter Brueggemann suggests, "This psalm shows the move from communal affirmation to individual appreciation, which is what we always do in biblical faith" *(The Message of the Psalms;* Minneapolis: Augsburg Publishing House, 1984, p. 139).

## 2 Timothy 2:8–15

For North American Christians at the end of the twentieth century, hearing someone described as having "left the church" is a regular feature of conversation. However much the phenomenon grieves us, and however much we ponder its causes, we are no longer shocked by the fact that people decide to leave the church.

The author of the pastoral epistles operates out of a different framework, one in which such decisions are nothing less than abandonment. Earlier in 2 Timothy, he refers to those who have "turned away from " Paul, presumably because of his imprisonment (1:15). Just following the present lection, he refers to the impact of those such as Hymenaeus and Philetus, who have not only effectively "left the church" by their false beliefs, but have taken others with them (2:17b–18).

In the face of such abandonment, whether of basic tenets of the Christian faith or of an apostle of Jesus Christ, the author writes a stern word about faithfulness to the gospel. It begins already in 2:1 with the admonition to "be strong in the grace that is in Christ Jesus." The examples of the soldier, the athlete, and the farmer all serve to reinforce the need to remain constant in one's convictions and actions.

With v. 8, the subject matter turns to the theological basis for such faithfulness: "Remember Jesus Christ, raised from the dead, a descendant of David—that is my gospel." Two central items of early Christian proclamation serve here as a terse summary of the entire gospel. Both appear in a variety of contexts, although Rom. 1:3–4 provides the closest parallel. The order in which they appear here is puzzling, since the relationship of Jesus to the house of David logically and chronologically precedes his resurrection. In view of the emphatic reminder of God's faithfulness later in the passage, the reference to David *might* stand last to connect it more closely with

God's faithfulness, since Christians see God's promise to David fulfilled in Jesus.

Verse 9 of 2 Tim. 2 returns to the suffering of Paul (see 1:8–12), which for the author of the pastorals seems to belong as a kind of adjunct to the kerygma itself. Over and over, he recalls the suffering of Paul and Paul's response to that suffering. That is, Paul's own faithfulness in the face of his imprisonment serves to remind this particular circle of Christians in the Pauline tradition of their own need to remain faithful.

Even if Paul wears chains, God's word remains free (v. 9). This pithy assertion recalls not only the experiences of Paul but the many occasions in Acts when attempts at silencing Christian preaching fail. Luke speaks of the word of God advancing, often in contexts when that seems most unlikely (for example, Acts 12:24).

The conviction that God's word is "not chained," that God's word could not be chained, enables Paul to endure for the salvation of others. His imprisonment serves not his own ends, but those of God's "elect," indeed, those of God alone.

Second Timothy 2:11 introduces what may be a liturgical fragment (vs. 11b–13), although its appropriateness for this particular context is impressive. The introductory formula, "The saying is sure," elsewhere in the pastorals serves to draw attention to some emphatic assertion about the nature of salvation (see 1 Tim. 1:15, for example). The four "if-then" statements that comprise this passage move from positive claims about Christian behavior to warnings against abandonment of the faith.

The first statement closely parallels Rom. 6:5, and reflects Paul's own understanding of Christian baptism. In baptism, the believer dies with Christ and will be raised to live with him (the future tense being extremely significant here). Second Timothy 2:12 restates this connection between the believer and Christ, although this time in terms calculated for the context. Those who endure, like Paul (v. 10) and unlike Hymenaeus and Philetus and their colleagues (v. 17) will "reign" with Christ.

Verse 12b puts the matter negatively. Those who deny Christ will in turn be denied by him. First Timothy 5:8 declares that those who do not provide for their family members have "denied the faith." Second Timothy 3:5 equates certain behaviors with denying the power of godliness. Titus 1:16 also characterizes some "rebellious people" (1:10) as denying God with their actions. Here the consequences of that behavior emerge.

We might well expect 2 Tim. 2:13 to follow this same logic: "If we are faithless, he will also be faithless." Such a claim cannot be made, however, even in the face of the most odious faithlessness on the part of human beings. So much does God's faithfulness partake of God's very being that God is incapable of being other than faithful. Here human hope resides, for even the most faithful of believers will fall short; all must rely completely on God's own promises.

The final two verses of the lection pair together a warning (v. 14) and an exhortation (v. 15). Timothy's people are warned against "wrangling over words." The specific character of this "wrangling" comes into focus in v. 18 and in 2:23; it is not talk or debate in general that concerns the author, but the kind of talk that contradicts the truth. By contrast with the warning about bad speech, the author admonishes Timothy to present himself as one who knows how rightly to teach "the word of truth." In this way, not only does Timothy himself remain strong (see 2:1), but he participates in the strengthening of others.

## Luke 17:11–19

This beautifully fashioned story of the leper who returned to give thanks has an irresistible appeal. We like gracious people who know how to acknowledge gifts given them and who find appropriate ways to express gratitude to the giver. As my mother often said, "It shows good breeding." The story is a favorite for services of worship during the Thanksgiving weekend.

Yet the text is much more than an illustration of the importance of writing thank-you notes. Ironically, the one in the story who returns to give thanks is not, from the vantage point of the narrative, well-bred, but a person of mixed breed, who may have been the least likely of the group of lepers to do what he does. The story is richer, more multifaceted, than merely an example story for gratitude.

Consider three critical themes that emerge in the text. First, the bottom line is that the leper who returns becomes a model of faith (Luke 17:19). In the previous section of the narrative, the disciples are faced with the warning not to be a stumbling block to others and the challenge to forgive repentant persons an unlimited number of times (17:1–4). Overcome with such a demand, they plead, "Increase our faith!"—only to be told by Jesus that faith is not to be quantified. The simple reality of trust, small as the size of a mustard seed, is sufficient (vs. 5–6).

Now the disciples get a further instruction in faith. The leper models it. Healed by Jesus and told to go to the priests and tend to what is prescribed in the law for cleansed lepers (Lev. 14:1–9), he stops on the way, turns back, praises God with a loud voice, falls at Jesus' feet, and thanks him. All ten lepers are healed, and, though we are not specifically told, the other nine presumably go to the priests and do what Jesus directed them to. Whether this lone leper ever gets to the priests or not, we do not know. What he does, however, singles him out for Jesus' commendation.

The NRSV with its rendering of Luke 17:19 ("Your faith has made you well") fails to get the full impact of the Greek verb *sōzō* (better, "Your faith has saved you"). The leper experiences more than the other nine experience, more than a liberation from his leprosy. His whoops and hollers of praise to God and his gratitude to Jesus in a posture of obeisance are the essence of faith. He is able to see beyond his whole body to the one who makes it whole. His actions of delight and gratitude, which distinguish him from the others, demonstrate his trust in Jesus, God's agent of healing.

The second theme of the story takes us by surprise. After all the local color of the setting (17:11), the proper approach of the lepers (vs. 12–13), the simple account of the healing (v. 14), and the detailed description of the grateful leper's response (vs. 15–16), we read the terse statement, "And he was a Samaritan" (v. 16). A story of healing, and even of faith, takes a dramatic turn.

The original listeners and readers were no doubt jolted by this bit of information which undermines the stereotypes they held about Samaritans. Earlier in the narrative they may have been angered, but would not have been surprised by the rejection of Jesus by a Samaritan village (9:52–53). But like the parable of the good Samaritan (10:30–37), the news that the grateful leper is a Samaritan occasions some rethinking. Even for us later readers, who are removed from the dynamics of the ancient racism, the point is reinforced by Jesus' reference to him as "this foreigner" (17:18). The model of faith turns out to be the ultimate outsider.

The third theme of the story is the indictment made of the nine lepers who do fail to praise God. Jesus' three rhetorical questions of vs. 17–18 are haunting. Were the other nine of Jewish birth? Probably, since they are sent to the priests and are contrasted with "this foreigner." But their Jewishness is not the point of Jesus' questions, only their lack of gratitude and their failure to praise God. Non-Jewish readers are hardly less probed by Jesus' questions than are Jewish readers.

We are made poignantly aware that not all who are helped by Jesus come to faith. Some take the help, perhaps, as sign of what they deserve, a just recompense for their years of suffering. Others are perhaps too busy with the new possibilities for a restored life to engage in the unbounded response of the Samaritan. Whatever their reasons, the nine are impoverished by their lack of the joy of praising God, by their failure to discern the One from whom restoration has come. They become models (of a sort) of what faith is not.

The passage, then, confronts us with more than a push for the common courtesy of saying our thank-yous. It gives us an outsider whose unrestrained and spontaneous appreciation (much like the sinful woman who anoints Jesus' feet in Luke 7:37–38) dramatizes the essence of faith and who disrupts an otherwise easy perception that we know who the real insiders are.

# PROPER 24

Ordinary Time 29

*Sunday between
October 16 and 22 inclusive*

The place of the Bible in the people of God is a theme that needs periodic attention from the pulpit in most congregations. Parishioners often find themselves caught, on the one hand, between a fundamentalism that flattens out the biblical text and ignores its historical and literary character and, on the other hand, a liberalism that tends to avoid the Bible entirely or that dwells only on texts that support a particular ideology. In addition to help in reading the Bible for themselves, Christians also want help in understanding the significance of the book they read. Three of the texts designated for this Sunday provide the occasion for such reflection. The fourth (the parable of the persistent widow and the ruthless judge) directs us to the essential companion to the study of the Bible—prayer.

Psalm 119 delights in the instruction of Yahweh. The text of the Torah is valued, not as a legal document, but as an occasion for meditation and for the shaping of values, intuitions, and sensitivities. The repetitive pattern and the formal structure of the poetry underscore its essential role as God's gift to Israel.

The reference to scripture in 2 Timothy continues both of these critical themes: scripture as the gift of God and for the practical life of God's people. For Timothy it serves as a source and resource "for salvation through faith in Christ Jesus" (3:15). Its instructive role equips believers for every good work.

Jeremiah 31 anticipates the time when God will write the law on the hearts of the people, and reminds readers that at the core of "the law" is the covenant relation God establishes: "I will be their God, and they shall be my people" (31:33). Again, the Bible is more than a collection of ancient wisdom, no longer applicable to the complex problems of a modern society. The God met in the pages of the text is the living God who forgives sins and grants the covenant partners a brand-new beginning in life.

## Jeremiah 31:27–34

The cycle of lectionary readings from Jeremiah comes to a conclusion with perhaps the most hopeful passage to be found in the entire book. As if to remind one that Jeremiah was not simply a prophet of destruction and death, 31:27–34 looks forward not only to the restoration of the people to the land (vs. 27–30), but to an even more radiant future, in which the life of the people will be characterized by a profound knowledge of the presence of God (vs. 31–34).

Some scholars suggest that passages such as the lectionary text for this day are not genuine oracles of the historical prophet from Anathoth. One may wish to consult one of the many fine critical commentaries on Jeremiah as to details. Yet, however one decides the issue for him- or herself, it is beyond dispute that such texts play a crucial role in the book of Jeremiah as we know it in the canon of the Hebrew Bible.

Chapters 30 and 31 have been named by some the Book of Consolation, because many of the passages contained in this section speak of Yahweh's outpouring of grace on the people. In many of these smaller units the image that is brought into focus is that of the coming Day of Yahweh. At least since the time of Amos, a century and a half before that of Jeremiah, the Day of Yahweh had been paradigmatic—in some quarters, at least—of the coming judgment by God (compare Amos 5:18–20). But in the Book of Consolation this negative image is transformed into a positive one. Nowhere is this clearer than in Jer. 30:23–31:6, where the phrases "the latter days" (30:24) and "at that time" (31:1) signify both Yahweh's judgment and Yahweh's restoration-beyond-judgment.

In 31:27–34, "the days are surely coming" clearly signals the advent of a bright and glorious time in the life of the people before God (vs. 27 and 31; compare v. 38). The phrase constitutes the opening words in each of the two sections of the lection.

The first section (vs. 27–30) carries one back to the original summons by Yahweh that Jeremiah should assume the prophetic role. In 1:10 (see Proper 16) the newly appointed prophet is commanded

> to pluck up and to pull down,
> to destroy and to overthrow,
> to build and to plant.

In 31:27–30 those words are recalled, some in the past tense, some in the future. "The days are surely coming" when destruction will be a thing of the past ("I *have* watched over them to pluck up," emphasis added) and restoration will be the story of the future ("I *will* watch over them to build and to plant," emphasis added). The land that will soon lie desolate (or perhaps already does) will again teem with both animal and human life. (It is of interest that, while classical Hebrew can sometimes be fuzzy in the matter of the tenses of verbs, the contrast between past and future tenses is clearly evident in the Hebrew text of 31:28.)

Incidentally, a further link with the narrative of Jeremiah's call is the use of the verb "to watch" *(šāqad)* both in 1:11–12, where it is the subject of the wordplay, and in 31:28, where the verb appears twice.

As evidence that a new day is dawning, the prophet cites a couplet that must have assumed the status of a well-known proverb among some Hebrews, in that it is also cited in Ezek. 18:2. In the time to come children will no longer be responsible for the sinfulness of their parents, but each person will live or die according to the measure of her or his own life (Jer. 31:29–30).

In the second section (vs. 31–34), the vision of the prophet grows even more expansive. No mere reclaiming of lost real estate is at issue here, but a new covenant, a new compact, to be extended by Yahweh to the people. The exodus and the giving of the law on Mount Sinai obviously form the background to this exhilarating promise made to *all* the people ("the house of Israel and the house of Judah"). The old covenant was characterized by the failure of the people to live up to its provisions, but the new covenant will be a covenant that operates from within. It will be etched not on tablets of stone, but on the innermost being of the people, on their hearts.

The metaphor involved in the phrase "knowledge of God" is, of course, sexual (compare Hos. 2:16–20). Yahweh has been Israel's partner in marriage all along, but until now the people have spurned Yahweh's love (Jer. 31:32) and have failed to consummate the union. But in "the days [that] are surely coming" Yahweh and the people will be "one flesh" (Gen. 2:24). Sin and judgment will be a thing of the past (Jer. 31:34).

So fundamental is the image of the new covenant that, for early Christians, it became emblematic of their encounter with Jesus Christ (1 Cor. 11:25; 2 Cor. 3:6; Heb. 9:15). In this sense Jer. 31:27–34 looks forward to the celebration in the not-too-distant future of the birth of Him who is the embodiment of the promise of the New Covenant. But the passage also looks beyond Christmas and, indeed, beyond all human history to the Second Advent when, and only when, the promise of vs. 31–34 will be realized.

Advent means "coming." And the joy of the season arises from the realization that "the days are surely coming," days of grace and redemption.

## Psalm 119:97–104

Psalm 119 has been aptly called "a literary monument raised in honor of Yahweh's revelation . . . to Israel" (Leslie Allen, *Psalms 101—150*, Word Biblical Commentary 21; Waco, Tex: Word, 1983, p. 141). Like most impressive monuments, some people like it and some do not. Many scholars, for instance, consider Ps. 119 tedious and boring, while others detect "a freshness of thought and a felicity of expression" throughout the psalm (Mitchell Dahood, *Psalms III, 101—150*, Anchor Bible 17A; Garden City, N.Y.: Doubleday & Co., 1970, p. 172).

Psalm 119 is obviously repetitive, and it follows a formal structure. It is an acrostic; that is, every line in the first section (vs. 1–8) begins with the first letter of the Hebrew alphabet, and each succeeding section utilizes the next letter of the alphabet in the same way. The eight-line format probably corresponds to the eight repeated synonyms for "law," although few sections contain all eight. Twenty-two letters times eight lines equals 176 verses. As Claus Westermann puts it, "If a person succeeds in reading this psalm's 176 verses one after the other at one sitting, the effect is overwhelming" (*The Psalms: Structure, Context, and Message*, trans. R. D. Gehrke; Minneapolis: Augsburg Publishing House, 1980, p. 117). This is precisely what the author intended—that is, to convey the overwhelming importance of God's "law." In short, the repetition and formal structure create and reiterate the message of the psalm. God's "law"—that is, God's "instruction" or "word" or "revelation" (see below)—is all-encompassing and all-important for humankind.

The lection consists of only one section of Ps. 119, but it is an important one. Will Soll has identified vs. 97–104 as the center of the psalm. It follows two sections that are the "nadir" (vs. 81–88) and "zenith" (vs. 89–96) of the psalm, and it articulates the psalmist's joy "derived from preceding consolation" in vs. 89–96 (*Psalm 119: Matrix, Form, and Setting*, CBQ Monograph Series 23; Washington, D.C.: Catholic Biblical Assn., 1991, p. 109). Thus, vs. 97–104 lie at the heart of Ps. 119, both structurally and theologically.

Verse 97 features the most frequently used and most important of the eight synonyms—*torah* (twenty-five times; see v. 1 and others). In fact, Ps. 119 is often categorized as a torah-psalm (see also Ps. 1:19). The NRSV retains the traditional translation, "law"; however, the connotations of the word "law" are too narrow. The Hebrew word means "instruction." What the psalmist loves is God's "instruction," at least some of which is embodied in written formulations that we would call "law." More broadly, however, *torah* suggests "scripture" (the Five Books of Moses, the first division of the Jewish canon, are known as the Torah), or even "revelation."

The psalmist's life is an example of what Ps. 1 calls "happy." He or she is constantly open to God's instruction (see Ps. 1:2; the Hebrew words for "meditate"/"meditation" are different in the two verses, but are essentially synonymous; see also 119:15, 23, 27, 78, 99, 148). The psalmist eschews autonomy (literally, "self-law") and lives instead to praise God (see v. 175). This orientation to life does not guarantee outward ease or material prosperity (see vs. 81–88 and 107–110, for example). Rather, happiness consists in being connected to the true source of life (see above on Ps. 1, Sixth Sunday After Epiphany). The benefits of this kind of happiness are described in the next three verses.

In vs. 98–100 of Ps. 119 the words "commandment" (v. 98; see Ps. 19:8; Ex. 24:12), "decrees" (Ps. 119:99; see Ps. 19:7; Ex. 31:18; 32:15, NRSV "covenant"), and "precepts" (Ps. 119:100; see Pss. 19:8; 111:7; the word is used only in the Psalms) more clearly suggest written forms of God's instruction. In each verse, a word from the wisdom tradition is used to describe the benefits of God's instruction—"wiser" (Ps. 119:98; see Ps. 19:7); "more understanding" (Ps. 119:99; see Pss. 2:10; 14:2; 94:8, NRSV "wise"); "I understand more" (Ps. 119:100; see v. 104; Ps. 94:8; Hos. 14:9). Instructed by God (see Ps. 119:102), the psalmist need not be intimidated by foe (v. 98) or friend (vs. 99–100). The authority figures in his or her life—"teachers" and "the aged" (or better, "the elders"; see Ex. 24:1)—are subordinated to Yahweh's ultimate authority.

The wisdom words in Ps. 119:98, 100 appear also in Deut. 4:6, where Moses tells the people that the "statutes" (Deut. 4:5; Ps. 119:83, 112, for example) and "ordinances" (Deut. 4:5; Ps. 119:102, for example) they are receiving "will show your *wisdom* and *discernment* to the peoples" (emphasis added). In short, "this entire law" (Deut. 4:8) is to govern the people's life in the land. The psalmist is a personal witness and example of what it means to heed God's instruction (see Deut. 4:9–10; 6:6–10; Josh. 1:8–9, for example).

In vs. 101–102 of Ps. 119 the psalmist affirms again that he or she is not self-directed, but God-directed. The word "ordinances" is a plural form of a word that in the singular means "justice." God's instruction reveals a way of life that makes for justice and righteousness, and it is this way that the psalmist pursues.

Verse 103 is reminiscent of Ps. 19:10 (see Prov. 24:13–14). The language is downright sensual (see S. of Sol. 2:3; 4:11; 5:1, 16; 7:9). The psalmist has an emotional attachment to God's instruction, indicative of a personal commitment to God. Not coincidentally, perhaps, this section opens and closes with feeling words—"love" for God's instruction (Ps. 119:97) and "hate" for "every false way" (v. 104; see v. 128).

The psalmist's commitment to discerning and doing the will of God anticipates the life of Jesus, who even as a boy could be found "among the teachers" (Luke 2:46; see Luke 2:41–52, and note especially "understanding" in v. 47 and "wisdom" in v. 52). Jesus upheld the torah (see Matt. 5:17–20). He was not bound to specific formulations (see, for example, Matt. 12:1–8 or 15:1–20) but rather sought to extend the torah to represent God's sovereign claim on all of human life (Matt. 5:21–48). In short, Jesus was no legalist, nor should the psalmist be understood as a legalist. Rather, he or she was open to God's instruction in whatever form it could be perceived and received—scripture, tradition, and ongoing human events and experiences that reveal God's way and represent God's claim on humankind.

In our scientifically oriented, education-obsessed culture, Ps. 119 is a crucial reminder that true knowledge is not achieved through detachment and "objectivity." Rather, the wisdom that ultimately matters begins with passionate involvement with God and commitment to God's values (see 1 Cor. 1:18–2:16). As people of God, we believe in order to understand.

## 2 Timothy 3:14–4:5

Up to the point at which this lection appears, 2 Timothy consists largely of discussions of Paul's own experience offered as example and discussions of false teachings offered as warning. In this passage, which serves as the summary of instructions, the subject turns to Timothy. Formally, the "But as for you" at the beginning of 3:14 marks this change of subject matter, and the "As for you" at the beginning of 4:5 marks its conclusion (note that v. 6 moves to "As for me . . .").

The imperative at the outset of the passage provides an apt summary of 2 Timothy: "Continue in what you have learned and firmly believed." Throughout the letter, the theme of persistence in faith runs strong. The author begins by urging Timothy to "rekindle" God's gift (1:6). Timothy is to "hold to the standard of sound

teaching" (1:13), "guard the good treasure" (1:14), remain "strong in
the grace that is in Christ Jesus" (2:1). He is also reminded of the
need for endurance, and warned about those who do not remain
faithful (2:11–13).

This particular exhortation takes on a new specificity, however, as
the author recalls the sources from which Timothy learned the
Christian faith. Timothy knows "from whom you learned." Regret-
tably, English translation has no good, noncolloquial way to reflect
the fact that the "whom" here is plural rather than singular. Given
the general content of the letter, we know that Timothy learned from
Paul, but he also learned from others, especially from Lois and
Eunice (1:5). The reference to his childhood in 3:15 further underscores the context in which Timothy first encountered Christian
faith, that of his family.

Timothy also learned and continues to learn from scripture, or the
"sacred writings" (a phrase that appears also in Philo and Josephus).
Scripture itself, which here certainly refers to the Jewish scripture,
instructs "for salvation through faith in Christ Jesus" (v. 15). This
assertion seems entirely consistent with what has previously been
said about Timothy's early teaching; both his family and scripture
served to teach him the Christian faith.

The additional statement in v. 16 has received enormous attention
in the discussion about biblical authority, as the commentaries will
indicate. What precisely does it mean to say that "all scripture is
inspired by God"? The Greek is ambiguous, as *pasa,* which the NRSV
translates "all," can also be translated "every." In addition, "scripture" here could refer to a single verse, to a given book (that is, the
book of Genesis or Deuteronomy), or to the entire collection of
scriptural writings. However the phrase is translated, the assertion
that all or every scripture is "inspired" raises a number of questions,
most of which cannot be answered by careful examination of the
wording, especially since the Greek word *theopneustos* ("inspired")
is exceedingly rare.

Whatever discussions of biblical authority make of this passage, it
is important to bear in mind that the context itself does not concern
biblical authority per se. What is at stake here is not the ontology of
scripture but its purpose in the Christian community. Scripture
provides a basis for "teaching, for reproof, for correction, and for
training in righteousness" (v. 16). As Timothy has learned from it
since his childhood, he and "everyone who belongs to God" (v. 17)
continue to learn from it and may do so with confidence that it bears
God's Spirit.

Having recalled for Timothy his rootedness in Christian teaching, the author turns in 4:1 to the present task. By calling on the presence of God and Christ Jesus as witnesses, the writer makes the charge an extremely solemn one. Here Jesus is described, not by reference to his descent from David or his resurrection (as in 2:8), but by reference to his eschatological role. Jesus will be judge of "the living and the dead" and will appear with "his kingdom." The urgency of that expectation necessitates an urgent response to the call of ministry to "proclaim the message" (4:2).

What stands out in v. 2 is the admonition to "be persistent whether the time is favorable or unfavorable." Since the Greco-Roman philosophers taught the importance of knowing when the time was "right" for a particular action or speech, this flagrant disregard for conventional wisdom would seem odd to them. It also might strike us as highly impractical, since preaching or teaching at an "unfavorable" time risks wasting energy and opportunity.

The context suggests that there are reasons for taking such risks. To begin with, the judgment referred to in v. 1 will not wait indefinitely, so proclamation is more important than practicality. In addition, v. 3 anticipates a time when Christians will take up every sort of bad teaching and will be impatient with solid Christian instruction. Other passages in 2 Timothy, of course, clearly indicate that these times are already at hand (2:16–18, 23–26; 3:1–9). Persistence is the only stance available to the preacher of the truth.

The final word to Timothy summarizes his own responsibility as a minister of the gospel. He is to remain "sober," or alert and sound in his judgment. He is to "endure suffering," as Paul himself has been forced to do for the sake of the gospel. He is to engage in evangelism and service ("ministry" in the NRSV), drawing on the resources available and watchful for the needs of his community.

## Luke 18:1–8

The delightful and humorous story of the persevering widow and the ruthless judge provides enough clues within itself to its own meaning. Yet it is set in a literary context in Luke's narrative that gives it even greater depth and urgency. For example, the parable is made a part of the preceding discourse about the eschatological crisis (17:22–37). Jesus warns the disciples about the frantic days just prior to the coming of the Son of man, days comparable to the time of the Flood and the judgment on Sodom. In the meantime, the parable directs the disciples to pray and leaves them with the question: "When the Son of Man comes, will he find faith on earth?" (18:8).

The inclusion of the parable in the larger discourse provides a new definition of faith—fervent and persistent prayer.

Furthermore, the parable that immediately follows the story of the widow and the judge is addressed "to some who trusted in themselves that they were righteous and regarded others with contempt" (18:9). By contrasting the prayers of the Pharisee and the tax collector, the parable exposes the arrogance of the self-righteous and points to the faith expressed by an unlikely source, namely, the tax collector. Prayer is the occasion for honesty about oneself and generosity about others.

When the early Christians repeated this story of the widow and the judge to one another, the accent sometimes fell on one character and sometimes on the other. Sometimes they paid special attention to the widow, with whom they felt they could empathize rather easily. They knew how she felt in her defenseless predicament. She had no clout in the community. She did not know the mayor of the town or any of the county commissioners who might pull strings for her to get her case on the docket. All she could do was to go back time and again and hound the judge. She turned up regularly at the gates of the city where he held court, and pursued him on the streets and in the shops. She would not let him rest until he granted her justice. Finally, exasperated, the judge gave in. "Otherwise this widow will keep after me until she gives me a black eye!"

The widow became a model for the early Christians, to teach them "to pray always and not to lose heart" (18:1). She was a reminder in days of crisis and moments of despair to continue to pray. Prayer was not a last resort when all the plans and programs and power plays had failed; prayer was, rather, the first and primary task of Christians. Her prayerful pursuit of justice became an expression of deep faith, the kind of faith the Son of man seeks.

But there were days when, in repeating this story, the early Christians reflected on the ruthless judge. One of his primary tasks was to see to the protection of the vulnerable people in society, especially the widow, the orphan, and the alien (compare Deut. 24:17–21; 27:19). They comprised the group in whom God had a special interest (compare Ps. 68:5; 146:9). Still, this judge had a well-earned reputation of being corrupt. It was not that he was underhanded or conniving; he simply had no conscience and was impervious to shame. The only way he could be reached was by the peskiness of the widow, who refused to give him a moment's peace until he granted her justice.

The early Christians thought about the judge. Look, they reasoned, if an unscrupulous person like this heartless judge gave in to the unceasing pleas of the widow, how much more will God listen to his people as they cry day and night for justice in the world? God can be counted on to vindicate the oppressed. God won't turn a deaf ear to our prayers.

The unjust judge in many ways parallels the begrudging neighbor who refuses to help his friend at midnight until he realizes the shame he might otherwise bring on himself (Luke 11:5–8). They both represent contrasting types for God. By their unsavory qualities they call attention to the opposite attributes of God—one to be trusted, one responsive to requests, one who sees that justice is carried out. Their stinginess and reluctance to help is more than matched by the lavish generosity of God.

But the two characters (widow and judge) also belong together. Persistence in prayer is rooted in the character of God. There is no reason to continue to pray unless the one who prays has at least an inkling of confidence (no more than a mustard seed?) that the one who hears prayers will answer them. Otherwise, exhortations to persevere can result only in frustration and discouragement.

Moreover, the character of God—just, holy, merciful, responsive—determines the answer to persistent prayer. The widow only asks for justice (18:3) and what God grants is justice (18:7, 8). The parable is not a commitment that God will give us whatever we want, unless what we want is in line with the character of God. What more could we want?

# PROPER 25

Both readings from the Hebrew scriptures declare the salvation of humankind and insist that the initiative for that salvation comes from God alone. Following the lament with which the book of Joel opens, Joel 2:23–32 anticipates the time when Israel will repent (see 1:13–20) and God will redeem Israel. As so often in the Hebrew scriptures, that redemption is imagined first in terms of the abundance of food ("You shall eat in plenty and be satisfied," 2:26) and then in terms of pride (vs. 26b–27). Finally, the prophet looks forward to the day when all Israel's sons and daughters will become as prophets in the land.

Psalm 65 is a psalm of thanksgiving for the "God of our salvation" (v. 5). The language of this psalm persistently reminds its hearers that God is, in every sense, the author of salvation. God is the one who "forgive[s] our transgressions" (v. 3) and who chooses human beings and brings them "near to live in your courts" (v. 4). God's salvation extends even to the earth itself; its creation and sustenance stem from God alone (vs. 5–13).

At first glance, the "Paul" who speaks in 2 Tim. 4:6–8, 16–18 appears to have forgotten the divine initiative in salvation, for here "Paul" elevates his own achievements by means of athletic imagery (vs. 7–8). The reading concludes, however, with an acknowledgment that strength and deliverance have come and will come from God (vs. 16–18). (In addition, if the writer of 2 Timothy is actually a student or disciple of Paul, he employs Paul's faithfulness here as an example for others.)

The familiar story of the prayers of the Pharisee and the tax collector in Luke 18:9–14 serves as something like a morality play on the perils of ignoring the fundamental truth of Joel 2 and Ps. 65. True, the Pharisee, a representative of the respectable and committed religious people of his (and every) day, does offer thanksgiving to God, but even his thanksgiving presumes that his achievements are his alone. The tax collector lives at the margins of respectability, but he knows that prayer begins and ends with a cry to God for mercy.

## Joel 2:23–32

There is one ultimate, overarching word that the Lord has for the community of faith, one word that extends above all others and that will serve as the Lord's final stamp on the story of human life. That word is redemption!

There are few better examples of the enduring nature of God's grace than the prophet Joel. Although the specific context in which this postexilic prophet labored is something of a mystery, it is clear that his initial work was in response to a devastating invasion of locusts, who swarmed both the crops in the field and the people in their houses (Joel 1:4; 2:3–9). For Joel this ruinous visitation is emblematic of the judgment of Yahweh. Drawing on the concept of the Day of Yahweh, first raised by Amos (5:18–20), Joel sketches the need for the people to repent and to cast themselves on Yahweh's mercy:

> Yet even now, says the LORD,
>    return to me with all your heart,
> with fasting, with weeping, and with mourning;
>    rend your hearts and not your clothing.
> Return to the LORD, your God,
>    for he is gracious and merciful,
> slow to anger, and abounding in steadfast love,
>    and relents from punishing.
>                                        (2:12–13)

We are not given the details of the people's response, but in Joel's view it seems to have been favorable, for with the coming of the autumn rains the prophet begins to speak of a new crop, which will take the place of that which the locusts devoured and which will fill the lives of the people with plenty once again. (It will be remembered that in Palestine the beginning of the autumn rains was the time for the planting of cereal crops, which were harvested in the spring.) Just as the locusts had served as a paradigm of Yahweh's judgment, the autumn rains now symbolize Yahweh's mercy (2:23–25; v. 25 implies that the locust invasion had lasted for more than one season).

Then, almost without the reader's notice, the language of the prophet begins to suggest an eschatological perspective. In 2:10–11 the description of the locust plague had been nuanced so as to suggest something of the nature of Yahweh's final judgment ("the sun and the moon are darkened," "the stars withdraw their shining").

> Truly the day of the LORD is great;
> terrible indeed—who can endure it?

In a similar manner, the prophet's anticipation over the newly sprouting crop is transformed into a promise concerning the people's ultimate redemption. "You shall eat in plenty and be satisfied" (v. 26) becomes "my people shall never again be put to shame." The significance of this enduring promise is emphasized by its repetition (vs. 26–27). The reason that the prophet may be so confident is that Yahweh is indwelling Israel's life.

If we have suspected an eschatological shift in vs. 26–27, that transition is made clearer still in vs. 28–32. "Then afterward" is unmistakably a pointer toward some moment beyond the present restoration of the people. (Note how this phrase becomes "In the last days" in Peter's noted citation of this text in Acts 2:17–18.) In this "after" time the Spirit of Yahweh will endow all conditions of people: young and old, women and men, bonded and free—"all flesh" will be bathed in the Spirit.

Then the text cites signs which had earlier been identified as the portents of the Day of Yahweh in Joel 2:10, except that these are now enhanced so as to be all the more frightful (v. 31). The moon is not just "darkened," but it is turned "to blood." Indeed, blood, fire, and smoke characterize this dreadful time. Yahweh's judgment, painfully described in the earlier passages of Joel, is revisited with heightened intensity. "The great and terrible day of the LORD" is surely coming.

Yet the prophet's words concerning redemption (vs. 24–29) have not been spoken idly. Even in the midst of judgment there is deliverance for all who invoke the name of Yahweh (v. 32). There is, in fact, to be a mutual invocation: just as those who call "on the name of the Lord shall be saved," "among the survivors shall be those whom the LORD calls." In other words, those who look to Yahweh for help will experience Yahweh's response.

(The problem raised by the phrase "among the survivors" has been noted by various commentators, in that it seems to suggest that not all the survivors will be called by Yahweh. The helpful suggestion of the editors of *Biblia Hebraica Stuttgartensia*, the standard critical edition of the Hebrew Bible, is that the word "Jerusalem" has been dropped out of the text and that the line should thus read "And in Jerusalem shall be survivors on whom the Lord calls" [see p. 1022]. The Septuagint translators had problems with this crucial sentence also; they render it: ". . . and they that have glad tidings preached to them, whom the Lord has called.")

The gist of the passage: No matter how dark the present moment, no matter how real the justice of God—and for Joel it was very real—judgment does not have the final word. God's final and gracious word is one of redemption. As the end of the present church year draws nearer and Advent looms ahead, this reality becomes all the more evident.


## Psalm 65

Psalm 65 is another affirmation of the theme sounded in the "theological heart" of the book of Psalms: "The LORD reigns!" (see Pss. 96; 97; 99). As H.-J. Kraus suggests, "The psalm fits best in the situation of the prostration before the creator and king of the world . . . , who is enthroned on Zion and is worshiped in hymnic adoration (Pss. 95:6; 96:9; 99:5, 9)" (*Psalms 60—150,* trans. H. C. Oswald; Minneapolis: Augsburg Publishing House, 1989, p. 28).

Scholars have often detected discontinuity in Ps. 65, even suggesting that vs. 9–13 should be treated as a separate psalm. There are, however, unifying features. For instance, God is addressed directly throughout the psalm, and various aspects of God's activity are celebrated. Verses 1–4 direct attention to God's answering of prayer, including forgiveness. Verses 5–8 broaden the focus, recalling both God's saving and creating activities. Verses 9–13 narrow the focus to one area of God's "awesome deeds" (v. 5) or "signs" (v. 8)—the provision of rain, which leads to the earth's productivity. As James L. Mays recognizes, "Each of these three parts of the psalm is concluded by a description of the effect of God's works (on the congregation, v. 4; on the world, v. 8; on the earth, vs. 12–13)" (*Psalms,* Interpretation series; Louisville, Ky.: John Knox Press, 1994). The "gateways of the morning and the evening" (v. 8), as well as the "pastures of the wilderness" and "the hills" and "the meadows" and "the valleys" (vs. 12–13), join "all flesh" (v. 2) in offering God the "praise . . . due to you" (v. 1).

The psalm begins in an unusual way, with the prepositional phrase "to you" (v. 1a). The phrase is repeated at the beginning of the second poetic line (v. 1c), and a similar phrase begins the third

poetic line (v. 2b, also translated "to you"). The effect is to direct
attention to God from the beginning of the psalm, an effect that is
reinforced by the appearance of the emphatic pronoun in v. 3b: *"you*
forgive our transgressions" (emphasis added).

The people gather to praise God and keep their promises to God
(that is, perform their vows; see Pss. 22:25; 61:8; 66:13; 116:12–14,
17–18), because God is the one who has heard and responded to their
prayers. Apparently this has been the case even when the people's
distress was a result of their own "transgressions," a word that
carries the sense of willful rebellion (v. 3). The word translated
"forgive" occurs in the Psalms only here and in Pss. 78:38; 79:9. It is
much more frequent in Exodus and Leviticus, where it often involves ritual activity and is translated "atone" or "make atonement." In any case, ritual or no ritual, the emphasis is on God's
gracious initiative (see Luke 18:9–14, the Gospel lesson for the day).
It is God who acts to "choose and bring near" so that people "shall
be satisfied" in God's place (note "Zion" in v. 1 and "courts,"
"house," and "temple" in v. 4). God is the gracious host who brings
people in to live and to eat at God's table (see Ps. 23:5–6; Matt.
26:26–29).

The mention of "all flesh" in v. 2 anticipates the broadening of
perspective in vs. 5–8. Although God has a place to which people are
invited, God's influence and power are felt to "the ends of the earth"
(v. 5, see "earth's farthest bounds" in v. 8). The mention of God's
"awesome deeds" recalls the exodus (see "awesome" in Ex. 15:11),
where God proved to be the "God of our salvation" (Ps. 65:5; see Ex.
15:2). As suggested two weeks ago (see Ps. 66:1–12, Proper 23), the
exodus was a public event that was not simply for Israel's benefit but
was intended, rather, to fulfill God's creational purposes. Thus, it is
not surprising that the "power" God revealed to Pharaoh (Ex. 9:16)
is mentioned in Ps. 65:6 (NRSV "strength") as that which has
"established the mountains." The chaotic waters and the unruly
peoples are subject to Yahweh's sovereignty (v. 7; see Ps. 46:10,
where God is exalted over the nations and the earth, which 46:3, 6
have described using the same word translated as "tumult" in 66:7).
As God was the security of God's invited guests in vs. 1–4, so God is
the "security of all the ends of the earth" (v. 5, author's translation;
NRSV "hope of . . ."). Thus, the creation joins in praising God in
recognition of God's gracious sovereignty (v. 8).

One way that God provides satisfaction (v. 4) and security (v. 5) is
by making the earth productive, a process that is described in vs.
9–13. As Mays suggests, we have here a remarkable poetic portrayal
of God as a "cosmic farmer," who carefully tends and waters the

earth (vs. 9–10) so that it produces abundantly (vs. 11–13). The word "bounty" (v. 11) is from the same root as "goodness" in v. 4. In God's place and throughout God's wide world, God is the gracious provider. In recognition of God's role and rule, the created elements offer their joyful praise (v. 13c).

Several scholars suggest that vs. 9–13 have a polemical intent; that is, the role of the Canaanite fertility God, Baal, is clearly occupied by Israel's God (see Hos. 2:8, 16–20). As at the beginning of the psalm, so at the end attention is clearly directed to God rather than to the gods or to human achievement. This pervasive and intensive focus on God as the object of thanksgiving offers a much-needed corrective to what often passes for gratitude in our secular culture but is actually self-congratulation. In terms of security, we are convinced most of the time that *we have things under control*. As for our prosperity, we are convinced that *we have earned it*. From this perspective, praise is due not to God, but to ourselves. In essence, we exalt ourselves, and the results are humbling (see Luke 18:9–14). As Walter Brueggemann suggests, "The loss of wonder, the inability to sing songs of praise about the reliability of life, is both a measure and a cause of our profanation of life" (*The Message of the Psalms;* Minneapolis: Augsburg Publishing House, 1984, p. 136).

## 2 Timothy 4:6–8, 16–18

Thoughtful preachers and teachers appreciate the many perils involved in self-reference. On the one hand, personal experience has an immediacy that lends itself readily to genuine communication between a speaker and a group of listeners. On the other hand, overuse or misuse of personal experience transforms preaching of the gospel into preaching of the self.

In the seven letters of Paul whose authorship is not in dispute, we see Paul employing self-reference with great care. He understands the rhetorical impact involved in referring to his own vocation or to the difficulties of his own labors. When he does refer to himself, he usually does so because he needs to offer a specific example of the working of the gospel. The focus is on what God has done through and for Paul, rather than what Paul himself has achieved.

The closing lines of 2 Timothy are startling when read against this customary method of working, for here Paul's own accomplishments and needs come very much to the foreground. If, as many scholars agree, the pastorals were produced by students of Paul or members of the Pauline circle some time after his death, this heightened use of reference to Paul makes excellent sense. First, it gives the letter an air of authenticity by referring to individuals and incidents from Paul's life that might have been familiar to many. Second, it consolidates the nurturing relationship between Paul and the figure of Timothy, demonstrating the caring nature of Christian friendship. Most important, it offers the reader a vivid and powerful example of Christian life.

The lection begins with "As for me," signaling the transition from discussion about Timothy's situation to discussion of Paul's own situation, namely, his impending death. Verses 6–8 dramatically portray Paul's impending death, piling up imagery drawn from his own letters. "I am already being poured out as a libation" recalls Phil. 2:17 (see also Num. 28:7). If that reference to the imminence of death does not suffice, the second half of 2 Tim. 4:6 is more explicit: "The time of my departure has come."

The phrases that immediately follow remind readers of the nature of Paul's life: "I have fought the good fight, I have finished the race, I have kept the faith" (v. 7). The language of 1 Cor. 9:24–25 and Phil. 3:12 is played again here, summoning up letters that might have been known to readers. Whether or not they were familiar with Paul's own use of such imagery, of course, athletic imagery was commonly drawn on in the first century—as it is in our own. People understood the discipline and endurance necessary for such competitions.

Second Timothy 4:8 turns to the prize that is anticipated, "the crown of righteousness." In God's role as judge, God will bestow that on Paul *and* on all "who have longed for his appearing." Here the author's use of Paul as example slips into view, for what reader would not wish to be among those who receive the crown?

Verses 9–15, which are omitted from the lection, turn to specific reports about individuals and instructions to Timothy. Prominent here is reference to Demas's desertion (compare 1:15). Perhaps Crescens and Titus have not simply left for other regions but have also deserted Paul, although that is difficult to ascertain with any certainty. The concluding notice regards a certain Alexander, who has also done some harm to Paul, and concerning whom Timothy must be warned. Lodged as they are, between the anticipation of Paul's death (4:6–8) and of his vindication (vs. 16–18), these brief notices serve as a powerful warning about the consequences of betraying the faith.

The "first defense" referred to in v. 16 might be an early trial in Jerusalem (see Acts 23:1–11) or some preliminary procedure in connection with his current imprisonment (see 2 Tim. 1:8; 2:9).

Identifying the situation precisely is less significant than understanding the theological claim being made here. Despite the abandonment of all, Paul was not alone. God stood with him in order that
the mission might not fail (see 4:17). As a result, he was "rescued
from the lion's mouth" (see Ps. 22:21).

As he was rescued then, Paul confidently affirms that he will be
rescued by God "from every evil attack" and saved "for his
heavenly kingdom." Given the clear evidence that vs. 6–8 anticipate
Paul's death in the immediate future, it seems clear that the delivery
looked for here is not to be equated with release from prison or
escape from human judgment. Instead, Paul remains confident that
God will finally vindicate him in God's "heavenly kingdom."

Here again we may catch a glimpse of the nature of the author's
implicit use of Paul's life as an example for other Christians to
imitate. Paul's endurance and confidence in the face of suffering,
even in the face of betrayal by fellow Christians, offers a powerful
model for those who may themselves endure profound discouragement and pain.

## Luke 18:9–14

Throughout the church, people look for help with the practice of
prayer. Knowing somehow that it characterizes the Christian experience, many feel guilty because they pray only spasmodically or are
frustrated because their requests never seem to receive answers.
Others get the notion that praying is reserved for a certain type of
Christian with a special aptitude for it, like those who sing in the
choir or teach a class. Ministers often are reluctant to address the
issue, either because they are only too aware of their own shortcom-
ings or because they relegate prayer to a priority secondary to social
or charitable activity.

Somewhat surprisingly, since it is usually distinguished as the
Gospel narrative giving most attention to the outsiders and to social
responsibilities, prayer turns out to be a prominent theme in Luke's
story. From the praise hymns of the birth narrative (1:46–55, 68–79;
2:29–32) to his intercession on behalf of his murderers (23:34), Jesus'
ministry is distinguished by prayer, particularly at critical moments.
His disciples are given a model prayer (11:2–4) and are invited in
their petitions to rely on God, who graciously hears and answers
prayer (11:5–13; 18:1–8). Communion with God lies at the heart of
discipleship, and faith can even be defined in terms of persevering
prayer (18:6–8). The long season of Ordinary Time, when Luke is the

assigned Gospel, provides unparalleled opportunities for the congregation (and preacher) to be instructed by Luke's rich and varied texts on prayer.

The lesson assigned for this Sunday consists of the parable of the two men who go to the Temple to pray (18:9–14). Its initial setting, outlining the intended audience for the parable (18:9) and the concluding application, repeating a theme from 14:11 (18:14), make the message indelibly plain. It is hard to miss the point. Yet a close reading of the passage is necessary so as not to overlook the significant details that give such force to the story.

Readers are already conditioned to the contrast between Pharisees and tax collectors (for example, 7:29–30) and can anticipate who in the story will be the good guy and who will be the bad guy. They are not disappointed. Immediately the Pharisee is described as "standing by himself" as he prays (NRSV), suggesting an aloofness from his unclean companion and an audible prayer. A better translation might read that he prays "thus within himself" (RSV), suggesting a narcissistic soliloquy, in which he talks mainly to himself. (A textual problem as well as a translation dilemma stand behind the Greek phrase *pros heauton*.)

His prayer, while in the form of a thanksgiving, turns out to be an implied request that God confirm what the Pharisee has already decided, namely, that he is "not like other people" and that his rigorous piety is exceptional. In fact, regular fasting and tithing *were* exceptional and well beyond what was required! Perhaps the recitation of his devotion to God seems not so unusual until we encounter the excessive number of first-person-singular verbs ("I," "I," "I") and the arrogant comparison to others less religious than he. His specific mention of his companion in prayer ("even like this tax collector") pits the two characters against each other in an intense fashion.

In contrast ("But"), the tax collector puts himself in a posture of contrition and remorse. He stands at a distance, cannot bring himself to look up toward heaven, and pounds his chest. Interestingly, the breast-beating is a traditional gesture of women in the Middle East, and is practiced by men only when in deep anguish. Unlike the Pharisee, the tax collector is clearly aware of the divine judgment, of the gap that exists between himself and God, and he throws himself on the divine mercy.

The closing comment declares that the tax collector's prayer is accepted by God, attesting to the paradox that "all who exalt themselves will be humbled, but all who humble themselves will be exalted" (18:14). It may be that the paradox at times works itself out in different ways, such as a tax collector-turned-Pharisee. "God, I thank you that I am not like this Pharisee, self-righteous and arrogant, who thinks that his good works set him apart from the rest of us ordinary folks and make him special. You and I both know that his prayer will never be accepted."

Luke 18, then, supplies readers with three models of people who pray. First, there is the widow, who hounds the unjust judge until she is granted justice (18:1–8). She reminds us to persevere in prayer and not become quickly discouraged. Then there is the Pharisee, who rehearses his virtues and downgrades others not measuring up to his standard of piety. He warns us about our presumptuousness in the presence of God. Finally, there is the tax collector, whose petition is simple (note no long list of failures): "God, be merciful to me." He personifies the one essential prerequisite for praying—an honest recognition of our place before the justice and mercy of God.

# PROPER 26

The opening lines of Habakkuk seem as contemporary as the evening news. In common with most of us, Habakkuk stands aghast at the "destruction and violence" all around (1:3) and wonders how it is that justice seems never to conquer. Within the confines of the lection, this profound longing to understand the human situation finds no direct answer. Yet the shadow of an answer comes at the end of the reading, as God contrasts the proud, whose spirit "is not right in them," with the righteous, who live by faith. That is, what must be understood first and last is the necessity to live out of confidence in God.

Read in conjunction with the passage from Habakkuk, Ps. 119:137–144 may seem glib. Here the psalmist delights in God's righteousness and in the commandments of God, and the longing of Hab. 1 seems far removed. Despite the confidence of the psalm, however, the psalmist admits that "I am small and despised," and that "trouble and anguish have come upon me." Understanding also is sought, but here the conviction that comes to expression is that the very discipline of living by God's law provides comfort to those who live constantly in the presence of injustice.

The psalmist's "trouble and anguish" appear in 2 Thess. 1:1–4, 11–12 also, but here the "persecutions and the afflictions" endured by the faithful serve a very particular end, in that they stand as signs that the eschatological future, the return of Jesus Christ, is imminent. That imminence, in turn, serves the important pastoral function of encouraging a community that might otherwise falter.

If the concern of 2 Thessalonians is with salvation in the eschatological future, at least one concern of the Gospel reading is with salvation in the present: "Today salvation has come to this house," Jesus tells Zacchaeus. Not only does this story engagingly depict the concern of the Lukan Jesus for the way in which believers treat possessions, it also reminds us that the righteous who live by faith are not necessarily the socially or religiously acceptable. Tax collector and sinner may be how Zacchaeus is seen through the eyes of his peers, but in the eyes of Jesus he merits the title "son of Abraham."

## Habakkuk 1:1–4; 2:1–4

Although not all the material in the book of Habakkuk is the composition of a single hand (for example, the entire third chapter appears to have been unknown to the author of the celebrated Habakkuk Commentary discovered at Qumran), the heart of the book seems to have been prompted by one of the several Babylonian invasions of Judah in the late seventh and early sixth centuries B.C. Its author had every reason to be discouraged, as his nation's defenses, and those of Judah's neighbors, were pushed aside. But Habakkuk also had an uncommon amount of frankness and courage, and he was bold enough to put to God those questions which must have been in the hearts of many devout Jews. Chief among these: Granted the sinfulness of God's people, why does God allow an even more sinful alien folk to oppress them? When one remembers that Habakkuk was a contemporary of Jeremiah, a prophet who went to great pains to assert that the Babylonian king, Nebuchadnezzar, was an agent of God (Jer. 27:6), his questioning of God's motives is all the more remarkable.

The core of the book consists of a series of conversations with God, in which the prophet first interrogates God and then God replies. The manner in which the present lection is structured captures the dialogical nature of the material, in that Hab. 1:1–4 represents the prophet's questioning of God, while in 2:1–4 God responds.

If 1:1–4 strikes one as similar to other Old Testament laments, that is not accidental. The opening complaint, "O LORD, how long . . .?" is echoed in a number of texts (compare Pss. 13:1; 62:3; Job 19:2) and is somewhat confrontational in nature. Destruction and violence (Hab. 1:2–3) are abroad in the land, and God seems unconcerned. Law and justice are forfeit—disorder prevails at every hand. We learn from 1:6 that the wicked ones who "surround the righteous" (1:4) are none other than the feared Chaldeans (or Babylonians), whose skills at terror are legendary (note vs. 6–11). The prophet cannot understand how Yahweh, Israel's God, would allow such horror while still claiming to be a righteous God (see v. 13).

In the face of such incomprehensible behavior on the part of Yahweh, the prophet defiantly positions himself to hear Yahweh reply to his protest (2:1). When Yahweh does speak, the message is accompanied by indications that it is very, very important, as shown by the prophet's instruction to write down what he has learned in characters so large and legible that even a passing runner (a refugee from the Chaldeans?) may read it (v. 2). It may appear to ordinary mortals that Yahweh takes a very long time to make the divine will known; but one must not be impatient, for the truth will come (v. 3). And the truth is this: Whereas the proud live their lives by principles of falsehood ("their spirit is not right"), "the righteous live by their faith" (v. 4).

In other words, a spirit of trust and dependence characterizes the lives of God's faithful people. The problem caused by so much evil in the midst of a world presided over by a righteous God does not admit a solution based on logic. Rather, insight into this problem comes to women and men who are confident that God has certain purposes in human life and that those purposes are full of love and grace—even if God's people do not always understand in detail what God is up to. The faith of such people is not a conceptual matter (as in the proposition "I believe that God exists"). It is rather a casting of oneself on God in the conviction and hope that God does what is right by God's world and by God's people. The word in 2:4 translated "faith" may also mean "faithfulness."

If the matter seems less than fully resolved—if all the questions have not been completely answered—that is part of the human condition. When all is said and done, the nature of life before God is one of trust, and the hope based on that trust.

This text from Habakkuk has played a significant role in the faith of the church. Quoted several times in the New Testament (Gal. 3:11; Heb. 10:38), its most significant citation is perhaps in Rom. 1:17. Here Paul cites Hab. 2:4 as an illustration of his assertion concerning the centrality of faith in the life of the Christian: "The one who is righteous will live by faith" (or, as the NRSV margin has it, "The one who is righteous through faith will live").

Martin Luther, at a critical time in his own life, was profoundly influenced by Hab. 2:4 when he read Paul's quotation of the text in Rom. 1:17. Luther is reported to have written the Latin word *sola* ("only") in the margin of his Bible beside Rom. 1:17, a significant early expression of what became for him the important Reformation doctrine of justification by faith alone.

## Psalm 119:137–144

As was the case for Proper 24, the lection is one of the twenty-two sections of Ps. 119 (see Proper 24 for an introduction to the psalm).

Despite the fact that many scholars view Ps. 119 as tedious and redundant, it is clear that vs. 137–144 are quite different from vs. 97–104. To be sure, the same synonyms occur here as throughout Ps. 119, but the supporting vocabulary is unique.

For instance, the dominant word in vs. 137–144 is "righteous"/ righteousness." It occurs five times (vs. 137, 138, 142 (twice), 144; the word "right" in v. 137 is a different Hebrew root), including three times as the first word in a line (vs. 137, 142, 144). Yahweh is "righteous" (vs. 137, 142; see Pss. 7:9, 11; 11:7; 116:5; 145:17, NRSV "just"; Deut. 32:4, NRSV "just"), and Yahweh's "decrees are righteous" (Ps. 119:144; see v. 138 as well as vs. 7, 62, 75, 106, 160). In fact, the word "righteousness" is a key word elsewhere in describing the policy that God enacts as ruler of the universe (see Pss. 89:14; 96:13; 97:2, 6; 98:2, NRSV "vindication"; 98:9; 99:4). In keeping with an understanding of Yahweh's universal reign, the psalmist proclaims that Yahweh's righteousness and righteous will are "everlasting"/ "forever" (119:142–144).

As is appropriate for one who recognizes Yahweh's universal and eternal reign, the psalmist describes himself or herself in relation to Yahweh as "your servant" (v. 140; see vs. 17, 23, 38, 49, 65, 76, 84, 124, 125, 135, 176). As a faithful servant, the psalmist is bothered by the same thing that bothers Yahweh—disloyalty. For instance, the word "zeal," which describes the psalmist's response when people "forget your words" (v. 139), is the same word that is used to describe Yahweh as a "jealous" God who will tolerate no rivals (see Ex. 20:5; 34:14; Deut. 4:24; 6:15; Ps. 79:5). Others may forget, but the psalmist is a faithful servant who does "not forget your precepts" (Ps. 119:141; see vs. 16, 61, 83, 93, 109, 153; Deut. 4:23; 26:13; and others).

The same verse that proclaims the psalmist's loyalty to God also contains the psalmist's complaint: "I am small and despised." Complaint is voiced again in Ps. 119:143; and indeed, several scholars prefer to categorize Ps. 119 not as a torah-psalm (see above, Proper 24) but as a lament/complaint (see Will Soll, *Psalm 119: Matrix, Form, and Setting,* CBQ Monograph Series 23; Washington, D.C.: Catholic Biblical Assn., 1991, pp. 59–86). Regardless of how one categorizes Ps. 119, one must agree with H.-J. Kraus's description of the psalmist (*Psalms 60—150,* trans. H. C. Oswald; Minneapolis: Augsburg Publishing House, 1989, p. 420; emphasis added):

> The obedient person is surrounded by trials and hostility. He is a *suffering servant* of God, who must prove his conduct amid the scorn and mockery of the ungodly. He *waits* and *looks for* Yahweh's effective word of power.

In short, the psalmist's perspective is eschatological. Trusting God and open to God's instruction, the psalmist experiences already "delight" (v. 143; see vs. 24, 77, 92, 174). But there is a "not-yetness" to this experience, for the psalmist lives with "trouble and anguish" (v. 143) and the reality of opposition (vs. 139, 141). So, as Kraus suggests, the psalmist "waits and looks for" Yahweh's word.

The posture of the psalmist in Ps. 119 recalls the beginning of the Psalter. Psalms 1:1–2 and 2:12 declare "happy" those who are open to God's instruction and "who take refuge" in God. But subsequent psalms of lament/complaint make it clear that such happiness is experienced amid opposition (see 3:1–2) and suffering. Thus, the people of God always live both delighting in God as refuge and awaiting the consummation of God's reign—already and not yet.

Due to the similarity between the psalmist's perspective in Ps. 119 and the rest of the Psalter, James L. Mays concludes that Ps. 119 "is a clue to the way the rest of the psalms are viewed" ("The Place of the Torah-Psalms in the Psalter," *JBL* 106/1 [1987]: 7). Mays further concludes (p. 12):

> The torah-psalms [Pss. 1; 19; 119] point to a type of piety as setting-in-life for the Psalms, a piety that uses the entire book as prayer and praise. That means this piety was quite different from any self-righteous, single-minded legalism. Its basic religious commitments were devotion to the instruction of the Lord [see Ps. 1] and trust in the reign of the Lord [see Ps. 2]. . . . Its way was faithfulness through study and obedience and hope through prayer and waiting.

In essence, the psalmist affirms that he or she *lives* by the word of God (v. 144), thus anticipating the life of another suffering servant, who articulated the motive for his faithful, hopeful obedience in words drawn from the Torah (Matt. 4:4; compare Deut. 8:3):

> One does not live by bread alone,
>     but by every word that comes from the mouth of God.

## 2 Thessalonians 1:1–4, 11–12

Although the pulpit is no place for a lecture on questions of authorship or the historical circumstances that produced any given letter, the preacher must have some understanding of each lest the text appear to have floated down from the heavenly places. Arriving at some sense of the authorship and circumstances behind 2 Thessalonians is particularly difficult, as a survey of commentaries will readily indicate. This letter has many formal elements in common with the other Pauline letters, especially with 1 Thessalonians, which suggests to some scholars that Paul also wrote 2 Thessalonians. Others call attention to the substantial conflicts between the two letters, particularly regarding the time of the Parousia (compare 1 Thess. 4:13–5:11 with 2 Thess. 1:5–12), and conclude that 2 Thessalonians was written in order to counter a kind of misguided eschatological fervor. The latter argument accounts better for the differences between the two letters, but scholarly opinion remains deeply divided on this matter.

In addition to this set of historical problems that plague any reading of 2 Thessalonians, the editors of the lectionary have created another problem by their decision to confine the reading to 1:1–4, 11–12, excising vs. 5–10. Even a quick glance at these verses reveals the probable reasoning of the editors, for they make claims about retribution and eternal punishment that can be misleading and difficult. Eliminating them, however, results in serious distortion of the text.

In the first place, in Greek all of vs. 3–12 constitute a single complex sentence. English translations cannot reflect that structure without producing something virtually unreadable, but the section represents a single unit of thought, so that excluding this central section is difficult to support. In the second place, and more important, vs. 5–10 introduce what is certainly the central topic of the letter, the Parousia of Jesus Christ. However uncomfortable we may find vs. 5–10, then, we probably should include them in considering this lection.

Following the customary salutation, identifying the church with God and with Jesus Christ, the thanksgiving (vs. 3–12) first lifts up the growing faith and love of the Thessalonians. This recalls the passionate thanksgiving of 1 Thessalonians, with its celebration of their "work of faith and labor of love and steadfastness of hope" (1:3); it also recalls 1 Thess. 3:12, Paul's prayer that the Thessalonians would continue to "increase and abound in love for one another."

Because of this growth, Paul and his colleagues are able to "boast" about the Thessalonians. Despite Paul's strong cautions about boasting on the basis of one's own accomplishments (see, for example, Rom. 3:27 and 1 Cor. 1:29, 31), he regards boasting about the churches as right and proper, indeed, as a means of proclaiming the work of the gospel (2 Cor. 8:24) and as a basis for eschatological hope (1 Thess. 2:19).

The particular basis for boasting here moves us toward the central concern of 2 Thessalonians. Paul boasts of them because of their "steadfastness and faith" in the face of their "persecutions" and "afflictions" (v. 4). Both the context and the use of this language elsewhere in the New Testament strongly suggest that these "persecutions" and "afflictions" are to be understood eschatologically. Mark 13:3–37 and its parallels express this connection narratively, but it appears also in Paul (for example, Rom. 8:18–25). While no timetable may be deduced from such sufferings, early Christians do identify them as signs of the eschaton.

The grammatical connection between 2 Thess. 1:5 and what precedes is ambiguous, for it is unclear whether "this" refers to the church's faithfulness, to the persecutions themselves, or perhaps to both. Whichever alternative is in view, the writer quickly moves to the expectation of the glorious return of Jesus. Both the detailed depiction here ("when the Lord Jesus is revealed from heaven with his mighty angels in flaming fire") and the anticipation of retribution toward unbelievers require careful handling. Because contemporary preachers know the damage inflicted when such passages are read literally and judgmentally, we often wish to ignore them altogether. Their insistence on the faithfulness of God to God's own people, the final protection afforded humankind by God, and the ultimate triumph of God belong among the fundamental elements of Christian proclamation.

The topic of the Parousia and the appropriate attitude toward it will dominate the second chapter of this letter. For the time being, the thanksgiving concludes with the prayer that God will make the Thessalonians worthy of their calling. The focus here is not on the attitude Christians are to have toward outsiders, but on their own worthiness, itself a gift of God. The final aim, of course, is the glory of Jesus (v. 12).

## Luke 19:1–10

The story of Zacchaeus is found only in Luke's Gospel, and for good reasons commentators are inclined to label it a masterpiece. The way the details subtly hint at Lukan themes and invite comparison with other characters, the colorful connections drawn within the story itself, make for an interesting text. Even the gaps in the story tantalize the reader. (Why is Zacchaeus so interested in Jesus? How does Jesus know Zacchaeus's name? What transpired to prompt Zacchaeus to make such excessive restitution to the poor and to victims he may have defrauded? When is Zacchaeus's speech in Luke 19:8 made—on the way to his house or after Jesus' visit?) The homiletical richness of the passage is hard to overestimate.

We shall indicate three possible approaches to the story, none of which excludes the others. First, Zacchaeus seems a perfect antitype to the rich ruler of 18:18–23. The one is genuinely respectable and religious, honored in the community. His question about inheriting eternal life no doubt reflects a sincere restlessness, a desire for something more in life than his present situation offers. His problem lies in his attachment to his riches, and, when instructed by Jesus to contribute his money to the poor, he becomes "sad." Jesus' response is that nothing short of a divine miracle will enable rich people to enter the kingdom of God.

Zacchaeus, then, represents the miracle. Like the ruler, he too is rich and yet clearly unhappy with his lot in life. Dishonored in the community, he takes the initiative in seeking out Jesus, despite the obstacles of a large crowd and his short stature. He is only too happy to welcome Jesus into his house. (The Greek says, "He welcomed him, rejoicing.") Unlike the ruler, Zacchaeus's encounter with Jesus enables a distancing of himself from his riches. He gives to the poor and promises restitution to any he may have cheated.

The similarities, but mainly the contrasts between the two characters, are remarkable, particularly regarding the matter of wealth—the idolatry of the one versus the freedom of the other, the sadness of the one versus the joy of the other. According to 18:24–27, what explains the difference is the powerful action of God, Luke's only reason for extraordinary occurrences (compare 1:37). Zacchaeus's response to Jesus illustrates that the miracle *can* occur, that the wealthy *can* gain freedom from possessions that possess them, just as the blind come to see, the lame to walk, the demon-possessed to be restored, and the dead to be made alive.

A second approach to this story pays attention to the gift of salvation pronounced by Jesus. The repeated use of "today" (19:5, 9) indicates that this is not an eschatological hope Zacchaeus is being given, but a change in his immediate life, an experience of salvation now.

What does this salvation entail? Four dimensions of the experience stand out: (a) Zacchaeus welcomes Jesus, implying hospitality and friendship. In a sense, by doing so Zacchaeus cooperates with the divine will, since the urgency of Jesus' intent to come to his house includes a "must." (The impersonal Greek verb *dei* ["it is necessary"] in 19:5 is an example of Luke's characteristic expression for God's will.) (b) The mood of the experience is joy. (c) Zacchaeus is restored.

The crowd unanimously has labeled him "a sinner" (19:7), a common and understandable designation for a chief tax collector who profits from the tolls he (over)charges. He is excluded from the community and is to be avoided at all costs. In a curious aside to the crowd (since the third person is used), however, Jesus declares Zacchaeus "a son of Abraham" (19:9b; compare 13:16), making him part of the community and an heir of all the promises given to Israel. (d) Zacchaeus makes more than adequate restitution, symbolizing his independence from his money.

A third approach to the story highlights the strange paradox of salvation. At the beginning, Zacchaeus is depicted as a seeker. "He was trying" (also translated "seeking") "to see who Jesus was" (19:3). He is not deterred by his inability to peer over the heads of the throngs who line the road, but finds a way to catch a glimpse of Jesus. As an adult, especially one the object of disdain, Zacchaeus no doubt presents a comic figure sitting in the branches of a sycamore tree. But he persists.

At the end of the story, however, we learn that it is the Son of man who seeks and saves the lost (19:10). The divine "must" that sent Jesus to Zacchaeus's house (19:5) coheres with this declaration of Jesus' purpose and mission. Reading the story in this light, one is reminded of the anonymous old hymn:

> I sought the Lord, and afterward I knew
>    He moved my soul to seek him, seeking me;
> It was not I that found, O Savior true;
>    No, I was found of thee.

# PROPER 27

Three of the readings for this week touch on the ways in which human beings persist in testing or assessing God. For the contemporaries of Haggai, the rebuilding of the Jerusalem Temple became a kind of test of God's promise. When they looked on the incomplete reconstruction, they remembered only the glory of the first Temple. The prophetic word in response insists on courage and labor. It also comforts them with the reminder that God's Spirit is already present among them and points toward the future, when the splendor of the Temple will be even greater than it had been.

Second Thessalonians emerges in a very different setting, one in which some Christians have grown extremely agitated by claims that the "day of the Lord" has already come. These Christians also may be said to test God, in the sense that they are judging God's very faithfulness on the basis of the arrival or nonarrival of the Parousia. The conclusion of the passage, with its reminder of what Jesus and God have already accomplished, insists that God's future may also be trusted.

The story of the Sadducees' attempt to trick Jesus in conversation does not fit easily within the rubric of "testing God," except that Jesus is sent by God and the Sadducees also presume to test his wisdom. Jesus' response confutes them, not merely by its cleverness (their question also is clever), but by its truth. The eschatological future cannot be understood simply as an extension of the present, except in one profound sense: God is Lord both of the present and of the future.

This profound truth demands the praise to which Ps. 145 calls all creatures. The reading opens with the praise of the psalmist alone ("I will extol you . . . and bless your name"), but it quickly moves to the praise of God by many generations ("One generation shall laud your works to another"). Not even the praise of all human generations suffices, however, for the psalm culminates in the acknowledgment that all living things owe their lives to God. When the individual psalmist speaks again in v. 21 ("My mouth will speak the praise of the LORD"), it is joined by that of "all flesh," for the praise of God is incumbent on nothing less than all of creation.

## Haggai 1:15b–2:9

The apparent failure of God to fulfill divine promises—those moments when human prayers seem to go completely unanswered—is not the only cause of spiritual despondency. Women and men of faith also experience the seeming distance of God when God's promises are fulfilled, but in ways that are less expansively proportioned than the believers had hoped for. That is the crisis which the present text addresses and, although the prophet's words are intended for a very specific historical moment, they overarch that moment and speak to the community of faith in all generations.

It would have been quite difficult to be cheerful in the Jerusalem to which the first groups returned from Babylonian exile. Ringing in their ears (or at least in the ears of some) were the grand promises of the Second Isaiah (see Isa. 55:1–11), which would have led many Jews to expect that their new Jerusalem would be a land of milk and honey. Instead they found ruins and deprivation so vast that the most strenuous effort was required to scratch a living from the land. In addition, quarrels with their neighbors (Ezra 4:1–5) made life uncomfortable and required constant watchfulness on the part of the settlers (note Neh. 4:21).

The most immediate objective to which many of them bent their efforts—once their houses had been made habitable—was the restoration of the house of God. Interference from others (Ezra 5:1–5) and the poverty of the Jews themselves delayed the restoration of the Temple for almost two decades, so that it was not until the arrival of the Davidic prince Zerubbabel about 520 B.C. that the new Temple was completed and services of worship reinstituted (Ezra 6:13–22).

And what a shabby Temple it was—at least in comparison to the great edifice on which Solomon had lavished such treasure! When the foundation of the second Temple had been laid, it was apparent from the size of the stones and the outline of the building on the ground that this sanctuary would only hint at the beauty and grandeur of its predecessor:

But many of the . . . old people who had seen the first house on its foundations, wept with a loud voice when they saw this house, though many shouted aloud for joy, so that the people could not distinguish the sound of the joyful shout from the sound of the people's weeping. (Ezra 3:12–13)

It is precisely to these weepers that Haggai speaks in the present text. Perhaps the prophet too is among those who feel great disappointment over the new house of worship. It was Haggai who had urged upon the newly arrived Zerubbabel that the work on the Temple must proceed as quickly as possible (Hag. 1:1–11). Perhaps in his view the new sanctuary simply did not come up to the standards one would expect for the house of Israel's God. Or perhaps he wished to mollify any wounds inflicted on Zerubbabel and his priestly colleague Joshua by those who were so vocal in their feelings of disappointment.

In any event, Haggai's message is basically this: Poor beginnings do not mean poor endings, when Yahweh of hosts presides over the fortunes of the people. The God who brought Israel out of Egypt so many years ago still stands behind all the ancient promises (2:5). Just as the Spirit of Yahweh was present in the pillars of fire and cloud (Ex. 13:21–22; 14:19–20), so "my spirit abides among you" here and now. The Second Isaiah had been quite straightforward in comparing the return from exile with the exodus from Egypt (note Isa. 43:15–17; 48:20–21), and Haggai draws upon this analogy also, with the same result: fear must be replaced by joy, for Israel's God is at work in the life of the nation and in the life of the world in ways that no one can quantify.

It is quite likely that the shaking of "all the nations" (Hag. 2:7) which the prophet expects is somehow connected with the wave of social and political unrest that appears to have swept the Persian Empire during the first years of Darius's reign (1:15b–2:1a). These convulsions will upset the normal order of things so that Judah, now an impoverished vassal state, will become a center of commerce and wealth into which the riches of the nations pour. A particular beneficiary of this new wealth will be the Temple which, although modest and unspectacular at the moment, will ultimately exceed even the greatest expectations. "The latter splendor of this house shall be greater than the former, says the LORD of hosts; and in this place I will give prosperity" (2:9).

The historical record makes it clear that, in materialistic terms, this promise was never completely realized (although the Temple as rebuilt by Herod the Great beginning in 20 B.C. was a very magnificent edifice). So it was natural that this text, along with certain others, should begin to be understood in eschatological terms. This new Temple vision is part of the biblical vision of the new Jerusalem, a city beyond time and place where the people of God dwell eternally (compare the vision of the new Temple in Ezek. 40—48). It is in this sense that the author of the Letter to the Hebrews understands this passage (and quotes part of it: Heb. 12:26). That which Israel's God has not done within history will be done beyond history, and of this new Jerusalem Jesus Christ is the pledge and symbol (Heb. 12:22–29).

In the face of all those promises of God that have not come true or that have come true only in fragmentary and partial ways, the prophet's word stands forth: Do not fear! (Hag. 2:5). The God who is Lord of both history and beyond-history is in the midst of the people of faith. God's promises will be consummated in ways that outreach all imaginings.

## Psalm 145:1–5, 17–21

Psalm 145 is a song of praise that serves as a prelude to a final collection of songs of praise, Pss. 146—150 (note that each of these begins and ends with "Hallelujah"—"Praise the LORD!"). It is not surprising that the end of the book of Psalms clearly echoes the affirmation that lies at its "theological heart"—"the LORD reigns!" (see Pss. 96; 97; 99). Psalm 145 opens by addressing God as "King," and the word "kingdom" occurs in the exact structural center of the psalm (v. 11) as well as three more times in vs. 12–13 (see also Pss. 146:10; 149:2).

In keeping with the character of songs of praise throughout the Psalter, Ps. 145 presents praise as the vocation not just of individuals, but of all persons and indeed all creatures. The structure of the psalm moves the perspective from individual to universal (see Leslie Allen, *Psalms 101—150*, Word Biblical Commentary 21; Waco, Tex.: Word, 1983, pp. 295–96):

| | |
|---|---|
| vs. 1–3 | the individual psalmist ("I"; vs. 1–2) |
| vs. 4–9 | "one generation . . . to another" (v. 4) |
| vs. 10–13ab | "all your works" and "all your faithful" (v. 10) |
| vs. 13c–21 | "all flesh" (v. 21) |

The first three sections consist of a call to or announcement of praise (vs. 1–2, 4–7, 10–12) followed by a description of the reasons for praise (vs. 3, 8–9, 13). The final section reverses this order. Here an extended statement of reasons for praising God (vs. 13c–20) issues in a culminating announcement of praise, which serves as an inclusion for the whole (note "bless" and "name" in vs. 1–2, 21, as well as "praise"/"be praised" in the title and vs. 2–3, 21).

The universality of the final two sections is reinforced by the repetition of the words "all" and "ever," which occur only three times in the first two sections but *sixteen* times in vs. 10–21. Furthermore, the structure outlined above occurs within an overarching acrostic pattern (see Ps. 119:97–104, Proper 24), which also reinforces the attempt of the psalmist to communicate all-inclusivity. God reigns over all peoples and things, and every person and every thing finds its destiny in praising God.

The word "Praise" in the title sets the tone for the whole. As the psalmist addresses "my God and King" in vs. 1–3 he or she announces three actions, each of which communicates the recognition of God's sovereignty: "extol" (see Ex. 15:2, NRSV "exalt," and compare Ex. 15:18; Ps. 99:5, 9), "bless" (Ps. 96:2; compare 96:10), and "praise" (Ps. 22:26; and compare 22:28, where "dominion" is from the same root as "King" and "kingdom" in 145:1, 11–13, and also compare "King" in 149:2). The mention of God's "name" (145:1–2) anticipates the attention that will subsequently be given to God's character (vs. 8–9), including God's activity (see "works"/"made" in vs. 4, 9, 10, 17; the word "fulfills" in v. 19 also represents the same Hebrew root). For the moment, however, the psalmist is content to declare that Yahweh is "great" and that Yahweh's "greatness is unsearchable" (v. 3). This affirmation also communicates the recognition of Yahweh's sovereignty (see Pss. 47:2; 48:1; 95:3; 96:4; 99:2).

In Ps. 145:4–9, while the individual psalmist remains in view (vs. 5b, 6b), he or she is joined by the generations who will "laud" and "declare" (v. 4) and "celebrate" and "sing aloud" (v. 7). What is being celebrated and declared is God's activity—"works" and "mighty acts" (v. 4), "wondrous works" (v. 5; the word "meditate" can also imply communication; see "tell" in Judg. 5:10; Ps. 105:2), "awesome deeds" (145:6). Yahweh's work reveals Yahweh's sovereignty, which is also indicated by the phrase in v. 5, "glorious splendor of your majesty" (see v. 12: the same three words appear in Ps. 96:6–7, NRSV "honor," "majesty," "glory"), as well as by "greatness" in 145:6 (see above on v. 3).

Even before the reasons for praise are stated in vs. 8–9, v. 7 suggests that Yahweh's sovereignty consists not simply of raw power. Rather, Yahweh's power serves the purposes of "goodness" and "righteousness." In short, Yahweh's power is always exercised in relationship, which means that Yahweh's power is ultimately manifest as grace, mercy, and steadfast love (v. 8; see Ex. 34:6). The reasons for praise in Ps. 145:3 had highlighted Yahweh's "great-ness." The reasons for praise in vs. 8–9 more specifically define that greatness. As in v. 3, a word is emphasized by repetition—namely, "compassion" (v. 9; the word "merciful" in v. 8 is from the same Hebrew root), or even more accurately, "motherly compassion" (another form of the Hebrew root means "womb"). The way God's power is made known is like the way a mother loves her children.

The two occurrences of "all" in v. 9 anticipate the universalistic perspective in the second half of the psalm (vs. 10–21). The words "made" (v. 9) and "works" (v. 10) are the same in Hebrew. Because God shows compassion over all God has "made," all God's "works" respond with gratitude. Like the psalmist and the generations in vs. 4–7, all God's "works" and all God's "faithful" serve as witnesses (vs. 11–12) to God's sovereignty, which we already realize takes the form of compassion.

The final section of the psalm (vs. 13b–21) reinforces this message. The repeated term here is "gracious"/"kind" (vs. 13c, 17b, Heb. ḥasîd, the adjectival form of the noun translated "steadfast love"; see v. 8). Yahweh shows faithful love by lifting up the oppressed (v. 14; see Ps. 146:8) and providing for all creatures (Ps. 145:15–16; see 104:27–28). Without contradicting the universalistic perspective of 145:10–16, vs. 17–20 focus more narrowly on those who explicitly recognize Yahweh's sovereignty—those who "call on," "fear," "cry" to, and "love" Yahweh. They will experience God's presence (v. 18), provision (v. 19), and protection (v. 20).

Verse 20b seems to contradict v. 9. The sharp distinction between the wicked and those who love God recalls Ps. 1, and what was said above about Ps. 1 is pertinent here (see Sixth Sunday After Epiph-any). The happiness or prosperity of the righteous is not so much a reward as it is their experience of being connected to the true source of life—God. Similarly, the destruction of the wicked is not so much a punishment as it is the result of their own choice to cut themselves off from the source of life. The compassionate God does not will to destroy the wicked, but their own autonomy gives God no choice.

The psalmist's choice is clear. He or she "will speak the praise of the LORD" (145:21). It is this vocation that the psalmist also envisions for "all flesh," for acknowledging God's rule and one's own insuffi-ciency is ultimately the way to life. Augustine opens his *Confessions* by quoting Ps. 145:3. In the opening paragraph, he asserts that because human beings are God's creation, they cannot experience contentment apart from praising God, "because you made us for yourself and our hearts find no peace until they rest in you" (trans.

R. S. Pine-Coffin; New York: Penguin Books, 1961, p. 21). The psalmist knew this great truth, and Ps. 145 invites us and "all flesh" to know it as well.

## 2 Thessalonians 2:1–5, 13–17

This lection stands at the heart of 2 Thessalonians. Because it also contains apocalyptic imagery and expectations that may be elusive and complex, contemporary readers may miss the urgent pastoral worries that drive the passage. When the author, whether Paul or a later writer, refers to the possibility that the Thessalonians have been "shaken in mind or alarmed," he refers to a situation of considerable anxiety. "Shaken in mind" may be translated a bit more literally as "shaken out of mind," as if they were quite distraught. It is not surprising, then, to find strong language being used in the pastoral response (for example, "we beg you," in v. 1; "Let no one deceive you," in v. 3; "Do you not remember . . . ?" in v. 5). Whatever the cause or the exact fears, the author believes that the Thessalonians are beside themselves.

The precise contours of the problem are hidden from our view, although it clearly concerns not only the Parousia of Jesus but the disposition of believers as well ("our being gathered together to him," v. 1). Somehow the Thessalonians have been instructed that this "day of the Lord" is already at hand. They may have been informed by some supposed prophetic utterance ("by spirit"), by some argument in the community ("by word"), or by a letter, whether 1 Thessalonians misinterpreted or a forged letter from Paul ("by letter").

Verse 3 begins to counter these fears with a reminder about previous teaching. First, the Day of the Lord is to be preceded by "the rebellion" and the appearance of "the lawless one." Several strands within the New Testament anticipate a rebellion (literally, "apostasy") prior to the Parousia of Jesus. Matthew 24:11–14 refers to the false prophets who will mislead the faithful and the time when "the love of many will grow cold." The pastorals likewise connect deceptive teachings with the last times (1 Tim. 4:1; 2 Tim. 3:1–5). Jude 17 recalls that the apostles themselves predicted that "scoffers" would appear in the last days.

The expectation that a period of increased lawlessness and opposition to Christ will precede the Parousia likewise occurs elsewhere in the New Testament (see, for example, Matt. 24:23–24; 1 John 2:18;

Rev. 13). The identification of this lawlessness with a particular figure ("the lawless one") is almost certainly influenced by Old Testament passages such as Isa. 14:12–15, with its celebration of the fall of the king of Babylon, or Ezek. 28:1–10, with its indictment of the king of Tyre. That the lawless one exalts himself but acts in accord with a divine timetable recalls Dan. 11:36 and its polemic against Antiochus IV.

The details of 2 Thess. 2:6–12 (which, of course, stands outside the limits of the lection) serve as further verification that the Parousia has not yet occurred. What precisely the author means about the restraint on the lawless one or by the "mystery of lawlessness" being "already at work" remains completely unclear. Does he refer to some figure or event commonly known to the community? Or is this a general reference to evil in the environment, evil that impinges on the life of the church? Whatever the precise nature of the situation, the author understands it to be a means of testing the community, "so that all who have not believed the truth but took pleasure in unrighteousness will be condemned" (v. 12). This period of trial serves to divide true believers from false.

Verse 13 abruptly returns to the language of thanksgiving. The sudden transition heightens the contrast between the faithful and the unfaithful. What awaits those who are led astray by lawlessness need not be frightening to those who remain faithful. They give thanks to God, confident in God's love, in God's choice of them "for salvation through sanctification by the Spirit and through belief in the truth" (v. 13). Unlike the Pauline letters, where we would expect to see salvation through belief or faith in Jesus Christ, here it is important to identify the faith with truth, as distinct from untruth.

The thanksgiving yields, in v. 15, into an exhortation to steadfastness to what has previously been taught "by us, either by word of mouth or by our letter." As with the earlier designation of faith as "belief in the truth," here also the particular kind of teaching becomes important. Not all teachers who purport to be Christian may be trusted. This central section of the letter concludes with a prayer-wish that focuses on the comfort of believers and their strength in "every good work and word" (v. 17).

Few contemporary pastors will have encountered an anxiety quite like that addressed in 2 Thessalonians. Even the eschatological fervor that occasionally manifests itself in the assigning of a particular date and place for the Parousia does not claim that "the day of the Lord is already here." This lection may nevertheless be helpful to pastors and teachers who encounter the various forms of anxiety that are born of misunderstanding—whether concerning eschatology or some other aspect of Christian faith. Here the teacher (Paul or someone else) moves straightforwardly, first naming the anxiety for what it is, then recalling the teaching previously offered on this topic, reminding of God's fundamental love and salvation, exhorting to confidence, and praying for growth. Taken together, these steps make for a powerful response to fear and alarm.

## Luke 20:27–38

The twentieth chapter of Luke contains the remarkable stories of controversy between Jesus and the religious authorities, stories found also in Mark and Matthew but here adapted to Luke's purposes. Jesus' triumphal entry into Jerusalem (Luke 19:28–40), his tears shed over the blindness of the city (vs. 41–44), and the expulsion of the money changers from the Temple (vs. 45–48) set the stage for the dramatic encounters—three questions put to Jesus with hostile intent (20:1–2, 20–22, 27–33), and one question of Jesus put to the religious authorities (20:41). The chapter concludes with a denunciation of the scribes for their pretentiousness (20:45–46) and a vivid contrast between their foreclosing on the houses of defenseless widows and one widow who elicits extravagant praise from Jesus for her gift at the Temple (20:47–21:4).

There are at least two tacks the preacher could take in preaching this assigned lesson. First, the context invites careful attention to the conflict between Jesus and the religious power structure. This is the third time in the Temple a trick question has been put to Jesus in hopes of shaming him before the people. The questioners this time are Sadducees, described as "those who say there is no resurrection." Josephus tells us they were the urban aristocrats, conservative in their beliefs and claiming a connection with Zadok, a priest during the time of David (2 Sam. 8:17). Their query is no genuine seeking of knowledge, since it assumes what in fact the Sadducees explicitly deny. Furthermore, the question turns out to be a rather complex riddle that contains an absurd scenario (the deaths of seven brothers), a surefire strategy to embarrass Jesus.

As with the chief priests and scribes who challenge Jesus' authority (Luke 20:1–2) and with the spies sent by the chief priests and scribes to trap him with the tax issue (20:20–22), Jesus uncovers the insincerity of the Sadducees. The riddle is easily solved. The narrator concludes the vignette by noting that the religious authorities "no longer dared to ask him another question" (20:40). Their strategy of posing trick questions had not only failed, it had backfired, leaving Jesus as the lone authoritative figure.

In a culture where the honor of an individual is attacked by challenges like these, the importance of a retaliatory retort is critical. The narrator presents Jesus as a master of riposte, cleverly throwing the question back to the questioners (20:3–4) or offering answers that expose the perverted intent of the question (20:34–36). Here in Jerusalem in the court of the Temple, on the home turf of the chief priests, scribes, and Sadducees, the questioners turn out to be no match for Jesus.

But Jesus' answer is more than merely clever. It shows the Sadducees as belonging to "this age," so preoccupied with the details of the levirate marriage system that they are unable to contemplate something radically new, the miracle of the resurrection. Their question ties them to a period that ultimately must give way to "that age," where there is no death and where the children of the resurrection are children of God.

A second tack that might be taken with this passage is to focus on Jesus' teaching about the resurrection. In moving in this direction, of course, one must recognize that we simply do not have the language or concepts to depict what life "in the resurrection from the dead" will be like. Literalism with the text will not work. Nevertheless, it is instructive to follow the line Jesus takes in answering the question of the Sadducees. It encompasses the themes of both discontinuity and continuity.

Initially, Jesus calls attention to the difference between life in the here and now and life after the resurrection (20:34–36). In this world people regularly die, and the future of the human race is sustained by sexuality. Beyond the resurrection, however, there is no more dying and thus no more need for the same type of sexual relationships that now pertain. (Describing the children of the resurrection as being "like angels" and as "children of God" merely depicts them as immortal.) Jesus' point is simply that God's future cannot be understood as an extension of our present existence. It is not the case that we can take what we like out of our current life, raise it to the nth power, and call it heaven. Resurrection entails transformation.

Then, using a rabbinic form of interpretation, Jesus makes a case for the resurrection based on the account of Moses' experience at the burning bush. The declaration that "I *am* the God" of patriarchs who have died (Ex. 3:6, emphasis added) means that in some sense they still live; "for to him all of them are alive" (Luke 20:38). The proof of resurrection, then, is the living God. While there is a radical discontinuity between the present and the resurrection, the continuity is to be found in God, the One who transcends death.

To be sure, the themes of discontinuity and continuity will not satisfy the curiosity of those who wonder about the particulars of life in the resurrection and who long to see parents and loved ones who have died before them. But such speculation is exactly what the Sadducees would like to have heard from Jesus. He would have been an easier target to combat.

Ordinary Time 33

*Sunday between
November 13 and 19 inclusive*

The omnipresent hyperbole of advertising, with its promise of new products or at least newly improved products, not only makes us wary of any claims to newness but perhaps renders us unable to recognize the new when it does appear on the horizon. The Old Testament lesson assigned for this week celebrates that which is genuinely new. Isaiah 65:17–25 looks forward to God's creation of "new heavens and a new earth." Jerusalem itself is not to be restored but created anew, a place in which life will be revered and protected, and in which God will permit no harm to any of creation.

If the newness anticipated in these lections stirs the spirit to strain toward the future, the New Testament lessons remind us of the reality—the sometimes painful reality—of the present. Second Thessalonians 3:6–13 warns against the disorderly conduct of those who believe that the newness of the eschatological future permits them license in the present. Such behavior is utterly irresponsible, because it places undue burdens on others in the community. It also misunderstands the future as somehow canceling the present.

Luke 21:5–19 provides a different element, one of sobriety, to the singing of new songs and the expectation of a new future. The eschatological future does not come without turmoil and testing. It necessitates that the faithful bear witness to God's future in the present, precisely when the new future cannot be seen, and even when it seems most improbable.

## Isaiah 65:17–25

The women and men who lived in Jerusalem at a time around, let us say, the year 475 B.C. were not to be envied. Two generations had passed since their ancestors, with much rejoicing, had set out from Babylon to repopulate the city of David. Those were exciting days—yet frightening. Their prophets had sung of how Yahweh would lead the people home from exile as all creation rejoiced (Isa. 40:1–11) and had spun visions of a glorious new Temple set within a sparkling city (Ezek. 40—48). These images must have danced in the heads of the returning Jews, yet as other Jews chose to remain within the safe precincts of Babylon, that was a reminder of the sorry state of the ruined city to which these were returning. There was still much distance between the vision and the reality!

That had been almost half a century, yet the brick-and-mortar Jerusalem was little changed. To be sure, there was a restored Temple, but it was shabby when compared with the great edifice of Solomon, which had stood on the same spot before the Babylonian invasion. There were as yet no city walls, and much rubble remained where houses and markets had once teemed with people. Those who returned but now doubted the grand promises of yesteryear could hardly be blamed.

In this despairing situation, however, certain individuals began to raise their heads and to sing the old songs of joy and hope, but in a new key. The ancient promises had been true all along, they insisted, but in a far grander way than anyone had realized. Women and men had thought about the new Jerusalem in all-too-tangible terms—the city of bricks and stones their ancestors had inhabited since the days of David. But that was not quite right, these individuals began to understand. The new Jerusalem that Yahweh had in mind far transcended the new Jerusalem of the merchants and traders and housewives who called the city of David home. Yes, *that* Jerusalem had been restored—somewhat, at least. But God's eye was on another Jerusalem also—a Jerusalem not of bricks and mortar, but of the human heart. God's ideal was not just a new Jerusalem, but a New Jerusalem!

The person(s) who is responsible for this day's Old Testament lection from Isa. 65 is one of those who understood the larger dimensions of Yahweh's plans for humankind. In fact, it is not just a new Jerusalem that Israel's God is about to create, but "new heavens" and a "new earth" (v. 17). The very order of existence is about to be turned on its ear. Within the context of this new order of being, the new Jerusalem will be "as a joy" and its people "as a delight" (v. 18). Sorrow will be banished from God's city, and the only emotion permitted to remain will be that of very great happiness (v. 19).

The prophet now recalls some of those perennial problems that plague humankind and that foster sorrow and despair: infant mortality and premature death, to name but two. Such causes for distress are to be banished forever from the new creation, the new Jerusalem (v. 20).

The horrors of war are recalled, those terrible times when families build their homes and farms only to have them overrun by the enemy, their possessions lost (note Deut. 20:1–9). In the new creation, the new Jerusalem, such disasters will be no more, for those who build will survive to enjoy the fruits of their labor (vs. 21–22).

The special vulnerability of youth is recalled, and perhaps the words of Jeremiah were on the prophet's mind here:

> [Jerusalem's] widows became more numerous
>     than the sand of the seas;
> I have brought against the mothers of youths
>     a destroyer at noonday;
> I have made anguish and terror
>     fall upon her suddenly.
>
> (Jer. 15:8)

Such a state of affairs will be foreign to the new Jerusalem, for Yahweh will answer the prayers of anxious mothers even before they are uttered (vs. 23–24). (The literal rendering of v. 23b, "bear children for sudden terror"—so NRSV marginal notation—draws the connection to the Jeremiah text even closer.)

The passage ends (v. 25) with an abbreviated version of the great "peaceable kingdom" vision of Isa. 11:6–9. All nature will be at peace with itself, as a reflection of the character of Israel's God.

It would perhaps be tempting to say that the inspired poet who is responsible for these words simply realized that the Jerusalem of his day would never fulfill the wonderful promises of the Second Isaiah and others, and that, if one wished to avoid despair altogether, one might as well assume that those promises would be realized at some unspecified point in the future. In other words, it would be simple to dismiss this text as a kind of pie-in-the-sky utopianism.

Such an explanation would not only miss the point, it would fail to account for the wonderful joy that courses through this poem. The prophet is convinced that God *is* in control and that all things will achieve the ultimate destiny for which God intends them. There is a new Jerusalem. But more importantly, there will be a New Jerusalem.

As a long church year draws to its close, with so many challenges yet unmet, and as a new Advent is about to dawn with all of its anticipation and hope, the prophet's vision of the new Jerusalem casts all other things into perspective.

## Isaiah 12

See the discussion of this passage under the Third Sunday of Advent.

## 2 Thessalonians 3:6–13

"Anyone unwilling to work should not eat." Preachers may cringe when they read this lection, knowing that they are entering a minefield. The moralism that constantly threatens to turn the Christian faith into a rulebook waits anxiously to take over a sermon on this particular text. Congregations eager for some answer to massive homelessness and hunger may see this passage as a step toward addressing those social issues.

Before we flee to some safer territory, several aspects of the text need to be noticed. First, and perhaps most important, 2 Thess. 3:6–13 concerns matters *within* the Christian community. On this point, there is no ambiguity. Verse 6 introduces the problem with a command to "keep away from *believers* who are living in idleness" (emphasis added). The use of the example of Paul's own behavior reinforces this conclusion, for it is precisely Christians—and only Christians—to whom Paul serves as an example. Although vs. 14–15 fall outside the lection proper, they also pertain to the same problem, and there again it is clear that this is an issue within the Christian community ("Do not regard them as enemies, but warn them as believers," v. 15). The problem here is how Christians treat one another, not how hungry people in the world are to be fed. (That is not to say that the Bible is indifferent to hunger, but that we need to turn elsewhere for those discussions.)

Second, the words "idle" and "idleness," which certainly reinforce our tendency to moralize on this passage, may not be the best translations of the Greek. The word *ataktos* primarily describes behavior that is insubordinate or irresponsible; perhaps these are individuals who rebel against the community itself, chafing at the constraints imposed by the needs and wishes of others. Apparently, one form that irresponsibility takes is that they eat the food of others "without paying for it" (v. 8) and are unwilling to work. We would rightly refer to this as idleness or laziness, but the underlying problem may be their rebellion against the church itself.

The passage does not hint at the reasons for such behavior. Some have speculated that fervent eschatological expectations, such as the author feels obliged to correct in 2:1–12, have fueled a kind of retreat from engagement with the world. If Jesus is coming back at any moment, the logic might run, then why would Christians continue to labor for food, when they know that their needs will be met?

Whatever the cause of this behavior, the response is sharp and unequivocal. If the author is Paul, then Paul calls on earlier tradition (perhaps similar to 1 Thess. 5:14); if we assume the author is a later follower of Paul, this follower employs Paul's example forcefully. The response opens with the language of command, and this "in the name of our Lord Jesus Christ" (v. 6). Those who engage in such behavior have violated "the tradition that they received from us."

The appeal quickly turns to the need to imitate Paul. Interestingly, Paul does often urge believers to imitate him (as in 1 Cor. 4:16; 11:1; Phil. 3:17; 4:9; 1 Thess. 1:6), but that imitation generally is an imitation of attitude and disposition rather than of specific behaviors. And in 1 Cor. 9, where Paul speaks about his own pattern of self-support (v. 15), he insists that he has the right to be supported by the congregations but refuses to take advantage of that right. Here, Paul's tradition of self-support and his admonition to imitation come together in a new way in order to address a new situation.

The reasons for such a sharp response become clear in 2 Thess. 3:8 and especially in v. 12. Those who eat the bread of others, as v. 8 suggests is occurring, place an unnecessary burden on the community. Other Christians are being harmed by this undisciplined behavior. Verse 12 concludes that all must "do their work quietly" and "earn their own living." The little adverb "quietly" speaks loudly here. Christians who do not live "quietly" may attract the sort of attention that compromises the community as a whole.

Initially, this passage seems remote from the nature and experience of contemporary Christian churches, for our massive individualism would not permit a situation in which Christians could choose not to work and count on other believers to feed them. Examined more closely, however, the perspective of these Thessalonians looks more familiar. Faith has become, for them, an excuse for irresponsible behavior. This particular form of irresponsible behavior is idleness of body, but we know also idleness of mind and spirit, that attitude that manipulates faith, expecting it to supply the missing pieces of life.

The stern response of this early Christian writer, whether Paul or another, insists that faith may not become an excuse for our own idleness. Faith does not wait for another to labor, for another to think, for another to pray. Faith plunges us into the reality of everyday life, even as it also insists that this life is not the whole story.

## Luke 21:5-19

Jesus' speech about the razing of the Temple and the city and the coming of the end-times is not an immediately accessible text for preaching, whether one chooses the report by Matthew, Mark, or Luke (Matt. 24—25; Mark 13; Luke 21:5–36). Contemporary congregations tend to find talk about the destruction of the Temple, times of severe persecution, and the coming of the Son of man distant from their own struggles. Even so, the speech occupies a critical place in the Gospel narratives, and in Luke stands alongside the Sermon on the Plain (6:20–49) as a major block of Jesus' teaching. For that reason, the speech ought not to be ignored, especially on a Sunday when all the designated lessons point toward God's promise of a re-created world.

The Temple is the controlling context of Jesus' activities from the time he makes his triumphal entry into Jerusalem (Luke 19:28–40) through this speech made at the Temple's entrance. Jesus cleanses the Temple (19:45–48), encounters hostile questioners in the Temple (20:1–40), raises the issue of the Messiah in the Temple (20:41–44), denounces the scribes in the Temple (20:45–47), and points to the generosity of the poor widow in the Temple (21:1–4). The Temple is where Jesus belongs by virtue of who he is, and yet where he is most unwelcome because he challenges its corruption and pretentiousness.

It is not a surprise, then, for the reader to hear Jesus respond to a comment about the Temple's beauty by announcing its destruction (21:5–6). We are prepared for the downfall of an institution blind to its own intended mission. Misguided and obtuse religious display, no matter how aesthetically pleasing, comes to a sad end when it ignores the very One for whom it exists.

Luke's version of Jesus' speech, however, does not present the sequence of events in chronological order. It is instructive to list them as they happen:

(a) The present, a time of witness (vs. 12–19)
(b) The destruction of the Temple and the city (vs. 5–11, 20–24)
(c) The coming end-times (vs. 25–36)

The immediate present is a time of testing and strife. Jesus points to this throughout his ministry, with the result that when Luke's audience reads about it they are able to find meaning amid their own predicament. Harassment by both religious and secular authorities is not unexpected. Betrayal by family and friends comes with the job.

Hostile responses can be counted on in a world where God's rule is not only rejected but seen as a threat. But faithfulness in the time of testing carries with it the assurance of divine protection ("not a hair of your head will perish," 21:18; compare 12:7) and eternal life ("you will gain your souls," 21:19; compare 9:24). Those being victimized are reassured they are not forgotten.

Furthermore, the time of testing is to be seen as an opportunity to bear witness (*eis martyrion*, 21:13). Where else can the community find such access to kings and governors? How better can the community exercise its vocation of mission? Rather than having a prepared defense that anxiety renders ineffective, the faithful can count on the presence and gifts of God—gifts of wisdom and eloquence that confound the accusers and do not contradict the gospel (21:14–15; compare 12:11–12).

While the text projects for Luke's readers (and Acts confirms) a fearful and distressing time, the text also reminds modern readers of the massive rejection from a sometimes complacent, sometimes hostile culture when the gospel is faithfully witnessed to. Inevitably God's reign poses a serious threat to established power structures. Reactions in North America are normally not so violent or dramatic as those in other times and places, but we are deceived if we think our power structures are any less resistant.

Both the predictions of a time of dire testing and the destruction of the Temple and the city will in fact have reached their fulfillment by the time Luke's audience hears and reads his Gospel. Readers then are confirmed in their realization that Jesus is a prophet to be trusted, one whose understanding of history and reality can be relied on. The moments of anguish and refusal lose their ultimacy when viewed in light of Jesus' speech at the Temple.

Moreover, beyond the present time of trial lies the coming of the Son of man "with power and great glory" (21:27). For the faithful who have borne their witness, the Second Advent becomes, not a time of fear and uncertainty, but one of encouragement and hope ("stand up and raise your heads"). It depicts a time beyond the travail of the present and the trampling down of Jerusalem, when God's redemption is drawing near (21:28). No reason to doubt Jesus on this promise as well.

# CHRIST THE KING OR REIGN OF CHRIST

Proper 29
Ordinary Time 34

*Sunday between
November 20 and 26 inclusive*

As is appropriate for the celebration of Christ the King Sunday, each of the passages for this day concerns the nature of kingly power. Although the contexts and the language employed change from one passage to the next, each reading addresses the ends served by divine power. Jeremiah 23:1–6 begins by castigating the "shepherds" of the people who have used their power to scatter the flock rather than to protect it. By contrast, God will gather the remnant of the flock and will send a "righteous Branch," whose kingship will be characterized by wisdom, justice, and safety. The exercise of kingly power, then, is on behalf of God's people rather than over against them.

The reading from Colossians praises the cosmic dimensions of Christ, who is "firstborn of all creation," "the head of the body, the church," and in whom "all the fullness of God was pleased to dwell." If the hymn does not explicitly call Christ a king, that designation is assumed in the introductory reference to his "kingdom" (v. 13), and it is implicit in the very imagery of the hymn itself. Even in this cosmic description of Christ, however, the exaltation of Christ is not an end in itself, for the task of Christ is one of reconciliation (v. 20; see also v. 13).

The goal of Christ's kingship moves to center stage in the Lukan lection. The bystanders and one of the criminals executed with Jesus know what it means to be a king, and so they taunt Jesus with the demand that he use his power to save himself. For Jesus, however, a king is not one who saves himself, but one who saves others, as Jesus' declaration to the repentant criminal indicates.

603

## Jeremiah 23:1–6

One of the vexing questions the people of ancient Israel sometimes faced had to do with the problem of distinguishing true
prophets from false. The celebrated incident involving Micaiah ben
Imlah (1 Kings 22:1–40) is but one example of quandaries that must
have arisen whenever prophetic voices clashed.

The Old Testament lection for this, the last Sunday in the church
year, is similar, except that it involves not the question of who is the
true prophet, but who is the true king.

The initial section of this passage (Jer. 23:1–2) is a denunciation of
Judah's rulers. For reasons noted below, the conclusion of many
interpreters is that this oracle dates from the reign of King Zedekiah
(597–587 B.C.), the last of the Davidic monarchs to exercise political
power from Jerusalem. That there was already some debate about
the legitimacy of Zedekiah's rule is attested by Ezek. 1:2, which
reflects the view doubtless held by many that Judah's only authentic
king was young Jehoiachin. This grandson of good King Josiah had
inherited the revolt against Babylonian rule led by his father,
Jehoiakim, upon the elder man's death, and for his pains Jehoiachin
was carried off to Babylon after the collapse of the insurrection in
597. Although Jehoiachin's uncle Mattaniah was installed on the
vacant throne by the Babylonians and renamed Zedekiah ("Yahweh
is righteousness"), not a few continued to look on the distant
Jehoiachin as Judah's legitimate monarch.

In the mind of the prophet, then, Zedekiah and those around him
("the shepherds who destroy and scatter the sheep of my pasture,"
v. 1) were subverting the well-being of the nation. Just when it
became clear to Jeremiah that Zedekiah would lead a second
fruitless revolt against the Babylonians—culminating in even
greater destruction, dislocation, and death than the first revolt—is
not clear, but the prophet from Anathoth began to view the king
with suspicion very early in his reign (note Jer. 28:1–11). Jeremiah
23:1–2 appears to be a reflection of this deep distrust.

The second section (vs. 3–4) looks forward to the day when those
who have been routed from their homeland will be returned. The
shepherds of the people having failed their flock, Yahweh promises
to be their new shepherd. Note that Yahweh assumes responsibility for the dispersal of the flock ("where I have driven them,"
v. 3), an understanding that is consistent with what the prophet
says elsewhere, namely, that the exile is Yahweh's response to
the people's sin (compare Jer. 27:1–8). But that in no sense exonerates
the unfit shepherds. Their leadership has helped corrupt the peo-

ple's lives and precipitated the scattering of the flock. Yahweh will undo their wrongs, first by shepherding the people himself, and second by raising up human shepherds who will guide the flock correctly.

The final and climactic section (23:5–6) carries Yahweh's promise one step farther by identifying the agent of Yahweh's gracious care. The word-root righteous/righteousness predominates here, and, moral considerations aside, the emphasis lies on the fact that this agent is the right and proper Davidic king, in contrast to the false rulers, those "shepherds who destroy" of v. 1. This king is to be a "righteous Branch" (language reminiscent of Isa. 11:1), a genuine shoot off the Davidic tree, who shall "execute justice and righteousness in the land." The name of this king is to be Yahweh-Zidkenu, "Yahweh is our righteousness." That this is a wordplay intended to reflect negatively on the present Davidic king, Zedekiah, can hardly be doubted.

(One view has it that Jer. 23:5–6 is somehow related to a coronation hymn for Zedekiah, which the prophet has now turned against that monarch.)

The church year is now very late in Ordinary Time, and the faith community cannot help reflecting back on the past—both its past and all human past. The monuments to sin and error lie strewn across the landscape for all to see, reminders that even the very best human efforts (to say nothing of the worst human efforts!) often lead to disillusion and despair. Where is one to turn for hope? for grace?

This text stands as witness that those qualities come from the Lord. It is the Lord's gracious intervention in our lives that saves us from ourselves, from all the havoc we impose on our own lives and happiness. Just as no flesh-and-blood Davidic king ever realized the grand promises vested by God in that royal house, so we all fail to be what God designed us to be, what God longs for us to be. Jesus Christ, however, is the one Davidic king who did realize the promises of the Lord. Jesus Christ is the one human life that lived out its full potential.

So the church looks forward to Advent as the emblem of God's loving intervention into human life, that gracious invasion which alone has the power to save us. Our anticipation, fueled by our own sense of inadequacy and failure, begins to rise, and we sense that soon, very soon, God's promises will be renewed. In this way we reiterate the experience of those so long ago who yearned for the birth of the Messiah. We also—in and for ourselves—yearn for the consummation of God's grace, that Second Advent of which the First was both promise and rehearsal.

## Luke 1:68–79

See the discussion of this passage under the Second Sunday of Advent.

## Colossians 1:11–20

Although it has already appeared earlier in Year C, this passage has particular relevance for Christ the King Sunday (see the discussions of Col. 1:1–14 under Proper 10 and Col. 1:15–28 under Proper 11). As the church celebrates the reign of Christ over all creation, the early Christian hymn found in the second section of this lection (Col. 1:15–20) asserts Christ's priority through a variety of images. First, along with other passages in the New Testament, the hymn asserts that Christ bears the very image of God (see also 2 Cor. 3:18; 4:4; Phil. 2:6; Heb. 1:3). Second, and more elaborately, the hymn proclaims Christ's connection with creation itself: he is firstborn (Col. 1:15b), he is an agent of creation (v. 16a), he is the origin and goal of creation (vs. 16b–17). Third, Christ is the head (or origin) of the church and the firstborn from the dead (v. 18).

Verses 19–20 move from these assertions about the priority of Christ to take up more directly his salvific role. It is through Christ that God reconciles "to himself all things, whether on earth or in heaven, by making peace through the blood of his cross." The theme of reconciliation returns to the reason for introducing the hymn in the first place, namely, the reference in the thanksgiving to God's rescue of human beings through God's son (v. 13).

Taken together, the two parts of this lection draw attention to both the reign of Christ in all creation and the implications of that reign for humanity. Through Christ, God transfers humankind from "the power of darkness" and into "the inheritance of the saints in the light" (v. 12). The commemoration and celebration of that transfer carries with it, of course, the obligation to gratitude and endurance (see vs. 11–12).

## Luke 23:33–43

The account of the crucifixion of Jesus in Luke abounds with themes characteristic of the whole Gospel, so much so, in fact, that commentators wonder whether Luke has reworked a Markan source or has used an entirely different source. Since the twists and turns of the narrative seem strategic and rich in meaning, they provide a plentiful lode to be mined by the preacher who is interested in more than relating bare facts.

For example, on this Sunday labeled "Christ the King" it is instructive to trace through the narrative the royal motif. Already the narrator has related the political charges brought against Jesus— that he perverts the Jewish nation, advocates a tax revolt against Rome, and calls himself "the Messiah, a king" (Luke 23:2). The hearings before Pilate and Herod exonerate him of the accusations, but nevertheless lead him closer and closer to crucifixion (vs. 1–16). A murderous political insurrectionist is released instead of Jesus (vs. 18–25).

It is in the mocking words of the scoffers—the leaders (v. 35), the soldiers (vs. 36–37), and an unrepentant criminal (v. 39)—and in the inscription put over the cross (v. 38) that readers are faced with the true nature of Jesus' Kingship. On the one hand, the repeated demand, "Are you not the Messiah? Save yourself and us!" functions as yet another temptation for Jesus. Just as the devil had earlier challenged his vocational identity three times and offered him a different, less painful option (4:1–11), so now Jesus is being invited to save himself, to avoid the cross, and in the process to save the criminals as well. He is being tempted to choose another vocation, to be a different sort of King from his distinctive calling, perhaps a political figure not unlike the one depicted in the false charges brought against him. By his lack of response to the scoffers, however, Jesus clearly remains steadfast in fulfilling the divine will.

On the other hand, the words of the scoffers ironically pose the paradox of his kingly mission. He is a Messiah who saves others only by not saving himself (v. 35). He is resolutely committed to God's plan, which includes betrayal and death (22:22, 37). Only in the powerlessness of the cross can he demonstrate the authority that ultimately rescues criminals, scoffers, and religious leaders. Refusing the voices of temptation, Jesus then defines for us what sort of King he really is.

This means that the constituting event of the Christian faith is not a power play that follows the rules and logic of most of the power plays we know—retaliation, competition, self-protectiveness, and the like. Instead, Jesus dares to trust and obey the divine will that takes him to the cross—and beyond.

There is, perhaps, irony here in that the religious authorities lead the cries for Jesus' death, whereas the one person in the text who perceives the truth and dares to speak it is the second criminal being crucified alongside Jesus (23:40–43). He acknowledges that he justly deserves his punishment, in contrast to Jesus, who is innocent. Furthermore, he sees that Jesus will enter his kingly realm not by coming down from the cross, but by dying. His request, "Jesus, remember me when you come into your kingdom" (v. 42), is a plea not to be forgotten. Yet it is also a confession of faith and an indication that he has understood the mystery of the gospel—that mockings, insults, floggings, and crucifixion are necessary to the prophetic plan that leads to resurrection (18:31–34). While other actors in the drama suppose that Jesus' fortunes are coming to an end (albeit for some a tragic end), the second criminal perceives that God will vindicate the King and will bring him into his proper rule.

A critical verse underlying the interchange with the criminals unfortunately remains, textually speaking, an uncertain one (23:34a). It is omitted in some ancient and trustworthy manuscripts and included in others. The notion that Jesus forgives his murderers because they are ignorant of what they are doing is certainly appropriate to the Lukan story. A case can be made for the theory that it is more likely that a scribe (who would tend to be anti-Jewish?) in copying would have omitted the verse than that he would have made it up. (See the critical commentaries for a fuller discussion.)

If the verse belongs in the text, then it becomes a watershed for the two criminals. They are specifically introduced in 23:32–33; then Jesus speaks these words of pardon on his crucifiers. One criminal "kept deriding him" and joined the group of scoffers. But the other criminal hears in the words something more and different—the words of a King, whose authority is like no other, who prays for those who spitefully abuse and persecute him. He seeks a place for himself in a realm where the keynote is pardon and not recompense, where condemned criminals can be fully restored.

# ALL SAINTS

*November 1 or the
first Sunday in November*

In the commemoration of All Saints, the church pays particular attention to the connection forged in the body of Christ, a connection that transcends the limitations of time and space. Part of that connection involves Christians of the present recalling the faithfulness of past generations and the heritage we receive from them. Each of the lections for All Saints assists us in focusing on that faithfulness and its importance for the present.

The visions of Daniel may be utterly remote from contemporary experience, but the encouragement to steadfastness recalls for the present generation those saints who remained constant in their faith so that we might receive it from them. In addition, the promise at the end of the lection is that God's "holy ones," or God's saints, will eventually triumph, no matter how bleak the present may be (Dan. 7:18).

Psalm 149 also promises "glory for all his faithful ones" (v. 9), although here the glory consists in their own present commitment to support God's work in the world. Read in the context of All Saints, of course, the "new song" of v. 1 includes the praise of God not only "in the assembly of the faithful" but *for* the assembly of the faithful. That is, among God's mighty deeds is the creation of this community of believers throughout history.

In Eph. 1:11–23, the writer (whether Paul or another early Christian) reports that he has heard of the Ephesians' love "toward all the saints" and demonstrates his own love in the prayer on their behalf. That love stems, not from a social or psychological connection, but from the conviction that the church is nothing less than Christ's body (v. 23). As such, love for "all the saints" is a theological given.

The blessings and woes of Luke 6:20–31, in the context of the celebration of All Saints, provide an example of the kind of life that is expected of the faithful. Theirs is not always the life of comfort and security, for faithfulness regularly leads to rejection. As we recall the

609

saints of ages past, we do so with gratitude for their endurance and with renewed commitment to follow their examples.

## Daniel 7:1–3, 15–18

Apart from those Christians who approach the matter with what appears to many, at least, as excessive zeal, most interpreters seem wary of the Bible's apocalyptic elements. Daniel, Revelation, Mark 13, and other apocalyptic texts are often passed over in favor of more easily digestible passages when the preacher arises to address her or his Sunday morning congregation. This is undoubtedly due, in part, to the fact that there is a long history of serious misinterpretation of apocalyptic, including such tragic episodes as those involving James Jones of Jonestown and David Koresh of the Branch Davidian compound in Texas. But this reluctance on the part of many to listen to the apocalyptic voice within the Bible is also due to the fact that, for people who tend to view the world in "common sense" terms, the apocalyptic message often seems irrelevant. It simply does not square with the world as we know it.

It may, therefore, strike one as highly unusual that the lectionary should turn to Daniel for, of all occasions, All Saints' Day. What does this anthology of tales and visions, set in long-ago Babylon, have to do with the company of faithful Christian men and women, living and dead, who constitute the church?

The answer, of course, lies in the book of Daniel's understanding of the struggle between good and evil, and in its understanding of how that conflict will be resolved.

The Old Testament lection for All Saints' Day is comprised of only seven verses of Dan. 7, but they occupy a particularly important place within the scope of the book. Daniel 7:1 marks the beginning of the second of two major sections within the book, the first (chs. 1—6) having to do with the stories of Daniel and his friends and their conduct in an alien environment, the second (chs. 7—12) consisting of four visions of Daniel in which he foresees the collapse of the present evil world order and the coming of the rule of God. Daniel 7:1–3, then, introduces the first of these visions, that of the four beasts (ch. 7).

Although they are not part of the vision proper, one must consult vs. 4–12 in order to understand the "four great beasts" of v. 3. These beasts represent the four great kingdoms with which the author(s) of Daniel are concerned: the Babylonians, the Medes, the Persians, and the Greeks. (One may wish to consult a good critical commentary on

Daniel for information concerning the worldview of the author[s] of Daniel, as well as for information concerning the nature of events in early second-century-B.C. Judah, the time and place of the writing of Daniel.) The Greek kingdom (more specifically, the Greek-speaking Syrian kingdom of the Seleucids) is destroyed by God, along with its arrogant ruler, presumably Antiochus IV Epiphanes, who ruled 175–164 B.C. (vs. 9–12).

Verse 13 introduces a transcendent agent of God who, relying on the power of the "Ancient One," establishes the rule of God. The dominion of this agent is to be a permanent one, for "his kingship is one that shall never be destroyed" (v. 14).

At this point the reader may well expect a statement concerning God's Messiah, the ruling Davidic king who will come in glory to judge the living and the dead. But Daniel is devoid of a messianic expectation, at least as the scriptures often understand messiahship (Isa. 9:2–7; Ezek. 34:20–24). Rather, the view here is that those who are faithful to God, the "holy ones" of v. 18, will exercise authority in the coming kingdom of God. It is they who will be God's triumphant agents when evil is overthrown and God's righteous rule is set in place.

> The kingship and dominion
>> and the greatness of the kingdoms under the whole heaven
>> shall be given to the people of the holy ones of the Most High;
> their kingdom shall be an everlasting kingdom,
>> and all dominions shall serve and obey them.
>
> (V. 27)

(Compare v. 22: "The time arrived when the holy ones gained possession of the kingdom.")

To the extent that Daniel describes a messiah, that messiah is the faithful people of God!

The first and second books of the Maccabees make it quite clear that the time in which Daniel was written was one of great suffering for many women and men who wished to remain faithful to the God of Israel and faithful to those traditions (observance of torah, for example) associated with Israel's God. Thus it was the purpose of Daniel not only to encourage faithful people in their devotion to the ways of Israel's God, but to assure them that God was in control of the affairs of their lives, in spite of much evidence that suggested the contrary. It was also the purpose of this book to promise that, when all the conflict had passed, the people of God would endure!

As the church looks back over the centuries of its life, it may identify much of which it can never be proud. At the same time, however, it is able to celebrate the faithfulness of many men and women who guided their lives by no other star than a trustworthy God, who promised never to abandon or forsake them. On All Saints' Day the church celebrates these women and men, and it celebrates also the God who inspired them—the God who has made them "rulers of the kingdom."

## Psalm 149

Psalm 149 starts like a typical song of praise—the invitation to praise (vs. 1–3) followed by reasons for praise (v. 4). The renewed invitation to praise in v. 5 is also fairly typical, but then vs. 6–9 present "an unparalleled departure" from the usual form (Leslie Allen, *Psalms 101—150*, Word Biblical Commentary 21; Waco, Tex.: Word, 1983, p. 319). These verses have proven puzzling to scholars and a source of difficulty for many readers who are offended by the call to vengeance. When these verses are heard figuratively, however, they present a radical call for the "faithful" (vs. 1, 5, 9) to enact and embody the reign of God that is celebrated in vs. 1–4, thus making Ps. 149 particularly appropriate for All Saints' Day ("faithful" is sometimes translated as "saints"; see, for instance, KJV).

Although the structure of the psalm is debatable, it is most likely that it consists of two main sections, vs. 1–4 and vs. 6–9, joined by v. 5, which should be understood as a "pivot," or hinge (see Anthony R. Ceresko, "Psalm 149: Poetry, Themes [Exodus and Conquest], and Social Function," *Biblica* 67 [1986]: 185; see also Allen, pp. 320–21). Verse 5 is the exact center of the psalm, and, along with vs. 1 and 9, it contains one of the three mentions of the "faithful." In addition, it belongs equally well with vs. 1–4 or vs. 6–9, and thus serves as a link between them.

Ceresko (pp. 179–80) argues that the conceptual unity of Ps. 149 lies in its allusion to two key historical events—the exodus (vs. 1–4) and the conquest (vs. 6–9; see below). He suggests that "Maker" in v. 2 refers not to creation but rather to God's formation of Israel as a people, and the constitutive event was the exodus (the root of "Maker" occurs in Ex. 14:31, NRSV "did"). The people's immediate response was to sing (Ex. 15:1; compare Ps. 149:1). Several other verbal links lend plausibility to this interpretation—"praise" (Ps. 149:1; Ex. 15:11, NRSV "splendor"), "dancing" (Ps. 149:3; Ex. 15:20), "tambourine" (Ps. 149:3; Ex. 15:20), "victory" (Ps. 149:4; Ex. 15:2,

NRSV "salvation"). In addition, the word "reign" in Ex. 15:18 is the same Hebrew root as "King" in Ps. 149:2.

In fact, the culmination of the exodus account is the affirmation that Yahweh "will reign forever and ever" (Ex. 15:18), and the assertion of Yahweh's sovereignty also underlies the call to praise in Ps. 149:1–4. As suggested concerning Ps. 145 (see Proper 27), it is not surprising that the conclusion of the Psalter explicitly returns to the theme that lies at its "theological heart"—"the LORD reigns!" (Pss. 96; 97; 99). In addition to the title "King" in 149:2, the invitation to sing "a new song" recalls Pss. 96:1 and 98:1 (see also Pss. 33:3; 40:3; 144:9; Isa. 42:10). The recognition that God rules the world opens the way for the possibility of "new things" (see Isa. 42:9; 48:6; compare 43:19; 65:17; Jer. 31:31) and calls for "a new song" (see Rev. 5:9; 14:3; compare Rev. 5:10; 11:15; and others).

It is likely that Ps. 149:5a invites the public recognition of God's reign (see "exult" in Ps. 96:12), while v. 5b encourages the recognition of God's sovereignty in every sphere of life including the private (see "sing for joy" in Pss. 96:12; 98:8, for example). Perhaps the same distinction between the private and public spheres is found in Micah 2:1 ("on their beds") and 2:5 ("in the assembly"; see Ceresko, pp. 156–87).

It is likely, as Ceresko suggests, that Ps. 149:6–9 alludes to Israel's conquest of the land. The phrase "the judgment decreed" (v. 9, literally "the judgment written") seems to allude to an earlier written tradition, perhaps the book of Judges (see especially Judg. 3:16–23, where Ehud uses "a sword with two edges" to kill King Eglon of Moab, as part of the consolidation of the conquest of the land; see also Deut. 7:1–6, and Num. 31:2–3, another episode in the possession of the land). If indeed Ps. 149 alludes to the book of Judges, it is crucial to note that Judges explicitly gives credit for Israel's victories not to its own leaders, but to Yahweh. Gideon refuses kingship (see Judg. 8:22–23), and the parable of the trees suggests the theological rationale—only Yahweh is king (9:7–20). In short, the possession of the land was another manifestation of Yahweh's sovereignty.

In this regard, it is important to note that Ps. 149:6–9 also recalls Ps. 2 and its concern with the rebellious "nations" and "peoples" (2:1; compare 149:7) and "kings" (2:2, 10; compare 149:8). Psalm 2 is ultimately an affirmation of Yahweh's sovereignty (see especially 2:11–12), and so is Ps. 149. It asserts that those who attempt to exercise their own sovereignty (see 2:3) will finally be called to account (2:10–12; 149:7–8), and things will be set right (149:9, which could be translated, "to do with them the justice decreed"). In short, Ps. 149 recalls both the "theological heart" of the Psalter (Ps. 93—99) and the beginning of the Psalter. Thus, the concern throughout the book of Psalms is to affirm that "the LORD reigns!" As the sweep of the Psalter reveals, this claim is made in the midst of circumstances that make it appear that Yahweh does *not* reign (see, for example, Ps. 3:1–2; note the pervasive presence of enemies, foes, and adversaries of God and the righteous). In short, like Pss. 2 and 93—99, Ps. 149 is eschatological. It proclaims God's reign, and it calls for a decision.

In this case, the call to decision is a portrayal of "the faithful" (vs. 1, 5, 9) participating with God in the enactment of God's claim on all peoples, nations, and kings. This sharing in God's rule is the "glory" of "the faithful" (v. 9; see Ps. 8:5, where the "honor" of humanity involves participation in God's dominion over the earth). To be sure, the war imagery is problematic and even positively dangerous if taken literally as a call to arms. But if understood figuratively as an invitation to join God at God's work in the world, vs. 6–9 of Ps. 149 are an eloquent call to discipleship. The value of the battle imagery is to convey the certain opposition that "the faithful" will face in representing God's policies in the world (see Eph. 6:10–17). As Jesus put it, the call to follow is a call to bear the cross (Mark 8:34). As John Calvin concludes about Ps. 149, citing Eph. 6:17, "As to the Church collective, the sword now put into our hand is of another kind, that of the word and spirit" (*Commentary on the Book of Psalms*, vol. 5; Grand Rapids: Baker Book House, 1949, p. 316). As "Christian soldiers" waging peace (see Eph. 6:15), we are in for a struggle; because we live in a "world [that] has declared war upon the gospel in the most subtle of ways" (Stanley Hauerwas and William H. Willimon, *Resident Aliens;* Nashville: Abingdon Press, 1989, p. 152; the authors are commenting on Eph. 6:13–20). The battle will mean for us what it meant for Jesus—suffering. The good news is that such suffering is our "glory" (Ps. 149:9; see Rom. 8:17).

## Ephesians 1:11–23

Previous discussions of this lection have focused on the major motifs of doxology and the ascension (see the discussions for the Second Sunday After Christmas and for Ascension). Reading the passage in the context of All Saints, however, draws attention to another element, that of the relationship among Christians.

When the passage opens in the middle of the letter's thanksgiving, it does so with a claim about the inheritance believers receive in Christ (Eph. 1:11). That inheritance enables Christians to "live for the praise of his glory" (v. 12), but it also at least implies a common bond among Christians. Those who inherit together share the inheritance.

Verse 15 turns to Paul's prayers (or those imputed to him by the author of Ephesians) for the community, and begins by recalling not only their faith but also their "love toward all the saints." As elsewhere in the New Testament, the term "saints" here refers to those whom God has called and thereby made holy (see 1 Cor. 1:2, for example). In all likelihood, then, it refers to believers in the present rather than to what we think of as the "communion of saints." Nevertheless, it celebrates the love of Christians for all the saints, whether past, present, or even future.

The prayer quickly turns to Paul's deepest longings for the Ephesians, namely, that they may have wisdom and revelation and hope (Eph. 1:17–18). Within that hope lie the "riches of his glorious inheritance among the saints" (v. 18). The precise nature of the riches is unclear, as is appropriate for a context that anticipates a future so glorious that it defies description. Within that future, however, the "glorious inheritance among the saints" again assumes that the saints of God belong together. When the church today confesses its faith in the "communion of saints," it acknowledges this profound connection among Christians of all generations, forged by the gospel of Jesus Christ and fully realized only in the eschatological future.

## Luke 6:20–31

Most of the time we are inclined to assume that the declaration and demands of the gospel are meant to help people live a normal, healthy human life. Like a balanced diet and regular exercise, the gospel enables folks to make the most of life, to take advantage of its opportunities and to cope with its downsides. Then along comes Luke's story of Jesus, repeatedly affirming a reversal of values (see Mary's Magnificat, 1:51–53) and offering an upsetting list of "blessings" and "woes" (6:20–26). Its alternative perspective on the nature of existence under God's reign, full of risk and insecurity, raises all sorts of questions about our normal, healthy human life.

Luke's Sermon on the Plain (6:20–49) presents a vivid picture of what life is like in the reign of God, and the section assigned for this Sunday functions in a subversive and threatening way. It begins with four beatitudes that invite the reader to take delight in the fact that the plight of poor, hungry, grieving, excluded people will be reversed in and by the rule of God (6:20–23). Who can help rejoicing in the change of circumstances for such unfortunate folks?

But then the four beatitudes are paralleled by four woes declared on the rich, the full, the happy, and the well-thought-of (6:24–26). The deliberate structure of the verses makes them even more forceful. Readers who have not found themselves included among those "blessed" (the poor, hungry, grieving, and excluded) are set to wondering about their place among the groups bemoaned. What in the world does the text mean?

Clearly there is no exaltation of poverty or hunger or grief or victimization as if these were virtues to be sought. The beatitudes are not exhortations, but promised blessings declared on people whose condition in the present would hardly seem to be favored. The future tenses ("you will be filled," " you will laugh") point to their ultimate circumstances. In turn, the woes are spoken on those whose current situation looks to an outsider to be fortunate, but whose ultimate life is quite the contrary.

The point is that those who prosper under the present structures of human life, who are self-satisfied and at ease with the ways things are, who benefit and are honored by the system, are in fact to be pitied. God's reign does not consist of a divinely offered promise of health and happiness which entails a simple adjustment to the present. Instead, it calls for an alternative manner of life that invariably means swimming against the stream. Those of Luke's original audience who found themselves included in 6:22 knew exactly how much at odds with the present system the reign of God put them and how violent the response could be.

Given this character of the gospel as counterculture, the text goes on to talk about how one lives and operates with avowed opponents (6:27–31). Instead of retaliation, the call is to love one's enemies, to do good to the adversaries, to bless and pray for the opposition.

The four examples of nonretaliation that follow (6:29–30) are striking in that they all have to do with physical abuse (a slap in the face) or material possessions (theft of one's coat, begging, and taking one's goods). Recompense is not to be sought, and in two cases the victim is to offer even more (the other cheek, one's shirt). On the one hand, the examples serve to draw attention to the point that in the reign of God love, rather than retaliation, prevails. On the other hand, the very particularity of the examples makes it impossible to turn them into new laws. Instead, readers are invited to reflect on the sweeping demands of love, especially in relation to hostile adversaries.

The content of 6:20–30 sets the Golden Rule of 6:31 into an

interesting context. No longer a general maxim to be universally applied, it becomes a specific counsel for dealing with one's enemies. Rather than responding to violence with violence, one is directed to treat the opposition as one would like to be treated. The section that follows continues the description, rooting the attitude and behavior toward the enemy in the very character of God: "Be merciful, just as your Father is merciful" (6:36).

For many of us these verses read like some indecipherable foreign language. In fact, for us the gospel never creates opposition. It simply makes adjustments with the prevailing culture to enable believers to remain rich, full, happy, and adulated. Any "enemies" we encounter are merely those with whom we have personality difficulties. The passage, however, has the power to undermine any easy truce we have negotiated with the culture and to wake us to the sharp demands of life under God's reign. It is a precarious, risk-filled existence, but one the text calls "blessed."

# Index of Lectionary Readings

## Old Testament

**Genesis**
15:1–12,
  17–18      200–202
45:3–11, 15      152–53

**Exodus**
12:1–4 (5–10)
  11–14      249–50
34:29–35      171–73

**Deuteronomy**
26:1–11      190–92

**Joshua**
5:9–12      220–21

**1 Samuel**
2:18–20, 26      67–68

**1 Kings**
17:8–16
  (17–24)      372–74
18:20–21
  (22–29) 30–39   362–64
19:1–4 (5–7)
  8–15a      392–94
21:1–10 (11–14)
  15–21a      382–84

**2 Kings**
2:1–2, 6–14      402–4
5:1–14      412–14

**Nehemiah**
8:1–3, 5–6,
  8–10      113–14

**Psalms**
1      144–46
5:1–8      384–86
8      354–56
14      510–12
19      114–17
22      259–61
23      298–300
25:1–10      4–5
27      202–4
29      95–98
30      288–90
32      222–23
36:5–10      106–7
37:1–11, 39–40      154–55
42—43      394–96
47      325–26
50:1–8, 22–23      462–64
51:1–17      183–84
52      432–34
63:1–8      212–14
65      569–71
66:1–12      549–51
67      316–18
71:1–6      125–27
72:1–7, 10–14      86–88
77:1–2, 11–20      404–6
79:1–9      520–22
80:1–7      32–34
80:1–2, 8–19      472–74

81:1, 10–16      489–92
82      422–24
85      442–44
91:1–2, 9–16      192–94
92:1–4, 12–15      163–65
96      41–43
96      364–66
97      51–52
97      333–36
98      59–61
99      173–75
104:24–34,
  35b      344–46
107:1–9, 43      452–54
116:1–2, 12–19      250–52
118:1–2, 14–24      269–70
118:1–2, 19–29      241–43
119:97–104      559–61
119:137–144      578–80
126      231–33
137      538–40
138      134–37
139:1–6,
  13–18      499–502
145:1–5,
  17–21      588–91
146      374–76
147:12–20      77–79
148      69–71
149      612–14
150      278–80

**Proverbs**
8:1–4, 22–31      352–54

Isaiah
| | |
|---|---|
| 1:1, 10–20 | 460–62 |
| 5:1–7 | 470–72 |
| 6:1–8 (9–13) | 132–34 |
| 9:2–7 | 40–41 |
| 12:2–6 | 22–24 |
| 43:1–7 | 94–95 |
| 43:16–21 | 229–31 |
| 50:4–9a | 239–40 |
| 52:7–10 | 58–59 |
| 52:13–53:12 | 258–59 |
| 55:1–9 | 210–12 |
| 55:10–13 | 161–63 |
| 60:1–6 | 84–86 |
| 62:1–5 | 103–5 |
| 62:6–12 | 49–50 |
| 65:17–25 | 596–98 |

Jeremiah
| | |
|---|---|
| 1:4–10 | 123–25 |
| 1:4–10 | 480–82 |
| 2:4–13 | 487–89 |
| 4:11–12, 22–28 | 507–10 |
| 8:18–9:1 | 518–20 |
| 17:5–10 | 141–44 |
| 18:1–11 | 497–99 |
| 23:1–6 | 604–5 |
| 29:1, 4–7 | 546–48 |
| 31:7–14 | 76–77 |
| 31:27–34 | 557–59 |
| 32:1–3a, 6–15 | 528–30 |
| 33:14–16 | 2–3 |

Lamentations
| | |
|---|---|
| 1:1–6 | 536–38 |

Daniel
| | |
|---|---|
| 7:1–3, 15–18 | 610–12 |

Hosea
| | |
|---|---|
| 1:2–10 | 440–42 |
| 11:1–11 | 450–52 |

Joel
| | |
|---|---|
| 2:1–2, 12–17 | 181–82 |
| 2:23–32 | 567–69 |

Amos
| | |
|---|---|
| 7:7–17 | 420–22 |
| 8:1–12 | 430–31 |

Micah
| | |
|---|---|
| 5:2–5a | 30–32 |

Habakkuk
| | |
|---|---|
| 1:1–4; 2:1–4 | 577–78 |

Zephaniah
| | |
|---|---|
| 3:14–20 | 20–22 |

Haggai
| | |
|---|---|
| 1:15b–2:9 | 586–88 |

Malachi
| | |
|---|---|
| 3:1–4 | 11–13 |

# New Testament

Matthew
| | |
|---|---|
| 2:1–12 | 90–92 |
| 6:1–6, 16–21 | 186–88 |

Luke
| | |
|---|---|
| 1:39–45 | 36–38 |
| 1:68–79 | 13–14 |
| 2:1–14 (15–20) | 45–47 |
| 2:(1–7) 8–20 | 54–56 |
| 2:41–52 | 73–74 |
| 3:1–6 | 17–18 |
| 3:7–18 | 26–28 |
| 3:15–17, 21–22 | 100–2 |
| 4:1–13 | 196–98 |
| 4:14–21 | 119–21 |
| 4:21–30 | 129–31 |
| 5:1–11 | 139–40 |
| 6:17–26 | 148–50 |
| 6:20–31 | 615–17 |
| 6:27–38 | 157–59 |
| 6:39–49 | 167–69 |
| 7:1–10 | 368–70 |
| 7:11–17 | 378–80 |
| 7:36–8:3 | 388–90 |
| 8:26–39 | 398–400 |

| | |
|---|---|
| 9:28–36 | |
| (37–43) | 177–79 |
| 9:51–62 | 408–10 |
| 10:1–11, 16–20 | 416–18 |
| 10:25–37 | 426–28 |
| 10:38–42 | 436–38 |
| 11:1–13 | 446–48 |
| 12:13–21 | 456–58 |
| 12:32–40 | 466–68 |
| 12:49–56 | 476–78 |
| 13:1–9 | 216–18 |
| 13:10–17 | 484–86 |
| 13:31–35 | 206–8 |
| 14:1, 7–14 | 494–96 |
| 14:25–33 | 504–6 |
| 15:1–3, 11b–32 | 225–27 |
| 15:1–10 | 514–16 |
| 16:1–13 | 524–26 |
| 16:19–31 | 532–34 |
| 17:5–10 | 542–45 |
| 17:11–19 | 553–55 |
| 18:1–8 | 563–65 |
| 18:9–14 | 573–75 |
| 19:1–10 | 582–84 |
| 19:28–40 | 245–47 |
| 20:27–38 | 593–95 |
| 21:5–19 | 601–2 |
| 21:25–36 | 7–9 |
| 23:33–43 | 606–8 |
| 24:44–53 | 328–30 |

John
| | |
|---|---|
| 1:(1–9) 10–18 | 81–83 |
| 1:1–14 | 63–65 |
| 2:1–11 | 109–11 |
| 5:1–9 | 320–21 |
| 10:22–30 | 302–4 |
| 12:1–8 | 235–37 |
| 13:1–17, | |
| 31b–35 | 255–56 |
| 13:31–35 | 310–12 |
| 14:8–17 | |
| (25–27) | 348–50 |
| 16:12–15 | 358–60 |
| 17:20–26 | 338–40 |
| 18:1–19:42 | 264–65 |

| | | | | | | |
|---|---|---|---|---|---|
| 20:1–18 | 272–74 | Galatians | | 1 Timothy | |
| 20:19–31 | 282–84 | 1:1–12 | 366–68 | 1:12–17 | 512–14 |
| 21:1–19 | 292–94 | 1:11–24 | 376–78 | 2:1–7 | 522–24 |
| | | 2:15–21 | 386–88 | 6:6–19 | 530–32 |
| Acts | | 3:23–29 | 396–98 | | |
| 1:1–11 | 323–25 | 5:1, 13–25 | 406–8 | 2 Timothy | |
| 2:1–21 | 342–44 | 6:(1–6) 7–16 | 414–16 | 1:1–14 | 540–42 |
| 5:27–32 | 276–78 | | | 2:8–15 | 551–53 |
| 8:14–17 | 98–100 | Ephesians | | 3:14–4:5 | 561–63 |
| 9:1–6 (7–20) | 286–88 | 1:3–14 | 79–81 | 4:6–8, 16–18 | 571–73 |
| 9:36–43 | 296–98 | 1:11–23 | 614–15 | | |
| 10:34–43 | 267–69 | 1:15–23 | 326–28 | Titus | |
| 11:1–18 | 306–7 | 3:1–12 | 88–90 | 2:11–14 | 43–45 |
| 16:9–15 | 314–16 | | | 3:4–7 | 52–54 |
| 16:16–34 | 332–33 | Philippians | | | |
| | | 1:3–11 | 15–17 | Philemon | |
| Romans | | 2:5–11 | 243–45 | 1–21 | 502–4 |
| 5:1–5 | 356–58 | 3:4b–14 | 233–35 | | |
| 8:14–17 | 346–48 | 3:17–4:1 | 204–5 | Hebrews | |
| 10:8b–13 | 194–96 | 4:4–7 | 24–26 | 1:1–4 (5–12) | 61–63 |
| | | | | 4:14–16; 5:7–9 | 262–63 |
| 1 Corinthians | | Colossians | | 10:5–10 | 34–36 |
| 10:1–13 | 214–16 | 1:1–14 | 424–26 | 11:1–3, 8–16 | 464–66 |
| 11:23–26 | 253–54 | 1:11–20 | 606 | 11:29–12:2 | 474–76 |
| 12:1–11 | 108–9 | 1:15–28 | 434–36 | 12:18–29 | 482–84 |
| 12:12–31a | 117–19 | 2:6, 15 | | 13:1–8, 15–16 | 492–94 |
| 13:1–13 | 127–29 | (16–19) | 444–46 | | |
| 15:1–11 | 137–38 | 3:1–11 | 454–56 | Revelation | |
| 15:12–20 | 146–48 | 3:12–17 | 71–72 | 1:4–8 | 280–82 |
| 15:19–26 | 270–72 | | | 5:11–14 | 290–92 |
| 15:35–38, | | 1 Thessalonians | | 7:9–17 | 300–302 |
| 42–50 | 155–57 | 3:9–13 | 6–7 | 21:1–6 | 308–9 |
| 15:51–58 | 165–67 | | | 21:10; | |
| | | 2 Thessalonians | | 21:22–22:5 | 318–20 |
| 2 Corinthians | | 1:1–4, 11–12 | 580–82 | 22:12–14, | |
| 3:12–4:2 | 175–77 | 2:1–5, 13–17 | 591–93 | 16–17, 20–21 | 336–38 |
| 5:16–21 | 224–25 | 3:6–13 | 599–600 | | |
| 5:20b–6:10 | 185–86 | | | | |